CAMBRIDGE READINGS IN
THE LITERATURE OF MUSIC

*General Editors: John Stevens and Peter le Huray*

Music in European thought 1851–1912

# CAMBRIDGE READINGS IN THE LITERATURE OF MUSIC

Cambridge Readings in the Literature of Music is a series of source materials (original documents in English translation) for students of the history of music. Many of the quotations in the volumes will be substantial, and introductory material will place the passages in context. The period covered will be from antiquity to the present day, with particular emphasis on the nineteenth and twentieth centuries. The series is part of *Cambridge Studies in Music*.

Already published:
Andrew Barker, *Greek Musical Writings, Volume I*
James McKinnon, *Music in Early Christian Literature*
Peter le Huray and James Day, *Music and Aesthetics in the Eighteenth and Early-Nineteenth Centuries*

# Music in European thought

# 1851–1912

*Edited by*
Bojan Bujić

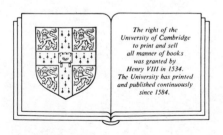

The right of the
University of Cambridge
to print and sell
all manner of books
was granted by
Henry VIII in 1534.
The University has printed
and published continuously
since 1584.

## Cambridge University Press

*Cambridge*
*New York   New Rochelle   Melbourne   Sydney*

Published by the Press Syndicate of the University of Cambridge
The Pitt Building, Trumpington Street, Cambridge CB2 1RP
32 East 57th Street, New York, NY 10022, USA
10 Stamford Road, Oakleigh, Melbourne 3166, Australia

First published 1988

Printed in Great Britain at
the University Press, Cambridge

*British Library cataloguing in publication data*
Music in European thought 1851–1912. –
(Cambridge readings in the literature
of music).
1. Music – Europe – Theory – 19th
century – Sources  2. Music – Europe
– Theory – 20th century – Sources
I. Bujić, Bojan
781'.094  MT6

*Library of Congress cataloguing in publication data*
Music in European thought, 1851–1912.
(Cambridge readings in the literature of music)
Bibliography.
Includes index.
1. Music – Europe – 19th century – Philosophy and
aesthetics – Sources.  2. Music – Europe – 20th century –
Philosophy and aesthetics – Sources.  I. Bujić, Bojan,
1937–  . II. Series.
ML3845.M973  1988  780'1  87–25612

ISBN 0 521 23050 0

*To the memory of my father*

# Contents

vii

Contents

# Preface

Not unlike a compiler of a dictionary, an editor of an anthology may easily become haunted by the feeling that the more he gathers in, the more material still remains outside his grasp. Any period of intellectual history, if it is to be documented exhaustively and meaningfully, requires that attention be paid to a variety of personalities and works and not only to the thought of the most distinguished intellectual lights of the time. Numerous lesser figures who often voiced short-lived though urgent concerns of a small intellectual community, followers of a belief, belligerents in critical disputes – all should have their say. Such a complexity of critical and philosophical themes is easy to recognize in any age but is exceedingly difficult to document. It may therefore sound like a veiled admission of defeat if at the outset I say that it is not the aim of this volume to paint a complete picture, but rather to offer a representative sample of some of the main tendencies in the aesthetics of music during the second half of the nineteenth century.

In chronological terms the volume succeeds Peter le Huray's and James Day's *Music and aesthetics in the eighteenth and early-nineteenth centuries*. The accent is on the material from the second half of the nineteenth century and the first decade or so of the twentieth century which in its themes and concerns still belongs to the intellectual currents of the preceding one.

Whereas le Huray and Day felt able to construct their *Music and aesthetics* around the concept of romanticism as a unifying factor of an extended period, such a central theme is lacking in the second half of the century. A style or an artistic trend in the making initially acts cohesively and draws to the central current a wealth of individual concerns. The full maturity, if a notion of such neat flow can at all be accepted as a historical norm, brings to the fore the feeling of fragmentation and parting of ways. Assuming a threefold division into the nascent, classical and declining phase of romanticism, Ernst Kurth saw the transition into the last phase as a long-drawn crisis, the examples of which were for him provided by Wagner and *Tristan und Isolde*.[1] More recently H. G. Schenk, Nietzsche's spirit peeping over his shoulder, identified 'a histrionic element in Wagner' which to him suggested 'a perversion or even a travesty of Romanticism'.[2] Carl Dahlhaus put it

[1] Ernst Kurth, *Romantische Harmonik und ihre Krise in Wagners 'Tristan'* (Berlin 1920).
[2] H. G. Schenk, *The Mind of the European Romantics* (London 1966), p. 212.

differently suggesting that 'the "neo-Romanticism" of Wagner and Liszt might well be defined as the musical survival of Romanticism in a positivist epoch'.[3] Elsewhere he questioned the validity of the term 'romanticism', not by proposing to do away with it but rather by re-defining the nature of the relationship of nineteenth-century music to its cultural and intellectual environment.[4] This enabled him to introduce the term 'realism', not as a straight borrowing from literary theory but rather as a concept with its own meaning in music history. The substance of this case need not concern us further here, it mainly helps to underline the fragmented nature of the consciousness of a style and its historical position in the second half of the nineteenth century. The lack of cohesion thus, seemingly paradoxically, makes it possible to identify a number of continuous schools of thought and these are best dealt with if the excerpts are united in thematic groups.

German authors of the second half of the century are by far the best represented group, understandably, since the aesthetics of music during this period was largely a German concern. The French and the English authors are often presented in relation to their German contemporaries in order that various interchanges of ideas could be more clearly demonstrated. Certain areas, important in themselves, were judged to be outside the scope of the volume since its main stress is on aesthetics. The development of historiography, theoretical works accompanying the emergence of schools of musical nationalism in Slavonic lands, Hungary, Scandinavia, and Spain, trends in music criticism and reviews of concerts are in themselves enough to fill a large volume. It is also true that during the early years of the twentieth century a number of philosophers, critics, theorists of literature, art, and theatre looked Janus-like to the past – in this case to the aesthetic and critical theories of the mid-nineteenth century – as well as to the future, providing as they did cornerstones of new intellectual edifices. The present volume shows the first aspect of their activity whereas the other more modern issues are left out and properly belong to a different volume in the Readings series, one dealing with the twentieth century. Sometimes such aspects are merely hinted at: the emergence of phenomenology, Heinrich Schenker's analytical thought, the systematizing nature of musicology; other significant themes, such as the connection between psychologism and expressionism, the impact of Freud, or the emergence of futurism are not touched upon at all.

It would be an easy way out to claim that the criteria for inclusion of some authors and exclusion of others were determined by their relevance to the modern reader, if this would not beg the further question of how that relevance is to be established. Some names remain of undisputed importance to a cultural historian, music historian and general reader: those of Wagner, Nietzsche, Baudelaire, Berlioz or Darwin; others, such as Eduard Hanslick, Eduard von Hartmann, Charles Lalo, Jules Combarieu or Guido Adler, are

---

[3] John Deathridge and Carl Dahlhaus, *The New Grove Wagner* (London 1984), p. 93.
[4] C. Dahlhaus, *Musikalischer Realismus* (Munich 1982); English transl. (Cambridge 1985).

likely to be known only to specialists. A happy mixture of names from the two categories would guarantee a degree of fairness but would not necessarily remove the difficulty of distinguishing between cause and effect. When dealing with French or German authors one is aware that the need to make their work accessible prompted translators to work, but on the other hand, the realization of their stature was largely brought about by the very existence of translations. This approach excludes less well-known names and establishes criteria of relevance on the basis of present-day needs, neglecting the fact that a meaningful characterization of an age requires familiarity with ideas or works which, although not having always stood the test of time, are an integral part of the cultural environment from which they sprang.

It is with all this in mind that certain editorial decisions have to be defended. E. Hanslick, for instance, is represented by a long excerpt from *Vom Musikalisch-Schönen* on the grounds that this, one of the central texts of nineteenth-century aesthetics of music, has hitherto been available only in Gustav Cohen's unreliable English translation. In comparison, Wagner's share in the volume may appear rather meagre. One has to bear in mind, though, that Wagner is almost always long-winded and repetitive, his thought unsystematic and diffuse, yet so strangely hypnotic, that a fair representation of his ideas within an anthology is hard to achieve. To this may be added the absence of a critical edition of his prose works in the original German on the one hand, and on the other, the continuing signs of a remarkable resurgence of Wagner scholarship in recent years, which is very likely to result in the availability of reliable German texts and equally reliable English translations. In short, Wagner, alongside with Nietzsche, stands a good chance. Working on the anthology, I felt that one may easily allow the whole period to be dominated by the figures of these two men. Without denying them their stature, one has to bear in mind that in the long run such a chance is unlikely to present itself to Friedrich Theodor Vischer, Otakar Hostinský, Friedrich von Hausegger, or Charles Beauquier. They all represent aspects of late nineteenth-century thought, hitherto little known in the English-speaking world and are needed in order to complete the picture.

Does all the philosophizing that is to be found on the pages of this volume drive towards achieving answers to the questions of what music is, what it stands for, or what it can achieve? Only perhaps in an incomplete manner. Indeed, a professional music historian may at times find himself irritated by inconsistencies or a philosopher's imperfect grasp of some or other technical aspect of music, so that, encouraged by his technical knowledge, he may delude himself that comprehension of the technical aspect guarantees a full understanding of a work of art. Put mildly, this may be seen as a fallacy, though Theodor Adorno, hardly known by mildness of manner, went as far as to assert that 'it is only rising barbarism that limits works of art to what meets the eye'.[5] In less urgent terms, it is still necessary to recognize that, as

---

[5] Theodor W. Adorno, 'Bach Defended against his Devotees', in *Prisms*, tr. Samuel and Shierry Webber (Cambridge, Mass. 1981), p. 138.

the title of the volume suggests, the relationship is a twofold one: not being only an object of explanation, music enters the world of philosophy as a catalyst. It informs a philosopher's thought process, acts as one of the bridges between himself and the world that he tries to explain: it is, to adapt the ancient dictum, *ancilla philosophiae*. Such a position of music in relation to philosophy certainly obtains in the second half of the nineteenth century, and it is an open question whether the weakening of the link, to be recognized in the period that followed, is not a testimony, however disturbing, in favour of Adorno's assertion.

In most cases the texts included in this volume are of some length, since it was felt that a short passage of a few pages only cannot present an author's case at all clearly.

As has already been mentioned, German and Austrian authors provide the greatest number of excerpts. Only a few of them are given in nineteenth- or early twentieth-century translations (Ambros, Helmholtz and Busoni), while Nietzsche and Schenker appear in established modern translations. All the other German texts have been newly translated by Martin Cooper who, sadly, did not live to see the volume in print. The translator's task was not an easy one. Most German authors seem to suffer from the Hegelian malaise of long and often extremely complex sentences, and in translating them into English it is difficult to avoid the horns of the dilemma of whether to reshape them into easily flowing English prose or to retain something of their original flavour. Since the complexity appears to have been a consciously adopted norm it seems wrong to avoid it at all costs; if some sentences seem tortuous to an English-speaking reader, he can console himself with the thought that they have a similar effect on a German-speaking one too.

Words difficult to translate into English adequately (such as *Geist* or *Vorstellung*), as well as whole phrases, appear in brackets in the original language whenever it was felt that they could alert the reader to the difficulty that faced the translator. In a number of places I felt that I had to alter Martin Cooper's translations, either for the sake of consistency throughout the volume, or because repeated readings of the original disclosed nuances of meaning difficult to detect on first acquaintance. In some of such cases I indicated that the translation is not entirely Martin Cooper's work. Needless to say, the final responsibility for all the texts remains mine.

Only three French texts are taken from existing translations: J. Combarieu's *Music, its Laws and Evolution*, Berlioz's account of Wagner's concerts in Paris from early twentieth-century publications, and Baudelaire's essay on Wagner from P. E. Charvet's modern and well-established English version. The rest of the French material has been translated by Jennifer Day and Rosemary Lloyd.

Nearly all of the sources, German as well as French and English, contain frequent indications of rhetorical stress, shown in the originals by italic or by some other typographical device. In most cases they are little else than mannerisms of the time and their use has been severely limited.

All editorial additions and excisions are indicated by square brackets; numbers in square brackets at the ends of passages indicate the pages of the original from which they were taken. Editorially added footnotes, also enclosed within square brackets, have been interposed between the original ones which therefore had to be re-numbered. The re-numbering of footnotes was also carried out in those texts which were taken from previously published translations with already existing editorial footnotes. Different origin of such footnotes is in all cases clearly acknowledged. In a number of cases throughout the book footnotes, either incomplete in detail or incorrect, have been expanded or altered; such small interventions were thought to be essentially questions of style rather than substance and therefore not acknowledged. This does not apply to the footnotes containing clearly erroneous statements, such as some original ones by Wagner or Combarieu, where editorial comment in square brackets explains the nature of the error.

In some cases quotations proved difficult to track. German authors especially, as educated humanists, assumed their readers' familiarity with the classical authors, Goethe or Schiller, and seldom provided clues about the origin of the material they quoted. I have done my best to furnish adequate indications, but had to give up in some cases, thus dangerously revealing my ignorance to the reader. It is heartening to discover that the gods are fallible too: Guido Adler, purporting to quote Chrysander, only paraphrases him (see below, p. 353).

The year in brackets in the heading of each excerpt refers to the date of the first edition, even if the source used came from a later one. In the case of German publications I have on the whole followed the authority of both series (1700–1910 and 1911–65) of the monumental *Gesamtverzeichnis des deutschsprachigen Schrifttums* (for details see bibliography). The two different spellings, *Aesthetik* and *Ästhetik*, are there in order to indicate the version used in the original editions. All quotations from Wagner's prose works have an indication of their location in the second edition (Leipzig 1887–8): this one has the virtue of providing a ready cross-reference to the first edition of 1871–3.

The expertise needed in order to deal adequately with the material contained in various texts embraces many disciplines and my editorial task would have been an impossible one without generous help of friends and colleagues. Mr P. L. Gardiner and Sir Malcolm Pasley patiently listened to my queries about aspects of German philosophy and literature and gave me valuable help. My forays into the history of nineteenth-century science and psychology would have yielded little result but for the help of Professor L. Weiskrantz, Professor B. S. Rosner and Dr L. E. Sutton. Dr A. W. Raitt not only advised me in matters relating to French literature and thought of the late nineteenth century, but also, as well as Gloria Cigman and my wife Alison, helped to straighten in places my wayward Slavonic English. Dr F. W. Sternfeld, Dr D. E. Olleson and Dr M. Rosen helped with translations of tricky passages from Dessoir, Adler and Dilthey, and in general displayed great patience whenever confronted with my unexpected questions. A large share of my gratitude goes to someone who has not been directly associated with this book: Dr Ivan Focht, formerly of Sarajevo University, Yugoslavia, who taught me philosophy and aesthetics when I was an undergraduate there, transmitted to me some of his enthusiasm for nineteenth-century aesthetics of music, and, with his uncanny understanding of the complex prose of German authors, opened to me the way into a field of study in which without him I might not have persisted. Persistence, though of a different kind, was required of Rosemary Dooley and Penny Souster of Cambridge University Press who for over seven years between them encouraged me and urged me on, and were always ready to offer a sympathetic ear to my excuses.

*Magdalen College*                                              BOJAN BUJIĆ
*Oxford*

*September 1986*

# Acknowledgments

I wish to thank the following publishers for granting permission to print extracts from copyright material: F. Nietzsche, *The Birth of Tragedy* and *The Case of Wagner*, tr. with commentary W. Kaufmann, by permission of Alfred A. Knopf and Random House, Inc.; H. Berlioz, 'Concerts of Richard Wagner' from *Mozart, Weber and Wagner with Various Essays on Musical Subjects*, tr. Edwin Evans, by permission of W. Reeves, Bookseller Ltd., London; C. Baudelaire, 'Richard Wagner and *Tannhäuser* in Paris' from *Selected Writings on Art and Artists*, tr. P. E. Charvet, by permission of Cambridge University Press; H. Schenker, *Harmony*, ed. and annotated Oswald Jonas, tr. Elisabeth Mann Borgese, by permission of the University of Chicago Press.

# Abbreviations

| | |
|---|---|
| GS | R. Wagner, *Gesammelte Schriften und Dichtungen*, 2nd edn. (Leipzig 1887–8), 10 vols. in 5 |
| HC | E. Hanslick, *The Beautiful in Music*, tr. G. Cohen (London 1891, repr. Indianapolis and New York 1957) |
| HMS | E. Hanslick, *Vom Musikalisch-Schönen*, 8th edn. (Leipzig 1891) |
| le Huray and Day | P. le Huray and J. Day, *Music and Aesthetics in the Eighteenth and Early-Nineteenth Centuries* (Cambridge 1981) |
| NZM | *Neue Zeitschrift für Musik* |
| PW | *Richard Wagner's Prose Works*, tr. and ed. W. A. Ellis (London 1892–9, repr. New York 1966), 8 vols. |

# General introduction

The enthusiastic hopes for swift advances in forming a theory of music which I as a youngster pinned on Helmholtz's discoveries as I found them in Poggendorff's *Annalen der Physik* have not so far been realized. On the contrary, no progress of any kind has been made, owing to the fact that the theory constructed by Helmholtz in his work on sound-sensations and based on his experiments, had led to the false trail of the Sensualists.[1]

These words of Eduard von Hartmann, dating from the penultimate decade of the last century, do not only describe the disappointment of his generation, they also reflect the main intellectual dilemma which characterized the outlook on music during the second half of the nineteenth century. In spite of a cliché which is often applied to descriptions of nineteenth-century music, emphasizing its emotionalism, reliance on fantasy, the cult of the virtuoso and a certain transcendental tendency, the century was also the period of immense advances in the sciences. Scientific progress, combined with national aspirations and economic enterprise, gave a particularly 'dynamic' quality to the second half of the century; the attitudes to music, whether as a living art or a historical phenomenon, went along with the inquiring spirit of philosophical and scientific writing. When he suggested that the aesthetics of music should 'approach as nearly as possible the method of the natural sciences',[2] Hanslick did not have in mind only the quality of systematic investigation so dear to all followers of the classical German philosophical tradition. His appeal was as much to an application of judgement which proceeds from a careful consideration of facts relating to a specific phenomenon, and then builds the picture stage by stage in a way similar to that of a scientist who carefully investigates related phenomena one by one and aspires to discover the scientific truth.

Whereas in the first half of the nineteenth century speculations about music centred mainly on discussion of its expressive power and emotional properties, the scientific climate of the century exerted its influence on philosophical aesthetics during the second half of the century and, in the work of several authors, philosophical speculation was so mixed with the scientific mode of thinking that it is often difficult to distinguish between these influ-

---

[1] Eduard von Hartmann, *Philosophie des Schönen* (1887). See below, p. 166, n.1.
[2] Eduard Hanslick, *Vom Musikalisch-Schönen* (1854, 8th edn 1891). See below, p. 12.

ences. In theory at least, such a combination of influences could only serve to strengthen the arguments and, by bridging the gap between the arts and sciences, provide a model for a new understanding of the world. There is some utopian naivety in this and, indeed, some of the writings from the period are curiously dated, precisely because their optimism at discovering the scientific or artistic truth was too great. But they are a part of the intellectual history of the second half of the nineteenth century; and, if the doctrines have not survived unshaken, they are important because they often demonstrate that ideas, like comets, tend to return and that many trends and thoughts in the aesthetics, philosophy and theory of music, which at first may appear to be twentieth-century phenomena, are in fact ideas or modes of thought which were tried out before, were found wanting, and, having been once abandoned, are taken up again. The passage of time often confirms their relevance, if not the manner in which the ideas were treated during the first attempt.

If giants such as Hegel and Schopenhauer dominated philosophical aesthetics in the first half of the nineteenth century, the second half produced epigones and pupils, none of whom managed to come close to their teachers, and the philosophy of Robert Zimmermann, Friedrich Theodor Vischer, Eduard von Hartmann and Richard Wagner's texts with philosophical aspirations do not come close to the original thought of Kant, Herbart, Hegel or Schopenhauer. It is perhaps significant that the most original philosophical mind of the second half of the century, Friedrich Nietzsche, is an 'impure' philosopher: impure in the sense in which the German tradition sees philosophy and the building of complete philosophical systems. It is Nietzsche who, with his ambition to become a philologist, with his temperament of an artist – poet and musician – and with his refusal to construct a full system of philosophy conceived in delineated disciplines, shows the decline of the grand philosophical systems of the past.

In the eighteenth century the systematizing nature of philosophers like Wolff and Baumgarten ensured the foundation of philosophical aesthetics and made possible its significant development in the early part of the nineteenth century. The whole of the nineteenth century is seen as a great age of aesthetics and music is certainly privileged among the arts in having been debated so vigorously by the philosophers. The reasons for this are sometimes seen in the peculiar social conditions of the time. After the decline of the aristocratic patronage of music in the nineteenth century, the members of the newly emerging bourgeoisie became the new patrons and to them music and its secrets had to be explained. However, this is only one part of the truth. A sociological explanation of an intellectual and philosophical phenomenon can be only partially successful simply because philosophy often pursues modes of thought which form a part of its own inheritance and survive over and above sociological categories or changing social conditions. Philosophical inquiry into music acquired its prominence because the ability of music to move the human mind while operating with tonal combinations which have laws of their own and do not have any significance in a non-artistic context afforded the philosophers a unique bridge between the material and the spiritual (in the sense in which the terms *Geist/geistig* are understood in German). The material element is undeniable in the physical phenomenon of sound and the superstructure of a loosely defined or undefined 'content' hovers above the physical appearance of sound. The value of the non-physical content, and the possibilities of its existence are seen in music as being essentially different from any other artistic reality, which in all other art forms is communicated through a set of verbally definable means. Music thus becomes a 'philosopher's art' quite independently of the need of any one social group for its explanation.

The desire to create complete systems of philosophy, characteristic of German classical philosophy, meant that aesthetics quite early abandoned investigations of either sensuous phenomena or taste, and concerned itself with various aspects of art which have some relevance for the study of metaphysics or epistemology, and as is the case with Herbart, ethics. It thus became the bridge between philosophical disciplines and ultimately provided philosophers and non-philosophers alike with an area of study which afforded an illusion of systematic completeness. Art, epistemology and ethics had already been linked in the work of Schopenhauer and by the time of Nietzsche the philosophy itself started to aspire to the condition of art.

Nietzsche often uses poetry in order to make statements that contain elements of a wider system of thought, just as he resorts to statements of poetic breadth in prose texts whose original intention is to argue a specific set of points in the form of an essay. The forms of expression and the context in which they appear, Nietzsche argues, should challenge the established order of elements, in art as well as in philosophy, and, not surprisingly, he assigns to Richard Wagner the task of demonstrating how this is to be done:

[Wagner] shows how the genius must not fear to enter into the most hostile relationship with the existing forms and order if he wants to bring to light the high order and truth that dwells within him.[3]

Instead of scientific exactness and the overpowering dullness of all striving towards systems, Nietzsche offers the notion of life as a source of wisdom and knowledge:

To understand the picture one must divine the painter – that Schopenhauer knew. Nowadays, however, the whole guild of the sciences is occupied in understanding the canvas and the paint but not the picture; one can say, indeed, that only he who has a clear view of the picture of life and existence as a whole can employ the individual sciences without harm to himself, for without such a regulatory total picture they are threads that nowhere come to an end and only render our life more confused and labyrinthine. Schopenhauer is, as I said, great in that he pursues this picture as Hamlet pursues the ghost, without letting himself be led aside, as scholars are, or becoming enmeshed in abstract scholasticism, as is the fate of rabid dialecticians. The study of quarter-philosophers is enticing only so as to recognize that they make at once for the

[3] Friedrich Nietzsche, 'Schopenhauer as Educator' (1874) in *Untimely Meditations*, tr. R. J. Hollingdale (Cambridge 1983), p. 137.

places in the edifices of great philosophies where scholarly for and against, where brooding, doubting, contracting are permitted, and that they thereby elude the challenge of every great philosophy, which as a whole always says only: this is the picture of all life, and learn from it the meaning of your own life.[4]

While Nietzsche was directing his attention towards this poetic notion of life, the same term stood both explicitly and implicitly at the very centre of Darwin's preoccupation with a theory which would explain the living world in terms of biological sciences. The complex of biological, evolutional and social factors which forms the main area of study of the Darwinians and evolutionists in general rests on an underlying principle that all causes of the living world are to be found in adaptation, change and satisfaction of needs. Nietzsche, standing for poetic truth, and Darwin, seeking truth in biological factors, signify the outer limits of the intellectual diversity of the second half of the nineteenth century. Across this broad span of intellectual themes and pursuits music repeatedly appears either as an area worthy of concentrated study or as a touchstone against which some general theories are to be tried. Physics, psychology and history are often being harnessed as aids in an attempt to define the essence of music – the very notion of 'essence' depending on the basis of the investigator's approach. It is both ironic and inevitable that the more the answer to the question of what music is slips through the net of general philosophical theories, the more a systematic study of music comes into its own. The roots of modern musicology are thus to be found in the philosophical and critical theories of the last third of the nineteenth century. In his *Ästhetik*, written during the Second World War and published posthumously, Nicolai Hartmann (1882–1950), possibly the last of the systematic philosophers of the German mould, wrote that it is the fate of aesthetics that it should disappoint.[5] Many of the writings contained in this volume, including excerpts from some of Nietzsche's 'quarter-philosophers', bear witness both to that disappointment and to various persistent efforts to overcome it.

[4] Nietzsche, 'Schopenhauer', p. 141.
[5] 'Es ist das Schicksal der Ästhetik dass sie enttäuschen muss.' Nicolai Hartmann, *Ästhetik* (Berlin 1953), p. 450.

# Part 1: German aesthetics of music in the second half of the nineteenth century

# 1.1   Music as an autonomous being

## Introduction

In his anthology of texts dealing with the aesthetics of music entitled *Musik-Ästhetik in ihren Hauptrichtungen*,[1] Felix Gatz introduced a firm division of aesthetic writings into two groups according to the basic criterion of whether an author believes that music does or does not possess the power to express the emotions. Such a rigid division is unadvisable as a system, but the two groups may be cautiously accepted as a scheme which could help to organize an anthology.

As all rigid divisions, the grouping of philosophical theories into two opposing camps of the aesthetics of content and the aesthetics of form does not reckon with the possibility of a considered critical approach beyond the boundaries of dogmatism. Yet, and in a seeming contradiction with the caveat expressed above, division into groups is not only useful but seems to stem from the nature of the speculation. Music seemed to have allowed even the ancient Greek philosophers only two possible paths of approach. One was taken by all those who, following Plato and Aristotle, saw in music a vehicle for the transmission of an ethical content, and the other who, like the Epicureans and particularly Philodem of Gadara assumed a sceptical position. In the early phase of German classical philosophy Kant, without reviewing the implications of the ancient division, and given the fundamental aim of his evaluation of art forms, recognized the poor use of music in a system which is founded on the premiss that the arts have a cognitive role. Music, because of the vagueness of the concepts which may be detected in it, is simply not able to fulfil the task and the lowly position assigned to it among the arts is not a criticism of music as such but the criticism of music as far as its intentionality is concerned. Both Hegel and Schopenhauer rejected this highly critical attitude of Kant's and by affirming the cognitive role of music came close to the romantic notion of vagueness as a virtue, instead of seeing it as a fault which for Kant with his rationalistic background was an inevitable conclusion. J. F. Herbart was the only philosopher of the early nineteenth century who was able to free himself from both the romantic infatuation with vagueness and from the Kantian cognitive position. His insistence on relationships as the constitutive elements of art made him an exception among the philosophers of his age and thus limited the attraction of his rationalist philosophy. Those who did take notice of Herbart's critical and reductionist

[1] Felix M. Gatz, *Musik-Ästhetik in ihren Hauptrichtungen* (Stuttgart 1929), pp. 11–13.

7

thought were certainly in the minority and are, like Eduard Hanslick, nowadays mainly seen as the belligerents in the Wagnerian controversy. Although Wagner may have been a useful goal against which to direct some of the polemical fire, it could be argued that the position taken by Hanslick would have been expressed in very much the same conceptual frame had the figure of Wagner not been there. The fundamental nature of Hanslick's writing consists not so much in his Herbartian inspiration as in his recognition of the specific nature of aesthetic inquiry. He drew on Kant, but by not insisting on the cognitive aspect of music or of art in general, understood the position of aesthetics as a unique philosophical discipline which investigates the nature of art once Occam's razor has been applied to remove the categories of emotion or morality. These may be important, and may have been seen by Hanslick to be important in a general or historical sense, but not in the sense in which he wanted to explore the specific quality which determines music *qua* art. As he was not a professional philosopher his advantage was precisely in that he was free from the limitations of a dogma or an established school. He was a Herbartian with a sense of history and a genuine understanding of the process of artistic creativity.

The dedicatee of several of the editions of Hanslick's *Vom Musikalisch-Schönen*, Robert Zimmermann comes much closer to one's idea of a dry and pedantic nineteenth-century German philosopher. Yet even he declines for himself the name of a formalist (see below, p. 48). The issue which was obviously close to the heart of both of these men was a clear statement of the unique position of music as an art form in which the organization of the material is the supreme challenge, or indeed, the only challenge for a composer. One art should not be judged according to the standards of another nor should critical tools be transferred from one art to another. This is a simplification of much of what Hanslick was concerned with but it is precisely the quality of his writing that prevented his treatise from becoming dated. His ideas reappear later as the foundation of the argument in the writings of Busoni, Schoenberg and Stravinsky.

Hanslick is often uncritically labelled as a formalist and the label is used to imply a certain insensitivity to art, or a simplification of a complex interplay of psychological motivation of the creator and the specific nature of the artistic material so that only a bare structural shell is understood as being important to the critical observer. This is mainly due to an incomplete understanding of the link between Hanslick's and Herbart's thought and a failure to recognize that there is a divide between Hanslick's intellectual position and the position taken by some of the more ardent disciples of Herbart, among whom Zimmermann occupies a prominent position.

Herbart's philosophy of art was formed in opposition to the emotionalist climate of his time. Art which is seen as an expression of a given content or a mental state must necessarily become only a transitional phase on the way to something which lies beyond art. This, in spite of the depth of understanding with which the case is presented, is the background to Hegel's view of art as a transitional phase of the manifestation of the Spirit, and in a different context is to be detected in Schopenhauer's relationship between art and the concept of the will. Herbart attempted to show that the importance of the art and the greatness of artworks lie ultimately within the domain of the art itself. It was A. G. Baumgarten's notion that art has a cognitive function and is thus a form of imitation. Thus aesthetics, dealing with art, which allows for a fanciful alteration of external stimuli, and is not clearly reducible to concepts, becomes identified as an inferior type of cognitive capacity (*gnoseologia inferior*, as he called it in the opening sentence of his *Aesthetica* of 1752). Herbart rejected the notion of any imitation and denied that any aesthetic theory could be constructed to accommodate the principle of imitation.[2] Instead, he turned his attention to the internal structuring of the artwork. As the emotionalist notion of a 'content' as a hidden substance to which an artwork ultimately leads only helps to underline the division between the 'content' and the structure, or the 'form', Herbart's continued acceptance of the division created a polarity between the concepts and this polarity was inherited, and held on to with some rigidity, by his disciples. The problem rests with the definition of the concept of 'content'. Herbart was quite right to insist on limiting, or indeed denying the importance of a content which is merely the presentation of a 'story', but by denying the importance he did not at the same time deny the possibility of the presentation of such content thus unwittingly aiding his opponents to go on maintaining the division. The beginnings of a schematized form—content opposition may be noticed in his writings and are then stressed in the work of his followers, who, battling against the content seemed to be on the point of excluding the specifically artistic content of an artwork, as opposed to its merely presentational, narrative level. Robert Zimmermann is usually taken to be the most characteristic Herbartian, demonstrating as he does in his work the rigidity which is, to an extent, shown in the way in which his text is organized. The division into numbered paragraphs, which he took over from Herbart (and ultimately from Kant), aspires to scientific exactness and may be seen as an illustration of that enthusiasm for the scientific method which characterized the thought of the second half of the century. On the other hand, the division demonstrates the rigid understanding of form as building bricks, or available shapes, which can be detected from his argument in paragraphs 73 and 651 of his *Allgemeine Aesthetik als Formwissenschaft* (see below, pp. 42 and 46).

Even a cursory glance at Hanslick's treatise reveals a much finer perception of the relationship between form and content. For Herbartians content becomes almost a necessary evil which somehow has to be tolerated, while the attention is directed towards the form: the two categories are kept separate. Hanslick adopts an analytical, almost phenomenological method in order to define different aspects of the term 'content'. The first two chapters of his treatise are devoted mainly to the process of exclusion of those aspects

[2] J. F. Herbart, *Kurze Encyclopädie der Philosophie* (1831), in *Sämtliche Werke*, vol. 9 (Langensalza 1897), p. 108.

of the term which are inapplicable in music, so that in the rest of the text he is free to use the term in that specific sense in which he feels it ought to be used in music. Since Hanslick does not understand the form as a rigid system of immutable factors, but rather as a system of changing relations which have to be perceived in their total complexity, form in music becomes an organism, which, understood by the sense of hearing leaves an impact on the mind. The mind thus becomes aware of the specifically musical aspect of music, its content. Hanslick does not despise the sensuous element in music, and does not deny its value precisely since he attaches no cognitive function to music. The form with its internal relationships excludes the need for any conceptual layer and leads directly to the spirit which forms itself from within (see below, p. 20). It is interesting to observe that, however much he set himself against Hegel, Hanslick unwittingly makes use of Hegel's notion that a concept may change its substance by being elevated onto a different level of meaning. The shallow concept of 'content' is thus seen gaining in depth when understood as a specifically musical spiritual quality emanating from the form as a living and active agent, rather than a passive structure. Hanslick's greatness lies in the extraordinary ability with which he was able to understand aesthetic currents of his time and rid the aesthetics of music of peripheral and unimportant issues. For these reasons it is one of the seminal texts in the aesthetics of music and this explains why it has been allowed such generous space in this volume.

# Eduard Hanslick (1825–1904)

## Vom Musikalisch-Schönen (1854)

Hanslick was born in Prague of German-speaking parents and received his musical education there as a pupil of V. Tomašek. Following a common pattern in the Austrian Empire he opted for a respectable legal career and studied law in Prague and Vienna. In 1849 he joined the civil service and, apart from a spell in Klagenfurt in 1850–2, spent the rest of his life in Vienna. He started writing music criticism while a student in Prague and continued to do so in Vienna, becoming in 1855 the music critic of the influential *Presse* (later re-named *Neue freie Presse*). In 1856 he became a *Privatdozent* at the University lecturing on the aesthetics and history of music and in 1861 was made a full professor. It was only then that he retired from the civil service thus breaking the pattern of hectic and curiously disparate everyday activity: he himself described his days as having been divided between the ministry in the morning, lectures at the University in the afternoon and the opera or concerts in the evening.

In his youth Hanslick showed an open and inquisitive mind. He admired the philosopher Herbart and the Herbartian link was strengthened through his friendship with Herbart's pupil Robert Zimmermann. However, he was also interested in the Hegelian ideas of F. T. Vischer. Together with A. W. Ambros, nine years his senior, he was in his early years influenced by Schumann's *Neue Zeitschrift für Musik* and admired Wagner. Later his consistently autonomist stance in aesthetics distanced him from Ambros and made him an opponent of Wagner, who was largely responsible for creating the image of Hanslick as a conservative 'formalist'. After the early *Vom Musikalisch-Schönen* Hanslick did not publish another extended theoretical work, concentrating entirely on reviews and shorter essays. It was through these that he became established as one of the foremost music critics in the German-speaking world during the second half of the nineteenth century.

## On the musically beautiful

### Source:

*Vom Musikalisch-Schönen. Ein Beitrag zur Revision der Aesthetik der Tonkunst*, 8th edn (Leipzig 1891). Chapter i Die Gefühlsästhetik, pp. 1–19; chapter iii Das Musikalisch-Schöne, pp. 72–116; chapter vii Die Begriffe 'Inhalt' und 'Form' in der Musik, pp. 203–21. Translated by Martin Cooper.

*Vom Musikalisch-Schönen* was first published in 1854 and by the end of the century went through eight more editions. Hanslick revised the main text, in some cases substantially, for the second edition (1858), and continued to add and expand footnotes in subsequent editions. Our text follows in the main the eighth edition, but takes into account some of the important features of the first edition. Some of the later added footnotes are merely anecdotal or quote at length from Hanslick's and other people's writings, and have been omitted whenever they are not closely tied to the argument of the main text.

*For further reading:*

The complete text of the treatise under the title *The Beautiful in Music*, tr. Gustav Cohen (1891, reprinted Indianapolis and New York 1957), though unreliable in many details, cannot be ignored. See also bibliography under Glatt and Abegg.

## Chapter I: The aesthetics of feeling

Up to now the treatment of musical aesthetics has suffered from a subtle misconception of its true concern, which has been represented as being with describing the feelings aroused by music rather than with scrutinizing the nature of what we mean by 'beauty' in music. Such enquiries correspond exactly with those earlier systems of aesthetics which considered beauty only in relation to the feelings that it arouses in us; and that of course gave the philosophy of beauty its name as a daughter of feeling (*aisthesis*).

Not only are such theories of aesthetics essentially unphilosophical, but when applied to the most ethereal of the arts they introduce a downright sentimental note, that may well be found comforting by tender hearts but provides the enquiring mind with very little illumination. Those who wish to understand the nature of music want precisely to escape from the dark realm of feeling and not constantly to be referred back to it, as happens in most reference works.

The search for a maximum objectivity in our understanding of the world which marks all departments of knowledge today, cannot fail to make itself felt in the investigation of beauty. This investigation can only hope to succeed if it abandons a method which starts from subjective feeling and returns – after a poetical tour round the outlying areas of the subject – once again to feeling. If it is not to be entirely illusory, it will have to approach as nearly as possible the method of the natural sciences: that is to say, it must try to grasp the object of enquiry in its essence and determine its objective, unchanging nature apart from the myriad changing impressions that we receive from it.

Poetry and the visual arts are far ahead of music in this matter of aesthetic investigation. Scholars in those fields have for the most part rid themselves of the illusion that it is possible to base the aesthetics of any art on a mere adaptation of a general metaphysical concept of beauty, since each art is distinguished by a set of individual features. This slavish dependence of each art's aesthetic on the overruling metaphysical principles of a general aesthetic theory is increasingly yielding to the conviction that every art must be known through its own technical definitions and understood by itself. 'System' is gradually being replaced by 'investigation', which is based on the principle that the aesthetic rules governing each art are inseparable from the individual characteristics of the material of that art and its technique.[1]

The aesthetics of literature and the visual arts, and their practical branches, the criticism of the arts, already adhere to the rule that in aesthetic enquiries the matter of investigation is the object itself and not the subjective feelings that it arouses.

Only music seems not as yet to have been able to achieve this objective attitude, and there is a firm distinction made between the rules of musical theory and grammar on the one hand and aesthetic enquiry on the other – the former stated as dryly and intelligibly as possible, while the latter goes to the opposite extreme of lyrical sentimentality. It seems to have been an insurmountable effort for the aesthetics of music to define its content clearly as an independent species of beauty. Instead of this the 'emotions' raise their old spectre in broad daylight. Beauty in music continues to be regarded from the angle of the subjective listener, and in books, criticisms and conversation insistence is laid on the emotions as being the only aesthetic basis of music and the only criterion for determining the scope of musical judgements.

Music, we are assured, cannot, like poetry, engage the intelligence by means of concepts or the eye by visible forms, as do the visual arts; and its task must therefore be to effect men's feelings. 'Music has to do with the feelings' – and this 'having to do' is one of the expressions most typical of musical aesthetics up to our own time. Those who use such expressions leave us entirely in the dark as to the actual connection between music and feeling, between individual works and individual emotions, the laws governing this connection and its operation. One must accustom one's eyes somewhat to this darkness before one can succeed in discovering that in the prevailing system of musical aesthetics feelings play a double role.

In the first place the purpose and intention of music is said to be to arouse feelings, or 'beautiful feelings'. In the second, feelings are designated as the content which music represents. The similarity between these two statements lies in the fact that the one is as false as the other. To disprove the first (generally the opening sentence in any musical reference work) need not

---

[1] R. Schumann has caused a lot of trouble by his observation (*Collected Works*, vol. 1, p. 43) that 'the aesthetics of one art is the same as that of another, only in a different medium'. Grillparzer's opinion is very different and much nearer the truth (*Collected Works*, vol. 9, p. 142): 'The greatest disservice that could be done to the arts in Germany was to lump them all together under the name "art". No doubt there are of course many points of contact between them, but the means they employ are different in innumerable instances, and so are the basic conditions in their execution. A striking example of the fundamental difference between music and poetry is the fact that the effect of music springs from a delight of the senses, a complex nervous phenomenon; and, once the feelings are roused, it is only at most in the very last instance that the spirit is touched. In poetry on the other hand feelings are only aroused by ideas and the senses only participate in the very highest – or the very lowest – instance. Each art, therefore, is the obverse of the other in its method of working. The one represents the spiritualization of the physical, the other the embodying of the spiritual.'

detain us long. Beauty has absolutely no purpose, being pure form, which can be put to the most diverse purposes according to the content with which it is filled but has in fact no other purpose but itself. If pleasant feelings are prompted in the beholder by the contemplation of beauty, this as such does not concern beauty. I can, of course, show the beholder a beautiful object with the definite intent of giving him pleasure, but this intention has nothing whatever to do with the beauty of the object. Beauty is and remains beauti-ful even if it arouses no feelings, indeed if it is neither seen nor contemplated – that is to say, only for the delight of the beholder, not on account of that delight. There can therefore be no talk of a purpose in this sense, when speaking of music, and the fact that this art has a lively connection with our feelings in no way justifies the assertion that its aesthetic significance resides in this connection. In order to scrutinize this relationship we must first make a clear distinction between the concepts of 'feelings' and 'sense-perceptions', often innocently confused in everyday speech.

Sense-perception is the perceiving of a particular sense-quality: a musical note, a colour. Feeling is the consciousness of a positive (heightening) or negative (lowering) change in our emotional state, something that is either pleasant or unpleasant, that is to say, if I observe the smell or taste of an object with my senses, then I feel them, if sorrow, hope, good humour or hatred either raise or depress my normal emotional state, then I feel.[2]

Beauty first strikes our senses. This is not a unique peculiarity of beauty, but one common to all phenomena. Sense-perception is the origin and con-dition of aesthetic pleasure and forms the first basis of feeling, which always presupposes a relationship, and often a most complex set of relationships. There is no need of art to originate sense-perceptions: a single note, a single colour can do as much. As has been observed, the two terms are arbitrarily confused, but for the most part older writers call sense-perception what we mean by feeling. So it is our feelings, according to these writers, that music should stir, filling us in succession with devotion, love, exultation and sor-row. In fact, however, such is not the end of this or any other art. The first concern of art is to represent the beautiful. The organ with which we register beauty is not feeling but imagination, in the activity of pure 'beholding' or 'contemplation'.[3]

It is an interesting fact that musicians and aestheticians of the old school in general only concern themselves with the contrast between feelings and intelligence, as though it were not precisely in the middle of this apparent

[2] Earlier philosophers agree with modern psychologists in this specification of ideas, and we must unquestionably prefer these to the terms used by the Hegelian school, which of course distinguishes interior and exterior impressions [Empfindungen].

[3] Hegel has shown how the investigation of impressions (or, in our terminology, 'feelings') aroused by an art remains vague and indeed actually refuses to consider the concrete content. 'What is felt', he says, 'remains enveloped in the form of the most abstract individual subjectivity, and therefore differences between feelings are also completely abstract, not differences in the thing itself.' (Ästhetik, vol. 1, p. 42). [The passage is quoted here as translated by T. M. Knox in G. W. F. Hegel, Aesthetics, Lectures on Fine Art, vol. 1 (Oxford 1975), p. 32.]

dilemma that the heart of the matter lay. A piece of music arises out of the artist's imagination and directs itself to the imagination of the listener. Of course imagination in the presence of a beautiful object is not simply a matter of beholding but of intelligent beholding i.e. presentation and judgement the latter reached, naturally, with such speed that we are not conscious of the isolated steps by which we come to our conclusions, and have the illusion of immediacy, whereas in fact there are many mediating mental processes. The word 'contemplation' [*Anschauung*], which has long been transferred from the visual to the other sense-phenomena, corresponds perfectly to the act of attentive hearing which in fact consists in a successive contemplation of musical forms. In this, imagination is by no means a closed field; for just as the imagination drew its vital spark from sense impressions, so in its turn it swiftly imparts its rays to the activity of the intelligence and the feelings. These are still only frontier areas for the true apprehension of beauty.

In pure contemplation the listener enjoys the sonorities of a musical composition, every material interest must be forgotten. Among these, however, is the tendency to allow the feelings to be stirred. An exclusively intellectual response to beauty is a logical rather than an aesthetic relationship, while a predominantly emotional response is even more questionable, in fact definitely pathological.

All that the development of general aesthetic theory has established in the past is equally true of beauty in all the arts. If music, therefore, is to be treated as art, the imagination rather than the feelings must be recognized as the aesthetic court of appeal concerned. This modest premise seems to us advisable in view of the weighty emphasis that is perpetually laid on the role of music as a soother of human passions, with the result that it is often difficult to decide whether music is being discussed for its value to the police, the pedagogues or the medical profession.

Musicians themselves, however, are less prone to the mistake of making all the arts dependent on the feelings, since they regard this rather as something specifically true of music. In fact they believe that what distinguishes music from the other arts is precisely this power and tendency to arouse emotions of all kinds in the listener.[4]

Little, however, as we have acknowledged this effect to be the object of the arts in general, we cannot to any greater degree see in it the specific nature of music either. If it is once established that the imagination is the faculty actually concerned with beauty, then in every art we shall find a secondary effect on the feelings. Does not a great historical painting stir us as strongly as an actual event? Do not Raphael's madonnas move us to religious devotion and Poussin's landscapes to a nostalgia for travel? Does the cathedral of

---

[4] If 'feelings' are not even distinguished from 'impressions' there can be no question of making more accurate distinctions among 'feelings' themselves: sensuous and intellectual feelings, their chronic form as 'mood', their acute form as 'emotions', inclination, passion and the individual nuances of the Greek 'pathos' and the later Latin *passio*. All these have been levelled down to become roughly equivalent, and it has become customary to say of music simply that it is *par excellence* the art of stirring the feelings.

Strasburg, say, really have no effect on our state of mind? There can be no doubt of the answer, which is equally valid in the case of poetry, and indeed of a number of activities beside the aesthetic e.g. religious edification, oratory etc. We can see that the other arts affect the feelings with similar force. Ostensibly, therefore, the chief difference between music and the other arts must be sought in the degree of this secondary effect. Such a solution, which is in itself quite unscientific, would imply that it depends entirely on the individual whether stronger and deeper feelings are aroused in them by a Mozart symphony or a Shakespeare tragedy, a poem by Uhland or a rondo by Hummel. If on the other hand one is of the opinion that music acts 'directly' on the feelings, whereas the other arts act through the agency of concepts, we are only acknowledging defeat in other terms; for, as we have seen, beauty in music appeals primarily to the imagination and only secondarily to the feelings. Writers on music repeatedly draw on the analogy, which is indeed very real, between music and architecture. Yet has it ever entered the head of an intelligent architect to suppose that the object of architecture was to arouse feelings, or that feelings constituted the content of architecture?

Every true work of art will establish some kind of relationship with our feelings, but in no case will that relationship be an exclusive one. In fact no general characterization of music by its effect on the feelings tells us anything decisive about the aesthetic principles of the art – any more, indeed, than the man who gets drunk establishes anything about the nature of wine. The whole question lies in the specific manner in which music arouses our feelings. We must therefore turn our attention away from the vague, secondary effect of musical phenomena on our feelings and penetrate further into the nature of music in order to explain the specific power of the impressions that it makes, in terms of the inherent laws of the art. There can hardly be a painter or a poet who still believes that he has given a satisfactory account of the beauty of his art by examining the 'feelings' aroused by his landscape or his play: he will rather try to discover the compelling power that accounts for the popularity of a work and the exact nature of its appeal. That this enquiry, as we shall see later, is far more difficult in the case of music than in that of the other arts – and is indeed only feasible to a certain degree – is no kind of justification for those critics who directly confound the stirring of the feelings and musical beauty, instead of keeping the two as separate as possible according to the methods of science.

If the feelings can in general be said to provide no foundation for the laws of aesthetics, there are still further weighty objections to the dependability of musical feeling. We are not concerned here simply with the conventional bias to which our feelings and imagination are often subjected by texts, titles and other purely fortuitous associations – particularly in ecclesiastical, martial and dramatic music – which we often mistakenly attribute to the music itself. It is rather that, generally speaking, the connection between a musical composition and the feelings that it arouses is not essentially a causal one, but these feelings vary according to the nature of the listener's musical experience and impressions. We are often at a loss to understand how our grandparents could regard some individual succession of notes as the expression of a given emotional state. There is an excellent example of this in the extraordinary difference between the emotional effect of many works by Mozart, Beethoven, and Weber on their contemporaries and on listeners today. How many works of Mozart's were declared, when they first appeared, to be the boldest, most ardent and impassioned expressions of feeling that it was possible to conceive! It was common to contrast the sense of comfort and sheer well-being radiated by Haydn's symphonies with the violent explosions of passion, the mortal struggles and the bitter, agonizing grief in Mozart's music. Twenty or thirty years later one had to decide in the same manner between Beethoven and Mozart.[5] Beethoven succeeded Mozart as the representative of violent, overwhelming passion, and Mozart was promoted to the same classical heights as Haydn. Any observant musician will register over the years similar changes of attitude in himself. Yet this difference in emotional effect does not, in itself, have the smallest effect on our musical evaluation of these works which were once found so exciting, or on the aesthetic delight still caused by their beauty and originality. The association of individual musical works with individual emotional states is therefore in no way universal, essential or absolutely compelling, but is in fact incomparably more variable than in the case of any other art.

The effect of music on the feelings, therefore, has neither the necessity, the exclusiveness nor the immutability characteristic of any phenomenon which can form the basis of an aesthetic principle.

It is not that we should in any sense underrate these strong feelings which the sound of music arouses from their slumber, all those tender or painful moods into which she lulls us between sleep and waking. This power of art to cause such stirrings without any earthly cause, but directly by the grace of God is one of the most beautiful and beneficial of mysteries. It is only against the unscientific exploitation of these feelings as aesthetic principles that we must be on our guard. Pleasure and pain can be roused, in the highest degree, by music; that is certainly true. Not perhaps to a still higher degree by winning a lottery or by the mortal illness of a friend? If one refuses to accept this as a reason for classing a lottery-ticket with the symphonies and a medical bulletin with the overtures, one must also refuse to accept feelings aroused by facts as a specific aesthetic quality of music in general or of an individual composition. It all depends upon the specific manner in which music arouses such feelings. In chapters 4 and 5 we shall pay special attention to the manner in which music affects the feelings and shall examine the positive aspects of this remarkable relationship. Here, at the beginning of our

---

[5] There are especially some sayings by Rochlitz about Mozart's instrumental music, which today sound rather strange. This same Rochlitz describes the graceful Menuetto capriccio from Weber's Sonata in A flat as an 'uninterrupted, gushing outpouring of a passionate and violently excited soul, and yet held together by miraculous steadfastness'.

study, it is the negative aspect – the protest against an unscientific principle –
that cannot be too strongly emphasized.

To the best of my knowledge Herbart was the first person to attack this
'aesthetic of feeling' in chapter 9 of his encyclopaedia. After declaring war on
the far-fetched 'interpretation' of music he continues

Astrologers and interpreters of dreams have for thousands of years refused to recognize that a person dreams because he sleeps and that the constellations appear now in
one position and now in another because they are in motion. So it is that even
knowledgeable musicians still argue as though the basis of music were not the
universal laws of simple or double counterpoint, but the emotions that music may well
arouse, and for the expression of which, should the composer so wish, it may hence be
employed. What was it that those artists of ancient time strove to express when they
explored the potential of fugue, or, again, those of still remoter times when, by their
skill, they created the various architectural orders? They did not wish to express
anything at all; their ideas were limited to an investigation of the art itself. But those
who rely on interpretations betray their distrust of man's inner nature and a preference for outward appearances.[6]

Unfortunately Herbart does not go into any closer detail when he makes this
timely protest; and side by side with these brilliant observations there are a
number of others which reveal an incorrect understanding of music. However
that may be, we shall soon see that his words as quoted above never received
the attention which was their due. [pp. 1–19]


## Chapter III: The musically beautiful

Hitherto our approach to the subject has been negative: we have simply
sought to counter the assumption that beauty in music can consist in the
representation of feelings. It is now our duty to give a positive content to our
scheme by answering the question 'what is the nature of beauty in music?' It is
something specifically musical – by which we mean a beauty that lies entirely
in musical sounds and their artistic arrangement, something independent of
any exterior content. Individually pleasing sounds in significant relationships
to each other, in harmonic concord and contrast, in flight and pursuit,
alternatively swelling and dying away – these, presented to our imaginations
in free-moving shapes, delight us by what we call their beauty. The basic
element of music is euphony, its essence is rhythm: both rhythm in general, as
the correspondence of parts in a symmetrical structure, and rhythm in particular, as the changing motions of individual elements of the tempo of a
work. It is not possible to imagine the wealth of the material at the composer's
disposition, for it consists of nothing less than all the notes of the gamut with
their inherent melodic, harmonic and rhythmic potentialities. The primary
and fundamental form of musical beauty, namely melody, has never been
exhausted and is in fact inexhaustible. Harmony with its myriad transforma-

---

[6] [ J. F. Herbart, *Kurze Encyclopädie der Philosophie aus praktischen Gesichtspunkten
entworfen* (1831). Quoted here as translated in le Huray and Day, p. 454.]

tions, reversals and re-enforcements offers perpetually new patterns, while the two combined are set in motion by rhythm, the pulse of musical life, and coloured by the charm of countless different timbres.

To the question, what is musical material supposed to express? the simple answer is musical ideas. A fully realized musical idea is already something absolutely beautiful and self-sufficient, neither a means nor a material for the representation of feelings or thoughts. The content and object of music consist of forms set in motion by sounding.[1] How music can present beautiful forms without any emotional content may be suggested by an analogy with the visual arts – that branch of ornamentation known as the arabesque – a pattern of lines first gently falling and then boldly rising, meeting and separating, forming large and small curves balancing each other, apparently disproportionate but in fact always well articulated, a collection of details and yet a whole. Now imagine an arabesque that is not lifeless and static, but perpetually renewing itself before our eyes. How the light and the heavy lines seem to pursue each other, how they rise from a small curve to a towering height, then sink again, grow broader, join together and ceaselessly surprise the eye by the meaningful alternation of tension and repose! Thus the design grows steadily in stature and nobility. If we clearly picture such a living arabesque as the active production of an artistic imagination, ceaselessly transfusing its whole wealth into the veins of this organism – shall we not in fact discover something not wholly unlike music in the impression it makes on us?

All of us must, as children, have enjoyed the play of shifting shapes and colours in a kaleidoscope, and music is just such a process on an infinitely higher, ideal plane. Like the kaleidoscope, music also presents us with a ceaselessly unfolding procession of beautiful shapes and colours, with delicate transitions and sharp contrasts, always self-consistent yet always new, wholly independent and self-renewing. The chief difference lies in the fact that this kaleidoscope of sounds presents itself to the ear as the direct production of a creative imagination, whereas the ordinary kaleidoscope is simply an ingenious mechanical toy. It is the attempt to achieve the step from colours to music not simply in the imagination but in reality – and thus to apply the means of one art to the effects of another – that leads to such trivial absurdities as the 'colour-keyboard' [*Farbenklavier*] or the 'eye-organ' [*Au-*

---

[1] [The original German sentence reads: 'Der Inhalt der Musik sind tönend bewegte Formen' and its full implications are difficult to realize in an English translation. In the first edition of the treatise, published in 1854, the sentence was slightly different and longer ('Tönend bewegte Formen sind einzig und allein Inhalt und Gegenstand der Musik.') and the one preceding it contained a clause which was subsequently deleted. The passage thus read originally: 'A musical idea, completely demonstrated, needs nothing more to be beautiful; it is its own purpose and not at all merely further means and material for representing emotions and thoughts; yet at the same time music can possess that symbolic significance, mirroring grand cosmic laws, which we find in everything artistically beautiful, and in just as high a degree. Forms moved in sounding are the sole and single content and object of music.' The English translation of the passage is quoted here as it appears in C. Dahlhaus, *Esthetics of Music*, tr. W. Austin (Cambridge 1982), p. 32.]

*genorgel*] – inventions which nevertheless demonstrate the basic formal similarity of the two phenomena.

Sentimental music-lovers may find such analogies damaging to music, but the question is surely whether the analogy is correct or not. Nothing can be damaged by being better understood. It is the characteristic of movement, of development in time, that presents the chief analogy between music and the kaleidoscope. If we leave that aside, a higher analogy with beauty in music can be found in architecture, in the human body, or in landscape – all of which present a fundamental beauty of outlines and colours, quite apart from any spiritual expression, from the 'soul'.

It is the undervaluation of the sensuous nature of musical beauty that is largely responsible for its misunderstanding. Aestheticians in the past have preferred moral and emotional considerations, or what Hegel speaks of as the 'idea'. Each of the arts is rooted in the senses which are the natural element of all art. The 'aesthetics of feeling' fails to take this into account, passing over 'hearing' and speaking directly of 'feeling', as though music were meant for the heart and the ear were something beneath their notice.

Of course when we speak of 'the ear', Beethoven certainly did not compose for the membrane of the tympanum or the aural labyrinth. But the action of the imagination on our aural perceptions is something quite different from that of a mere sieving of superficial phenomena: it experiences a conscious sensuous delight in sound-patterns and tonal structures, which it contemplates in a manner which is both immediate and uninhibited.

To give a picture of this self-consistent beauty, this specifically musical character of beauty in music, is exceptionally difficult. Since music does not copy anything in the natural world and has no conceptual content, we can speak of it only in one of two ways – in dry technical terms or in poetic metaphors. It can indeed truly be said that the kingdom of music is 'not of this world'. All the fanciful descriptions, characterizations or paraphrases of a musical composition are either figurative or misconceived. What is in every other art 'description' is in music no more than metaphor. Music must in fact be grasped simply as music and can only be understood in its own terms and only enjoyed in its own way.

This 'specifically musical' character is by no means to be understood simply as acoustical beauty or symmetry of proportions: these are subsidiary elements which it includes. Still less can there be any question of 'ear-titillating plays of sound' or similar phrases commonly used to emphasize an absence of spiritual engagement. Our examination of music does not exclude spiritual content, but rather seeks to determine the conditions. We do not in fact recognize any such thing as a beauty devoid of all spiritual content. But by regarding beauty in music as essentially a matter of forms we have already adumbrated a very close connection between those forms and a spiritual content. The concept of form has a unique realization in music. Forms created by musical sounds are not empty but filled, no mere linear outlines describing a vacuum but the appearance of the spirit being shaped from within. Compared with the arabesque, therefore, music is in fact a picture, but a picture of something that cannot be described in words or subordinated to our concepts. There is sense and coherence in music, but it is musical sense and musical coherence; music is a language that we can speak and understand but are unable to translate. There is a profound recognition of this in the fact that we speak of musical 'thoughts' and that a trained judge can easily distinguish between genuine 'thoughts' from mere verbiage. In the same way we recognize the rational separateness of a group of notes when we speak of a 'phrase'. In fact we feel exactly the same as we feel at the end of a logical period, where the meaning demands a break, although it is impossible to compare the 'veracity' of the two.

The intellectual satisfaction that is the very essence of some musical constructions is founded on certain primitive laws which nature has implanted in the human mechanism and in the external phenomena of sound. The basic principle of 'harmonic progression', which may be compared to the circle in the visual arts, is the most noteworthy source of musical development and provides the explanation (though itself, unfortunately, still unexplained) of the different musical relationships.

All the elements of music are related to each other by connections or 'elective affinities', which may be mysterious but are none the less founded on natural laws. These elective affinities exercising an invisible power over rhythm, melody and harmony must necessarily be observed in human music, and any ignoring of this necessity is felt to be arbitrary and ugly. Such ignoring is instinctively recognized – though not necessarily consciously and scientifically by every trained listener, who has only to listen to a group of notes to know whether it is organic and intelligent or self-contradictory and unnatural. No recourse need be had to any logical concept as a criterion or to any *tertium comparationis*.[2]

This negative, internal rationality is assured to the tonal system by natural laws and is the foundation of that system's ability to admit of a positive 'beauty content'.

Composition is a mental activity in material that lends itself to such an exercise. The material of music is, as we have seen, itself rich and in the same way it reveals itself as malleable and penetrable by the artistic imagination. The composer does not build, like the architect, out of rough, resistant stone but out of the effect of musical notes which have already sounded. No other art is constructed of such delicate, immaterial elements as these sounds, which seem to offer themselves to every idea the composer may wish to

---

[2] 'Poetry may up to a point freely use the ugly (unbeautiful). Since the effect of poetry reaches the feelings only through the concepts which it raises, the representation of the purposefullness will dampen the impact of the ugly (unbeautiful) to such an extent that as a stimulus or a contrast it may bring a strong effect. The sense (of hearing) accepts and enjoys musical impressions without a mediator, and the approval of the intellect comes too late to smooth down the disturbance caused by what is displeasing. Hence Shakespeare could go as far as the hideous, while Mozart limits himself to the beautiful.' (Grillparzer, *Werke*, vol. 9, pp. 141–2.)

formulate. Since the series of notes, whose relationship to each other constitutes musical beauty, are not determined mechanically but by the free play of
the composer's imagination, it is the mental power and the individuality of
this imagination that gives a composition its character. As the creation of a
thinking and feeling mind a musical composition can itself, potentially,
communicate thought and feeling. We shall demand this spiritual content of
every work, but it cannot be traced to any source other than the musical
structures themselves. Our view of the position of spirit and feeling in a
composition bears the same relationship to that generally received as the
ideas of immanence and transcendence. The object of every art is to give
exterior expression to an idea born in the artist's imagination. In the case of
music this idea is itself musical and is not a conceptual notion which must be
translated into sound. The point of origin from which everything else in a
composition springs is not the intention to portray a given passion in musical
terms, but the invention of a melody. By means of that primitive and mysterious power, whose workings never have been – and never will be – plain to
the human eye, the composer's imagination conceives a theme, a motif.
Beyond the genesis of this cell it is impossible for us to extend our search: we
must simply accept it as a fact. Once it has appeared in the artist's imagination, he can set about his work;[3] and this has as its constant aim the
presentation of the original idea in all its relationships, making it the starting-
point of his creation and repeatedly referring to it. The beauty of a simple,
self-subsistent theme is perceived by the aesthetic faculty with an immediacy
that is inexplicable except, at best, by pointing to the essential inevitability of
the phenomenon and to the harmonious ordering of its component parts
without reference to any external factor. It delights us by itself in the same
way as an arabesque, a column or some natural feature, such as a leaf or a
flower.

Nothing is commoner or more mistaken than the distinction between
'beautiful music' with and without 'spiritual content', for it implies a far too
limited conception of beauty in music. By presenting artistically constructed
form and the 'soul' infused into it as two separate entities, this theory divided
musical compositions into full and empty champagne bottles. Musical champagne, on the other hand, has the property of growing with the bottle.

A given musical idea is in itself a phenomenon of the spirit or it is nothing. If
we take a final cadence, for instance, its dignity can be destroyed by changing
two notes. We are perfectly justified in calling a musical theme magnificent,
graceful, full of feeling, commonplace, trivial; but all such designations
describe the musical character of the passage. In order to denote the character
of the musical expression of a motif we often choose ideas drawn from our
own interior disposition such as 'proud, despondent, tender, bold, yearning'.

[3] [The original reads: 'Ist es einmal in die Phantasie des Künstlers gefallen, so beginnt
sein Schaffen . . .', and Hanslick suggests that the idea has literally 'descended' or
'fallen into' a composer's conscience as if from an already existing ideal sphere. Such
Pythagorean allusions can be found elsewhere in Hanslick's treatise. See above, p. 19,
n. 1, and below, p. 39.]

We can, however, select designations from quite different areas of experience and speak of music as 'scented, springlike, cloudy, frosty'. Our feelings are therefore only one set of phenomena that provides designations of musical character. One may employ epithets of this kind in full awareness of their metaphorical nature, and it is in fact impossible to avoid them. What we must guard against is saying 'this music portrays pride' etc.

A careful study of all the determining musical features of a theme will convince us that, although the final ontological foundations may be beyond our ken, there are still a number of proximate reasons closely connected with the spiritual expression of a musical work. Each element (i.e. every interval, every timbre, every chord, every rhythm etc.) has its own physiognomy, its own precise mode of affecting the listener. The artist may be unfathomable, but we can still fathom his creations.

A theme will sound quite different when played above a triad from what it sounds above a sixth chord. The interval of a seventh in a melodic line is quite different in character from that of a sixth. The specific colour of a motif will be changed by the loudness or softness and the individual timbre of the accompanying rhythm. In fact each individual factor necessarily contributes to the precise emotional effect of any passage on the listener. What makes Halévy's music strange or Auber's graceful, and how do we recognize a work as Mendelssohn's or Spohr's? The answers to these questions can be reduced to purely musical definitions without any recourse to those enigmatic 'feelings'. On the other hand, of course, neither psychology nor physiology can answer the question why Mendelssohn's frequent use of six-five chords and narrow-spaced diatonic themes, Spohr's preference for chromatic and enharmonic passages, Auber's short binary rhythms etc. each produce their own definite, unmistakable impression.

If however we go on to the next determining cause – which is the most important in artistic matters – the passionate effect of a theme does not arise from any extravagant grief that we are to imagine in the composer, but from the extravagant intervals in his music, not from the trembling of his soul but from the rolls of the timpani, not from his nostalgic yearnings but from the chromatic nature of his harmony. The connection between the two things should by no means be ignored, but rather examined more closely. What must be borne in mind, however, is the fact that the only firm, objective facts in the scientific examination of a theme's effect on the listener are these musical factors, and not the supposed mood of the composer at the time of writing. By arguing directly from such a mood to the effect of a work on the listener, or from the latter to the former, a conclusion may be reached that could conceivably be correct, but the most important middle term of the argument – namely the music itself – is passed over.

A practical knowledge of each musical element is the possession of every competent composer, whether consciously or instinctively. Even so, the scientific explanation of the various musical effects and impressions demands a theoretical knowledge of these factors, from the richest combinations down to the smallest element that can be distinguished. The definite impression by which a melody captivates us is not simply 'enigmatic, mysterious wonder' that we can only 'feel' and 'sense', but the inevitable consequence of musical factors which make their effect in this individual connection. A rhythm that is precise or free, progressions that are diatonic or chromatic – such things have their own characteristic physiognomy and their own particular appeal to the listener. For this reason a good musician will get a far clearer idea of an unfamiliar work by being told that it contains a lot of diminished sevenths and tremolando passages than by any description of the emotional crises that the music may have caused in his informant.

The thorough study of the nature of each single musical element and its connection with a distinct impression (of the fact, not its final cause) and the referring of these detailed observations to general laws – this would constitute the 'establishment of a philosophical basis for music' desired by so many authors, who at the same time fail to make clear to us exactly what they mean by the expression. The psychic and physical operation of any given chord, rhythm or interval is not explained by speaking of 'red', 'black', 'hope' or 'despair' but only by subsuming specific musical qualities under general aesthetic categories and these categories in turn under one overriding principle. Once each single factor has been explained in isolation, we should then have to proceed to show how each affects and determines the other in the most various combinations. Most musical experts grant harmony and contrapuntal accompaniment a leading part in determining the spiritual content of a composition, but this claim has been made in too superficial and disconnected a fashion. Melody has been represented as the inspiration of genius and as the sensuous and emotional agent in music, the Italians winning high marks in this field. As against this, harmony has been said to contribute vigour of content, something that can be learned and the product of conscious thought. It is curious that so jejune a system should have been regarded for so long as satisfactory. There is some truth in both assertions, but neither is generally valid nor can the two elements be isolated in this way. The power of invention is one and indivisible, and so too is the musical imagination of a composer. The melody and harmony of a theme spring simultaneously, and in the same armour plate from the composer's brain. Neither the law of subordination nor the law of contrast applies to the relationship of harmony to melody. Each can display in one passage a simultaneous power of development, while in another one may voluntarily play a secondary role to the other – in either case the highest spiritual beauty can be achieved. Can we really maintain that it is the harmony (actually nonexistent) that gives the main themes of Beethoven's *Coriolanus* and Mendelssohn's *Hebrides* overtures their expression of profound thoughtfulness? Would Rossini's air 'O Matilde!' or a Neapolitan folksong be more 'spiritual' if the bare harmonic skeleton were replaced by a basso continuo or a complex chord-sequence? No, each of these particular melodies was essentially conceived with its own specific harmonization, rhythm and timbre. The spiritual content is the product of the sum of all these features, and the maiming of one limb mars the effect of the others. If in any passage the chief interest lies in the melody, the harmony or the rhythm, it is in the interest of the passage as a whole, and it is pure pedantry to attribute all the 'spirit' of one passage to its chords and all triviality of another to their absence. Camellias have no scent and lilies no colour, while roses delight both senses – there can be no question of 'transferring' the characteristics of one to another; and yet each of the three is beautiful.

The first study needed to establish a 'philosophical basis for music' would therefore be to discover the exact spiritual characteristics necessarily connected with each element of music, and how they are associated. This double demand – for a strictly scientific framework and an extremely resourceful psychology – makes the task a formidable one, but its difficulties are by no means insurmountable. We should in fact be on the path towards the ideal of a science of music as 'exact' as chemistry or physiology.

The manner in which instrumental music is composed provides the most reliable insight into the specific nature of musical beauty. In the first place a musical idea occurs to the composer's imagination and he develops it – the process of crystallization continues until, almost unknown to him, he has the main outlines of the whole work before him and all that is needed is the process of realization in detail, with all its experimenting, calculating and correcting. The instrumental composer does not give a thought to the portraying of any definite content; or if he does, his attitude is mistaken and 'para-musical' rather than musical, in which case his work will be the translation into music of some programme unintelligible to those who do not possess the key. If in this connection we mention the name of Berlioz, it is not to misunderstand or to underestimate his brilliant gifts. Liszt followed his example with his much weaker 'symphonic poems'. Just as the same marble serves one sculptor for the creation of fascinating shapes and another for clumsy bunglings, so the same scale becomes in different hands either an overture by a Beethoven or one by a Verdi. Wherein lies the difference between the two? Is it that one portrays nobler feelings than the other? or that one portrays the same feelings with a greater truth of nature? No, it is neither; but simply that the musical shapes of the one are more beautiful than those of the other. It is only this that makes music 'good' or 'bad' – the fact that one composer starts with a brilliant theme and the other with a commonplace one; that the one discovers perpetually changing and significant relationships in developing his theme, while the other makes his original theme even worse than it was, if possible. The one discovers numerous and original modulations while the other remains rooted to the spot from sheer poverty of invention; and whereas the rhythms of the one constitute a vital pulse, those of the other resemble a tattoo.

In no other art are so many forms exhausted so swiftly as in music. In a matter of fifty years, even thirty, modulations, cadences, progressions and harmonic sequences become so well worn that no original composer can use them any longer: he is perpetually compelled to invent new purely musical features. There are a whole heap of compositions, very much superior to the general level of their time, of which it may justly be said that they were once beautiful. The ingenious composer will discover the subtlest and most recondite of the mysterious fundamental relationships between the musical elements and their innumerable possible combinations. He will create musical forms which at first appear absolutely arbitrary, but prove in fact to be necessarily connected by a fine invisible band. Works or details of this kind can unquestionably be called 'ingenious' [geistreich]; and this explains Ulibishev's[4] mistaken assertion that no instrumental music can be called 'ingenious' because 'ingenuity' [Geist] 'consists for a composer simply and solely in the employment of his music for some programme, direct or indirect'. In our opinion it would be absolutely correct to call the famous D sharp in the Allegro of the Don Giovanni overture, or the descending unison passage in the same work, 'ingenious' traits. But Ulibishev has absolutely no ground for saying that the former represents 'Don Giovanni's hostile attitude to the world' and the latter 'the fathers, husbands, brothers and lovers he has seduced'. All such interpretations are in themselves mistaken but doubly so in the case of Mozart, who was the most musical nature in the whole history of music and transformed everything that he touched into music. Ulibishev also sees the G minor Symphony as the story of a passionate love-affair, in four distinct phases. But the G minor Symphony is music, and nothing else. Surely that is enough. It is no use searching musical works for representations of distinct emotional processes and events: if one searches before all else for music itself, one will have the enjoyment of that which music provides to perfection. Should musical beauty be lacking, its place will never be supplied by some sublime interpretation thought up by a clever commentator and absolutely otiose if the work is in fact beautiful. Such attempts in any case completely misdirect any attempt to understand music. The same people who wish to vindicate the claim of music to be one of the revelations of the human spirit – a claim which is, and always will be, unjustified, because music is not capable of communicating convictions – have also popularized the use of the word 'intention'. There is no such thing in music as an 'intention' that can make up for lack of invention. Anything that fails to appear in music is quite simply not there; and what actually appears can no longer be called 'intention'. To say of a composer that 'he has intentions' is generally considered laudatory, but to me it seems quite the reverse – to mean, in fact, in plain language that the composer 'would if he could, but he can't'. The word Kunst (art) is derived from können (to be able): the man who 'cannot' has 'intentions'.

The beauty of a composition resides simply in its musical definitions [Bestimmungen] and these also provide the laws of its construction. There are a great many vague and mistaken notions on this point, only one of which is

---

[4] [Alexander Dimitryevich Ulibishev (Oulibicheff) (1794–1858), Russian music critic, author of a study of Mozart (Nouvelle biographie de Mozart, Moscow 1843).]

worth our attention, viz. the commonly accepted theory of the symphony and sonata based on the idea of 'music and feeling'. According to this the composer has four emotional states, distinct yet connected (one wonders how?), and these are portrayed in the four movements of a sonata. In order to account for the undeniable connection between these four movements, the listener is fairly compelled to identify definite feelings as the content of each movement. Such an interpretation is indeed sometimes applicable, though more frequently not and never with any kind of necessity. What is always, and of necessity, applicable is that four musical movements are combined to form a whole and that, according to the laws of musical aesthetics, they must complement each other and grow to a climax. We are indebted to the imagination of the painter Moritz von Schwind for an attractive visualization of Beethoven's Piano Fantasia op. 80, the movements of which are presented by the artist as a series of events in the life of a single character. The music is interpreted in terms of scenes and figures, in the same way as the listener may interpret it in terms of feelings and events. In each case there is indeed a certain connection, but it is a fortuitous rather than a necessary connection, and scientific laws are only concerned with connections that are necessary.

It is often argued that Beethoven designed a number of compositions with definite events or emotional moods in mind. But when Beethoven, or any other composer, followed such a practice it was simply as a subsidiary means of assuring the musical unity of a work by attaching to it some objective event. Berlioz, Liszt and others were deceiving themselves when they imagined that a poem, a title, or an event could be anything more than just this. The organic connection between the four movements of a sonata lies in the unity of their musical atmosphere, not in a connection with some (extramusical) object in the composer's mind. When he denies himself the use of such guidelines and creates in purely musical terms, the unity of the component parts of his work will be found to be purely musical. From the aesthetic point of view it is a matter of indifference whether Beethoven chose definite programmes or not: if we do not know of them they – from the musical point of view – do not exist. It is the work itself, without any commentary, that concerns us; and as the lawyer regards as nonexistent anything not contained in his brief, so the critical judgement admits the existence of nothing beyond the actual work itself. If we perceive a unity in the movements of a work, this relationship can be founded on nothing but what can be defined in musical terms.[5]

We should like finally to counter one possible misunderstanding by affirming our conception of 'beauty in music' on three counts. In the specific sense outlined already 'beauty in music' is not confined to 'classical' art, nor does it imply any preference for this rather than for 'romantic' music. It is equally applicable to both, to Bach as well as to Beethoven, to Mozart as well as to Schumann. There is therefore no hint of partisanship in our theory. The

[5] [Footnote omitted.]

whole tenor of the present investigation is alien to the consideration of how things ought to be and is concerned simply and solely with what is. It is impossible to deduce from our theory any definite ideal of musical beauty: it merely claims to establish exactly what it is that constitutes that beauty in the works of any and every school and era.

It is only in the last few years that works of art have begun to be considered in relationship to the ideas and events of the period at which they were created. There is no doubt that a connection of this sort does exist, in the case of music as of the other arts. As a manifestation of the human spirit music must of course stand in a mutual relationship to other human activities – to the literature and visual arts of the day and to the poetic, social and scientific circumstances as well as to the experience and convictions of the individual artist. An examination and demonstration of this relationship in the case of individual composers and compositions is therefore perfectly justified and of real value. It must nevertheless be always borne in mind that such drawing of parallels between artistic features and individual historical circumstances is the concern of the art historian and not of the pure aesthetician. There is a necessary methodological connection between art history and aesthetics, but each of these disciplines must be scrupulously distinguished from the other. In his apprehension of the main outlines of some artistic phenomenon the historian may well regard, let us say, Spontini's music as 'the expression of the Napoleonic imperial ideal' or Rossini's as that of the Restoration era. But the philosopher of art must keep his eyes fixed on the work itself and simply enquire what constitutes and causes its beauty. Aesthetic enquiry knows nothing – and is content to know nothing – of the personal relationships and the historical circumstances of a composer. The enquirer only has ears for what the work itself says and it is only this that concerns his intelligence. He therefore has no need to know Beethoven's name or his life-story in order to discover that his symphonies are impetuous, full of struggle and unsatisfied longing. But the features which throw light on the symphonies from the art historians' point of view – that the composer had republican sympathies, was unmarried, deaf and so forth – cannot be gathered from the music, nor have they anything to do with its evaluation. To compare the different life-philosophies of Bach, Mozart and Haydn and to trace the difference between their works to this difference of attitude may well be thought an entertaining and valuable undertaking; but it is extremely complex and will be exposed to the danger of false conclusions in proportion to the strictness of the demand for the establishing of a causal connection. The danger of exaggeration is particularly great in such an undertaking as this. It is very easy to represent the slightest influence of contemporary events as an inner necessity and to interpret the untranslatable language of music to suit one's own convenience. It will depend on the ready application of one and the same paradox whether it appears as a sage observation in the mouth of an intelligent man or a piece of nonsense in that of a simpleton.

Even Hegel in his discussion of music has often said misleading things by involuntarily confusing his own attitude – largely that of the art historian – with that of the aesthetician, and pointing to explicit certainties that music, as such, has never possessed. Of course the character of a composition has a connection with that of the composer; but this connection is not manifest to the aesthetician, and the idea of a necessary connection existing between all phenomena can easily be pushed to an absurdity in concrete instances. At the present time it needs little less than heroic strength of mind to oppose this piquant, wittily formulated type of criticism, and to insist on a clear distinction between 'historical understanding' and 'aesthetic judgement'.[6] The following remain objective certainties: firstly, that the difference of expression in different works and schools rests on a radically different arrangement of the musical elements, and second, that what is truly pleasing in any work – whether it be the strictest of Bach's fugues or the most ethereal of Chopin's Nocturnes – is musically beautiful. Beauty in music is to be identified with the architectural even less than with the classical. The architecture of a work forms only a part of its beauty. The rigid grandeur of superimposed figures and the ingenious interweaving of many parts – none of which is free and independent because all are – have their own immutable justification. And yet the polyphonic monuments of the old Italians and Netherlanders, with all their gloomy loftiness, constitute only a single province in the world of musical beauty, in exactly the same way as do the admirable Sebastian Bach's countless finely-wrought salt-cellars and silver chandeliers.

Many aestheticians consider that musical enjoyment is sufficiently explained by our delight in regularity and symmetry, though this is never in itself enough to create beauty as such, let alone a specifically musical beauty. The most insipid theme may be perfectly symmetrical in construction. Symmetry is of course a relative conception and provides no answer to the question what it is that in fact appears symmetrical. It is easy – and precisely in the most worthless compositions – to point to the regular arrangement of lifeless, hackneyed phrases. Musical thought demands symmetrical formations that are for ever changing.[7]

Oersted has recently developed this Platonic theory in relationship to music, taking as an example the circle, a form for which he claims objective beauty.[8] He can surely never have experienced the frightfulness of a perfectly circular composition.

It may be just as well, though it can hardly be necessary, to add in conclusion that beauty in music has nothing to do with mathematics. Many non-musicians (including some sentimental writers) cherish the belief that mathematics plays an important part in composition, though they are very vague as to the precise nature of that part. They are content with the fact that

[6] We should like to mention in this connection Riehl's *Musikalische Charakterköpfe* [Stuttgart and Tübingen 1853] and express our gratitude for this witty and stimulating book.

[7] [Footnote omitted.]

[8] [Hans Christian Oersted (1777–1851), Danish physicist, now known for his work in the theory of magnetic fields.]

sound-vibration, intervals and (what we call) consonance and dissonance are all based on mathematical relationships, and they are therefore convinced that the beauty of a composition has a numerical basis. In fact they regard harmony and counterpoint as a kind of kabbala, the study of which will enable a composer to 'calculate' his work.

Investigation of the physical element in music does indeed provide a key that is indispensable; but its significance for the composer can easily be exaggerated. Mathematical calculations play no part in any composition, good or bad. Creations of the human imagination are not mathematical 'sums'. Monochord experiments, vibration-figures [*Klangfiguren*], interval-proportions etc. are irrelevant to the aesthetician, whose task only begins where these elementary relationships have ceased to be significant. Mathematics controls only the elementary material on which the imagination works: its presence in the simplest relationships is a hidden one, and the musical idea comes to birth without that presence making itself felt. I confess that I fail to understand Oersted's question 'would the life-spans of several mathematicians suffice to calculate all the beauties of Mozart's symphonies?'[9]; what is there to calculate? the proportion between the vibrations of each note to its neighbour, perhaps, or the comparative length of individual phrases? What constitutes the difference between a composition and a series of physical experiments is the fact that the latter is a free manifestation of the human spirit and therefore incalculable. The part played by mathematics in musical composition is no larger and no smaller than in the other branches of the arts. For in the last resort mathematical rules must guide the hand of the painter and the sculptor, mathematical symmetry determines the length of the poet's lines and verses, the constructions of the architect and the figures of the dancer. Mathematics, in fact, must play a part in every field of exact knowledge, viz. that of the active intelligence; only we must guard against assigning to mathematics, as the philosophers among the musicians (the conservatives among the aestheticians) are inclined to do, any real, positive creative power. In fact the position of mathematics very much resembles the stirring of 'feelings' in the case of the listener – a universal phenomenon in all the arts but a source of polemical discussion only in music.

Attempts have also been made to draw a parallel between music and language, and to apply the rules of the latter to the former. By its very nature song is closely allied to speech, both physiologically and by the fact that both are exteriorizations of man's inner being by means of the human voice. In fact the analogies between the two are too obvious to require any detailed examination here. It must, however, be expressly conceded that although music is simply a question of the subjective exteriorization of an inner impulse, the laws governing human speech are at least in part applicable to singing. Thus, the voice of an impassioned orator will rise and then, as the orator calms down, fall: sentences of particular import are spoken slowly,

[9] [Oersted.] *Geist in der Natur*. tr. Kannegiesser, vol. 3, p. 32.

while unimportant matters are spoken fast – these and similar considerations will be taken into account by the composer of vocal, and particularly of dramatic music. Many aestheticians have unfortunately not been content with these limited analogies, and they have regarded music itself as a more delicate, less precise form of language, and attempted to deduce the laws governing its beauty from the nature of speech. Every characteristic and effect of music has been referred to its similarity to speech. It is our opinion, however, that in the investigation of what is specific to any one art the similarities between that art and other related disciplines are of less importance than those features that distinguish it from those disciplines. In fact these analogies, beguiling as they often are, are not relevant to the real essence of music and must therefore be shunned by the philosophical investigator, who must press on indefatigably to the point where music and speech finally part company. It is only after that point has been reached that we can hope to discover definitions that really assist us in the understanding of the nature of music. The essential difference between music and speech resides in the fact that in speech sound is only a sign i.e. a means of expressing something that is in itself quite alien to that means, whereas in music the sound is an object, that is an end in itself. The self-subsisting, independent beauty of musical forms on the one hand, and on the other the total subordination of sound (as a means of expression) to sense – these two principles are so completely incompatible that any intermixture of the two is a logical impossibility.

Speech and music have, as it were, essentially different centres of gravity; and it is around these that all their other characteristics are grouped. All specifically musical laws radiate from the self-sufficient significance and beauty of sounds in themselves, whereas all the laws governing speech are concerned with the correct use of sounds for the purpose of expression.

The attempt to understand music as a kind of language has given rise to the most mischievous and confusing theories, which have practical results that can be daily observed. Naturally enough it is mostly composers of inferior creative ability who have regarded as a false and materialistic principle that self-sufficient musical beauty that they are unable to create; and have proclaimed meaning as the characteristic of music. Quite apart from Richard Wagner's operas, we often find in the smallest instrumental works instances of the melodic flow being interrupted by abrupt cadenzas, passages of recitative etc. which disorientate the listener by their apparent significance, although what they in fact signify is nothing but non-beauty [*Unschönheit*]. In modern works where the main rhythm is repeatedly interrupted in order to obtrude mysterious additions or a mass of contrasts it is generally claimed that the composer is aiming at extending the narrow frontiers of music and elevating it to the status of a language. We have always found praise of this kind highly ambiguous. The frontiers of music are by no means narrow, rather, they are firmly determined. There can never be any question of 'elevating' music to the status of language – 'lowering' would be more accurate from the musical standpoint – since music must manifestly be considered as itself an elevated form of speech.[10]

This is something that our singers forget when, at moments of supreme emotional tension they employ a *quasi parlando* style for individual words, and even whole phrases. They think that in so doing they achieve the maximum expressiveness of which music is capable, and fail to realize that any transition from singing to speech is always a descent, just as the highest pitch of the normal speaking voice always seems lower than even the lowest pitch of the singer. Equally disastrous – and perhaps even more so, since they cannot be tested in practice – are the theories which attempt to foist on to music the grammar and syntax of speech. In the past this was done at least partially by Rousseau and Rameau, who have been copied in our own day by the disciples of Richard Wagner. Such attempts stab the true heart of music –

[10] It cannot be denied that one of the greatest works of genius of all time has contributed by its glamour to this popular error of modern music criticism, namely 'the inmost impulse of music to achieve the explicitness of the spoken word' and 'to shake off the bonds of mere eurhythmy'. Beethoven's Ninth Symphony is one of those artistic watersheds which are visible from afar and form an unsurmountable barrier between the currents of opposing convictions. Those musicians who attach most importance to greatness of 'intention' and the spiritual significance of an abstract idea place the Ninth Symphony in the very front rank of musical works. On the other hand the little band of those who cling to the old-fashioned conception of beauty and fight for the cause of purely aesthetic considerations are more reserved in their admiration. The chief bone of contention is of course the last movement. No observant and experienced listener is likely seriously to dispute the noble beauty of the first three movements, despite occasional imperfections. In the finale, however, we ourselves have never been able to see more than the giant shadow of a giant frame. It is perfectly possible to understand and appreciate the loftiness of the idea – a great spirit driven almost to despair by the sense of isolation and dreaming of universal human reconciliation in the spirit of joy – and yet to be unable to call the finale, despite its character of genius, 'beautiful'. We are quite aware of the universal disapprobation incurred by this negative judgement. When in 1853 one of Germany's most intelligent and versatile scholars undertook in the A[ugsburger] Allgemeine Zeitung to criticize the fundamental idea of the Ninth Symphony, he humorously acknowledged the necessity of referring to himself at the very outset as 'a limited intelligence'. He cast a searching light on the aesthetic monstrosity of finishing a three-movement instrumental work with a chorus, and compared Beethoven to a sculptor carving legs, trunk, chest and arms of a statue in colourless marble and then proceeding to colour the head. It might have been thought that the entry of the voices would have caused a similar sense of unease in any sensitive listener, since here the work's centre of gravity suddenly shifts, threatening to throw the listener off his balance. It was almost ten years later that, to our delight, the 'limited intelligence' removed his mask and revealed himself as none other than David Strauss.

On the other hand, the highly intelligent Dr Becher – who may serve here as representative of a whole class of writers – published in 1843 an essay on the Ninth Symphony in which he described the last movement as 'one to which originality of conception, grandeur of design and boldness of individual ideas give a unique place among the creations of Beethoven's genius'. And he went on to assure his readers that 'it rises among its peers – King Lear and perhaps a dozen other creations of the human spirit at its most poetical – as the peak of Dhavalagiri towers above the rest of the Himalayas'. Like the great majority of those who share his opinion, Becher gives a detailed account of the symphony's four movements and the profound symbolism of their content without even mentioning the actual music; and this is absolutely characteristic of this whole school of music criticism, which prefers to avoid the issue of whether a work is beautiful by referring to the grandeur of its significance.

self-subsisting formal beauty – in the search for some imagined significance. Any philosophy of music must therefore have as its chief object the ruthless and radical distinguishing of the essential difference between the nature of speech and music and the establishing – with all its logical consequences – of the principle that in treating of what is specifically musical analogies with language are totally irrelevant. [pp. 72–116]

## Chapter VII: The concepts of 'content' and 'form' in music

Has music a content? This has been the most hotly disputed question ever since the day when our art was first subjected to intellectual analysis, and both negative and affirmative answers have been given. Foremost among those whose answers have been negative have been the philosophers – Rousseau, Kant, Hegel, Herbart,[1] Kahlert[2] etc. Among the many physiologists who have been of the same opinion the most outstanding are Lotze and Helmholtz, both excellent musicians. Those who have answered the question 'has music a content?' in the affirmative, who form the very great majority, include the writers who have a strong feeling for music; and they have the general public on their side.

It may well seem strange that precisely those who have a good technical knowledge of music have not been able to liberate themselves from an opinion that contradicts that same knowledge and would be more pardonable in an abstract philosopher. This anomaly is explained by the fact that many writers about music are concerned in this matter with what they believe to be the honour of their art rather than with the truth. They oppose the doctrine of 'music without content' not as a mistaken opinion but as a heresy, seeing in their opponents nothing but gross misunderstanding and outrageous materialism. 'Is the art that ennobles and inspires us, the art which can serve the highest ideals and to which so many great souls have devoted their lives, to be under the curse of non-significance and reduced to mere sensuous pattern-making, an empty jingle?' Such familiar questions as these – strung together, though there is no connection between the two constituent clauses – neither prove nor disprove anything. What is at stake here is not a point of honour or a party slogan but simply the recognition of the truth; and in order to attain this, the first necessity is to have a clear picture of one's opponents' ideas.

The lack of clarity in the actual subject of the dispute itself has always been due to a confusion between the meanings of content, object and material. Each writer employs either a different word for the same idea or the same word for different notions. The real, original meaning of the word 'content' is

[1] [In the first edition instead of 'Herbart' stands 'Vischer'.] Following Herbart, Robert Zimmermann has recently in his *Allgemeine Aesthetik als Formwissenschaft* (Vienna 1865) applied the formal principle in a strict manner to all the arts, including music.
[2] [K. A. T. Kahlert (1807–64), German philosopher, historian of literature and music critic. Later in this chapter Hanslick refers to his *System der Aesthetik* (Leipzig 1846). See also le Huray and Day, p. 559.]

of course 'that which a thing contains or holds in itself'. In this sense the sounds of which a composition consists – the parts of which it is the whole – are the content of that composition. The fact that no one is satisfied with this as an answer (which is dismissed as self-evident) is due to the common confusion between 'content' and 'object'. In any discussion of the 'content' of music the writer is actually thinking of the 'object' (material, *sujet*) – the idea or ideal, as opposed to the 'material components' i.e. the actual notes. A 'content' in this sense i.e. a 'material' in the sense of an 'object handled' is something that music does not in fact possess. Kahlert rightly makes this very point – that, unlike a picture, a composition cannot be described in words (*Ästhetik*, p. 380), although he is mistaken when he goes on to assume that a verbal description of this kind can ever provide 'a substitute for aesthetic appreciation'. The question of what actually constitutes musical 'content' would automatically be answerable if the composition really had a content (i.e. an 'object'). An 'indeterminate content' that each listener can imagine differently from his neighbour, that is only felt and not expressed in words, is in fact no 'content' in the ordinary sense of the word. Music consists of scalar and other figures and shapes composed of notes, and these have no other content but themselves, again recalling architecture and the dance, both of which similarly present us with pleasing relationships that have no definite content. Everyone is free to experience and describe the effect of a composition in his own individual way; but the actual content of the work is nothing but the musical shapes, since music does not simply speak by means of notes; it also consists of nothing else but notes.

The best informed champion of musical 'content' against Hegel and Kahlert is Krüger,[3] and he maintains that music simply presents us with another facet of the same content that we find in the other arts e.g. painting. 'Every plastic shape', he says (in *Beiträge*, p. 131), 'is static: it does not show us action itself, but action completed in the past or, the essence of an action. That is to say, a picture does not portray Apollo conquering, but Apollo as conqueror, as wrathful fighter etc.' On the other hand 'music adds the verb, as it were, to the static, plastic substantives, the activity, the inner flow; and if in a picture it is the true static content – wrath, love – that we recognize, in music it is no less clearly the actual content of the movement of raging, loving, rushing, surging, storming'. This, however, is only half true; for although music is indeed capable of 'rushing, surging, storming' it is not capable of 'raging' and 'loving', passions that are simply attributed to the music from the [listener's own] emotional experience. We must here refer the reader to our second chapter. Krüger goes on to compare the particular content depicted and that expressed through music. 'The visual artist portrays Orestes pursued by the Furies. His whole exterior – eyes, mouth, brow, stance – reveals the sombre, desperate fugitive. By his side stand the shapes of the curse, who have

[3] [E. Krüger (1807–85), German music critic. Hanslick refers to his *Beiträge für Leben und Wissenschaft der Tonkunst* (Leipzig 1847). See also le Huray and Day, pp. 530 and 560.]

him in their power, terrible in their commanding majesty. They too are presented in static outlines, features and positions. The composer, on the other hand, presents the fugitive Orestes not in static outlines but in a manner which is not possible to the visual artist. He catches Orestes's agony and terror of mind, the agitation of the struggling fugitive' etc. This seems to me quite wrong. The composer cannot present Orestes in one way or another: he simply cannot present him at all.

It is useless to object that in fact the visual arts, too, are incapable of presenting a definite historical character, and that without a previous knowledge of the historical facts we should be unable to recognize any individual personage whatever. Surely, we do not here have Orestes, the man associated with such and such experiences and definite biographical events. Such a man can be portrayed only by the poet, because it is only the poet who is capable of narration. Even so a picture of Orestes does indeed show us a young man of noble appearance, in Greek clothes, with terror and despair in every feature and every gesture, pursued and tormented by the ghastly figures of the spirits of vengeance. So much is clear and unambiguous, a visual narrative, whether the man's name is Orestes or not. The only elements that the painter is unable to express are the young man's circumstances – the matricide and so forth. What has music to show that is comparable in precision to that visual content (leaving aside the historical circumstances) of the picture of Orestes? diminished sevenths, themes in the minor, restless bass figures etc. – in fact, musical shapes, which might 'mean' a woman rather than a man, a fugitive from the bailiffs rather than the Furies, a jealous man thirsting for revenge, someone tormented by bodily pain – in fact anything one cares to imagine if one is determined to make a musical work mean anything.

There is no need to refer back in detail to the principle established earlier, viz. that when we speak of music having a content, we can only be speaking of instrumental music. No one will be so oblivious of this as to quote Orestes in Gluck's *Iphigénie en Tauride*. This Orestes is not the creation of the composer: it is the librettist's text, the singer's appearance and acting ability and the stage-designer's costumes and sets that present the complete figure of Orestes. The contribution of the composer is perhaps the most beautiful element of all, but it is precisely the one that has nothing to do with the real Orestes – the music.

Lessing has analyzed with astonishing precision the potentialities of the story of Laocoon for the visual artist and for the poet. The poet, by means of language, can present Laocoon as a definite historical individual, whereas the painter and the sculptor present an old man with two sons (of a definite age, physical appearance and clothing) imprisoned in the folds of two hideous snakes and showing by their expressions, their postures and their gestures the anguish of an imminent death. Lessing says nothing about the musician – and very understandably, since for him Laocoon's story has not even a potential interest.

We have already suggested the close connection between the content of music and the relationship of the art to natural beauty. The musician has no model to work from comparable with those that guarantee the precision and recognizability of the other arts. An art which lacks any model in the world of natural beauty will be, properly speaking, disembodied. We can nowhere discover any original from which its various phenomena are taken and it therefore lies outside the field of our ideas as a whole. It does not present us with the likeness of any known, named object and therefore – according to our method of thinking in definite concepts – it has no content to which a name can be given.

One can in fact only speak of the content of a work of art when such a content can be already distinguished from form. The concepts of 'content' and 'form' are mutually dependent and complementary. If the mind cannot clearly distinguish the one from the other, then no independent 'content' exists. But in music content and form, the material and its shaping by the composer, image and idea form a mysterious and inextricable unity. This characteristic of music – the indivisibility of form and content – separates it clearly from the other arts, in which the same event can be presented in different forms. The story of William Tell, for example, served Florian for a historical novel, Schiller for a play and Goethe for an epic which he never completed. In each case the story is the same and can be analysed, narrated and recognized; but the form is different. In the same way the story of Aphrodite rising from the sea has been made the content of innumerable pictures and carvings which retain their unmistakable identity thanks to their different forms. In music this distinction between form and content does not exist because music has no form apart from its content. Let us observe the matter more closely.

In every composition it is the theme that provides the self-sufficient musical unity of thought, aesthetically speaking the unit incapable of further subdivision. The primary definitions attributable to music as such must always be traceable back to the theme, or musical microcosm. Take a main theme – that of Beethoven's Fourth Symphony, for example. What is its form and what its content? Where does the one begin and the other end? It is to be hoped that we have already shown that no definite 'feeling' can be the content of a movement, and this will become increasingly plain from this – and every other – concrete instance. What do people mean, then, when they speak of content? The notes themselves? Certainly, only it is they that already have a form. So what is form? Once again, the notes themselves – but they are form that is already realized.

Every concrete attempt to separate the form of a theme from its content leads either to contradictory or to arbitrary results. Let us take an example. In the case of a phrase being repeated by a different instrument or an octave higher, is the change one of content or of form? It is generally said to be the latter; but in that case it must be simply the series of intervals as such that constitutes the content of the phrase – the pattern of notes that meets the score-reader's eye. This, however, is an abstraction, not a musical reality. The case resembles that of a summer-house with windows of coloured glass, which enable the viewer to see the same countryside as red, blue or yellow, so that in fact neither form nor content change but simply colouring. These myriad changes of colour without changes of form, from extreme contrasts to the finest nuances, are absolutely characteristic of music and constitute one of the richest and most highly developed of its appeals.

A melody conceived for the pianoforte and later orchestrated is thereby given a new form but not a primary form: it was already a formed (musical) idea. Still less can it be claimed that by transposing a theme its content is changed while its form remains the same, for this would involve a double contradiction, the hearer being obliged to say that he recognized a familiar content, only 'it sounds different'.

It is of course common to speak of the form and the content of whole compositions, particularly those on a large scale. In such a case the two concepts are not used in their original logical sense, but with a specifically musical connotation. When one speaks of the 'form' of a symphony, an overture, a sonata, an aria, a chorus etc. what is meant is the architecture of the whole complex of individual movements and groups of which the work consists – in fact the symmetry of these subsidiary parts in their succession, the contrasts between them, their repetition and development. In that case the 'content' is said to consist of the themes employed as materials for this architecture. Here, therefore, there is no longer any question of content as 'object' but the word is used in a purely musical sense. When speaking of whole compositions, therefore, the words 'content' and 'form' are used not in their purely logical sense but by a kind of artistic analogy; and if we are to apply this to the idea of music [in general], it must be not to a complete work constructed on these principles, but to the smallest of all musical units, incapable of further subdivision i.e. the theme or themes, in which it is not possible in any sense to distinguish form from content. Anyone who wishes to specify the 'content' of a musical phrase has no choice but to play the phrase itself. In fact the 'content' of a musical composition can never be grasped objectively [*gegenständlich*] but only musically i.e. as the concrete sounds of which the work is composed. Musical composition follows certain definite aesthetic laws, and the course of a work is therefore no arbitrary improvisation, meandering according to no set plan, but an organic development that can be traced by the student and resembles the gradually unfolding of a wealth of blossoms from a single bud.

That single bud is the main theme of the work – the actual material and content (or 'matter') of the whole creation. Everything in the work is a free derivation and effect of the theme, which shapes and conditions, controls and fulfils every detail. The course of a musical development is analogous to a logical process; it is axiomatic that the satisfaction that the original theme gives the listener is spontaneous and immediate, but the intelligence demands to follow the argument with all its propositions and counter-propositions. The composer, like the novelist, presents his theme, the 'hero' of the work, in the most various situations and circumstances, in perpetually changing moods and events; and everything else, however strongly contrasted in character, is determined and shaped with reference to that theme.

Free improvisation, in which the player simply lets his imagination range through a series of chords, arpeggios and sequences without giving preference to any one independent phrase or figure – a form of relaxation rather than of creation – this may truly be said to have no 'content'. Free improvisation such as these are not individually recognizable or distinguishable, and we may well say that they have strictly speaking no content because they have no theme.

Thus the theme, or themes, of a composition are its actual content. Aestheticians and critics do not attribute sufficient importance to the main theme of a work. The theme alone immediately reveals the mentality of the composer. When Beethoven begins the *Leonore* overture this way, and Mendelssohn his *Hebrides* that way, each musician will sense the palace in front of which he stands before he has heard a note of the music's development. On the other hand a theme like that of Donizetti's overture to *Fausta* or Verdi's to *Louise Miller* tells us plainly and without more pondering that we are in the tavern. In Germany both theory and practice attach overwhelming importance to musical development as against thematic invention. But what is not, either actually or potentially, present in a theme cannot be later developed; and it may well be that the failure of the present age to produce orchestral works like those of Beethoven is due to a lack of symphonic power and fertility of themes rather than to any lack of skill in their development.

It is of particular importance when considering the question of a work's content not to use the word in a laudatory sense. The fact that music has no objective content does not mean that it has no substance [*Gehalt*]. 'Spiritual substance' is plainly referred to by those who argue with the zeal of partisans for the 'content' of music; and here we must refer the reader back to what has already been said in chapter 3. Music has the character of a game, but it is no mere playing. Thoughts and feelings are the life-blood that courses through the veins of the body of a composition, with all its beauties of symmetry and proportion; they are not identical with that body, nor are they visible, but they give it life. The composer invents and thinks, but he does so in notes, quite apart from all objective reality. It is necessary to repeat this commonplace here, because it is precisely those that recognize its truth in principle who all too frequently deny or abuse its consequences. They think of composition as a translation into sound of some imagined subject, whereas in fact it is the sounds themselves that form the basic language, which it is impossible to translate. The fact that the composer is obliged to think in sounds accounts for the fact that music has no 'content', since any notional content must be capable of being conceived in words.

However firmly we must insist, in our investigation of 'content' in music, that all works with literary texts in fact contradict the pure concept of music, we must never overlook the fact that the masterpieces of vocal music are indispensable in appreciating the substance [*Gehalt*] of music. From a simple song to an opera with all its dramatis personae and the ancient and venerable worship of the Almighty in the music of the church, music has never ceased to form the accompaniment – and thus directly to exalt – the deepest and most precious emotions of the human spirit.

In addition to vindicating the spiritual substance of music we must also draw particular attention to another aspect. The fact that beauty in music is purely formal and has no 'object' does not mean that individual works have no character of their own. Thematic invention and development are in each case so individual that there is no danger of their character being lost in a kind of noble generalization: each work is unmistakably itself. A phrase of Mozart's or Beethoven's is as clearly characterized and unmistakable as a line of Goethe's, an aphorism of Lessing's, a statue of Thorwaldsen's or a picture of Overbeck's. Self-subsistent musical ideas (themes) have the warrant-like quality of a quotation and the evidential character of a picture. Their personal, individual nature makes them immortal. For this reason it is impossible for us to share Hegel's view that music has no substance; and he seems to be even more mistaken in allowing music to be no more than the expression of 'an inner world that lacks all individuality'. Hegel overlooks the truly formative, objective activity of the composer and regards music as a voluntary self-abandonment to subjectivity; but even this point of view does not necessarily imply any absence of individuality, as the creative artist is essentially individual, even if wholly subjective.

We have already suggested in chapter 3 the way in which a composer's individuality is manifested by his choice and use of the various constituent elements of music. In answer, therefore, to the charge that music has no content we maintain that it has indeed a content, but that it is a purely musical one, and no less a spark of the divine fire than we find in the beauty of the other arts. The truth is that we can rescue the 'substance' of music only by insisting on our denial of any and every other 'content'. The spiritual significance of music cannot be deduced from those vague feelings on which such 'content' is at best based, but from clearly and beautifully defined sound-shapes, freely created by the human spirit from material that lends itself to working by the imagination.[4] [pp. 203–21]

In the mind of the listener this spiritual content connects beauty in music with all other great and beautiful ideas. For him music acts not merely and exclusively through its own beauty, but also as a tonal representation of the great movement in the cosmos. Through deep and innermost connections in nature the meaning of music is raised high above itself and allows us to feel at the same time the infinity in the work of the individual human talent. Thus the elements of music: sound, notes, rhythm, strength, frailty, are to be found in the whole universe, and thus man finds the entire universe in music.

---

[4] [The paragraph that follows appeared only in the first edition of 1854. It was then shortened in the second edition (1858) so that only its first sentence remained, and it in turn was omitted from subsequent editions.]

# Robert Zimmermann (1824–1898)

## Allgemeine Aesthetik als Formwissenschaft (1865)

Zimmermann studied philosophy in Göttingen under Herbart and in Prague under Franz Exner. He obtained his doctorate in Vienna in 1846 and from 1849 taught at the University of Olomouc as well as being an unsalaried lecturer (*Privatdozent*) in Vienna. He became Professor of Philosophy in Prague in 1852 and then moved to a chair in Vienna in 1861.

A follower of Herbart, he saw himself as a champion of the anti-Hegelian stream, directing his polemics against F. T. Vischer. According to Zimmermann, philosophy is an investigation of abstract ideas needed in order to establish norms for scientific, aesthetic and ethical investigations. Forms are, according to him, primary categories which underline all aspects of mental activity. In radicalizing some of Herbart's postulates he contributed towards Herbart's unjust fame as a dry formalist, as some of Zimmermann's views were uncritically attributed to his teacher. He exerted some influence on Hanslick.

## General aesthetics as a theory of forms

*Source:*

*Allgemeine Aesthetik als Formwissenschaft* (Vienna 1865) Erstes Buch. Erstes Kapitel: Die Vorfragen §21, 25, 26, 28, 29, 30, 31, 32, 73, 74, 76, 77, 78, 79, 80. Zweites Buch. Zweites Kapitel: Der schöne Geist §275, 276, 277, 280, 299. Drittes Kapitel: Die idealen Kunstwerke des Vorstellens §649, 651, 653, 654, 655, 656, 661, 662. Translated by Martin Cooper.

### Book 1, chapter 1: Introductory questions

§21 [Aesthetic ideas] are nothing else but simply images, and their presence in the thinker's mind provides justification neither for the theoretical extension of presentation to knowledge nor for a practical extension of such knowledge to a judgement or transformation of the object. It justifies only an additional activity [*Zusatz*] within the individual presentation – the constatation of pleasurable or unpleasurable feelings, preference or rejection. Concepts of this kind are called aesthetic concepts. [p. 10]

§25 Since aesthetic concepts are simply images and not copies, it follows automatically that the additional activity cannot be defined by the truth or falsehood of their content. This depends on the relationship of the presentation to the object, whereas the additional aesthetic activity depends on the presentation alone. 'Cognition' [*Erkenntnis*] and 'imagination' [*Einbildung*], history and fairy tale, are equally valid as far as the aesthetic function is concerned. Were we to disregard science and continue to regard the sky as a hollow sphere surrounded by innumerable flames, this would fly in the face of scientific theory but would, from the aesthetic point of view, be by no means an unacceptable idea. Scientific theory and the world of aesthetic vision are concerned with quite different things. [p. 11]

§26 The additional activity accompanying the image in the subject is called feeling, in the most commonly accepted sense of the word. When this is absent, we have pure presentation and the imagining (presenting) agent could then be said to be indifferent. The clearest case of this is the attitude of the scholar towards the presentation that he conceives. His gaze is directed entirely on the object and he has eyes only for that which, in the content of his presentation, reflects the object. The most exquisite flower is for him nothing more than the outer covering of a plant's sexual organs, with so many stamens and so many styles. The anatomist has no more time or inclination to admire the hand that he is about to dissect than has the doctor who is about to amputate it. He is not concerned with any 'additional activity' of his imagination that does not arise from the object, and the object alone. Should such things occur to him spontaneously, he strenuously rejects them from his mind. [pp. 11–12]

§28 As a string awaits the bow, so does the additional activity expect the presentation that has caused it. This alone is sufficient to demonstrate that feeling is not a primary state, any more than desire. Both presuppose the presentation and are states of the presentation. If these are absent, there are no feelings and no actions. [p. 12]

§29 Feelings, however, often seem to arise when the presentations are not at hand. In such cases we say that we feel, but cannot say what it is that we feel; we may call the feeling 'vague'. More accurately it is only 'what we feel' that is vague. We are quite clear in our minds about the additional activity of approval or disapproval, pleasure or un-pleasure caused by what we imagine; it is only the content of what we imagine that is unclear. We may well be unable to say which tooth it is that aches, but that we have toothache is unfortunately often only too clear to us. [p. 12]

§30 Not knowing the content of our presentation makes the feeling itself seem undefined. The same additional activity may well have the most varied presentational content. In fact, it would seem that an identical effect must arise from identical conditions: the same presentation must produce the same additional activity. But if the content of the presentation i.e. the presentation itself remains unknown, who is in a position to say that the presentation is identical in two different instances of the feeling arising? [pp. 12–13]

§31   In addition to this there is another difficulty. The aesthetic concept arises when the additional activity is joined by the image. The concept arises in, and perhaps through, the subject. In the latter case the aesthetic idea depends on the changeable condition of the subject, even when the causative presentation has the same content; and it is therefore itself changeable. If, as has been described above, it is hard to determine 'what' has been felt, then – as we said before – 'who' has felt it appears doubtful. But the aesthetic idea is a function of the two. [p. 13]

§32   Aesthetics as a science is a doubtful proposition, not from any lack of concepts but from the lack of knowledge about those concepts. There are as many aesthetic concepts as there are causative presentations – contents which, having entered the subject's mind, bring additional activities of pleasure and un-pleasure. Feeling continues at all times and in all places: but if it is impossible to know either what is felt or by whom, it is impossible to found any science on this double ignorance. [p. 13]

§73   Aesthetics as a pure science of forms is a morphology of the beautiful. By showing that it is only forms that give, or fail to give, pleasure, aesthetics demonstrates once and for all that everything that gives, or fails to give, pleasure does so by means of forms. Try to think of form apart from its pleasingness: pleasure itself vanishes. I can separate in my mind the metre or the euphony from a line of poetry, but not the symmetry of ideas, the poetic imagery – or if I do, I immediately rob the line of its specifically aesthetic character. Conversely, if there are unambiguously pleasing forms, they must be pleasing in every context and to every person for the very condition of 'pleasing' – that of being perfectly imagined – to be in any way fulfilled. It is not permissible to enquire whether these forms are suitable to any particular material; since they are indifferent to materials, they are suited to all. It is superfluous to ask whether the form can explain this indifference; as every material, whatever it may be, is a matter of aesthetic indifference, the form can only spread its lustre over indifferent materials. Just as the sun shines without distinction upon the just and the unjust, so pleasing form hovers over dead material and imparts to it soul and interest. [p. 30]

§74   The first part of aesthetics as a science of forms, the general theory of form, is devoted to the search for forms which are universally and of necessity pleasing or unpleasing. We shall have to see whether one, or several or a complete enumeration of these forms is possible; it is self-evident that it would be impossible if the material were not indifferent to the form imposed upon it. For the quantity and variety of that which can in any way become part of an aesthetic relationship is limitless, even if we consider species of material alone – e.g. colours, a field in which words, and even, beyond a certain point, our senses themselves – are insufficient to determine every individual nuance that may be brought into harmonious or unharmonious relationship with another (one). The question of which colour-blendings are pleasing and which are not belongs to the material, the terms of relationship and the answer – insofar as experience permits of an answer – must be given by the special theory of colour-harmony, which forms one of the rudiments of the art of painting.[1] The only question to which aesthetics, as the science of forms, must answer is – 'by what sort of forms i.e. what sort of "ensemble", do blendings of colour please or displease us?' Harmony is that form and disharmony is its opposite. [pp. 30–1]

§76    Aesthetics is an a priori rather than an empirical science inasmuch as it deals only with those forms by which every material capable of receiving forms of any kind (that is to say every homogeneous material) gives, or fails to give, pleasure. It is only the material which falls into those forms that is empirical. The issues connected with the form can be explained without knowing the whole range of the material, which has hitherto proved inexhaustible. It would be rash to maintain that no composer in the future will discover new harmonies, but by no means rash to feel sure that musical beauty will always have to include the harmonious. Any enrichment that aesthetics may hope to obtain not only from increased experience but from pioneers of the new in art, can only be in the realm of the material: the forms which are essentially and universally pleasing will be found to be eternal and everywhere the same. No one can prophesy the desires and actions of our descendants, but the forms which make the desires and actions pleasing or displeasing are immutable. [p. 32]

§77    This a priori nature of aesthetic forms enables them to serve as norms in judging all that demands judgement. Aesthetic forms are not commandments and prohibitions. They are simply what is absolutely pleasing and absolutely displeasing. Anything that presents itself to the aesthetic judgement as pleasing or displeasing can only do so by the fact that its forms are copies of aesthetic forms. The artist who wishes to give pleasure must make aesthetic forms the norm of his art, and the critic who wishes to judge correctly must take aesthetic norms as the standard of his criticism. They are the basic forms that please or displease, and for that very reason the pleasure that they give, or fail to give, is irrational [*grundlos*]; and since it is the effect of images that occur in relationship to each other, it is called absolute, or unconditional. [p. 32]

§78    The second part of aesthetics as the theory of forms embraces the particular forms that arise by applying general forms to the main categories of being, nature and spirit, individual and social. Of the latter as such aesthetics knows nothing, but borrows her concepts from ontology [*Wissenschaft vom Seienden*]. Inasmuch as they resign the responsibility for their correctness and validity to the latter (i.e. ontology), they are for the aesthetician no more than simple images, pleasing or displeasing according to their conformity with

---

[1] [It is most likely that Zimmermann here has in mind Goethe's theory of colours as explained in his *Farbenlehre*, an extensive study on which Goethe worked between c. 1790 and 1810.]

aesthetic forms, leaving aside the question whether an object does or does not correspond to them as beautiful or ugly images. This object has therefore three parts – the first concerned with the absolute pleasingness of the image, the second with the absolute pleasingness of the individual spirit and the third with the absolute pleasingness of the social spirit. The object gives a general idea of these images simply as images i.e. without any assertion of either their reality or their unreality. [pp. 32–3]

§79    In so far as aesthetic forms appear at the same time as norms, they form the major premises of artistic theory, of practical aesthetics which in an empirically given material show the way to their realization. The number of these aesthetic forms depends on the variety of the empirical material in which the forms are to appear. Whereas the theory of forms is not concerned with material, this is of prime importance to artistic theory. That is to say, it depends on the material how far the intention – the realization of the forms – can be successful. While, therefore, the theory of forms is concerned with what is pleasing or displeasing, regardless of whether this is existent or non-existent, artistic theory concerns itself with the same matter in so far as it is either something that is not yet in existence but should be or, on the other hand, with something that is in existence but should not be. The goal of artistic theory is the existence of the pleasing, the non-existence of the unpleasing. [p. 33]

§80    Inasmuch as aesthetics is the science of forms, it is allied to logic as a science of forms. But whereas the latter deals with the forms of presentations [*Vorstellungen*] in so far as these become genuine and valid concepts by means of logic, aesthetics does this in so far as the forms of presentations are, pleasing or displeasing, simply presentations. Logic as a science of forms seeks to shape those forms as true copies, aesthetics as a science of forms seeks only to shape those forms into pleasing images. Logical forms are directed to being and knowing, aesthetic forms to pleasing. The two belong to quite separate areas, and the parallel between them is only justified by the fact that logical forms are norms for conceiving truth [*das richtige Vorstellen*] in the same way as aesthetic forms are norms for conceiving what is pleasing [*das gefällige Vorstellen*] and, in addition to this, for feeling and volition, for which there exists no analogy in the case of logic. [pp. 33–4]

## Book 2, chapter 2: The spirit of beauty

§275    It is an axiom that spirit is related to nature in the same way as the conscious (or the potentially conscious) is related to the unconscious (or for that which has no potential consciousness): and because this axiom concerns being, aesthetics borrows it from the science of being that we call metaphysics. It is the province of metaphysics to decide whether this concept be valid: aesthetics simply asks by what means anything corresponding to this idea, when conceived as an image, arouses pleasure or displeasure. Aesthetics sketches an aesthetic mental image in the same way as it has sketched an aesthetic natural image. [p. 136]

§276    In the idea of spirit the emphasis lies on (its) consciousness. It has the quality of existing in common with nature, the quality of appearing in common with phenomena [*Erscheinungen*]. The difference lies in the fact that Nature, being unconscious, is unaware of her own phenomena and unable to perceive the expression of absolute approval or disapproval embodied in the aesthetic judgement, whereas spirit, being conscious, is capable of both. Nature is judged i.e. compared with absolute standards of pleasingness and displeasingness, whereas spirit judges itself. Its phenomena are exposed to its own gaze, whereas Nature's are exposed only to the gaze of others. Spirit cannot make its appearance without imagining that appearance; it cannot imagine that appearance complete without making a judgement of it, whether favourable or unfavourable. Although it may escape being judged by others, it cannot escape its own self-judgement. [p. 136]

§277    Spirit perceives the voice of the aesthetic judgement, it knows what is absolutely pleasing or displeasing. It is conscious i.e. it appears, if to no one else, at least to itself. But what it appears (to be) to itself i.e. the image that it has of itself, either corresponds or fails to correspond to that which it knows as the absolutely pleasurable or unpleasurable. In the former case it praises, in the latter it blames itself. It is its own image that appears to it. The praise or blame is its own. [pp. 136–7]

§280    In the idea [*Begriff*] of spirit as something conscious is necessarily included the idea of it being an artist, exactly as the idea of the aesthetic nature includes that of something endowed with soul, something that reveals itself as both law and knowledge, spirit and volition i.e. as artist. Nature as such is by definition unconscious: nature as affording pleasure seems to be spirit, consciousness. Spirit is by definition conscious: not only phenomenal [*erscheinend*] but also conscious of its phenomenality; not only perceiving the voice of the aesthetic judgement but judging its own phenomenality according to the norms of that voice – at one moment encouraged by its own approval and at another cast down by the disapproval – that it cannot refuse to itself. [p. 137]

§299    'Put nothing into this section that does not belong here.' This warning, made by Herbart on a comparable occasion, seems to be relevant here. All that we are discussing is the means by which a phenomenon of the spirit satisfies its own demands in a completed work of the presentation [*im vollendeten Vorstellen*] – the forms of the phenomenon, that is to say, not the phenomenon itself, not its content, which is a matter of indifference. We know nothing about spirit except that it is that which exists consciously, just as nature is that which exists unconsciously. We are not concerned here with what else forms its content. To aesthetics it is a matter of indifference what it appears to itself, but not how it appears. If a phenomenon of the spirit has an 'ideal content', this is absolutely irrelevant to the forms of that phenomenon. Whatever the nature of the content, the phenomenon whose content it forms pleases us, or fails to please, by means of its forms, not its content. [p. 146]

### Book 2, chapter 3: The ideal presentational works of art

#### Section ii: Composite works of art

§649   [. . .] The beautiful takes the shape either of form, sensibility or thought, and from these arise in succession metrical, linear, planar and plastic variations of beauty on the one hand, and on the other beauties of rhythm, light, colour, modulation, sonority and thought. [. . .] it is one of the first conditions of an aesthetic relationship that its constituent parts are capable of being compared, and so it comes about that the constituent kinds of beauty mentioned above cannot be mingled, but at most combined i.e. united to form a single whole, yet always in such a way that constituents of an identical nature together form a unity of that nature. And what is more, this will the more easily happen the closer the connection (from higher points of view) between constituents that are in any case heterogeneous and therefore appear more compatible. [p. 346]

§651   The only incompatibility is between those pairs in which the gaps in the presentation have to be filled by two different, disparate spheres of the presentation, say, painting and poetry, or music and poetry. In the former case the gaps in the spatial form are already filled by visual sensations, and cannot therefore be filled a second time by thoughts. In the latter case the gaps in the temporal form are already filled by auditory sensations, and cannot therefore make room a second time for definite presentations. Simultaneous empty formal presentations may well include colour-sensations in the intervals [*Zwischenräume*], while successive empty rhythmic presentations may well include musical or poetic sensations, but not both together, and always in such a way that each affirms its own validity and unites with other elements of the same kind to form an aesthetic whole. One or the other, the visual sensation or the thought, the musical or the poetic, must then be reduced to forming a simple medium, a representative of the other i.e. become a sign instead of being itself significant. [p. 347]

§653   [. . .] the sonorous element in poetry is quite different from the sonorous element in music. In music it is the ultimate consideration, while in poetry it appears against a wider background, viz. the thought of which it is, as a word, the sign. The sonorous element in music can claim independent validity, while the same element in poetry has only a validity subordinate to the thought. In fact it is not simply a sign – and indeed, since we are speaking only of the phenomenon of spirit for itself, not of that phenomenon for others – it is not yet even a communication sign and can be considered as a sound, indeed as sound; the sonorous imagination, which unites with the thought-imagination to form the poetic, appears as sound-imagination filling in the temporal gaps in the rhythmic form. Nevertheless, because thought-imagination fills the same temporal gaps, only with thoughts, it is a question which of the two – sound-presentation or thought – has to make way for the other. There can in fact be no doubt of the answer. Poetry in which the thought is subordinate to the sound is doggerel, while poetry in which the sonorous element is reduced to mere indifferent sound-marks [*Lautzeichen*] and has no individual beauty of its own, is 'unmusical'. Three elements in fact, are required to form a poetic whole – thought, sonority and rhythm. Like music, poetry is addressed to the ear: it is the bard who first brings a poem to life, as it is the virtuoso who first gives life to a musical work; the poet hears his poem just as the composer hears his composition. There lies the advantage that 'musical' languages (i.e. those in which the sonorous element is in itself beautiful) have over those that are unmusical – the Romance languages over the Germanic, the older forms of the German language over the newer. If in addition to this a language possesses a beauty of modulation – something commoner among southern and, generally speaking, more primitive peoples than among northerners, with their modern outlook and more complex civilization – it is easy to understand that the poetry of the 'musical' peoples will lean more towards pure euphony, while among the peoples whose languages are unmusical the thought-element will be all the more strongly emphasized – in fact pure sound will be predominant in the former case, and sense in the latter. [pp. 348–9]

§654   For this reason a trend which, even in music, tends to emphasize the thought (in the poetical sense of that word) can only be prejudicial to the sonorous (i.e. specifically musical) element in music. Thoughts are easily paired together, but this is not true of thought and music. In that case we have a marriage in which one of the two – thought or music – becomes henpecked. If the thought is not a function [*Zeichen*] of the music, the music is inevitably reduced to being a function of the thought. The former is only justified in the way it has been done by the Minnesingers and Mastersingers, in a folk-song (the *G'stanzl'n* of the Alpine folk), or happens even today in the Italian opera when a single melody is fitted with any number of different texts. The text is there for the music, and music pays no attention to it. What unites them is a common rhythmic form that allows both to pursue their ways in the same rhythm. In the reverse case, on the other hand, the independent beauty of musical sound is abolished and this leads logically to the spoken word. With corresponding logic the aria predominates in the one case, easily tending towards the wordless vocalise, while in the other we have recitative easily tending towards the *parlando*. Each is an instance of a union between music and thought, not the substitution of the sonorous for the poetical. That is something altogether unthinkable because the sonorous is simply and solely sound-sensation, while the poetic is thought-presentation (aesthetic contemplation, a perceptional image, imagination directed to an object). [pp. 349–50]

§655    It is psychologically false to confuse perception (i.e. sense-perception) with feeling – that is to say, a psychic condition belonging to the presentation – with a condition that presupposes the imagination; and it is only a psychological error of this kind that could lead to the attempt to express feelings by musical sounds in the same way as presentations are expressed in words. This mistake leads furthermore to the belief that because feelings are attached to presentations, the music which gives expression to the one must of necessity give expression to the other. Perceptions are indeed a form of presentation but quite different from actual thoughts – musical imaginings, for instance, are simply pure musical perceptions – and this must be clearly realized if one variety is not to be represented by another [. . .] [p. 350]

§656    Does it follow from the fact that the purely sonorous can never replace thought, that music is therefore simply a 'game with sound forms', as it has been called by some? It must be clearly borne in mind that what we call 'music' does not reside in the sonorous alone, but in the union of sonority with rhythm and modulation. The two latter form the link between music and the series of imaginative acts with which, purely *qua* sonority, it has nothing to do. Vague or clearly defined feelings, desires, emotional states and passions, temperamental conditions and motions which, as such, depend entirely on the activity of the imagination [*Vorstellungsverlauf*], show not only certain degrees of intensity but also rhythmical relationships in their ebb and flow: a rise and fall, regular or irregular acceleration or retardation, a tranquil persistence or hasty interruption, gradual increase and momentary cessation, sudden emphasis and fading into the imperceptible. It is the rhythmic and modulatory elements in this psychic life of the presentation that music can make its own and unite [them] with the purely sonorous; and in this way it becomes possible for music to represent mental events [*das Psychische*] in so far as these are exteriorized 'in simple forms of flow' i.e. forms of movement. But the ideas that find themselves in that flow (i.e. in the 'how') are in fact the 'what', the stuff of the inner life of the psyche, and these can never be reproduced by music as such. [pp. 350–1]

§661    [The] union of the plastic chromatic with the dramatic [. . .] forms the theatrical imagination. It is thus that a playwright mentally sees and hears his work simultaneously, and would not be worthy of the name of playwright if it were not so. Only a work that springs from the theatrical imagination is viable in the theatre – otherwise it may well be a dramatic poem, but it is certainly not a stage-play. This is one of the most complex combinations of the human imagination, because it is concerned at one and the same time with the simultaneous and the successive, with the statuesque, the picturesque and the poetic, with ideas and effects of their expression, both rhythmic and sonorous. Of course the composer, too, imagines himself, baton in hand, on the platform and he hears his music, seeing the full orchestra grouped round him, but in this case the chromatic-plastic impression is an unreal one. The visual effect of the performance does not belong to the work's essence, whereas in the theatrical imagination the chromatic-plastic element is a part of the work; what is seen is as important as what is heard, and the play that is not acted is only half a play. It is for this reason that orchestral musicians rightly appear in the simplest clothes; it would be best if they were not visible at all, as Goethe's 'Uncle' suggested,[2] since the musical imagination is not concerned with anything visible, whereas for the theatrical imagination what is seen is at least as important as what is heard. Thus every classical stage-play must necessarily benefit from being performed by good actors – actors, that is to say, who enter completely and objectively into the parts they play – while many a dramatic poem necessarily loses something by even the best performance. On the other hand a dramatic poem loses less by even the most miserable performance than a good stage-play loses by poor performance, because the play forfeits half its individuality – the visual half – while the dramatic poem preserves its most important individuality, which is the audible. [p. 354]

§662 The character of the musical–poetic imagination varies according to whether the poetic element is lyrical, epic or dramatic [. . .] The song, the romance and the cantata are relevant examples. Associated with the chromatic-plastic imagination the first becomes a stage-song, the second a stage-romance and the third an operatic fantasy, which bears the same relationship to the musico-dramatic as the theatrical to the dramatic. The operatic fantasy contains all the difficulties associated with the relationship between simultaneous music and thought; and these difficulties are greatest in dramatic poetry, where thought is the most important element i.e. where there is an insistence on the laws of logical causation. Since there is no solution of this difficulty, all that can be achieved is a continual compromise or the contrasting of two alternatives – the music dominating the word or the thought dominating the music. The latter alternative was described by Gluck in the letter in which he dedicated his *Alceste* to the Grand Duke of Tuscany:

music plays the same part as that played by the brilliance of colours in a good, well-designed drawing, and by a well-chosen chiaroscuro, which serves to give life to the figures without damaging the overall contours.[3]

The contours must therefore seek to make up in some other way for the musical beauty sacrificed to the thought, and only two means are possible – one directed to the ear and the other to the eye. If the ear is chosen, we have the great instrumental operas of Mozart, Gluck or Beethoven, in which any purely musical loss noticeable in the vocal sections is made up by the overture, by introduction and rich accompaniments. If the eye is chosen, we have spectacular operas like Spontini's and like Wagner's *Rheingold*. On the other hand, if music is the dominating element, as in the case of Italian and many

---

[2] [The reference here is to a character and an episode in Goethe's *Wilhelm Meisters Lehrjahre*, book 8, chapter 5.]

[3] [For the full text of the dedication see O. Strunk, *Source Readings in Music History* (New York 1950), p. 673.]

French operas, no need is felt either for independent instrumental music or for spectacular staging: all the interest is concentrated on the singing, and less on the singers' interpretation than on their actual voices – the purely sonorous element. Aria and coloratura play, as it were, the leading roles. [pp. 354–5]

# 1.2   Music as an expressive force

## Introduction

Hegel's system of aesthetics exercised an enormous influence on German philosophy and theory of criticism in the nineteenth century, either by inspiring followers, often unoriginal ones, or by provoking a reaction or determining a stance conditioned, at least in part, by Hegel's powerful intellectual presence. Yet what of Hegel appealed to the nineteenth-century critics was not so much the complex system of philosophy in which individual parts cannot be taken separately, and where, for instance, aesthetics cannot be fully understood without a reference to his logic or the philosophy of history, but rather the most readily intelligible hierarchic system of the arts. The hierarchy is built on an investigation of the relationship between the spiritual content and the sensuous material within three stages which Hegel called the symbolic, classical and romantic. In symbolic art (architecture) the universal Idea is still very much imprisoned by the material of the medium; an equilibrium is reached in the classical art (sculpture), and then in the final stage are grouped the romantic arts, those 'whose mission it is to give shape to the inner side of personal life'.[1] This group includes painting, music and poetry. Music, although high in the hierarchy, has to yield to the supremacy of poetry, for the vagueness of the content of music, 'the abstract inner life of feeling'[2] prevents the Idea from being fully revealed. That revelation is achieved in poetry which is capable of 'unfolding the totality of an èvent, a successive series and the changes of the heart's movements, passions, ideas, and the complete course of an action'.[3] Music has a form and a content and this division would in itself not suffice to distinguish Hegel from those who, like Herbart, may be seen as his philosophical opponents. Hegel's content is 'a spiritual feeling felt by the heart'[4] which is somehow added to the material of music, to its harmonic and contrapuntal dimension, and this extra-musical quality makes Hegel view the repetition and variation of thematic material with some suspicion, since in repetition the meaning that resides in a theme simply appears again.[5] Variation and repetition belong to the technical, formal element of music and thus by implication the form and content in music appear in an uneasy rela-

---

[1] G. W. F. Hegel, *Aesthetics, Lectures on Fine Art*, vol. 2 (Oxford 1974), p. 625.
[2] Hegel, p. 960.
[3] *Ibid.*
[4] Hegel, p. 908.
[5] Hegel, p. 896; le Huray and Day, p. 341.

51

tionship. This may be a side issue in Hegel, and indeed, elsewhere he goes some way towards acknowledging the interconnectedness of form and content.[6] The division is nevertheless there and the criticism of it in the early twentieth century demonstrated the coincidence of the anti-romantic aesthetics and the anti-Hegelian attitude of German philosophy of the time.

What of course appealed to the romantics most, were Hegel's statements that music is 'the art of the soul',[7] that it works especially on the 'heart as such'[8] and that it deals 'with a concrete inner life'.[9] Such detached statements, rather than the full system of Hegel's aesthetics became the themes of much of the criticism of music in the nineteenth century and their presence in Wagner's writings betrays a link with Hegel. Categories in which Hegel argued the significance of each individual art within his hierarchic system were closed ones, and although some transitional phases or border areas, like the one between music and poetry, were envisaged, the transformation of one art into another was not described nor was a combining of the arts encouraged. This is to be expected, since each category is based on a closely argued investigation of the relationship between the material and the content.[10] The connection between the material and the art form was in the preceding century discussed by G. E. Lessing in his *Laokoon* (1766).

The appearance of a certain Hegelian desire to discuss all the arts as belonging to a system is discernible already in the first of Wagner's theoretical works, *The Artwork of the Future* (1849). The Hegelian succession of architecture, sculpture and painting is taken over complete, but Wagner gives a prominence to a group of arts which are, of course, close to him as an operatic composer. The 'three original arts: Dance, Music and Poetry' represent an extension of Hegel's system, since dance, according to Hegel, 'an imperfect art',[11] is accorded prominence. Whereas with Hegel music mediates between painting and poetry, Wagner presents it as an art mediating in the chain between dance and poetry, but with Wagner the mediation itself has a different quality about it. Instead of Hegel's closed categories Wagner presents a fluctuating world in which the arts transform themselves. It is not a world of conceptual clarity, but one of dynamic change, supported by the instinct and sensibility of an artist rather than the analytical thought of a philosopher. Hegel's influence is even stronger in the *Opera and Drama* (1851), where the mediation of music between dance and poetry gives way to an upward surge towards poetry by which the hierarchy of Hegel's system has been given a certain dynamic impulse. This is partly achieved through an adroit twist of using the possibilities afforded by the German language for creating new words. *Dichter* (a poet) is linked to *Tondichter* (a circumlocu-

[6] Hegel, p. 906.
[7] Hegel, p. 891.
[8] Hegel, p. 904.
[9] Hegel, p. 941.
[10] Hegel, *Aesthetics*, vol. 1 (Oxford 1975), p. 82.
[11] Hegel, vol. 2, p. 627.

tion for a composer) so that the two are fused. This fusion is central among the several themes of *Opera and Drama*.

It was after *Opera and Drama* that Wagner became acquainted with the philosophy of Arthur Schopenhauer. Although philosophically opposed to Hegel, yet like him treating the arts as a cognitive activity, Schopenhauer offered a hierarchy of the arts which on the outside is superficially similar to Hegel's. The important difference is that Schopenhauer places music after poetry at the top of his hierarchy since music 'is by no means like the other arts, namely a copy of the Ideas, but a copy of the will itself, the objectivity of which are the ideas'.[12] This supremacy of music appealed to Wagner and in his essay on Beethoven (1870) he attempted a partial revision of his earlier thoughts in the light of his reading of Schopenhauer. There is no explicit mention of any attempt at revision and the argument strikes one as an uneasy mixture of musical, historical and literary reflections.

Wagner may have been attracted to Schopenhauer not only by the latter's esteem of music, but perhaps more strongly by the appearance in Schopenhauer's philosophy of a strong element of fantasy and wilfulness betraying an artistic sensibility. That same sensibility pervades the thought of Friedrich Nietzsche. Nietzsche's aesthetic views are most clearly expressed in his first work, *The Birth of Tragedy* (1870). It was originally intended as a study in classical philology, but its real significance lies in Nietzsche's argument about the nature of a work of art as well as the nature of creativity. Drawing his inspiration from the rich sources of German classical philosophy, Nietzsche, with a characteristic twist of originality and an inclination towards powerful images, asserted that in art the spirit of ecstasy and unbridled creative urge (Dionysian element) is checked and controlled by the sense of order, form and contemplation (Apollonian element). The equilibrium of these elements ensures great art, although for Nietzsche it is the Dionysian element which always remains the more important one. And, as in ancient Greece the tragedy was born from the musical, Dionysian element of the chorus, so in his day Richard Wagner is the person who was capable of uniting the power of myth and tragedy and the ecstasy of music. The text which starts as a philological treatise thus ends as an apologia for Wagner's art and uses that art as a paradigm for an aesthetic theory.

The second of Nietzsche's texts should, ideally, not belong to this section of the book. It is appended here for the sake of convenience, but should otherwise form a part of an argument tracing the development of the existentialist attitude to music. Nietzsche's approval of the Dionysian impulse, his contention that art springs out of life, and that the Apollonian sense of beauty and of form is essentially something that is imposed upon the original creative urge, leads him to distrust not only any formal organization, but also any desire of the artist to use the artwork as a means to an end, whereby he becomes only an actor. Wagner's elaborate structuring of myth, particularly his use of

[12] A. Schopenhauer, *The World as Will and Representation*, tr. E. F. J. Payne (New York 1969), vol. 1, p. 257.

Christian symbolism in *Parsifal* demonstrated to Nietzsche that Wagner had merely become a grand actor and was enslaved by the trappings of form. *The Case of Wagner* (1888) contains the main thrust of Nietzsche's criticism, while *Nietzsche contra Wagner* (1888, not included here) elaborates on the subject.

None of the other authors represented in this section exercised such a strong influence on thought in the second half of the nineteenth century as did Wagner or Nietzsche. Friedrich Theodor Vischer belongs to a stream of Hegel's heirs who followed him by imitating the general layout of his system as more or less skilful commentators, adding here and there their own alterations. Like Hegel, Vischer accepted that art was an imperfect stage of the objectification of the spirit, reserving the ultimate place for philosophy, but unlike Hegel, he saw religion only as an area preparatory for the arts. He does not insist on the Hegelian characterization of music as a language of feelings and shows in general more understanding towards the requirements of the process of composition. He nevertheless classes music as a 'subjective' art form, reserving the title of the 'objective' art form for painting.

All the other texts from this section demonstrate the extent to which literary or musical historians were developing their theories under the influence of the philosophical doctrines of the time. The influence must not always be understood as a conscious application of a philosophical system. Rather, in several instances it may be seen that the cultural tradition from which the works come had thoroughly absorbed some of the philosophical arguments and made them into recurrent themes that characterize an age. Georg Gottfried Gervinus is by his conservatism perhaps the least representative of the time, yet his belief that music has to be turned into a vehicle for expression by addition of a definable content qualifies him as an adherent of the aesthetics of content. Both August Wilhelm Ambros and Friedrich von Hausegger show the grasp on the one side of the Hegelian system, and on the other the Wagnerian belief. The very title of Ambros's work owes something to the Hegelian categories seen in the dynamic manner of Wagner. Ambros repeatedly feels the need to justify the addition of poetry to music, whether as a text or as an 'idea', as if afraid that the lack of a definable content would cause music to collapse from within. Friedrich von Hausegger, writing later in the century, is aware of the advances made by his time in the study of the psychology of listening and although it is his intention to warn the reader against the belief that music can imitate in the Aristotelian sense, its definition as an art of expression raises more questions than it answers. The answer is then sought in a Wagnerian simplification of Hegel whereby art is equated with religion.

It is not easy to disentangle the influences on Kretzschmar's theory of musical hermeneutics. The term itself reminds one of Dilthey, but the belief that an art of interpreting the sound-patterns of music helps to bring out the meaning encapsulated within music and striving to break out, may be traced to Hegel's discussion of the differences between music and poetry.[13] Kretz-schmar then attempts to reverse Hegel's description of the 'absorption of the inner life into the realm of notes'[14] without appealing to the higher category of poetry, by devising a system for revealing the hidden meaning of music.

Mies's text demonstrates the extent to which the theories of emotion and content are taken over by a musicologist who, without an investigation of the theory of significance or expressivity, simply considers the various options open to a listener for whom, at the beginning of the twentieth century, programme music is simply a given genre.

[13] Hegel, vol. 2, pp. 962–3.
[14] Ibid.

# Richard Wagner (1813–1883)
## Oper und Drama (1851)

As an author of poetry, essays, criticism, extended theoretical works and various texts of autobiographical nature, Wagner is probably the most prolific among composers. His earliest essays date from 1834 and he continued to write regularly and copiously until his death. His writings contain important ideas on the nature of poetry, drama, *Gesamtkunstwerk* and creativity in general and occasionally show deep insights into psychology of art and artists. However, they are also inconsistent, contradictory, repetitive and often full of prejudice. His style suffers from verbosity and hyperbole, and nearly all of his prose works are shot through with a feeling of self-importance. It is a mark of their significance that in spite of these shortcomings they are regarded as a remarkable intellectual achievement.

The first edition of Wagner's collected works (1871–3) was put together under his instructions, and later editions, which included subsequent writings, continued to use Wagner's chronological rather than thematic organization. There is as yet no reliable critical edition of the complete prose works. The following are most often quoted and consulted:

*Gesammelte Schriften und Dichtungen* (Leipzig 1871–3), 9 vols., 10th vol. 1883; reprinted 1976. 2nd edn, 10 vols. in 5 (Leipzig 1887–8).

*Richard Wagner's Prose Works*, tr. and ed. W. A. Ellis (London 1892–9, reprinted New York 1972), 8 vols.

Two modern editions deserve to be mentioned:

*Oper und Drama*, ed. K. Kropfinger (Stuttgart 1984). A detailed critical edition with commentary.

*Dichtungen und Schriften*, ed. D. Borchmeyer (Frankfurt 1983), 10 vols. Not a complete edition, but includes all the major poetical and prose works.

# Opera and Drama

Source:

*Oper und Drama* in *Gesammelte Schriften und Dichtungen*, 2nd edn, vol. 4 (Leipzig 1887). Teil iii: 'Dichtkunst und Tonkunst im Drama der Zukunft'. Chapter iv, pp. 157–60; chapter v, pp. 173–6; 182–5. Translated by Martin Cooper.

(The first edition of the treatise, published by J. J. Weber in Leipzig bears the date 1852 but the book was in fact issued in November 1851.)

## Part III: Poetry and music in the drama of the future

### Chapter IV

[.    .]

Our modern music may be said to have developed from harmony alone. It has been determined arbitrarily from an inexhaustible wealth of possible choices presented by root-basses and the chords derived from them. In so far as this music has remained absolutely true to its origins, the impression that it has made on the feelings of listeners has been only one of stupefaction and confusion, and its most highly-coloured manifestations have appealed only to a certain conscious delight in solving musical problems, which is common among our artists but not among the laymen who do not understand music. Music lovers in general, with the exception of those who lay claim to some understanding of the art, have concerned themselves only with the most superficial aspect of melody and the purely sensuous charm of the human voice.[1] Such people counter the lovers of 'absolute' music by saying 'I do not understand your music, it is too erudite for me'. Yet in the instance of harmony as it should be – the purely musical determinant and foundation of the poetic melody which it supports – it is not a case of 'understanding' in the sense in which the exceptional musician 'understands' and the layman does not. In performance the listener's attention should by no means be drawn to the effectiveness of the harmony as such, but to its silent power of determining the characteristic expression of the melody and yet, by its very silence, enormously complicating the understanding of the expression – making it in fact only fully within the grasp of the attentive musical scholar. Thus the actual sound of a harmonization will render the abstract, disturbing activity of the musical intelligence unnecessary and will make evident the musical and emotional content of the melody, something that can be grasped without any distracting trouble and is easily and quickly communicated to the feelings.

If, therefore, musicians have hitherto construed, as it were, their music on a harmonic basis, composers will now consider not only the melody as determined by the poet's verses but another essential musical consideration inherent in this first one – namely the harmony which reveals the full implications of the melody itself. The poet's melody already includes its harmony, only implicit rather than explicit and secretly determining the expressive significance of the sounds that the poet designed for the melody. This expressive significance was already in the poet's ear, though he was not aware of it, and already determined the harmony, of which it was the clearest utterance; but this manifestation existed only in the poet's mind and was not yet perceptible to his senses. It is to the senses, as to the immediately perceptive organs of the feelings, that he turns for his salvation and it is to them that he must communicate the melodic manifestation of the harmony and the conditions

[1] I am reminded of the gelder's knife.

of that utterance; for an organic work of art is only that which includes simultaneously the conditioning factors and what is already conditioned. Until now harmonic conditions have been provided by the absolute music: the poet would communicate in his melody only that which was stipulated and he would therefore remain as unintelligible as a composer who did not completely communicate to the listener the harmonic conditions of the melody as warranted by the poet's verses.

It was, however, only the musician that could discover the harmony, not the poet. We saw the poet invent the melody from the spoken lines but, as a harmonically conditioned melody, it was in fact discovered rather than invented. The right conditions for the composer's melody must be present before the poet could consider his melody validly conditioned. It was the composer who laid down the conditions of this melody before the poet discovered it and found his redemption – and these conditions belong to the musician's most personal possessions. He presents the melody to the poet as one that is harmonically justified: and it is only the melody which is made possible by the very nature of modern music that will save the poet and both stimulate and satisfy his poetic impulse.

In this matter the poet and the musician resemble two travellers who set out from the same point and go in opposite directions, observing a straight line. At the opposite point on the earth's surface they meet again, each having covered one half of the planet. They question each other and each man recounts what he has seen and encountered. The poet speaks of the plains, mountains, valleys, meadows, human beings and animals that he has seen during his long travels by land. The musician explored the seas and recounts the wonders of the ocean, his near escapes from shipwreck, the great deeps with their strange monsters that inspired him with a pleasurable horror. Each man is excited by the other's account and each is absolutely determined to experience in person all the things described by the other. Once again they part, each to complete his journey round the world. Finally they meet again at their original parting-place: this time the poet has explored the oceans and the musician the dry land. They do not separate again, as each now knows the world: each has now practical experience of what he had previously only dreamed or imagined. They are at one, since each shares the other's knowledge and feelings. The poet has become a musician and the musician a poet: both are now complete artistic human beings.

At their first meeting, after traversing one half of the world, the conversation between poet and musician was that melody which we are now considering – the melody formed by the poet from his innermost longings, themselves conditioned by his experiences. When both men took leave of each other the second time, each had in his imagination things that he had himself not yet experienced, and it was in order to obtain this convincing experience that they parted again. Then let us observe the poet possessing himself of the musician's experiences in his own person, but guided by the musician, who had already crossed the oceans boldly, had found his way safely back to dry land and could give him exact information about safe routes to take. On this new journey we shall see that the poet becomes identical with the musician travelling over the other half of the world's surface on the instructions of the poet: so that the two journeys can now be considered identical.

If the poet now sets out for the vast open spaces of harmony in order, as it were, to obtain proof of the veracity of the melody 'narrated' to him by the musician, he will no longer find the trackless deserts of sound encountered by the musician on his first journey. Instead, he will be delighted by the marvellous boldness of design, the strange novelty and infinitely delicate detail, combined with giant strength, of the seagoing vessel built by his predecessor and now serving to carry him safely over the waves. He has been instructed by the musician in the handling and use of the rudder, the principle of the sails and all the strange and ingenious knowledge needed in order to steer a safe course through wind and weather. At the helm of this ship, as she makes her majestic way through the waves, the poet will forget his painful plodding over hill and dale in his delighted awareness of man's unlimited powers. Seen from her high deck, even the mightiest waves appear to him as loyal and willing agents of his own noble destiny, the destiny of poetic intention. This ship is the powerful instrument which enables him to carry out his most far-reaching and ambitious desires, and his mind turns in warm gratitude to the musician, who invented the vessel to save himself from shipwreck and has now entrusted her to his hands – for this trusty vessel is master of the limitless sea of harmony: the orchestra. [pp. 157–60]

[.    .    .]

## Chapter V

The orchestra is unquestionably possessed of the faculty of speech, as has been revealed by the creations of our modern instrumental composers. In Beethoven's symphonies we have seen this faculty of speech developed to a point at which it felt impelled to give expression even to that which, by its nature, it is unable to express. In the verbal melody of the poet [*Wortversmelodie*] we have now conferred on the orchestra precisely that to which it could not give expression and provided it, as bearer of this related melody, with the ability to express – with complete freedom – precisely that which by its nature it is unable to express; and we can therefore precisely identify this faculty of speech of the orchestra as the power of uttering the verbally inexpressible.

This phrase must not be understood in a purely ideal sense, but as something absolutely real and concrete. We have seen that the orchestra is not a kind of complex of vaguely similar sonorous potentialities, but that it consists of an almost infinitely extendable confederation of instruments, each an individual personality and required to give an individual quality to every note that it is asked to produce. A body of sound without this definite individual quality in each component part does not really exist in fact, and can at most be imagined. As we have seen, this individual quality is determined by the special characteristics of each instrument, which gives a distinctive, consonantal timbre, to the vowel-sound of each note it produces. As this consonantal timbre can never achieve a significance conditioned by the understanding of the feelings comparable to that of a consonant in ordinary speech, and moreover has not the same ability to change and thereby alter its influence on the vowel, the musical language of an instrument cannot possibly achieve the exclusive expressiveness of human speech, which is the organ of the intelligence. On the other hand, as organ of the feelings, it expresses precisely and exclusively that which language, by its very nature, is unable to express and is therefore, from the point of view of the human intelligence, quite simply inexpressible. The instruments of the orchestra make it quite clear that this 'verbally inexpressible' is not something essentially inexpressible, but simply something beyond expression by the organ of the human intelligence and therefore not a mere intellectual fiction but something real. Each instrument in isolation makes this manifest, and infinitely more so in alternating action with other instruments.[2]

Let us now take into consideration the inexpressible which the orchestra has managed to express with great certainty, and indeed in association with another thing inexpressible – the gesture.

Physical gestures, as determined by the significant moving of the limbs most capable of conveying expression and of the features of the face denoting emotions, may be said to be something completely unutterable insofar as language can only describe and interpret them, whereas the emotions concerned can only really be expressed by precisely those gestures and those facial features. Anything that can be conveyed completely by language, that is, anything that is to be communicated from one intelligence to another, has no need of any gesture to accompany or reinforce its sense – in fact the communication might well be disturbed by any unnecessary gesturing. As we saw earlier, in a communication of this kind the physical organ of reception, the ear, is not in any way excited: it serves simply as neutral agent. The communication of anything which language cannot convey with complete conviction to the feelings to which it is addressed, i.e. an expression issuing in the affective system of the listener, certainly needs reinforcing by an accompanying gesture. We see therefore that in cases where the ear is to be stimulated to important physical sympathy recourse is automatically had to the eye: ear and eye together must mutually assure each other of a more elevated form of communication to make their message convincing to the emotions. Gesture, however, in its necessary communication to the eye was conveying to the eye only that which language was no longer able to convey – if it were

---

[2] This easy explanation of what is meant by 'inexpressible' might with justice be extended to the field of religious philosophy, where that which is declared absolutely 'inexpressible' from one point of view is in essence perfectly capable of expression, provided that the right organ of expression be employed.

otherwise, the gesture was superfluous and disturbing. Gesture stimulated the eye in a manner different from the corresponding counterpart of the communication as addressed to the ear. This counterpart, however, is necessary in order to make the impression absolutely intelligible to the feelings. The verse which emotional stimulation has caused to become melody transmutes the intellectual content of the original verbal communication into an emotional content. The moment exactly corresponding to that at which gesture communicates the message to the ear is not yet present in this melody which, as the most highly charged form of verbal expression, first led to the intensification represented by gesture, as a reinforcement. The melody stood in need of this precisely because it could not yet contain that which precisely corresponded to the moment of reinforcement represented by the gesture. The verse-melody consequently contained only the antecedent condition for the manifestation of the gesture. The melody is still incapable of that which gesture must justify (or rather interpret) to the feelings, as the line of verse is vindicated by the melody or the melody by the harmony. Springing from the line of verse, the melody retains an essential, indispensable though only partial connection with language, incapable of expressing what is peculiar to gesture and therefore turning to it for help, yet still unable to communicate the exact equivalent to the listening ear. Consequently that which could not be expressed by gesture in the language of vocal music found expression in a language totally divorced from words, namely that of the orchestra, capable of communicating to the ear what gesture communicated to the eye.

This power of communication was achieved by the orchestra through its role as accompanist to the most sensuous of all gestures, namely the dance which by its very nature needed this accompaniment in order to make its message intelligible. The gestures of the dance, like all gestures, stand in relationship to orchestral melody rather as verbal poetry stands to the vocal melody which it determines; so that gestures and orchestral melody only together form an intelligible whole like that of vocal melody. The point at which dance-gestures and orchestra meet in a way most plain to the senses, the one in space, the other in time, one directed to the eye, the other to the ear – that is to say, the point at which they show themselves as equal, interlocked and mutually dependent – is in rhythm. In moving away from this point both must necessarily fall into the background, in order to remain or become intelligible in rhythm which reveals their deep relationship. It is from this point that both orchestra and gesture equally develop that power of speech which is the most essential feature of both. On the one hand gesture reveals by this power to the eye what gesture alone can express, while on the other it communicates to the ear that which corresponds precisely to its own form of manifestation, just as, at the outset of their relationship, musical rhythm made clear to the ear that which was manifest in those moments of the dance which made the most direct appeal to the senses. The alternate rise and fall of the dancer's foot strikes the eye in exactly the same way as the alternation of strong and weak beats strikes the ear; and in the same way a rapid instrumental figure forming a melodic link between strong beats affects the ear in exactly the same way as the eye is affected by the movement of the feet or other expressive limbs of the dancer between the alternations which correspond to the strong beats in the music. [pp. 173–6]

[.    .    .]

Anything that we cannot express, however much we may wish to, by any of our organs of communication, or any composition of those organs, is nonexistent, a nothing. Everything for which we can find expression, on the other hand, is something real, and we acknowledge this reality when we explain to ourselves the expression that we automatically select. The term 'thought' [*Gedanke*] is quite easy to explain by going back to the root of the word. A 'thought' is the picture of something real but absent, that appears [*dünkend*] as we resort to memory [*Gedenken*].[3] This absent something is in origin a real object that has presented itself at some other time and in some other place to our senses and made a distinct impression on them. This impression has taken possession of our sensibilities, and in order to communicate this we have had to discover an expression corresponding to the impression made by the object, according to the universal human ability to make classifications. We can only receive this object according to the impression that it makes on our sensibility; and it is this impression, as determined by our sensory faculty that is the image which appears to our memory as the object itself. Memory and recollection are therefore the same thing: and in fact a thought is an image that recurs to our memory in the form determined by our sensory faculty, since it is the impression made by an object on that faculty. It is then vividly presented by the thinking memory to our sensibility, as a kind of echo [*Nachempfindung*] of the original impression – evidence of the lasting power of sensibility and the depth of the impression made upon it. We are not here concerned with the development of the faculty of combining in an orderly fashion [*bindende Kombination*] all images, whether directly or indirectly experienced, of objects not actually present but stored in the memory. That is the 'thinking' that we encounter in philosophical science; but the poet's path leads from philosophy to the work of art, which is the realization of thought in terms of the senses. Only one thing remains to be precisely established. We are unable to 'think' of anything that has not first made an impression on our feelings [*Empfindung*], and that first experience of the feelings determines the

[3] Similarly we can conveniently explain the term *Geist* [spirit] from the related root of *giessen* [to pour out]: in a natural sense it is something that 'pours out of us', in the way in which the scent spreads out and pours out of a flower. [Wagner's explanation is based on the associative value of sounds in the two pairs of words. Etymologically there may be a distant connection between *Gedanke* and *dünken*, but there is no connection whatsoever between *Geist* and *giessen*. See F. Kluge, *Etymologisches Wörterbuch der deutschen Sprache*, ed. W. Mitzka, 19th edn (Berlin 1963). Schopenhauer displayed a similar weakness for unfounded etymological speculation when he claimed that the German word *schön* is related to the English 'to show'. See A. Schopenhauer, *Parerga and Paralipomena*, tr. E. F. J. Payne, 2 vols. (Oxford 1974), vol. 2, §211, p. 424.]

form of the thought that is searching for expression. A thought is therefore prompted by feeling and must necessarily issue again the feeling, for it is the link between a feeling that is not actually present and one that is present and seeking exteriorization.

The poet's verse-melody in a sense materializes before our eyes the thought i.e. transforms the earlier feeling presented by our thinking into a feeling that is actually and really perceptible. In simple verbal verse the feeling includes the earlier feeling as presented, thought and described from memory and determining the shape of the second. In the case of pure musical melody, on the other hand, it contains the new, actual, determined feeling in which the former feeling – having passed through the thinking-process and now acting as the stimulus – is resolved into something cognate and newly realized. The feeling to which utterance is given in this melody has visibly developed from the thought of an earlier feeling which forms its justification; it is immediately perceptible to the senses and unfailingly determines our sympathetic reaction. It is a phenomenon that belongs to those to whom it is communicated quite as much as to him that communicates it; and we can retain it as a thought i.e. a memory, just as it occurred in the first instance to its originator. If he feels impelled when thinking of this phenomenon to give expression to a new and similarly actual feeling, he now returns to it in thought simply as a past moment in his imagination lightly indicated by his memory and intelligence. The process is similar to that of the verse-melody, the expression of a melodic phenomenon now only remembered, where he used the thought of a former feeling, now weakened by the passage of time, as a stimulus for a new feeling. We, as listeners, can retain in our musical memories this feeling which now exists only in the mind as a purely melodic statement. It has become the property of music itself; and presented to our sense-perceptions with fitting expression by the orchestra, it appears to us as an actual realization of what was only a thought in the composer's mind. Such a melody, communicated to us as the exteriorization of the performer's sensibility, realizes for us – in any properly expressive orchestral performance, at a moment when the performer only preserves that feeling in his memory – the thought of that performer. Indeed even in cases where the actual communicator of that feeling appears to be no longer conscious of it, its characteristic sound in the orchestra can arouse in us a sensibility which – in order to complete a connection and make a situation clearly intelligible by interpreting motifs contained in this situation but unable to emerge completely in their representable moments – becomes for us a thought. In itself, however, it is more than that, for it is the emotional content of the thought made present to our consciousness.

Thanks to the orchestra the composer's power is almost limitless, if it is used to realize the poetical intention at the highest possible level. Without being conditioned by the poetical intention, the pure musician has up till now supposed that he was working with thoughts and combinations of thoughts. If purely musical themes were called 'thoughts', this was either due to a careless use of the word or evidence of a delusion in the composer. He called a theme a 'thought' but although he himself no doubt did 'think' something when setting it down, it was something that was not intelligible to anyone but a friend to whom he described his thoughts in simple words and thus invited him to have the same thoughts about the theme as himself. Music cannot think, but it can substantialize thoughts i.e. express their emotional content as something not merely remembered but re-lived [*vergegenwärtigt*]. Yet music only has this power if its own message is conditioned by the intention of the poet, and this in its turn not merely thought but clearly expressed by means of the organ of human intelligence, namely speech. A musical motif can only produce an emotional effect that is precise and relates to a definite mental activity if the feeling expressed in the motif was presented to the imagination by a definite individual in relation to a definite object and itself clearly defined and properly conditioned. In the absence of these conditions a musical motif presents itself to the feelings as something vague: and however often something vague may recur within the same phenomenon, it remains for us simply a recurrent vagueness that we cannot justify by any sense of its inevitability and that we cannot therefore attach to anything else. On the other hand a musical motif into which a dramatist's line, with all its intentions, has been as it were dissolved before our very eyes – is something conditioned by necessity. When it recurs we are sensibly aware of a definite feeling, and what is more – the feeling of the artist who is himself compelled to give expression to a new feeling derived from that earlier one which, though not now expressed by him, is made perceptible to our senses by the orchestra. The simultaneous sound of that motif connects, in our minds, an earlier experience conditioning the present experience, which it has both conditioned and brought into existence. Thus, by making our feelings the enlightened witnesses of the organic growth of one definite feeling out of the other, we give those feelings the power of thought – or rather in this instance, something superior to thought, namely the instinctive knowledge of a thought as realized in feeling. [pp. 182–5]

# Richard Wagner

# 'Beethoven' (1870)

*Source:*

'Beethoven' in *Gesammelte Schriften und Dichtungen*, 2nd edn, vol. 9 (Leipzig 1888), pp. 97–112. Translated by Martin Cooper.

[.   .   .]

It is impossible to grasp Beethoven as a man without immediately including in our consideration Beethoven the astonishing musician. We have seen how the instinctive direction of his life coincides with that of emancipating the art of music. Just as he himself could never be the servant of luxury, so his music too must be liberated from any mark of subjection to frivolous taste. Furthermore, we have a clear proof that his optimistic religious faith went hand in hand with this instinct to broaden the sphere of his art in his ninth symphony with choral finale; and we must take a closer look at the genesis of this work if we wish fully to understand the astonishing connection between these two fundamental tendencies in the great man's nature.

The same impulse that guided Beethoven's intellectual perception to the formation of the idea of the good man also guided him in his restoration of the good man's melody. Melody had lost its innocence in the hands of professional musicians, and it was Beethoven's desire to restore that innocence in all its purity. We need only recall Italian operatic melody of the previous century to recognize that it was no more than a trivial musical spectre wholly subordinate to fashion and to fashionable purposes. Music had in this way been brought so low that novelty was all that wanton taste demanded, since last year's melody was already intolerable. Our instrumental music, too, was dependent on this melody, and we have already pointed to its use for the purposes of a social existence lacking in all nobility of character.

It was Haydn who had direct recourse to the robust and hearty dance-melodies of the common people and his borrowings from Hungarian peasant dances – the music closest to hand – are often easy to recognize. This circumstance restricted the sphere of his music within humble and comparatively narrow, local bounds. But from what sphere was a composer to borrow this natural kind of melody if he wished it to impart a nobler, durable character? The attraction of these peasant dance-tunes of Haydn's was that of a piquant specialty rather than that of a pure human type of art with permanent validity. It was certainly not possible to borrow anything from the higher spheres of the social order, for it was they that waxed enthusiastic over the opera-singers and ballet-dancers with their effeminate, over-ornamented melody, for which there was nothing to be said. Beethoven followed Haydn's example; but instead of using these popular melodies to provide entertainment to a nobleman's dinner-table, he transmuted them in an ideal sense for the common man. He recognized that innocent nobility of which he dreamed in Scottish, Russian and old French folk tunes, and it was as homage to that nobility that he conceived his whole art. In the last movement of his A major Symphony he used a Hungarian dance-melody to include the whole of Nature; and any man witnessing the dance of Nature to this music would think that he was beholding a new planet in this huge circling round-dance.

The problem, however, was to find the original type of innocence, the 'good man' of Beethoven's idealistic faith, in order to unite this ideal with his other belief, that 'God is love'. The composer might almost be said to be close to defining him in the 'Eroica' Symphony, where the unusually simple theme of the finale – which he used also in other contexts – should, it seems, have served him as a kind of groundplan. But the captivating melodic charm of these variations is still too close to Mozart's sentimental cantabile, though broadened and developed in so individual a manner by him, to be considered an achievement in the sense now under discussion. There is clearer evidence of this search in the exultant finale of the C minor Symphony, where the naive appeal of the simple march-tune – with its almost exclusive use of tonic-dominant harmonies solemnly succeeding each other in the natural scales of horns and trumpets – is all the more appealing because it seems to be the conclusion for which all the rest of the symphony was preparing us emotionally – like the sun's brilliant rays breaking through after a storm or clouds dispersed by gentle breezes.

Here we must make what may well seem like a digression, but one which has in fact an important bearing on the subject in hand. This C minor Symphony holds our attention as one of the stranger of Beethoven's conceptions – the initial mood of painful and passionate involvement soars, through moments of consolation and spiritual elevation into the final outburst of confident, victorious joy. The lyrical pathos lies very close to that of an ideal drama in the more precise sense: and it might seem dubious whether this does not in itself involve some prejudicing of the pure musical conception, since it must lead to the admission of ideas entirely alien to the spirit of music. But it must be recognized that Beethoven was not guided here by any irrelevant aesthetic speculation but purely by an absolutely ideal instinct rooted in the very nature of music itself. This instinct coincided, as we showed at the end of our last enquiry, with the impulse to rescue (or perhaps to restore to human consciousness) the belief in the original goodness of man's nature despite all merely superficial arguments from experience. Such ideas as these, springing almost entirely from a spirit of exalted serenity, belong (as we saw above) mostly to that period of spiritual isolation when total deafness seems to have removed him entirely from the world of suffering. It may be unnecessary to explain the frequent recurrence of depressive moods in some of Beethoven's greatest works by supposing a decline in that spirit of serenity; for we should certainly be mistaken if we were to suppose that the master could create in any other spirit but one of deep interior serenity. The spirit expressed in his creations must therefore belong to that idea of the world comprehended by the artist and manifested in his work. Since, however, we have definitely accepted that music reveals the idea of the world, the composer himself must be a primary feature of this idea, and his utterance is not simply his view of the world but the world itself, with its alternations of joy and grief, pleasure and pain.[1] This world also included the doubts which, as we know, Beethoven felt as a man. He is thus speaking directly, and not as the object of reflection, when he gives expression – as it were – to the world, as he does in his Ninth Symphony, in which the first movement shows his idea of the world in its most horrible light. Yet it cannot be denied that it is precisely in this same symphony that the higher ordering of the will of that world's Creator prevails. This finds immediate expression in the answer – like a word spoken to a man waking with a cry of anguish from a hideous dream and near to madness after every silencing of his recurring despair – and the ideal meaning of that answer is none other than 'man is good in spite of everything'.

Not only critics but all unprejudiced men of feeling have always been offended by the way in which the master here suddenly to some degree deserts music – as though he could be seen stepping outside the magic circle that he himself has drawn – and turns to a faculty of the imagination quite foreign to the musical conception. In fact this event, which has no precedent in the art, does indeed resemble the sudden waking from a dream. But we are immediately made aware of its beneficial effect on the tortured dreamer, for never before had a composer communicated the agony of life with such sustained horror. It was therefore indeed a despairing leap made by the divinely naive composer, conscious only of his magic, into a new world of light; and it was from the ground of that world that there sprang up to meet him the melody for which he had searched so long – the divinely sweet melody of humanity, in all its innocent purity.

It is with that same ordering will which we have mentioned above and which led him to this melody that we see the master boldly comprehending [enthalten] in music, as the idea of the world; for it is not in fact the sense of the words that strikes us at the entry of the human voice but the character or that voice itself. It is not even the ideas expressed in Schiller's verses that concern us from this point onward, but the intimate sound of the choral music in which we feel invited to join, like the congregation of some ideal liturgy – as in the chorales of the great Passions of S. Bach. It is quite evident that Schiller's words were only later added – with some difficulty and not even very skilfully – to the chief melody. For this melody has first been fully

[1] [Wagner here condenses and paraphrases several of Schopenhauer's sentences. See A. Schopenhauer, *The World as Will and Representation*, tr. E. F. J. Payne (New York 1966), vol. 1, pp. 260–1.]

developed in its own right, played by the orchestra alone, and in that form has stirred us with the unspeakable joy of paradise achieved.

Great art can show nothing simpler, from the artistic point of view, than this tune with its childlike innocence, and it fills the listener with a kind of awe at its first appearance, whispered by the lower strings in simple unison. It then becomes the cantus firmus, the chorale of a new congregation of believers, round which the other parts are woven contrapuntally, as in S. Bach's church chorales. There is nothing quite comparable to the deep fervour aroused by each part that is added to this primal song of purest innocence until every ornament, all the splendour of heightened emotion unite and lose themselves in that song, like the breathing world around the final revelation of the doctrine of Perfect Love.

If we glance for a moment at the advance achieved by Beethoven in the history of music, we can express it briefly as the achieving of a new potentiality hitherto, as it seemed, denied to the art. Thanks to this potentiality music has risen far above the realm of the aesthetically beautiful into the sphere of the sublime, where it is freed from all the restrictions of traditional and conventional forms, which are completely penetrated and revivified by the deepest spirit of music. This achievement is immediately manifest to every human spirit in the most fundamental of all musical forms, namely melody, in the form given to it by Beethoven. It was he who reclaimed its character of natural simplicity and rediscovered the source from which melody can be renewed, at every time and in every place, and nourished so as to blossom in the highest and richest variety. This can be grasped as a single, universally intelligible idea: Beethoven emancipated melody from the influence of fashion and changes in taste and raised it to a pure human type, valid to all eternity. Beethoven's music will be intelligible to every age, while the music of his predecessors will for the most part be understood only by means of historical reflection.

There remains still another advance visible on the same path along which Beethoven sought the final ennobling of melody, and that is the new significance of vocal music in its relationship to purely instrumental.

This significance was unknown to the mixed vocal and instrumental music of the past, most familiar to us in ecclesiastical works and unhesitatingly regarded as a degenerate form of vocal music inasmuch as the orchestra is here employed merely to reinforce or to accompany the voices. S. Bach's great compositions for the church can only be understood through the choral passages which are already handled with an orchestral freedom and elasticity suggesting orchestral reinforcement and support. As the spirit of church music progressively decayed, this blend of orchestra and voices led to the insertion of Italian operatic music with orchestral accompaniment in the taste of each succeeding age. It was reserved for Beethoven's genius to employ the artistic whole formed by these various insertions simply as an orchestra with greater potentiality. In his great *Missa Solemnis* we have a purely symphonic work in the purest Beethoven spirit. The voices are here treated exactly like human instruments – arbitrarily, as Schopenhauer rightly observed. It is not the notional meaning of the sung text in these great church compositions that holds our attention. These texts serve simply as material for the voices, and they do not serve as distraction to our musical receptiveness simply because they stir no kind of intellectual activity in our minds but simply move our feelings – as is proper in church music – by the impression of familiar symbolic formularies of faith.

When we realize by experience that music loses nothing of its character when put to the most diverse texts, it becomes clear that the relation between poetry and music is entirely illusory. For we can establish that in vocal music it is not the poetical thought that is grasped by the listener – in choral music the text is not even intelligible to him – but at best what the composer found musical in that thought and inspired him to compose. Any union of music and poetry must therefore always result in poetry taking an inferior place; and one cannot cease to wonder how it is that even the greatest of our German poets continue discussing, and even attempting to solve, the problem of combining the two arts. They have clearly been influenced by the effect of music in opera, and certainly this seemed to be the only field in which a solution of the problem should be sought. Whether the expectations of our poets were based more on the formal structure of the opera or the deep emotional effect of the music, one thing remains clear – that they could only have been concerned with employing the powerful auxiliaries that opera appeared to offer them in order to give their poetical expression a more precise and penetrating expression. They may well have thought that music would willingly do them this service if they were to provide a serious poetic conception in place of the trivial theme and language of the general run of operas. It may also well have been that what repeatedly held them back from making serious efforts in this field was a vague but in fact well justified doubt as to whether such a contribution on their part would ever in fact be noticed when in conjunction with music. Careful consideration of the matter can hardly have failed to convince them that apart from the music nothing in opera claims the audience's attention except the visual events on the stage, not the poetical idea behind those events; and that in the last resort opera was a matter of alternate listening and watching. Neither of these receptive faculties can achieve complete aesthetic satisfaction for the reason that I have already given. Operatic music does not, in fact, produce in the listener that spirit of almost devout concentration which alone is proper to music, reducing the visual faculty to a point at which the eye no longer perceives objects with its normal intensity. On the other hand we were forced to admit that, in the case of opera, we are only superficially moved by the music, excited rather than possessed, and led on to hanker for visual satisfaction – but certainly not for anything intellectual. We are in fact robbed of the faculty for any kind of intellectual activity by precisely this contradiction in our desires for entertainment, as a result of a distraction fundamentally concerned with overcoming boredom.

These considerations have given us sufficient insight into Beethoven's exceptional nature to make his attitude to opera immediately intelligible, his summary and absolute refusal to set any operatic text of a frivolous nature. He recoiled with horror from the idea of providing music for ballet, processions, fireworks, erotic intrigues and anything of this sort. His music must be able absolutely to penetrate a complete, high-minded and passionate drama. What poet was there able to co-operate with him in such an undertaking? In his single operatic essay he was faced with a dramatic situation which at least had nothing of the frivolity that he so much disliked. Moreover the glorification of feminine fidelity corresponded well with a leading feature of his humanitarian creed. On the other hand, the subject comprised so much that was alien to music, so much that music was unable to assimilate, that Beethoven's ideal understanding of the drama is only made absolutely clear to us in the great *Leonore* Overture. No one who has heard this great work can have failed to be fully convinced that the music contains in itself the most complete drama. Is the stage action of *Leonore* in fact anything but an almost repugnantly weakened version of the drama experienced in the overture, rather like some dull exegesis by Gervinus of a scene in Shakespeare?[2]

What forces itself upon the feelings of every perceptive person, however, can only become clear to the intelligence if we return for a moment to the philosophical explanation of music.

Music does not present ideas taken from everyday phenomena, but is rather itself a comprehensive idea of the world, automatically including drama, since drama again expresses the only idea of the world on the same level as that of music. Drama passes beyond the barriers of poetry in exactly the same way as music passes beyond the barriers of every other (and particularly every plastic) art, by the fact that its effect lies solely in the field of the sublime. Just as the drama does not portray human characters but causes these characters to portray themselves, so musical motifs present the character of all external phenomena [*alle Erscheinungen der Welt*] in their quintessential form. The motion, formation and variations of these motifs are, by analogy, not only uniquely related to the drama: it is only by means of such motions, formations and variations of musical motifs that it is possible to understand with complete clarity the drama of ideas. Indeed we should not be far wrong were we to regard music as the a priori qualification of the human personality in the shaping of drama in general. Just as we construe the phenomenal world by employing the laws of time and space, which are a priori models in the human brain, so this conscious presentation of the idea of the word in the drama would be modelled by those inner musical laws which made themselves felt in the playwright, though without his knowledge, precisely as the laws of causality unconsciously employed in our apperception of the phenomenal world.

It was a presentiment of this that captivated our great German poets; and it

[2] [For Gervinus see below, p. 90. Wagner had in mind Gervinus's *Shakespeare* (Leipzig 1849–50).]

may be that here they had also hit upon the mysterious foundation of Shakespeare's genius, inexplicable on any other assumption. This prodigious playwright cannot be understood by analogies with any other poet, and for this reason aesthetic judgements of his work have remained to this day completely without foundation. His plays appear to us to present such a direct picture of the world that we simply do not notice the part played by art in the presentation of the idea, nor indeed have critics been able to identify it. For this reason these plays have been admired as the productions of a superhuman genius and have served our great poets, in almost the same way as the wonders of nature, as objects of study in their search for the laws determining such creation.

The distance separating Shakespeare from the poet as such often finds almost crude expression in the quite exceptional veracity of every trait in his characters – as for example in the scene in *Julius Caesar* where Brutus and Cassius quarrel and the 'poet' is treated as a foolish creature[3] – whereas we never encounter the so-called 'poet' Shakespeare himself except at the core of the characters of his plays. There was therefore absolutely no standard by which to judge Shakespeare until the German genius produced in Beethoven a figure only explicable by analogy when compared with him. If we try for a moment to call up the total impression made on our deepest sensibilities by the whole world of Shakespeare's dramatis personae and the quite extraordinary intensity of the characters that it contains – and then do the same with the world of Beethoven's themes, with their irresistible force of penetration and clarity of outline – we cannot fail to perceive that the two worlds are identical, each enclosed within the other, however great the apparent difference between the two spheres in which they move.

It may serve to facilitate this image if we take the example of the *Coriolanus* overture, in which Beethoven and Shakespeare have handled the same subject. Let us try to recall the impression made on us by the figure of Coriolanus in Shakespeare's play and, since the plot is a complicated one, concentrate our attention on one detail – what it was in fact that could have made a lasting impression on us simply because it concerned the chief character of the drama. What will stand out above all the confusion will be the figure of the defiant Coriolanus at odds with the voice of his own conscience [*seine innerste Stimme*], a voice which speaks to his pride with greater power and urgency from his own mother's lips; and the dramatic development that holds our imaginations will be simply the overcoming of this pride by that voice, the breaking of an inordinately powerful man's defiance. It is these two leading themes, and these alone, that Beethoven chooses for his drama; and they impress on us the fundamental nature of both characters more effectively than any intellectual presentation. Let us now first conscientiously trace the movement that develops from the single confrontation of these two motifs and belongs completely to their musical characters, and then savour the purely musical detail – the manner in which these two motifs are made to play equal

[3] [Wagner refers to *Julius Caesar*, act v, scene 3.]

or subordinate roles, are first separated and then intensified. We shall find that we are in fact tracing at the same time the course of a drama which, in its own form of expression, contains all that arouses our sympathy in Shakespeare's own drama, with its complicated plot and the friction between the subordinate characters. What seized us immediately in the play with something like the force of actual personal experience, seizes us in Beethoven's music as the actual kernel of the drama. In the play this was made explicit by the interplay of characters endowed with the quality of natural forces, and in Beethoven's music by the themes which operate in those characters and are fundamentally identical with them. The only difference lies in the different laws governing movement and development in the two spheres.

If we spoke of music as a revelation of the most intimate vision of the nature of the world, then we might call Shakespeare a Beethoven who carries over that vision into the world of waking reality. The two spheres are separated by the formal conditions laid down by the laws of apperception valid in each sphere. The most perfect art-form must therefore grow from the frontier-point at which these two sets of laws first meet. The incomparable, indeed incomprehensible, quality of Shakespeare lies in his ability so to penetrate with new life the forms of the drama which determined the individual artistic character of plays – from those of the great Calderon down to the most frigid and conventional productions – that they seem to us to have been completely swept away by Nature herself. We seem to have before our eyes real human beings rather than products of art, and yet they remain so incredibly remote that any real contact with them must seem as impossible as if they were ghosts. Beethoven exactly resembles Shakespeare in his attitude to the formal laws of his art and his penetration of them with a new spirit of freedom. We may therefore hope to identify most clearly that frontier-point where their two spheres of action meet by once again turning to our philosopher as our immediate guide and returning to the final aim of his hypothetical theory of dreams, namely the explanation of ghostly apparitions.

Our immediate concern is with the physiological rather than the metaphysical explanation of what is known as 'second sight'. Our philosopher supposed the organ of dreaming to be active in that part of the brain which is stimulated by impressions of the organism busied, though in deep sleep, with its interior concerns.[4] This stimulation was analogous to that exercised by waking impressions of the external world on that part of the brain which is now completely passive, directed outward and connected directly with the organs of sense. The dream-communication conceived by means of this inner

[4] ['Our philosopher' is, of course, Schopenhauer. Wagner's sentence may refer to Schopenhauer's words: 'Thus the world must be recognized, from one aspect at least, as akin to a dream, indeed as capable of being put in the same class with a dream' etc. (*The World as Will ...*, vol. 2, chapter 1, p. 4.) The 'ghostly apparitions' to which Wagner refers in an earlier sentence, are dealt with by Schopenhauer in his 'Essay on Spirit Seeing and everything connected therewith' in *Parerga and Paralipomena*, tr. E. F. J. Payne vol. 2 (Oxford 1974), pp. 227–309.]

organ could be transmitted only by a second dream immediately before waking; and this second dream could only transmit the real content of the first in allegorical form. This was the case because the imminent, and then actual waking of the brain to full consciousness inevitably brought into play the modes of knowledge proper to the phenomenal world i.e. time and space and with this an ability to construct only such images as were in complete accord with the common experiences of life. We have compared the work of the composer to the sight of the clairvoyant sleep-walker as the immediate copy of the first, original dream [*Wahrtraum*] seen by him and now exteriorized in a highly excited state of clairvoyance; and we found the path [*Kanal*] to this communication of the composer's on the way to the origin and formation of the world of sound.

Let us now compare the physiological phenomena of somnambulistic clairvoyance, which we chose as an analogy, with the phenomenon of seeing ghosts, once again using Schopenhauer's hypothesis that this is a form of waking clairvoyance. By this he meant a diminishing of the waking power of sight, and the inner urge to communicate to the consciousness, already on the verge of waking, making use of this already impaired sight to produce a clear image of the figure that has appeared in the first, original dream. This figure, projected to the sight from within, can in no sense be said to belong to the real world of phenomena, and yet for him who sees it there is no characteristic of a real being that is absent. We believe that Shakespeare's works are examples of this strange and rare phenomenon – the successful projection by the inner will of an image seen by it alone but now projected before the eyes of a man fully awake. Thus we could account for Shakespeare as a kind of visionary or necromancer able to produce before his own eyes and ours figures of human beings, of all periods of history, as they have shown themselves to his intuitive perception, so that they seem really to come to life before us.

Once we have acquainted ourselves with this analogy and all that it implies, we are in a position to point to Beethoven – whom we have already compared to a clairvoyant sleepwalker – as the active subsoil [*wirkender Untergrund*] from which the visionary Shakespeare springs. What Shakespeare's imagined characters project is the same as what is projected in Beethoven's melodies: and they will mutually interpenetrate each other's beings to the point of achieving absolute identity, if we can make the composer's entry into the world of sound coincide with his entry into the world of light. This would occur in a manner analogous to the process which accounts on the one hand for the seeing of ghosts and on the other for the sleepwalker's clairvoyance. This supposes the reverse of the impression made from outside on the waking brain, i.e. an interior excitement penetrating the brain from within outwards and eventually striking the organ of the senses, thus exteriorizing and objectifying the interior event. We have already established as an undeniable fact that while mentally engaged in listening to music our power of vision is so reduced that we no longer perceive objects with the normal intensity: thus this would be a state aroused by deep interior dreaming which, as reduction of the power of vision, made possible the appearance of a ghostly figure.

We can use this hypothetical explanation of an otherwise inexplicable physiological event, by regarding it from several points of view, in order to explain the artistic problem now confronting us, and we arrive at the same conclusion. The figures of Shakespeare's imagination would be brought to musical expression by the complete awakening of the interior organ of music. Or, to express it in another way, Beethoven's themes would stir the reduced power of vision to a clear perception of those figures embodied in which these figures now moved before our eyes, now endowed with clairvoyant power. In either of these virtually identical cases an enormous power proceeds, against the laws of nature, from within outwards in the accepted sense of forming an apparition; and this power can only arise from a deep sense of affliction. This affliction would probably be identical with that expressed in ordinary life by the cry of distress uttered by a man suddenly waking from a deep sleep in which he had had an oppressive dream. Here, however, it is the case of something altogether exceptional in significance, something that shapes the life of human genius; and the sense of affliction leads to waking in a new world only to be revealed by this waking, a world of the clearest knowledge and the highest potentiality.

We experience this same sense of waking from a sense of affliction at the remarkable transition from instrumental to vocal music in Beethoven's Ninth Symphony. This has remained offensive to the majority of aestheticians and formed the starting-point of this long digression in our discussion of the work. At this point in the symphony we are aware of a certain feeling of excess, a powerful impulse to exteriorize, wholly comparable to the sleeper's impulse to wake from an oppressive dream. The significance of this for the artistic genius of humanity lies in the fact that this impulse in Beethoven's case prompted an actual artistic deed which procured for that genius a new potential ability to create the greatest work of art.

What we may infer from this work of art is that the most perfect drama must be something far beyond a work of actual poetry. We may make this inference after recognizing the identity of Beethoven's and Shakespeare's drama and supposing that its relation to opera is the same as the relationship between a play of Shakespeare's and a literary drama or between Beethoven's symphonic and operatic music.

We should not be misled in our judgement of that remarkable transition from instrumental to vocal music by the fact that Beethoven in his Ninth Symphony is simply returning to the form of the choral cantata with orchestra. We have already examined the significance of this choral part of the symphony and recognized it as belonging to the most individual field of music. Apart from the introductory exaltation of melody the movement contains nothing unprecedented in the matter of form: it is a cantata in which the relationship between music and text is no different from that in any other cantata. We know that music cannot be determined by the poet's words, even though these be Goethe's or Schiller's, but only by the drama. Even then it is not the dramatic poem, but the actual drama that unfolds before our eyes as the visible counterpart of the music where word and speech belong simply to the action and not the poetic idea.

We should therefore not regard Beethoven's work as the peak-point in the development of his genius but the unprecedented artistic achievement that it contains. In fact the work of art entirely penetrated and shaped by this achievement must also present us with the most perfect art-form i.e. one in which everything merely conventional, whether dramatically or more parti-cularly musically speaking, has been set aside. This would then represent the new art-form, both the only form corresponding completely to the German spirit so powerfully and individually expressed by our great Beethoven, and an achievement in the purely human sense yet at the same time deeply original and personal to him. This is the form which, in comparison with antiquity, our modern age has hitherto lacked. [pp. 97–112]

[.    .    .]

# August Wilhelm Ambros (1816–1876)
## *Die Grenzen der Musik und Poesie* (1855)

Like Hanslick, Ambros came from the German-speaking community in Bohemia, but unlike him showed more sympathy towards the emerging Czech nationalism. He studied law in Prague, graduating in 1839, and acquired a thorough knowledge of music, partly under the influence of his uncle, the music historian R. G. Kiesewetter. He joined the civil service, working first in Prague and then moving to Vienna in 1872. During his last two years in Prague he taught music history at the University, and continued to do so in Vienna, at the Conservatory as well as the University.

Ambros was an industrious and untiring worker. During the 1860s he was engaged on the preparation and publication of his extensive *Geschichte der Musik* which involved long periods of study in the Austrian, German and Italian archives. His knowledge of art history helped him to conceive of the history of music as a part of the intellectual and cultural history. In this he was aided by his knowledge and interpretation of Hegel's philosophy of history. In his youth in Prague he was close to Hanslick, but their paths began to diverge in the early 1850s, Ambros advocating a strongly heteronomist approach to aesthetics. His *Die Grenzen der Musik und Poesie. Eine Studie zur Ästhetik der Tonkunst* (Leipzig 1855) closely followed the appearance of Hanslick's *Vom Musikalisch-Schönen* and its purpose was to counteract the impact of Hanslick's work. The title may have been consciously modelled on the subtitle of Lessing's *Laokoon: Über die Grenzen der Malerei und Poesie*.

# The boundaries of music and poetry

Source:

*The Boundaries of Music and Poetry. A Study in Musical Aesthetics*, tr. J. H. Cornell (New York 1893), pp. 9–12; 51–4; 181–3; 184–6.

**Introduction**

[.　.]

Music, ever striving conformably to its nature after more definite expression and more distinctly stamped individuality, has at length attained a standpoint which, in itself belonging to the art of the intellect, seems to push to its outermost boundary, because it tries to represent, on the stage of inner soul-life, what speech alone can illustrate perfectly – some external event, some object to be grasped by the senses – thus trespassing upon another domain. Take Berlioz, for example. In his *Sinfonie fantastique* it is always the interior morbid traits of a young artist's soul-life that he displays to us; it is, therefore, like the *Lear-Overture*, one of his works continuing the preceding development of art. In *Romeo and Juliet*, on the other hand, it is no longer simply the yearning, the happiness, the sorrow of the lovers for which he seeks suitable tones; he adopts wholly external events as they appear in Shakespeare's tragedy – the dispute of the servants, the pacificatory entrance of the princes, the ball at Capulet's etc. This music might perhaps be designated as the art of speech resolved into music.

In short, music acts toward the adherents of mere play with forms, pretty much as Diogenes did to the philosopher who denied motion, in that he, when the latter was proving that there was and could be no motion, arose and actually walked to and fro.

Nevertheless, attention has lately been called with great satisfaction by the Herbartian philosophy to a book by Hanslick, *Of the Musically Beautiful*,[1] in which a musician is said to have reached the same conclusion by way of empiricism as they by way of speculation.

His conclusions are, briefly, the following: Hanslick rejects as unscientific the standpoint of the aestheticians, with whom 'the feelings, at least in the domain of music, still disport themselves in broad daylight as of old, after the time of those aesthetic systems, which have examined the Beautiful with reference to the feelings thereby awakened, has gone by in all other domains'.[2] Feelings, he says, are not the aim, or the subject-matter, of music, because music by no means possesses the means of representing or exciting any determinate feeling whatsoever, and the 'representation' of 'indeterminate' feelings involves a contradiction in itself; consequently, music has to describe neither determinate nor indeterminate feelings – its only subject-matter is forms set in motion by sound, and how music can furnish beautiful forms without the subject-matter of a determinate feeling is shown us 'very appositely' by a branch of ornamentation in plastic art, the arabesque (!). We ought not to undervalue the sensual element, with the older aestheticians, in favour of 'morals and the heart', nor with Hegel, in favour of the 'idea' – every art springs from sensuality and breathes therein. But the Musically Beautiful is not founded upon the pleasure felt in symmetry, it has nothing to do with architecture or mathematics. The subject-matter of a piece of music is only its musical theme and its development, according to the different relations of which it is, musically, capable.

Thus far Hanslick as to the main point; but he, too, seeks for the real charm of music on physiological lines in the 'elementary nature of tones', in the excitement of the nerves; which is of such a nature that we are accustomed to regard the essence, the mind-product, the form, as an external thing, a secondary matter, whereas that which is purely physical, the charm of the

---

[1] [See above, p. 11.]
[2] [Ambros here paraphrases rather than quotes Hanslick. See above, p. 13.]

sound, the stimulation, is held to be the essential subject-matter of a piece of music.

And thus, after music, if we accept Marx's historical presentation,[3] has actually passed through its process of development up to the point indicated by us, we are still disputing whether it was allowable to do such things, or even possible to do them (that they have actually been done is of no consequence); we are still actively disputing about its first principles; if we wish to draw the line between music and poetry, we must – there is no help for it – undertake the labour of Sisyphus, of reinvestigating (if possible, by the empiric method also) how far right these absolutely mathematical, physiological and formal standpoints are. With equal reason it might be said that plastic art has to do exclusively with the representation of beautiful corporeal forms. In that case there would exist no point of contact whatever with poetry, and Lessing need not have written his *Laokoon*, and we, too, might as well abandon, once and for all, our investigation as to the point where poetry and music separate. For where every analogy, every intellectual connection, is lacking, there is no necessity of seeking for boundaries. [pp. 9–12]

[.    .    .]

## [Chapter iii] The ideal feature of music

[.    .    .]

And as we before spoke of the body of music, and said that it demanded a soul, we feel that we are led to the conviction that poetry alone is able to breathe this soul into it. We were right in calling music a poetic art.

But what is the boundary between it and poetry?

## [Chapter iv] The points of contact between music and poetry

Where a boundary is to be drawn between two domains, a point of contact between them must, in general, first be ascertained. The point of contact common to poetry and music lies in the excitement of moods. This power is – as will be shown later – in a high degree peculiar to poetry, not only to the lyric, whose peculiar domain is to be sought for here, and the dramatic, but, up to a certain degree, even to the didactic, epic, and even the epigrammatic, in which the point, unexpectedly springing forth, can express the effect of the humorous up to the provocation to laughter – to the satirical, in which, e.g. Horace fills us, so to speak, with his graceful waggishness (*Vafer Flaccus circum praecordia ludit*),[4] Juvenal with his profoundly moral indignation.[5]

[3] [The reference is to Adolf Bernhard Marx, *Die Musik des neunzehnten Jahrhunderts und ihre Pflege: Methode der Musik* (Leipzig 1855).]

[4] [The passage should read properly: *omne vafer vitium ridenti Flaccus amico/tangit et admissus circum praecordia ludit*. Persius, *Satura* i, lines 116–17.]

[5] [Presumably referring to *si natura negat, facit indignatio versum*. Juvenal, *Satura* i, line 79.]

The effect of music likewise consists essentially in this, that it awakens moods in the hearer, and indeed, moods of very determinate colouring. Mozart's *Figaro* has, as yet, hardly disposed anyone to solemn seriousness, his *Requiem* hardly anyone to a cheerful love of life. If one should play, in front of a bridal pair going to the altar, a funeral march, it would excite laughter, just as it would give rise to no little scandal if the band of music at a funeral should strike up – say – the merry, frivolous gallop from Auber's *Masked Ball*. Thus, in Schiller's *William Tell*, Rudolph commands Harras to stop the music of the bridal procession in the presence of mortally wounded Gessler, and the gloomy choral of the 'Brothers of Charity' takes its place.

States of mind are, in general (for insofar as they are in any way the result of the morbidly excited bodily organism, they cannot here be taken into consideration), the result of a series of definite ideas. These latter can be expressed in definite, clear words, the former cannot. If the word joy, love, anger, pity etc. be spoken, it is an empty sound, appealing only to the hearer's power of recollection, as far as he is familiar with these states from experience, but giving him no idea of them if they are not experimentally known to him. The Spartan perhaps knew not the paralyzing effect of fear – the coward, on the contrary, will never understand the hero. When Thomas à Kempis relates of his friend Arnold von Schoonhofen that, while praying, he gave utterance to joyful sounds of ecstasy, a man of earnest religious feeling, to whom, as to the youthful Faust, prayer is 'bliss', can well imagine what he felt – to the cold atheist it can never be explained what called forth those sounds of ecstasy.

Now, music conveys moods of finished expression; it, as it were, forces them upon the hearer. It conveys them in finished form, because it possesses no means for expressing the previous series of ideas which speech can clearly and definitely express. The charm of music, which one is so very much inclined to ascribe to sensuous euphony alone, lies, in a great measure, if not for the most part, in this contrasting of finished states of mind, concerning whose previous series of ideas it gives us no account; for we speak of charm when we see powerful results produced whose causes remain enveloped, as far as we can see, in mysterious obscurity. Now, the state of mind which the hearer receives from music he transfers back to it; he says: 'It expresses this or that mood.' Thus music receives back its own gift, and thus we perceive how the best intellects, on the one hand, could claim for music, as a fact beyond doubt, so to speak, the 'expression of feelings', while the advocates of the mere 'pleasure in the play of forms', on the other hand, deny to it such ability, because, forsooth, tones set up in order eternally remain in that order, but never can become love, sorrow, joy etc. With the expression 'music awakens moods', there is no infringement of it, nor is the matter pushed too far into the subjectivity of the hearer, for the resources of the real poetry of sentiment, of lyric poetry, also extend no further. It is only in the same improper sense as of music that we can say of lyric poetry that 'it expresses feelings'. A versified dry statement of joy or sorrow excites no mood at all, therefore bears none in itself, and cannot lay claim to the name of a lyric poem, for the reason that it is no poetry at all. [pp. 51–4]

[.   .   .]

## [Chapter ix] Final conclusions reached by investigation

[. .] In its ideal feature music keeps within its natural boundaries, so long as it does not undertake to go beyond its expressional capacity – that is, so long as the poetical thought of the composer becomes intelligible from the moods called forth by his work and the train of ideas stimulated thereby, that is, from the composition itself, and so long as nothing foreign, not organically connected with the music itself, must be dragged in, in order to assist comprehension. It is, therefore, no objection that the purely musical expression of a song becomes essentially modified by the words to which it is set, or would even become unintelligible if the words were omitted, for here the words that are sung form a component part of the music itself; the word has been changed into music, the connection of both has become so intimate, rather so inseparable, that the separation (by omitting the words e.g. by executing the voice-part by a clarinet or a flute), can be only a purely external or, so to speak, mechanical one.

Thus the music accompanying a poem can also not be set down in this category, since this spoken poetical language and the accompanying music ought, according to the composer's intention, to form together only a single art-work, hence the connection between the two is an organic one. As a matter of course, this is not so in the case of a program; it is foreign to the music, and remains foreign to it, even when it is reduced to verse and set to music, like the prologue to *Romeo and Juliet*. When composers, to render their music more intelligible, have recourse to a motto, to a title for a single movement or of an entire piece of music, this is not necessarily a mistake – if only this subject of the music, that is, the given title, the motto etc. appears merely advantageous, but not entirely indispensable, to the composition. The delicate tone-painting of the 'Scene by the Brook', taken together with the mood of this movement, would hardly allow a misunderstanding, even if the four words did not stand over it. On the other hand, it is no excuse, if an incapable composer from the class of profound forcing-house geniuses would fain justify the lack of organic development of a confused piece of music, in the case of which heaven only knows what particular thing he was thinking of from measure to measure, by means of some motto or other from Goethe's *Faust*, and the like, or even attempts to deceive, and (by omitting the program, or even the last lodestar in the shape of a motto) wishes to make the false impression that his music is genuine and true, whereas in truth he has gone far beyond its boundaries. Such a piece might be called: 'Music with a suppressed program'.

The objection that, by means of a principle like that thus far established, the measure of the expressional capacity of music is estimated too much according to the hearer's capacity for understanding it (thus being based on a very shaky foundation, the subjective perceptive faculty of each individual), loses its significance in view of the fact that the same objection applies with equal force to all the other arts. [pp. 181–3]

[.    .    .]

[The] subjective point, dwelling in the recipient of the art-work, cannot be set aside; it is not to be treated as something accidental, having nothing to do with the art-work itself, and to be waived. For the artist embodies his ideas in the art-work in order that they, through the medium of the latter, may become the ideas of other men also. The painter counts upon a spectator, the musician upon a hearer, the poet likewise upon a hearer or at least a reader. That which is to bring the three into relation with one another is something spiritual, something incorporeal, the idea. The art-work forms, in this connection, the conducting, sensuous medium. To the man that is intellectually blind, a picture is present in hardly any other sense than it is to one physically sightless. If a composition is not understood, it is the same as if it were not played. The composer will rightfully feel this more deeply and painfully than a noble, well-justified pride allows him to show outwardly – even Beethoven, whose thoughts were surely high-souled enough, is said to have shed tears over his grand C major overture to *Fidelio*, because no one would understand it – neither the public, who received it with icy coldness, nor the critics, who listened to it with Midas-ears, and consequently pronounced Midas-judgements; nor even Cherubini, who complained that he had not been able even to distinguish the fundamental key. We hardly need to observe, that since that time the comprehension of this overture, which Schumann justly calls 'as high as heaven and as deep as the sea', has become accessible. Therefore let no artist lose courage – if his artistic conscience says to him that his art-work is genuine, he may also hope that it will be understood, either at once, or at least later.[6] [pp. 184–6]

[.    .    .]

---

[6] Of course, this consolation is one with which proud, self-sufficient incapacity flatters itself.

# Friedrich Theodor Vischer (1807–1887)

## Aesthetik oder Wissenschaft des Schönen (1857)

Vischer studied philology, philosophy and theology at Tübingen from 1825 to 1830 and graduated in theology. He became strongly attracted to Hegel's philosophy and in 1832 obtained a doctorate in philosophy. His interest in Hegel was further intensified when in 1833 he attended in Berlin lectures by the distinguished Hegelians Gaus, Michelet and Hotho. In 1836 he obtained his licence to teach at a university (*Habilitation*) and in the following year was appointed extraordinary and in 1844 full professor of aesthetics at Tübingen. Close to the left-wing Hegelians, he offended the university authorities by his inaugural lecture which was judged too subversive. He was suspended from office in 1845 and in 1848 was a member of the Frankfurt Parliament sitting on the united left. In 1855 he went to teach at the Zurich Polytechnic Institute, returned to Tübingen in 1866 and at the same time taught at the Polytechnic Institute in Stuttgart. In 1870 he became a member of the Württemberg State Council.

In his early works, especially in his *Aesthetics*, he was strongly influenced by Hegel, but later moved cautiously towards positivism and psychologism. He is credited with the introduction of the term *Einfühlung* into German philosophical terminology.

Vischer felt that he lacked detailed knowledge of music and in the third volume of his *Aesthetik oder Wissenschaft des Schönen* wrote only the first, general section (§746–66). The rest (§767–832) is the work of Karl Reinhold von Köstlin (1819–94). Köstlin studied theology, philosophy and art history in Tübingen and from 1849 taught there, first theology and later philosophy, aesthetics and the history of German literature. At first under Hegel's influence, he too, like Vischer, later moved away from Hegelianism, accepting some ideas of the experimental and psychological aesthetics.

## Aesthetics or the science of the beautiful

*Source:*

*Aesthetik oder Wissenschaft des Schönen*, ed. Robert Vischer, 2nd edn (Munich 1923), vol. 5: Kunstlehre: Musik. Zweite Gattung. Die subjektive Kunstform oder die Musik. a) Das Wesen der Musik. α. Überhaupt §746, pp. 1–4; §749, pp. 17–19. β. Die einzelnen Momente §767, pp. 79–83. Translated by Martin Cooper.

Vischer worked on his *Aesthetik* over a long period during the 1840s and 1850s. The first volume to appear was *Die Metaphysik des Schönen* (Reutlingen and Leipzig 1846) and the part dealing with music is contained in the third volume, *Die Kunstlehre* (Stuttgart 1857).

## The second type. The subjective artform: music

### a. The essence of music α. In general
### §746

The step towards the dissolution of objectivity, which has been announced in the field of painting, must be carried through, the object entirely swallowed by the subject and identified with that subject's inner mobility [*innere Bewegtheit*]: only thus will subjectivity come into its full rights. Only thus too will it be possible at a later stage — and one in any case demanded by the concept of the beautiful and its foundation in the very laws of our being [*Lebensgesetz*] — for the object now to proceed once more from the human spirit as a new creation.

Music's entry into the system has been so prepared by painting that it may be said that her step can be heard at the door. All the essential points in musical theory make it clear that music is on the borderline of the plastic arts. In the first place this is generally true owing to the principle of music's method of representation, which is to throw a mere appearance of things onto a flat surface. Then the predominance of expression, the protean action, the borrowing of media that present themselves spontaneously [*die Aufnahme der elementarisch ergossenen Medien*] and most noticeably the magic of colour — all these seem to point to the volatilization of objectivity. This elucidation is contained particularly in the passages quoted, where we read of 'subjective mobility having penetrated to such a degree that it is within an ace of outweighing objectivity'. Hegel puts it in a striking way when he speaks of the magic of colour 'already beginning, as it were, to undermine objectivity' and its effect as being 'something no longer quite material'.[1] Only painting is and remains still a plastic art, which still presents an ideal vision of the world, over and against the subject, as something that has a real objective existence in space, though it lacks the ability to move. We have already seen what important deficiencies spring from these circumstances, even for the richest of the plastic arts. However warm the feelings aroused by a painting may be, a wall still exists between it and the viewer: the exclusive nature of space separates them. This is not the place to examine once again the many things that painting cannot, with its means of representation, provide, or to argue directly from that the necessity of choosing another method of presentation. We must first say something of the act of creation [*der geistige Akt*] and basic general laws. We have already found these laws (§537), which are the foundation of the division of Art into separate arts, in the progress from objectivity to subjectivity and the higher union of the two, the same category on which repose the stages of the system: natural beauty — imagination — art.

[1] ['Yet colour is available to make spatial forms and figures visible as they exist in actual life only when the art of painting has developed to the magic of colour in which what is objective begins as it were to vanish into thin air, and the effect scarcely comes about any longer by means of something material.' G. W. F. Hegel, *Aesthetics, Lectures on Fine Art*, tr. T. M. Knox, vol. 2 (Oxford 1974), p. 889.]

The artistic instinct [*der Geist der Kunst*] first produces an objective copy in space of its inner vision, and the viewer encounters it as an object of natural beauty. This gives it all the sharpness and clarity of outline of a confrontation, but it also loses so much that in its own field it must retrace the path taken by the imagination when faced with art, first consuming the naturally beautiful object, digesting it and transforming it into a purely internal image. An artist mentally cherishes and penetrates the material of what is to become a picture or a sculpture before he separates himself spatially from his work; but this mental penetration is not complete, only an antithesis in the synthesis, and the viewer will be aware of the alien residuum, since all spatial being has the character of exclusiveness. There must be a still more intimate, a total penetration, in which confrontation remains floating identification, and what is produced and exposed still remains profoundly the artist's own property. What is more, this must be true of the inmost act where, for that very reason, the individual who enjoys the work enters that work with his profoundest self or, vice versa, feels the work entering his profoundest self, and the two become one. At §551 on p. 176 we read that in a second art-form following the plastic arts there will be a fusing of object and subject, more intimate but more obscure than the relationship in the plastic arts, something both more and less than that with the following subjective form. The definiteness of the confrontation between natural beauty and the artist, and the artist and his work, is just as much a prolonging of Nature's influence, the need of one element in the antithesis. 'The heart's absorption of the world', which that subjective art will have to achieve, will mean the end not only of the clarity of the counterblow, but also of this obsession with the object: it will prepare the reinstating of the object and that reinstating will be accompanied by incomparably clearer consciousness. Of the two sides important in these theories the one that is of course first to be emphasized is that from which this new step in art appears as an enormous advance. This art must now adopt the standpoint of the subjective idealists, sharing their errors but also – which is all-important here – their insights. It was essential to destroy philosophic realism, and to exaggerate the truth that the subject forms the content, the measure and the aim of everything. Indeed that exaggeration had to be carried to the point at which it was impossible to reconstruct an object from the subject which had devoured everything, before philosophy could find a way to rebuild its world, the world of ideal realism. Just the same is true of art. In the plastic arts the mind must be first confronted with the stable object; and the truth – that every object is only what it is for the mind – must be exaggerated to the point of devouring everything before it can rise again, new born, from this tomb, determined and penetrated by the human mind [*der Geist*]. On the other hand this cannot of course be done without stating frankly the element of error in this point of view. For this reason it is stated in the same paragraph that the entrance of art into the principle of pure subjectivity is a necessary stage on the road to a further, higher understanding of the subject; and that this is demanded by the idea of Beauty and its foundation in the very laws of our being [*Lebensgesetz*]. Beauty is an idea in limited, phenomenal form: the visible is the essential phenomenal form in which ideas appear. The idea is life, and life is the mobilizing of the powers inherent in the human body; the existence of the idea is therefore before all else its 'incarnation' or 'embodiment'. In organic bodies a delicate structuring of material matter leads to the sparking of inner spirit [*Geist*] – something infinitely more than any physical matter, and more properly regarded as the truth of all such matter, but not so radically different that matter is not still its foundation and its organ. Art may therefore now desert the world visible to the physical eye [*das Sichtbare der Körperwelt*] in order to seek it again, for it will not have extinguished but merely concealed that world. From this it follows that any art-form based on this attitude will have an individual, double character: it will point forward to another, higher stage of development rather than possess an independent nature that is its own justification. This idea is one that must be further developed and then stated with the same maximum of explicitness. The deficiencies of each art point to the other arts; and of none of the arts is this truer than music. [pp. 1–4]

### §749

[.    .    .]

Subjectivity of feeling is [. . .] variable, and should one wish to pin it down, almost inevitably a relationship to some object establishes itself. Thus, for example, fear is a feeling that is not pure but accompanied by consciousness, since all fear is related to some object. If I remove the object, I am left with a vague apprehensiveness on the horizon of which hangs, cloud-like, the object causing apprehension, always threatening to grow and become more formidable. This apprehension has no object but threatens at any moment to become objective. Let us for a moment suppose that feeling finds its own art-form which serves it as a language without the necessity of words. In that case the perpetual consciousness of the proximity of the conscious, objective world will result in anyone who hears [*vernimmt*] this language of the feelings finding that at the same time his more definite mental faculties are brought into play – the inner eye of the imagination will conjure up figures whose vague outlines float, as in a dream, on the waves of feeling, and memories, definite images will spring up unbidden – and he will give the feeling expressed a definite object. There are as many different images as there are listeners – and every image that is at all compatible with the nuances of expression in the emotion that characterizes the composition will occur to one listener or another and will accompany the music like a band of spirits, each listener believing that the special secrets of his individual breast are being laid bare. And this, far from being any clouding of the feeling represented, is on the other hand simply the realization of its inherent ability to spread in all directions into the form of an image with definite content. Music presents the listener with a whole world wrapped in feeling and the listener unwraps it in a thousand different ways.

We have already referred earlier to an absolutely fundamental difference in the art-form itself, and this now explains itself. Feeling that is pure i.e. not accompanied by consciousness, is experienced empirically simply as a fleeting moment, and by its very nature is always on the point of transferring itself to the definite mental world that exhibits objects. The same is true in art, where we find a tendency for another, object-naming art-species coming to the aid of [music's] obscurity and giving it a definite content. Thus we shall see vocal music establishing itself as distinct from pure (i.e. instrumental) music. In this connection the feeling of a conscious content, an object, becomes conscious. 'At last', we say, 'I know what it is that makes me feel sad or liberated, melancholy or cheerful. At last I am done with the problem of trying to define in words something that eludes verbal description, and in future listeners will be informed of the imagery with which they must accompany their emotional experiences.'

At §698 we spoke of landscape as that branch of painting most nearly akin to music, and observed that it was not possible to express in words the 'feeling' of a landscape. One could only say 'it feels' so bare, so rough, so sultry, so lowering, so damp etc. It is the same with instrumental music, where we look for words and choose those referring to obscure, half-psychological circumstances of atmospheric life – gentle, stormy, gloomy, cloudy, clear, energetic, faint, tense, relaxed, stealthy, like a bird. With the help of such words, moods whose essential quality is so hard to define exactly take on body and content, and the riddle is solved. In §748, however, we saw that feeling is only pure when divorced from any accompanying consciousness; and this faces us with the difficult choice between pure feeling that needs complementing by some interpretation to make up for its lack of object, and interpreted feeling, related to any object and therefore no longer pure. [pp. 17–19]

[.    .    .]


## §767

From considering individual points in the nature of music we can now pass on to examine the *material* of music, that which conditions the art of composition. Music in fact has no material in the ordinary sense of the word i.e. no external, already existing elements or material means such as the plastic arts possess. There is in music no external objectifying of images created by the imagination, by means of the technical working of given elements of the physical world. The material *in* which music works is simply the inner, mental world of the hearer's imagination into which music introduces her images; and the material *with* which she creates those images is similar – something that has indeed been elicited from matter [*die Materie*] and conditioned by the quality and structure of material bodies, but is in itself immaterial and only created by human agency and by the artistic shaping of the element of sound. The material of the plastic arts is already in existence, but music fashions her own, by first creating and then ordering and combining sounds, in order to produce a material that can be used for composing. This whole process is the proper work of the musical imagination.

To understand the material of the art is more important in the case of music than in that of the plastic arts. These use their material simply as matter, whose quality is of much less importance to them than in the case of music; and they therefore feel free to impose on their material forms and shapes taken from elsewhere, either from the imagination or from external nature (natural beauty). Only painting has, in colour, a predetermined, specific material element that cannot be arbitrarily modified, but can only be used and worked in different ways. In music, on the other hand, the whole artistic process consists of nothing other than 'com-posing' the sound-material in different ways. Unlike painting and the plastic arts, music does not transfer shapes borrowed from other sources to a material that is indifferent to those shapes. She does not as architecture does, use inorganic, shapeless masses to construct buildings which are formally independent products of the imagination, however necessary it may be to consider the nature of substance used. Music cannot create objectively or produce figures, in the proper sense of the word: she can only set sound-material in motion and produce sound-combinations of various kinds. Her 'structures' are merely successions and webs of sounds: they never attain plastic objectivity or individuality, and their production depends on the quality of the actual material employed i.e. on a series of relationships between intervals, chords, consonance and dissonance. All these are based on the physical organization of the human ear and are therefore immutable natural circumstances determining the activity of the composer. The material of music is neither undifferentiated nor shapeless: it possesses its own interior laws and a wide variety of fixed forms and relationships. These permit of a vast number and variety of sound-combinations and in that sense provide the composer with the greatest freedom and play, but they are nevertheless absolute preliminary data which he can never disregard. Just as the painter has simply to accept the characters and relationships of colours as they are in nature, so the composer has to accept sound-relationships as they are in nature; he must in every case base his work on them and can only make his effects by means of them. In the rhythmical disposition of sounds he is free, but not in their combination. Musical composition is simply the complex practical employment of the different relations of sounds to each other, as pre-determined by nature; and a knowledge of these relationships, of the natural constitution and characteristics of the sound-material is therefore an essential preliminary to understanding the nature of composition itself. The knowledge of colours is not nearly so important to the understanding of painting in which, in the main, the design does not depend on the material and may be anything.

Beside this principle, however – that 'the material of music determines composition' – we must place another, which appears to contradict it i.e. that sound-material is determined by the musical imagination, which must in the first place bring it to birth and then prepare, organize and shape it to the artistic purpose of the composer. The material of music is not an empirical datum like the material of the plastic arts, which in the main find their material ready to hand when they set to work. It is simply something present in nature and to be developed from nature, but not something finished. It is an art-product itself, a creation of the musical imagination, which is stimulated by the awareness of the musical potentialities of human bodies and bodily organs and thus produces, orders and develops the sounds and combinations of sounds which are the basis of music. This explains more particularly the strange fact that the scope and nature of the material of music are essentially dependent on the standard of development of the [composer's] musical imagination. The more highly developed art of painting will seek new colour-materials in order to satisfy the artistic requirements and demands of an advanced society; and the same occurs in music to an even more marked degree. There have been epochs and countries in which what we call the sound-material was either not known or not explored, and was therefore never developed as it can be in various modes, harmony and rhythmic shapes. Before sound-material is really of use to the composer, it has to go through a series of transformations which are by no means self-explanatory. The simple empirical datum is in the first place nothing but a quite indeterminate, chaotic mass of individual sounds and notes with no internal relationships of any kind. As it is, this could never be used to produce a work of art that had beauty of form or any definite content and character. This primitive chaos must be stripped down and converted into an ordered, flexible system. A precise and pleasing basic scale [*Tonfolge*] must be established, with charac-teristic intervals and relationships, for without these the sound-material would not offer any scope for complex combinations or concrete formations. For instance, higher and lower pitch-ranges must be established, the charac-teristics of the different intervals and harmonic relationships clarified; and finally rhythm must be organized and articulated. It is only after all this that the composer's material can be said to be actually there and ready for use. Such things as harmonic and interval-relationship are of course founded in Nature and, as it were, pre-existent in the nature of the human ear and the human psyche [*das Gehör und das Gefühl*]; but they are not by any means necessarily present as yet to the human consciousness. Everything had – indeed still has – to be discovered gradually by the action of the imagination, carrying on the development and determining increasingly the individual points. This creative shaping of the sound-material preliminary to composi-tion is by no means so clearly indicated in nature that it automatically suggests itself as certain and complete to the composer's imagination. The different tonal systems of different epochs and peoples make it clear how unstable everything becomes once we descend to details, such as the span of scales and the normal size of intervals. Harmony, and rhythm in its modern form, are for the most part fairly recent inventions. Everything is inherent in nature, but not everything is presented empirically, by nature, in its perfect state, or so rigidly determined as to exclude deviant conceptions of individual points and occasional difficulties in demonstrating the origin in nature of some feature or other (such as, for example, our major scale). This labile, uncertain character of details in the formation and articulation of the sound-material presents the aesthetics of music with a double task. In the first place it must analyse the constitution of the sound-material, its development over the years and its significance for the composer; and secondly it must trace its root in the nature of the human ear and the human psyche, explore the acoustic and psychological laws of aesthetics and thus achieve a theory of the sound-material that is based on nature itself. [pp. 79–83]

[.   .   .]

# Georg Gottfried Gervinus (1805–1871)
## Händel und Shakespeare (1868)

On leaving school in 1819 Gervinus went into business but in 1826 entered the university in Giessen to study philosophy and philology, continuing his studies at Heidelberg. In 1830 he became a *Privatdozent* and in 1835 extraordinary professor of history at Heidelberg, moving in 1836 to a full professorship at Göttingen. The following year he was suspended from duty because of his political activity, but in 1844 resumed lecturing as an honorary professor. He was one of the founders in 1847 of the *Deutsche Zeitung* which advocated German unity and severing of the links between Germany and Austria. His interest in Handel was shown in a public-spirited way in forming the *Deutsche Händel-Gesellschaft*, planning with Dehn and Chrysander the publication of Handel's complete works and initiating the action for the Handel monument in Halle which was unveiled in 1859.

Although primarily a historian and the author of an influential history of the nineteenth century (*Geschichte des 19. Jahrhunderts seit den Wiener Verträgen*, 8 vols., Leipzig 1855–66), Gervinus also wrote on German literature and on Shakespeare. Mussorgsky claimed to have been influenced by Gervinus in formulating his own view of the relationship of music and speech.

# Handel and Shakespeare

*Source:*

*Händel und Shakespeare. Zur Ästhetik der Tonkunst* (Leipzig 1868). i. Aus der Geschichte. Die reine Instrumentalmusik, pp. 157–61. ii. Aus der Natur der menschlichen Seele. Die Tonkunst die Sprache der Gefühle, pp. 199–202. Translated by Martin Cooper.

**Pure instrumental music**

[.　.　.]

Mozart was buoyant by nature, perceptive in the extreme and gifted with natural delicacy of feeling. His early familiarity with music of all descriptions and his phenomenal memory meant that he was completely saturated with music and permanently under its influence. His mind was flooded with musical forms which occurred to him mostly at night when there was nothing either to stimulate or to distract him and the creative process was undisturbed, as in a wonderful vivid dream. Hints such as these reveal and explain the fascinating technical ease with which he handles the vast wealth of musical material at his disposal and waiting to be formed and moulded, and also that fearless search for ever newer and bolder forms and designs that was characteristic of all those masters. Bach himself had been dismissed by his contemporaries as turgid, over-complicated, incorrect and excessively ingenious; Beethoven was blamed in the same way for being uncouth, shocking, fantastical, monstrous, cyclopean; and even the sober Mozart, who seems to us today the very personification of harmoniousness, was found odd and complex. At this point in the history of instrumental music we seem to have reached the extremest point of achievement and of risk. It was only in this field, and not in that of vocal music, that it was possible to embark on those voyages of discovery to ascertain the real limits of music and to plot the full extent of its potentialities; for in instrumental music every experiment, however bold, was permissible and every attempt, however impossible in practice, might be considered rewarding. Every crazy idea, every excess in the means employed and the effects aimed at, could be in some way justified for the information that it provided. Yet all such things, though willingly and even proudly welcomed as technical miracles, are not necessarily artistic miracles, as the most unprejudiced of the great masters themselves – such as Mozart – would have admitted. Domenico Scarlatti was very far from maintaining that there were 'deep intentions' in his sonatas. All these brilliant experiments were perfectly justified among professionals; but had it been possible, it would also have been preferable, to restrict them to the classroom and to private performance, as was done at the time of the contrapuntal composers and also initially by instrumental composers, when professional players performed such works for themselves and not for the public, for their own instruction and delight and not commercially.

Times have of course changed in this respect. Virtuoso performers have achieved high professional standing and are not willing to hide their lights under bushels; and the popularity of the pianoforte has increased the number of amateurs to such a degree that it is now quite possible to imagine whole audiences consisting of the musically semi-educated. In fact, however, the situation has not fundamentally changed. The semi-educated listeners of today are a doubtful factor, none of them having gone through the strict training of the past; and it may even be doubted whether today's audiences can be compared with the devout and unprejudiced lay listeners of earlier times. It is easy to forget that intelligent contemporaries of Mozart regarded it as indecent to give large gala concerts at which his piano quartets and his wind quintet with piano were performed – works that could be fully appreciated only by those with technical knowledge and which either seemed boring or unintelligible to the inexperienced layman or else met with an affectation of admiration which was quite insincere. Every instrumental work has every claim on every kind of respect, provided that it is addressed exclusively to the only audience deserving of it, namely the *cognoscenti* – those who 'know' and are in a position to judge its formal worth and the solidity of its construction from a technical, scientific point of view, the only valid standard by which such things can be judged. Any work of art written to please the uninformed public almost inevitably suggests that it is not meant for serious criticism. The most recent instrumental music has by its technical perfection lost sight of the natural objects of musical imitation (in so far as such a thing is at all possible) and removed them as unrecognizable, from the innocent eye of the beholder. If, however, there is no natural object of imitation, there can also be no objective evaluation, no artistic criticism: if there can be no comparison with real objects, there can also be no ideal; and when both are absent, there can also be no real art and no real work of art.

At the peak of its development instrumental music was itself aware of its non-imitative character, of the fact that it lacked an object and therefore a content; but its efforts to repair this fault might almost be called the tragi-comic episode of musical history. From the time when music written for pastime first began to aim beyond the purely educational and technical use and to aspire to artistic effect of however humble a kind – some giving of pleasure and satisfaction – it has always selected objects to imitate. The dances of the old suites were not concerned with poetry and words, but with familiar plastic movements. Another form of imitation was borrowed from song-accompaniments, namely musical painting. But although this was ad-mirable in cases where words provided signposts to indicate the scenery intended, it inevitably became ridiculous in the absence of words when com-posers attempted, without any preliminary indication, to imitate aimlessly everything audible and visible, everything that did or did not lend itself to imitation, whether it resulted in beauty or ugliness: sunrise and sunset, animal calls, the sounds of daily life, or instances where one instrument is aping indiscriminately the sounds of another. The next stage was the representation of exterior events and actions, the notorious 'programme-music', which Ambros compared to those medieval paintings in which the figures have written labels coming out of their mouths. It would be possible to draw up a formidable list of all this 'representational' music by Froberger, Kuhnau, Buxtehude and Dittersdorf – starting with Allemandes representing battles, biblical stories in sonatas and Ovid's *Metamorphoses* in symphonies, and ending with Berlioz's programme-symphonies such as *Roméo et Juliette*, in which he attempts to reproduce in music the whole action of Shakespeare's play. It was a step towards greater interiorization – though not necessarily greater naturalness or practicability – when other composers tried to illus-trate more interior subjects, as when Haydn suggested in one of his sympho-nies God's rebuking of a hardened sinner and later composers attempted to represent in music travel impressions in an intellectualized landscape. In the meanwhile there was a lengthening list of works by the greatest composers, who made no claims of this kind and were guided by purely technical, formal principles, yet suggested in their music a content that went beyond the purely mechanical – inexpressible thoughts, facts that had no objective reality and representations that were not simply superficial but rather an emotional content, a mental atmosphere or psychological portraits such as we find in vocal music only here reproduced, almost unconsciously, without words. Academically correct thematic music has already revealed that all music, whether consciously or not, is the spontaneous expression of some state of mind or feeling, every musical phrase unconsciously forming part of a language of the feelings which varies in intelligibility. Speaking of the instrumental works of Mozart and Haydn, Kant at least believed that these formed a language of the feelings that needed no words, only modulations:[1] and that by adhering to a given theme that communicated the chief emotional character of the work a carefully proportioned disposition of the feelings in its handling would express the aesthetic idea of a coherent whole. If we were to ask a Mozart how his instrumental works were given an emotional expressiveness of this kind, he would be content to refer it to spontaneous inspiration and refuse to offer any closer explanation. [pp. 157–61]

[.    .    .]

### Music as the language of the feelings

There is an old observation of Cicero's to the effect that every motion of the soul has its own natural glance, tone of voice and gesture;[2] glance and tone have often been called the mirror and echo of the inner feelings, 'tone' more particularly being regarded as the actual material for the expression of feeling, the voice as the perfect tool for this expression. It was very early in man's development that he observed the specific power of tones to express with deep conviction and perfect intelligibility the emotional circumstances of the soul. If we take as an example the more strongly contrasted feelings and the vigorous or mute expressions of pleasure or pain, happiness or sadness, the natural man whose senses have not been artificially blunted must have associated these with rising musical phrases growing in intensity, with falling phrases expressing dejection and with all the intervals that are perpetually changing in the restless ways of the passions. It must have dawned on him that in all this ebb and flow, this whole chiaroscuro of vital spirits and vital evidences, there was a relationship between music and emotion, and furthermore that the relationship of each to the other was that of cause and effect, reality and appearance. Music thus seized on this natural characteristic of tones and made the emotional elements in man's constitution an object of imitation, translating these deep and powerful moments of emotional excitement from the real world to the ideal. For this reason music has always been called the language of the heart, a revelation of the world of feeling; and its task has been to represent and – if the music is sufficiently sincere and the listener sufficiently sensitive – actually to excite movements of the spirit.

[1] [I. Kant, *The Critique of Judgement*, §52. Kant, in fact, does not refer to any composer by name. See also le Huray and Day, p. 222.]

[2] [Cicero, *Orator*, §17, section 55.]

What Goethe says to poets – 'what you do not feel, you will not achieve'[3] – and what he says of the poet – 'I create a full heart, a heart full of one single feeling'[4] – is even truer and apter of the composer than of the poet. That music is the expression of the feelings of the soul is a Chinese proverb that dates back to more than two thousand years before the Christian era. The Greeks, as we know, valued music as one of the most important elements in education owing to its cleansing effect on the emotions, and they insisted on the spiritual aspect of even the smallest details. In the Middle Ages this characteristic power of music was partly denied by the learned musicians of the Scholae but never by the natural singers among the people. The theoreticians from the end of the sixteenth century who were connected with the musical renaissance followed what the Greeks had said; and the practical thinkers of the seventeenth and eighteenth centuries – the complete opposite of the old arithmetical schoolmen – were united in regarding music as essentially the language of the feelings, and in seeing it as a practical school of the feelings in the same way as Bacon regarded poetry as a practical school of morality and worldly wisdom. Rousseau's only opponent, the Realist Chabanon, found the natural sounds by which we express our feelings – laughing and crying, in fact – 'unaesthetic' and unworthy of imitation, and thus arrived long before the theoreticians of the present day at the conclusion that music is in principle independent of anything that can be imitated.[5] But even Chabanon spoke in the same breath of 'feeling' as the principle of music and had to admit that owing to some inexplicable inner analogy music corresponded to the different human emotions. All practising musicians from Handel to Beethoven and Mendelssohn have agreed that the essence and purpose of music are the expression of emotions. All vocal composers, even the most wretched ballad-singers, allow themselves to be guided consciously or unconsciously, and with varying degrees of success, by the mood of their text. All the latest aestheticians of our own nineteenth century have, almost without exception, followed this traditional view and have always, like our forefathers, unconsciously used these entirely spiritual terms even when discussing individual elementary musical constituents and means. The larger, stronger intervals of diatonic music were found best suited to cheerful music and the smaller, weaker chromatic intervals to funeral dirges. The difference between major and minor was described as a difference between what is clear, bright and well-defined and what is dark, veiled or uncertain. There might be disagreement over the possibility, or actuality, of each key possessing an individual character, but there was a general agreement in the practical use of any particular key for any particular purpose, always founded on – or

[3] ['Wenn ihrs nicht fühlt, ihr werdets nicht erjagen.' Goethe, *Faust*, part i, line 534.]
[4] ['So fühl ich denn in dem Augenblick, was den Dichter macht, ein volles, ganz von *einer* Empfindung volles Herz!' Goethe, *Götz von Berlichingen*, act i, scene 5.]
[5] [Michel-Paul-Guy de Chabanon, *Observations sur la musique, et principalement sur la métaphisique de l'art* (Paris 1799) and *De la musique considérée en elle-même et dans ses rapports avec la parole, les langues, la poésie et le théâtre* (Paris 1785). See le Huray and Day, pp. 379–80.]

returning to – the premiss of a conformity existing between musical forms and emotional states. For three thousand years this belief about the nature of music remained unchanged and unattacked and had seemed armed against all objections. It has remained for the present age, with all its excessive cleverness, to see this maiden castle assailed and – in the opinions of many – easily forced to surrender. The first to teach the new doctrine was a philosopher (Herbart), saying that although music could perhaps be used to express feelings, that was not its true essence, but rather that he saw it as something much more to do with the rules of simple and double counterpoint.[6] A practical man (Dehn)[7] varied this by formulating it in another way which needed a certain amount of interpreting – music he said, was concerned not so much with the expressing, as with the arousing of feelings. We saw that the theory of the most recent Formalists was more logical and more positive – music, according to them, had neither to express nor to arouse feelings and could and should be used for neither purpose. This is perhaps not really so strange as it seems. The formal, technical side of music is of such great scientific importance that composers and scholars who are exclusively concerned with its study and practice may easily go astray. Who, moreover, would maintain – however much he may take the relationship between music and the world of the emotions for granted – that everyone must discover the emotional content of a piece of music, and that this must always and everywhere stir the feelings of every listener? Even supposing that there is no denying that all music must, whether intentionally or not, express some feeling, who is to say that every listener possesses the feeling in question? Is the superficial social world, that goes to concerts in order to see and to be seen, supposed to understand, or even be ready to listen? And what of the small Civil Service employees, whose purely mechanical head-work has narrowed or twisted their sensibilities, or the adding-machines of the commercial world, eternally concerned with the mathematics of the material world, are these to be expected to penetrate the mathematics of music and to discover, behind them, emotional relations? What of those who seek for nothing more in music than entertainment, those whose listening powers are as remote as possible from their powers of feeling (if indeed there is any connection whatever between the two) – are they to be asked to look for 'sensibility' in music? Not to speak of those insensitive, temperamentless people who are incapable of registering purely organic changes, even those due to alterations in their own feelings, let alone those due to alterations in other people's feelings or to artistically modelled expressions of feeling! Without a consciously sentient, warm and sympathetically-minded human being the spiritual power of music extends no further than the outermost tips of the listener's ears. [pp. 199–202]

[.    .]

---

[6] [J. F. Herbart, *Kurze Encyclopädie der Philosophie* (1831). See le Huray and Day, p. 454.]

[7] [Siegfried Wilhelm Dehn (1799–1858), German music theorist and teacher.]

# Friedrich Nietzsche (1844–1900)

## Die Geburt der Tragödie (1872)

Nietzsche was educated at the distinguished school in Pforta near Naumburg and studied classical philology and theology in Bonn. In 1865 he gave up theology and went to Leipzig, following there his Bonn teacher, the classical scholar Ritschl. When in 1869 the chair of classical philology at Basle fell vacant, Ritschl recommended him so strongly that he was appointed to it although he had not written a doctoral dissertation. He gave up the chair in 1879 and, having been granted a pension, lived for the next ten years in northern Italy and on the Riviera. His creative life was terminated by insanity in 1889 and during the remaining years he was cared for in asylums and by his sister Elisabeth Förster-Nietzsche.

As a philosopher Nietzsche strongly differs from the tradition of philosophizing as established in Germany in the eighteenth and nineteenth centuries. He did not build a complete philosophical system, preferring instead to direct his attention in an intense manner to certain issues of moral philosophy and aesthetics. His style is aphoristic and his works, although philosophical in nature, are characterized by a passionate poetic quality.

Nietzsche first met Wagner in Leipzig in 1868, became his ardent and devoted supporter, and during the early years of his professorship at Basle was a frequent visitor to the Wagner household at Tribschen. *Die Geburt der Tragödie* (1872), his apologia of Wagner's art, was followed in 1876 by the essay 'Richard Wagner in Bayreuth' forming a part of his *Unzeitgemässe Betrachtungen*. Already at that time he began experiencing his disillusionment with Wagner's ideas and by the end of the decade the breach with Wagner was complete. Nietzsche's arguments against Wagner are contained in *Die fröhliche Wissenschaft* (1882) and especially in *Der Fall Wagner* (1888) and *Nietzsche contra Wagner* (1889). Nietzsche was a very accomplished pianist and a capable composer.

## The birth of tragedy

Source:

The Birth of Tragedy in The Birth of Tragedy and The Case of Wagner, tr. Walter Kaufmann (New York 1967). Section 1, pp. 35–6, 37–8; section 21, pp. 125–30. The footnotes are by the translator, unless otherwise indicated.

Nietzsche's manuscript of The Birth of Tragedy originally ended with section 15, the remaining sections, where Wagner is discussed, having been added by Nietzsche as a second thought. The title of the first edition was Die Geburt der Tragödie aus dem Geiste der Musik, but Nietzsche shortened it for the second edition (1878).

*For further reading:*

*The Portable Nietzsche*, ed. W. Kaufmann (New York 1954). F. Nietzsche, *The Gay Science*, tr. W. Kaufmann (New York 1974). F. Nietzsche, *Untimely Meditations*, tr. R. J. Hollingdale (Cambridge 1983). See also Bibliography under Silk and Stern, and Hollinrake.

**Section 1**

[.    .]

This joyous necessity of the dream experience has been embodied by the Greeks in their Apollo: Apollo, the god of all plastic energies, is at the same time the soothsaying god. He, who (as the etymology of the name indicates) is the 'shining one',[1] the deity of light, is also ruler over the beautiful illusion of the inner world of fantasy. The higher truth, the perfection of these states in contrast to the incompletely intelligible everyday world, this deep consciousness of nature, healing and helping in sleep and dreams, is at the same time the symbolic analogue of the soothsaying faculty and of the arts generally, which make life possible and worth living. But we must also include in our image of Apollo that delicate boundary which the dream image must not overstep lest it have a pathological effect (in which case mere appearance would deceive us as if it were crude reality). We must keep in mind that measured restraint, that freedom from the wilder emotions, that calm of the sculptor god. His eye must be 'sunlike', as befits his origin; even when it is angry and distempered it is still hallowed by beautiful illusion. And so, in one sense, we might apply to Apollo the words of Schopenhauer when he speaks of the man wrapped in the veil of *māyā*[2] (*Welt als Wille und Vorstellung*, I, p. 416):[3] 'Just as in a stormy sea that, unbounded in all directions, raises and drops mountainous waves, howling, a sailor sits in a boat and trusts in his frail bark: so in the midst of a world of torments the individual human being sits quietly, supported by and trusting in the *principium individuationis*.'[4] In fact, we might say of Apollo that in him the unshaken faith in this *principium* and the calm repose of the man wrapped up in it receive their most sublime expression; and we might call Apollo himself the glorious divine image of the *principium individuationis*, through whose gestures and eyes all the joy and wisdom of 'illusion', together with its beauty, speak to us. [pp. 35–6]

[.    .]

[1] *Der 'Scheinende'*. The German words for illusion and appearance are *Schein* and *Erscheinung*.

[2] A Sanskrit word usually translated as illusion. For detailed discussion see e.g. *A Source Book of Indian Philosophy*, ed., S. Radhakrishnan and Charles Moore (Princeton, N.J., Princeton University Press, 1957); Heinrich Zimmer, *Philosophy of India*, ed. Joseph Campbell (New York, Meridian Books, 1956); and Helmuth von Glasenapp, *Die Philosophie der Inder* (Stuttgart, Kröner, 1949), consulting the indices.

[3] This reference, like subsequent references to the same work, is Nietzsche's own and refers to the edition of 1873 edited by Julius Frauenstädt – still one of the standard editions of Schopenhauer's works.

[4] Principle of individuation.

Under the charm of the Dionysian not only is the union between man and man reaffirmed, but nature which has become alienated, hostile or subjugated, celebrates once more her reconciliation with her lost son,[5] man. Freely, earth proffers her gifts, and peacefully the beasts of prey of the rocks and desert approach. The chariot of Dionysus is covered with flowers and garlands; panthers and tigers walk under its yoke. Transform Beethoven's 'Hymn to Joy' into a painting; let your imagination conceive the multitudes bowing to the dust, awestruck – then you will approach the Dionysian. Now the slave is a free man; now all the rigid, hostile barriers that necessity, caprice or 'impudent convention'[6] have fixed between man and man are broken. Now, with the gospel of universal harmony, each one feels himself not only united, reconciled, and fused with his neighbour, but as one with him, as if the veil of *māyā* had been torn aside and were now merely fluttering in tatters before the mysterious primordial unity.

In song and in dance man expresses himself as a member of a higher community; he has forgotten how we walk and speak and is on the way toward flying into the air, dancing. His very gestures express enchantment. Just as the animals now talk, and the earth yields milk and honey, supernatural sounds emanate from him, too: he feels himself a god, he himself now walks about enchanted in ecstasy, like the gods he saw walking in his dreams. He is no longer an artist, he has become a work of art: in these paroxysms of intoxication the artistic power of all nature reveals itself to the highest gratification of the primordial unity. The noblest clay, the most costly marble, man, is here kneaded and cut, and to the sound of the chisel strokes of the Dionysian world-artist rings out the cry of the Eleusinian mysteries: 'Do you prostrate yourselves, millions? Do you sense your Maker, world?'[7] [pp. 37–8]


### Section 21

[.    .    .]

Tragedy absorbs the highest ecstasies of music, so that it truly brings music, both among the Greeks and among us, to its perfection; but then it places the tragic myth and the tragic hero next to it, and he, like a powerful Titan, takes the whole Dionysian world upon his back and thus relieves us of this burden. On the other hand, by means of the same tragic myth, in the person of the tragic hero, it knows how to redeem the greedy thirst for this existence, and with an admonishing gesture it reminds us of another existence and a higher pleasure for which the struggling hero prepares himself by means of his destruction, not by means of his triumphs. Between the universal validity of

[5] In German, 'the prodigal son' is *der verlorene Sohn* (the lost son).
[6] An allusion to Friedrich Schiller's hymn *An die Freude* (to joy), used by Beethoven in the final movement of his Ninth Symphony.
[7] Quotation from Schiller's hymn.

its music and the listener, receptive in his Dionysian state, tragedy places a sublime parable, the myth, and deceives the listener into feeling that the music is merely the highest means to bring life into the vivid world of myth. Relying on this noble deception, it may now move its limbs in dithyrambic dances and yield unhesitatingly to an ecstatic feeling of freedom in which it could not dare to wallow as pure music without this deception. The myth protects us against the music, while on the other hand it alone gives music the highest freedom. In return, music imparts to the tragic myth an intense and convincing metaphysical significance that word and image without this singular help could never have attained. And above all, it is through music that the tragic spectator is overcome by an assured premonition of a highest pleasure[8] attained through destruction and negation, so he feels as if the innermost abyss of things spoke to him perceptibly.

If these last sentences have perhaps managed to give only a preliminary expression to these difficult ideas and are immediately intelligible only to few, I nevertheless may not desist at this point from trying to stimulate my friends to further efforts and must ask them to use a single example of our common experience in order to prepare themselves for a general insight. In giving this example, I must not appeal to those who use the images of what happens on the stage, the words and emotions of the acting persons, in order to approach with their help the musical feeling; for these people do not speak music as their mother tongue and, in spite of this help, never get beyond the entrance halls of musical perception, without ever being able to as much as touch the inner sanctum. Some of them, like Gervinus,[9] do not even reach the entrance halls. I must appeal only to those who, immediately related to music, have in it, as it were, their motherly womb, and are related to things almost exclusively through unconscious musical relations. To these genuine musicians I direct the question whether they can imagine a human being who would be able to perceive the third act of *Tristan and Isolde*, without any aid of word and image, purely as a tremendous symphonic movement, without expiring in a spasmodic unharnessing of all the wings of the soul?

Suppose a human being has thus put his ear, as it were, to the heart chamber of the world will and felt the roaring desire for existence pouring from there into all the veins of the world, as a thundering current or as the gentlest brook, dissolving into a mist – how could he fail to break suddenly? How could he endure to perceive the echo of innumerable shouts of pleasure and woe in the 'wide space of the world night', enclosed in the wretched glass capsule of the human individual, without inexorably fleeing toward his primordial home, as he hears this shepherd's dance of metaphysics? But if such a work could nevertheless be perceived as a whole, without denial of individual existence; if such a creation could be created without smashing its creator – whence do we take the solution of such a contradiction?

[8] An allusion to Faust's last words in lines 11,585ff. of Goethe's play.
[9] G. G. Gervinus, author of *Shakespeare*, 2 vols. (Leipzig 1850), 3rd edn, 1862; English tr., *Shakespeare Commentaries*, 1863. [For Gervinus see above, p. 90.]

Here the tragic myth and the tragic hero intervene between our highest musical emotion and this music – at bottom only as symbols of the most universal facts, of which only music can speak so directly. But if our feelings were those of entirely Dionysian beings, myth as a symbol would remain totally ineffective and unnoticed, and would never for a moment keep us from listening to the re-echo of the *universalia ante rem*.[10] Yet here the *Apollinian* power erupts to restore the almost shattered individual with the healing balm of blissful illusion: suddenly we imagine we see only Tristan, motionless, asking himself dully: 'The old tune, why does it wake me?' And what once seemed to us like a hollow sigh from the core of being now merely wants to tell us how 'desolate and empty the sea'.[11] And where, breathless, we once thought we were being extinguished in a convulsive distension of all our feelings, and little remained to tie us to our present existence, we now hear and see only the hero wounded to death, yet not dying, with his despairing cry: 'Longing! Longing! In death still longing! for very longing not dying!' And where, formerly after such an excess and superabundance of consuming agonies, the jubilation of the horn cut through our hearts almost like the ultimate agony, the rejoicing Kurwenal now stands between us and this 'jubilation in itself', his face turned toward the ship which carries Isolde. However powerfully pity affects us, it nevertheless saves us in a way from the primordial suffering of the world, just as the symbolic image of the myth saves us from the immediate perception of the highest world idea, just as thought and word save us from the uninhibited effusion of the unconscious will. The glorious Apollinian illusion makes it appear as if even the tone world confronted us as a sculpted world, as if the fate of Tristan and Isolde had been formed and moulded in it, too, as in an exceedingly tender and expressive material.

Thus the Apollinian tears us out of the Dionysian universality and lets us find delight in individuals; it attaches our pity to them, and by means of them it satisfies our sense of beauty which longs for great and sublime forms; it presents images of life to us, and incites us to comprehend in thought the core of life they contain. With the immense impact of the image, the concept, the ethical teaching, and the sympathetic emotion, the Apollinian tears man from his orgiastic self-annihilation and blinds him to the universality of the Dionysian process, deluding him into the belief that he is seeing a single image of the world (Tristan and Isolde, for instance), and that, *through music*, he is merely supposed to see it still better and more profoundly. What can the healing magic of Apollo not accomplish when it can even create the illusion that the Dionysian is really in the service of the Apollinian and capable of enhancing its effects – as if music were essentially the art of presenting an Apollinian content?

[10] The universals before (antedating) the thing.
[11] [This and the previous quotation come from Wagner's *Tristan and Isolde*, act iii, scene 1.] *Wie 'öd und leer das Meer'*, also quoted from *Tristan und Isolde* by T. S. Eliot in *The Waste Land* (1922), line 42.

By means of pre-establishing harmony between perfect drama and its music, the drama attains a superlative vividness unattainable in mere spoken drama. In the independently moving lines of the melody all the living figures of the scene simplify themselves before us to the distinctness of curved lines, and the harmonies of these lines sympathize in a most delicate manner with the events on the stage. These harmonies make the relations of things immediately perceptible to us in a sensuous, by no means abstract, manner and thus we perceive that it is only in these relations that the essence of a character and of a melodic line is revealed clearly. And while music thus compels us to see more and more profoundly than usual, and we see the action on the stage as a delicate web, the world of the stage is expanded infinitely and illuminated for our spiritualized eye. How could a word-poet furnish anything analogous, when he strives to attain this internal expansion and illumination of the visible stage-world by means of a much more imperfect mechanism, indirectly, proceeding from word and concept? Although musical tragedy also avails itself of the word, it can at the same time place beside it the basis and origin of the word, making the development of the word clear to us, from the inside.

Concerning the process just described, however, we may still say with equal assurance that it is merely a glorious appearance, namely, the aforementioned Apollinian *illusion* whose influence aims to deliver us from the Dionysian flood and excess. For, at bottom, the relation of music to drama is precisely the reverse: music is the real idea of the world, drama is but the reflection of this idea, a single silhouette of it. The identity between the melody and the living figure, between the harmony and the character relations of that figure, is true in a sense opposite to what one would suppose on the contemplation of musical tragedy. Even if we agitate and enliven the figure in the most visible manner, and illuminate it from within, it still remains merely a phenomenon from which no bridge leads us to true reality, into the heart of the world. But music speaks out of this heart; and though countless phenomena of the kind were to accompany this music, they could never exhaust its essence, but would always be nothing more than its externalized copies.

As for the intricate relationship of music and drama, nothing can be explained, while everything may be confused, by the popular and thoroughly false contrast of soul and body; but the unphilosophical crudeness of this contrast seems to have become – who knows for what reasons – a readily accepted article of faith among our aestheticians, while they have learned nothing of the contrast of the phenomenon and the thing-in-itself – or, for equally unknown reasons, have not cared to learn anything about it.

Should our analysis have established that the Apollinian element in tragedy has by means of its illusion gained a complete victory over the primordial Dionysian element of music, making music subservient to its aims, namely, to make the drama as vivid as possible – it would certainly be necessary to add a very important qualification: at the most essential point this Apollinian illusion is broken and annihilated. The drama that, with the aid of music, unfolds itself before us with such inwardly illumined distinctness in all its movements and figures, as if we saw the texture coming into being on the loom as the shuttle flies to and fro – attains as a whole an effect that transcends *all Apollinian artistic effects*. In the total effect of tragedy, the Dionysian predominates once again. Tragedy closes with a second which could never come from the realm of Apollinian art. And thus the Apollinian illusion reveals itself as what it really is – the veiling during the performance of the tragedy of the real Dionysian effect; but the latter is so powerful that it ends by forcing the Apollinian drama itself into a sphere where it begins to speak with Dionysian wisdom and even denies itself and its Apollinian visibility. Thus the intricate relation of the Apollinian and the Dionysian in tragedy may really be symbolized by a fraternal union of the two deities: Dionysus speaks the language of Apollo; and Apollo, finally the language of Dionysus; and so the highest goal of tragedy and of all art is attained. [pp. 125–30]

# Friedrich Nietzsche
## Der Fall Wagner (1888)

## The case of Wagner

Source:

The Case of Wagner in The Birth of Tragedy and the Case of Wagner, tr. by Walter Kaufmann (New York 1967). Sections 1 and 2, pp. 157–9; section 8, pp. 172–4. The footnotes are by the translator.

### Section 1

Yesterday I heard – would you believe it? – Bizet's masterpiece, for the twentieth time. Again I stayed there with tender devotion; again I did not run away. This triumph over my impatience surprises me. How such a work makes one perfect! One becomes a 'masterpiece' oneself.

Really, every time I heard *Carmen* I seemed to myself more of a philosopher, a better philosopher, than I generally consider myself: so patient do I become, so happy, so Indian, so settled. – To sit five hours: the first stage of holiness!

May I say that the tone of Bizet's orchestra is almost the only one I can still endure? That other orchestral tone which is now the fashion, Wagner's, brutal, artificial, and 'innocent' at the same time – thus it speaks all at once to the three senses of the modern soul – how harmful for me is this Wagnerian orchestral tone! I call it *sirocco*. I break out into a disagreeable sweat. *My* good weather is gone.

This music seems perfect to me. It approaches lightly, supplely, politely. It is pleasant, it does not *sweat*. 'What is good is light; whatever is divine moves on tender feet': first principle of my aesthetics. This music is evil, subtly fatalistic: at the same time it remains popular – its subtlety belongs to a race, not to an individual. It is rich. It is precise. It builds, organizes, finishes: thus it constitutes the opposite of the polyp in music, the 'infinite melody'. Have more painful tragic accents ever been heard on the stage? How are they achieved? Without grimaces. Without counterfeit. Without the *lie* of the great style.

Finally, this music treats the listener as intelligent, as if himself a musician – and is in this respect, too, the counterpart of Wagner, who was, whatever else he was, at any rate the most *impolite* genius in the world (Wagner treats us as if – he says something so often – till one despairs – till one believes it).

Once more: I become a better human being when this Bizet speaks to me. Also a better musician, a better *listener*. Is it even possible to listen better? – I actually bury my ears under this music to hear its causes. It seems to me I experience its genesis – I tremble before dangers that accompany some strange risk; I am delighted by strokes of good fortune of which Bizet is innocent. And, oddly, deep down I don't think of it, or don't know how much I think about it. For entirely different thoughts are meanwhile running through my head.

Has it been noticed that music liberates the spirit? gives wings to thought? that one becomes more of a philosopher the more one becomes a musician? – The gray sky of abstraction rent as if by lightning; the light strong enough for the filigree of things; the great problems near enough to grasp; the world surveyed as from a mountain. – I have just defined the pathos of philosophy. And unexpectedly answers drop into my lap, a little hail of ice and wisdom, of *solved* problems. – Where am I? – Bizet makes me fertile. Whatever is good makes me fertile. I have no other gratitude, nor do I have any other *proof* for what is good.

### Section 2

This work, too, redeems; Wagner is not the only 'redeemer'. With this work one takes leave of the *damp* north, of all the steam of the Wagnerian ideal. Even the plot spells redemption from that. From Mérimée it still has the logic in passion, the shortest line, the *harsh* necessity; above all, it has what goes with the torrid zone: the dryness of the air, the *limpidezza*[1] in the air. In every respect, the climate is changed. Another sensuality, another sensibility speaks here, another cheerfulness. This music is cheerful, but not in a French or German way. Its cheerfulness is African; fate hangs over it; its happiness is brief, sudden, without pardon. I envy Bizet for having had the courage for this sensibility which had hitherto had no language in the cultivated music of Europe – for this more southern, brown, burnt sensibility. – How the yellow afternoons of its happiness do us good! We look into the distance as we listen: did we ever find the sea smoother? – And how soothingly the Moorish dance speaks to us? How even our insatiability for once gets to know satiety in this lascivious melancholy!

Finally, love – love translated back into nature. Not the love of a 'higher virgin'! No Senta-sentimentality![2] But love as *fatum*, as fatality, cynical, cruel – and precisely in this piece of nature. That love which is war in its means, and at bottom the deadly hatred of the sexes! – I know no case where the tragic joke that constitutes the essence of love is expressed so strictly, translated

---

[1] Limpidity, clarity.
[2] Senta is the heroine of Wagner's *Flying Dutchman*.

with equal terror into a formula, as in Don José's last cry, which concludes the work:

'*Yes. I have killed her,*
*I – my adored Carmen!*'

Such a conception of love (the only one worthy of a philosopher) is rare: it raises a work of art above thousands.[3] For on the average, artists do what all the world does, even worse – they misunderstand love. Wagner, too, misunderstood it. They believe one becomes selfless in love because one desires the advantage of another human being, often against one's own advantage. But in return for that they want to *possess* the other person. – Even God does not constitute an exception at this point. He is far from thinking, 'What is it to you if I love you?'[4] – he becomes terrible when one does not love him in return. *L'amour* – this saying remains true among gods and men – *est de tous les sentiments le plus égoïste, et par conséquent, lorsqu'il est blessé, le moins généreux.* (B. Constant.)[5] [pp. 157–9].

**Section 8**

[.  .  .]

The actor Wagner is a tyrant; his pathos topples every taste, every resistance. – Who equals the persuasive power of these gestures? Who else envisages gestures with such assurance, so clearly from the start? The way Wagner's pathos holds its breath, refuses to let go an extreme feeling, achieves a terrifying *duration* of states when even a moment threatens to strangle us! –

Was Wagner a musician at all? At any rate, there was something else that he was more: namely, an incomparable *histrio*,[6] the greatest mime, the most amazing genius of the theater ever among Germans, our *scenic artist par excellence*. He belongs elsewhere, not in the history of music: one should not confuse him with the genuine masters of that. Wagner *and* Beethoven – that is blasphemy and really wrongs even Wagner. – As a musician, too, he was only what he was in general; he *became* a musician, he *became* a poet because the tyrant within him, his actor's genius, compelled him. One cannot begin to figure out Wagner until one figures out his dominant instinct.

[3] Compare Nietzsche's admiration for Shakespeare's characterization of Brutus in *Julius Caesar* (discussed with quotations in Kaufmann's *Nietzsche, Philosopher, Psychologist, Antichrist*, Princeton 1950, rev. edn. New York 1956 – see Index under Brutus) and Oscar Wilde's *Ballad of Reading Gaol* (1898): 'For all men kill the thing they love . . .'

[4] Goethe, *Dichtung und Wahrheit*, book 14; cf. *Wilhelm Meisters Lehrjahre*, book 4, chapter 9 (*Theatralische Sendung*, book 6, chapter 4), where the wording is ever so slightly different. In his autobiography Goethe links these words with Spinoza's famous dictum: 'Whoever loves God cannot will that God should love him in return' (*Ethics*, book 5, proposition 19).

[5] 'Love is of all sentiments the most egoistic, and, as a consequence, when it is wounded, the least generous.'

[6] Actor.

Wagner was *not* a musician by instinct. He showed this by abandoning all lawfulness and, more precisely, all style in music in order to turn it into what he required, theatrical rhetoric, a means of expression, of underscoring gestures, of suggestion, of the psychologically picturesque. Here we may consider Wagner an inventor and innovator of the first rank – *he has increased music's capacity for language to the point of making it immeasurable*: he is the Victor Hugo of music as language. Always presupposing that one first allows that under certain circumstances music may be not music but language, instrument, *ancilla*[7] *dramaturgica*. Wagner's music, if not shielded by theater taste, which is a very tolerant taste, is simply bad music, perhaps the worst ever made. When a musician can no longer count up to three he becomes 'dramatic', he becomes 'Wagnerian'.

Wagner almost discovered how much magic is still possible with music that has been dissolved and, as it were, made *elementary*. His consciousness of that is downright uncanny, no less than his instinctive realization that he simply did not require the higher lawfulness, *style*. What is elementary is *sufficient* – sound, movement, color, in brief the sensuousness of music. Wagner never calculates as a musician, from some sort of musician's conscience: what he wants is effect, nothing but effect. And he knows those on whom he wants to achieve his effects. – At this point he is as free from qualms as Schiller was, as every man of the theater is, and he also has the same contempt for the world which he prostrates at his feet. – One is an actor by virtue of being ahead of the rest of mankind in one insight: what is meant to have the effect of truth must not be true. The proposition was formulated by Talma;[8] it contains the whole psychology of the actor; it also contains – we need not doubt it – his morality. Wagner's music is never true.

But *it is taken for true*; and thus it is in order.

As long as we are still childlike, and Wagnerians as well, we consider Wagner himself rich, even as a paragon of a squanderer, even as the owner of huge estates in the realm of sound. He is admired for what young Frenchmen admire in Victor Hugo, 'the royal largesse'. Later one comes to admire both of them for the opposite reasons: as masters and models of economy, as *shrewd* hosts. Nobody equals their talent for presenting a princely table at modest expense.

The Wagnerian, with his believer's stomach, actually feels sated by the fare his master's magic evokes for him. The rest of us, demanding *substance* above all else, in books as well as in music, are scarcely taken care of by merely 'represented' tables and hence are much worse off. To say it plainly: Wagner does not give us enough to chew on. His *recitativo* – little meat, rather more bone, and a lot of broth – I have called *'alla genovese'* – without the least intention of flattering the Genoese, but rather the *older recitativo*, the *recitativo secco*.[9]

[7] Handmaiden.
[8] François Joseph Talma (1763–1826) was a celebrated French actor.
[9] Dry.

Finally, as far as the Wagnerian 'leitmotif' is concerned, I lack all culinary understanding for that. If pressed, I might possibly concede it the status of an ideal toothpick, as an opportunity to get rid of *remainders* of food. There remain the 'arias' of Wagner. – And now I shall not say another word. [pp. 172–4]

# Friedrich von Hausegger (1837–1899)
## *Die Musik als Ausdruck* (1885)

Austrian music critic. Hausegger studied law at Graz and received a thorough musical education as a pupil of C. G. Salzman and O. F. Dessoff. He was a music critic of the *Grazer Zeitung* and from 1872 taught the history and theory of music at Graz University as a *Privatdozent*. As an admirer of Wagner he sought to counteract Hanslick's aesthetic theory with his *Die Musik als Ausdruck* in which, apart from Wagner's ideas, may be detected influences of evolutionism and biologism.

## *Music as a form of expression*

*Source:*

*Die Musik als Ausdruck*, 2nd edn (Vienna 1887). Section v, pp. 149–52; section vi, pp. 209–12, 215–16; section vii, pp. 234–7. Translated by Martin Cooper.

**Section V**

[.    .]

Music may be said to consist of sounds. A sound can be considered without reference to its source, its effect or the historical circumstances determining its use and its effect. Considered thus, purely physically, it is by no means without interest. Suppose now that this sound is heard in relation to other sounds; comparisons between them will reveal relationships determined by certain laws. In music we find these laws realized. In fact, music consists of sounds arranged according to certain definite laws. Sounds themselves, however, are only the effects produced in our ears by sound-producing causes. We can only grasp them as sonorous sensations. Thus it is with sonorous sensations that music is concerned. The effect of musical sounds [*Töne*] is not restricted to the organ that receives them, in isolation. That effect is communicated to the whole nervous system and provokes specific conditions in that system: it influences our sensibilities [*Empfindungsleben*]. If our attention was previously concentrated on the phenomena of vibration, we must now turn it to the physiological effects of these phenomena. We enquired into the nature of musical sound by consulting first exterior objects set in vibration and then into our own organs as affected by those vibrations. But we are far from having plumbed the depths to which this extraordinary phenomenon leads our attention. A musical sound is determined by the proportions of its vibrations [*Schwingungsverhältnisse*] not only as regards pitch: these produce still another entity [*Wesenheit*] which, in its turn, depends on the object which is the source of the musical sounds. Timbre, or tone-colour, gives that object significance. Nature itself achieves a language in musical sound [*Töne*], by which she reveals characteristics to the ear and in further impulses to the nervous system, thus entering into sympathetic contact [*Fühlung*] with human sensibility. We can thus not dismiss as dreamers those who maintain that nature discloses her soul to us in music. If she imparts herself to our eyes as something which has come into existence [*ein Gewordenes*], music is a means by which she can reveal herself to us in the very process of becoming into existence. She discloses herself from a new angle, decomposing what we were accustomed to know as our world, dissolving its torpor, conjuring up before our senses a new world of fresh creative activity and drawing us into its life – a world of vital truth by the side of which the external world appears as no more than a phantom. Little wonder that this activity once communicated to our nervous systems has a productive effect on our imaginative faculties! This effect will have to be taken properly into account in considering the essence of music. Can it be that what we designate as music is nothing but an effect produced on our nervous systems and is there not perhaps reason to reject this effect as irrelevant to the essence of music, or to allow it only secondary significance? To insist on restricting ourselves to concrete phenomena will lead us into dangerous waters. Such phenomena depend not only on the state of our nervous systems under the impression of certain musical sounds, but on a number of circumstances which can neither be observed nor calculated. The mistake of those who believe that music is able to communicate concrete ideas lies, therefore, not in the fact that the arousing of such ideas has nothing to do with the essence of music, but in the belief that it is the task of music to communicate unambiguously to the listener a deliberate imaginative content. There are of course means by which the composer can direct or detain the listener's imagination, thus narrowing and directly guiding the course of his associative process. Music affects us by means of symbols but to understand that affect symbolically is to touch only the surface and by no means to exhaust the subject.[1] [pp. 149–52]

[.  .  .]

[1] Wundt maintains (*Vorlesungen über die Menschen- und Tierseele*, vol. 2 (Leipzig 1863–4), p. 60): 'For no art has symbol a greater importance than music. Without a symbolic significance of form there can be no significance in a composition. Form and content are absolutely identical in music. A musical composition reflects only on the most general agreement of the intellectual organization.' We believe it to be rather the agreement of the physical organization that must be presupposed in understanding a musical composition, and this understanding by no means depends in the first place on the mind's faculty of comparison but on immediate perception.

**Section VI**

The essence of music is expression – expression refined and raised to the highest power of effectiveness. So much is the outcome of our investigations. It is in expression that we have the revelation of the full value of this art, something frequently misunderstood. The mere pleasure of the sense furnished by playing with sound could never justify the status generally allowed to music. That status can indeed be traced back to a pleasant nervous titillation which does not become any more valuable from the fact that the medium which it provokes is something invaluable and owes its existence to the most singular complexities. In this connection music can indeed have deleterious effects. Many have pointed, and with good reason, to the wakening, enervating, demoralizing effect of practising an art concerned primarily with exploiting the power of sound as a stimulant of the senses. It would, however, be unjust to hold the noble art of music responsible for something which is alien to its true nature. That multifarious ability so to occupy our senses that all other impressions are thrust into the background and our imaginations are thus free to construct their own dream-world as a momentary escape from reality may surely be regarded as a particular advantage of music. Only it is one that she must share with alcohol and narcotics: this peculiarity cannot be made the basis for any higher claims on her behalf.

More significant is the expenditure of ingenuity, constructional ability [*Combinationsgabe*], skill and diligence demanded in the handling of musical material. The immediate impression made by the composition, however, has nothing to do with the pleasure which it gives as the result of the employment of these qualities. That pleasure can only be enjoyed after examining a composition for evidence of these qualities and requires the employment of intellectual abilities that have no immediate connection with the composition as a sensuous phenomenon. Pleasure of the same kind, and in a higher degree, can be obtained from activities to which no one would give the name of art – the answering of riddles, for example, or the solution of mathematical problems. And in fact listening to music has been called an unconscious mathematical activity [*unbewusstes Rechnen*].[2] *Musica est disciplina quae de numeris loquitur qui inveniuntur in sonis* – this was Alcuin's definition.[3] This attitude, however, could only have any significance if what was really being sought was an explanation of the fact that, in listening to music, tonal and rhythmic order could clearly be stated in mathematical terms. But this is by no means the case. The pleasure given by a work of art does not depend on a revelation

---

[2] [The reference is to Leibniz's words: 'Music charms us, although its beauty consists only in the harmonies of numbers and in the counting (of which we are unconscious but which nevertheless the soul does make) of the beats or vibrations of sounding bodies [. . .]' *Principles of Nature and Grace* (1718). English translation in Leibniz, *Monadology and other Philosophical Writings*, tr. and ed. R. Latta (Oxford 1898), p. 422.]

[3] ['Music is a discipline dealing with the numbers to be found in sounds.' See M. Gerbert, *Scriptores ecclesiastici de musica*, vol. 1 (St Blasien 1784), p. 26.]

of this kind. The listener's attention is directed towards quite other things, not on proportions or the like. It may well be that the most primitive sequence of notes gives a much higher pleasure than the most ingenious harmony [*Ton-combination*]; and as for 'an unconscious mathematical activity', it is hardly possible to imagine anything in more total contradiction to the facts of listening to music. The essence of mathematical activity lies precisely in the clear consciousness of relationships; it is an intellectual activity as opposed to a sensuous impression. Anything entrusted by the senses to the intellect ceases thereby to be unconscious, while anything that escapes the intellect remains a simple sense-impression and cannot be called mathematical activity. There is not the smallest doubt that we experience tonal and rhythmic relationships, only they bring us no nearer to discovering the nature of the pleasure we experience from music.

Sounds are not simply phenomena that please or displease our senses; nor have we exhausted their essential nature when we state that they stand in interesting relationships to each other. The fact that they are a revelation of characteristics of the natural world lends them a higher interest. The sounds produced by a vibrating object are not simply sense-impressions correspond-ing to the number of vibrations which determines the pitch. The sense-impression is further qualified by an essential feature of the object, which determines the 'colour', or timbre, of the sound emitted. As Helmholtz has demonstrated, timbre depends on the relative strength of the upper partials. This relative strength varies according to the object vibrating and thus the timbre of a sound serves as a guide to the nature of that object. The pitch and intensity of a sound are influenced by circumstances that have nothing to do with the nature of the medium [*der leitende Körper*] e.g. the length of the column [of air] set in motion, the intensity of the blow creating the sound; the character of timbre is determined by the object from which the sound eman-ates. It is in timbre that nature herself finds a voice. In a composition, therefore, we are in communication not only with the relationships imagined by the composer, but with nature herself, as it were roused from her silence and revealing qualities of the most wonderful kind. [pp. 209–12]

[.    .    .]

Any attempt to apply to music Aristotle's theory that the principle of all the arts is imitation can only lead to embarrassment for nobody can fail to observe that the task of music is something very much more than the mere imitation of the audible phenomena of the natural world, and that this forms only a minute and inessential part of what music is called upon to express. Nor did Gervinus's attempt to explain music as an imitation of human speech meet with any greater success.[4] According to Westphal when Aristotle speaks of 'imitation in the art of music', he means 'musical veracity and scrupulous-ness in reproducing the sensations to be represented'; and for Aristotle the most perfect music was that which represents any image either of man's

[4] [For Gervinus see above, p. 90.]

emotional life in passionate agitation, or alternatively of the stilling of those passions.[5] From our own point of view we believe that we have discovered a quite definite original for this 'imitation' that cannot be regarded as the mere reproduction of an object; and it is an original that in fact corresponds to that supposed by Aristotle – that is to say, the combination of speech-sounds and expressive gestures characteristic of human beings. A sound-picture that comes within the meaning of the term 'music' is recognized by us as a form of imitation i.e. we know the original to which it must in essence conform. On the other hand the activity which creates that sound-picture cannot in any sense be called imitation. [pp. 215–16]

[.    .    .]

**Section VII**

[.    .    .]

Only a complete misunderstanding of the essential nature of art can lead anyone to suppose that art could ever be ousted or replaced by science. Each satisfies needs of entirely different kinds. As science spreads its influence more and more widely and attempts with increasing success to comprehend life from without, so too the impulse to know grows stronger – to rediscover our own voice in the stifling mass of phenomena that besiege our senses and to accentuate the creative power of all existence by revitalizing the depths of our own personalities. It is science that is capable of error, not art, and science rather than art that is subject to superstition. The shapes and forms of the creative life may be mutable, but art does not rest on these. The true work of art, as Richard Wagner rightly observes in *Das Kunstwerk der Zukunft*, is 'the satisfaction in life of our need for life'.[6] 'Should that familiar arbitrary way of thinking really come to dominate life entirely', he continues, 'and should it prove able to seize the vital instinct itself and employ it for any other purpose than the satisfaction of our bare necessities, this would be a negation of life itself, which would become indistinguishable from science [*in Wissenschaft aufgehen*]; and science has in fact dreamed of such a triumph.'[7] Elsewhere he writes: 'But as soon as thought, abstracting from reality, attempts to construct a future reality, it cannot produce knowledge but takes the form of supposition [*Wähnen*], something very different from unconsciousness.'[8] Thus there is an unbridgeable gulf between the essential nature of art and the essential nature of science. Art is essentially a matter of producing, and only needs external objects in order to submit them to the process of creation. Science is essentially a matter of demonstrating, and avails itself of inner

[5] Rudolf Westphal, *Die Musik des griechischen Alterthumes*, (Leipzig 1883), p. 15.
[6] [Richard Wagner, *Das Kunstwerk der Zukunft, GS*, vol. 2, p. 46; *P W*, vol. 1, p. 73.]
[7] [Wagner, *Das Kunstwerk . . .*, *GS*, vol. 3, p. 46; *P W*, vol. 1, p. 74.]
[8] [Wagner, *Das Kunstwerk . . .*, *GS*, vol. 3, p. 52; *P W*, vol. 1, p. 79–80.]

impulses for strictly determined ends. Any exchange of roles would involve each abdicating its own essential nature.

Both the task and the supreme value of art thus reveal themselves, as it were spontaneously. Art owes its existence and its development to that power which, in relation to any given object, we call love. It springs from that universal feeling that it also fosters by providing a common sensation uniting human hearts. This sensation finds expression in forms of the greatest refinement which, as they are perceived, exercise a softening purifying and ennobling influence. In this sense art serves to purify the passions, embodying in us an ideal of humanity that raises us above the impressions of everyday life and work towards our perfecting. It does this not by any moralizing tendency, which is alien to the nature of art, but by taking possession of our innermost impulses and raising them to its own beauty. It is therefore not a charge of lacking moral tendencies that should be brought against a so-called artistic school that believes that the task of art is best performed by a faithful picturing of life as it is, by taking into account men's most primitive impulses and allowing them a place in the picture. What such a 'school' does indeed lack is the ennobling influence of true artistic creation; if it assumes the cloak of morality, it only recalls those lascivious representations of the chaste Susanna bathing that are not uncommon. Your aims in life, your merits and your true vocation are all revealed by your art. Woe unto you if your art does not point upwards but borrows its sounds and images exclusively from the miseries and trivialities to which the primitive impulses of everyday life expose the noble image of humanity! For it is to artists that the jewel beyond price is entrusted, they who are the keepers of the everburning lamp to illumine human existence and preserve it from wretchedness and despair. In their hands lie consolation for the present and hope for the future. They are called upon to be mankind's priests, for true art is true religion. [pp. 234–7]

# Hermann Kretzschmar (1848–1924)
# 'Anregungen zur Förderung musikalischer Hermeneutik' (1903)

Kretzschmar studied composition in Dresden and Leipzig and musicology in Leipzig, graduating in 1871. He held various conducting, teaching and administrative posts in German cities before returning to Leipzig in 1887 as the director of music at the university. In 1904 he moved to a professorship at Berlin.

Both as a scholar and as a practical musician he was an active promoter of baroque music. His series of guides for the general musical public, *Führer durch den Konzert-Saal*, first published between 1887 and 1890 went through many editions and achieved a great popularity in the German-speaking world. Although in the early years of this century he was considered as one of the foremost German musicologists, his reputation did not last as well as that of Riemann or Adler.

## A stimulus to promote a hermeneutics of music

*Source:*

'Anregungen zur Förderung musikalischer Hermeneutik', *Jahrbuch der Musikbibliothek Peters für 1902*, vol. 9 (1903), pp. 47–53. Translated by Martin Cooper.

*For further reading:*

Werner Braun, 'Kretzschmars Hermeneutik', *Musikalische Hermeneutik*, ed. C. Dahlhaus (Studien zur Musikgeschichte des 19. Jahrhunderts, vol. 43) (Regensburg 1975), pp. 33–9.

It is now some time since the German public and German booksellers have become familiar with literary introductions to musical works. Musicians themselves, however, seem uncertain of their attitude towards this innovation. A number of renowned composers have themselves contributed – Heuberger, Humperdinck, Müller-Reuter, Vollbach and Weingartner for instance.[1] Heinrich Zöllner, on the other hand, has rejected these analytical

---

[1] [Richard Heuberger (1850–1914). Composer, conductor and music critic; succeeded Hanslick on the *Neue freie Presse* in 1901. Engelbert Humperdinck (1854–1921). Composer and critic; opposed Hanslick's views. Theodor Müller-Reuter (1858–1919). Conductor and composer. Fritz Vollbach (1861–1940). Conductor, composer and writer on music. Felix Weingartner (1863–1942). Conductor and composer.]

essays out of hand, and treated them humorously regardless of their character;[2] and an increasing number of critics and journalists are following him in adopting a hostile attitude to what they consider a kind of *pons asinorum*.

It may then be just as well to point out that theorists should refrain from jokes of this kind, unless they are short-sighted enough to wish to cut off their own noses. The fact is that the field which is being worked by these famous or infamous gentlemen is in fact a very important area of musical theory, in a sense the conclusion – the last and richest harvest – of all musical theory as such. It is called musical hermeneutics.

Hermeneutics – the art of interpretation – was first developed by the theologians, but was soon transferred to philological studies, both ancient and modern, and thence to all intellectual and artistic studies. In every field its aim is the same – to penetrate to the meaning and conceptual content enclosed within the forms concerned, to seek everywhere for the soul beneath the corporeal covering, to identify the irreducible core of thought in every sentence of a writer and in every detail of an artist's work; to explain and analyse the whole by obtaining the clearest possible understanding of every smallest detail – and all this by employing every aid that technical knowledge, general culture and personal talent can supply. As far as the arts are concerned the significance of interpretation lies in the significance of the great masterpieces; for if these represent the most important supports and pillars of an art, any serious attempt to obtain a thorough understanding of them will be of the first importance. This applies equally to creative artists and their public. The nature of our relationship to these masterpieces does not really in the last resort depend on whether we personally live our lives through the arts – in fact, have a creative concern with them – or whether we regard them as something outside ourselves which nevertheless plays a determining part in our lives. For the latter the creations of great artists – presupposing a sympathetic understanding that may amount to a form of real, if secondary, creation – are the highest reward of study, while for the former they represent an indispensable juncture on the path of their own achievements. For this reason both artists and art-lovers are united in regarding works of interpretation in the fields of poetry and the visual arts – always supposing that they are of high quality – as the summit of theoretical wisdom. Their gratitude to those who have increased their understanding of great artists and masterpieces is at least as warm as their gratitude to the writer of a grammar or a technical guide, or to a poet or painter of the second rank. If works of musical interpretation meet a different, hostile reception from musicians, it can only be for one of two possible reasons – either music must need no interpretation or it permits of none.

The first supposition may be rejected out of hand. More than any other art music needs aids to its understanding, aids that go beyond mere questions of form: and this is because in music there are none of those direct relationships

[2] See his essay 'Loreley' in *Musikalisches Wochenblatt*, 1902.

with the external world that, in poetry and the visual arts, are normally sufficient to explain the 'content' [*Hauptsache*]. The greatest creations in the field of instrumental music, so important nowadays, leave the uninstructed listener absolutely puzzled. If he is gifted, he will now and again be struck by a powerful but simple melody. Generally speaking, however, he will not get further than sensuous impressions, either of pleasure and admiration or of dislike and amazement. That uninstructed listeners include quite a number of professional musicians – as C. Stumpf once insisted – can be proved in this case too. Only a minority of listeners leave a concert with a really clear conception of an instrumental work and an understanding of its chief ideas and their detailed development; and only very few find themselves able to discuss a good sonata or symphony in the way that they can discuss a poem or a picture. It is because interpretation has been neglected by musicians that it has fallen into the hands of amateurs, for the most part philosophers with insufficient musical training, who have decided that the content of instrumental music is something vague and unconscious or even nonexistent. If they were right, we should do better to follow the ancients and their medieval followers, who regarded independent instrumental music as a threat to society. Fortunately, however, these would-be philosophers are refuted by musical practice. It is of course possible for a pianist to go on for hours playing a passage mechanically without asking himself what it means, the sense of the notes on the page in front of him; but with an orchestra this is not possible. If Beethoven writes, without comment:[3]

the violins are obliged, for purely technical reasons and in order to obtain a homogeneous performance, to have a clear idea of the character of the figure. The same is true in all instrumental music: hardly a bar can be performed correctly – or as will be shown, listened to with pleasure – without an understanding of its sense. Instrumental music demands, always and everywhere, an ability to penetrate beyond the printed page – it demands, in fact, of its performers the gift of interpretation [*Auslagen*].

In vocal music much, though by no means all, is explained by the text. In the first movement of his *Grande messe des morts* Berlioz gives the sopranos the following phrase on the word *dona* (*eis requiem*):

do   -   -   na

---

[3] [Beethoven, Symphony No. 3 (*Eroica*), first movement, b. 65.]

It needs someone with a gift of interpretation – with the ability, that is to say, to discover the image that this rocking figure represented in the composer's imagination. Without that gift a listener might take this figure for a kind of waltz-rhythm, which would be tasteless and offensive in the context; and he might be confirmed in this by a bad performance. This is only one example of something that is true of all vocal music, where technical training and literal accuracy alone provide no satisfactory insurance against gross errors and abuse of works of art.

If it is performing practice that provides evidence of the need for an understanding of music that goes deeper than a mere understanding of its forms, it is performing practice too that makes such an understanding possible. When an orchestra plays that Beethoven figure firmly and aggressively, and a choir sings the Berlioz figure as though in a gentle dream, then factual evidence is provided that it is possible to achieve agreement on the sense and character of individual features of a composition, a clarity that will also cover another need when it arises. In accordance with the laws of addition it must therefore follow that a whole composition can be explained in this way. It must be possible to explicate the spirit of a whole work and the smallest details of its individual parts – in fact there must exist a form of musical hermeneutics. The majority of musicians do in fact consider this possible, since they make judgements on whole compositions and passages, even though these judgements are for the most part very summary. On a more serious level such a form of musical interpretation has in fact been questioned in our own times only by so-called 'aestheticians of form'. These constitute a philosophical school of great antiquity and have found, with the rise of the New German School of composition, a representative in Eduard Hanslick whose brilliant dialectical wit and perceptive observations and comments certainly put all Pythagoreans, all Artusis and Ulybishevs in the shade. It is he, and he alone, who has given the musical world to believe that the establishment of new forms with a new content is inadmissible, that music has no content but is simply a sequence of notes. That this belief is untenable is shown by the attempt to apply it to the other arts. Thus the content of poetry would consist in sequences of syllables, the content of paintings and sculptures in colours and canvas, marble and bronze. Paradoxes, however, have their uses and Hanslick's boldness has been beneficial in reducing the altogether excessive claims for the boundless powers of music such as are common today. It still has the effect of compelling those who on principle oppose the aesthetics of form to recognize the differences between the expressive power of music and that of the other arts.

In some directions music is less powerful than the other arts, in other directions much more powerful. Music cannot objectify or present unaided exact images or concepts. With all the notes in the gamut at his disposal no composer can produce an unambiguous image of a wood or a lake, such as the poet can give in a word and a draughtsman with a few dozen strokes of his pen. On the other hand, with the aid of a text or a title music can suggest the solemn or secret character of a wood more quickly, more immediately and more grippingly than any poem or painting. Music is by nature an ancillary art whose intentions must be communicated to the intelligence and the imagination, and whose objects must be previously agreed. Music has no organ for dealing with names and specifications; it is, as M. Hauptmann says, a kind of algebra, a calculation with unspecified quantities. To the initiate music gives uniquely rich and delicate images of the nature and interior life of objects. Next to music comes poetry and the two together form the group of the 'speaking arts' [*Die redenden Künste*]: non-musicians even speak of tone-poems, the 'language' of music and compositions that 'say' nothing, or 'say' a lot to them. The chief value of music does indeed lie in its eloquence, its power to 'speak', and the great musical reforms and revolutions of recent musical history – the appearance of monody at the end of the Renaissance and the New German School in the nineteenth century have had as their object the restitution and development of this prime feature. This 'power of speech' is not the same in music as it is in words. It is less independent and less clear. But in fact the two can accommodate each other very well. Music continues when words have no more power; the composer is able to catch in a moment, and in all their fullness and individuality, those movements of the human soul – the smallest as well as the greatest – which a poet can only partially communicate in long paraphrases and circumlocutions. The dependence of music is a lack, a kind of grammatical fault, but it is one with which, in view of its advantages, we are quite willing to put up and even compound. The aestheticians of form are obstinate in emphasizing and exaggerating this lack, but they forget that the rest of a listener whose eye and ear are engaged is not dead. Wherever man is present, it is the human spirit that hears and sees. All art, and all individual works of art, depend for their full effect on the goodwill of the recipient and the ability of his imagination to co-operate. Remembering this, we shall find an essential reduction of the 'indefiniteness' of music, even in the case of instrumental works. Thus, it is inconceivable that any educated person, who may wonder what the overture to Mozart's *Magic Flute* has to do with a magic flute, should interpret that overture as depicting the chattering of market-stallholders. It is the same with all other operatic overtures and indeed all instrumental works in which title or programme provide the intention of the music: these and all vocal works are virtually wide open to 'interpretation'. Not only that, but fugues, sonatas, symphonies, concertos and all instrumental works generally reckoned as 'pure' music – in so far as they rise above the level of simple craftsmanship – are capable of being understood in a more general, human sense in certain circumstances and up to a certain point: they conceal a general spiritual content of which the musical form, whatever it may be, is as it were the husk or shell. It is this content, or the kernel or core, that forms the chief interest of a work to the real connoisseur, and it is he who is in a position not only to appreciate this 'core' but to suggest or describe in words at least its essential features. Composing and listening to music have nothing to do with somnambulistic circumstances and powers: they form an activity which demands the highest degree of mental clarity. Philosophers and aestheticians who hold other views on the subject must expect musicians to retort with 'a cobbler should stick to his last' [*ne sutor ultra crepidam*].

There are two main questions in any 'explication' of instrumental music without a title. The first is 'how far this explication can be pushed without abandoning solid ground?' and the second 'how far must the explication be carried if it is to have any significance?'

The answer to the first of these questions must begin with an admission: the limits of what can be precisely demonstrated are in fact fairly narrow when we are speaking of instrumental music without a title. They are determined by what our forebears used to call the 'affections' [*Affekte*] i.e. the characteristic qualities of sensations, images and ideas. It is these 'affections' that are, so to say, incarnate in musical phrases, themes and figures, either in isolation or in associations and amalgamations such as are possible only in music. It is the task of hermeneutics to distil these 'affections' from the music and to describe in words the basic pattern of their development. This may well seem a poor sort of undertaking, a kind of shadow-play, but it is in fact a valuable service! Anyone who can penetrate behind the notes themselves, and their configurations, to the feelings, is elevating sensuous pleasure and raising purely formal workmanship to an activity of the spirit; and he is thus protected from the dangers and disgrace of a purely physical way of listening to music. If he is gifted with imagination and that degree of artistic talent presupposed by any concern with the arts, he cannot fail to perceive the basic emotional pattern of a work which will, as it were, come to life with all his own subjective memories and associations – figures and events from his past, from poetry, from his dreams and his vague aspirations. Such a listener will see, as in a lightning-flash, the place of mind and heart in the music which he is interpreting. His close observation of the 'affections' will prevent him from falling into mere reverie, while the obligation of tracing their developments and checking the composer's art and logic will ensure him against any excessive appeal to him at the moment. Why, he will ask himself, does the music suddenly shift at one moment from the majestic to the tender, at another from tranquillity to excitement? Is there a reason for these unusual transitions, or are they designed simply to dazzle the listener? Anyone who is capable of following this play of the 'affections', is in that sense a critical listener and his enjoyment is critical; but his activity resembles that of Socrates rather than that of Beckmesser. It is a distinguishing between light and shade, points of excellence and points of weakness; and without this ability to distinguish, admiration is valueless and easily becomes self-deception or hypocrisy.

As I hope to demonstrate later, such an understanding of the affections is something that can be taught; and there is therefore no doubt that the listener – or the man who undertakes this 'explication' – is on firm ground in seeking to understand the character of individual passages in an instrumental work, and hence the larger sections composed of these passages.

To identify the affections is the least of his tasks, and the duty of going thus far is incumbent on all but those who are content to enjoy music simply as such and to relinquish all association between music and the life of the human spirit. In the case of music a particularly large part may be allowed to the spirit (δαίμου) that presides over all artistic creation; the question of the moods and ideas that prompt the composer to write can be left to him, since it is in his imagination that music sings and resounds. But a large composition will never become a work of art unless the composer goes beyond his first ideas and penetrates from the sphere of the unconscious to a clear understanding of the nature and true end of those first ideas. Philosophers repeatedly overlook this cardinal point in the composer's activity, and in so doing they reveal their ignorance of the very essence of creative activity. This was pardonable in Hegel's day, but not since historical research has revealed such a quantity of material from the workshops of the great composers – Beethoven's sketch-books, for instance, and the many different versions of works by Handel, Bach, Mozart and Schubert. Historical research of this kind makes it clear that exceptional results are the outcome of calculation and conscious invention rather than mere inspiration. And the same is true of the listener too. It is only enthusiastic amateurs who are content to make their enigmatic character the distinguishing feature of musical impressions. Such an attitude denotes neither knowledge nor talent, but only that indispensable preliminary – enthusiasm. Any serious and gifted music-lover must progress beyond that first stage, both in his listening and in his attempts to understand what he hears. Even a knowledge and understanding of musical forms of all kinds is no more than a step on the road. Forms are means of expression. What is to be expressed is something spiritual which must – unless the composer is a charlatan – be made manifest in and through the various musical forms and be clear, at least in its main outlines, to the listener – namely the affections. The belief that the effect of music is something uniquely musical must be abandoned, and delight in 'pure music' must be recognized as an example of muddled thinking, aesthetically speaking. In the sense of an exclusively musical content there is no such thing as absolute music! It is a phantom, like pure poetry i.e. words in rhyme and metre, but no thoughts. Even in the case of instrumental works without a title the art of 'explication' will often go beyond the identification of the affections and will be able to point to, or guess, the objects to which the affections refer. Biography and history provide the means for this. If, for instance, these reveal the circumstances in which Mozart wrote his late symphonies in E flat and G minor and Beethoven his symphony in B flat, it is not merely permissible but a matter of conscience to examine whether there exists any connection between the affections expressed in those works and the facts of the composer's life. An acquaintance with the atmosphere and tendencies of the period and its individual musical attitudes and usages will often disclose more about the content, the object, of instrumental works. [pp. 47–53]

[.   ·   .]

# Paul Mies (1889–1976)
## Über die Tonmalerei (1912)

Mies studied musicology in Bonn graduating in 1912 and for most of his life taught at Cologne. His doctoral dissertation on tonal painting attracted the attention of Max Dessoir, who published it in part in his *Zeitschrift für Ästhetik und allgemeine Kunstwissenschaft*.

## On tonal painting

*Source:*

*Über die Tonmalerei* (Stuttgart 1912), pp. 2; 3–4; 7–9; 11–13. Translated by Martin Cooper.

[.   .]]

The effect of vocal music on a listener consists of two elements: the contents of the text is expressed through the words, it is a concrete quality, and further, the text can awake in us a certain feeling from which follows a mood.[1] We then speak of the emotional content of the text. The music which is connected with words arouses likewise a mood in us. A deeper quality of the mood and an intensified effect on the human mind will also result if the words and the sounds share the same emotional content. [p. 2]

[.   .]]

The possibility of a correspondence between word and sound has always been taken for granted in any music that has progressed beyond the primitive. Exactly how this concord is achieved has never been satisfactorily explained, as we have seen, any more than a general agreement has been reached as to the mode of its occurrence – whether it is merely in the realm of mood, feeling or indeed ideas.

We are accustomed to consider a poem or a picture against the background of everyday life and its phenomena. In the case of painting we are assisted by perception, in that of poetry by the firm link between words – whether written or spoken – and ideas or images. Music, on the other hand, does not appeal to our perceptions in the same way as painting nor is there any

[1] E. Hanslick, *Vom Musikalisch-Schönen*, 11th edn (Leipzig 1910), p. 25.

unambiguous link between musical sensations and ideas, or images. At first sight it would therefore seem pointless to attempt to represent in music any image, whether it be that of an object in the exterior world or a sequence of mental states.

Suppose that we adopt Hanslick's point of view and reduce to a minimum the representation in music of any extra-musical content. Even then there still remains a way of establishing a kind of relationship between musical sensations and the imagination. If we encounter in a musical work, or a single phrase of that work, a definite dynamic moment of feeling – whether it be gay, vivacious, turbulent or violent – it is possible in certain circumstances that this may stimulate a definite feeling e.g. joy, enthusiasm, anger and so forth. Since, however, a dynamic moment of this sort can belong to a whole series of different feelings, the transition from one to the other cannot be achieved by music: it must be brought about by extra-musical means such as a text, a title, some particular circumstances or emotional mood. Furthermore, since – as Hanslick explains – feeling has an intelligible core consisting of a complex of images and judgements,[2] a definite image belonging to this complex may in certain circumstances enter our consciousness: and this of course again presupposes an extra-musical stimulus. From this it follows that one and the same piece of music can prompt quite different feelings, and even evoke quite different images in us according to circumstance. In this case therefore there can be no question of a musical representation of definite feelings or images. This explains the origin of many of the titles of piano pieces by Schumann, Grieg and in earlier times Couperin. The emotional content of title, music and even the feelings aroused in the listener may all be in agreement, yet the selective power of the composer's imagination implicit in the formulation of the title is so arbitrary that in Schumann's case, for instance, 'Leid ohne Ende' (op. 124) might really have equally well been given the title of 'Erster Verlust' (op. 68) or 'Fast zu ernst' (op. 15). The emotional content is the same, and only the image that prompted it is different.

Here I should like to observe that we are not for the moment concerned with the question of whether beauty in music depends on a connection between definite musical sensations and corresponding moods, feelings or images. Our task is to discover whether in fact such a connection exists and how far this can be established. [pp. 3–4]

[.    .    .]

The rhythmical element plays an important part in music as well as the sonorous. Every creation of the musical imagination of which rhythm is an element can, by this fact alone, serve as a stimulus for musical representation. Obvious examples are the trotting of horses – the musical representation of which will be dealt with more fully later – and the call of the quail, most remarkable for its rhythm, though also of course for its actual note. Generally

[2] Hanslick, p. 22–3.

speaking we cannot make a hard and fast distinction between these two areas, since most rhythms are connected with definite noises or sounds which, even if not accurately pitched, are nevertheless linked with distinctive pitches and timbres. Take for example the hammer-blows of a smithy as translated into musical terms; and it immediately becomes clear that any musical phrase in which the similarity to some external phenomenon is only rhythmical is far less significant than one in which the reference lies also in the actual notes.

A great number of other such 'illustrations' depend on movement in the wider sense – fast and slow, heavy and light, falling and rising. We have already taken the example of a butterfly's flight and found that the chief characteristics in any musical suggestion were speed, lightness and zigzag rising and falling. The 'illustration' of such words as 'rising' and 'falling' is much less complicated. All musical illustration not based on rhythmic or sonorous analogy can be explained on this principle. The subordinate species of movement quoted above determine the overall movement of an event. If therefore any image to be conveyed in musical forms has a distinctive motion of this kind, it is possible to translate that image into musical terms. Let us call such a translation an analogy by movement [*Bewegungsanalogie*].

Ideas of 'height' and 'depth' i.e. rising and falling are used, though not very frequently, to depict objects in musical terms. In such a case a succession of notes must correspond to simultaneity in the external world, and the analogy is confined to upward or downward movement. Representation of objects of this sort has been rare in music, and this suggests that it is neither satisfactory as a means of denotation nor really effective musically, even as a means of illustration. There are examples to be found in the works of Haydn (the branched head of a deer), Wagner and Mattheson (the rainbow).

One and the same movement may be included as an element in a number of different images – at least this is so if the movement is only generally represented, as is necessarily the case in music. If we take an image which can be represented with the help of an analogy of movement, it is hardly ever possible to make this unambiguous. When in such cases it is essential that the listener's intelligence be directed to a definite image, a verbal hint in the score will be needed in small pieces devoted to a single subject, while larger works will need a text which the listener can absorb at the same time as he is listening to the music. In fact the text must be clearly audible, as in vocal music, or each individual phrase must be accompanied by the words which the composer wishes to be understood.

In all the examples that we have so far discussed the analogy between image and musical phrase is to be found by comparison, which is an activity proper to the intellect. In the purely physical sense music addresses itself simply to our power of hearing, which apprehends musical sounds according to their pitch (including chords), their dynamic force, their rhythmic pattern and the speed with which they succeed each other. From this we can draw the conclusion that analogies by sonority, rhythm and movement are – purely physically speaking – the only possible ones, and all 'tone-painting' must rest on them. We therefore reach the following definition: *The term 'tone-painting' is rightly applied to music in which images are so conveyed that the connection between image and music can only be established and expressed in words by means of analogies of sonority, rhythm or movement and by intellectual process of comparison.* This does not, of course, mean that there may not also exist a similarity of emotional content between image and music, but this cannot be recognized by purely intellectual means. [pp. 7–9]

[.   .   .]

The instrumentation of a work may also be regarded as a means of tone-painting. Natural sounds and noises can be imitated by individual instruments or by a combination of several. Thus in Saint-Saëns's *Danse macabre* the rattling of skeleton bones is represented by the xylophone,[3] and Strauss in his *Don Quixote* suggests the bleating of a flock of sheep by an ingenious use of wind instruments.[4] The imitation of the wind by a wind-machine, also in *Don Quixote*, is certainly a form of representation, but cannot rightly be called tone-painting, since the means employed are mechanical rather than musical and no pitched notes are involved. All these examples of tone-painting fall under the heading of analogy by sonority. On the other hand, Berlioz uses the viola for the theme symbolizing the hero's melancholy in *Harold in Italy* because he finds the viola's tone dark and melancholy;[5] and this is an aesthetic judgement rather than a sense-impression and cannot therefore be counted as an example of tone-painting.

Another kind of tone-painting has been used by composers in the past and is used even more frequently today. This is not based on the physical or aesthetic effects of music but on certain intellectual speculations about music and musical processes. Thus Kuhnau represents Laban's deceiving of Jacob by false progressions,[6] and R. Strauss employs similar means to represent Don Quixote's mistaken and illogical conclusions.[7] Under the same heading may be classed the passage in the seventh variation of *Don Quixote*,[8] where the pedal-note in the bass is meant to show that although both the Don and Sancho Panza believe that they are flying through the air, they have in fact never left the ground.[9] In the same way the theorists' criticisms of the Hero in *Ein Heldenleben* are represented by parallel fifths in the bass, symbolizing the academic misdemeanours of which the Hero is accused. On this point we agree with M. D. Calvocoressi, who allows a wide scope to programme music but rejects representations of this kind as unmusical and childish.[10] Vincent d'Indy's symphonic variations *Istar* provide a similar instance. These varia-

[3] O. Klauwell, *Geschichte der Programmusik* (Leipzig 1910) p. 296.
[4] Klauwell, p. 263.
[5] Klauwell, p. 109ff.
[6] Klauwell, p. 43.
[7] Klauwell, p. 260ff.
[8] Klauwell, p. 265.
[9] Klauwell, p. 272.
[10] M. D. Calvocoressi, 'Esquisse d'une esthétique de la musique à programme', *Sammelbände der Internationalen Musikgesellschaft* vol. 9 (1907–8), p. 424ff.

tions become increasingly simple to symbolize Istar's shedding of her garments, and the theme emerges with increasing clarity, so that it eventually stands naked, like Istar herself.[11] Interesting as the music is in itself, the idea must be regarded musically as a mistake.

In the examples that we have been quoting the image to be conveyed and the musical phrase conveying it are indeed linked, however loosely. It remains for us to consider the case in which the relationship between the two is absolutely arbitrary – as in 'tone-symbolism' such as we find in most of the leitmotifs of Wagner, Berlioz and Strauss. The arbitrary nature of such imagery makes it quite impossible to understand the composer's intention without some text or programme.

If we now examine all the points that we have been considering, we shall find ourselves able to come to the following conclusion. Looking for an image that precisely matches a musical phrase, we shall find perhaps only one that is absolutely unambiguous, namely the call of the cuckoo. In every other instance there is a greater or lesser degree of ambiguity in all tone-painting as defined by us. In vocal music the relevant image is supplied by the text accompanying the music, and the analogies between the two, if such exist, are not difficult to discover. Instrumental music depending on a programme is another matter. Listening to music with a knowledge of the programme involves a matching of music and programme moment by moment, if we are to understand the work. In order to make this possible the analogies between the successive images of the programme and the music must be as precise as possible. Owing, however, to the imprecision and ambiguity of all events in music it will be difficult for any listener without a previous knowledge of the programme, as well as the music and their mutual relationship to synchronize the two correctly. It may indeed well happen that even a musical listener discovers himself to be still in the middle of the programme when the music comes to an end. The only remedy for such an unfortunate state of affairs would be to show a film of the programme simultaneously with the performance of the music. This experiment has indeed been made,[12] though what it has to do with the enjoyment and understanding of music must be left for others to decide. [pp. 11–13]

---

[11] Klauwell, p. 304ff.
[12] Klauwell, p. 206. Klauwell makes many references to the impossibility of representing definite programmes in musically recognizable form.

# 1.3   The eclectic tendency

## Introduction

The dividing line between the aesthetic views of the authors in this and the preceding section is not a sharp one. Indeed, it is in the nature of any eclectic tendency to avoid demarcation and manifest itself in an unpredictable range of sources and intellectual causes which may be espoused by any one author. Eclecticism is above all an illustration on the one hand of the weakening of the grip of the prominent philosophical systems of the late eighteenth and the early nineteenth centuries, and on the other, of the continuation of the belief that philosophy has to be presented as a complete system of which aesthetics is but a small part. Thus the weakening of the bond that ties aesthetics to philosophy results, quite predictably, in a belief that the discipline is not a speculative one and that, rather than serving a philosophical system, it can be practically applied. This is the view expressed by the music historian Franz Brendel who was himself close to the aesthetics of F. T. Vischer. However, Brendel's idea of the practical application of aesthetics does not show a direct link with the new scientific and experimental tendency, but it does owe something to the optimistic belief of the mid-nineteenth century that truth in aesthetics may be reached through a systematic investigation of separate issues: instead of constructing a speculative system an aesthetician should proceed gradually and construct a composite truth by addressing himself to a single problem at a time. Unwittingly Brendel exhibits a Herbartian mode of thought, although his attitude towards music and its expressive power makes him otherwise quite independent from Herbartian notions.

Herbartian influence is clearly visible in the work of Otakar Hostinský. The title of his treatise is surprising for it tries to unite the two opposites in the aesthetic theory of the time. It ought to be noted that Prague University, at which Hostinský studied and later taught, was through a good part of the nineteenth century a stronghold of Herbartism. The long line of Herbart's followers there stretched from F. Exner who taught philosophy at the university between 1832 and 1852, and Robert Zimmermann who succeeded him and taught in Prague until his move to Vienna in 1861, via Hostinský's teacher W. F. Volkmann, to Josef Dastich and Josef Durdík, the latter having been Hostinský's friend and colleague.[1] It is hardly necessary now to argue whether the synthesis attempted by Hostinský is possible or to judge the

[1] For a discussion of Hostinský's intellectual environment see Miloš Jůzl, *Otakar Hostinský* (Prague 1980).

degree to which he managed to convince his readers. Hostinský may have been led by desire to view Wagner from a Herbartian point of view in deference towards the prevailing orientation among Prague philosophers. The very attempt to provide a bridge between the Herbartian school and the theory of *Gesamtkunstwerk* is an interesting one since it helps to explain the weakness in Herbart's concept of form and content as expounded by Robert Zimmermann. If 'content' and 'form' are treated as two completely separate entities, then it was, of course, possible for Hostinský to indicate that the 'pure' instrumental music and vocal music make two separate categories distinguished only by the absence or presence respectively of a content. Whereas Hanslick's argument was directed against the dogmatic division of form and content, and the concept of a content was defined from within, Hostinský retains the notion of a separate feeling which arises as a concomitant of formal disposition: one and the same element, such as a leitmotif, may be viewed in its formal capacity, but may likewise serve a different, poetic function. At first sight this may appear as a reasonable or common-sense explanation, but it leaves unresolved the problem of the causal link between the musical meaning generated from within the material itself, which Hanslick argued for, and a symbolic interpretation which always leaves open the question of what the symbol is standing for. This latter aspect of the form-content relationship may be seen as a link that connects Hostinský, however tentatively, with Suzanne Langer's later symbolic interpretation of Hanslick.

H. A. Köstlin also starts, if not from a Hanslickian standpoint, then from a premiss which in the choice of words betrays an echo of Hanslick. Chapter 2 of his *Die Tonkunst* is meant to provide the answer to the question which is rhetorically put at the end of the preceding chapter: 'The content of music is the musically beautiful [*das Musikalisch-Schöne*]. But what is the musically beautiful?'[2] The answer which he provides is partly influenced by his vocation as a priest and his standing as a theologian, but more important than that it illustrates the tendency of the withdrawal of one stream of musical production and of criticism from the issues raised by the scientific advance in the late nineteenth century. Köstlin's argument combines in a true eclectic manner the wording of Hanslick, Hegel's belief in the supremacy of religion, and the early romantic infatuation with the idea of the artist as a divinely inspired individual revealing a universal truth.

Gustav Engel seems to be more aware of the advances in the field of psychology of music, and his own interest in physics, as well as his career as a singing teacher should distinguish him from the authors whose primary interest was strongly speculative. A mixture of speculative and scientific interest is present in his thesis that music is a 'rationally structured pure time'. The main weakness of his *Aesthetics of Music* is that he fails to argue this assertion consistently, preferring to shield himself behind themes derived from the influential sources of the time: Hegel's categories of art are given by him a 'dynamic' Wagnerian interpretation and the *Gesamtkunstwerk*

[2] H. A. Köstlin, *Die Tonkust* . . ., p. 274. See below, pp. 152–8.

appears as a central element in the construction of a system of interactions between the arts. Any scientific or psychological interest that seems to have been exhibited in the early part of his work disappears under the wash of diluted Hegelian speculation.

Among the nineteenth-century philosophers Eduard von Hartmann was the only one, apart from Nietzsche, who showed a keen interest in composing, although in his case this may have been only an amateurish juvenile pastime. At the beginning of the twentieth century Paul Moos refers to Hartmann as 'the greatest aesthetician of our time',[3] but already at the time he was writing this the interest in Hartmann's philosophy began to wane. This was largely due to the fact that in the early twentieth century he was seen as an epigone in the tradition of the great philosophical systems of the past. In a sense he may be seen as an eclectic who took over Hegel's system of philosophy and imbued it with Schopenhauer's pessimism: God's creation of the world is a form of alienation whereby God, seen as Schopenhauer's will, is threatened by destruction. The task of philosophy, ultimately striving towards religion is to prevent this destruction. Inevitably aesthetics plays, however prominent, only one part in such an ambitiously conceived system. Hartmann's importance and his popularity, especially outside Germany, rested on his *Philosophy of the Unconscious* (1869), and if later in our century he was accorded any prominence it was done in recognition of his introduction of the notion of the unconscious in the philosophy of mind. His aesthetic theory is presented in a manner later made widely known by Benedetto Croce: a historical part is followed by a systematic one, the latter presenting the full argument of the author's revision of the German thought of the earlier nineteenth century. Hartmann combines the general thrust of Hegel's system with an artistic sensibility derived from Schopenhauer and develops a theory in which art becomes an embodiment rather than a mere reflection of the idea of beauty. His own musical interest and knowledge may have been responsible for his recognition of the formal, developmental aspect of music which Hegel viewed with a dose of reserve. Yet, there stands as a counterweight to this, and in the tradition of the adherents of the aesthetic of content, Hartmann's description of musical form as 'a representation of the shifts and mutations of our own emotional life' (see below, p. 173). This suggestion of an interaction, of a projection of our own emotional experience into the fabric of music, brings Hartmann close to Theodor Lipps's aesthetics of *Einfühlung*.

[3] Paul Moos, *Moderne Musikästhetik in Deutschland* (Leipzig 1902), p. 369.

# Franz Brendel (1811–1868)

## 'Die Aesthetik der Tonkunst' (1857)

Brendel studied philosophy and medicine in Leipzig, Berlin and Freiberg and obtained a doctorate of medicine in 1840. While a student in Leipzig he took piano lessons from Friedrich Wieck and later lectured on music history and aesthetics at Leipzig Conservatory. At the end of 1844 he succeeded Schumann as the editor of the *Neue Zeitschrift für Musik*, editing the journal until his death. In his youth he was influenced by Hegel's aesthetics and his subsequent writings showed a strong Hegelian bias. His *Geschichte der Musik in Italien, Deutschland und Frankreich von den ersten christlichen Zeiten an bis auf die Gegenwart* (Leipzig 1852) went through numerous editions throughout the second half of the nineteenth century.

## *Aesthetics of music*

*Source:*

'Die Aesthetik der Tonkunst', *Neue Zeitschrift für Musik*, vol. 46 (1857), pp. 185–6. Translated by Martin Cooper.

[ . .]

I believe that the time has come for the really serious consideration of musical aesthetics, not only from the strictly scientific standpoint or in books but rather empirically and in the daily press. What has hitherto been established should be brought to the common awareness and the public should be prepared for new discoveries and further achievements. In recent years there have been two stages in our understanding of music. The first of these was the psychological description of artistic impressions, a field of study which F. Rochlitz first explored, followed by others well into the 1830s. The second stage was chiefly characterized by the attempt to refer what earlier reached our consciousness only as vague feeling back to precise ideas [*Vorstellungen*]: to understand content not simply as feeling but as a directing of the mind [*Gedankenbestimmung*], and so to come nearer to understanding the complex of phenomena. This was the chief task that I set myself both in this journal and in my *Geschichte der Musik*.[1] The next step which must be taken,

---

[1] [Franz Brendel, *Geschichte der Musik in Italien, Deutschland und Frankreich von den ersten christlichen Zeiten an bis auf die Gegenwart* (Leipzig 1852).]

and with no delay, consists in grasping the nature of the creative impulse [*der künstlerische Geist*], not simply by subjective personal experience but by the objective shape of a composition, understanding the mental content of a work from its external, technical configuration. I stated this principle many years ago, and Hanslick has recently done so, though he has drawn false conclusions which, strictly speaking, invalidate each of his propositions. This, it may be observed in passing, in no way prejudices the excellence of his work (something that I have already acknowledged) or the scientific clarity with which he approaches the subject.[2] In scientific matters it is not exclusively a question of a single individual reaching the truth in a direct manner [*schon unmittelbar*]: it is a great achievement if someone puts a question in such a way that it prompts a better answer than has hitherto been forthcoming, or furthers the study of a problem by purely negative means. Hanslick does both of these things, the latter by his successful attack on fanciful notions that were accepted in the past. Now, however, the question is how to make progress along a path which has been proved to be the correct one, and how to guard against future deviations from that path, which in fact promises to reveal a new world to musicians. Hitherto much has been established as provisionally or partially true, and I regard it as one of the next tasks of this journal to promote this advance still further. It is in this sense that the abstracts from Vischer's *Aesthetics* are important: they have to introduce and prepare the subject and as far as possible orientate our readers. It is for this reason that I included [E. von Elterlein's] reports.[3]

The value of the aesthetics of music is not simply scientific, in the strict sense. It is not exclusively an intellectual inquisitiveness that it satisfies: its practical significance can be enormous, when it has come to maturity. Can there really be any doubt that a large proportion of our present disagreements would automatically cease immediately with the establishment, or more public familiarizing, of the aesthetic principles concerned? Let us take a single example. One of the most hotly disputed questions is that of form and content, a particularly knotty problem in music. Let us suppose that this question receives an adequate answer, tracing clearly how in music content creates its own form and is thus the primary element, but then appears only in that form and hence as merely secondary (as we shall have to show later, Hanslick's answers to these questions are quite unreliable). That question once answered, all doubts about the permissibility or impermissibility of formal variations e.g. in Liszt's tone-poems are resolved at a single blow. These variations are not only permissible, they are essential to the extent that we must welcome every new form provided it is beautiful and is not arbitrary,

---

[2] [A review of Hanslick's *Vom Musikalisch-Schönen* by Brendel appeared in the *NZM*, vol. 42 in three instalments (no. 8, 16 February 1855; no. 9, 23 February 1855; no. 10, 2 March 1855).]

[3] [A lengthy summary of Vischer's aesthetics of music by E. von Elterlein was published in the *NZM*, vols. 46 and 47 in eleven instalments between January and August 1857. A reference to Elterlein was made by Brendel in the opening paragraph of his article, omitted in the present edition.]

but grows naturally from previous forms. Such a step forward would come to be regarded like progress in any other field of human endeavour. A whole epoch is plagued by problems and doubts, with which it tries with all its might to grapple. Once the answer to the problem is found, that epoch is regarded with a condescending smile – it shrinks suddenly into insignificance. Now, if ever, is the time for us to press forward, since we could not progress until we had passed through the two stages mentioned above.

Of course our first concern is not with philosophical investigations; on the contrary, musical practice must provide the point of departure from which we embark on our search for more exact knowledge. This is the path trodden by all sciences today, and one that in the natural sciences has already led to great results. A similar method in the aesthetics of music promises that problems will be given their proper solution, one which we have been seeking for a long time. [pp. 185–6]

# Otakar (Ottokar) Hostinský (1847–1910)

## Das Musikalisch-Schöne und das Gesamtkunstwerk vom Standpunkte der formalen Aesthetik (1877)

Hostinský started studying law in Prague in 1865, but soon changed to philosophy. After a period in Munich in 1867–8, he returned to Prague, graduating in 1869. During the 1870s he was active as a contributor to and editor of several Czech-language periodicals. In 1877 he was appointed *Dozent* for aesthetics at Prague University, and when in 1882 the university divided into its German and Czech halves he became professor of aesthetics at the latter, lecturing also on the history of music and history of art. A champion of Smetana, he influenced several younger Czech musicologists, among whom Zdeněk Nejedlý and Otakar Zich.

## The musically beautiful and the Gesamtkunstwerk *from the standpoint of formal aesthetics*

Source:

*Das Musikalisch-Schöne und das Gesamtkunstwerk vom Standpunkte der formalen Aesthetik* (Leipzig 1877). Chapter v (pp. 111–37); chapter vi (pp. 148–60). Translated by Martin Cooper.

### Chapter V

We must now examine more closely what we have established about the relationship between music and the other factors in the *Gesamtkunstwerk*. The most important of these will of course be the connection with poetry, as being the art which provides both the material and the form of the whole. Let us therefore consider once again the three conditions which determine unity in any alliance between one art and another.

1. As far as the harmony of content [*Übereinstimmung*] is concerned, it is clear that we must definitely deny the possibility of such a harmony as regards a content that is peculiar to poetry. The whole province of ideas communicable by means of language is unattainable by music as such — there can therefore in this sense be no 'harmony' between music and poetry. Yet there are nonetheless apparent exceptions in which music reproduces — for what-

ever the reason may be – a thought-content with a greater or lesser degree of explicitness, and we certainly cannot ignore such exceptional instances. Certain short horn-passages suffice to say 'hunting' to us; a trumpet-call over a drum-roll says 'battle'; long held trombone chords with bells say 'funeral'; a brazen fanfare with drums 'banquet' or 'king'; a few guitar chords 'serenade' and so forth. These are not so much sound-painting as simple quotations of musical shapes, the conventional accompaniment of these or other scenes, in fact imitations of music-making in actual life. There is really hardly any objection to the use of such quotations, which in certain cases naturally find an organic place within the poetic plan of the *Gesamtkunstwerk* and must therefore harmonize with the poetic content of the drama. Moreover, they form only isolated representational passages and their connection with the rest of the work can only be established by means of words. The quotation of a chorale or a song with a familiar text represents a more substantial loan from the world of ideas. Such a melody has only to appear in the orchestra for the hearer automatically to supply the text in his mind and to receive an identical impression. There is something essentially questionable about a quotation of this kind, which breaks through the frame of the work of art and seeks a direct connection with real life. It can be considered aesthetically valid only if it is not accompanied by any wish to arouse extra-artistic interest and is used simply as a touch of historical or national colour. The aesthetic independence and isolation of a work would be better guaranteed if in such instances a knowledge of an already existing song were not actually taken for granted in the listener and the whole song, with its text, were to be used at a suitable juncture before any passage from which it is quoted. In that case the key to its understanding and the reason for quoting it would lie, as is proper, within the actual work. In such cases, however, it is obviously a matter of indifference, from the purely artistic point of view, whether the song-fragment in question exists elsewhere than in the work and is thus already familiar. The artist has an inalienable right to make full use of the power of music to refer to the text of a song, and all the ideas with which that text is associated, by repeating simply the melody of a passage that has already been sung, whether that melody is his own or not. This applies to the so-called leitmotifs which have achieved such significance in modern opera thanks to Wagner's use of them and his theoretical exposition of their importance.

Such leitmotifs may serve a double purpose, purely musical or poetic–dramatic. Of the purely musical purpose we shall speak later; for the moment we must remark on the conditions in which such a leitmotif may serve the drama. Here the decisive point lies in the conditions governing the most effective automatic recall. To achieve this, the first essential is a profound amalgamation of words and music, that is to say correct declamation and characterization, which facilitate and accelerate the process of recall. The second essential is that the first appearance of the passage in question must occur at a point marked by a certain musical and dramatic emphasis, thus concentrating the full attention of the listener. It need not, of course, always be a vocal melody that serves as a leitmotif: it may equally well be an orchestrated melody that accompanies a certain situation or the appearance of a certain character, or more generally some significant scene. In either case the reappearance of the leitmotif will automatically communicate to the listener a definite mental concept. It is not, to be sure, the content of the music as such that is here expressed, but simply the content of the poet's works or the stage scene. A happy amalgamation of these with the accompanying melody has converted these into a powerful 'aid to recall' and, by this exterior association, they have become in a certain sense the property of music.[1] If we may once again make use of Fechner's terminology for our own purposes,[2] music is here making its effect not simply by a direct method but also by means of the factor of 'association'.

As far as the use of leitmotifs goes, this can only of course be in perfect accord with the dramatic scheme, and this can be in one of two ways. The leitmotif may either serve simply to reinforce ideas communicated by words and gestures (or at least by the latter) or to convey to the listener ideas which would otherwise remain unexpressed. In the latter case the ideas may equally be secret, or at least unexpressed, ideas of one of the characters of the drama or those of the author himself, simply contributing to the clarification of certain relationships or to the connection between different points of the action. This action is often forwarded by the characters becoming more communicative; but even though there is no objection in principle to 'thinking aloud' on the stage, circumstances often arise in which the hero would do better to remain silent rather than open his heart to the audience, though this of course may be essential if the plot is to be intelligible. In any case the dramatic poet has a far more difficult task than the epic-writer, since the former can only speak through the mouths of his characters while the latter is by no means confined to direct speech: he can also use narrative and even interrupt the course of the actual story to interpose his own subjective comments. In the *Gesamtkunstwerk* these purposes are well served by the leitmotif which can recall to the listener without any recourse to word or gesture, what he has seen or heard earlier in the drama. It thus serves not only as a powerful support to the actor but also as a means of suggesting a character's thoughts in situations where acting itself is as good as useless. Thus it is that in the *Gesamtkunstwerk* the orchestra plays such an important role, illuminating the course of the action by its ability to recall what has gone before.

Finally tone-painting acquires in the *Gesamtkunstwerk* a significance that it can never have in pure music. It is not possible for a phrase to be beautiful because it attempts to imitate a gesture or a natural sound by means of music – its beauty depends solely on its specifically musical shape. Such a phrase may, on the other hand, be found apt when either word or picture has made

---

[1] See Wagner, *Gesammelte Schriften und Dichtungen*, vol. 4, pp. 229ff. [*GS*, vol. 4, p. 183; *PW*, vol. 2, p. 27].
[2] [G. T. Fechner, *Vorschule der Aesthetik* (Leipzig 1876). See below, pp. 284–91.]

unambiguously plain what the music is trying to imitate. It is only then that
the artist can count on a specific effect, only then that tone-painting loses that
vagueness and unreliability which are inevitable in pure music. The listener
no longer needs to be distracted from the path of pure artistic enjoyment by
the need to worry his head over the 'meaning' of illustrative phrases. 'Words
are like the rails at the top of a precipice, put there to prevent the public from
falling over the edge', as Beauquier says.[3] A mere glance at a piano score
without words will confirm this ability of word and image to particularize
and the weakness of pure music in this respect. Divorced from their verbal
and scenic context many phrases that seemed, in full orchestral performance,
to be the most striking musical illustration, prove to be highly questionable as
pure imitation. Here the listener only too often plays the part of old Polonius,
inclined to see every conceivable kind of shapes in the musical sky as soon
Prince Hamlet – that is to say, the text – suggests them. Thus the *Gesamtkunstwerk* in fact makes even more use of the ability of text and scenery to specify
objects or situations than of the power of scenery actually to 'paint' them. It is
easy to understand that no general prescription can be given for the exact
extent to which tone-painting may be valid. Only one norm might perhaps be
considered beyond dispute, since it is implicit in the very nature of the
*Gesamtkunstwerk*: tone-painting in music is indispensable inasmuch as
everything audible must in any case be translated into musical terms if that
appears in any way practicable. The establishing of this demand in fact brings
us already to our second instance, unity of content in the *Gesamtkunstwerk*.

The material element proper to music, the real fundamental 'content' of its
aesthetic shapes is the musical sound and this must be in absolute accord with
the corresponding acoustic elements of the other factors in the *Gesamtkunstwerk*. This specifically musical unity demands as a principle the exclusion of
all non-musical noises which can in any way be replaced by musical sounds,
and also the conforming of pitched sounds to the aesthetic tone-relationships
of contemporary music. Nothing can be worse than suddenly, in the middle
of a musical passage, to hear the noise of the theatre-machinery used for a
tempest, a rainstorm or a waterfall. The exclusive use of tone-painting, on
however modest a scale, is quite enough and certainly preferable to mechanical devices which can only act disturbingly on the artistic imagination by their
crassly prosaic imitation of natural sounds. Equally intolerable is the introduction into the music of bells, drums, anvils etc. unless these are toned down
so as not to interfere with the sound of the orchestra.

Among these non-musical sounds we must also include those of human
speech, the poet's means of communication. Speech varies in pitch and must
be similarly 'toned down' to match definite intervals of music. It is clear that
in this case speech-cadences must be adapted to that of the music rather than
vice versa: without clearly defined intervals there can be no aesthetic tone-
relationships, nothing musically beautiful, and such intervals are only to be

[3] Ch. Beauquier, *Philosophie de la Musique* (Paris 1865), p. 136. [See below, pp.
182–96.]

found in the artistic system of our music, not in the natural cadences of human speech. These contain innumerable intervals, including of course some that correspond to musical pitches. But the modulations of the speaking voice are characterized less by the precise measurement of the intervals, which are in any case very variable, as by the relative relationship between these intervals, the risings and fallings of pitch, or what might be called their melodic direction. Absolutely considered, the intervals in normal conversational speech are fairly small; they are of course larger in the speech of a naturally vivacious person and in moments of excitement. The main characteristic outlines of the 'melody' in human speech can therefore be perfectly well observed by comparing its variations with what we have spoken of above as 'stylization' – the process by which declamation passes into the field of the musically beautiful i.e. the unmistakably tonal. It goes without saying that many fine shades of declamation are lost in the process, though these are more than balanced by countless other means peculiar to music. For example, several intervals in the melodic line of the speaking voice may, though small, yet be sufficiently remarkable to change the impression made on the listener. In musical declamation these may all have to be represented by a single interval, yet this loss of variety can be concealed by the varying harmonization of the same interval, quite apart from the many other means represented by the different timbre and figuration of the orchestral accompaniment.

What we have said here applies only to one aspect of declamation, the melodic. The other, rhythmic–dynamic aspect is no longer a matter of according with the material i.e. an accordance between the sounds uttered by the voice and the intervals of the tonal system. It concerns rather the accordance of the temporal mode of appearance common to both speech and music.

[.    .    .]

It may be said in general that the relationship between music and poetry in the *Gesamtkunstwerk* is best understood by approaching it from the angle of the spoken drama and the halfway house of the melodrama rather than from the purely musical angle and the sacrifices implicit in any union between drama and music. Any attempt to bring pure, instrumental music nearer to natural declamation would involve the principle of 'imitating nature' and that we have been obliged to reject. We must therefore adopt the reverse policy and bring speech as close as possible to music, though of course without sacrificing the characteristic qualities of speech as a means of dramatic presentation. This is the path from spoken drama to sung drama and therefore involves no 'destruction of the musical element', the charge often wrongly brought against Wagner. In the last resort speech raised to the power of song cannot simply return to being mere speech. On the other hand such a descent from music to speech is in fact implicit in the frequent practice of 'pure' musicians who in their search for a 'characteristic' style, modify purely instrumental melodies to meet the demands of declamation. By doing this they in fact sacrifice the specific beauty of 'pure' melody without achieving the true dramatic expression of sung declamation; and the final result is an unstylish manner that is neither beautiful singing nor expressive speech-melody. The spoken word must be the natural, fixed point of departure, whereas the musical beauty of singing is the highest, ideal aim of the creative artist. To set out from pure instrumental melody in order to achieve characteristic declamation is like saddling Pegasus back to front.

Another gross misconception of this relationship between words and music is implicit in the attempt to achieve a maximum 'dramatic' effect by introducing the spoken word at an emotional climax, that is to say at the point of greatest musical tension. There is no denying the effect of this sudden contrast: it surprises and puzzles the listener – but it is absolutely inartistic. It is really hardly necessary to explain the unjustifiable nature – from the point of view of the musical unity indispensable to every union of poetry and music – of both the musical 'intermezzos' and the spoken link-passages which, for one reason or another, are imposed on poetic or musical works. It will at least be granted that in neither instance – musical intermezzos in spoken drama or spoken texts inserted in musical works – is the union of the two arts so complete that we feel ourselves faced with a single work of art. Nor does the alternation of song and speech represent a higher degree of artistic unity than we meet with in a print that is partly monochrome and partly coloured.

2. Unity of mode [*Erscheinungsform*] concerns the organization in time of all the factors in the *Gesamtkunstwerk*, great and small. In poetry syllables, words, phrases, sentences, scenes and acts are arranged in a great variety of ways according to definite aesthetic rules. The same occurs in music with notes, phrases, passages, periods and movements, and in the theatre with gestures and facial expressions. Now let us consider once again the relationship between music and poetry. Once a mutually harmonious relationship has been established between the rhythmic–dynamic and the architectural patterns, it is essential to subordinate the spoken word – in which the divisions of time are by their nature irregular and difficult to measure – to a clear and regular beat without deforming their characteristic nature. In fact speech must become song. Here, too, as in the case of stylizing differences of pitch, tempi can only be relative and such as allow the composer a large degree of freedom.

Stress organizes the metrical lines by emphasizing the regular reappearance of certain groups, and therefore makes them rhythmical lines in the true sense; and it must coincide in the music and in the poetry. Musical stress is not of course to be understood as mere blind accentuation of each so-called 'strong' beat; it must observe all the liberties won by the magnificent development of the polyphonic orchestra in today's music. In speech it is represented not only by the verbal accentuation which plays an important part in singing, but also by the sense-accentuation, or emphasis; and if the composer ignores this, he can only impose on himself a major obstacle in his search for clear and effective expression of the inherent sense of a passage. Failing this, the poet must of course in similar fashion observe in his verses the rules of prosody in his treatment of sense-accentuation, particularly in closed lyrical forms where there is a question of the rhythmic parallels between individual distichs. Otherwise the composer, like the declaimer, must strip the verses of their artistic form and treat them like simple prose, in order not to be distracted by the artificialities of metre and to arrive at the natural, logical accentuation of a passage.[4]

Similarly again in the matter of diction, the pauses between subordinate clauses and whole sentences – respectively the largest and the smallest units of accentuation – demand gradual rise and fall and a corresponding organization of the vocal melody and consequently of the music in general, in order to avoid open contradiction between the two arts. The case is the same with dramatic–poetic compositions in general, where the structure of the music must correspond exactly. The whole dramatic architecture of the piece – the different insertions in the course of the action, the alternating entries or simultaneous appearances of the voices of the various characters, the transitions from one scene or act to another, their dovetailing and shaping to form a climax – constitutes a rhythmic–structural pattern, and this must be seen to coincide with the various dispositions of the overall musical form, if we are to be able to speak of an organic union between the two arts. It will be clear from what we said in the previous chapter that it is poetry that here provides both the material and its form.

People like to compare the acts of a play to the movements of a symphony and this is quite reasonable. But as soon as this comparison is extended to the acts of an opera, it becomes clear how far, from the purely formal point of view, operatic music has lagged behind instrumental music. There can really be no comparison between the act of an opera – composed of a series of independent 'closed' numbers which are only superficially jointed together rather than organically connected, and in many cases set in the two quite different and unconnected styles of 'recitative' and 'aria' – and a symphonic movement composed as a single unity. In music structural design has to be consolidated by the repetition of certain phrases and figures, and this has always been important. The mere repetition of vocal phrases, whether large or small, and the parrot-like repetition of words are certainly the most primitive expedients in this instance, and in addition they hardly remain effective beyond a single number. Any serious thought of unifying an operatic act like a symphonic movement will reveal the absolute necessity of thematic unity, not only of each single act but of the whole composition. The recurrence of themes, whether in their original form or in different guises, is not merely justified musically but absolutely imperative, and should they – as is right and proper – be brought into accordance with the poetic–dramatic scheme of the Gesamtkunstwerk, what we have is in fact the leitmotif. In this way it is possible for the orchestra to weave a musically unified web round the whole drama without disturbing the continuity of the sung dramatic dialogue. It is not R. Wagner who 'breaks the mould of the great musical forms',

4 See Wagner, vol. 4, p. 143 [GS, vol. 4, p. 113; PW, vol. 2, p. 249].

but those composers who, forgetting the glorious achievements of Beethoven's symphonies, regard operatic music as a mere patchwork composed of a number of pieces skilfully put together without any concern for interior, organic connection. The best we can hope for from such a method is a work consisting of twenty or thirty independent numbers more or less well matched with each other. It is therefore clear that it is precisely from the purely musical point of view and taking into consideration the great architectural forms of music that traditional opera is a very imperfect, disconnected piece of jobbery. Wagner's ideal, on the other hand, is not by any means confined to subordinating musical expression to the dramatist's purposes: it also includes the emancipation of music, as part of the *Gesamtkunstwerk*, from the shackles imposed by an obsolete taste which instrumental music has long since outgrown, and the free development of a more unified musical form. By the very nature of the matter this form will be something quite different from the traditional forms of pure music, which developed from those of the dance. The fact that in the *Gesamtkunstwerk* music has to adjust itself to the poetical form means that its form must be perpetually changing and modelled according to the essential nature of the drama, quite independently of any preconceived pattern. Of course it has been objected that this means imposing an alien element on the music, forcing it into the form of the poem. It should, however, be realized that the poet's rhythmic—architectural arrangement of his means of representation is determined by fundamentally the same aesthetic principles; and it is therefore not a question of any alien element but rather of one that is common to both poetry and music. After all we speak of the 'musicality' of a poem quite apart from the sensuous euphony of metre and rhyme. Music does indeed dispose of a much greater wealth of forms than poetry and is freer and more refined in rhythm and dynamics, though architecturally more rigorous. It is therefore an underrating of the composer's formal creative ability to suppose that the composer is helpless when faced by the poet's forms and unable to fit them properly to his own requirements. There is no satisfactory poetic creation whose structural pattern would not be capable of being successfully turned into music. Of course the poet must have prepared the way for the composer, in the sense that he must not have been content with a jejune or monotonous form or denied himself all formal charms: he should in fact aim at the greatest possible artistic beauty even in the exterior presentation. By 'form' we do not of course mean merely 'verse-forms' but the whole poetic composition. In modern drama both are treated rather ungenerously. Imagine a composer faced with a text written exclusively in ruthless iambic pentameters. Such a form cannot of course be respected by a composer unless he will consent to being quite intolerably tedious. He will split up one line into two or three parts, treat two parts of different lines as a unity or even, in cases where the existing text makes a properly polished form impossible, have recourse to the sorry method of repeating, inserting or omitting words to suit his purposes. If the resulting text is then written down in the form devised by the composer, there will no longer be any trace of iambic pentameters, but we shall have a free, practicable strophic form that may be more or less artistic but will be at any rate practicable. The composer has, to the best of his ability, corrected the poet who should in fact have done this preliminary work himself.

Although we have said that traditional instrumental and vocal forms should not be attempted in the *Gesamtkunstwerk*, this does not mean that their use in this context is never justified. It would be truer to say that no form, however strict or free, should be automatically excluded; all depends on the development of such forms being well-suited to the poetic structure. Consequently there will be many, particularly lyrical and dance-forms, that will appear here more seldom than is generally the case – their effectiveness will be all the greater for the rarity of their use. For instance, there is no objection in principle to polyphonic vocal writing, though what Hanslick has called 'the musical goose-step' must remain the norm for the very good reason that dramatic dialogue can be nothing else but 'a poetic goose-step'. On the other hand there are situations where a number of characters are engaged in the dialogue of a spoken drama (in lively popular scenes or where, for the sake of intelligibility, the same thing is repeated by different characters in succession, something better achieved by simultaneous speech as in the 'asides', in several simultaneous monologues, or even by several scenes running concurrently). It is in such instances that the polyphonic use of voices is more completely justified. Duets, choruses, ensembles etc. are not therefore rejected as such from the dramatic point of view, but only the use of polyphonic forms where these are out of place e.g. in the actual dramatic dialogue, where there is a mutual exchange of ideas between the characters concerned.

[.    .]

3. The unity of mood of music and poetry is what is primarily meant by 'dramatic expression' in the *Gesamtkunstwerk*. The poetry gives us groups of ideas, stimulated sometimes by a single word and sometimes by whole sentences or periods. The mutual relationship between these groups is determined by their notional content; and according as to whether they exercise a power of attraction or repulsion they produce in our consciousness a movement: it is the awareness of this that constitutes a mood. On the other hand music does not originate in us this movement that creates the 'mood'; it provides more than the impulse or stimulus to that movement, it provides the complete movement itself, in the series of notes that actually strike the listener's ear. It goes without saying that a mood is not created exclusively by the relationships between our successive reactions: a mood depends much more on the qualitative relationship of elements that appear simultaneously, their harmony or lack of harmony. Poetry can also, of course, affect us by such immediate data as the various forms of prosody (*Bewegungsformen*). These include, beside metre and rhythm, a whole host of ornamental turns and figures of speech consisting of repetition, gradation, connection, separation, contrast or similarity of imagery. On the other hand music can also

achieve similar effects only if stimulated by certain elements of association. Thus the 'quotations' mentioned above, leitmotifs and illustrative passages etc. can serve as introductions to different moods, but of particular importance is the similarity between certain melodic, rhythmic and dynamic passages and certain speech-cadences that we recognize as characteristic expressions of different moods. Pleading, commanding, questioning, sighing, longing – these are all simply formal–acoustic phenomena that can also appear in instrumental music; and they can provide in any case so many points of connection in the subjective activating of the listener's imagination. Finally the purely mechanical effect of music on the whole body of a listener – not merely his organ of hearing – is not to be underestimated. For instance, loud, deep orchestral sonorities make us clearly aware of the sympathetic vibration of membranes of the body – the solar plexus in particular – and in cases of illness the nerves of the skin of the head, even the brain etc. are directly affected when listening to music. Yet even when we are not aware of these shocks as such, it seems certain that there is an effect on our bodily awareness [*Körpersinn*] and thus on our general susceptibility [*Gemeinempfindung*], and this last is obviously important in determining our emotional mood [*Seelenstimmung*].[5] Indeed we shall not be far from the truth if we see in the elementary effect of musical sonority on the human organism the original point of departure from which the art of music has developed.

The demand that we must now make on the composer is simply this – that he shall try to do justice to the poetic mood of the work in every detail, following every slightest change of nuance and intensity and not contenting himself with generally matching the colour of the large sections. There is no limit to his obligation in this matter, an obligation which must either be accepted, with all its consequences, as absolute or else rejected. It is often said that music may contradict a text 'but not too blatantly', that it must follow 'at least the main outlines' although there is no hard and fast line between 'too blatantly' and 'not too blatantly' or between 'main point' and 'subordinate points'. Such a line is immensely variable and will depend partly on subjective factors in the individual composer and partly on objective principles, conventions rooted in the historical development of music, a fact already emphasized. Nobody can approve of music which he is convinced actually contradicts the text; the degree of his disapproval may well depend on the degree of that contradiction, but it can never become approval. This can only happen if one ceases to be aware of such a contradiction and it therefore ceases, for the listener, to exist. La Harpe found no contradiction in Alcestis singing an aria when she takes leave of Admetus – she is, after all, on the stage to sing – and he found it quite consistent to enjoy the beauty of the aria and at the same time to feel sympathy with Alcestis's fate. In this he was not so much differing from Gluck's principles in his attitude as disputing the application of

---

[5] *Körpersinn* and *Gemeinempfindung* are here taken in the sense employed by W. Volkmann, *Lehrbuch der Psychologie vom Standpunkte des Realismus und nach genetischer Methode* (Cöthen 1876), pp. 300 and 312.

those principles in a single concrete instance. When he was aware of any contradiction between music and text, he did not hesitate to condemn it – as in the case of the duet between Agamemnon and Achilles in *Iphegénie en Aulide*, of which he wrote 'that it was incompatible with the dignity of these two heroes to speak simultaneously'.[6] We cannot regard such things as a kind of fluctuation in aesthetic judgement. Contradictions are never in any circumstances acceptable; as soon as they are recognized as contradictions, it is impossible to approve or even to tolerate their presence. What fluctuates therefore is not the condemning of contradictions but simply the opinion as to whether any individual case involves contradiction. In French classical tragedy no king or prince could indulge in a natural uninhibited outburst of savage passion, since this would have been incompatible with the then accepted ideas of propriety and decency; yet no one was in the least disturbed by a Greek tyrant or a Roman emperor appearing in a wig, since a wig (according to those same ideas) was a very proper article of apparel for persons of such standing. And in spite of that – or rathèr for that very reason – it was the French who considered 'the imitation of nature' as the sovereign principle of art, although French art at this time contained so much that was unnatural and pompous. What we can learn from these considerations is this – that there cannot be even the slightest contradiction between music and poetry. Opinions may of course differ as to what constitutes such a contradiction, but not as to its admissibility.

The actual reason why excessive contradiction is forbidden rather than contradiction as such is in fact quite sensible: it lies in the fear that an unqualified condemnation of such contradiction may be reduced *ad absurdum* by the ostensible inability of music to observe such a ruling. This is in fact a quite mistaken idea. Music is a Proteus not so easily embarrassed by the poet. The usual objection, that music is far too cumbrous to keep in step with her agile sister poetry, rests quite simply on a misapprehension. A single savage phrase, a short expressive motif, even a single gripping chord is quite enough, in some circumstances, to transport the listener into a clearly-defined atmosphere of significant tension. Herbart, who most certainly understood music, even went so far as to maintain the exact opposite about the mutual relationship between poetry and music, and for the same reason, in which he found an obstacle to the union of the two. He says for instance – 'Musical ideas develop much faster, and music is therefore within a given space of time incomparably richer in such ideas, than poetry that is sung syllable by syllable. It is therefore quite pointless to try to make the two arts keep in step, or to attempt any real aesthetic unity.'[7] And in another passage – 'Music is the swiftest means of communicating an atmosphere.'[8] Hanslick also champions music in this connection – 'A few chords will transport us to an atmosphere in

---

[6] E. Hanslick, *Vom Musikalisch-Schönen. Ein Beitrag zur Revision der Ästhetik der Tonkunst*, 4th edn (Leipzig 1874), p. 41 [*HMS*, p. 66; *HC*, p. 43].

[7] J. F. Herbart, *Sämtliche Werke*, 2 vols. (Leipzig 1850–2), vol. 1, p. 348.

[8] Herbart, p. 590.

a way that a poet can only do by a considerable exposition, while the painter requires a sustained consideration of his work. On the other hand both enjoy this advantage over the composer, that they have at their disposal the whole world of imagery on which, as our intelligence tells us, feelings of pleasure and pain depend. The effect of music is not only swifter; it is also more immediate and more intense. The other arts persuade us, music takes us by surprise. It is in moods of excitement or depression that we experience most strongly this power over our emotional system that is peculiar to music.'[9] These last sentences of Hanslick's illuminate the whole situation. Two different conclusions have been drawn from the fact that moods aroused by music (and especially in association with words) are so incomparably more intense. One rests on the greater swiftness of its effect. The other is based on the ability of music to create a far broader sense of atmosphere, to sustain it longer and to increase its intensity by means of repetitions which by no means appear tautological to the listener. This has been used as an argument for the belief that music in fact takes longer than poetry to create an atmosphere. In fact both characteristics are among the advantages of music. The poet, too, needs only a few words to release a whole host of ideas in our consciousness and thus to conjure up a distinct emotion; but within the same space of time the composer can produce a still stronger and more violent effect. If the poet continues too long in a single mood, he runs the risk of becoming monotonous and wearisome; his charm will appear insipid and saccharine, his pathos hollow and bombastic. The composer, on the other hand, can deploy his effects over a much wider area without running the same risk. Music consequently disposes absolutely of the means of following poetry into every nook and cranny of the human heart. It is of course useless to demand individual word-painting from music, which can only conform with the sense of whole phrases i.e. with the mood that such phrases inspire. What concerns us most here is the point made by Hanslick at the end of the passage quoted above – that the effect of music varies in intensity according to the listener's susceptibility to the emotions concerned, and this susceptibility is at a maximum if the listener is already predisposed by other means e.g. poetry. Each emotion aroused by a work of art meets with a certain resistance and the struggle with it and its removal causes some of the effectiveness of the work to become fallow. If such resistance has already been removed, then art will naturally develop its full, unrestricted power. Thus music and poetry support each other in a felicitous alliance in affecting the listener's emotions and his sense of beauty, acting in fact as 'aesthetic aids',[10] always supposing that a complete unity of mood is sustained. This is the point made by Hanslick when he says that 'the union with poetry enlarges the power of music, but not its boundaries',[11] Wagner on the other hand means the same when he speaks of the 'raising' of poetic expression to the power of music. Dramatic diction is

[9] Hanslick, p. 81 [*HMS*, p. 130; *HC*, p. 77].

[10] See Fechner, p. 50ff.

[11] [*HMS*, p. 42; *HC*, p. 30.]

raised thereby to pathos – it is clear in what direction the poet should smooth the way for the composer. No *Gesamtkunstwerk* can be founded on a text with no atmosphere, or rather very weak atmosphere, one whose centre of gravity is purely notional; for such a text is by its very nature incapable of heightened expression. Only isolated and subordinate parts of the text may be allowed such a character, and the music that accompanies such passages must then (and this is quite possible) 'not indeed entirely hold its peace but conform to the conceptual element of speech so imperceptibly that, although in fact acting as a support, it gives full play to this element'.[12] Such moments are to be found chiefly in the *recitativo secco* of the old Italian opera, where French *opéra comique* uses conversational speech. These ideas are at the root of the familiar demand that an operatic text should be as 'lyrical' as possible – if the essence of lyricism is taken to be its effect on the feelings.

One more point must be mentioned. The pace, or time, of song is much lengthier than that of the spoken word. The reason for this lies partly in the heightening of the emotion, partly in a natural requirement of the human voice – hence the demand for a more concise, more compact diction in texts designed for music than is usual in spoken drama. Many more words can be spoken in a given space of time than can be sung. This concision naturally implies a reduction of the space between individual dramatic moments: and this in its turn means an increase in their immediate effectiveness. Fewer explanatory or preparatory stages means, to quote Wagner again, 'an intensification of motifs'. The slower the rhythm of a passage, the slower the gesture of the singer – this goes without saying. Should an operatic singer who is concerned with 'acting well' content himself with copying an actor's gestures as closely as possible, he will find that he has come to the end of his gesture before he has finished his phrase. He will then have no choice but either to make a pause in his gesture, simply to repeat it or to fill the gap with something in fact quite superfluous. Thus it comes about that among opera singers beginners act either too much or too little. They make use of a host of gestures where a good actor might have used perhaps only a few, but those few really significant; and the impression these beginners make by this piling up of means of expression is one of affectation and pretentiousness.

Unity of atmosphere is also necessary when music is combined with stage action, whether it is a question of the singer's gestures of the background against which he is playing, landscape or architecture. This is because both arts depend on poetry and therefore automatically possess a considerable guarantee of accord. In the course of a dramatic *Gesamtkunstwerk* there will now and then be moments at which music will be called upon to accompany a static scene. There is, however, no contradiction between this and our earlier assertion, that it is impossible to form an organic work of art by combining music with motionless visual art. What we have here is a moment of repose in the course of the dramatic development similar to a pause [.] in speech or

[12] Wagner, vol. 3, p. 189 [*GS*, vol. 3, p. 160; *PW*, vol. 1, p. 194].

stage-action, during which the emotional mood of the moment is first held and then eloquently developed by music. [pp. 111–37]

[. . .]

## Chapter VI

We have reached conclusions which in the main coincide with the theories of Richard Wagner, though without either abandoning Herbart's principles of aesthetic form or renouncing Hanslick's basic doctrine of beauty in music. Our method has not been that of an eclectic compromise between the two so much as a simple development of those principles and that doctrine in relation to the union of the arts in the *Gesamtkunstwerk*. One further task now remains – to examine the chief points of Wagner's theory (we are not here concerned with his works) in order to establish those in which we agree with him and those in which we feel obliged to differ.[1] Every art is limited by the specific nature of the means that it employs, and these determine purity of style in that art. These limitations may be regarded as either an advantage or a deficiency, according as to whether they are taken as safeguarding the specific character of the art concerned or as restricting its field. Those who value most highly elements specific to artistic beauty will see in these limitations the real wealth of an art and feel no obligation to go beyond its natural boundaries. There will be others, however, who fix their attention chiefly on what an individual art is unable to do and will be unwilling – for whatever the reason may be – to dispense with this. They have no alternative to the view that an art reveals its poverty in the restriction of the means at its disposal, and the demand for purity of style constitutes open acknowledgement of this poverty. Both schools are faced with a problem in any union of the arts. An insistence on purity of style leads necessarily to the reflection that any union of the arts must (or at least might) be subject to different stylistic rules from those governing a single art in isolation. The other school of thought is concerned with examining points in which the limited potentialities of each individual art may be extended and supported. Herbart belongs to the former school, to which we have given our unconditional allegiance, while Wagner belongs to those who regard the limitations of the individual arts as serious deficiencies. Neither party refuses to recognize these limitations, and in fact Wagner draws them even more narrowly than, for instance, Lessing. Thus, speaking of poetry, he maintains that it should in no case attempt representation [*Schilderung*] – as in the *Laokoon*, for example – and he regards lyric writing as the beginning and end of all poetry. He is equally emphatic about the natural limits of the other arts, including music, as we shall see in a moment. On this point Wagner's theory is generally misunderstood. Not only has his aesthetic

[1] Incidentally, the author will not conceal here that he actually no longer sees the highest ideal of the *Gesamtkunstwerk* embodied in Wagner's music drama (of what human achievement could this be claimed without any reserve?), but he still maintains that the Master from Bayreuth is not only on the right path towards that ideal, but also much closer to it than anybody before him.

principle nothing in common with negating all limitations of and differences between the individual arts, but it bases its real essence on the recognition of the absurdity of such tendencies. A glance at the *Artwork of the Future*, which contains something approaching a synoptic view of his theories, will reveal Wagner bitterly attacking 'the egoism of each individual art behaving as though it were art as such, whereas this in fact only weakens further its real individuality'.[2] It is precisely the recognition of each individual art's limitations that is at the root of the demand for their co-operation in a common work, in order that sterile hopes may be replaced by successful achievement. As for music in particular, Wagner's whole theory reposes on the idea that music is absolutely unable by her own means to realize any poetic intention whatever: to achieve this she must necessarily be united to a poetic text, which she must not imagine that she can replace. The most characteristic effect of pure music is to arouse vague premonitory feelings and this power becomes a weakness the moment such feelings need to be clearly identified.[3] The work of an absolute musician is 'to be described as altogether devoid of any poetic intention, as the feeling may have been stimulated, although not determined, by the purely musical expression'.[4] Any attempt to achieve poetic expression in purely instrumental music is, for Wagner, an attempt to achieve the impossible. He even characterizes as 'madness' the composer's 'anxiety to claim for himself and his powers things that in fact lie outside both – things that he can only take a part in creating with the assistance of powers belonging to another'.[5]

Innumerable other passages might be quoted, all of which would simply go to prove that Wagner does certainly not belong to the school of those who completely ignore the barriers dividing the different arts and believe them-

---

[2] Wagner, *Gesammelte Schriften und Dichtungen*, vol. 3, p. 87 [*GS*, vol. 3, p. 71; *P W*, vol. 1, p. 99].

[3] Wagner, vol. 4, p. 233 [*GS*, vol. 4, p. 187; *P W*, vol. 2, p. 331].

[4] Wagner, vol. 4, p. 247 [*GS*, vol. 4, p. 198; *P W*, vol. 2, p. 344].

[5] Wagner, vol. 3, p. 378 [*GS*, vol. 3, p. 307; *P W*, vol. 2, p. 101]. Wagner was evidently not in the least inclined to agree with e.g. Count Laurencin's outspoken and confident remarks in his controversy with Hanslick [*Dr. Hanslicks Lehre vom Musikalisch-Schönen* (Leipzig 1859)], p. 213: 'Of course, it is perfectly possible to define in words the identity of what constitutes beauty in music – and indeed in logical and, linguistically speaking, very precise words at that. It is easy, using words, to arrive at a definition of what music is, namely, its content: and all the stock phrases about the impossibility of expressing the content of a musical work and so forth, then vanish into thin air.' In contrast to this let us quote once again from Wagner's *Opera and Drama*: '. . . the musical language of an instrument cannot possibly achieve the exclusive expressiveness of human speech, which is the organ of the intelligence. On the other hand, as organ of the feelings, it expresses precisely and exclusively that which language, by its very nature, is unable to express and is therefore, from the point of view of the human intelligence, quite simply inexpressible. The instruments of the orchestra make it quite clear that this verbally "inexpressible" is not something essentially inexpressible, but simply something beyond expression by the organ of the human intelligence and therefore not a mere intellectual fiction but something real. Each instrument in isolation makes this manifest, and infinitely more so in alternating action with other instruments' (Wagner, vol. 4, p. 218 [*GS*, vol. 4, p. 174; *P W*, vol. 2, p. 317; this volume, p. 60]).

selves justified in demanding everything from each of them. He does not require of any art that which it cannot perform, he respects the limitations of each. But he does see these limitations as constricting barriers which every art must strive to overstep. The only work of art that will ever overcome these barriers is one in which none of the potential effects of art as such is excluded, in fact a *Gesamtkunstwerk* like the music-drama. Compared with such a work, and with each other individually, each art by itself is limited, not free. A union of the arts is therefore an imperative consequence for those who recognize the limitations of each art and the barriers dividing them and consider these as a lamentable deficiency, an attitude nearer to over- than to under-valuation. To put it in a nutshell – it would be easier to find points of contact between Wagner's ideas and those of Hanslick than with those who champion the 'poetic content' of music. Similarly, Hanslick starts by trying to distinguish as clearly as possible the power of music from that of poetry, in order to render each of the two arts its due. Hanslick, however, ceases where Wagner may be said to begin – with the search for the terms of an alliance between the two arts, terms which are conditioned by their limitations and the barriers dividing them. If a composer strives for the perfect expression of a poetic idea by means of instrumental music, Hanslick and Wagner are at one in believing him doomed to fail. But whereas Hanslick would advise him to abandon the whole thing, Wagner would urge him to seek the assistance of the human voice. It is only at this point that the paths of the two go in different directions.

It will be necessary to remind ourselves for a moment of Wagner's view of art in general if we are to understand his opinions and ideal of a total, exhaustive artistic expression, and hence of a union of the arts in a stage work to which all contribute. For him the task of art, and its very essence, is to create 'a faithful imitation of man as he really is and of man's life as it must necessarily be, an imitation that reveals a deep human consciousness [*bewusstseinverkündende*]';[6] the achievement of this aim is essential if art is to realize its full potential and perform its true function. The 'highest object of art, and that most worthy of communication' is man; and man can only appear in his full, unspoilt and untrammelled beauty in a total communication 'according to the whole wealth of his power of appeal to the most exalted conception'[7] – that is to say, to our eyes and ears by means of gesture, speech and music. According to Wagner, therefore, the true purpose and the real, all-embracing ideal of art is 'not the celebration of artistic creativity as such, but the celebration of humanity itself in art as a whole'.[8] The artistic sense consequently finds complete satisfaction only in a great *Gesamtkunstwerk* – 'embracing all species of art in order to consume and, in a sense, to annihilate each of these species individually as a means to realizing the united purpose of their alliance i.e. the immediate and unconditional representation of per-

---

[6] Wagner, vol. 3, p. 55 [*GS*, vol. 3, p. 44; *PW*, vol. 1, p. 71].
[7] Wagner, vol. 3, p. 185 [*GS*, vol. 3, p. 156; *PW*, vol. 1, p. 189].
[8] Wagner, vol. 3, p. 178 [*GS*, vol. 3, p. 150; *PW*, vol. 1, p. 184].

fected human nature'.[9] Such a work can plainly consist only of something which is present to our senses, namely a drama actually performed on the stage and one in which each art makes its richest contribution. For Wagner this dramatic *Gesamtkunstwerk* is something more than the noblest bloom, the sublimest peak of human art. He describes its purpose as 'the only true artistic purpose that can in fact be realized; any other must necessarily lose itself in vagueness, unintelligibility and limitation'.[10]

We cannot of course give our assent to these theories. We must, however, recognize them as a necessary consequence not only of Wagner's personal philosophy of art and of the world, but in essence of every aesthetic system in which the aim of art is regarded not simply as the creation of beauty but as the representation and realization of an ideal content valid in its own right – that is to say in the material rather than the formal element [*Moment*] of art. If the artist's concern is less with creation of beautiful shapes (in any object) than with the representation of an object (in beautiful shapes), there can be hardly any doubt that the whole universe presents no 'higher' object and 'none more worthy of communication' than man himself and his life, both exterior and interior. In fact even the notion of divinity does not achieve its place in the sphere of art or its full aesthetic value except in becoming humanized, in the Incarnation! The artist must therefore, logically, consider any representation that includes only one aspect of the human ideal as limited and imperfect, more or less one-sided and therefore unsatisfying; and he will extend at most a provisional tolerance to any kind of art which is either concerned only indirectly with, or able to present only one side of humanity. He will not grant such an art any absolute validity. It is clear that, in justice, many theories of aesthetics according to which beauty resides in the 'substantial idea' rather than in absolute pleasingness of shape must eventually issue in the Wagnerian *Gesamtkunstwerk*, which is the negation of 'pure' art. This is best shown by the many gradations and different evaluations noticeable everywhere in assigning its exact place to each art. It cannot of course be denied that such a view of art is justified with regard to the general cultural interests of humanity; but this should not for a moment be confused with the aesthetic consideration of art, and still less should it be allowed as an exclusive substitute for such consideration.

Formalist aesthetics puts aside the content and the cultural element of art and demands beauty above all. From this point of view a work of art is aesthetically justified provided that it is beautiful, whatever it may represent – and even if it represents nothing whatever. The artist is free to choose what he offers and is only bound to give a beautiful form to whatever he may choose. The material, the object presented, is only important inasmuch as it influences the artistic shaping of the work – that is to say, it falls under the heading of practical aesthetics in each artistic discipline. There is clearly a large province of art in which 'beauty of form' will be expressed primarily in the

[9] Wagner, vol. 3, p. 74 [*GS*, vol. 3, p. 60; *PW*, vol. 1, p. 88].
[10] Wagner, vol. 3, p. 189 [*GS*, vol. 3, p. 159; *PW*. vol. 1, p. 193].

phenomena of human nature and human life; and furthermore within this same province there will be a significant area devoted to the representation of human existence in all its variety, both physical and spiritual. The 'immediate and unconditional representation of perfected human nature addressed to eye and ear' therefore seems to us to be only one of the many possible aims, rather than the sole aim of art. It stands, from the aesthetic point of view, on a level footing with other possible aims rather than above them. Consequently the theory of the dramatic *Gesamtkunstwerk* will certainly form an integral part of practical aesthetics i.e. technique – so to say, its coping-stone – but it will not constitute the whole of technique or indeed the whole of aesthetics.

We have now succeeded in showing that in this connection the aesthetics of form cannot arrive at any conclusion materially different from that of Wagner; and that it is therefore necessary to incorporate the final results of his theory of the *Gesamtkunstwerk* into a practical aesthetics of form. It may come as a surprise at first glance that we find ourselves compelled to reject his theory of the individual arts just as decisively as we accepted his theory of the *Gesamtkunstwerk*. A closer consideration will resolve this apparent contradiction; starting from different premisses he arrives at the same conclusion – or rather, by a reverse process, arrives at other premisses from the same conclusion. That is to say, his exceptional and varied gifts and his sharp critical discernment led him to the truth about the collaboration of the arts in the theatre, and he then looked for a theatrical justification for his ideas which he eventually found in his doctrine of the nature and function of art set forth earlier in this chapter. Nevertheless, like all aestheticians, Wagner found it difficult to come down from the consideration of general problems and difficulties to the simple forms of art and their implications, and in fact he did not succeed in this, though it must be admitted that his approach was logical. Since in the last resort he acknowledges no other art but one in which all the arts are combined – and this means giving preference to the drama – he can only grant validity to each individual art insofar as it contributes to the realization of his basic ideal. This ability to be absorbed in the *Gesamtkunstwerk* is therefore for him the measure and criterion of each art, and he regards everything not directly connected with this as alien to the true nature of art, as at best a historical stage or some kind of preparatory step – in any case something purely conditional. In the case of music he emphasizes its privileged position in achieving the dramatic aim of the *Gesamtkunstwerk*: it is able, by its subjective effects, to arouse emotional states. Wagner therefore finds the essential character of music in this faculty. The sound of the human voice is for him the immediate expression of feeling, the 'organ of the human heart', whose 'artistic langugage is music'; and music is therefore for him an 'art of expression' that 'answers a fundamental spiritual need'.[11] This is equally true of both vocal and instrumental music, and the 'speaking power' of the orchestra plays a very important part in the *Gesamtkunstwerk*. It is

[11] Wagner, vol. 3, pp. 79, 99, 106, 343 etc. [*GS*, vol. 3, pp. 64, 81, 87, 277 etc.; *PW*, vol. 1, pp. 92, 110, 116, vol. 2, p. 71 etc.].

therefore true that in this matter Wagner adheres to the aesthetics of feeling,[12] although it should not be forgotten that this is territory in which we, too, have had to take into account the subjective impression made by music – and indeed by art in general – as a decisive factor. If we are to understand Wagner's adherence to the 'aesthetics of feeling' as a necessary consequence of his general view of art, this must appear doubly surprising where there is absolutely no question of denying each art a fully justified existence quite apart from the *Gesamtkunstwerk*. The subjective effect of music, its 'emotional facet' is after all not significant for music as such, but only for music as an ally of poetry in song, melodrama, programme music etc.

Finally there is another question which must at least be mentioned although it cannot be dealt with at length. It is in fact a question that may well have often forced itself on the attention of the reader. What is Wagner's attitude to so-called programme music, and what is our own to be? One thing has become clear to us in the course of our investigations, and it is this: we have no right to identify Wagner's ideals with the generally accepted notion of programme music as understood not only by the general public but by a large number of professional musicians. Wagner's aesthetic principle has nothing to do with any music which claims in its own right to be poetry and thus disputes the rights of poetry itself; a music that makes bold to 'represent' things that only the visual arts can represent. In his *Artwork of the Future* and *Opera and Drama* Wagner expresses himself frequently and unambiguously on the subject of programmes, attacking the selfish attempts of the individual arts – whether it be music or dancing – to communicate something that lies outside their own sphere and is unattainable by their means. He was therefore quite justified in later observing: 'I freely forgive all those who have hitherto questioned the possibility of a new instrumental form. I must confess that I shared their doubts and thus allied myself with those who regarded programme music as a most regrettable phenomenon, with the result that I found myself in the comic position of being counted among the composers of programme music and coming under the same condemnation as they.'[13] Wagner's championship of Liszt was nevertheless quite logical, as is shown by this last quotation, since he did regard Liszt in fact as the creator of a new form of instrumental music – and we ourselves must recognize him as such. The true concept of programme music i.e. the concept shared by Liszt and Wagner is not that of a music that seeks to express a poetic content by musical means and is merely supported by the programme, which simply seeks to express more precisely a literary content already provided by the music – that

[12] In his later writings, and especially in his essay on Beethoven (Wagner, vol. 9, pp. 74ff [GS, vol. 9, pp. 74ff.; P W, vol. 5, pp. 57ff.; this volume, pp. 65–75]) Wagner suggests that Schopenhauer provides a more profound speculative basis for his aesthetic views. As regards Wagner's theory of the *Gesamtkunstwerk* this is irrelevant, since Wagner developed this entirely independently of Schopenhauer's philosophy. Since we are concerned exclusively with this theory, we have no need to make any further reference to Schopenhauer's musical aesthetics.

[13] 'Über Franz Liszts symphonische Dichtungen', Wagner, vol. 5, pp. 235ff. [GS, vol. 3, pp. 182ff.; P W, vol. 3, pp. 235ff.].

would mean that the programme was either superfluous or nothing more nor less than an attestation of the poverty of music as an art. No, programme music is in fact an individual form of alliance between two independent and equal factors – poetry and music, and what we have established earlier about vocal music is fundamentally true of this alliance also. Certainly the connection between the music that strikes our senses by its irrefutable presence and the poetic idea that is present only in the listener's mind is a very loose one. Indeed, considered from this angle programme music as such is a far more imperfect union of the arts than melodrama, and its only advantage lies in the fact that it does not involve any conflict between audible speech and instrumental sound. Even so, the chief importance of programme music lies not so much in this uniting of music and poetry in the moment of aesthetic pleasure as in the fact that poetry stimulates the composer's imagination to create a great variety of new musical forms. A closer discussion of this subject would involve repeating, almost word for word, much of what has already been said. Liszt himself certainly had no desire to 'destroy' or to 'blow up' the form of the symphony, only to reshape it and to develop it in the direction of a higher unity in the purely technical, musical sense. The parallel with Wagner is exact, though we cannot pursue it here. The special task of this present study does not include the problem of programme music, but is already determined, and limited, by the title – the investigation of beauty in music in relation to the *Gesamtkunstwerk*, from the point of view of formal aesthetics.

It must be emphasized that our study makes absolutely no claim to being even a brief theory of musical aesthetics or of the *Gesamtkunstwerk*. It must, however, be clear that the author has not submitted to the temptation of following a 'golden *via media*' and carefully avoiding extremes on either side. There can be no question of muting or toning down ideas of such fundamental importance as those with which we have been dealing: they must be either rejected out of hand or followed to their logical conclusion. In the present instance it has only been possible to enquire whether – and if so, within what fields – the two opposing philosophies, Hanslick's of the 'musically beautiful' and Wagner's of the *Gesamtkunstwerk*, with all their logical consequences, can be considered aesthetically justified. The results of this enquiry must be left for the friendly reader to judge. [pp. 148–60]

# Heinrich Adolf Köstlin (1846–1907)

## Die Tonkunst. Einführung in die Aesthetik der Musik (1879)

Köstlin studied theology in Tübingen graduating in 1868 and then spent a short time in Paris as a private tutor. Having served as an army priest during the Franco-Prussian war, he returned to Tübingen and for a while taught music history at the seminary. From 1873 to 1883 he served as a parish priest and then until 1891 taught at the seminary in Friedberg. There followed a period of higher church appointments and from 1895 to 1901 he occupied the chair of practical theology at Giessen University. He was an active promoter of church music and involved himself in the activities of various church music societies.

## Music

> Source:
>
> *Die Tonkunst. Einführung in die Aesthetik der Musik* (Stuttgart 1879). Dritter Abschnitt: Die geistige Seite der Tonkunst; 2. Das Wesen des Musikalisch-Schönen, pp. 274–5; 286–8; 289–95. Translated by Martin Cooper.

The beauty of a musical work imposes itself on any mind susceptible to beauty in music. A feeling of artistic well-being floods our whole personality with magnetic warmth when we hear a composition that glows with beauty, and at first blush there is no mediating reflection – the effect is one of lightning speed at the very moment of contact between the receptive mind and the ideal life inherent in the music.

This contact between the mind and sonorous beauty, however, is not as immediate as one might at first suppose. It is mediated in a number of different ways; the effect of music is not simple but complex.

A musical composition addresses itself in the first place to the sense of hearing, since every art springs in the first place from the senses. Every musical pleasure is based on the sense of hearing. Although experienced musicians are able to appreciate and estimate the beauty of a composition simply by reading the score, yet this reading is – properly considered – a hearing in the imagination. Thanks to long years of practice the aspect of a musical text is vividly associated with the actual sounds, and a score reader will find himself automatically humming phrases and melodies to himself.

The beauty of a composition – its full effect on the hearer – will therefore be essentially conditioned by the fact that it is possible for sonorous sense-impressions formed by sounds penetrating the aural mechanism [*das Gehör*] to be perceived with absolute clarity and without disturbance of any kind. On this depends what we might call the elementary side of musical beauty.

Listening to music or the pleasure afforded by a musical work is further-more mediated by thinking, an activity of the mind – whether our music enthusiasts like it or not. If the impression made by musical beauty were immediate, the beauty of e.g. Beethoven's Ninth Symphony would be as immediately perceptible to the first yokel as is the beauty of a simple folksong. The feeling of well-being experienced by the mind when consciously contem-plating a beautiful object – including the pleasure afforded by musical beauty – depends on an act of thought, an aesthetic judgement formed no doubt with lightning speed, but itself the end-product of complex exercising and school-ing in musical thought. [pp. 274–5]

[.  .  .]

It is therefore quite understandable that the preparation of the actual material of music and the establishment of a musical system are only achieved by the artistic spirit. Even the simplest and most obvious musical relationships, the practical distribution of the whole realm of music and that which corres-ponds best to the creation of various forms, the most judicious and favour-able classifications of pitch – all these were the outcome of long searching and experiment. In the same way it was long before the musical sense was sufficiently educated to select for the purposes of musical creation only that which conformed to the system, and to reject all other musical sensations.

Once the principles of pitch and of the octave are established, and accepted by every listener as forming the creative material serving the composer for the free creation of musical forms, no attention will be paid to any music that fails to conform with the system, with these pitch-divisions and relationships. Knowledge of that system and familiarity with the pitch-relationships which it involves are essential to the understanding of today's music. No one would maintain that the ancient Greeks lacked a fine ear for music, but they would not understand what there was to admire in a Beethoven symphony. This was not because they had no ears for the beauty of harmony – the aural apparatus is after all identical in human beings – but because they had been brought up in a completely different musical system, and one in which the musical dimensions of Beethoven's works had no place. They therefore had quite different standards of comparison, quite different ideas of musical rela-tionships and quite different basic musical attitudes. For example, a D major triad was impossible in their system because it includes the Pythagorean third. To understand any music more complicated than a simple rhythmic succes-sion of notes needs experience in handling the material of music, familiarity with the musical relationships inherent in the system concerned.

Let us take an example – the recognition of a scale or succession of notes as forming a melody i.e. something arranged according to definite rules and dimensions and representing a musical idea. The listener, in order to recognize this, must have an absolutely firm mental grasp of the diatonic system to enable him automatically to classify the succession of notes as he hears it: it is only by reference to this that his musical sense perceives what is characteristic and delightful in this particular succession and rhythm of sounds. In order to sing with correct intonation and expression, a singer must be master of the notes of the scale, so that he can hold each note of the melody accurately on whichever degree of the scale he wishes: the more successful he is in this, the more impressively will what is original in this melody be brought out – the more 'expressive' will his performance be. But the listener, too, must have a firm aural grasp of the scale and its relationships if he is to appreciate the beauty and originality of a melody.

Furthermore, in order to understand a whole procession of sounds i.e. a sequence of harmonies, and to be immediately aware of their inner relationship to each other, the listener needs a firm observation-post from which he can review the march-past of these harmonies, like a general reviewing his troops on parade. Or, to put it another way, his ear must always and everywhere retain a consciousness of the basic triad to which all subsequent harmonies stand in a definite relationship. Unless the harmonies are unconsciously related to this basic triad, they will appear to stand in no intelligible relationship to each other, to present no shape, and no unity and to form no whole.

Thus a musical system is presupposed by any formal understanding, as it is by musical forms themselves. [pp. 286–8]

[.    .    .]

All musical understanding consists of an activity of the musical sense, which makes comparisons and unconscious adjustments: and for this reason the understanding of any artistic musical form presupposes an accurate knowledge of the ground-plan [*Schema*], or law of construction, underlying it. The originality and unique beauty of a melody and the individual character of an artistically-shaped phrase dawn on the listener by a lightning-swift mental relation to the succession of notes in a scale and in the same way the unique formal beauty of a fugue, a rondo or a sonata only stands out clearly and distictly to the listener who has a conscious knowledge of the laws governing the constructions of a fugue, a rondo or a sonata. No commonly received opinion is more mistaken, or more convincingly disproved by actual experience than that of the universal effect of music – at least insofar as real musical art-forms are meant. The only universal feature of music is the pathological effect of rhythm: the effect of music itself, in the work of art, depends on the understanding.

The beauty of a Bach fugue is by no means so obvious that it must strike anyone with a little sense of musical beauty. You need to have heard – indeed to have played – many fugues i.e. to have become fully conscious of the laws of fugal construction, to be able to appreciate the individual beauty and the original strength of a Bach fugue. For both make themselves felt to the listener only by his comparing the living, sense-stirring and power-exerting individual example with the pale, lifeless pattern of fugue as such. Why did the nobleman who was no mean connoisseur of chamber music tear up the score of Mozart's C major string quartet?[1] Simply because he could not understand it, because Mozart's originality did not conform to the model existing in the gentleman's consciousness. Why indeed is it necessary for even an experienced musician to play works that fit into no familiar pigeon-holes several times before he 'understands' them? Because he has to discover and assimilate the basic pattern underlying the notes, before the work is clear and intelligible to him.

If the scale, the designation and disposition of the degrees may be said to be a matter of more or less fortuitous agreement – in fact, to a certain degree, a matter of conventional acclimatization – this is still more true of actual music forms. Beauty in music does not depend on, and is not confined to any one musical form: no limits can be set to genius in its search for new forms. The laws of formal beauty demand only one thing – that a composition shall have a form as a self-subsistent musical whole, a clearly and firmly defined sound-picture, a combination of harmonies and melodies not only ordered according to definite rhythmic, melodic, symmetrical and modulatory principles, but also dominated by a single creative idea. These conditions are fulfilled only when the development and presentation of a musical idea conform with the general laws of form inherent in the nature of musical sensibility and musical perception, and also with the laws of symmetry – in fact when the development and presentation of a musical idea prove themselves consistent and natural. The eye that observes an architectural work of art, a statue or a picture has no difficulty in doing so with a very high degree of accuracy: the object observed is stationary in space and the eye can return as often as it needs to describe the outlines of the whole and its constituent parts, thus impressing the object on the viewer's consciousness.

Listening to music – like writing or performing it [*Tonerzeugung*] – takes place in time and is only perceived in temporal form. Musical forms, too, present themselves to the musical sense only fleetingly [*zeitlich*]: they are quickly gone and only appear once, so that the listener has not the viewer's advantage and cannot return repeatedly to contemplate the outlines of the whole and its constituent parts until his intelligence has fully mastered them. For this reason the musical form in which the composer has shaped some given impulse needs a special law by which the chief features essential to and characteristic of the form (motif, movement, part etc.) are presented more than once, in periodic repetition. This is the law of symmetry. Of the in-

[1] [The incident concerns the 'Dissonance' quartet, K. 465, and the nobleman is Count Grassalkowitsch (Kražalkovicz). See Georg Nikolaus von Nissen, *Biographie W. A. Mozarts*, 2nd edn (Leipzig 1828), p. 490. Nissen took the story over from the *Allgemeine musikalische Zeitung* of 11 September 1799. It is later taken over by Jahn and Abert.]

numerable varieties of musical form none has absolute or unique validity; but whatever the form may be, it must somehow achieve symmetry – symmetry in the whole and in its constituent parts, symmetry overall and in details. This is the fundamental principle of all musical form, which cannot otherwise be apprehended as form, as a unity, an independent sound-picture but resembles rather a noise, which gives the impression of an aggregate of sounds which have either no interest for, or actively repel, the musical sense. There is no definite law as to how this symmetry should establish itself for the hearer. It may be simply rhythmically i.e. by the return of certain rhythms, or melodically i.e. by the repetition of certain phrases that play a determining part in the work as a whole; or it may be the two together. All that matters is that the whole should immediately strike the musical sense as a symmetrically ordered pattern; for that sense is not content with floating sounds but demands the delight of beautiful forms and beautiful ideas.

The formal beauty of a composition, therefore, depends on the symmetry of the whole and its parts, but it does not consist in that symmetry. It consists rather in the immediate delight of individual forms, in naturalness and logical coherence, in the development of a basic idea. The condition always presupposed, the *sine qua non*, is symmetry in time.

Of course beauty of form, indeed the sense of form itself [*Formgemässheit*] would vanish and be replaced by mere formalism, the mere conformity to pattern [*Schematismus*] were it not for that spiritual something which is the soul of form, of the whole sound-structure [*Klangleib*], were it not for the resemblance of the basic idea to the formula according to which a crystal is formed and a curve shaped – or better, to the life-bearing seed shed by an organism and forming the origin of new life.

Suppose that we hear two sonatas in both of which the architectural idea of the sonata is clearly and immaculately exposed, the musical craftsmanship irreproachable, development, harmonies and modulations correct. We find ourselves unable to call one of these sonatas 'beautiful' though we have no right to speak of it as 'not beautiful', while the other seems to us to be the fullest expression of beauty in music, which it radiates to perfection, engaging our interest and riveting our attention. Of the first sonata we are inclined to say that it is 'dull' – correct in workmanship and irreproachable in pattern (it would be wrong in this case to say 'form') but 'with nothing significant to say', thin and insignificant. Of the second we say that it shows intelligence in every detail, is in every way significant, pregnant with meaning. What do we in fact mean when we speak in this way? Both works are examples of sonata form – or, more accurately, of the formal plan of the sonata i.e. that architectural grouping of movements and periods distinguished by the name 'sonata-form' from other groupings and organizations of movements. The essential difference between the two works lies in their different melodies, harmonies and modulations – in fact, in everything that does not belong to the superficial pattern of sonata form.

In the one sonata these are only superficially related to each other, not clearly welded into a unity; or the themes and movements have nothing novel about them, they are commonplace or completely insignificant. In the other everything, from the opening of the movement to the coda, springs as though by an inner necessity, from the generative impulse of the original musical idea, like an organism in full-blossoming life. Every feature and every element is closely connected, there is nothing otiose, nothing lacking significance; and however spontaneous the melodies and motifs may seem, however uninhibited the harmonies and modulations, everything is nevertheless novel and attractive and unfamiliar in this particular context, with this particular significance and in this particular light. In fact the two sonatas are identical as far as their formal organization goes, but totally different from the first appearance of the opening creative, generative idea. They are like two trees, both of which exemplify the idea of 'tree' though one exemplifies the idea at its finest and most developed and the other in stunted form. The music of the one sonata is thin and tedious, hardly more than the skeleton, the dry groundplan of sonata form. That of the other appears as a vital organism breathing beauty. The one is a sonata-formed construction painfully built up of poor-quality fragments. The other work bears the imprint of an original mind, one which casts its creative ideas in forms which recall Goethe's vision of 'gold buckets'.[2] These forms seem to be inherent in the ideas themselves, to grow naturally and necessarily from them as the only natural, only possible and nevertheless unique representation of precisely these musical ideas. That sensitive thinker E. T. A. Hoffman has put it most compellingly – 'It is only the spirit, with its arbitrary control of the necessary means, that exercises irresistible power in masterpieces. Spirit understands only the language of spirit.' Spirit is to be found in every motif, every theme – in fact at its most concentrated in these (just as the spirit is found at its most concentrated in the organ of thinking, the brain) – as in the work as a whole, in its development and unfolding. It is heaven's gift to the artist, his share of divine grace, to plunge his musical ideas into the element of Beauty and to imprint the seal of a unique originality on the nobility of form. This is a case of 'no man can rob himself without heaven making good the loss'. This beauty, which some call substance [*Gehalt*] and others content [*Inhalt*] is, in Goethe's words, 'a mystical something, both outside and above the object and content'[3] of an art-work: a spiritual fluid that fills Bach's gothic fugues, Beethoven's Fifth Symphony and Chopin's tender and melancholy waltzes and mazurkas; that casts a halo round Mendelssohn's *Elijah* and *St Paul* and a warm, magnetic glow round Schumann's *Kinderszenen*. It is ideal beauty in sonorous form, musical beauty itself in its truest shape and beyond any further definition, a moment of eternity incarnate in forms that ring in our ears. To the question of

---

[2] [Goethe, *Faust*, part I, line 450. See below, p. 163.]

[3] [*Dieses Schöne – . . . ist – mit Goethe zu reden – 'ein Mystisches ausser und über dem Gegenstand und Inhalt des Kunstwerkes.'* The quotation has proved elusive and the words may not be Goethe's, as his attitude towards mysticism is known to have been a critical one: 'Mystik: eine unreife Poesie, eine unreife Philosophie' (*Maximen*, no. 905).]

where genius finds those creative ideas which gleam with unfading loveliness, there is perhaps no profounder or wiser answer than that which we find in the biblical text – 'Eye hath not seen, nor ear heard, neither have entered into the heart of man, the things which God hath prepared for them that love Him.'[4]

Beauty is an eternal idea, and with the ideas of goodness and truth it forms the first, original, individual possession of the human spirit. There is a beauty that can only be represented in sound, a sonorous life of the spirit – and that is the content of music. [pp. 289–95]

[4] [I Corinthians 2:9.]

# Gustav Eduard Engel (1823–1895)

## Aesthetik der Tonkunst (1884)

Engel was somewhat of a polymath: a philosopher, scientist, music critic, singer and singing teacher. He studied philology at Berlin University, graduating in 1847, and music with A. B. Marx. While a student he sang tenor parts in concerts and in 1846 joined the Cathedral choir. After a short spell as a schoolmaster he was appointed music critic of the *Spenersche Zeitung* in 1853 and in 1861 succeeded Ludwig Rellstab on the *Vossische Zeitung*. From 1862 he taught singing, first at Kullak's Academy, and then at the *Königliche Hochschule für Musik*.

His writings show a mixture of influences coming both from the older German speculative tradition and from the modern scientific approach inspired by positivism and Helmholtz's theories.

# Aesthetics of music

Source:

*Aesthetik der Tonkunst* (Berlin 1884), Vierter Abschnitt: Das Gesamtkunstwerk und die Einzelkünste, pp. 264–7; 284–8. Translated by Martin Cooper.

## Chapter IV

### The *Gesamtkunstwerk* and the individual arts

In the same way as music and poetry show a tendency on the one hand to independence and on the other to amalgamation, so do the equivalents of music and poetry when intended for the eye. The sculptor and the painter can give more nearly perfect, and more durable, form to the ideal glimpsed by their imagination than to the actual human form, with its dependence on an empirical limitation, and in that sense their art, too, strives for independence; on the other hand movement can only be represented by actual human beings. There are furthermore a number of facts so manifest that they really stand in need of no elaboration or explanation, viz. that a live human being making expressive movements reveals the reason of those movements if he accompanies them with words; that words themselves stir stronger feelings if they are accompanied by gestures; and that the whole process is rendered more nearly ideal if words are used in association with music. It follows from this that we can take it for granted that the individual arts in isolation are no less contradictory in nature than is their union in *Gesamtkunstwerk*, which is what we must call opera – for the individual art provides no satisfaction for the impulses to amalgamate and the *Gesamtkunstwerk* suppresses the impulse towards a full, interior development of a single, fundamental idea. There can therefore never be any question either of the *Gesamtkunstwerk* ousting the individual arts or of these making the existence of the *Gesamtkunstwerk* impossible. All we can ask ourselves is whether the individual arts have the same value as the *Gesamtkunstwerk* or which is the more valuable.

We shall be nearer to giving an answer to this question if we examine more carefully a difference in aim between the individual arts and the *Gesamtkunstwerk*. We have seen in our earlier discussion that the essence of music consists in the shaping by the organizing intelligence of the world of sound [*das hörbare Dasein*]. Symmetry of conscious and unconscious rhythm, pitch-relations and the development of all possible consequences of this basic principle – that is what music is. The material of poetry lies in the human imagination, in human feeling and desire and it is the poet's task to strain off all that is fortuitous, irrelevant, jejune and imperfect. In the visual arts the sculptor or painter presents to the view a visible area of space in a manner purified of all the chance circumstances of empirical existence. In both music and the visual arts the idea itself is immanent in the sensible experience [*das sinnliche Dasein*]. For even if the imagination of the listener or viewer is inclined to import a mental significance to what he hears, the statues of the gods and pictures of everyday life, the final justification for this – the explanatory word, which alone provides confirmation – is still missing. It is different with poetry, insofar as it addresses itself simply to the reader: it can call up sensory imaginations, but it can provide no sensory experience. In the one case, therefore, we have the idea not developed to perfect clarity, and in the other the external, sensory presence [*Dasein*] not completely achieved. So it is only in the drama, and most especially in the opera, that the idea is veritably and totally an idea and the outer form real, ideal sensory experience. In the *Gesamtkunstwerk*, therefore, we have an essential change of fundamental aim.

In all the arts that unite themselves in the opera we find the basic principle to be the relationship between the idea and the sensory phenomenon; and we may therefore well ask whether we can make use of the thought of realizing an idea in order to complete our enquiry as to whether artistic beauty can be shown to be an independent area of existence. But the simple execution of an idea is something common to all human activities. If we take such a deliberately trivial example as cobbling, it is the idea of providing a covering for the human foot that is realized. However little the individual cobbler may be aware of this idea, for cobblers as a whole this remains the idea that informs them – an idea which partakes of the geographical, the ethnographical, the historical, the practical and indeed, to some extent, even the artistic. Take billiards or cards etc. and we find that each is a realization partly of the idea of play as such, and partly of the particular game involved. The mere fact of realizing an idea, therefore, does not justify us in allowing architecture, music etc. any unusual place in the list of human activities.

It now concerns us to observe that, in speaking of the realization of any one idea, a distinction can be made between the realization of the idea and the idea itself. But this 'pure' idea could only be grasped as the idea underlying all existence [*das Weltdasein überhaupt*], the very idea of being itself. This, however, we find already realized; and it is a modest portion of this that we are concerned to transform. In order to make ourselves complete masters of this we have only, on the one hand, our empirical knowledge and on the other that imaginary creation of it regarded provisionally, as the task of philosophy. If art, then, is to occupy a separate category of its own, we must find something that is neither the realization of some definite idea nor the realization of an idea as such [*des reinen Begriffs*]. [pp. 264–7]

[.　.　.]

Of the individual arts it is music that forms the neutral middle term. For in the case of musical sound the material is not stable as in the fine arts but vanishes before its sense [*Geist*] has been made clear. Just as in reality musical sound, appearing as the human voice, is the means by which intellect achieves its own form [*Selbstgestaltung*], so in the arts it is through music that their union first achieves perfect realization. Moreover in no other art is the gap so large between ideal artistic representation and natural reality as it is in music; and it is for this reason that music has been the last of the arts to achieve its true and definitive form, which it did only some three or four hundred years ago. It is possible to regard the arts as the culmination of man's attempt to improve the world; but it is equally possible to consider them as a renunciation of that effort. The artist is ready to abandon the hope of humanity becoming as beautiful as it appears in painting and sculpture, expressing its feelings with the nobility, liveliness and warmth or pursuing its purposes with the logic that we find in poetry. He simply represents human beings as they present themselves to his imagination. But this happens in another sense, too. For next to something that is simply beautiful no art can, or should, hold up its head: art enters into what is dissonant and indicative of character, and it only becomes false to its own nature when this dissonance and character try to become more than transitional phases. Just as in life, so in art the threat comes from both sides – the limited and the limitless are in perpetual opposition, with the Scylla of a dead formalism on the one hand and the Charybdis of a crude naturalism on the other. Although art may never wholly abandon the aim of really improving human existence, artistic ideals are meanwhile so far-reaching that they can only be presented as ideals. On the other hand, in representing everyday life art probes so deeply that here, too, its creations can be intended only as character-studies, as in the cases of Richard III and Falstaff, for instance.

No individual art, and no union of the arts as such, can furnish an example of absolute beauty, but it is only in the latter that we find the nearest approach [*das höhere*]. Absolute artistic beauty, therefore, is to be found only in the totality, and it is precisely in the mutual relationship of the individual arts to each other – their combining, separating or complementing each other – that we have the highest beauty. Such beauty, however, is something purely intellectual and is not experienced in a single moment, although if even conceived in the mind [*gedacht*] it may spread a beneficial influence over the whole life of a person gifted with real understanding and sensibility in all the arts, whether individually or in combination. This intellectual beauty will generally meet with resistance among those whose only idea of beauty is a momentary sense-impression furnished by the sense-organ concerned. Here, too, though, it is easy to persuade such people of how beauty can be transformed from something sensuous to something spiritual. If he begins with a general impression of, say, a painting or a sculpture, a more careful observer will go on to examine its individual features, and the work will then appear to him as a relationship between these parts – in fact as something intellectual [*geistig*], ideal. In the case of music a complete tiro may well be attracted in the first place by a single beautiful sound, such as a horn-note. But beauty of sound depends, according to our modern physicists, essentially on a harmonious relationship between a fundamental and a certain number of simultaneously sounding overtones. Once again, therefore, we have something not simple like a sense-impression but complex – a relationship.

There are of course such things as simple notes without overtones; these are produced by tuning-forks fitted to resonance-boxes. But here again what we hear is not simple. No human ear is capable of hearing a single vibration; even the lowest notes perceptible to the human ear produce in one-eighth or one-tenth of a second (i.e. the smallest unit of duration perceptible to human consciousness) several vibrations in succession, and the beauty of these notes lies in the similar duration of these vibrations i.e. once again in a relationship. The more advanced our examination of a work of art, the more clearly does beauty – which at first seemed a simple sense-perception – prove to be a relationship. Thus, in a melody the relationship is between a series of notes in succession. Unless we can remember the notes that have already been sounded and have an eager expectation of the notes still to come, we can neither understand nor enjoy the melody – in fact it makes no appeal to our sense of beauty. It is for this reason that repetition of a melody is a traditional feature of music, in order to assist the memory and thereby partly to strengthen the understanding and enjoyment and partly to call them into play [*erzeugen*]. Of course the addition of harmony or a polyphonic accompaniment is a further invitation to the intelligence to discover remote relationships. This is still truer in the case of large-scale compositions based on the artistic development of one or two basic ideas and demanding a constant comparing of present with past musical events, in order fully to appreciate their quality. In vocal music the comparison is between the emotional state evoked by the poet and the forms of musical expression chosen by the composer. It is hardly necessary to point out that the same is true of poetry, which is in any case the most intellectual [*geistig*] of the arts. But it may be pointed out in passing that the most gripping scenes and situations in a play – those that prepare the actual denouement – depend for their effect entirely on the memory of what has gone before in the drama.

If then, as we have demonstrated, the whole realm of artistic beauty is formed by the different arts – either in isolation or in combination – their mutual complementing of each other involves a relationship which arouses in the comprehending mind a feeling of harmony, and hence of beauty. Only in this kind of beauty the sensuous element gets a raw deal. For instance, in the longest composition, in a play or a novel, it is relationship i.e. the intellectual element that is repeatedly finding partial expression in immediate sensuous effects. This sensuous substratum, however, is not absent even from the idea of the artistic whole [*das Kunstganze*], since it is present in all real art. We must add in conclusion that the whole concept of artistic beauty can only be grasped by those who are gifted with understanding and sensibility in all the arts and at the same time do not exercise this multilateral sensibility without consideration, but with the philosophical insight to realize that this is in fact the way to mastery of this whole province of artistic beauty. For it is only through this insight that they can grasp that point of unification [*Einheitspunkt*] which forms the only foundation of the most profound understanding – both in the arts generally and in music, for instance in the grasping of a theme or in the more detailed knowledge of its development. Goethe makes it clear that considerations of this kind may well suggest themselves to the artist, when he writes in the introduction to *Faust*:

> Into one Whole how all things blend,
> Function and live within each other!
> Passing gold buckets to each other
> How heavenly powers ascend descend!
> The odour of grace upon their wings,
> They thrust from heaven through earthly things
> And as all sing so *the* All sings![1]

And at the end of the Second Part:

> A swamp along the mountains' flank
> Makes all my previous gains contaminate;
> My deeds, if I could drain this sink,
> Would culminate as well as terminate:
> To open to the millions living space,
> Not danger-proof but free to run their race.
> Green fields and fruitful; men and cattle hiving

[1] [Goethe, *Faust*, part I, lines 447–53. Here quoted after: *Goethe's Faust, Parts I and II*, an abridged version tr. L. Macneice and E. L. Stahl (London 1965), p. 21.]

Upon this newest earth at once and thriving,
Settled at once beneath this sheltering hill
Heaped by the masses' brave and busy skill.
With such a heavenly land behind this hedge,
The sea beyond may bluster to its edge
And, as it gnaws to swamp the work of masons,
To stop the gap one common impulse hastens.
Aye! Wedded to this concept like a wife,
I find this wisdom's final form:
He only earns his freedom and his life
Who takes them every day by storm.
And so a man, beset by dangers here,
As child, man, old man, spends his manly year.
Oh to see such activity,
Treading free ground with people that are free!
Then could I bid the passing moment:
'Linger a while, thou art so fair!'
The traces of my earthly days can never
Sink in the aeons unaware.
And I, who feel ahead such heights of bliss,
At last enjoy my highest moment – this.[2]

In the first of these passages the poet is inspired by the idea of the interaction between natural and supernatural, in the second by the perpetual evolution of the human race which depends on struggle and liberty. It is this that gives rise to that 'highest moment', that brings Faust's life to an end. In each case the 'beauty' involved is purely spiritual, and in a much wider sense than we find it in the mutual relating of the arts. [pp. 284–8]

[.    .    .]

---

[2] [*Faust*, part II, lines 11559–86, tr. Macneice and Stahl, p. 287.]

# Eduard von Hartmann (1842–1906)
## Philosophie des Schönen (1887)

Son of an army officer, von Hartmann followed his father's career and on leaving school entered army service in 1858. He left the army in 1865 for health reasons and devoted himself to a study of philosophy. Having established his reputation with his *Philosophie des Unbewussten* (1869), he received offers of chairs at Leipzig, Göttingen and Berlin, which he declined pleading his ill health (a stiff knee as a result of an injury from his army days), though more likely in order to preserve his philosophical independence.

In his philosophy von Hartmann wove together various strands of the German speculative philosophy, combining some of Hegel's ideas with Schopenhauer's notions of fantasy and dream. The term 'concrete idealism' is sometimes used to describe von Hartmann's philosophy as distinguished from Hegel's 'abstract idealism'.

# The Philosophy of the beautiful

*Source:*

*Philosophie des Schönen*, 2nd edn, ed. Richard Müller-Freienfels (Berlin 1924). Chapter ii. Die Konkretionsstuffen des Schönen; section 1d: Das sinnlich Angenehme der Klänge und Farben, pp. 79–81. Chapter x. Die einfachen freien Künste; section 2a: Die Instrumentalmusik, pp. 632–6; 637–9. Chapter xi. Die zusammengesetzten Künste; section 2a: Die binären Verbindungen, p. 770–1; 771–2; 773–4. Translated by Martin Cooper.

**Chapter II: The degrees of concretization of the beautiful**

**Section 1d: The sensually pleasing quality of sounds and colours**

It is a fact that, in so far as we are aware of tempo and rhythm, we class them under the heading of formal beauty; and it is equally a fact that, when notes form a chord, we have the choice between regarding the component notes of that chord either individually or as together forming a single unit. Moreover our consciousness of the relationship between the total impression and the component notes of the chord depends entirely on our own changing attitudes, whereas we need artificial aids to distinguish between the fundamental and the overtones of a single note. We class our understanding of a chord in relation to the notes composing it, under the heading of formal beauty, whereas we class our understanding of a single note, which we cannot analyse without artificial aids, under the heading of what pleases our senses. On the other hand no one will deny that there is an element of the sensually pleasing in the impression made by a chord which the ear can analyse unaided; and it is a matter of common experience that with long practice the ear can be taught to analyse certain individual notes into their component parts without artificial aid. It is therefore clear that the borderline between the sensually pleasing and the formally beautiful is not a stable one, and that the two overlap according to whether the unconsciousness of the relations between the different pleasurable components [*Reizkomponenten*] of the sensually pleasing is penetrated by consciousness, or the formal beauty of even the more composite structures remains impenetrable to the less practised ear.

The instability of the borderline between the sensually pleasing and formal beauty has long been observed in the field of music, but we are indebted to Helmholtz for an exact description of the facts.[1] In the same way it is a matter of common knowledge that formal beauty is founded on the rationality and simplicity of relationships that are clear to our consciousness: from this we may conclude that the sensually pleasing as such (i.e. apart from its psychophysical side-effects) is founded on the rationality and simplicity of relationships that are concealed from our consciousness. The rationalist aesthetics of Euler and Leibniz assumed that the sensually pleasing consisted in an unconscious mental arithmetic – an unconscious perception of the rational relationships between the different pleasurable components without conscious apperception; so that in fact the immediate cause of pleasure lay not only in the conscious rationality of formal beauty but in the unconscious rational element existing in the sensually pleasing. On the other hand sensualist aesthetics assumes that the only reason why simple rational relationships make a sensually more pleasing impression is because they are free of any disturbance that might irritate the ear; and concludes from this that conscious rational relationships also appear to us beautiful only because we recognize them as the cause of the sensual pleasingness of the impression.

The sensualist theory as stated by Helmholtz is untenable in the first place because it conflicts with actual experience. From this we know that chords with a high proportion of disturbing elements (unstable overtones and combination tones) may nevertheless possess more formal beauty than other chords with many fewer disturbing elements: it will depend upon the pitch, high or low, and the saturation [*Sättigung*] of the chord or its need of resolution.[2] Apart from this, the positively beautiful as such remains an illusion for sensualist aesthetics, which reduces the problem to two elements –

---

[1] The enthusiastic hopes for swift advances in forming a theory of music which I as a youngster pinned on Helmholtz's discoveries as I found them in Poggendorff's *Annalen der Physik* have not so far been realized. On the contrary, no progress of any kind has been made, owing to the fact that the theory constructed by Helmholtz in his work on sound-sensations, and based on his experiments, has led to the false trail of the sensualists.

[2] See Gustav Engel, *Aesthetik der Tonkunst* (Berlin 1884), pp. 306–15.

on the one hand the pleasure of shared feeling [*Gemeingefühl*] i.e. the pain-free use of the organs concerned, and on the other the counter-pleasure associated with the restoration of a disturbance-free sensation after the pain caused by disturbing sensations. The pleasure of shared feeling in the pain-free use of organs can by no stretch of the imagination be considered spiritual or aesthetic: it is something physical, a purely bodily euphoria caused by the intensification of vital awareness, and as such incapable of providing any explanation of formal beauty. But since the sensually pleasing and formal beauty perpetually overlap, it can also provide no explanation of what is sensually pleasing to eye or ear; and this is the more certain because the 'pleasure of shared feeling in the pain-free use of the organ' itself reposes on a fiction. There does not in fact exist any organic sensation without disturbance of any kind; there is no such thing as consonance without relative dissonance, no simultaneous harmony of musical notes without concomitant overtones or combination tones. All that remains for the sensualists, therefore, is to retire to their second line of defence, and to maintain that aesthetic pleasure is to be explained as a counter-pleasure between more and less 'disturbed' sensations. According to this, music could be defined as 'the least unpleasing of all noises', though unpleasing it must still be accounted – not only by reason of the many disturbing sensations with which it is contrasted, but also on account of the less disturbing sensations which provide that contrast. Music would thus resemble the self-inflicted tortures of the ascetics who flogged themselves alternately with scourges and scorpions and then with simple birch-rods, explaining that they experienced the rods as a counter-pleasure and were satisfied with the sum-total of their 'impressions'. In which case, of course, it would really be wiser to abandon both music and flogging.

What must be sought, therefore, if we are to explain the positive pleasure afforded by music (which is by no means merely a 'counter-pleasure') is a positive cause; and since the sensualist aesthetic is not in a position to provide this, we shall be forced one way or another to return in some sense to the rationalist aesthetic. The mistake of the earlier rationalists consisted only in their identifying the fundamental principle on which they based their explanation with the immediate, proximate cause, overlooking the necessity of physical, physiological and psychological intermediate steps. For if the rational relationships between the different pleasurable components were in any way perceived, they would automatically enter our consciousness even if it were not the reflected consciousness of observant apperception; and this is put out of court by the smallness of the time-elements concerned as well as by the empirical impossibility of distinguishing them subsequently from the totality of the perception. If on the other hand the rational relationships between the different pleasurable components are to remain unconscious (in the proper sense of the word), they cannot as such enter perception, but can only play a part in the physiological and pre-conscious, psychological originating of perception. In that case what needs to be explained in more detail is the nature of that part. The attempts to solve this problem which have been made by Hauptmann, Oettingen, Riemann and others still seem to me a long way from succeeding, although they are valuable as signposts to their successors. It is in fact a matter of indifference that the majority of these attempts have been directed to explaining the first principles of formal beauty (major and minor triads etc.), since any solution in this field would also provide a key to the problems of single notes and their sensual pleasurableness, owing to the instability of the borderline separating the two areas. [pp. 79–81]

## Chapter X: The single free arts

### Section 2a: Instrumental music

[...] — Side by side with [the] musical forms that spring from already existing melodies (songs or dances) are those which have developed from *elements* of the melody itself, especially from the theme or motif worked contrapuntally or in imitation. Closed forms of this kind include canon and fugue, but motivic development is a much wider field. The musical 'working' of a melody very commonly includes the working of individual phrases or motifs which occur in that melody; or alternatively whole melodies may be worked canonically or fugally. A third species of purely musical forms is one consisting entirely of harmonic progressions, with no melodic interest or definite rhythm. As an independent form this seems to our modern taste the most remote, since we are too aware of the absence of that melodic and rhythmic interest to which we are accustomed to be fully captivated by the expressive power of harmonic progressions in themselves (Palestrina). On the other hand this same expressive power plays the largest and most important part as an immanent factor in all other musical forms where, from the purely formal point of view, it is held in reserve. This is seen most clearly in free variations on a song-melody, where the harmonic progressions of the original eventually form the only solid and unchanging framework and (particularly with the greatest composers) there is scarcely any other connection with the original theme. All these different varieties of musical forms, elaborated in successive eras of musical history, interpenetrate each other in modern instrumental music and form a solid kernel discernible even in works, such as elaborate preludes or 'fantasias', where all form seems to have been dissolved.

It always appears as though the great masters have been the most impatient with traditional forms, but this has in fact only been due to their wish to amalgamate already existing forms in new, more advanced combinations. Lesser men deliberately seek to dissolve or destroy existing forms without replacing them by anything better. All the great composers have shown themselves able to express the highest content within existing forms, which did not in fact inhibit them. Smaller men feel the more frustrated by formal limitations the less they have to say, and they lay the blame for what is in fact their lack of creative ability on the restrictions imposed by existing forms. True freedom is always exercised within formal prescriptions, not without, and only exceeds existing forms if they can be replaced by those that are higher. The false freedom, which acts arbitrarily and not according to law, does not seek to replace existing forms by higher ones in the cause of progress, but simply in order to be free of formal restrictions altogether. This is on an exact par with their poverty as creators, which they thereby make abundantly plain to everyone. The more intricate and comprehensive the forms, the more significant must be the content filling them; the freer their use, the surer and more delicate must be the tact of the artist who wishes to master them. On the other hand simple and precise forms, that permit of little freedom in their use, are easier to fill and to master, and therefore better suited to conceal any poverty of artistic creation behind traditional beauty of form.

[. . .] Of all the liberal arts music is the one in which the formal beauty of specific art-forms has the greatest significance. If there were a hope for aesthetic formalism anywhere, it would be in music; and it is therefore easy to understand why the theories of those aestheticians who base themselves chiefly on music tend more than others towards formalism, if they are not caught up in sensualism. The significance of the sensually pleasing is greater in music than in any other art; differences in sensual impressions form the whole basis of a composition, whereas they form only one element in painting – namely, colour. On the other hand, mental content occupies an even more obscure position in music than in the other arts, as far as consciousness is concerned – it can neither be touched by hand nor described in words, but must be felt; nor is it possible to demonstrate its existence to those who maintain that they are unaware of it.

It is the important part played by the sensually pleasing in music that makes it the most popular of all the arts; the public enjoys having its ears tickled and its nerves shattered, and behaves as though it were on art's account. The physiological and pathological stimulation of the sense of hearing is more effective than that of the sense of sight; and for this reason music is more threatened than painting by the danger of degenerating into real emotional self-indulgence [*reale Gefühlsreize*], just as painting in its turn is more threatened than are the plastic arts. The whole area of emotional excitement stimulated by the nervous effects of musical sounds still lies outside the province of art; and its significance for art consists simply in the possibility of repressing these real excitements by an emotional reflex and making use of that emotional tendency as a connecting link [*Bindeglied*] in the production of aesthetic shadow-feelings [*Scheingefühle*] of the same, or similar, kind. Music's power of expression has its natural basis in the natural connection between certain nerve-stimulations through physiological effects of sound and an inclination to real emotional excitement, though music's power of expression is owed to other factors as well. This is the psychological basis of musical symbolism, ensuring it against arbitrariness and guaranteeing its universal intelligibility. Any listener, too, who has not yet achieved awareness of the fact that music, like the other arts, has a mental (ideal) content, will be involuntarily captivated and overcome by this musical symbolism, with its philosophical foundation, once he has arrived at understanding a composition as a work of art rather than as actual sensual pleasingness i.e. once he has achieved a purely aesthetic attitude towards it, divorced from all objective and subjective reality.

This aesthetic attitude is achieved by grasping the formal beauty of a composition, even when the unconsciousness of the mental content implicitly perceived in the sensually pleasing and the formally beautiful persists, or may even harden into an explicit denial of anything of the kind. From this we can see the great aesthetic value of a formal musical education to anyone who wishes to enjoy music. It is only this that will ensure an aesthetic attitude towards the superficial impressions that assail the ear and the ability to rise above the sphere of physical (real), neuropathic excitement, thus indirectly enabling a listener unconsciously to grasp the immanent mental content of a work. If perhaps eighty per cent of the normal concert- and opera-going public may be counted as philistines [amusisch] who are there for other than aesthetic reasons and are content with a non-aesthetic excitement, some eighteen per cent will belong to a different class. Whether they are dilettanti, artists or art-scholars, they will have had a formal musical education of one sort or another and they will have a special, conscious interest in musical forms; and thus will in fact transfer to the aesthetic sphere the sensual pleasingness of their random aural experience. According to their powers they will to some degree enjoy the mental content of the work, even if they are unaware of the fact and consciously suppose that their enjoyment comes purely from the musical forms with their sensually pleasing charms. Such an attitude resembles that of someone who maintains that he only enjoys listening to poetry because he is interested in the different species of versification and the musical quality of language. On the other hand, anyone who looks in music for nothing but the actual emotional excitement released by the physical effect on the senses resembles a man who is uninterested in poetic forms and only loves poetry for its power of arousing laughter, terror, breathless suspense and gloating delight in quick succession – in fact because poetry gives him a good cry or a good laugh.

Only a few members of the musical public avoid both the Scylla of non-aesthetic sensualism and also the Charybdis of empty formalism, and these few are able to understand that their pleasure in understanding musical forms from a purely aesthetic point of view is nevertheless essentially conditioned by the fact that concrete, phenomenal forms of expression do in fact conform with a mental content grasped implicitly and determining them as their immanent principle. Of course elementary rhythmic, melodic and harmonic forms and such specifically musical processes as part-writing and motivic development have a certain independent formal beauty, like that of versification. This is on the concrete level of the sensually pleasing, the mathematically or dynamically satisfying. But even though the low-grade formal beauty of these forms and processes is partly independent, and fills out the space left free for development by the content which is the principle determining the form, they must still conform to the content, both in their totality as a formally beautiful frame and in detailed development, as formally beautiful music. They must be in direct harmony with that content and, indirectly through their harmony, with the formal constituents and elements immediately determined by the content.

As we have repeatedly emphasized, the mental content is – as it is in all beauty without exception – objectively unconscious, and the subjective, implicit perception of it in concrete, phenomenal forms is also unconscious; it is therefore not surprising that this is so in the case of music. Nevertheless, it is more difficult in the case of music than in that of the other arts to discover and point to the natural channel by which certain groups of notes become the legitimate and universally intelligible expression of definite mental contents. Despite all the work done in this field by theoreticians of music we are still on the threshold of the subject. Even so, our relative ignorance of how such an association takes place need not prevent us from recognizing, fully and completely, the fact itself as such. A careful consideration of our own experience will show us that, in music as in the other arts, an implicit, unconscious grasp of the mental content of a work occurs on the emotional plane; and that, even objectively speaking, that mental content consists exclusively of emotional states and emotional impulses, whereas this is only partially true of the other arts. There are cases in which music attempts to give expression to a nonhuman or subhuman mental content, for instance the sorrowful sound of the Holy Grail lost in the desert, the statue of Memnon, the song of the dying swan or the imaginary emotional life of the vegetable world such as the lotus-flowers, the freezing pinetree and the sun-drenched palm, or the harmony of the spheres. But even these are always subjective emotional states, feelings transferred either by analogy or by borrowing to the music which serves as their vehicle.

Music is therefore pre-eminently an art of feeling, able to express only the emotional aspect of its mental content, whereas other arts include the mental in their sphere as well. Music can express ideas only in so far as these have assumed for the emotions the form of subjectivity, or inwardness; and music is therefore pre-eminently also the art of subjectivity, whereas in the other arts ideas may be established in an objective as well as in a subjective form. Even the subjective species, such as landscape-painting and lyric poetry, must be considered more objective than music, inasmuch as they do in fact transfuse the subjectivity of their content into a mode of vision, whether it be actual vision or in the imagination that is concerned – which is either wholly or partially objective. The only means of expression open to music, on the other hand, are sense-impressions and networks of impressions [*Empfindungskomplexe*], which lack both spatial perceptibility and perceptible objectivity. On the other hand, it is erroneous to speak of music as not simply pre-eminently, but exclusively, an art of feeling or subjectivity, or to think that the feelings and subjective inwardness receive less indirect expression in the sense-impressions and networks of sense-impressions characteristic of music than in the visual or imaginary modes of vision – or alternately the association networks of sensations and ideas – in the other arts. [pp. 632–6]

[.    .    .]

Every art expresses the content which it represents – quite precisely as far as its own special aspect is concerned, but imprecisely and only by suggestion in the case of the other aspects unless, indeed, these lie quite beyond its reach. The aesthetic appearance [*Schein*] of every art, therefore, is in one sense a definite representation of the mental content, in another sense a vague suggestion, and in other respects pointless stammering and vain striving to say something that cannot be said in this particular language. It is precisely those aspects of a mental content that are quite beyond the power of one art to express, or can only be vaguely suggested, that in another art are expressed with the greatest precision, and vice versa. Thus music can represent the emotional life in the clearest and most concrete manner, whereas words fail the poet, and the actor can only suggest it approximately, in momentary flashes, without involving his public in a detailed maze of argument. If we mean by 'precision' intellectual precision alone, music's content is of course absolutely imprecise; but intellectual precision is by definition that kind of precision that does not enter the aesthetic sphere at all and can never provide a standard for the concrete precision of the beautiful. The mental precision of poetry only appears to us as 'precision' in the highest sense because its fixation in language makes a translation of this into terms that are intellectually precise (i.e. the mental description of the poetical content) easier than in the case of any other art. Such a description, however, is not the real mental content of the work, but simply its counterpart in non-aesthetic terms. In the art of mime, which dispenses with words, the mental content of beauty is already more difficult to describe than in poetry, and in music more difficult still; but that is in no way prejudicial to the precision of the mental content in either case, since even in poetry the mental content, *qua* mental of beauty, is destroyed and replaced by something else, as soon as any attempt is made to describe it in any words other than those of the poet.

Music and mime – the languages of sound and gesture – have conventional components, but nothing like as many as speech, which is almost entirely conventional; so that a poem has to be translated from one language to another, while music and mime are universal and therefore universally intelligible. But this is also the reason why music and mime must be careful not to load themselves with conventional components which destroy the natural laws and universal intelligibility of their symbolism. The conventional mimed language of the deaf-and-dumb is as non-aesthetic as 'programme' music, only the former fulfils a real need and lays no claim to beauty whereas the latter fulfils no need and does lay claim to beauty. Symbolism in music is only aesthetically justified if it confines itself to the 'musical language' aspect of the mental content, subjective emotions in fact. It forfeits all justification if it attempts to communicate objective images, opinions [*Anschauungen*] or ideas, in which case musical beauty is reduced to a non-aesthetic signal, the musical phrase becomes a label, a stamp or a seal superficially denoting some definite imaginative content by means of an arbitrary convention. So-called 'tone-painting' is only justified if it can arouse subjective aesthetic shadow-feelings [*Scheingefühle*] and not objective images [*Vorstellungen*]. The *ranz-des-vaches* does not 'represent' the Alps and their herdsmen, any more than the flute represents a flock of sheep with their shepherds or a horn fanfare represents huntsmen with hounds and horses. What they do is recall the feelings normally aroused by such spectacles, and it is purely by chance, not by necessity nor aesthetically relevant, if the association existing between these musical elements and the relevant feelings and moods is also incidentally accompanied by objective images [*Vorstellungen*] of the objects concerned.

All musically genuine tone-painting is therefore the representation of feelings by means of musical figures or symbols, and not the representation of objects by those means. Even musically genuine tone-painting suffers from a serious disadvantage: that is to say the association of definite feelings with definite musical figures, if not an arbitrary convention, is nevertheless determined by cultural, historical circumstances and is thus marked by an element of fortuitousness. On the other hand there is no such element of fortuity in natural musical symbolism, which is based upon a law of natural necessity, namely the interdependence of the physical and the psychic, the senses and the mind, and the analogies that automatically suggest themselves between the laws governing the shifts and mutations of each. Thus we find a representation of the shifts and mutations of our own emotional life in the inflections of musical forms, with their transitions and contrasts, their dissonances and resolutions, their changes of pitch, key and mode etc.; and in the interplay of themes or polyphonic parts we discover symbols either of opposing feelings and aspirations in the individual himself or the struggle between the feelings and aspirations of different individuals or groups of individuals.

It is not to the intelligence that music – like other arts – makes these revelations and representations of the content of the emotional life, with all its varying obscurity. Once again it is to the feelings and their obscure interplay, upon which the intelligence throws little light; and the organ of perception is the same as that in which mental content has achieved its subjectively concrete definiteness. But what thus achieves definite, though only partial representation as immanent mental content in musical beauty is nothing other than the idea at the stage of individuality. For the inner, emotional life, more particularly of human beings, is only one side of the concrete individual idea, which as such includes the idea at the stages of inner vivacity and the emotional laws proper to each genre. The composer reveals to us in the first place his own subjective personality, but still only as strengthened and illuminated through the aesthetic appearances. After that, though, thanks to the power of his clairvoyant imagination, he becomes an interpreter of the emotional life of all other human individuals, and indeed of animals and plants and the whole interiority [*Innerlichkeit*] of the natural cosmos. As all this passes through his subjective musical imagination it does indeed take on a special individual colouring, a subjectivity at second remove, though without sacrificing the objectivity of its idealistic truth. Just as a poet can write lyrics based on the emotional life of a character he does not know, so the composer, too, can make music out of the emotional life of a man he does not know e.g. reveal an inner understanding of the feelings of a child, a girl or a mother. In this sense music is just as objective as other arts, although it is the objectivity of the subjective emotional life of concrete, individual characters that music plunges into the composer's subjectivity, from which it arises in the form of intensified idealistic truth.[3] [pp. 637–9]

## Chapter XI: The combined arts

### Section 2a: Binary links

[.    .]

The combination of lyrical poetry and expressive singing in vocal music does really produce an organic unity. Both arts enter our consciousness through the sense-impressions of the same organ, the ear; both show a preponderance of feeling over rational notions; and both are essentially successive in character. In fact both present an essentially similar spiritual content by means of expression that are formally cognate. This does not of course prevent each of the two arts presenting the same content from a different angle and by different means of expression, so that the two do not exactly coincide, each excelling in its own way. Music reveals ineffable depths of the emotional life, such as poetry simply cannot express, whereas poetry presents not only the emotion itself but a perception of the situations, characters and actions that determine the emotions. If the unity of the two is to remain undisturbed, the music must not represent any feelings not also suggested by the poem: it must confine itself to the deepening, purifying and more delicate realizing of the feelings alluded to in the poem. On the other hand the poem must not concern itself with considerations that do not at the same time find an emotional echo in the music. Both arts must pull together and keep close to the matter in hand, avoiding all side-tracks. [pp. 770–1]

[.    .]

Music, or at least vocal music, must relinquish from the start any attempt to reflect through symbolical word-painting the intellectual content of the

---

[3] For a theory of specifically musical forms one should refer to Marx, *Kompositions-lehre*, 4 vols.; to amplify on the old strict style of the church modes to Bellermann, *Der Kontrapunkt*, 2nd edn (Berlin 1877), or to Bussler, *Kompositionslehre*, 2 vols. For the history of music refer to A. von Dommer, *Handbuch der Musikgeschichte*, 2nd edn (Leipzig 1878) and to Ambros's detailed history of music which remained incomplete but is continued by Langhans, *Geschichte der Musik des 17. und 18. Jahrhunderts*. Further see the extensive *Musikalisches Lexikon* by A. von Dommer, and as a reliable handy reference work, Riemann's *Musik-Lexikon* (Leipzig 1882).

text, and must confine itself simply to employing its own means of expression in order to deepen and intensify the emotional content of the poem concerned. Music must therefore never attempt to follow or illustrate any changes of attitude [*Anschauung*] in the poem, unless these are accompanied by an emotional change, rather than a simple change in the angle from which the original emotion is considered. What music has to take into account is always, and only, a change in the emotions; she is not in any way concerned with the changed attitudes by which the poet represents that change in the emotions. This explains the fact that different verses of the same song can be sung to the same tune without aesthetic contradiction, even though the content of their attitudes may be entirely different. It is quite enough that they serve to represent one and the same basic emotion, and that the structure of the verses repeats similar emotional contrasts. Even so, the uniform continuation of a single basic emotion throughout several verses will always be the mark of a certain simplicity and monotony in the emotional life, such as we find in folk-songs. The verses of an art-song will normally exhibit a pattern of dialectic shifts and contrasts which the composer will be bound to follow.

The essential nature of the *Gesamtkunstwerk* will never be grasped by those who start with the mistaken idea that it depends on a perfect mechanical balancing of the different arts concerned. A balance of this kind is pure fiction and no more exists in reality than does a balance on the scales, where there are always greater or lesser divergences. It is in fact no more possible to find two dissimilar objects that weigh exactly the same than it is to find two similar objects that do so. That such a demand as this should in fact crop up is sufficient proof that in these matters the influence of abstract idealism is still strong. In any organic unity it is impossible to point to any component that is exclusively dominant or exclusively ancillary: all are mutually dependent and each has a claim on the services of all. The microcosmic significance of an organism does not increase with the similarity or equality of its members, but with their differentiation i.e. with their different character and importance. The greater the importance of a member to the whole, the greater of course are the claims that it can make on the services of the other members; but these greater claims are only justified by greater performance i.e. greater services done by this member on behalf of the whole. The balance of an organism does not arise from all parts of that organism being of equal significance to the whole, but from the correlation of pre-eminence and superior performance, rights and duties, the claiming and the performance of duties, the demanding and granting of consideration. The same is true of a work in which several arts co-operate, where the aesthetic balance is in no way disturbed by the hierarchical relationship between those arts, but only by one of the arts concerned attempting to dominate the scene in a manner which does not correspond to the role which that art plays in the total impression made by the work. [pp. 771–2]

[. . .]

Since poetry and music have now succeeded in developing to a higher degree, poetry has been obliged to forego the sensuous enchantment of music, with its overwhelming appeal to the listener, and to develop along its own path. On the other hand music has sought to exploit its advantage, to thrust poetry into the background or merely to tolerate it as a means of developing the sensuous beauties of vocal music. Such a relationship contradicts the relative positions of the two arts in the scale of abstract values and cannot therefore be regarded as the ideal of their association. Recent reforms in the province of the lied and the ballad, as well as in that of opera, have therefore tended to approach more nearly to the ideal stated earlier.

Poetry, as the aesthetically superior art, must therefore in association with music play a dominant and determinant role mentally [*ideell*], though this does not mean that the poet does not serve the composer by taking into the most exact account all the claims that music of its very nature makes. On the other hand music will always be the dominant factor in this co-operation, so far as the senses are concerned: it will at every moment demand the lion's share of the listener's attention, though continuing to serve poetry and using its means of expression to represent, describe and elucidate only that which is, either expressly or by implication, present in the emotional content of the poem. Generally speaking the impression made by a poem should not be exhausted at a first reading or hearing, but should grow in power and depth with repetition; and such repetition will be indispensable in the case of poems set to music, if the poetic effect is to be fully developed. For this reason listeners procure the text of a song before hearing it, so that their response to the mood of the poem may be more prompt; and they re-read the text after the performance in order fully to grasp the poetic import for the first time, in retrospect. This is the same process as that with which we are familiar in a picture-gallery – looking at a picture for the first time and after obtaining a more intimate acquaintance with its details returning to relate these to a comprehensive vision of the picture as a whole. It is only after hearing a number of performances of a *Gesamtkunstwerk* that the listener can really appreciate the organic interplay and musical effects; and although at a first performance the sensuous effect of the music may have been predominant at the expense of the poetry, further performances will allow the poem to establish its predominant position as determining the content, overriding the sensuous predominance of the music, and establishing even in the realm of subjective experience the ideal organic balance of the two arts. [pp. 773–4]

[.    .    .]

# Part 2: Aesthetics of music in France and England

## 2.1 France

## 2.1.1 General works

## *Introduction*

Unlike the Germans, the French, in the second half of the nineteenth century, were not the direct heirs of a weighty and systematic philosophic tradition. The great French tradition of the eighteenth century had become subsumed into established intellectual history, and there existed no bond between philosophy and the art of romanticism such as existed in Germany. Nevertheless, the recurrence of certain themes in French authors reveals the presence of a continuing national habit of thought. These later Frenchmen may have differed from the encyclopaedists in their attitude to language and poetry, but the investigation of the connection between music and language or, more precisely, music and poetry still remains central to their preoccupations. Apart from that, there was no pattern to which they felt obliged to conform, and indeed a sense of being independent of philosophical systems eventually led them to regard aesthetics as a self-contained discipline, closely related to history and sociology and completely divorced from metaphysics. Positivism undoubtedly contributed to this autonomy of aesthetics and helped to found a method of aesthetic analysis. Auguste Comte, the father of positivism, never addressed himself specifically to aesthetics, but Hippolyte Taine (1828–93), one of the most influential thinkers of the positivist persuasion, did devote much attention to the philosophy of art. The most durable of Taine's theories was that which regarded the artist above all as part of a national and cultural continuity, but it is unfortunately weakened by the excessive importance it attributes to environment, and the desire to provide biological explanations ultimately led him to pay more attention to the causes of art than to art itself.

Charles Beauquier can hardly be called an archetypal positivist, since his work does not contain the detailed historical classifications and frequent comparisons which characterize positivism. Admittedly his *Philosophie de la musique* is lucidly expounded, starting from the particular, in the first part of the book (investigation of sound, melody and harmony) and moving towards the general, in the second part (the relationship of music to feelings and intelligence, and the characteristics of vocal and instrumental music). This gradualist approach may perhaps be a personal attitude, but it brings him close to the positivists, even if it would be going too far to see him as one in the full sense of the word. Hanslick, too, advocated a scientific method in aesthetics, without ever defining its structures, and this aspect of his work results from that widespread admiration for science so characteristic of the time and from that desire for a clearly structured system which Herbart and his followers had in common with the positivists. It is hard to be certain how strongly Beauquier was influenced by Hanslick, but at least one early twentieth-century author classed him as a French Hanslickian.[1] Beauquier takes a very critical view of Lacépède's description of music as a vehicle for the feelings, but the weightiest part of his treatise deals with the relationship of music and language, resurrecting a typically French eighteenth-century theme in the light of the autonomist aesthetics of the mid-nineteenth century.

The influences which one can only guess at in Beauquier's case are more easily visible in the work of Jules Combarieu. His studies with Spitta in Leipzig in the 1880s familiarized him with the historical tendency of German musicology and may have been partly responsible for turning him towards the study of the relationship between music and poetry (though that was of course a favourite theme of the French tradition, too). Although he does not expressly identify himself with the positivists when he mentions them at one point in his *Rapports de la musique et de la poésie*, their influence plays a significant part in the foundation of his aesthetics and in his view of history. At the same time, one must remember that Combarieu was a skilful eclectic, taking from current aesthetic theorizing whatever seemed to him best suited to justifying his dictum that 'music is the art of thinking in sound'. The concision of the definition reminds one of Hanslick, and that in itself was enough for some authors to classify Combarieu as a 'formalist'.[2] However, whatever one may think of formalism, there is one substantial difference between Hanslick and Combarieu, in that the positivist way of relating the development of art to social conditions is crucial to his thought – indeed, the very title of his book *La musique, ses lois, son évolution* (1907) demonstrates his concern to discover laws, whether historical or sociological, governing the evolution of music. As the positivist zeal for going back to ultimate origins leads him into the prehistory of music, he attempts to define the initial force that makes music possible and sees it in the efforts of primitive man to establish a relationship between himself and his natural surroundings. In that first phase of its existence, Combarieu associates music with magic, and argues that it gains its eventual independence when the requirements of magic cease to be operative. That, so he contends, is where it is closest to poetry, to which it is indissolubly linked. Interestingly, in the course of this speculation, Wagner is only mentioned in passing, though the connection with German thought is undeniable.

Combarieu had already discussed the link between music and poetry at length in his earlier study, *Les rapports de la musique et de la poésie* (1894). At that stage he had not yet formed his own theory of musical evolution and an echo of Wagner's ideas is not difficult to detect. *Les rapports* is often inconsistent in its treatment of the relationship between music as an auton-

---

[1] See Fausto Torrefranca, *La vita musicale dello spirito* (Turin 1910), p. 415.
[2] F. Sparshott, 'Aesthetics of Music' in *The New Grove Dictionary of Music and Musicians*.

omous art and the non-musical, textual elements which threaten to destroy its autonomy. But because he is here expounding his views at length, Combarieu is able to provide a detailed discussion of the relations between the two arts, and that is what legitimizes the inclusion of substantial passages in this anthology. Though the later work, *La musique*, may be a more significant illustration of the way in which positivism influenced musicology in France, the very fact that Combarieu, in the positivist manner, wanted to include a wide-ranging account of musical technique as well as an examination of the links between music, social life, magic and the laws of nature, meant that stimulating ideas are often not investigated in depth. Nods in the direction of Wagner and Nietzsche here and there in the book may, however, be more than mere remnants of Combarieu's German apprenticeship, since the rationalizing positivist attitude which seeks to proffer an explanation for all the factors in the equation is given a strongly irrational twist. It appears almost as a reversal of the positivist assurance when the continuity of music is presented as persisting beyond magic or any human historical reality and as becoming part of a Pythagorean cosmic entity, 'as the world, floating in space, is wrapped in harmony'.[3] This link between rational appearances and suprarational eternity is echoed by Busoni in his *Entwurf einer neuen Aesthetik der Tonkunst* (1907): both cases seem to suggest an obscurely felt unease at the over-confident mood of positivism.

Charles Lalo's activity stretched well beyond the period covered by this volume, but his early works show strong connections with the intellectual legacy of positivism. He started as a critic of the experimental method in aesthetics of Fechner and Wundt (in *L'esthétique expérimentale contemporaine*, 1908), rightly pointing out that psychological investigations lie outside the domain of aesthetics, to which at best they form a preparatory stage. But this did not exempt him from the weakness inherent in the positivist desire to explain art in terms of forces lying outside the work of art itself. For the psychological element in Fechner and Wundt, Lalo simply substitutes a sociological element, arguing that there is a general principle of aesthetics in the process of selection operated by society and in the evolution of social forces. The result is a narrowing of outlook, compared to the broader span of Combarieu's ideas.

³ See below, p. 215.

# Charles Beauquier (1833–1919)

# *Philosophie de la musique* (1865)

A native of Besançon, Beauquier studied law in Paris as well as palaeography at the distinguished *Ecole des chartes*. He started as a journalist, regularly contributing articles on politics, music criticism and aesthetics to the *Figaro, Tribune, Revue moderne, Gazette musicale* and *Monde musical*. During the 1870s he was active in politics in Besançon and in 1880 was elected to the Parliament sitting on the extreme left. He supported a number of radical and anti-clerical causes and retired from politics in 1914. His interests were varied and besides music and politics embraced literature, folk customs and history. His opposition to Wagner became apparent in his *La musique et le drame* (1872). He also wrote a number of opera librettos.

# *Philosophy of music*

*Source:*

*Philosophie de la musique* (Paris 1865). Deuxième section: Effets de la musique sur l'homme, considéré comme être sensible et intelligent. Chapitre vii. La musique et le sentiment, pp. 74–7, 80–1; chapitre viii. La musique et l'intelligence, §1. La musique exprime-t-elle des sentiments?, pp. 82–6, 90–1; §2. La musique n'est pas née du langage, pp. 91–4, 98, 99–102; §3. Du symbolisme musical, pp. 102–9, 113–14. Translated by Jennifer Day.

### Chapter VII: Music and emotion

There is perhaps no opinion that has given rise to fewer objections than the following: *music is the art of emotion*. It is one of those ready-made opinions that we pass on to each other, like a currency that everyone considers sound and that no one ever thinks of testing against the touchstone. But it is basic to our subject not to accept this without enquiry and we are going to try to unravel how much is truth and how much is fallacy in this statement.

Before anything else, we must find out what we mean by feelings.

Man has included under the name of emotion a good part of his life, perhaps the largest, everything that is to him joy or sorrow, affections, emotions, passions of every kind, whether they be the charm or the torment of his existence. It would be wasted effort to list the names of all the emotions, so numerous are they and of infinite variety, and so often do they differ one from the other by nuances that escape analysis. Nearly all are composed of a multiplicity of elements, of facts deriving from physical sensibility mixed with intellectual facts, whether in the domain of pure reason or the domain of the imagination.

But at bottom they all derive from physical sensibility. Their substance, their essence, and this is what distinguishes them from pure ideas, is nothing more than organic activity modified in different ways by understanding, imagination or memory. Thus anger, attributed to the blood, the bile, the humours, is over-excited activity, along with an idea or collection of ideas. Love, now languishing, fickle, and enervated, now violent and impetuous, dwells essentially in the organism, but is characterized by the ideas of every kind which transform human love into an emotion above that of a brute, in which it is only a sense, a physical function.

Therefore, taken as itself and setting aside the particular characters that can be assumed with the help of ideas, this physical activity, which is the *substratum*, the basis of moral sensibility, gives us pure unadulterated emotions, which are general situations of the soul closely allied to the physical life and independent of the will, unaware of either the object or the cause.

After retiring to bed one evening in a most cheerful mood, I am well able to awaken next day sad, morose, irritable without knowing why. I do not know the cause of this indeterminable feeling I suffer, an emotion without object and consequently neither desire nor hatred; for if I love or hate, I know very well the object of my hatred or love. These general dispositions of the soul stem from a host of causes and especially from the state of the body, from its internal motions, from the good or ill health of some part or other of the organism, from the regularity or otherwise of its functions, from that unconscious life we have lived in our slumbers of which the echoes live on in our waking hours. These dispositions of the soul may stem from the combination of fleeting judgements, from the reawakening of vague, dormant and indistinct impressions, from the amount of electricity in the air and its effect on our constitution, that is to say, from the atmosphere surrounding us, from the brightness or dullness of the light, from the temperature, in a word from the manifold action of a host of differing agents, external or internal, from a thousand influences that our sensibility defers to without our being aware of it.

Any art can only act in two ways upon moral sensibility. Either it acts as one of the agents we have just listed and modifies the physical sensibility, resulting in the creation of indeterminate states and general and unconscious dispositions; or it passes through the intelligence and awakens ideas which give determination to the emotions. Painting, sculpture, by nature of the subjects they deal with, are arts destined for this determination of the emotions, and so is poetry especially.

As we shall see in the following chapter, music on the other hand, because of its powerlessness to furnish the mind with clear and sharply-defined ideas, is confined to pure and unspecific emotion.

Since the vibration of bodies is subject to particular laws, sensibility, being merely the echo of this vibration, obeys the same laws. It is the soul itself in its material life that is in motion and it is frequently the nature of this motion that brings about moral situations. Thus, if one considers the sound in itself in isolation, the faster the vibrating movement is, that is to say the higher the pitch becomes, the greater the increase of vital energy, and consequently the more lively is the impression of well-being and contentment, resulting from activity in its highest degree. That is why high-pitched sounds have a more joyful effect than extremely low-pitched ones. So with low-pitched notes, as we have already said, the vibratory life is less marked. It is the state of the matter as it approaches as near as it can to what we call inertia, and consequently it is the least liable to produce an impression upon the body. Precisely because of this a very low-pitched sound is frightening; we do not easily connect it with the manifestation of life, with movement. It surprises us with its revelation of the essence of matter in a form which is the furthest removed from us. All quick-moving things are pleasing to us, we call them lively and we consider the greatest activity as the ultimate perfection among beings. If we saw an animal which seemed to us to be completely motionless and corpse-like, and which, however, we establish to have moved in a way that escaped our notice because of its slowness, it would arouse in us invincible terror, because it would overthrow all our ideas on life, with which we always associate a certain degree of activity. [pp. 74–7]

[.    .    .]

Music does not create [the emotions], nor express them by characterizing them, but simply places the body in a certain situation the consequence of which is a general disposition of the soul. This is doubtless much, but it is all. If, after hearing a powerful melody with a strong rhythm, a man feels capable of facing death, will one pay tribute to the music for this fine emotion? Does not this effect presuppose in the first place a natural reserve of courage? If music counts for anything in it, it is simply because of the vibration, movement and rhythm. And yet can one say that noise would be more powerful in its effect? Look at the acrobats at fairs when they want to attract the public to their pitch. They shout, yell, break their drums, bray on their brass instruments, so the crowd may be besotted by noise and feverish with the movement. In certain operas it is the reason for their success: choruses are sung at the top of the voice and accompanied by a great din from the orchestra. Violent effects can be produced simply by stirring the sensibilities forcefully, which perhaps will be less moved by the order and discipline of the music than by the speed, abruptness and harshness of the noise. The sounds of the brass, the shouting, the brouhaha, the striking of the wood of the instruments, carry you out of yourself and thrust you into the action. It is not without reason that military bands are for the most part composed of brass instruments. Quintilian has already said that it was to this type of music that the Roman militia chiefly owed its reputation for bravery. The Spartans, tough nation of warriors, always made use of them. Violent sounds are as intoxicating as heady wines. But, since music is a powerful force in the incitement to battle, if one concludes that it inspires courage, one should therefore recognize the same power in the art of the distiller. By its excitation of the nervous system brandy, too, produces the same agitation, the need for action and certain soldiers, as one knows, can only fight when topped-up with alcohol.

We suppose it is useless to pursue this point any longer and sum up our chapter by this proposition which seems to us demonstrated: music in itself and reduced to its own resources, does not directly produce clearly-defined emotions, but only moral situations and general emotions. [pp. 80–1]

## Chapter VIII: Music and the intelligence

[. . .]

To represent the various emotions painting and sculpture have the signs of the natural language: posture, facial expression, the external circumstances that go with the emotions and which serve as a framework for the development of the passion. The great emotions of the soul have in general a particular and easily recognizable physiognomy. Are not students of drawing required to follow courses in expression, where it is indicated to what degree the eyebrow should be raised or lowered, the mouth pursed, what muscles should be prominent to express fright, anger, disdain, arrogance etc.? If poetry wishes to portray an emotion, apart from the right word [*mot propre*], a conventional device that gives the idea straight away, but once all vagueness about the idea has been removed, a device which seems crude like the impression of a coin that has passed through too many hands, it [poetry] describes the diverse circumstances that accompany this emotion in reality and the connected ideas that follow in its wake, the gestures, the facial features of a person undergoing the emotion, and by a daring personification, poetry even invests inanimate and detached nature with a physiognomy, an expression. Remember the famous account of Théramène which deals with the sorrow of Hippolyte.[1] A word conveyed the idea, but how feebly compared with the picture the poet places before our eyes: we see the young hero, lost in thought, allowing the reins to dangle on the neck of his steeds, his guards imitating his silence and the very horses seeming to defer to his sorrowful thoughts.

Has pure music, not set to words, but music in itself, similar resources for awakening in the soul or in the imagination specific emotions? If one were to rely on the most general opinion, the question would soon be settled. 'Music, language of emotion' is an opinion that has nearly become an axiom, but we shall not allow ourselves to be impressed by the authority of the *res judicata*. It is worth appealing against the judgement.

[1] [Translator's note: Racine, *Phèdre*, act v, scene 6.]

## §1    Does music express emotions?

The qualification 'language of emotion' has no significance if it does not mean that music makes use of a collection of signs able to give an exact representation of the emotions. A language in fact can be nothing other than a system of signs.

Three types of languages are usually recognized, characterized by the signs they use: the natural language that expresses emotions and ideas through outward bodily indications, the artificial language in which the signs are completely conventional and the symbolic language which allows one to glimpse the idea beneath concrete forms.

If we only consider sound as we find it in the voice, we can say that it is one of the principal elements of the natural language, because the sounds of the voice are of necessity bound up with certain emotions.

The voice is the chief sound of the body when considered as an instrument of the nerves. Should some violent commotion of the physical or moral order shake our sensibility, we cry out, just as matter gives out a sound when an impact sets up a vibration. The voice is essentially the organ destined to make our fellow-beings join in the spectacle of our inner life. One could call it a window that we open on a world outside and through which the soul can be glimpsed. All the emotions we experience are shown to different extents in the voice and they modify some part of this complicated and delicate instrument. The vocal cords are stretched now a little, now more, the glottis distends or tightens, letting variable quantities of air pass, the tongue strikes this air with irregular beats. During emotion, the constituent molecules of the vocal apparatus undergo modifications in their cohesion that cause variations of tone. In this way physical pain makes the voice louder, raises or lowers it several tones according to the nature of the suffering and the temperament of the patient. Mental suffering makes the voice tremulous, stifles it, chokes it with sobs; fear deepens the voice, admiration lengthens it, anger makes it hoarse, joy gives it a sparkling tone. During calm emotions, the sounds become soft and faint. We are so in the habit of deducing inner phenomena from these outward phenomena, that from a distance and without hearing the words, we can make out from the intonation alone the emotions that animate people while they are speaking. It is for this reason that, setting aside the differences in articulation during the formation of the words, the organ in itself holds such a great fascination for orators: by their tone alone do they move the audience, disposing it to anger or to pity. In declamation, if we express sad emotions, our voice is lowered and slows its pace, and on the other hand it rises and quickens for cheerful emotions. From the tone of voice can be recognized kindness, disdain, haughtiness, pity, anger etc. One could say that every emotion has its natural accent. Though a person is an old hand at dissimulation, yet he often has difficulty in counterfeiting the accent of the emotions, and this shows through the supposedly impenetrable mask. 'It's the tone that makes the song', the people say, with that intuitive common sense that goes as deep as does analysis.

Let us add that if certain emotions are habitual, the voice as a result acquires, just as does the physiognomy, a different character which may help us to pass judgement on our fellows. In certain countries the nature of the voice is specified in the passports. It is evident that we would form a very different opinion of two men, if one had a loud, curt, staccato voice and the other a feeble, slow and ponderous voice with a dead and monotonous tone. The relationship between voice and character is so well-established that blind people, whose sense of hearing is keener, can judge character from the voice as surely as we do from the physiognomy. It is known that Hippocrates predicted illnesses and even death from the sounds of this organ. While waiting for a Lavater of the voice to be revealed amongst us, each individual makes use of this clue to some extent in order to judge a man's moral attitudes and his habitual passions. As we have already said, man in fact does not have a dual personality: when he is dominated by a passion, it is expressed in him in all things – his voice, physiognomy, actions, in such a way that this expression of the emotion is merely one of the characters of the emotion itself.

Considered thus, the sounds of the voice are therefore legitimate signs of the natural language, just as much and in the same way as are gestures and physiognomy. But can one confuse the sounds of the voice with music, and draw the conclusion that music is the language of emotion? This is what we claim to be inadmissible, no more than one could say on the basis of this fact that gesture also expresses emotions, affections, and passions, that dance is the language of the emotions. [pp. 82–6]

[.    .    .]

Without wishing to deny the aptitude of the sounds of the voice to act as auxiliary to the natural language, is it necessary to demonstrate that a series of inarticulate sounds is neither closely nor remotely connected with the art of music? Is it possible seriously to uphold that one will shape a melody by exactly noting the sobs of a man who has lost his mate, or by imitating a burst of laughter? Certainly there is a succession of notes in sobbing and laughter, but would any succession of sounds or other suffice to make a melody? It is just as if one ventured to say that a succession of colours suffices to make a picture.

And moreover the inarticulate cries of powerful emotions do not figure on a scale. Their intervals are much more narrowly spaced than those that the art of music, and I am not talking only of modern music and of the diatonic genre, but of those that any kind of art has had to select as materials to work upon. Do they move in that regular scale of notes that generate each other according to fixed and inviolable laws? Do they have a measured and cadenced rhythm; is their melodic line proportioned, composed of equal phrases, reappearing at almost symmetrical intervals etc.? Briefly, do they obey the laws of regularity, proportion, tonality and rhythm which alone can constitute the motif? Quite clearly not. So there is nothing musical about them. They are means of expression for the natural language and nothing else.

Wanting to give them a musical sense is just like claiming that pedals and mutes constitute instruments. It is understood that in an opera, along with the determination of the words, some time one might chance to make use of the inarticulate cry of emotion, for example the cry of fright uttered by Leporello, on opening the door to the statue of the Commendatore, but it is only an accident, a fantasy of the composer, which could not form the basis for any theory. [pp. 90–1]

## §2   Music does not spring from language

Lacépède [. . .] placed the origin and the aim of music in the imitation of the inarticulate cries of the passions.[2] Others went still further. They claimed that this art was nothing but the imitation of the various intonations of language, with the articulation of the words removed, and they consequently made out of it a language, a much better one, the language *par excellence*.

This system has formed the basis of music criticism up till now and is still in great favour, although from the philosophical point of view it is not worth discussing. This system, because of the weight carried by its historical author-ity, obliges us, however, to study the relationships between music and spoken language.

In a language, setting aside the articulation which gives the words their true and strictly speaking their only character of signs, by the very fact that it contains sounds, the sounds have different qualities of pitch, intensity, timbre etc. These different qualities, when combined with movement, constitute what is called the 'tune' or 'intonation'.

Most of the time intonation is found to be connected with emotions and ideas. It serves as accompaniment and additional expression to the words, and varies according to their sense. Let everyone remember what he hears round about him: 'He's a thickset, burly fellow, with an enormous paunch', people say, ponderously stressing every syllable. On the other hand 'he's a dry little fellow, exuberant and sharp-eyed', is uttered with all the dryness and liveliness that can be put into each word. Should one wish to indicate some remote spot, one repeats the word several times in order to prolong the time taken, in a drawling voice that dies away just as if to imitate a sound heard in the distance: 'It's far off, far off, far off, over there.'

These varying intonations, which form a sort of tune in the language, increase the significance of the words, and often they even provide it, like the ironical or menacing tone given to a phrase, which, taken literally, would not have this meaning. Cannot a host of meanings be put into the same word by nuances of intonation? Thus, to quote just one example, this simple phrase:

2   [Lacépède (la Cépède), comte de (Bernard German Etienne de la Ville sur Illou), *La poétique de la musique*, 2 vols. (Paris 1785). See le Huray and Day, p. 179.]

'You will not go'[3] can, according to the tone of voice, contain a threat, a challenge, a taunt, a question etc. It is this strange abundance of expression that makes the spoken language superior to the written.

Besides these different intonations, which are not arbitrary but spontaneous and nothing but the signs of the natural language and which give expression to speech as do gestures and physiognomy, languages also have a conventional tune that goes with the words and gives them a meaning that is so to speak purely grammatical. So we have in French the rising of the voice in questions. This particular rising is conventional, for foreigners who are not over-familiar with our language often take an interrogative or doubtful phrase as affirmative.

In order to place them outside the scope of our study, it is also necessary to draw attention to other intonations which do not always carry significance. There is a particular tune and cadence whose only aim is to avoid monotony of delivery. This pitch and rhythm are to a great extent determined by the natural movement of the vocal sound as it rises and falls, like the vibratory movement of bodies, and like all kind of movement. In this way the phrases of speech generally finish on a low tone, a kind of fundamental tone that leaves nothing else to be expected after it. This is why punctuation offers so to speak several musical characters. The full stop is like the tonic of a phrase, conceding that the phrase has a kind of tonality, and it is on this tonic that the voice rests. The comma is similar to the leading-note; as the intonation rises it inevitably calls for a complement to the phrase. The semi-colon is like the dominant, the intermediary sound before the tonic etc.

As can be seen from what we have just said, there is nothing to prevent the conventional creation of new accents, signs of new intonations expressing a greater number of senses. What advantages would not be gained from this? Were it only to convey the tone to those interpreting the dramatic writers, to the actors, and thus avoid countless repetitions? Music has for its expression its fortes, pianos, decrescendos; why not similar markings in literature? It is affirmed that Molière had that idea.

If we turn from our consideration of whole phrases to words in particular, we shall find in the pronunciation of the same word differences of pitch, less marked in French but extremely obvious in other languages, establishing what is called the tonic accent, which is also of the utmost importance in the physiognomy of language. This accent, which puts differences of length and intensity into the words, constitutes a sort of cadence, of rhythm, which in certain languages forms one of the bases of poetry. Everyone knows that the principal charm of Greek verse lay in the different ways of accentuating the words, nuances which have been lost in the more barbarous organizations of northern peoples, the conquerors of the ancient world. In France our system of prosody is differently based; however with a little study and attention, we

---

[3] [Translator's note: The French expression 'Vous n'irez pas' expresses the English phrase 'You will not go' and 'You shall not go', hence the phrase can be neutral in tone or overlaid with a variety of emotions.]

can get an idea of the cadence of that ancient poetry, and of that type of song composed of the different pitches of the voice, rising or falling according to the accents of the syllables. [pp. 91–4]

[.    .    .]

One understands that the Greeks, who had such rhythmic poetry, never did properly separate the art of verse from the art of music. They undoubtedly had a way of pronouncing verse by making the emphasis according to the different accents and making the movement felt, with the result that poetry had the same value when simply declaimed as when sung. And as the rhythm directly imparts movement to the sensibility and acts in the manner of the passions, one easily understands that they were led to give a moral value to music, a moral value which seems to us today greatly exaggerated.

But what we are saying about the ancient art cannot apply to the present-day art. Modern artists have almost totally lost the feeling for rhythm in poetry. Who amongst us comprehends the beauties of the different feet of Greek or Latin verse? In our prosody we have only two musical elements, the metre of the syllables and the rhyme or assonance which is only a variety of the rhythm that it accentuates, which it does more strongly, after the fashion of percussion instruments. None of that delicacy that distinguished the ancient public has been transmitted to our more vulgar organizations. We merely ask that a strong and striking impression be made on our ears. Rhyme, that drumbeat at every line end, or alliteration, is there not something savage about them? It is a vestige of barbaric literature. [p. 98]

[.    .    .]

If one has been convinced of the childishness of the doctrine of Lacépède, who placed the origin of music in the inarticulate cries of the passions, one will all the more have to recognize the spuriousness of that other theory which only differs from the first in the slightest degree and which consists of placing the origin and aim of music in the imitation of the intonations of language. Do we need to repeat it: what constitutes the art of music is above all tonality, the connection and interdependence of sounds with relation to a fundamental sound, which are conditions not found in the sounds of a language. These, distorted by articulation, have no inherent musical qualities. In articulation the teeth, the tongue and the lips put obstacles in the path of the sound; they break it up, choke it, frustrate its natural emission, so as to give it that great number of different characters that go to form the words and make of them the vehicles of ideas.

It is a childish pursuit to wish to establish an other than metaphorical connection between music and language. There is no conclusion to be drawn from the fact that music, just like a language, uses sounds that differ in pitch, intensity and timbre. These characteristics belong to the very nature of sound. There is no conclusion to be drawn either from the fact there are seven sounds in a scale, as there are seven vowels in a language. I will not speak of those who claim that each letter of the alphabet represents a note of the enharmonic scale and that consequently one could write down a musical equivalent of any word. To argue thus is to show oneself up as far too scornful of common sense.

What does it matter then that we have a memory for musical sounds like that for words, a memory for tunes like that for sentences, that we imagine musical forms, that is to say, that we can combine sounds inside ourselves as we do ideas. That does not prove that music is a language. A theory relying on such errors as these is doomed to powerlessness and futility. Gluck, Rousseau and Rameau only escaped ridicule by violating the laws that they themselves put forward, concerning the analogy of music with a language and the necessity of applying the rules of construction of language to the art of music.

Is it possible to call music a language when the slightest attempt at reflection shows us the truth of Condillac's definition that languages are methods of abstraction and generalization?[4] What! would music analyse the workings of thought and express abstract ideas? And since a language is so confused with intellectual faculties that one cannot distinguish the one from the other, could one say that one thinks in music and writes philosophical books in music? It is the height of absurdity and yet that has been maintained, doubtlessly *quia absurdum*. A host of critics have seen in the compositions of Beethoven cosmogonic and philosophical poems. Does not Wagner claim that where the word finishes music begins and expresses to the intelligence the most abstruse mysteries of the creation? Certain German writers speak with the most unshakeable seriousness of the psychological problems to which Beethoven puts forward the solution in his symphonies, and they place the composer from Bonn on the same level as Hegel and Kant as a philosopher. They naively suggest to modern musicians that they tackle history, as Beethoven tackled philosophy, and they foresee plentiful laurels to be won in those fields still unexplored by instrumental music. So we shall soon have an influx of 'symphonist historians' from beyond the Rhine. I can understand the battle of Prague on the piano, in which the striking of notes in the lower octaves aims to recall the firing of cannon, but I imagine with difficulty what a symphony would be like that was presenting a picture of the Middle Ages or the age of Leo X.

It is clear that, since a conventional language can be formed with all kind of signs, one could also be formed with music, making B D signify bread, G A wine, etc., or agreeing that such and such a melody, such a musical phrase shall have a specific sense. There is here a telegraphic medium as good as any other for carrying warnings or commands a great distance, when an articulated voice could not be used. Hunting calls, such as the 'hare', the 'roebuck', the 'tally-ho', the various 'at bay' calls, are examples everyone knows. It is the

---

[4] [Condillac's assertion, in fact, is that languages are methods of analysis. See *Course d'études pour l'instruction du Prince de Parme* (1775), part ii, chapter vi, in *Oeuvres philosophiques de Condillac*, ed. Georges le Roy, vol. 1 (Paris 1947), p. 442; and *La logique* (1780), part ii, chapter iii, in *Oeuvres philosophiques*, vol. 2 (Paris 1948), p. 398.]

same with the calls used in the regiments of infantry and cavalry, calls which all bear a characteristic name: the 'cookhouse', the 'boots and saddles', the 'reveille', the 'lights-out'. A cavalry regiment has thirty or so different tunes which constitute a true conventional language. It is a mnemonic device which can be extremely useful, but there is no connection between the trumpet-tune and the thing it signifies. The cookhouse call could just as well have announced the lights-out if so desired. Moreover, I do not suppose that it was such a system of arbitrary signs that was the matter under discussion for those to whom music is a language. [pp. 99–102]

### §3     On musical symbolism

Music therefore is not a language like that which we speak, neither does it spring from human language. Notes cannot be signs as words are. It could not be said either that it is a natural language, this qualification only being applied to gestures and the voice, and not to an art which is easy to understand quite apart from the human voice.

But there also exists another kind of language; the symbolic language, and those who term music a language take refuge here as their last ditch stand to support their opinion. It is from here that they must be flushed out.

A symbolic language is one which expresses ideas to the intelligence by means of signs, either conventional ones or ones linked by some necessary connection to the things they represent. Thus there is a conventional symbolism and a natural symbolism. As an example of the former, we shall cite the language of flowers, which is pure convention. It could not have been a question of this kind of symbolism, I think, in the case of music. Never has it been agreed that such and such a phrase of an instrumental theme, such a modulation, or such a tonality should signify virtue, God, a plant etc. So there only remains natural symbolism, that is, a language depicting the ideas it wants to express by signs that of necessity call them to mind.

Therefore if we consider sounds separately from the voice, which has its special role as the organ meant for relating events, rather than as a musical instrument, it is a matter of seeing in what things sounds can express emotions and ideas to the intelligence.

Taken in itself sound, as a phenomenon perceived by one of the sensory organs, is not *representative*, no more than is smell or taste. It is almost exclusively *emotional*.

Pitch conveys no idea to the intelligence, not even of the number of vibrations which remains imperceptible to the hearing. Sounds doubtless have, according to the pitch, a general effect on the emotions, disposing us to joy or to sadness, to activity or lethargy, but they cannot give us any precise notions. Could one say what a high-pitched sound expresses? By really searching, perhaps one would find that it gives rise to a feeling of serenity in us, just as low notes produce a feeling of anxiety or mystery. On hearing one of these latter sounds, the ear, we have already said, is as if surprised to perceive such slow vibrations; it would seem that the ear has a vague intuition of the latent movement that animates matter, which so to speak forms its essence, and this quick glance cast at the infinite gives rise to a certain terror in us.

We find an almost similar emotion expressed by intensity, this second quality that we have distinguished in sound. As sound represents force, matter in its essence, it is natural that a sound of great intensity frightens us, because it seems to indicate that this latent force can suddenly break out and put our existence in danger. Slight, hesitant sounds, faintly murmured and intermittent, the mysterious buzz of the orchestra, these inspire anxiety by their very vagueness. One senses a brooding force that at any moment could break out and the emotion experienced resembles that aroused when the eye is confronted by a dim light, mist or moonlight, blurring the shapes of things in a mysterious atmosphere which gives free rein to the imagination.

Likewise, in melodrama, when the dramatic situation is about to reach its greatest tension, and when the author wishes to inspire in his public that quivering anxiety, that vague fear that opens them to emotion, the orchestra plays a muted tremolo, whilst the footlights are dimmed. The two means are equivalent.

If we now examine the third characteristic of sound, timbre, we see that it is almost exclusively emotional. To the imagination, it represents in absolute terms only the instrument that is resonating, granted, however, that this instrument in its material form is already known to us, just as the scent recalls the shape of the flower or the taste that of the fruit. Since the timbre, taken as a sign, corresponds only to the form of the instrument, this element of sound can in no way be turned to advantage as regards symbolism.

It is not the same case with respect to the *movement* and *rhythm* of a series of sounds. These characteristics in fact are general, and a host of analogies can be found for them in nature and in man. It is only a question of knowing if these analogies are constant and exact enough to serve as symbols, or to put it another way, if by the movement fashioned from sounds one can represent clearly to the intelligence and the imagination emotions and passions or natural objects which are animated by movements.

Passion is not conceived without a movement of the nervous sensibility. The two are so confused that passion is often viewed as the movement itself. Anger, love, desire, hope are just so many agitations of the soul that are translated materially into the blood rushing through the heart. They are even capable in their paroxysm of bringing about congestion of certain organs and causing fatal lesions. Emotions and movements thus have a natural analogy. In this case what spiritualists call the soul, forms such a close alliance with the body that it is very difficult to distinguish the two principles that they wish to separate by such a deep abyss. In his emotion man is a whole: the inner movement that shakes him is revealed outwardly by actions and physiognomy. In this way the mind has become used to associating certain emotions with certain movements, although they are not always united by the bond of cause and effect.

But we are going to see that the movement is too general to serve as a transparent symbol for the idea. So it is rather as a simple metaphor than as a precise sign that it can be used.

Primitive man, in contact with nature but still ignorant about it and cast upon this mysterious stage in the middle of speechless characters who live their own lives and play roles with which he is completely unfamiliar, only knows himself, is only aware of his own personality. Since he is unable to conceive of anything beyond this limited notion, he lends to everything outside himself the same life as the one he feels teeming within his breast. He humanizes everything: the rushing, roaring torrent is *furious*, the animal devouring its prey *cruel*, the lamb *gentle*, the sea *treacherous* etc. Not content with this perpetual metaphor which causes him to carry his life, ideas and emotions over into the world outside him, he generalizes the mysterious facts that strike him, the movements of matter outside him, and he passes progressively from metaphor to deification. The life-giving river becomes a god, the inexhaustible spring a nymph, the vegetative force is personified in dryads and hamadryads etc. These unknown powers that seem so different from him frighten him, throw him into a mysterious wonderment, he worships them and he creates a religion which is simply an immense and splendid metaphor – polytheism.

Polytheism or at least anthropomorphism is found at the dawn of all civilizations. It is the first stage of intelligence. Man lends to everything he does not know his own form or his intimate nature, his ideas and emotions.

But as knowledge increases, that is as truth is discerned behind falling veils, the mind of man rids itself of these egoistic forms through which nature was perceived and begins to consider nature as being more outside him. Following him on this superficial view which only gave him inconsistent analogies, man analyses and this is when that naive freshness which is the principal charm of antiquity found in a Hesiod or a Homer, is lost in the arts. This slow evolution from the subjective to the objective, whereby man has managed to detach himself from the world outside and which leaves a well-marked trail in all the arts, is most easily perceived in music.

Since the impression of sounds on the sensibility is very lively and excites the movements of the body, and since on another hand passion goads it on to the same outward manifestations, men have established from the outset comparisons between music and the passions, and have made out of the art of music a symbolic language that expresses the emotions.

These metaphors were natural ones. One could not deny that without any effort we associate sad emotions with slow movement and low sounds, and joyful emotions with rapid movement and high-pitched sounds. But if sounds, as we have seen, can quite easily signify to the intelligence general situations because sounds produce them directly in the sensibility, the art of music does not provide those necessary characteristics that clarify those situations nor give them the physiognomy of particular emotions. In order for this to be otherwise, it would be necessary for *movement* to be able to express clearly the incidental ideas of general emotions. Unfortunately, for movement to represent this, to *signify* this exactly is impossible.

Although it may be obvious there is a rapid movement of blood and of nervous matter in connection with anger, to propose that a lively movement of sounds expresses anger, is to go beyond the bounds of induction. Why should not such a movement not equally well convey a tempest, a battle, the bounding of a lion, a rushing torrent etc.? I well know that all these instances, all these movements stem from something similar to the emotion of anger, but that analogy is merely in the violence and the speed and it is of this generality alone that music can give an idea. Exactness could only come from other causes outside music itself. To maintain the contrary is to hold that Matteson is right in claiming that the sarabande expresses respect, the courante hope: it is to fall into the subtlety of Chinese music where the different modes represent the Empire, the majesty, the minister and his boldness in wielding power, submission to and respect for the laws, or even the swiftness of government affairs.

We have just seen that neither ideas nor emotions are expressed by the movement in sounds; but can objects be represented? This is what we are about to examine. At first glance, it seems that nothing could be simpler than to recall to the imagination the movements of nature with the help of sounds. But still one does not think that music can imitate movement except in an abstract manner, and that consequently in moving objects there will always be the form, that is, the thing which constitutes the object itself and of which music is powerless to give the idea. Comparing in them the facts of the physical and moral order, for they offer the same movements, is as if one wished to establish analogies between objects of the same colour. What an amusing error! One would end up like a certain Spanish commander who was extremely well-known in Paris in former times and who had an unfortunate passion for natural history, putting in the same genus the leopard and the thrush, because they are both spotted.

This imitation of objects by music is the dream of a diseased brain. Music does not speak sufficiently to the intelligence because it only expresses a very general character, a too remote analogy with the imitated object itself of which it cannot consequently give a precise idea. [pp, 102–9]

[.   .   .]

For myself, I do not really see what aspects of nature could have been useful to man for creating the art of the Mozarts, Beethovens and Rossinis. I am not one of those who believe in the 'concert of nature'. The habit of hearing them often repeated, has made these people take the poets' most daring metaphors as words from the Gospel, and they have created a philosophy of art, adapted from these forms of speech, just as the primitive poets created mythology by exploiting words: *numina nomina*, the proverb says.

We shall not stop at demonstrating that nature presents only discordant sounds, fine for a part in a hullabaloo; its so-called concert is simply a colossal exaggeration. There is something slightly musical in the moaning of fir-trees or the whisperings of reeds, when the wind, like a vast bow, passes over these resonant plants. All other noises merely create a cacophony which can have a certain poetic pleasure. If, above this jumble of noises, there occasionally stands out a clear, pure sound that comes within the scale of sounds pleasant to the ear, it is never more than an isolated phenomenon. If we only consider organized beings, the much overrated song of the nightingale has nothing musical about it. No trace of melody at all will be found in the song of any bird. They only produce noises, which are somewhat similar to musical sounds, that is all.

If the laws of the vibration of sounds have their origin in nature, one could not say as much about the art of music. This is a creation of man which supposes the ear and intelligence of man, and which has no reality outside him. In nature, you will find sounds in combination with movements, but nothing of what constitutes music. What one calls the *song* of the bird does not merit this qualification; whereas if man sings, whether he be a ploughboy or his name be Mozart, he always produces something artistic, that is to say musical sounds, an arrangement worked out by his intelligence and adapted according to his organization. The song our peasants call out at the top of their voices in the evening when they bring their cattle home is not *natural*, it is not an effect of the mechanism of their larynx as is the action that one has agreed to call the *song* of the bird. It is art, naive, that is true, but art.

By the very fact that man lives in nature, that he is part of it, that he has a body, and organs that relate to the world outside, it is evident that he can do nothing completely apart from nature. But from the fact that for a work of art he combines the elements around him, sounds and movement, for example, it does not follow that he imitates nature. Art does not imitate nature: quite the contrary, since nature must resemble art to be worth anything to our ears. Does not one say when speaking of a lovely voice: 'It's true music.'? Music is thus the ideal with which one compares reality. [pp. 113–14]

[.    .    .]

# Jules Combarieu (1859–1916)

## Les rapports de la musique et de la poésie (1894)

French musicologist and critic. Having studied at the Sorbonne and under Spitta in Berlin, he obtained a doctorate in Paris with his *Les rapports de la musique et de la poésie*. He taught at Parisian *lycées* and at the College de France and contributed music criticism to various French papers and periodicals. In 1901 he founded the *Revue d'histoire et de critique musicales* (later *La Revue musicale*). His aesthetic attitude and his method in music history show a mixture of the French positivist tendency and German speculative orientation.

## The relationship between music and poetry

Source:

> *Les rapports de la musique et de la poésie considérées au point de vue de l'expression* (Paris 1894). Première partie – Chapitre premier: Les sons et le language instinctif de l'émotion, i, pp. 23–5. Chapitre quatrième: La pensée musicale, iii, pp. 168–74. Troisième partie – Chapitre troisième: Fondement et conditions diverses de l'union de la musique et de la poésie, pp. 339–40; 342–5. Conclusion, pp. 419–23. Translated by Jennifer Day.

**First part – Chapter I: The sounds and instinctive language of emotion**

All instruments are human voices.

(R. Schumann)

Declamation should be thought of as a line, and song as another line winding over the first . . . It is up to the animal cry to dictate the line that befits us.

(D. Diderot, *Rameau's Nephew*)

### Section i

The human voice – the common origin of poetic language and musical language – possesses, quite apart from any artistic training, a threefold power of expression. It can be at different instances or at the same time: 1. a representation of feeling; 2. a representation of certain external and material objects; 3. a representation of thought. In the first case, it takes the form of a

197

cry and all its nuances; in the second, the form of onomatopoeia and all its sophistications; in the third, the form of actual language, such as is reproduced in writing. These three faculties can be distinguished by their origin and their degree of intelligibility. Instinct is their common origin; but the first two can be the work of pure instinct, whereas the last derives for the most part from convention. Moreover, when the human voice is a spontaneous product of the emotion or an echo of external sounds, it acts directly upon the physical sensibility of the listener, and its means of expression, because of their realism, are intelligible to all men. When the human voice is evidence of thought, it speaks to the reason, it has an ideal sense, and its means of expression, because of their conventional nature, are limited in their intelligibility. Let us occupy ourselves with the first two cases, that is, with the purely instinctive natural language, and first of all with its power to convey feeling.

How is it possible for language to translate feeling thus? Between the life of the soul and that of the body, there is an abyss for philosophic reason; this is not the case for nature. Common experience shows us this astonishing and at the same time commonplace miracle: the voice makes emotion sensible to the ear, just as facial expression makes it visible. It has been said that Condé bore victory in his eyes; it would be equally true to say that a general bears it in the tone of his harangue before battle. Between feelings and tones or inflexions of the voice, there is a relationship of cause and effect so close and so obvious that we instinctively transform this into the close connection of likeness and almost into total similarity.

To follow a Ciceronian image, the voice vibrates under the impact of the passions like the chords of the lyre under the musician's fingers, and it follows the most delicate shades of emotion with a suppleness whose limits know no bounds. The ancient proverb: 'It is through the heart that one is an orator', rests on a simple observation of the language of instinct and its effects.[1]

One can distinguish the following elements in the sounds of the human voice: their intensity, their pitch, the intervals (together with their range and their direction) which separate them, their length, their timbre, and the movement of the sequence of sounds. We must bear in mind the expressive

[1] In the poem entitled *La Parole*, Sully-Prudhomme spoke with a great felicity of expression about the natural language, only known to the earliest men:

> Pain and pleasure found utterance in cries;
> Terror stammered out wild prayers;
> On the lips sighing spelt an exchange of souls;
> Joyful wonder burst forth in laughter
> And when words failed the answer was in the eyes.

Cicero had said less poetically: 'Delivery is a kind of bodily eloquence when it comes from the voice and the motion. Changes of the voice are as many as those of the passions.' (*Orator*, §17, section 55) And Quintilian says: 'This quality (appropriate delivery) is in the main supplied by the emotions themselves, and the voice will ring as passion strikes its cords.' (*Institutio oratoria*, §11, section 3, subsection 61) One knows how Montaigne one day through a series of connected facts recognized that his travelling companion was a Huguenot: 'It seemed to that poor man that through his mask and the crosses on his tabard one could read his secret intentions right within his heart.' (*Essais*, book 2, chapter V)

value of these diverse characteristics of the natural language and show that they have always been used in song, the point of departure for instrumental music in moving towards identical effects.[2] [pp. 23–5]

[.    .    .]

## Chapter IV: Musical thought

### Section iii

Have we indicated the great originality of music by saying that it has the privilege of a thought peculiar to itself? Not yet.

[2] The sounds used by music have a natural analogy with the cry, and all the nuances of natural language. It is scarcely necessary to prove such a certain yet misunderstood matter. 'Musical sounds', Lessing says, in a supplement to *Laokoon*, 'are not signs. They express nothing; it is merely the succession of musical sounds that can express or arouse the passions.' [This sentence comes from Lessing's annotations to *Laokoon* known as 'Materialen zum "Laokoon"' or 'Entwurfe zum "Laokoon"'. See Gotthold Ephraim Lessing, *Gesammelte Werke*, vol. 5 (Berlin 1955), pp. 301–2.] According to this opinion the sound could be compared to the geometrical point, which, on its own, is nothing, but which, taken together with other points, forms a line. Such a judgement is refuted by the evidence; sound is not an abstraction, it is always characterized and only exists as such. Darwin has said that all the sounds of nature from the buzzing of the insect even to the crash of thunder and the utterances of man could be linked with a victory or a defeat in the battle of life. This idea carries a deep meaning, but we do not need to explore the question any further. Suffice it to say that there is no musical sound without certain characteristics. Now these characteristics resemble those of the human voice, and are consequently elements of expression.

Hanslick has put forward a contrary opinion to that of Lessing, but a much stranger one. According to him, sounds offer a symbolic meaning, comparable to that given to colours. 'Green', he says, 'is often taken as a symbol of hope, blue as a symbol of fidelity etc. . . . but, when they are combined in a unified work, the colours can no longer have any significance. Thus, in a historical picture, blue no longer represents fidelity, green hope etc. . . . It is the same with sounds: taken separately, they can be considered as signs of various feelings, but when combined in a symphony, their significance is nil.' [Combarieu misunderstands and misrepresents Hanslick, so that his subsequent criticism of Hanslick is unfounded. See *HMS*, p. 34, *HC*, p. 25.] One is amazed to find such ideas coming from the pen of one of the most celebrated critics in Germany. To compare here the tame and puerile symbolism of colours with the language of sounds, is to confuse the most arbitrary of conventions with nature. Where shall I go and find out, in order to know whether blue or green represents a certain feeling? To recognize the joyful or sad, the menacing or tender character of certain sounds, instinct is enough.

This simple observation allows us to reject this other idea of Hanslick's: 'The composer can borrow nothing from nature, nor transform anything; he is obliged to create everything from scratch.' [Again a slight misquotation of Hanslick. See *HMS*, p. 195, *HC*, p. 112.] Whatever the importance and wealth of resources that he finds in the special spirit of his art and his own genius, the musician cannot get rid of the original character of the elements he makes use of; and these elements are the cries and sighs of the human soul. He is obliged to use them, as the painter uses colours. There is a vital bond, which in spite of his fantasy and his most original structures, binds him to us. Neither is it true to say that 'the musician and the architect have had to create their art from start to finish'. This comparison is inadmissible. Stones mean nothing on their own, before they form part of a whole; they can equally well be used for a church, a prison, a town, a slaughterhouse etc. Sounds, on the other hand, prior to being used in combination, have a distinct value and meaning, because they have of necessity a certain colour, pitch and intensity.

To our mind, the whole secret of this art, the principle behind its marvel-lous power of expression, the cause of the so deep and moving effects it has on the listener − and, at the same time, the cause of so many contradictory theories that it has provoked in the field of aesthetics, is the close connection, the total similarity of the musical thought and the imitation or expression of the real world. We shall express this similarity by saying that (in good music, it is understood):

*All musical thought is, AT THE SAME TIME, an imitation of the external world or an expression of feeling;*

*All imitation of the external world or expression of feeling is, AT THE SAME TIME, a musical thought.*

The first of these propositions seems obvious to us. The musician can close his eyes to the material world; but, no matter what he does, he cannot suppress the analogy of the sounds he employs with those of the instinctive language. Berkeley said to Locke that it was impossible to imagine a triangle whose angles were neither right-angles, nor acute nor obtuse, and whose sides were neither equal nor unequal; it was impossible to imagine a horse that was neither little nor big nor medium-sized, nor of a definite colour, neither a saddle horse nor a draught horse. In the same way, it is impossible to imagine a musical phrase without registers, timbres, movement, intensity or definite intervals.[3] So, all these characteristics are already known to us; they are inherent in the human voice, and they express feeling. It follows from this that all music of necessity expresses a mood. There are those expressive sounds, for which the initial model was provided by the natural language and which we always instinctively connect with it; they are like colours for the painter, and the musician is unable not to make use of them. One cannot then see in music a sort of rainbow, suspended in the void. It is moreover highly unlikely that a work lacking in any resemblance to nature and to life could hold the slightest interest for us.

As for the second proposition, it is advisable to linger over it a little more. It seems to me that in pointing out this similarity between concrete imitation (or expression) and pure thought, in classical masterpieces, one notes the essen-tial originality of the music. Being an observer like all artists, the musician creates a work in which observation is completely at one with the act of reason which dominates it. Like some of the instruments he uses, he trans-

---

[3] 'Eine Musik ohne Melodie is gar keine.' [A piece of music without melody is not one at all.] (R. Schumann) In his *Philosophie de l'art* (vol. 1, p. 51) Mr. Taine has laid down a distinction, which, in spite of the amendment following it, is doubly inadmissible: 'For this side of the question (the analogy of sound with the cry) the art of music is similar to poetic declamation, and provides a kind of music (expressive music), that of Gluck and the Germans, in opposition to melodic music, that of Rossini and the Italians.' Firstly, this opposition of the Germans and the Italians, wrapping up each side in a single formula, prompts some in fact very easy objections; what could be more tuneful and Italian than certain operas from beyond the Rhine! Moreover, to contrast expressive music with melodic music, as if the latter is wanting in expression, is to contrast light with the sun.

poses what experience affords him. He is at the same time the slave and the master of the model placed before him.

It must not be thought that descriptive music is an exceptional and separate thing, distinct from music. The elements that we distinguished by analysis are in reality blurred. Look at the celebrated storm from the Pastoral Symphony. It has given rise to two distinct interpretations, because it has in effect a two-sided character. Berlioz sees in it a very 'picturesque' piece containing 'an inconceivable degree of *truth*'. He finds in it a gripping imitation of natural phenomena – wind, claps of thunder, etc. . . . . Weber derides this interpretation; he is particularly sensible to the 'grandiose and imposing character of the work', which, because of its musical value, and *although it is intended to depict a storm*, to him seems admirable.[4] Berlioz and Weber are both right. It is impossible not to see a 'storm' in the Pastoral Symphony, and if it were only a 'storm', it would be puerile. The work is both realistic and idealistic, at once imitation and musical thought; remove one of these two terms, and the work would no longer exist. The crash of the thunder and the whistling of the wind have become, through the composer's genius, the language of a thought, without ceasing for all that to represent the wind and the thunder. Into the noise made by things, Beethoven has put the music of the soul. From this springs that enthusiasm of Berlioz identifying the *truth* of the expression with the *sublimity* of art. 'Listen, listen to those rain-sodden gusts of wind, those dull grumblings of the basses, the strident whistling of the piccolo-flutes warning us that a terrible storm is about to break; the hurricane approaches, swells; a tremendous chromatic passage starting in the high registers of the instruments comes to search in the depths of the orchestra, picks up the basses, carries them along, and rises shuddering like a whirlwind that overturns everything in its path. Then the trombones burst in, the thunder of the cymbals grows twice as loud' etc.[5]

It is with a similar intention that elsewhere Berlioz can see 'one of the highest of Gluck's inspirations' in the imitation of the barking of Cerberus (scene in the underworld in *Orphée*) in these lines:

> A l'affreux hurlement
> De Cerbère écumant
> Et rugissant.[6]

The imitation uses the basses, who attack an F fortissimo, preceded by a volley of little notes. According to Berlioz's opinion this effect becomes, by its position in the score, an admirable 'thought'.

[4] [H. Berlioz, *Voyage musical en Allemagne et Italie*, (Paris 1844), pp. 291–5. However, nowhere in his writings does Weber refer explicitly to Beethoven's Pastoral Symphony. It has been generally assumed that a passage in his *Tonkünstlers Leben* (1809–20) alludes to it, although doubt has been cast on this. See Carl Maria von Weber, *Writings on Music*, tr. M. Cooper, ed. J. Warrack (Cambridge 1981), pp. 16 and 332–3.]

[5] J. W. von Wasielewski, *Ludwig van Beethoven*, 2 vols. (Berlin 1888), vol. i, p. 245.

[6] [To the dreadful baying/Of the frothing and howling/Cerberus.] H. Berlioz, *Traité d'instrumentation* (Paris 1844), p. 55.

The greatest composers have in this way associated the art of description and expression with the most lofty and independent views of musical reason. We are informed of this by the fact that the vast majority of works are characterized by a precise title, which may be detailed to a greater or lesser extent, occasionally summarizing a whole collection of scenes and episodes. A. César Bombet,[7] one of the biographers who knew Haydn personally, says that as he was composing, the author of the 'Symphonies' would often imagine a specific theme and sometimes a sort of novel (for example, one of his friends, father of a large family, whose business affairs were going badly, embarking for America to seek a better lot).[8] Beethoven, the great thinker and the one who most possessed the right genius for music, is also one of those who most sought after the expression of ideas and concrete feelings. A good number of his works that are without descriptive clues can be considered as having a programmatic base. I cannot prevent myself from believing that his imagination was following some grandiose scene from an epic when he wrote the sonata dedicated to the archduke Rudolf; that his heart was brimming over with tenderness when he wrote the sonatas dedicated to the great ladies of his time.[9] Nevertheless Beethoven is everywhere independent of the subjects he describes or expresses; he draws the entire substance of his work from one overriding thought, and which is of a different nature even though he is involved in a passion; he remains as Wasielewski says, 'an elemental force'. Likewise, Handel was able to imitate the leaping of frogs and the flight of flies, and Berlioz the jumping of the flea; both of them have remained great musicians.

Music resembles those fanciful, divine beings created by the imagination of the poets, who joined together in them forms and forces found in different orders, like the Echidna of antiquity, whose head and bust were those of a maiden, and the lower part that of a dragon with changing scales – an image of beauty which is superimposed on the life of passion – or like the Flower Maidens, those *Zaubermädchen* that surround Parsifal in the enchanted garden: on their lips and in their eyes glows the all-powerful charm of that higher life sought after by love; however they hold fast to the soil with deep roots.

Schumann says, 'When a composer wants me to read a programme before hearing his music, I say to him: "First of all, let me hear whether you have

[7] His letters on Haydn appeared in 1814. G. August Griesinger (*Biographische Nachrichten über J. Haydn*, Leipzig 1810, p. 117) gives a similar account; another contemporary, Dies (*Biographische Nachrichten über J. Haydn*, Vienna 1810, p. 128), relates that, having asked Haydn if his symphonies were not based on a descriptive theme, the master replied: 'Rarely, it is my custom in my instrumental music to leave the field open to my fantasy.' These various testimonies do not seem to us contradictory.

[8] The descriptive liberties that Haydn allowed himself without demeaning himself too much are too well-known to be called to mind here.

[9] See in Wasielewski the analysis of Sonata op. 109 (vol. 2, pp. 270–1), Sonata op. 31 (vol. 1, p. 343 onwards), the appreciation of the Adagio of the Fourth Symphony and that of the Fifth (vol. 2, p. 237 onwards) etc.

written beautiful music, then your programme will please me too." [10] He is perfectly right, in the sense that nothing can replace purely musical beauty; but he was wrong to treat the programme upon which that beauty is based disdainfully. Could he himself, in translating the poetry of Heine, Herder, Chamisso and Goethe consider the adaptation of the music to the words as incidental? Was it not an essential goal too to be exact in this adaptation? Hartmann, who cares little for the picturesque daring of the symphonic poem and the opera, gives the following reason for his repugnance; in the *imitation* the thought disappears. That is a capital error, to which one can put forward better objections than theoretical developments. Countless works belie this most strikingly. Such ideas only hit their mark with trashy music; but that stuff need not be bothered about.

One has so far seen nothing but shadows, and not art itself, if one does not feel that its originality stems precisely from linking together what seems to us incompatible. All music contains a double truth; music is the meeting-point of the senses and the reason, fused together into a unity which is the work of art, just as man is a combination of a soul and a body fused into a real unity which is life. It is what a German calls 'the harmony of the spirit and of nature'. One could apply to it Kant's comment: 'The sensible and the suprasensible are merely the same thing seen from two different sides.' [11] It comes from observation; it also comes from the far regions of the soul. It fuses the impressions of experience with the incommunicable dream of a Beethoven, and in this way it achieves the complete penetration of matter and thought which is precluded from the other arts.

As a result the chaos in which the aesthetics of music has found itself is only too apparent. Everyone is in the right, some preaching the exactitude of expression, others preferring pure inspiration; the idealists pursue long and loud the origin of musical beauty; the positivists bring it down to the most simple facts: Herbert Spencer and Darwin figuring as much as Herbart and Schopenhauer. Explanations of an empirical nature and those of a metaphysical nature are equally valid here. To reach complete truth they must be reunited. [pp. 168–74]

[.　.　.]

---

[10] 'Vor allem lass mich hören dass du schöne Musik gemacht, hinterher soll mir auch dein Programm angenehm sein.' (*Gesammelte Schriften*, vol. 1.) [The sentence occurs in a review of Spohr's Seventh Symphony, originally published in the *NZM*, vol. 18, no. 35, 1 May 1843, p. 140. See also L. Plantinga, *Schumann as Critic* (New Haven and London 1967), p. 154.] Engel (*Aesthetik der Tonkunst*, Berlin 1884, p. 53) writes: 'A detailed programme is of no real use, for it detracts the attention from the piece of music, which, to be understood as a whole, needs all that attention.' He only admits the need for a general title: *Mary Stuart, Julius Caesar, Coriolanus* etc.

[11] 'Das Sinnliche und Übersinnliche ist eins, nur von zwei Seiten angesehn.' (*Kritik der Urteilskraft*, §19). [These words do not appear in the place marked by Combarieu or indeed elsewhere in Kant's *Kritik der Urteilskraft*.]

### Third part – Chapter III: Basis of and various conditions affecting the union of music and poetry

> The secret and profound aspiration of poetry is to resolve itself finally into music.
> My goal is, before all else, to involve the public in the actual drama.
>                    (R. Wagner, letter of 15 September 1860 to M. François Villot)
>
> The searching of one rhyme for another is the most harmful thing of all to music.
>                                    (Mozart, letter of 13 October 1781)

[.    .]

When one stands before a monument and one dares to undertake a systematic judgement, the first duty of the critic is to have a good look and meekly to try to understand; it is only after gathering information by as many analyses as possible, that he can rise to some discussions of a general nature. He must still display prudence, in this last part of his task, the least interesting, I believe, for the true friends of the arts.

Is the union of poetry and music legitimate in itself, and does it in any way offend against plausibility? Is its basis purely of an aesthetic nature? Should one look for it in nature and in instinct? in the character of the two associated arts? in simple conversation? In this last case, what are the limits of this convention?

Can musical expression be applied to all poems? What type of verse is most suited to it? Are there types that are incompatible with it? Must the poet who works for the musician resign himself to making certain sacrifices, and does the union of the two arts, like all unions, mean that one of the two parties must become subordinate to the other? [pp. 339–40]

[.    .]

We have before our eyes today the proof of a transformation of language in the musical sense. The cross-fertilization of the two arts, affirmed at the beginning of this century as having vague common ground, as an elegant memory of the traditions of antiquity, an inoffensive metaphor hedged about by a vestige of classical taste against any attempt at realization, has become a *fait accompli* under the pen of certain innovators, or to put it better an ever-increasing danger. This situation, at first denied or sneered at as the result of a passing fancy, has already presented itself several times to the scrutiny of serious criticism. The confusion of genres, brought to a head by romanticism, was moderately revolutionary; now poetry, sick of its own riches, bored with hackneyed rhythms, driven on, too, perhaps by the secret envy of the weaker for the stronger, has attempted to unite with its all-powerful rival, no longer standing side by side, as up till now, fulfilling a loyal treaty by which each art remained itself while conspiring with its neighbour, but by stealing from its practices, through substitutions and 'absorption', as physiologists say. What are the decadents looking for? If one rids it of the puerile and contrived wrangling of certain phrases used for effect, the programme of our revolutionaries can be boiled down to two main points: a fresh orientation of the vocabulary; systematic distortion of the rhythm. They wanted to form an imitative or symbolic language, founded on instinct and steeped in naturalism. In the classical and romantic phraseology, the word was limited to translating the *idea* of things and not the things themselves; it seems that it is this intermediary of the idea that a group of writers (limited, I may add) is aiming to suppress today in order to translate impressions with directness and immediacy. In the second place they break up the line of verse and substitute for the old alexandrine, lines of very variable length, which it is impossible to sort out into regular groups. It is a sort of recitative, an equivalent of continuous melody.

Certainly, one could not condemn wholesale all the works that have issued from this twofold endeavour, and one must wish that a genius will make them work. *Exoriare aliquis*! It is the sincere wish of all who love literature. But while we await the appearance of the new Messiah, one can affirm that experience has condemned unfeasible pretensions. In borrowing from the language of the senses their imitative character or their symbolism, one no longer creates poetry neither does one make music; by replacing the alexandrines by lines of indeterminate length, one creates neither verse nor prose, but falls into unintelligibility or perpetual ambiguity.

Since poetry is obviously powerless to take on a form that is alien to it, but towards which it is propelled by an irresistible need, it has no alternative but to attach itself to that form as a simple auxiliary and without claiming to identify with it.

Equally there are cases where this union becomes necessary; a quick comparison of the expressive power of the two arts, taken separately in a special category, will show this.

There is a need to distinguish poetry that is read or declaimed, and dramatic poetry. The former does not claim to express things directly; the latter, on the contrary, intends to be a direct reproduction of reality.

Poetry when read or declaimed outside the theatre is in an indefinable way evocative and creates in our mind a free activity without precise bounds; for this reason, one cannot see what other art could be put forward in opposition as having a richer meaning. When the poet of the *Légende des siècles*[12] paints Boaz asleep; when he describes the sunrise in the *Satyre*, or when he paints the portrait of Satan:

> The terrifying gatherer of rags from the pit,
> With his pack on his back, full of souls, his sin
> Neath his bending wing, and in his dreadful fist
> His black hook gleaming, and in his eyes, the night . . .

there is no marble, nor painted canvas, nor symphony nor opera that can awaken in my mind images more numerous, more exact, more striking or

[12] [Victor Hugo].

more terrible. The poet in these conditions holds the universal chisel. The ideal expression of his language – for it is ideal and does not aim at any *imitation* – embraces and dominates all the direct expressions of reality. The very absence of any imitative ploy makes for its power. Being nothing, it is all. Instead of catching the eye or ear as does the painter or musician in order then to reach the reason, he at the first touches the reason, the very faculty that allows us to see and to hear, and through this he does what he wants with our sensibility and our imagination, since he is master of the site of our organism with the aid of which all the rest is governed.

In the theatre the situation is quite different. Poetry retains its superiority, it is true, with regard to rational expression. Thus Berlioz, Wagner and Gounod can very well paint the world-weariness of Faust; they cannot set forth the grounds for it. Goethe, on the contrary, analyses this mood, and describes its genesis. He quickly makes a critical review of the various human sciences, whose study procures neither knowledge nor happiness; he shows Faust studying in turn philosophy, jurisprudence, medicine, theology; he proclaims the vanity of studying history, eloquence, etc. . . . All this philosophical aspect of the matter is denied the musician. But, on the other hand, the indefinite power of suggestion that the poetry had in the book is found to be restricted by the rigid constraints imposed by theatrical imitation.

The object of dramatic poetry is action; but one can observe how poetry in the theatre is powerless to attain its objective to the full, and observe the constraints imposed on it on all sides in a domain in which, it would seem, dramatic poetry ought to reign supreme. Dramatic poetry can only set before one's eyes a mediocre action, watered down and cut about; whether from a question of suitability or from practical impossibilities, it most often remains half way from its goal. There are two sorts of events over which dramatic poetry has only a precarious and contestable power, or else it only manages to give expression to them by a circuitous route: certain feelings that have reached fever pitch, and the fantastic element. [pp. 342–5]

[.    .    .]

## Conclusion

Poetic language and musical language, travelling such different paths, search for each other, catch up with each other, and after a series of misunderstandings, gropings and difficulties, are united in order to collaborate on a grandiose work.

They develop first of all in opposite directions, more and more do they separate the two powers of expression contained in the original language, and end by creating two territories completely foreign to one another. The first, that of poetry, is the territory of the intelligible expressed by conventional signs, along with abstract images and a purely numerical rhythm. It is formed by *ideal imitation*. The second, that of music, is the domain of sensation expressed by instinctive signs, along with worked out images and rhythm; it is that of *real imitation*. Starting from the moment when its second historical evolution begins, the art of music seems to turn back to rationalism in creating a thought that will thenceforth give it its essential character and which cannot be reduced to any experimental notion. By this means, on the contrary, it strengthens its independence, affirms and ennobles its originality, since the thought that it is working upon has nothing in common with literary thought. It has sprung from a division of language, and it divides reason itself, and enriches psychology with a unique phenomenon.

And yet the two arts have need of each other; in transforming each other, they tend to rediscover each other. Even though her language remains ideal, poetry is already in the habit of transposing the ideas of reason into the impulses of sensibility, and the impulses of sensibility into the symbolism of imagery, that is into the indirectly reproduced sensation. At this point, poetry comes up against a barrier that worries her, and that she gradually, and with growing boldness and at the risk of a pitiful downfall, ends by wanting to cross. She strives to transpose her images into a direct imitation of the sensation itself. This tendency is borne out at first by the clumsiness of the imitative harmony of certain classical writers, then by the freely acknow-ledged pretensions of certain modern writers. With Lamartine, does not poetry flatter herself that she has become the 'universal' language and that she has taken hold of man 'by his total humanity', by his senses in the same way as by his imagination and his intelligence? To bring about this intention, the poet needs the help of the musician.

For her part, music likewise wishes to bring about a synthesis. What she lacks to achieve this, is precision. This is what satisfies common reason and what is usually to be found in literary language. She seeks to send a shaft of clear logic piercing into the realism and special thought in which she revels. The beginning of this evolution is believed to have been spotted in Beet-hoven's Ninth Symphony, hailed by certain critics as the dawn of a new era. In reality, there is not a single noted musician who has not required somewhat extensive help from the verbal language. Be that as it may, this tendency is daily becoming more pronounced. Music has abandoned those abstract regions in which she soared so high with certain great masters; she is approaching reality as if to gather it on to her wings. The fugue is no longer a scholastic exercise. The art of Bach from now on is turning towards the programmatic symphony and the drama. The musician needs the help of the poet fully to reach this goal.

Poetry and music can only form an effective union in existing side by side and not in substituting one for the other (according to the mistaken belief of the decadents and their predecessors). Also it could be said, in a general way and from a lofty standpoint, that this longed-for union implies, on both sides, a certain degeneration of the two languages. An art is at its peak when it has managed to give all possible independence to the resources of expression at its disposal, and especially when it has been able to create a mode of thought that is special to itself; it is in decline when it alienates its independence, even were it in order to replace convention by truth. We have seen what the poet and the musician have gained by their association, and also what they were losing or compromising in this two-sided game. The poet gives the musician objective clarity; the musician gives the poet real colour and movement, an expanded and definite rhythm, and the life that supports and complements the ideas. But to how many sacrifices and to what a subordinate role must the poet resign himself! The musician crushes him with his ringing voice, or subordinates him by imposing upon him a fresh idea which takes precedence; and supposing that the writer makes the necessary concessions without his part being torn to pieces, a great difficulty arises: it is the eternal bitter conflict between musical rhythm and poetic rhythm.

The musical genius is constructive; it cannot do without those symmetrical arrangements of phrases or groups of phrases that go to make up rhythm, in the lofty sense of the word. Not having of itself a meaning that is exact enough for the ordinary intelligence, it seems to make up for this by repeating phrases and fragments of phrases, which manage, thanks to their clever insistence, to convey a certain sense. But repeated phrases, except in some special cases, are repugnant to literary language; therefore it follows that one appears to be locked in the following dilemma:

Either music wishes to remain faithful to the laws of her rhythm, and then, not finding the literary text suited to the constructions she is fond of, she mocks it, treats it in a high and mighty manner, distorts it and turns it topsy-turvy in a thousand ways, in the manner of a Mozart, now fragmenting the line in order arbitrarily to repeat certain words or certain syllables, now gathering together a string of lines, in spite of their distinct meaning, into a rapid synthesis;

Or else music wishes to respect the poetic rhythm; then it is music's turn to give way; she loses what was charming to the ear, her relative clarity for the common intelligence, her higher interest in musical reason; she forsakes that beautiful organization which got the musician the name of 'composer'; she lapses into the monotonous dryness of the recitative or into the ambiguous compromise of the 'continuous melody'. She is like a statue of which we shall only ever have fragments.

For a long time, this conflict resolved itself to the benefit of the musician, by the systematic and complete sacrifice of poetic rhythm; in the theatre, by an error which was at the same time an injustice, concertos, trios, and quartets for voices were written, based on the unspeakable remains of vague versification. The conflict disappeared thanks to a scheme an example of which can be seen in the first scene of the *Damnation of Faust*: the tune alone – without ceasing for all that to be a melody – is sacrificed, that is, it agrees to follow the text faithfully and model itself on that; the orchestra keeps, among other functions, that of restoring to the music its freedom, and of offering to it wide enough scope for its rhythmic combinations. This arrangement has not merely the advantage of satisfying, by sharing things fairly, the exigencies of the two arts; it comes the closest to the truth, every time that the artist has to express certain strong passions. Melody, such as it was used in lyric drama even yesterday, had a capital fault, redeemed, it is true, by a peculiar charm: it suited the symphony extremely well, but it was scarcely dramatic.

Poetry and music are thus joined by a contract made of mutual concessions and compensations; they increase their power tenfold by the very diversity of two characters that complement each other; they are united in a synthesis of which analysis may find the mechanics extremely complex, but which offers grace, lightness, continuous and disciplined movement. And in this way they capture our ears, our reason now enriched by a new faculty, our better instinct, our heart. Their beneficial action has no precise limits – somewhat suspect perhaps in the view of the moralist, since the will is momentarily engulfed in such a total enjoyment – but it exalts our intelligence and gives their widest expansion to all our sympathetic faculties. A subtle cry, a true accent, a spot of colour, the rhythmic imitation of a detail, are all they need to make us thrill with that confused feeling of universal life. [pp. 419–23]

# Jules Combarieu

## *La musique, ses lois, son évolution* (1907)

## *Music, its laws and evolution*

*Source:*

Music, its Laws and Evolution (The International Scientific Series, ed. F. Legge, vol. 93) (London 1910). Introduction (pp. 5–9). First part – Musical thought and psychology – chapter V: Music and magic, §5 Conclusions of the first part (pp. 107–8). Conclusion (pp. 316–20).

### Introduction

[.  .]

If we wish to have an accurate idea of music, ought we not to formulate a system of study corresponding to what appears to be the normal order of facts; that is to say, to interrogate in turn these different sciences, each of which has the task of explaining a portion of our subject? We should, then, begin with acoustics, and end with what are called the moral sciences.

This method would be legitimate and fairly safe. A person who undertakes to speak or write on the art of music should begin by practising it; and, without going into too many details, we shall not fail to give here the substance of the programmes it suggests. But this order of research cannot form the plan of our work without three objections.

If we confine ourselves to tracing the material basis of music, from the moment when it is constituted outside ourselves to that in which it blossoms forth within us as a melody or a symphony, and to characterizing each stage of its evolution, we shall have at first nothing but juxtaposed ideas. The bird's-eye view needful to a 'scientific philosophy' would be lacking to us. In the second place, those ideas would appear contradictory to each other.

Lastly, we should run the risk of establishing our theory on very unstable foundations, because, in spite of the authority of the great scholars who have made so much progress in them since the eighteenth century, acoustics, and especially physiology, are yet very far from accepting, unconditionally, the principles with which these sciences have wished to supply the elementary grammar of music. Our first requirement, therefore, *in music* (and not in a sister-science such as acoustics) is an experimental basis of certainty.

A second method would be to consider the subject solely on historical lines, and to deviate from it only to draw conclusions. Beginning at the period of the earliest known appearance of music, its development throughout the ages could be described without troubling oneself about philosophic generalizations. Acoustics and physiology would be mere episodes in the path traversed; they would be introduced in their place in the succession of facts at the moment when they were formed into sciences – that is to say, rather late in the day. This long review once finished, an endeavour would have to be made to gain therefrom a bird's-eye view.

This last method is fascinating, because by it, instead of the theorist, the things themselves are, as it were, made to speak. It is, however, impracticable. If, before investigating any period of history, we do not begin by giving as exact an answer as possible to the question, *What is music?* how can we recognize, and, especially, how interpret the facts which interest us?

Our first task, then, must be to give a definition, and this we shall look for from the domain of psychology. Our starting-point can only be from the musical feeling itself, the state of mind, that is, of the average listener at the concert or the theatre during the performance of a symphony by Beethoven, Berlioz, or César Franck, an opera by Bizet or Wagner, one of Schumann's lieder or Chopin's nocturnes, one of those works, in fine, which, to use an old metaphor, 'inflicts on the soul a voluptuous wound and leaves the point therein'.

A good definition ought to be applicable only to the object defined. If, for example, we attribute to music any quality which may also be affirmed of poetry, our definition is worthless. What we ought to bring to light is the essential originality, or the *specific* difference.

We think that we shall satisfy this rule by stating that music is the art of *thinking in sounds*.

This primary notion, somewhat disconcerting to grammarians and psychologists of the ancient classical school, is arrived at, chiefly, by the use of contrasts, or by comparing thoughts expressed by music with those expressed by words. In everyday life, in literary work, or even when communing with ourselves, we use words; each of these words is the symbol of a concrete object, represented in our minds by an idea, or, as it is called in philosophy, a *concept*. If I say, 'the earth turns round the sun', I utter a thought made up of four concepts: the two material bodies, rotation on itself and movement round a point.

Our ordinary life is pervaded, filled, and directed by representations of a similar kind.

The originality of the musician consists in suppressing the concepts in the acts of the intelligence. Does he thus arrive at a vague formula? By no means. The elimination of words and the employment of the activity, pure and simple, of the mind in the linking together of sounds seems rather to favour the free exercise of thought, and sometimes even to allow it to become deeper. To the true musician music is more intelligible than speech; in fact, words may even obscure it. The sense of a beautiful passage from Bach or Handel can be rendered by no other language except that of sound, and in such manner only can it be properly grasped. Composers frequently write above a stave of music, for the guidance of the player, 'with expression'! – Expression of what? There is no need for such minuteness, and only mediocre musicians would condescend to such directions. Every good melody carries within itself its sense and its explanation.

To *think without concepts*, not for the losing sight of the objects the concepts represent, but rather to penetrate better their meaning; to dissolve that surface personality encumbered with words and turned outwards, which envelops and conceals one's true personality; to return to the state of nature, to the free disposal of oneself, to the ingenious and yet skilful use of our internal energies; to subtly intellectualize the sensitiveness and to pour into the intelligence a diffused emotion, so as to produce, as it were, a delicate emanation from both – such appears to me to be the privilege of music. [pp. 5–9]

[.    .    .]

## First part: Musical thought and psychology

### Chapter V: Music and magic

[.    .    .]

### §5    Conclusions of the first part

The conclusions to which this part of our studies brings us may be summed up as follows –

1st.  Music – a synthesis of sounds which must not be confused with purely sonorous phenomena – has a meaning untranslatable into verbal language; it is formed by a thought without concepts, rhythmically constructed, of which we cannot anywhere find the equivalent.

2nd.  It only translates emotions indirectly and by means of images organized in accordance with its proper technique.

3rd.  The only thing it is able to imitate or reproduce directly in passion is its dynamics; the power of expression which we attribute to it is founded on the following principle: Every movement represents to us the cause which produced it.

4th.  Primitive folk and the non-civilized races of today, in their magical operations, and, after them, the greatest philosophers and composers in Germany, have attributed to music a supernatural power which seems due to two causes: first to the absolutely special character, unique, and isolated in the internal life, of musical thought; then to the lofty generality of this emotional dynamics, which is not that of a certain given emotion, but that of life itself.

5th.  It is likewise true to say that music is a superior act of the intelligence and springs from the depths of feeling. As a matter of fact, emotion and thought are not clearly distinguishable.

We have thus ended the first part of our programme. We have defined music. We have now to explain it, to say whence it came, and how it came to be formed. As I said at the very beginning, it is, above all, the origins of the musical art and the rules of its use that are here in question [pp. 107–8]

## Conclusion

After so many incursions into fields where I must, at times, have shown more curiosity than actual knowledge or clearness, it is time to conclude.

In order to define music, we have taken as starting-point musical feeling, which has revealed to us that a melody, when really deserving the name, is a thought *sui generis*, without concepts, but as significant to the musician as is, to the literary man, a thought formed without concepts. From musical feeling we passed on to the study of sensation and of the physiological mechanism; there, two routes branched off which we have successively followed: on the one side, social life; on the other, objective nature. We have shown the relations of music to both.

Music is refractory to all analysis which wishes to explain its essence; it appears isolated amid the arts of painting and poetry. But if it be so, it is solely because it has connections, deep, and not superficial, with the individual, social, and cosmic life. The mystery which surrounds it is in no way due to its nature or its organization, it proceeds from life itself, which it expresses with deep penetration and in the most general form. It issues from a universal and deep-seated instinct of humanity; it is feeling and imagination; and it obeys those laws which rule things and living beings. If a part of its secret is hidden from us, it is that the secret of nature is unfathomable; even did we know it, we should be unable to express it in words.

We think, however, that we have established a clear principle founded on observation, and supplying in practice a sure criterion, by enunciating the following definition: *Music is the art of thinking in sounds.* If this be not granted, it will be impossible to understand a quartet of Beethoven, or any other musical composition; a phrase can no longer be distinguished from a simple, regular sequence of sounds; it cannot be explained in what way *Au clair de la lune* differs from an adagio of one of the great masters. Our definition embraces all the facts and sacrifices none. The composer of music-hall waltzes is a man who thinks in sounds as does a Bach or a Handel, only his thought is weak, superficial, trivial, poor and as far from that of Handel or Bach as that of an ordinary writer differs from the thought of a Leibniz, a Pascal, or a Bossuet. The Hottentot, who has only three or four notes in his melodies, also thinks in sounds, only his thought is (from our point of view) blurred, incomplete, and barbarous.

Many minds fashioned by classical education are loth to admit that thought is possible without the aid of words. Yet it is a fact which must strike an observer. I have endeavoured not to multiply the already very numerous points of view I have had to take up in this work, by examining the real value of verbal language as the expression of deep psychical life, but I will sum up my opinion in a few words: the *essential* nature of things (moral or material) cannot be defined; now verbal language, formed of very clear concepts, only acts by means of definitions. It, therefore, deforms all it touches.

Music, on the contrary, liberated from literary formalism and only borrowing from reality its most general dynamics, is more able to pass through the surface of things and to penetrate, more or less, into their inmost being. This causes it to be a very realistic and very valuable art, for, without it, many far-off phases of moral life would remain closed to us. But music is also a work of great imagination. It is not too much to say that it gives a plastic form to immaterial realities; without neglecting fundamental laws, it creates possible ones. It is flexible, diverse, and unequal; it is free, it has wings, like thought; in a word, it does what it will.

At every stage of our investigation – physiology, sociology, acoustics, mathematics – we have met with a system which claimed to stay us by forcing upon us its own explanation. But we simply, while keeping on our road, stored up 'contributions', and it is indispensable thus to set things right.

The student of acoustics who sought to explain musical art by that science alone would achieve very poor results. One might as well, in order to understand the poetry of Lamartine, simply study his manuscripts, note their caligraphic mannerisms, and interpret them after the manner of the graphologists. Sounds considered as mere matter certainly play, in a symphony, a more important part than the caligraphic style or the voice of the reciter does in poetry; but, however pure, agreeable, and regularly connected they may be, they do not, of themselves, constitute music.

The theory we are upholding – which, after all, only notes an evident fact, which we are unable to define fully – has no need whatever to call in metaphysical conceptions or to appeal to a vague mysticism. Musical thought is a form widely differentiated from our intellectual activity; but, by showing us its universality, history enables us to connect it with a primordial and persistent instinct of humanity, which is, no doubt, very apt for the dialectic of concepts, but has always required feeling, belief, and imagination for its existence.

We also know that the work of the musician, entirely permeated by social influences, is organized in accordance with general principles which overpass it and govern many other phenomena. We have discovered the same laws at various stages in life. We have, therefore, the right to draw conclusions as to the sentiment of one grand ensemble in which everything is connected by secret links.

In an article on music, in which all the conceptions of the Western world are again met with,[1] the Chinese Se-Ma-T'sien says: 'Music *comes from*

[1] *Mémoires historiques de Se-Ma-T'sien*, tr. with notes, Ed. Chavannes, Professor at the Collège de France (Paris 1889), vol. 3.

*within us* – music is *that which unifies*.' This twofold formula, in agreement with what has been said in former pages as to primitive magic and German philosophers, sums up the ruling thought of this book.

In a celebrated poem in his *Feuilles d'automne (Ce qu'on entend sur la montagne)*, Victor Hugo contrasts the voices of nature with those of humanity. Nature gives out a grand, peaceful and joyous music, and the world, floating in space, is wrapped in harmony. Humanity, on the contrary, gives forth a sound which grates, like one produced by a brazen bow on an iron lyre; it is no longer a symphony, but there are shrieks! A contrast easy to note, if in humanity we only view the conflicts of interests, mean passions, political storms, and social events, in fact, the superstructure, but if we penetrate to the permanent and universal base, there is no longer a dissonance, and there is a concert which should appeal to the poet's ear.

Without suspecting it we live, as guests of the cosmos, in the midst of a sublime harmony; and *it is not possible* for perfect accord not to exist between what is within us and what is all around us. The grandest function of music, by enlarging the ego and freeing it from all surface divagations, is to replace us in this harmony of which we have never the full consciousness, but to which we are insensible, because it is in us, and because without it we should not be. A lied of Schumann, a nocturne of Chopin, and a symphony of Beethoven, quite pure and without 'programme', have the privilege of emancipating us and plunging us again into the midst of universal harmony. An art such as this, in spite of the technical knowledge with which it has been enriched, is full of simplicity: it expresses, exalts, and magnifies the feeling of life which aspires to a higher state; and it is marvellous that so many things so coarsely indicated by analysis should be contained in a passing breath of air. . . . [pp. 316–20]

# Charles Lalo (1877–1953)

## Esquisse d'une esthétique musicale scientifique (1908)

French aesthetician. After studies and a doctorate at the Sorbonne, he was a schoolmaster and then from 1933 until his death held the chair of aesthetics at the Sorbonne. He was a founder of the Société française d'esthétique. Under the influence of positivism, he formulated his own 'integral aesthetics' – an approach to aesthetics which advocates investigations of the physiological, psychological and sociological components of a work of art.

## An outline of a scientific aesthetics of music

Source:

*Esquisse d'une esthétique musicale scientifique* (Paris 1908). Introduction – L'expression musicale (pp. 14–21). Translated by Jennifer Day.

### Introduction – Musical expression

#### Section 2

[.   .]

Sentimental or mystical aestheticians claim that the laws of a language are not part of, are not even the beginning of, the laws of poetry; and that perhaps the greatest poet is he who has never known what a line is. And in matters of aesthetics, from Plato right down to Tolstoy, mystics have been legion. Is the true poet the man who lives so deeply wrapped up in a dream world so profound and intense that nothing of it can reach us? It is a matter of definition. It is merely that since the man who lives in this inner world is not specially a poet rather than a musician or a painter or an architect, but he is all that at the same time and a lot of other things too; and since on the other hand that man of depth has more often than not no firm opinion on nor even any decided taste for all that is commonly called music, painting and poetry, we shall be excused from any further discussion about words.

There is no poetry outside language, music outside sounds, painting out-

216

side forms. So, language, sounds and forms are inseparable from their laws, because those are intrinsic to them and constitute their very nature. These essential elements are, on the contrary, readily separated from the accompanying feelings that they evoke: history would suffice to establish this by proving that their respective evolutions are not interdependent. The emotional states are not therefore essential to the aesthetic event.

Such is the thesis of the so-called formalist aesthetics in contrast with the mystical or sentimentalist doctrine of 'intuition' or 'expression'. The formalist theory is doubtless widespread, but it has never found a more justifiable application than in music.

It is not, however, that Hanslick's theory taken as it stands is satisfactory.[1] It consists of distinguishing two sides in the feelings said to be expressed in music: the ideas associated with them, and their dynamism, that is to say, the intensity or emotional impulse. Thus love differs of necessity from hate, regret or hope by descriptions linked with it: ideas of future or past, of attraction or repulsion in relation to a strange object. But these passions are incapable of differing in the slightest degree in intensity, in their development or in their unexpectedness, for example. Therefore these dynamic relationships are the only ones that pure music is able to express by the means that are special to it: sound patterns, intensity, timbre, or even rhythm. It follows that the so-called 'expressions' of hate and love, regret or hope, by pure music, will be absolutely indiscernible, or else their distinction will be essentially arbitrary and conventional. On the other hand, the violence, the persistence, the increase or the decrease, in short the dynamism of all these passions will be very well expressed; but it must be in the same manner for all indiscriminately.

This is why an untitled instrumental composition does not express any particular feeling: for that it would have to depict or describe objects or ideas. And a fragment of song in which the words have been changed immediately changes in expression without the slightest nonsense being apparent to a listener who had not been forewarned. 'I have *found* my Eurydice.' sang a joker to the famous tune of Orpheus lamenting the loss of his heroine. The most fervent disciples of 'expression', like Gluck, have themselves often put forward the examples of these palinodes or these misinterpretations; the history and success of their misadventures thus refutes their own theory by absurdity. So-called expression, being changeable, is quite subjective, arbitrary and secondary. Descriptive or evocative music, programme music, are the product of an impure taste, or even of an anti-aesthetic state of mind.

---

[1] E. Hanslick's *Von Musikalisch-Schönen*, approved of by Helmholtz in his *Lehre von den Tonempfindungen*, was followed in Germany by more or less direct adaptations of Herbart's general formalism: O. Hostinský (*Das Musikalisch-Schöne und das Gesamtkunstwerk*, 1877), Lazarus, Zimmermann, Siebeck, and Fechner (see P. Moos, *Moderne Musikästhetik in Deutschland*, Leipzig 1902, pp. 79–179), and in France by C. Beauquier (*Philosophie de la musique*, 1866, chapter vii; *La musique et le drame*, 2nd edn, 1884, chapter i).

In short the only truly musical interest lies in two single elements, according to Hanslick: the perception of the form, a sort of arabesque of sounds; that is formalism; and the perception of the dynamics, that is, of the intensity and evolution of moods that are indeterminate in their quality; that is dynamism. As for precise feelings, this third factor only comes into the question in the bad taste of those who do not understand music in itself and do not listen to it for itself.

The sentimentalists put forward, so it seems, two kinds of objections to formalism. The first is a blunt and rather ill-founded denial; the other is derived much more intelligently from the historical point of view.

The triple distinction of the form, the dynamism and the factors determining the feelings is, it is said, arbitrary and much too formal: those associations of ideas deemed to be secondary are in reality inseparable both from the dynamism and from the musical form itself. For example, we cannot prevent our universal experience from associating the idea of spatial height with the pitch of sound, or that of depth or intensity of a sound with that of mass or physical or moral strength. We thus of necessity associate certain images with the dynamic and also with the form of the musical elements. Certain feelings are even directly bound up with the phenomena of sound rather than with any other, as has been recognized since Aristotle; are not consonance, harmony and dissonance for example pleasant or unpleasant by themselves? Music is therefore able to describe or suggest; and not only can it do so, but it must do so, for here music has a far more lofty aim than the simple game of combining patterns of sound, which is not worthy of engrossing music totally. Formalism's only *raison d'être* therefore is simply a clever device, an arbitrary division of what, according to nature, cannot be divided.

This objection has no foundation: for the relative independence of the elements distinguished by formalism is an indisputable fact. The feeling expressed by the work of art, and in which so many aestheticians want in a confused way to see the whole of art itself, is trebly vague in comparison with that genuinely experienced by both the public, the composer and the performers. For the feeling can equally well represent: either the mood people are actually in at the moment; or a diversion, a sort of remedy for that actual mood; or their ideals, which by definition are not real. What is, what is to be, what is not; realism, idealism or game: there are the three psychological subjects of aesthetic activity. They can exist equally well, successively or perhaps even simultaneously in the same man, at any rate in the same public. A survey carried out on the audience of a big concert would be completely convincing in this respect, to the extent of being useless: for one can guess what diversity there would be in the response. A certain Beethoven symphony seems unequivocally to express unbounded joy; but the sketches for it and the composition are contemporary with the gloomiest periods of his life. It is pointless to give a multitude of examples. Apart from the three big categories of importance that we have pointed out, the art of music and perhaps the whole of art, is absolutely *vague* with respect to the feelings, moreover genuine ones, that it excites, soothes or inspires both in the public, the composer and the performer.

A handful of critics, being better informed, instead of persistently rejecting the movement in spite of the facts, have resolutely adopted the historical point of view: they show that changes of expression in the course of evolution, such as for instance those provided by the contradictions in the work of Gluck, do no more demonstrate the absence of any precise expression in the music, than the almost complete change in the meaning of certain words since the sixteenth century proves that the words have no definite expression. It has been said that not only is sentimentalism not put completely in the wrong by this evolution of feeling, but on the contrary it is formalism that is incompatible with this evolution; for the idea of an evolution of the moods awakened by music exactly supposes that in the first place the emotions play a fundamental part in musical life.[2]

This consideration is definitely a fruitful one; on condition, however, that one establishes this historical law, which people take care not to do and which we shall attempt. But the argument, excellent in itself, does not come down for or against formalism or sentimentalism. It only demonstrates the necessity for a historical viewpoint of evolution; we would rather say: a sociological viewpoint. This new factor alters the question considerably. And basically, what formalism has so far lacked in order to be able to explain all the facts is perhaps merely the sociological element.

This element in fact can help to settle the question. It introduces firstly the idea of society, then the idea of laws in evolution. What cannot be distinguished in psychological reality, can be so in aesthetic reality: because the latter is many-sided, and at the least two-sided: psychological and social. On the other hand, outside the material and rudimentary necessities, which are vital to any organism, what is aesthetically pleasing in one age may not be so in another. It is *natural* that a passage moving from low to high-pitched sounds awakens in us the idea of a physical or even a mental elevation. But that is not necessarily *aesthetic*. There are times when these sorts of picturesque or sentimental associations are judged to be in bad taste, that is, relatively ugly or unaesthetic: those are classical periods, when 'art for art's sake' is alone counted as beautiful. There are other times when on the contrary such effects are much sought after, when they alone are counted as aesthetic and when the simple play of sound patterns ceases to offer the slightest interest: those are the periods that follow and even in another sense precede the classical period.

Thus the psychological expression of sounds may be everywhere present by the fact of associations that have become practically inseparable. But it can be inartistic to evoke them; they can remain unaesthetic, repressed in the shadows of the 'aesthetic awareness'. They can also, on the other hand, form an integral part of the technique, and even become in themselves the goal of art, so much so that it conjures up their appearance or even supposes them to be

[2] R. Louis, *Der Widerspruch in der Musik* (Leipzig 1893), p. 14.

there where they are not, by some trick. Such is the leitmotif or verbal programme. But the existence or negation of such procedures is not a permanent question of principle, it is a question of age within evolution.

Consequently formalism and sentimentalism are not two theories of absolute value, revolving around a single fact and therefore incompatible; they are two notions of two different facts; two excessively abstract theories, which consist of setting up two facts to the status of laws, or two moments in time as absolutes. In reality, the first forms the theory of the classical school; the other of the romantic school. Both are true, but each for a different moment in history. It is true that precise suggestions really are and must be part of the aesthetic idea of the romantic; and it is equally true that this same suggestion would lessen the aesthetic value of a work, according to classical taste.

The fault of any partial theory is merely that of setting itself up as absolute. If one enriches each of these narrow-minded notions by superimposing on each the sociological point of view then the formalists are not necessarily 'atheists towards musical expression', as was commented by an 'enemy of music', who, believing he was exalting 'real music' to the level of a deity, was merely full of superstition; and sentimentalism is not necessarily superstitious, if it becomes aware of its rightful significance, which has its limits. When properly understood, the two opposing doctrines are reconciled in a superior synthesis: the integral aesthetic.

Thus the idea of evolution determined by laws and of sociological aesthetics brings a new clarity to this dispute and to a certain extent keeps the adversaries apart. This idea appeals at the same time to both atheism and superstition. However it does not, with idle amateurishness, leave the two theories face to face, by attributing to them a value that is necessarily equal. They keep themselves to themselves like the two ages they represent: classicism and romanticism; the one sound, normal and 'normative' – something like an ideal that has been realized – the other disorderly, excessive, morbid. In the matter of art as in all human things, it is always the sociological point of view that is the definitive one, because it is the synthesis of all the others.

If therefore formalism seems to us to be a superior doctrine, it is not particularly for personal reasons of taste, although when these are based on history they may have an objective value. It is most particularly because in its deliberate psychological vagueness, it allows full rein to the various possible sociological determining factors: thus on its own it can lend itself to the expression of all the historical facts.

Finding its doctrine limited, does one wish to make up for it by imagining that, for lack of precise feelings, music can express directly relatively vague moods, that have been narrowed down for example to the two extremes between which all emotive tonality evolves: joy and sorrow, with the neutral shades in between? Here are comparatively clearly defined states, since they are in no way interchangeable; and yet they are without precise purpose. Would not one have to be completely and utterly tone-deaf to confuse a funeral march with a triumphal fanfare?

However, the sociological facts must make the aesthetician extremely circumspect in face of these absolute affirmations, moderate though they may be. Too often, in fact, a historical knowledge of variations can alone make us guess at the presence of more than psychological forces. So, the direction given by social facts to psychic laws may go so far as to turn their position completely upside down. Just as we cannot say a priori where the action of the mental on the physical stops in the matter of suggestion, similarly we cannot put an arbitrary limit on the impact of sociological facts and the reciprocity of action that links them to individual events.

Too narrow and too absolute a theory of expression would make us believe that sadness is invariably linked to low sounds and slow rhythms, which is borne out by the usual practice of our funeral marches. Yet, it is a fact, the Ancients and the Orientals assign to the expression of sadness high-pitched voices and quick rhythms.

Similarly we readily believe that the minor is linked psychologically and absolutely with a feeling of sadness; modern dualism for example presents it in this way. Now the minor [mode] conveyed the calm and strength of the Dorian, the national mode of the Greeks; it seems in no wise to be connected with sadness in the Middle Ages and Renaissance, where it is still predominant. What is a normal part of technique will not do to express sorrow, which is the abnormal element in life above all else. The Dorian mode is still preponderant in the seventeenth century and even at the beginning of the eighteenth or in many popular songs, so can one say without being naive that it expresses sadness in the dance music of periods which have nothing particularly melancholy about them; or are certain peoples always supposed to be sad?

It is only when the cadences of modern harmony had positively established the major as more natural and spontaneous to our ears, that the minor became a less natural mode, almost abnormal. It is for this reason that it was once again preferred by a few sophisticates, like Chopin, Mendelssohn or Schumann, whose characters if not their art try to be romantic, and who consequently seek out the rare and the exceptional. The emotive tone of the minor, engendered by its predominant or rare use within a given technique, and not by an immutable property of the psychological elements, is therefore in spite of appearances of a sociological rather than a psychological nature.

Thus, perhaps the dynamism of Hanslick when well understood is the wisest and most liberal solution, because it allows one to make room for any well-proven historical variation. [pp. 14–21]

## 2.1.2    The impact of Wagner

## Introduction

This section is not intended to give a complete account of the reception of Wagner's music in France; the history of French musical criticism on Wagner is a separate issue – and an extremely complex one, considering all the intrigues, prejudices, differences of opinion, social and political factors involved in it. The aim here is rather to present an outline of what is known as *wagnérisme*, that is to say, Wagnerian influence exercised through an essentially literary infatuation with his ideas. But the first excerpt, Berlioz's 'Concerts de Richard Wagner', stands somewhat apart from this central theme; it is included to illustrate an individual response to Wagner, unaffected by any wider ideological issues, in contrast to the other contributions, in which literary or philosophical motives predominate.

The first significant French criticism of Wagner came from F.-J. Fétis in a series of articles in the *Revue et gazette musicale de Paris* in 1852, which were essentially an attack on his theoretical works. Fétis may have been right to warn his readers that Wagner was strongly inclined to self-adulation, but his description of Wagner as a positivist and his view that the *Gesamtkunstwerk* revealed a positivistic striving towards completeness were very wide of the mark:

All the evidence shows that M. Wagner is one of the followers of this philosophy of positivism of which the founder in France is M. Auguste Comte, and who has as his spokesmen in Germany some of the pupils of Hegel. Like him these philosophers suppress the genius and put in its place the action of the vital force, like him they reject the ideal and, finally, like him they want to limit tender emotions and imagination in favour of the clarity of ideas. Unity is the goal of the positive philosophy, this too is the unity which M. Richard Wagner is seeking in his fusion of music and poetry into one single language.[1]

His criticism of Wagner's music is concerned mainly with the novelty of its sound and its techniques, and this was also the line of approach taken by Berlioz some eight years later on the occasion of the three orchestral concerts of Wagner's works conducted by the composer in the Théâtre des Italiens in January and February 1860.

The fact that the article contains a mixture of approval and disapproval, that acceptance of some of Wagner's techniques is followed by rejection of

[1] F.-J. Fétis, 'Richard Wagner', *Revue et gazette musicale de Paris*, vol. 19 (1852), p. 259.

others, does not necessarily indicate that Berlioz was inconsistent or that he had failed to understand Wagner's aims. The essay is above all the spontaneous response of a practising artist to innovations adopted by a fellow-composer, so that dissent is inevitably registered when his own expectations are not fulfilled. Such criticism is no doubt severely restricted in its scope, but it has at least the merit of concentrating on Wagner's music without attempting to come to grips with his ideas.

Ideas rather than music were of crucial importance in attracting a number of important French literary figures to Wagner between the early 1860s and the late 1880s. These ideas, whether or not they were fully understood, coupled with the name of Wagner and the symbolic significance of Bayreuth in European culture, were frequently used in the protracted battle against positivism in those years, and all played a part in shaping the symbolist theory of art. Positivism had sought to inject scientific precision into criticism, and its view of art was largely determined by matters which are ultimately non-artistic, such as history, geography or social relevance. There were signs of a reaction against this approach among certain French idealists in the late 1850s, and Baudelaire's writings, both as poet and critic, stress the role of imagination, fantasy and freedom in artistic creation. Whereas the positivists tended to see Balzac as a realist and an observer, Baudelaire proclaimed: 'All his stories have the rich colour of dreams.'[2] The word 'dreams' (les rêves) is vital here, since it diverts attention away from the quasi-scientific representation advocated by the positivists and towards the understanding of art as the product of fantasy. Equally significant is the term rêverie, not only in Baudelaire (see below, p. 236), but also in the subtitle of Mallarmé's essay on Wagner (see below, p. 242), both instances being linked to the anti-rationalist tradition going back to Rousseau's Rêveries du promeneur solitaire.[3] However, dreams and fantasy in no wise denote anarchy in the production of a work of art. What must impress itself on the reader is the sense of freedom from constraint, the effect of a dream – but this must be brought about by scrupulous attention to detail in the process of creation. For a poet, this means a highly wrought and deliberate use of language: 'Handling a language with skill is to practise a kind of evocative witchcraft.'[4] This witchcraft is responsible for revealing hidden correspondences between words, colours, sounds. Baudelaire speaks of this in his essay on Gautier and it forms the theme of his sonnet Correspondances, the fourth poem in Les fleurs du Mal. Significantly, this poem is quoted in his essay on Wagner. Similarly, he quotes from programme notes by Wagner and Liszt, but does not take these as secondary products of a tendency to verbalize the effect of music; he sees them rather as proof that there exists a link between literature and music: Wagner's achievement was the realization of the yearning for correspond-

[2] Charles Baudelaire, 'Théophile Gautier', English tr. in Selected Writings on Art and Artists (Harmondsworth 1972), p. 274.
[3] See A. G. Lehmann, The Symbolist Aesthetic in France 1885–1895 (Oxford 1968), p. 81.
[4] Baudelaire, p. 272.

ences expressed in his poem. A connection was thus established between a particular type of literary sensibility and the music of Wagner, and when in the early 1880s German idealist philosophy and that of Schopenhauer in particular came to assume central importance for the anti-positivist literary avant-garde, Wagner was adopted as an intellectual and spiritual model. Yet this adoption did not mean that his ideas were fully comprehended by or that his music was entirely familiar to all the participants in the symbolist movement. Wagner became a label, a slogan with which to declare one's allegiance to a literary movement which emphasized the 'musicality' of poetry and sought to make poetry an expression of the 'Idea', a concept borrowed from Schopenhauer. The symbolist notion of the unity of diverse art-forms went further than Baudelaire's *correspondances*, but discussion of such distinctions belongs essentially to literary criticism.

If the first stage of the reception of Wagner in France is represented by Baudelaire's essay, the second may be seen in the reports on performances of Wagner's works which Catulle Mendès and Judith Gautier sent back from Germany in the late 1860s and early 1870s, as well as in the pages of the *Revue des lettres et des arts* which Villiers de l'Isle-Adam edited during its short run between October 1867 and March 1868. The third phase coincides with the publication of the *Revue wagnérienne* between 1885 and 1888 under the editorship of Édouard Dujardin (1861–1949). Dujardin, who was only twenty-four, adulated Wagner with all the enthusiasm of youth, but the appearance of his review came at the high point of the attempts to formulate the symbolist theory of art, with the result that he managed to gather around it a group of eminent men of letters, most of them much older than himself. What attracted the symbolists to Wagner was his use of myth and symbol and his concept of the *Gesamtkunstwerk*; this meant that his impact in France had such a predominantly literary flavour that any influence he may have exercised on French music was filtered through a layer of literary interpretation. In fact, several of the contributors to the *Revue* were only vaguely imbued with the 'spirit of Bayreuth', since few of them had enough German to read Wagner in the original, and at the time hardly any of Wagner's prose writings were available in translation – even among the operas, of the later works only *Tristan* and *Parsifal* had appeared in French (the *Ring* was not translated until the 1890s).[5] Consequently, the symbolists, in order to understand Wagner, had to rely mainly on two books in French, neither of them reliable guides to the maze of his ideas: Édouard Schuré's *Le drame musical* (1875) and Judith Gautier's *Richard Wagner et son oeuvre poétique, depuis 'Rienzi' jusqu'à 'Parsifal'* (1882). Apart from that, only Houston Stewart Chamberlain was readily accessible to them.

Since Wagner was a pretext rather than an object of serious study, the *Revue* offered some highly personal interpretations of Wagner's thought. Mallarmé, for instance, in the essay Dujardin persuaded him to write, shows

---

[5] See Léon Guichard, *La musique et les lettres en France au temps du wagnérisme* (Paris 1963), pp. 326–7.

extreme ambivalence. He recognizes that Wagner's attempts at artistic synthesis bring him close to his own aspirations, but he rejects his reliance on myth as an aspect of history because it imposes restrictions on the independence of poetic imagination, the French mind being in his view essentially abstract, hence poetic in his sense of the word. This veiled suggestion of the imperviousness of French art to German influence later receives a much more elaborate expression in Cocteau's *Le coq et l'arlequin*.

The literary critic and music historian Théodore de Wyzéwa took it upon himself to expound Wagner's ideas for the benefit of the readers of the *Revue*, but he often went so far as to attribute to the composer views which he did not in fact hold.[6] But it is interesting to note that Wyzéwa presented a historical interpretation in which the appearance of Wagner's music appears as the culmination of a long process: this historical angle is given more prominence than the unique and individual factor in artistic creation. This method seriously undermines Wyzéwa's attempt to provide a justification of the symbolist mode of thought, and on the whole it is, as A. G. Lehmann points out, too systematic to account for the complexity of symbolist reactions to Wagnerian music drama.[7] On the other hand, Wyzéwa's historicism helps him to avoid the danger besetting various other contributors to the *Revue*, who simply used Wagner as an excuse for pouring out their own subjective feelings: at least Wyzéwa relates him firmly to the development of opera from Lully onwards. By stressing the evolution of French music, he may in fact have contributed to the eventual decline of Wagner's influence in France, since it came to be felt that French music could only progress on the foundations of a French tradition. But it remains true that Wagner served as a catalyst in the formation of that belief by becoming not only an object of adulation but also a touchstone against which ideas had to be tested. This latter process is clearly visible in Debussy's career.

The eclectic nature of the *Revue* is well illustrated by the appearance in its pages of the article in which Émile Hennequin sought to establish a link between Wagner and Spencer's theory of art. Strongly influenced by a 'scientific' attitude to art in some ways akin to positivist pretensions, Hennequin was nevertheless *persona grata* among the symbolists, perhaps because of his preferences in literature, notably his interest in E. A. Poe, who, after being championed by Baudelaire, was one of the tutelary deities of symbolism. The application of Spencerian doctrine to Wagner is perhaps no more than an arbitrary ploy to attract attention to his own ideas by drawing the name of Wagner into the argument.

In themselves, the texts from the *Revue* make somewhat disappointing reading, since the main conclusion they lead to is negative, namely, that it is very difficult to reinterpret Wagner outside the context of mid-nineteenth-century German ideas; apart from that, they simply indicate that Wagner affected artistic sensibilities rather than scholarly and critical attitudes. At

[6] See Lehmann, pp. 194–206.
[7] Lehmann, p. 206.

best, the *Revue wagnérienne* is thus only an accompaniment to literary achievement of a much higher order, represented by the writings of Baudelaire, Villiers de l'Isle-Adam and Mallarmé. Moreover, it is through poetry that literary Wagnerism becomes an important influence on what, for want of a better term, is still labelled musical impressionism.

# Hector Berlioz

# 'Concerts de Richard Wagner, la musique de l'avenir' (1860)

In common with several other prominent nineteenth-century composers Berlioz possessed a fine literary taste and cultivated an expressive and flowing prose style. Unlike Wagner he never tried to establish his own aesthetic theory, and unlike Schumann he did not enjoy an extended period of editorial power. His experience as an editor was confined to a period of ten months, from August 1836 to May 1837, when he stood in for Maurice Schlesinger as the editor of the *Gazette musicale*. Between 1823 and 1863 he contributed essays, criticism and reviews to some sixteen Parisian periodicals. By far the largest number of his prose texts appeared in the *Journal des débats*. Three anthologies of essays appeared during Berlioz's lifetime and have since then been understood as entities: *Les soirées de l'orchestre* (1852), *Les grotesques de la musique* (1859) and *A travers chants* (1862). Berlioz often resorts to parody, dialogue, lively rhetorical exaggeration and satire, and the subtitle of *A travers chants: Études musicales, adorations, boutades et critiques* admirably sums up the nature of his writings.

# *Richard Wagner's concerts. The music of the future*

Source:

'Concerts of Richard Wagner' in H. Berlioz, *Mozart, Weber, and Wagner with various Essays on Musical Subjects*, tr. E. Evans (London 1918, repr. 1969) pp. 116–18; 119–21; 122–9. Berlioz's essay was first published in the *Journal des débats* of 9 February 1860 and later included in *A travers chants*. Wagner's response to Berlioz was first published in the *Journal des débats* of 22 February 1860. For the original French text see J. Tiersot, *Lettres françaises de Richard Wagner* (Paris 1935), p. 191–7; German translation in GS, vol. 7, pp. 82–6; English translation in *PW*, vol. 3, pp. 287–91.

[.   .   .]

He has ventured to compose the programme of his first concert exclusively of ensemble pieces; either choruses or overtures. This was, to begin with, a defiance of the habits of our public, who love variety. Under this pretext, they often show themselves ready to manifest a noisy enthusiasm for a little song, well sung; for an empty cavatina, well vocalized; for a violin solo, well bowed upon the fourth string; or for variations, well tongued upon some wind-instrument; after having given a kindly, but cold, welcome to some great work of genius. They evidently think that the king and the shepherd are equal during their lifetime.

There is nothing like doing boldly such things as are practicable at all. Wagner has just proved it; for his programme, although deprived of the sweets which allure children of every age to our musical festivals, was none the less listened to with a constant and very lively interest.

He began with the overture, *Der fliegende Holländer*, which is that of an opera, in two acts, which I saw performed at Dresden, under the direction of the composer in 1841;[1] and in which Madame Schroeder-Devrient played the principal part. This piece produced upon me the same impression then which it has just now done. It starts off with an overpowering orchestral burst, in which we fancy we at once recognize the howlings of the tempest, the cries of the sailors, the wind whistling through the rigging, and the stormy noises of the sea in fury. This commencement is magnificent; and it imperiously seizes the listener, and carries him along. But, the same method of composition being afterwards constantly employed, one tremolo succeeding another, and one chromatic-scale only ceasing in order to be immediately continued by another effect of the same kind, without a single ray of sunlight coming to break through these dark clouds charged with electric fluid, and incessantly pouring down their merciless torrents without the slightest melodious design coming to the relief of their black harmonies, the attention of the listener begins to wane, is then discouraged, and finishes by giving way. This over-ture, the development of which appears to me excessive, already manifests the tendency of Wagner and of his school not to take account of the *sensation*; and to recognize nothing but the poetical or dramatic idea required to be expressed, without troubling whether the expression of that idea obliges the composer or not to transgress musical conditions.

The overture, *Der fliegende Höllander*, is vigorously instrumented; and the composer has secured, at the onset, an extraordinary effect with the chord of the naked fifth. Presented in this way this sonority takes an aspect which is both strange and thrilling. [pp. 116–18]

[.    .]

The overture to *Tannhäuser* is, in Germany, the most popular of Wagner's orchestral pieces. Force and grandeur still reign supreme; but the effect of the method which the composer has chosen in this instance is, in my case at any rate, to produce an extreme fatigue. The overture commences by an andante maestoso – a sort of chorale of beautiful character, which, later on, towards the end of the allegro, reappears against a high accompaniment consisting of

[1] [Berlioz is in error here, he was in Dresden in 1843. See H. Berlioz, *Voyage musical en Allemagne et en Italie*, (Paris 1844), pp. 93–110, and *The Memoirs of Hector Berlioz*, tr. and ed. David Cairns (London 1977), pp. 302–3.]

an ostinato violin passage. The theme of this allegro, composed of two bars only, is but slightly interesting in itself. The developments to which it afterwards gives rise bristle with chromatic successions, and with modulations and harmonies of extreme harshness; precisely as in the case of the overture to the *Fliegende Holländer*. When, finally, the chorale reappears, its theme being slow and of considerable breadth, the violin passage which accompanies it right to the end is necessarily repeated so persistently as to be terrible to hear. It has already occurred 24 times in the andante; but, in the peroration of the allegro, we have it for 118 times more. This 'obstinate', or rather 'desperate', design figures, therefore, altogether, no less than 142 times in the overture. Is this not too much? It reappears again very often in the course of the opera, however; so that I am tempted to suppose that the author attributes to it some expressive signification relative to the action of the drama, which I am unable to guess.

The fragments from *Lohengrin* are distinguished by more striking qualities than the preceding works. It seems to me that they contain more novelty than those from *Tannhaüser*. The introduction, which takes the place of an overture for that opera, is an invention of Wagner producing a most remarkable effect. A visible idea of it is presented by the figure:

as it is, in reality, a slow and immense *crescendo*; which, after having attained its climax, follows the reverse progression and returns to the point from which it started, concluding with a harmonious murmur, scarcely perceptible. I do not know what relations exist between this form of overture and the dramatic idea of the opera; but, without concerning myself with this question, and considering it only as a symphonic piece, I find it admirable in every respect. There are no periods, properly so called, it is true; but the harmonic sequences which it contains are melodious and charming, whilst the interest never for a moment wanes, notwithstanding the extreme slowness of the *crescendo*, and that of the *diminuendo*. It is also a marvel of instrumentation, both in soft tints as well as in brilliant colours; and, towards the end, a remarkable feature is presented by the bass, which continues to rise diatonically whilst the other parts descend, and thus present an idea which is most ingenious. This fine piece, moreover, does not contain the least harshness; being as suave and harmonious as it is grand, strong and sonorous. I regard it as a masterpiece. [pp. 119–21]

[. . .]

I have not yet spoken of the instrumental introduction to Wagner's last opera, *Tristan und Isolde*. It is singular that the composer should have chosen to produce this at the same concert as the introduction to *Lohengrin*, considering that, in both, he has followed the same plan. Here, again, we have a slow movement, begun *pianissimo*, increasing gradually to *fortissimo*, and returning to the nuance of its starting point, without any other theme than a sort of chromatic sigh; but full of dissonant chords, the harshness of which is still further increased by extensive modifications of the real notes of the harmony.

I have read this again and again, besides listening to it with profound attention and an earnest wish to discover what it means, but am constrained to admit that I have still not the least idea of what the composer wanted to do.[2]

The above sincere account brings out sufficiently the grand musical qualities of Wagner, and seems to me to carry the conclusion that he possesses the rare intensity of feeling the interior warmth and power of will, as well as the faith which subjugates, moves and convinces. But it also implies that these qualities would have worked more effectively had they been united to more invention, less research, and to a more just appreciation of certain constituent elements of art. So much for the practical part of the question.

Now, let us examine the theories which are said to be those of his school – a school which is now generally designated by the name of 'music of the future' because it is supposed to be in direct opposition with the musical taste of the present time; and, also, certain to be found in perfect accord with that of a future period.

Both in Germany and elsewhere, opinions upon this subject have, for a long time, been attributed to me which I do not entertain. In the result, certain praise has been addressed to me which I could only interpret as blame; though I preserved a constant silence. But now, being in a position to explain myself categorically, no one I hope will consider that I ought still to keep silent, or halt in my profession of faith.

Let us proceed, therefore, with entire frankness, and avow certain precepts to which it may be hoped that the school of the 'music of the future' adheres.

'Music at the present day is in the force of its youth, is emancipated and free; is in a state of liberty to act.'

'Many old rules have no longer any force; having been formulated by inattentive observers or by plodding minds for the use of plodders.'

'Fresh needs have arisen; alike of the mind, heart and sense of hearing. These impose upon us new attempts; and even the occasional infraction of ancient precepts.'

'Several forms have been too much employed to allow of their being considered as any longer admissible.'

'*Everything is good*; or, *everything is bad*; entirely according to the use made of it, and the reason or motive by which such use is suggested.'

'In its union with the drama, or even merely with words intoned by the voice, music should always be in direct relation with the sentiment verbally expressed; with the character represented by the singer; and, often, even with the accent and vocal inflections which are most natural to the spoken word.'

[2] [Berlioz received from Wagner a copy of the full score of *Tristan und Isolde* in January 1860, at the time of Wagner's concerts in Paris. See Julien Tiersot, *Lettres françaises de Richard Wagner* (Paris 1935), p. 188.]

'Operas should not be written for singers; but singers, on the contrary, trained for operas.'

'Works written with the sole object of displaying the talent of virtuosi cannot aspire to be considered as compositions of more than secondary order, and of comparatively little value.'

'Executants are merely instruments; more or less intelligent, destined to reveal the form and intimate sense of works. Their despotism is at an end. The master remains the master. It is for him to command.'

'Sound and sonority are subservient to the idea. The idea is subservient to sentiment and passion.'

'Long, rapid vocalizations; ornamentations; the vocal trill; and a multitude of rhythms are irreconcilable with the general expression of all serious, noble and profound sentiment. It is therefore insensate to write for a *Kyrie eleison* (that most humble prayer of the Catholic church) passages liable to be mistaken for the vociferations of a group of topers round a tavern table. It is scarcely less insensate to employ the same music for an invocation to Baal by idolators, as for a prayer of the children of Israel addressed to Jehovah. It is most odious of all to take an ideal creation of the greatest poets, an angel of purity and love, and give it to a form of exclamation expressive only of depravity.' Etc.

If such is the musical code of the school of the future we belong to it, heart and soul, with profound conviction and the warmest sympathy.

But, then, everybody belongs to it. There is no one, nowadays, who does not more or less openly profess this doctrine; either entirely, or in part. Is there a master who does not write with full liberty? And who is there who believes in the infallibility of scholastic rules, unless it may be some timid old fellows who would be frightened at the shadow of their own noses?

But more still. It already has been so for a long time. In this sense, Gluck himself belonged to the 'school of the future'; for he says, in his famous preface to *Alceste*, that 'there is no rule that he has not felt justified in sacrificing readily in favour of effect'.[3]

And Beethoven, what was he, if not the boldest, most independent and the most impatient of all restraint amongst composers? Long even before Beethoven, Gluck had admitted the employment of 'upper pedals', or long sustained notes in the upper part; although they do not enter into the harmony and produce double and treble discords. He succeeded in drawing sublime effects from this act of boldness in the introduction of the infernal scene in *Orphée*; in a chorus of *Iphigenia in Aulide*; and, especially, in this passage of the immortal air of *Iphigenia in Tauride*: '*Mêlez vos cris plaintifs à mes gémissements*'.

M. Auber did the same, in the tarantella of *Muette*.[4] What liberties has

---

[3] [The whole text of Gluck's preface is in O. Strunk, *Source Readings in Music History* (New York 1950), pp. 673–5.]

[4] [*La muette de Portici*. The translation originally had the traditional Victorian title *Masaniello*.]

Gluck not taken with the rhythm? In the 'school of the future' Mendelssohn passes for a classic; but he, nevertheless, disregarded tonal unity in his beautiful overture *Athalie*; which begins in F, and finishes in D; though this was no more than Gluck, who commences a chorus of *Iphigenia in Tauride* in E minor, and finishes it in A minor.

We are all of us, therefore, in one respect, of the 'school of the future'.

But, if this school proposes to us the following precepts; the case would be different.

'We must always, always go contrary to the rules.'

'We are tired of melody, of melodic designs, of airs, duos, trios and of all pieces in which the theme is regularly developed; satiated with consonant harmonies; simple discords, prepared and resolved; and with modulations which are natural, and artistically regulated.'

'We have no concern with anything but the idea; and, therefore, care nothing for the sensation.'

'We despise the ear as a contemptible attribute, requiring to be tamed. The object of music has no reference to its pleasure. It must be accustomed to everything: to successions of diminished sevenths, ascending and descending, like troops of serpents, twisting and biting one another with a hissing sound; to triple discords, without preparation or resolution; to intermediate parts, obliged to go together without agreeing in respect of either harmony or rhythm, and which stand in one another's way; and to atrocious modulations, which introduce a tonality in one corner of the orchestra before the preceding tonality has departed from the other.'

'We should hold the art of singing in no esteem; not trouble about its nature or its requirements; and, in an opera, we need only think of the declamation, to the neglect of whether the intervals employed are unsingable, absurd or ugly.'

'No difference need be made between music destined to be read by a musician quietly seated at his desk; and that which has to be sung at heart, on the stage, by an artist obliged to give attention, at the same time, to his own dramatic action, and to that of the other actors.'

'We have not to concern ourselves with possibilities of execution.'

'If singers experience as much trouble in acquiring a part and accustoming their voice to it as if they had to learn a page of Sanscrit by heart, or swallow a handful of nutshells, so much the worse for them. They are paid to work and are slaves.'

'The witches in *Macbeth* were right: "Fair is foul, and foul is fair"; or, in other words, beauty is horrible, and ugliness beautiful.'

If the above correctly represents the new religion, I am far from professing it. I never have accepted such principles, nor do I now, nor shall I ever do so. I raise my hand, and swear: *Non credo.* [pp. 122–9]

[.    .    .]

# Charles Baudelaire (1821–67)
# 'Richard Wagner et *Tannhäuser* à Paris' (1861)

French poet and critic. After leaving the *lycée* Louis-le-Grand he spent some two years as a reluctant law student. His real education was gained through active contacts in the literary and artistic world of Paris. He started writing criticism in the mid-1840s and when his *Fleurs du Mal* appeared in 1857 he was probably better known as a critic than as a poet. Less than two years after the publication of *Fleurs du Mal* Victor Hugo wrote his celebrated appreciation of the poet in which he stated that Baudelaire's poetry had created 'a new kind of shudder' ('frisson nouveau'). His critical essays on Gautier, Delacroix, E. A. Poe, Flaubert, Wagner, Hugo and other contemporaries appeared in numerous Parisian periodicals (*Le monde littéraire, Le pays, L'artiste, Revue européenne, Revue fantasiste* etc.) and were posthumously collected in *L'art romantique* (1869) and *Curiosités esthétiques* (1868).

## Richard Wagner and Tannhäuser in Paris

*Source:*

'Richard Wagner and *Tannhäuser* in Paris' in *Selected Writings on Art and Artists*, tr. P. E. Charvet (Harmondsworth 1972, repr. Cambridge 1981), pp. 328–32; 342–5; 354–7). The essay was first published in *Revue européenne* of 1 April 1861 and later included in *L'art romantique*.

*For further reading:*

See Bibliography under Coeuroy, *Wagner* . . ., Guichard and Loncke.

I

[.    .]

I have often heard the opinion expressed that music could not claim to convey anything with precision, as words or paintings do. That is true to a certain extent, but it is not wholly true. Music conveys things in its own way and by means peculiar to itself. In music, as in painting, and even in the written word, which, when all is said and done, is the most positive of the arts, there is always a gap, bridged by the imagination of the hearer.

These are no doubt the reasons that led Wagner to look upon dramatic art

– that is to say the meeting point, the coincidence of several arts – as art in the fullest sense of the term, the most all-embracing and the most perfect. Now, if we disregard for a moment the help provided by plastic art, scenery, the embodiment in live actors of characters created by the imagination of the dramatist, and even song, it still remains beyond argument that the more eloquent the music is, the quicker and the more clear-cut will be the suggestions conveyed, the greater the chances that sensitive natures will conceive ideas akin to those that inspired the artist. Let me take the first example that comes: the well-known *Lohengrin* overture, of which M. Berlioz has written in technical language a splendid encomium; but for the moment I am proposing to content myself with testing its value by the ideas it gives birth to.

In the programme handed out at the time, at the Théâtre-Italien, occurs the following passage:

From the very first bar the pious solitary is waiting for the sacred vessel; his soul *soars to the infinite spaces*. Little by little, before his eyes unfolds an unearthly vision, which takes the shape of a body and a face. The outlines of the vision become sharper, and the *miraculous choirs of angels*, bearing the sacred cup in their midst, pass before him. The saintly procession comes nearer; his heart full to overflowing, God's elect is slowly uplifted in joy; his heart swells and expands; ineffable yearnings awaken in him; *he yields to a growing beatitude* as the *luminous apparition* comes even closer, and when at last the Holy Grail itself appears amidst the sacred procession, he *sinks in ecstatic adoration as though the whole world had suddenly vanished*.

Meanwhile the Holy Grail pours out its blessings on the saint as he kneels in prayer, and consecrates him its knight. Then the *brightness of the burning flame slowly softens*; in holy joy, the angel choir, smiling in farewell to the earth, ascends once more the heavenly heights, leaving the Holy Grail in the keeping of the pure in heart, *in whom the divine elixir is active*; what time the august choirs fade once more into the *depths of space*, whence they came.[1]

The reader will presently understand my purpose in italicizing some passages. But first let me take the book by Liszt, and open it at the page where the imagination of the celebrated pianist (who is both an artist and a philosopher) interprets in its own way the same piece:

This prelude contains and reveals the *mystical element* always present and always hidden in the work itself . . . So that we may learn the inexpressible power of this secret, Wagner first shows us the *ineffable beauty of the sanctuary* where dwells a God that avenges the oppressed and asks of those that believe in Him only *love and faith*. He reveals the Holy Grail to us; he displays to our gaze the dazzling temple built of incorruptible wood, whose walls are sweet-smelling, and doors of *gold*, whose lintels are of *greenish chrysolite*, whose columns are of *opal* and partitions of *cymophane*, whose resplendent portals are approached only by those of noble heart and unstained hands. Not in its imposing structural reality, but as if sparing the weakness of our senses, he shows it to us first reflected in *blue waters* or shimmering as though in an *iridescent haze*.

The effect at the outset is of a *broad slumbering surface* of sound, *an ethereal haze spread out* before us, so that our uninitiate eyes may see there the sacred vision; that

---

[1] [The text is related to, but not identical with, Wagner's programme note on the Prelude to *Lohengrin* in *GS* vol. 5, p. 179; *PW* vol. 3, p. 231.]

effect is entrusted exclusively to the violins, divided into eight sections, which, after several bars of harmonic tones, climb to the highest notes of their register. The theme is next taken up by the softest wind instruments; the horns and bassoons, joining in, prepare the entry of the trumpets and the trombones, which take up the melody for the fourth time, *with a blinding climax of colour*, as though at this unique moment the holy edifice *had shone* before *our blinded eyes*, in *all its brightness and radiating magnificence*. But the *sparkling brilliance*, brought gradually to this *intense degree of solar radiance*, dies down quickly, like a *faint celestial light*. The clouds, from the *transparent haze* they were, become opaque once more, the vision fades slowly in the same cloud of *iridescent* incense it had appeared in, and the music ends with a repetition of the first six bars, *more ethereal than ever*. The ideally *mystical character* of the prelude is particularly brought out by the orchestra's *pianissimo*, maintained throughout by the orchestra and scarcely disturbed by the brief moment when the marvellous outlines of the only theme the piece contains *shine forth* in the *clash of the brass*. Such is the image suggested to our senses, overflowing with emotion, as we listen to this sublime *adagio*.[2]

May I, in turn, relate, express in words, what my imagination inevitably conjured up from the same piece of music, when I heard it for the first time, with my eyes closed, feeling as though transported from the earth. I would certainly not venture to speak complacently of my reveries, were it not useful to bracket them with the preceding ones. The reader knows the aim we are pursuing, namely to show that true music suggests similar ideas in different minds. Moreover, a priori reasoning, without further analysis and without comparisons, would not be ridiculous in this context; for the only really surprising thing would be that sound could not suggest colour, that colours could not give the idea of melody, and that both sound and colour together were unsuitable as media for ideas; since all things always have been express-ed by reciprocal analogies, ever since the day when God created the world as a complex indivisible totality.

> La nature est un temple où de vivants piliers
> Laissent parfois sortir de confuses paroles;
> L'homme y passe a travers des forêts de symboles
> Qui l'observent avec des regards familiers.

> Comme de longs échos qui de loin se confondent
> Dans une ténébreuse et profonde unité,
> Vaste comme la nuit et comme la clarté
> Les parfums, les couleurs et les sons se répondent.[3]

[2] [Franz Liszt, *Lohengrin et Tannhäuser de Richard Wagner* (Leipzig 1851), pp. 48–50. German translation in F. Liszt, *Gesammelte Schriften*, vol. 3/2 (Leipzig 1899), pp. 90–2.]

[3] [Translator's note:] *Fleurs du Mal*. no. IV:

> Nature is a temple from whose living columns
> A sound of confused words comes forth;
> Man walks there in a forest of symbols
> Which look down upon him with familiar glances.

> Like echoes which merge in the distance
> Into a unity, dark and deep,
> As measureless as night, or day,
> Scents, colours and sounds correspond.

But to return to my theme, I remember the impression made upon me from the opening bars, a happy impression akin to the one that all imaginative men have known, in dreams, while asleep. I felt freed from the *constraint* of weight, and recaptured the memory of the *rare joy* that dwells in *high places* (be it noted that I had not at the time come across the programme notes I have just quoted from). Then, involuntarily, I evoked the delectable state of a man possessed by a profound reverie in total solitude, but a solitude with *vast horizons* and *bathed in a diffused light*; immensity without other decor than itself. Soon I became aware of a heightened *brightness*, of a *light growing in intensity* so quickly that the shades of meaning provided by a dictionary would not suffice to express this *constant increase of burning whiteness*. Then I achieved a full apprehension of a soul floating in light, of an ecstasy *compounded of joy and insight*, hovering above and far removed from the natural world.

You could easily establish the differences between these three interpretations. Wagner speaks of *a choir of angels bearing a holy vessel*; Liszt sees a *miraculously beautiful edifice*, mirrored in haze. My own dream is less adorned with material objects, it is vaguer and more abstract. But the important point in this context is to concentrate on the similarities. Even if they were few in number, they would still be proof enough, but by good fortune they are superabundant and striking even to excess. In the three versions we find the sensation of *spiritual and physical beatitude*; of *isolation*; of the contemplation of *something infinitely big and infinitely beautiful*; of an *intense light*, which is a joy to *eyes and soul to the point of swooning*, and finally the sensation of *space, extending to the furthest conceivable limits*.

No musician excels as Wagner does in *depicting* space and depth, material and spiritual. That is an observation that several of the most acute minds have often felt themselves compelled to make. He has the art of rendering by subtle gradations all that is excessive, immense, ambitious in both spiritual and natural man. Sometimes the sound of that ardent despotic music seems to recapture for the listener, against the background of shadow torn asunder by reverie, the vertiginous imaginings of the opium smoker.

From that moment, that is from the first concert, I was possessed by the desire to penetrate more deeply into an understanding of these singular works. I had undergone, or so at least it seemed to me, a spiritual operation, a revelation. My rapture had been so strong, so awe-inspiring, that I could not resist the desire to return to it again and again. My feeling was no doubt largely compounded of what Weber[4] and Beethoven[5] had already revealed to me, but also of something new that I was powerless to define; and that powerlessness produced in me a sense of vexation and curiosity mixed with a strange delight. [pp. 328–32]

[.    .    .]

---

4 [Translator's note:] 1786–1826.
5 [Translator's note:] 1770–1827.

**III**

[.   .   .]

At the beginning of this study I drew attention to the power with which in the overture to *Lohengrin* Wagner expresses the ardour of mysticism, the yearnings of the spirit towards God the incommunicable. In the *Tannhäuser* overture, in the struggle between the two opposing principles, he has shown himself no less subtle or powerful. Whence, one may ask, has the master drawn this frenzied song of the flesh, this total knowledge of the diabolical element in man? From the very first bars our nerves vibrate in unison with the melody; lustful memories are awakened sharply. Every well-ordered brain has within it two infinities, heaven and hell; and in any image of one of these it suddenly recognizes the half of itself. First come the satanic titillations of a vague love, soon followed by enticements, swoonings, cries of victory, groans of gratitude, then again ferocious howls, victims' curses, impious hosannas from those officiating at the sacrifice, as though barbarism must always have its place in the drama of love, and the enjoyment of the flesh must lead, by an inescapable satanic logic, to the delights of crime. When the religious theme, launching a renewed attack on sin let loose, gradually brings back order and gains the ascendancy, when it rises, in all its compact beauty, above this chaos of dying sensual joys, the whole soul feels refreshed and uplifted in redemptive beatitude; an ineffable experience which occurs again at the opening of the second scene, when Tannhäuser, after his escape from the grotto of Venus, finds himself back in life as it is, amidst the pious sound of his native bells, the humble song of the shepherd, the hymn of the pilgrims, and before him the cross planted on his road, emblem of all the crosses that have to be carried on every road. There is a power of contrast here that makes an irresistible impact on our minds and recalls the broad easy manner of Shakespeare. Shortly before, we were in the depths of the earth (Venus, as we mentioned, has her abode in the vicinity of hell), breathing a scented but stifling atmosphere, bathed in a pink glow that did not come from the sun; we were sharing the experience of the knight Tannhäuser himself who, satiated with enervating delights, *longs for suffering* – a sublime cry, which all professional critics would admire in Corneille, but which not one of them would care perhaps to recognize in Wagner. At last we are back above ground, breathing the earth's pure air, accepting its joys with gratitude, its sufferings with humility – poor humanity has been reunited to its homeland.

Just now, as I was trying to describe the sensual part of the overture, I asked the reader to close his mind to commonplace love songs such as a swain in high spirits might conceive them; and certainly there is nothing trivial here; rather it is the overflowing of a powerful nature, pouring into evil all the strength it should devote to the cultivation of good; it is love, unbridled, vast, chaotic, raised to the height of an anti-religion, a satanic religion. Thus in his musical interpretation the composer has avoided the vulgarity that too often accompanies the expression of the feeling, of all feelings, the most popular – I nearly said 'of the populace' – and to achieve that all he had to do was to express the overabundance of desire and energy, the indomitable, unrestrained ambition of a delicate soul that has taken the wrong road. Similarly in the plastic representation of the idea, he wisely discarded the irksome crowd of victims, the Elviras by the dozen. The pure idea, personified by the one and only Venus, conveys a clearer, more eloquent message. Here is no ordinary libertine, flitting from beauty to beauty, but man in general, universal man, living morganatically with the absolute ideal of love, with the queen of all the she-devils, the female-fauns and female-satyrs, banished below ground since the death of the great Pan; in other words the indestructible and irresistible Venus.

A hand more skilled than mine in the analysis of operatic works will, in this very number,[6] be offering the reader a complete technical description of this strange and unjustly neglected *Tannhäuser*. I must therefore content myself with general considerations, which, brief as they are, are nonetheless useful. Moreover, is it not more convenient, for certain types of mind, to judge of the beauty of a landscape by standing on a height, rather than by following in turn all the paths that run through it?

I merely wish to observe, to the greater glory of Wagner, that, in spite of the importance he very rightly ascribes to the dramatic poem, the overture to *Tannhäuser*, like that to *Lohengrin*, is perfectly intelligible even to the hearer unfamiliar with the poem; and further, that this overture contains not only the main idea, the duality of the soul, which constitutes the drama, but also the principal themes clearly emphasized, and designed to describe the general sentiments expressed in the body of the work, a fact that is clearly shown by the deliberate reintroduction of the diabolically sensual theme and of the religious theme or the 'Pilgrims' Chorus' each time the action requires it. As for the grand march in the second act, it long ago won the approval of the most rebellious minds, and the same praise may be applied to it as to the two overtures I have spoken about, namely that it expresses what it wants to in the most visible, the most colourful, the most representative manner. Who, one wonders, on hearing those rich proud accents, those graceful cadences and majestic rhythms, those royal fanfares, could imagine anything other than a feudal ceremony, a march-past of heroes, in gorgeous apparel, all of lofty stature, all men of will and simple faith, as magnificent in their pleasures as they are terrible in their wars?

What shall we say of Tannhäuser's narration of his journey to Rome, in which the literary merit of the piece is so admirably completed and sustained by the musical structure that the two elements combine to create an inseparable whole? Any fears one might have had about the length of the passage are dissipated by its invincible dramatic power, already noted. The sadness, the

---

[6] The first part of this study appeared in the *Revue européenne*; M. Perrin, the former director of the Opéra-Comique and well-known as a supporter of Wagner, is the review's music critic.

despondency of the sinner during his rough journey, his joy at the sight of the supreme pontiff who has the power to absolve sins, his despair when the latter shows him the irreparable nature of his crime, and at the end, the feeling, almost ineffable by its very terror, of joy in damnation; everything is told, expressed, translated by the words and the music in a manner so positive that to find another way of saying it all is well-nigh impossible. And so we can fully understand that a disaster of this magnitude can be reversed only by a miracle, and we can forgive the unfortunate knight for taking once again the mysterious path leading to the grotto, to recover at least the favours of hell at the side of his diabolical consort. [pp.342–5]

[. . .]

## IV

Setting aside for a moment, as can always be done, the systematic element which every great and deliberate artist inevitably introduces into his work, we then need to seek and assess the peculiar personal qualities that distinguish him from others. An artist, a man really worthy of that great name, must surely have in him something essentially *sui generis*, by the grace of which he is himself and not someone else. From this point of view, artists may be compared to a miscellany of flavours, and the store of human metaphors is not perhaps rich enough to provide approximate definitions of all known and all possible artists. We have already, I think, identified two men in Richard Wagner, the man of order and the man of passion. It is the man of passion, the man of feeling, I want to discuss here. In the least of his compositions his ardent personality is so evident that this quest for his main quality will not be difficult to pursue. From the outset, one point had struck me forcibly: it is that in the sensual and orgiastic part of the *Tannhäuser* overture, the artist had put as much power, had developed as much energy, as in the description of the mysticism that characterizes the overture to *Lohengrin*; the same ambition in the one and the other, the same titanic climbing of the heights, and also the same refinements, the same subtleties. What therefore appears to me to characterize above all, and in an unforgettable way, the music of the master is nervous intensity, violence in passion and in will-power. That music express-es, now in the suavest, now in the most strident tones, all that lies most deeply hidden in the heart of man. An ideal ambition, certainly, hovers over every one of his compositions; but if, by the choice of his subjects and his dramatic method, Wagner comes close to antiquity, by the passionate energy of his expression he is in our day the most genuine representative of modern man. And all the technical knowledge, all the efforts, all the strategy of this fertile mind are, in truth, no more than the very humble, the very zealous servants of this irresistible passion.

Whatever subject he handles, the result is a superlative solemnity of accent. By this passion, he adds to everything he touches an indefinable super-human element; by this passion he understands and makes others understand everything. Everything that is implied by the words will, desire, concentration, nervous intensity, explosion, is perceptible, may be apprehended through his works. I do not think I am deceiving myself or anybody else when I say that I see there the main characteristics of the phenomenon we call genius; or, at least, that in the analysis of all we have legitimately called *genius* until now, the very same characteristics are to be found. In matters of art, I confess I am not opposed to excess; moderation has never appeared to me the hallmark of a vigorous artistic nature. I like those excesses of robust health, those overflowings of will-power, which stamp themselves on a work like burning lava in the crater of a volcano, and which, in ordinary life, often accompany the phase, so full of exquisite delight, that comes after a great moral or physical crisis.

As for the reform the master wants to introduce in the application of music to drama, what will its result be? On that subject, it is impossible to make any clear prophecy. In a vague and general manner, we may say, with the Psalmist, that sooner or later those who have been humbled shall be exalted, and the exalted humbled, but nothing more than what is equally applicable to the known run of all human affairs. We have seen so many things, formerly regarded as absurd, that have later become models adopted by the crowd. The general public of today will remember the stubborn resistance met with, at the outset, by the plays of Victor Hugo and the paintings of Eugène Delacroix. Besides, as we have already observed, the quarrel which is now dividing the public was a forgotten quarrel, now suddenly revived, and Wagner himself had found in the past the first elements of the foundation on which to establish his ideal. What is certain is that his doctrine is just what is needed to rally all intelligent people long since tired of our Opera's errors, and it is not surprising that men of letters, in particular, should have shown sympathy with a musician proud to call himself both poet and dramatist. Similarly, the writers of the eighteenth century had acclaimed the works of Gluck, and I cannot help noticing that those who show the greatest dislike of Wagner's work also show a clear dislike of his precursor.

And when all is said and done the success or failure of *Tannhäuser* can prove absolutely nothing, nor even influence the chances for or against, in the future. Even supposing *Tannhäuser* to be a thoroughly inferior work, it could well have had a colossal success; and if we assume it to be perfect, it could just as well have been disliked. In point of fact the question of the reform of opera is not settled, and the battle will go on; there may be a lull, but it will flair up again. Recently I heard someone say that if Wagner scored a brilliant success with his opera, that would be a purely individual accident, and that his method would have no subsequent influence on the destiny and development of lyric drama. I feel entitled by my study of the past, in other words of the eternal, to say just the opposite, namely that a total failure in no way destroys the possibility of new experiments in the same direction; and in the very near future we might well come to see not only new authors but even men with established reputations profiting in some degree from the ideas expounded by Wagner and passing successfully through the breach opened by him. Where in history have we ever read of a noble cause being lost in one throw? [pp. 354–7]

# Extracts from Revue wagnérienne

## Stéphane Mallarmé (1842–98)

## 'Richard Wagner, rêverie d'un poëte français' (1885)

French poet. After leaving school he started as a clerical assistant, but at the age of twenty decided to become a teacher. During a stay in London in 1862–3 he obtained a certificate for teaching English and in the autumn of 1863 got his first teaching post as an English master at Tournon. After a spell at the *lycées* in Besançon and Avignon he moved to Paris in 1871 and taught there until his retirement in 1894. Behind this seemingly uneventful, even dull career was hidden a life of extraordinary intense literary activity. Mallarmé's output was relatively small but the intensity of his poetic expression and his inventive use of the French language make him the central figure of the symbolist movement in France in the late nineteenth century.

Mallarmé's criticism and his prose writings reveal the same quality of elusiveness and the intricate syntactical structure that characterize his poetry. The expression of the idea beyond the appearance of reality was for him the link that united music and poetry: 'Music and Letters are the alternative face, here extended towards the obscure; scintillating there, with certainty, of one phenomenon, the only one . . . the Idea',[1] said he in a speech delivered at Oxford and Cambridge in 1894 (later published as *La musique et les lettres*).

Mallarmé mentioned Wagner as early as 1862 in one of his essays and retained a life-long interest in Wagner's art and ideas. In a letter to E. Dujardin of 5 July 1885 he described his essay on Wagner as 'moitié article, moitié poëme en prose' ('half article, half poem in prose').

# Richard Wagner, a French poet's reverie

### Source:

'Richard Wagner, rêverie d'un poëte français', *Revue wagnérienne*, vol. 1 (1885), pp. 195–200. Translated by Rosemary Lloyd.

After its appearance in *Revue wagnérienne* the essay was included in its entirety in the collection *Pages* (1891), then in fragments in *Vers et prose* (1893) and then again in its entirety in *Divagations* (1897). This last version differs from the original one in small points of style.

### For further reading:

René Wellek, *A History of Modern Criticism 1750–1950*, vol. 4 (London 1965), pp. 452–63. See also bibliography under Austin, Bernard, Cooperman, Kravis (discusses in particular the style of Mallarmé's prose), and Lehmann.

[1] Translation taken from L. J. Austin, 'Mallarmé on Music and Letters', *Bulletin of the John Rylands Library Manchester*, vol. 42 (1959), p. 36.

A modern French poet, who, for a variety of reasons, is excluded from any participation in official displays of beauty, takes pleasure, as an outcome of a task undertaken – the mysterious refinement of poetry for solitary Celebrations – in reflecting on the sovereign pageantry of Poetry, such as cannot exist alongside the flood of banality borne along by the arts in our counterfeit civilization. – A Ceremony of a day which lies in the heart of the crowd, unknown to it: almost a Cult!

The certainty that neither he nor any of his contemporaries is involved in any such enterprise frees him from any constraints that might be imposed on his dream by a feeling of incompetence and the remoteness of the facts.

His gaze, untroubled in its integrity, penetrates the far distance.

It is easy for him, and the least he can do, to accept the heroic and solitary task of considering, in the proud coil of the consequences, the Monster-Which-cannot-Exist! Leaving in its side the wound of a pure, affirmative gaze.

Leaving aside his glimpses of the extraordinary but currently incomplete splendour of plastic figuration, among which Dance is outstanding at least in the perfection of its representation, for its elliptical writing alone can transform the fleeting and sudden into the Idea – such a vision includes entirely, absolutely entirely, the Drama of the future. If this art-lover considers what Music has brought to the Theatre, a marvel that music is best able to set in motion, he does not long remain immersed in his own thoughts. Already, with whatever bounds his mind leaps, it senses the colossal approach of an Initiation. Or rather, see if your wish has not already been realized.

What a unique challenge for poets, whose task he has usurped with the most candid and splendid bravura, this Richard Wagner!

The emotions inspired by this foreigner are complex, exaltation and veneration, but also a feeling of unease that everything should be done by other means than directly shining forth from the literary principle itself.

To reach a judgement one has to face the doubts and imperatives of perceiving what circumstances surrounded the Master's first attempts. He sprang up in the days of the only form of theatre which can be described as decrepit, so coarse are the elements of which its Fiction is formed: since that Fiction imposes itself directly and instantaneously, demanding that we believe in the existence of the character and the adventure – believe, simply, nothing more. As if that act of faith demanded from the spectator should not be the very result he extracts from the conjunction of all the arts giving birth to the miracle of the stage, which otherwise remains inert and void! you have to fall under a spell, to achieve which no means of enchantment implied by the magic of music is superfluous, in order to overpower your reason grappling with a simulacrum, and from the outset it is proclaimed: 'Let us suppose that all this really happened and you are right in the middle of it!'

Modern man scorns all demands to use his imagination; but since he is a past master at exploiting the arts, he expects every art to transport him to the point where a special power of illusion bursts forth and then he gives his consent.

Before the use of Music, Theatre was obliged to make its starting-point a concept which was authoritarian and naive, at the time when this new source of evocation was not available to its masterpieces, which, alas!, lay entombed in the pious leaves of the book, and none of which had any hope of surging forth from it at our celebrations. Theatre's mechanism remains attached to the past, or such that a popular representation would repudiate it because of that intellectual tyranny – for the crowd wants to remain master of its own belief, following the suggestions the arts provide. The simple addition of an orchestra changes the old theatre completely, annulling its very principle, and it is in a purely allegorical way that the current theatrical act, which is in itself empty and abstract, impersonal, must, if it is to move forward with any semblance of certainty, make use of the invigorating effluvia of Music.

The mere presence of Music is a triumph, provided it does not attempt to retain the old conditions, even with the aim of extending them sublimely, but bursts forth as the generator of all vitality. The audience will have the impression that if the orchestra stopped exerting its influence, the mime would instantly become a statue.

Was it possible for the Musician, the close confidant of his Art's secret, to confine its function to this simple initial aim? Such a metamorphosis demands the disinterestedness of a critic, who does not have behind him, ready to rear up with impatience and joy, the abyss of musical performance, which in this case is the most tumultuous a man has ever contained with his clear will.

This is what he achieved.

Going at once to what was most urgent, he reconciled an entire tradition, intact but on the point of falling into disuse, with what he divined to be welling up, pure and undetected, in his scores. Excluding perspicacity, that form of sterile suicide, the strange gift of assimilation existed in such lasting abundance in this creator in spite of all, that between two elements of beauty, mutually exclusive or at least unaware of each other, personal drama and ideal music, he was able to bring about a marriage. Yes, through a harmonious compromise, generating a precise theatrical phase which corresponds, as if by surprise, to the temperament of his race!

Although from a philosophical viewpoint it merely places itself alongside Drama, Music (I insist that someone intimate where it stems from, what its primary meaning is, and its destiny) penetrates and envelops Drama through the composer's dazzling willpower, and thereby links up with it. There is no candour or depth which, with an enthusiastic awakening, it does not pour forth to bring about that fusion, except that Music's own principle escapes.

What amazing sureness of touch to be able to fuse these diverse forms of pleasure on the stage and in the symphony without totally transforming either of them.

Now, indeed, a form of music which, apart from the observance of very complex laws, retains of that art at first only what is innate and elusive, blends the colours and outlines of the hero with the timbres and themes, in an atmosphere richer in Reverie than any earthly song, a deity clad in the invisible folds of a fabric of chords, or will carry the hero away on a wave of Passion, whose unleashing is too vast when directed at a single being, will hurl him and twist him and withdraw him from his notion, swept aside before that superhuman flood, only to make him seize it afresh when he dominates everything through song, a song which bursts forth, as it rends asunder the thought that inspired it. The hero, who treads not so much on our earth as on mist, will always be revealed in a distant prospect filled with the haze of laments, glories and joy emerging from the instrumentation, cast back by this means to the beginnings of time. He is effective only when surrounded, in the Grecian way, by that blend of stupor and intimacy an audience experiences when it is faced with myths which seem barely to have existed, so completely does their instinctive past melt away! But at the same time he constantly benefits from having the familiar outer forms of the human individual. Some forms even satisfy the intellect because they seem not entirely unconnected with random symbols.

Behold, enthroned on the stage, Legend.

With a prior piety, an audience on the second occasion since time began, the first being Greek, the second German, considers the theatrical representation of the secret of our origins. Some remarkable happiness, new and barbaric, establishes it: in front of that moving veil the subtle orchestration, magnificently decorates its genesis.

Everything is steeped anew in the primal stream: but without completely reaching the source.

If the French mind, which is strictly imaginative and abstract, and thus poetic, blazes forth, it will not be like this. In accordance with Art in all its integrity, for Art is inventive, the French mind is repelled by Legend. See how, from the days forever gone they retain no anecdote, enormous and rough hewn, as if they foresaw what Legend would bring, anachronistically, to a theatrical representation, the enthronement of one of the acts of Civilization.[1] That is, unless the Fable, devoid of any known place, time and character, appears, a product of the meaning latent in the concourse of all, the Fable inscribed on the page of the Heavens and of which History itself is merely a shadowy interpretation, namely, a Poem, the Ode. Could it be that the age, or our country, which exalts it, have dissolved Myths through thought, only to forge new ones! These are what the Theatre calls for, not myths which are fixed, or venerable or famed, but one, stripped of all personality, for it combines our manifold facets: and it is this myth that Art evokes, from the magic corresponding to our national behaviour, in order to reflect that behaviour in us. A Type without any preliminary name, so as to liberate a sense of surprise: his gestures draw together towards him our dreams of sites or edens, which the theatre of the past engulfs, in the vain

[1] Exhibition, Handing over of Powers etc. Do I see you there Brünnhilde, or what would you do there, Siegfried!

pretension of containing or depicting them. Do not think of the actor as an individual, or of the stage as having any precise location! (the double error, a fixed set and a real actor, in Theatre lacking Music): does a spiritual fact, the flowering of symbols, or their preparation, demand a place in which to develop other than the fictional focus of the crowd's gaze? Holy of Holies, but all in the mind . . . then, in some supreme burst of light, which arouses the Figure that is No one, there converges every mimic gesture that Figure seizes from a rhythm provided in the symphony, and setting it free! Then there come to breathe their last, as if at the feet of the incarnation, but an incarnation revealing a definite link between them and its humanity, those quintessences and natural summits which Music recreates, that ultimate vibrant prolongation of all things, like Life itself.

Man, and his true earthly abode, exchange reciprocal proofs.

Thus the Mystery is accomplished.

The City which provided a theatre for the sacred experience sets on the earth the universal seal.

As for its people, it was the very least they could do to testify to the august fact – I call as witness Justice which cannot but reign there – since that orchestration, which a moment since revealed the presence of the god, never produces anything other than the synthesis of those moments of delicacy and magnificence, immortal and innate, which are present unknown to all whenever a silent audience assembles.

That is why, Genius!, I who in my humility remain the servant of an eternal logic, o Wagner, I am filled with suffering and self-reproaches, in those minutes marked by lassitude, because I cannot count myself among those who, wearying of everything in their search for definitive salvation, go straight to the edifice of your Art, which for them is the end of the journey. That undeniable portico offers, in these days which are not times of jubilation for any people, welcome shelter from our own insufficiencies and the mediocrity of our homelands; it exalts some fervent devotees to the point of certainty; for them this is not the greatest distance towards the goal ever ordained by a human gesture, which they run with you as guide, but the completion of Humanity's voyage towards an Ideal. At least, for I want my share of the ecstasy, you will allow me to enjoy a moment of rest in your Temple, half-way up the holy mountain, whose sunrise of truths, the most comprehensive yet, fills the dome with its fanfare and invites, as far as the eye can see from the parvis, lawns trodden by the feet of your chosen brothers: it is as if the mind were set apart from our harrying incoherence, and sheltered from the too lucid obsession with that menacing pinnacle of the absolute, whose outline can be divined in the parting of the clouds on high, fulgurating, bare and alone: which looms above and beyond and which, it seems, no one is to scale. No one! the word does not strike remorse into the heart of the passer-by drinking at your convivial fountain.

# Théodore de Wyzéwa (1862–1917)
# 'La musique descriptive' (1885)

French literary critic and musicologist of Polish origin (his name was originally Teodor Wyzewski). He studied in Paris and Nancy and worked as a journalist and critic in Paris. He wrote not only on music but also on political affairs, literature, philosophy and art. In collaboration with Georges de Saint-Foix he embarked on a monumental biography of Mozart which Saint-Foix completed after Wyzéwa's death.

## Descriptive music

*Source:*

'La musique descriptive', *Revue wagnérienne*, vol. 1 (1885), pp. 74–7. Translated by Jennifer Day.

*For further reading:*

See Bibliography under Delsemme and Lehmann.

In a column published by *La France*, M. Saint-Saëns defends descriptive music. The musical work of art, he says, can and must be picturesque; thus it has been made by the great composers, and by Richard Wagner after them:

Richard Wagner combined description with lyric drama, according it a new phenomenal development. With the storm of the *Flying Dutchman*, which lasts a whole act, an unheard of *tour de force* brought off with brazen felicity, with the pilgrimage from *Tannhäuser*, with the flowing water of *Rheingold*, the flickering fire of the *Valkyrie*, the clamour of the forge and the rustlings of the forest in *Siegfried*, there is throughout all his work a veritable invasion of descriptive music; which does not prevent the Wagnerites from being in the forefront of the attack led by the enemies of the picturesque genre. Let anyone who can explain this anomaly!

(*La France*, 23 March [1885])

Yes, we Wagnerites, we are enemies of the picturesque genre in music; and we are grateful to M. Saint-Saëns, who gives us the opportunity to explain this anomaly.

Music, like any art form, must only do what she alone is able to. She must translate, through symphonic melody, our feelings and emotions, for the very reason that neither the novel, nor poetry but only music can express that deep-rooted emotional ground, at times situated beneath our ideas. Music must not reproduce natural sounds, nor the phenomena of matter, nor actions, that triple goal of descriptive music, because the machinery of theatre, and painting and literature can succeed in this as well, and better.

'Music', says Saint-Saëns, 'must not reproduce things, but create the illusion.' I confess I do not understand, and that the examples quoted by Saint-Saëns enlighten me but little. Does this mean to say that music should give merely the impression of natural facts? But any impression is already an emotion; it is either pain or pleasure aroused in us. Or else is it a matter of a purely acoustic and psychological illusion, like that, Saint-Saëns says, which makes us think that sounds are high and low, which are in reality shrill and dull?[1] In this case, the illusion is only concerned with the cause of the event reproduced; Saint-Saëns' restriction boils down to saying that music can portray thunder only with drums and not with electrically-charged clouds.

Descriptive music remains for us that which seeks to portray material facts, and we condemn it, because music has another objective. We could not care less about knowing, then, whether this portrayal may be perfect or not. Formerly, Spontini believed he had achieved the ideal of imitation in producing the sound of the organ by using brass instruments. Berlioz, Wagner, Saint-Saëns have come after him, who have shown many other marvels to be possible. Perhaps one day we shall hear symphonic poems in which the sounds of nature will be caught in full, even outdone in their realism. But we shall attend these performances with the same curiosity as the recent demonstrations of electricity or the imitations of birdsong by M. Fusier.[2] And, while admiring them, we shall keep the name of music for expressive works.

'Expression, a joke', says Saint-Saëns, 'a fashionable joke.' He cites the great masters of music – Haydn, Beethoven, Weber, Mendelssohn, who, all of them, were concerned with description. He forgets that the example of the greatest masters, in theory, does not weigh against the truth; he forgets, too, that these artists made scant use of description; that they never indulged in pure description, but only as a preface to expression; that *The Seasons* would still be a masterpiece without the rather thin imitations that they contain; that Haydn on his deathbed regretted having followed fashion in employing these imitations; that Beethoven, in the *Pastoral Symphony*, his weakest work, clearly wanted to depict the emotions of a lover before the rustic scene.

There remains the example of Richard Wagner: certainly, he made use of description, and boldly and felicitously (such boldness is unknown to Saint-Saëns). Pictures occur more frequently in his works than in the classical

---

[1] This image is extremely pleasing. Sounds, says Saint-Saëns, falsely appear to us to be high or low; in reality they are simply shrill [*aigus*] (that is sharp), or dull [*graves*] (that is heavy). [Translator's comment: *aigu* can be translated as 'high-pitched', 'sharp' or 'shrill'; *grave* means both 'low' or 'deep'.]

[2] M. Saint-Saëns, to defend description, calls upon public taste; but does he not know that, for this public, all orchestral effects appear crude in comparison with the vocalizations of M. Fusier? [Léon Fusier (1851–1901), popular actor and comedian.]

masters, and they are perfect. But it is enough to read his works to understand that, with him, as with Beethoven, the imitation is a means, not an end in itself, a dramatic necessity, not an essential outcome.

Yes, there is flowing water in *Rheingold* and flickering fire in the *Valkyrie*, and the clamour of the forge and the rustlings of the forest in *Siegfried*, and in all the dramas, prodigious paintings, giving, as Saint-Saëns wants, both an illusion and an impression; and we Wagnerites, enemies of musical description, find these descriptions of the Master necessary, as much as beautiful. But Wagner is not a musician, he is a dramatist, wanting to portray the whole of life, not this emotion or that. The symphonies of Beethoven, which are purely expressive, created feelings, but without telling the reason why; the complete, analytical and realistic drama was bound to account for the emotions by providing facts, and to keep the unity of the work, Wagner again used musical instruments to produce the illusion of these facts, summoned to explain the feelings.

Wagnerian description is also a means to other ends; the Master has observed that emotion is never homogeneous nor constant in us; again and again, in our most acute sufferings ideas appear, or some strange anxiety; and by almost material descriptive themes, Wagner has cut into the lyrical music, to put over the notion that the idea is reappearing and breaking through the emotion.

Richard Wagner has assessed the role, necessary to theatre, but not at all essential to music, of description. We understand it like him. Drama needs to show the events; and it must show them by all available means. But the descriptive music in this work is the work of the poet rather than of the musician. Saint-Saëns is not a poet, leaving this work to Gallet and Détroyat;[3] by admitting his powerlessness to feel musical emotions, he abandons the idea of becoming a musician.[4] We shall hope that he will give himself over entirely from now on to the invention of instrumental painting and imitation. The dramatists of the future, who are already able to discover so much mannered action in *Le déluge*, *Le rouet d'Omphale*, and *Étienne Marcel*, will be grateful to Saint-Saëns for giving them yet further secrets. If musical glory has been elusive, does not the glory of having enriched the machinery of drama hold its delights?

Nevertheless, however indispensable this intervention of machinery into art is today, we cannot prevent ourselves, Wagnerites, from being completely so; we dream of a moment when the threefold objective of the Wagnerian work shall be realized: the ideal work, which he has outlined so fantastically and which will be free of all decorative machinery, a complete psychological study and romance; the ideal theatre, not that of Bayreuth (the only one

---

[3] [Louis Gallet (1835–98), French poet, wrote librettos for Saint-Saëns, Bizet, Massenet and Gounod. Pierre-Léonce Détroyat (1829–98), French naval officer, writer and politician, wrote librettos for Saint-Saëns, Godard and Dubois.]

[4] Perhaps, all the same, Saint-Saëns did not intend to say that in his article. How right Wagner was in his demand that the musician should also be a man of letters.

possible today), but the delightfully realistic theatre of our imagination; finally the ideal public, capable of recreating this work, without any need of electrical or musical gadgetry, but by merely reading, and exerting the will.

We greatly fear that this public will not be as grateful as we are to Saint-Saëns for the progress he has made on behalf of description.

# Théodore de Wyzéwa

# 'Notes sur la musique wagnérienne' (1886)

## Notes on Wagnerian music

Source:

'Notes sur la musique wagnérienne', *Revue wagnérienne*, vol. 2 (1886), pp. 263–9. Translated by Jennifer Day.

[.    .    .]

## VI

Whilst modern instrumental music, created by J. S. Bach, was legitimatized for ever by the master Beethoven, another form, opera, born about the same time, was occupying many a memorable artist. To tell the truth, the difference was for the most part external: operatic music like instrumental music remained exclusively music. The addition of words to sounds was in no wise an intervention of literary art into music; for the words, all designed to be sung, did not express precise notions, they simply guided the emotion, indicating its precise nature. A Beethoven quartet suggests to us definite emotions; but the master has left us free to choose the seat of those emotions, the causes, the accompanying ideas that seem to us the most fitting. A Gluck opera, on the contrary, and without expressing anything except emotions, shows us by means of the words the state of the agitated soul and what is exciting it. The person suffering the agonies portrayed in the quartet is whom we will, Beethoven or ourselves; the person suffering the agonies portrayed in the opera is Orpheus, Alceste, the hero provided by the libretto.

Lully's aim was to recreate exactly real emotions by means of an established musical language. His naive language has become incomprehensible to us; but few kept such an admirable concern for strict expression. After him, Rameau, a far lesser artist, acquired for musical vocabulary somewhat fleeting meanings, soon lost. And as the emotions in the eighteenth century were delightfully simple and delicate, an operatic music was drawn up that was simple, exclusively melodic, but delightfully delicate and graceful and of consummate clarity: by Monsigny, Philidor, Duni, who translated the naive affections of their age and society, as Haydn and Mozart had done for Germany; but this was especially perfected by Grétry. One should read the arias from *Richard Coeur de Lion* such as 'Je crains de lui parler la nuit'[1] and 'La danse n'est pas ce que j'aime';[2] here the notes have the wonderful precision of words; and then it is a delicate and light-hearted age that is pouring forth, whilst the sweet phrases are being made anxiously to limp along.

The time of naive affectations is fled; increasingly grave do souls become as the century progresses. Here we find the strongest emotions expressed by Christophe Gluck; and already the language is richer; two parts, the singing and the orchestra, work together towards expression. Scrupulous attention is paid – and perhaps by none other as much as by Gluck – to seeing that the music recreates only the precise emotions of the personages on stage. Operas are strictly divided into two parts: one, entertainment (ballets, certain arias), the other, art; there is a depth of analysis so far unsuspected; with that, a very small number of emotions, the same ones portrayed over and over again and by the same means. And how grievously is Orpheus's heart broken when he suddenly sees Eurydice lost anew.

After Gluck, one man alone was able to create opera. Beethoven has constructed the ideal opera, hallowing this genre, as he did all genres. It was not *Fidelio*, a collection of lovable little songs, amongst which there shines an extraordinary page; the true opera of Beethoven is a solemn mass in D, composed for voices, orchestra and organ. It is a drama in five acts, the emotional drama of a pious soul:

Firstly, the memory of self before God; a complaint, the agitation of shame: have mercy on me, Lord! And it is the self-effacement, the total invasion of the heart by the dazzling Glory. An illusion, that, maybe! The soul violently declares its Faith. It *believes*, it wants to *believe*. Then there come words explaining the truths that must be believed; the music, recreating the depths of the soul, keeps on repeating the violent affirmation: the soul *believes*, wants to *believe*. Now it is ecstatic with the certainties that have been won: the soul is blessed and floats along on a gentle and rather slow stream. Wondrous joy, the soul is effaced: 'For I am a miserable sinner; Lamb of God, that takest away the sins of the world, see into my heart; have pity, Lamb of God. O, thanks be to Thee! Thou hast granted me the only heavenly good, rest!'

An opera in five acts or – what is better – in five words. All the ploys of the most erudite music have been used to recreate these five emotions, taking account of their deepest subtleties. Such a masterpiece, that psychologists could search in it and in the last quartets, too, for the scientific analysis of the passions.

I think that these marvels ought to have brought all music to a close; they at least bring so-called classical music to a close. Musical romanticism was being born.

---

[1] [Act I, no. 5; Laurette.]
[2] [Act I, no. 2; Antonio.]

## VII

Romanticism, introduced into all the arts from the same causes, had, in all the arts, the same characteristics. It was determined by the advent of democracy: souls underwent a modification: things appeared more in the light of sensibility: the feeling of their relationships faded: the feeling of their external forces grew. At the same time the emotions acquired a more vivid intensity; but they lost their intimate subtleties. It was a continual contrast of vibrant passions.

Under these mental influences romantic music was established. The emotions recreated by them are always very intense; sudden clashes, passages of poignant anguish alongside elation and ecstasy. There is no analysis of emotional details, rather a tendency to exaggerate. Then, haunted by those ardent sensations, music reached the point of wishing to escape from her purpose: she strove to become a painting, imitating natural sounds, the movements of living things, their colours.

The old language of the classical musicians, so precise and meticulous, was dangerously compromised: vulgarized, and diverted from its essential goal, polluted by the overwhelming and facile passions to which she had been enslaved. However romanticism had a valuable outcome: it created harmony.

Previous musicians, and Beethoven himself, only knew about melody: they had made it polyphonic, but it was still melody, for the different sounds, taken separately, had no distinct significance; only the way they were combined counted for expression. The romantic musician, used to the sensible aspect of things, clothed every sound with a distinct significance. Thenceforth, a few notes, even taken in isolation, had a meaning by themselves. And harmony brought in its wake the distinction between timbres: each instrument was recognized as having an emotional range particular to itself alone. Instruments were improved and their number multiplied.

But the romantics did not know how to put this progress at the service of art. They attempted to recreate emotions that were not real in everyday life, that were therefore powerless to provide life of a higher order. Carried away by a sudden frenzy, they gave up being realists: in this way they lost the power to touch the somewhat delicate souls. However, some of them were sincere: Schubert and Weber, both telling of their ardent passions, the former grievously distressed, the other bright and brash. Then there was Chopin, the only real sufferer from tuberculosis: today he rings lugubriously false: yet how greatly he desired to experience that languid despair of which he spoke [through music]!

Schumann was full of anxiety; his romances, of a pretentious ingenuousness, keep the fingers and voices of pale young ladies busy; but he has really no more expressed a true emotion in his serious works. Equally, Berlioz, incapable of emotion but an exemplary romantic dramatist, exhausted himself translating literary and verbal passions by music. He enriched musical language with timbres: but he made no artistic use of the terms he created.

Whilst the Italians were improvising some pleasant sentimental rubbish, whilst Boieldieu was prostituting the venerable comic opera of Grétry, and emptying it of all emotional meaning, Meyerbeer was taking on more skilfully the task that Berlioz had badly performed. With the knowledgeable flair of a merchant, he understood that music must, if she does not correspond to any emotions, and without any need for vain learned researches, be merely a ringing tremolo meant to keep the attention of the masses upon the actions of melodrama. He singled out some commonplace romances, for extremely sensitive souls, and scattered them about among a collection of deafeningly noisy and hollow snippets; all this was only so that people would not lose track of the puppet-like gestures and movements thrashing out some long-winded tale.

However, other romantics, imitating Berlioz and the academic Mendelssohn, embarked on some graceful deceits. There was oriental, Hindu, Jewish, Languedoc music.

Gounod introduced a new formula into the business, which was quickly paid court to: an anodyne mishmash of Bellini, Schumann and Meyerbeer, the whole nicely served up, even sprinkled, with a special graceful and vulgar languor.

Must I list the composer Jacques Offenbach among the romantic musicians? He, at least, has created a special life of emotions. His work, still shut away a short while ago from our intelligence by a barrier of silly adulation is today, for the learned races who appraise it, a very praiseworthy effort at restoring the collective passion of noisy Parisian souls. From between the two types of music, one of which expresses and analyses the emotions of an individual, and the other which recreates the collective emotions of the masses, Offenbach has constantly chosen the second. The characters in his operettas have no proper nature: the flat melodies that they take up in no way translate personal moods. But his work as a whole seems like the curious translation of what the men of the preceding generation enjoyed and suffered communally in the external life of Paris. *La belle Hélène, La Grande Duchesse*, are the quadrilles of vain and coarse souls, just as a certain finale of the symphonies of Beethoven was the waltz of passionate and naive souls. And I fully believe I would admire Offenbach if this master had not given certain extravagant composers of operettas, who are incapable of being either expressive or witty, the right to exist after him. Besides, is not Auber more responsible than Offenbach for Lecocq and Audran?

Romantic music, in its diverse forms, has seduced unsophisticated minds, as she must. Springing from democracy, she has become the favourite music of our democracies. She will still live long. Like drama and the serial novel in literature, she will satisfy the artistic need of countless similar souls. But for those rare folk who are different, for those who were accustomed by Bach, Grétry and Beethoven to the refined recreation of delicate emotions, that music remains valuable only in its accidental fabrication of new terms and useful procedures. She produced no work of quality, until the day when at last an intelligent master, Wagner, wanted to restore the subtle emotions of his soul by making use of her as well as all kinds of music.

I would like to tell as well of the heroic attempt of Wagner to rescue Music, and the value of the new musical forms that he has outlined.[3]

---

[3] [The last sentence implied that a sequel was to appear. In fact no continuation of this essay appeared in the *Revue wagnérienne*.]

# Émile Hennequin (1858–88)

# 'L'esthétique de Wagner et la doctrine spencérienne' (1885)

French literary critic. Born in Palermo of Swiss parents, he spent his youth in Paris, working first as a translator for a news agency and then as a newspaper editor. His output was prodigious, considering that it was confined to a short period between 1882, when he published his translation of E. A. Poe (*Contes grotesques*), and his death in a bathing accident six years later.

Although there are some positivist inclinations in his writings, he distanced himself from the mainstream positivists and the school of Taine. A sensitive and perceptive critic, he showed interest in Wagner, Poe, Berlioz, Russian novelists and Villiers de l'Isle-Adam. In a letter to Victor Margueritte of 15 July 1888 Mallarmé described him as 'une des seules intelligences de ce temps'. His most important critical essays were published posthumously.

## Wagner's aesthetics and the Spencerian Doctrine

*Source:*

'L'esthétique de Wagner et la doctrine spencérienne', *Revue wagnérienne*, vol. 1 (1885), pp. 282–6. Translated by Jennifer Day.

*For further reading:*

René Wellek, *A History of Modern Criticism 1750–1950*, vol. 4 (London 1965), pp. 91–6. See also Bibliography under Caramaschi.

One discourses upon aesthetics in terms of art or in terms of science. One can discuss it in a quite individual manner, according to one's taste, establish the relationships between the inclinations of the artist and those of the critic, appreciate, approve, denigrate, without any higher considerations intervening in the debate to disturb the particular opinions of the one who initiated it. One can also – and this is what we are trying to do – set about the examination of a work or a theory of art, starting from a collection of philosophical or scientific doctrines, which allows one to decide whether a certain aesthetic point conforms to and links up with the highest laws, if a certain book or symphony can synthetically be put into a category with a certain biological principle or mathematical axiom. For all those who consider the work as a natural hotchpotch, whose origin and properties, comparable to those of a flower or a crystal, are subject to the conditions of force, time and space that govern all kinds of matter, this sort of criticism is the only legitimate kind.

Wagner's aesthetic philosophy is a doctrine of condensation, that in principle proposes the co-operation of all the arts in bringing about the birth of the supreme genre, the music drama. In accordance with this affirmation, poetry, music, mime, and that area of pictorial art which deals with the beauty of stage décor and fine costumes, are all gathered together, and the master is led to produce new and imposing works which all those who enthuse about high art are constrained to admire. Herbert Spencer, in the so far unfinished series of his works, has promulgated the most comprehensive instruction that man could have contemplated since Aristotle. Starting from the latest principle of modern science – the axiom of the conservation of energy[1] – he thence deduces and confirms with a prodigious soundness of reasoning all the partial laws to be abstracted from all phenomenal manifestations of matter. His books contain the inorganic world and the organic, go from psychology to sociology and ethics, not without touching upon aesthetics, in the *First Principles*, the *Principles of Psychology*, and the *Essays*. It will appear fair to compare the most general and fruitful artistic doctrine of this century with this summary of all our positive knowledge.

It is pointless to expound the aesthetics of the German master to the readers of the *Revue wagnérienne*, just let this phrase from M. E. Dujardin's study be borne in mind: 'First of all a general principle that could be said to be the characteristic of Wagnerism: it is a mistake to take music, which is only an artistic means of expression, as the purpose of art, whereas only the action is the true purpose.'[2] It must be remembered that Wagner's aesthetics tend to put forward the laws of music drama, which is viewed as the supreme work of art, and not decree general rules on music and poetry. According to Wagnerian aesthetics, a new genre is being created, and the most elevated of all. By its very originality, this genre is answerable to the laws of development. And it is precisely the distinction of Spencerian philosophy to have fixed the laws of all evolution, from that of a nebula to that of a seed, and this will allow it to be determined whether the music drama is really the actual final conclusion of art.

The Spencerian formula for evolution is, in its marvellously concise form, the following: 'Evolution is an integration of matter, accompanied by a dissipation of movement, during which matter passes from an indefinite, incoherent homogeneity to a definite, coherent heterogeneity, and during which too the movement retained undergoes a similar transformation.' In more concrete terms, any combination of things deprived at the outset of

---

[1] [It was H. von Helmholtz who in 1847 drew attention to this law, basing his own observations on the work of J. R. Mayer concerning the equivalence of heat and mechanical work. The fundamental implication of this law is that 'although energy may be converted from one form to another it cannot be created or destroyed'. See S. Glasstone, *Textbook of Physical Chemistry* (London 1940), pp. 178–9.]

[2] [Edouard Dujardin, 'Les oeuvres théoriques de Richard Wagner', *Revue wagnérienne*, vol. 1 (1885), p. 66.]

cohesion and subordination, deprived, too, in its primitive unity of different parts, organs and types, still formless, indefinite, imprecise, becomes of necessity condensed and integrated, divided into special and dependent parts, takes on a form and a definition. The history of social institutions offers one of the clearest examples of this law. Individuals, who at first were nomadic and unrelated, grouped themselves into families and then these into tribes; tribes were formed into nations, just as kingdoms sprang from fiefs united into provinces. These grouped themselves into alliances which more and more are tending to embrace continents and races. There we have the transition from the incoherent to the coherent. But these human groups did not only unite; they became differentiated. Before the formation of tribes, there were few differences between men except that dictated by the difference in physical strength of the two sexes; the patriarchal system and more so the gathering together of families into tribes created the difference between the governors and the governed; at the same time, the occupations of the governed separate them, firstly into castes, then into trades, finally into specialists. And this transformation cannot be carried out without each group thus created becoming more and more clearly defined and distinct from the others; the authority, at first feudal, becomes monarchistic; institutions with initially vague prerogatives gradually take on definite attributions; each trade separates itself more clearly from all others; and the priest, who in the beginning was also warrior, doctor, architect and sage, is gradually narrowed down to being just a priest.

At first glance, it does not seem that Wagner's works satisfy any of these conditions. Historically, his aesthetic idea seems deliberately to tend towards reviving ancient Greek drama; in itself it apparently constitutes a system of condensation, but from another aspect it seems completely alien to progress by the specialization and definition of its parts. These initial impressions are incorrect.

Wagner's dramas bear only an outward similarity to Greek drama. In the latter poetry and dance were associated with music; but this union ordained by tradition could no longer be profitable, since the harmony was confined to a unison line and therefore only added to the words a monotonous threnody; so that with respect to music, poetry was then in an equal but inverse relationship to that which exists today between the libretti of Scribe and for example the music of Meyerbeer. There is no more similarity between the dramas of Aeschylus, of which almost all has been saved for us by the preservation of the words, and the dramas of Wagner, than between the *Ring* and the operas of Verdi.

In the same way that Wagner is ahead of his contemporaries, does he surpass and revitalize the artistic form which represents the final development of the Greek genius.

Even as regards the very basis, similar conclusions emerge. Using elements up till then either badly put together or not at all, Wagner has formed a new artistic organism, the music drama. And the parts from which he composes it, are not added as if they are lumps welded together, but are allied naturally with each other like related atoms. There is nothing closer nor more alike than words and music, the latter having been born of the other, and formed, according to Spencer's essay,[3] from all the elements of timbre, rhythm, accent and intonation that differentiate the emotion-filled word from the calm word. The German master has therefore created a superior integration of elements until then unrelated, in the way that a flower is formed of leaves allied and modified.

And just as this flower, formed of elements originally alike, combines them while differentiating and subordinating them, Wagner's aesthetics substitutes for relatively homogenous units, such as music, poetry, mime, pure spectacle, a more heterogeneous work, in which the individual features of the three arts, although harmoniously blended, increase its diversity, extend and complicate the emotion produced. The work in this way realizes this aphorism of Spencerian aesthetics: 'that the highest aesthetic feeling is one having the greatest volume, produced by due exercise of the greatest number of powers without undue exercise of any'.[4]

Finally, starting from an undefined combination, from the vague symphony because it lacks the precision of the word, from the still vague poetic word because it lacks the significance of accent, Wagner has defined the two sorts of vocal production each by means of the other. He has materialized the dream of the music through the real and human character of the action; he has completed and consequently confined the drama, by the latent mystery of the passions, which the word reveals but which the music alone suggests, thus providing in *Tristan and Isolde* the perhaps supreme image of all the bestiality and pure mysticism to be found in love.

Thus subjected to the laws of any development, Wagner's works confirm yet again one of the universal forms of any manifestation of force: rhythm. His works can thus be curiously aligned with the work of the English philosopher. Just as the star systems oscillate rhythmically on a vast scale between the limits of a variable equilibrium, or just as the variation of the seasons corresponds to the motion of oceanic swell, science and art are at one moment scattered among fragmentary specializations, at another condensed and brought back into monumental works of unity. Spencer fuses into one single and huge mass the infinity of notions acquired by centuries of painstaking work, till he reaches the point of fixing the meaning in a five-line formula. Wagner, the inheritor of two centuries of music, summarizing German poetry from the Minnesänger to Goethe, forms from it a double and simple work, which is like the contradiction of an immense rhythm of which previous art might be the expansion. It is the same unstable finishing point that is marked by the *Ring* and the *First Principles*. Each is the crest of a wave attained by the human spirit in its slow voyage towards the universal.

---

[3] [Herbert Spencer, 'On the Origin and Function of Music'. See below, p. 309.]
[4] [Herbert Spencer, *The Principles of Psychology*, vol. 2, §539.]

## 2.2 England

*Introduction*

Although English authors are represented elsewhere in this volume, this section contains the work of only one man, Edmund Gurney. It is impossible to characterize Gurney in the way in which some of his German or French contemporaries may be classified. He belongs to no tradition and no school, although his work shows understandable links with some of the tendencies in English philosophy of his time and betrays insights which he shares with Hanslick. Gurney's training in music and psychology must inevitably have conditioned his whole approach to the complex subject of the philosophy of music as he envisaged it in his *The Power of Sound*.

The approach to music in the works of the philosophers who belonged to the German tradition rested on the presupposition that music existed *per se* and hence in the early and mid-nineteenth century no significant theories of art were offered from the point of view of perception. It was left to the psychologists in Germany in the latter part of the nineteenth century to explore this aspect, and they usually did it by applying to aesthetics some of the results of the exact sciences. Gurney himself confesses that he had not read 'any of the German systems of aesthetics, general or musical'[1] which in a way might have contributed to the freshness of some of his ideas, but at the same time weakened his grasp of some of the implications of his own argument.

His standpoint is clearly defined at the beginning of the Preface where he states that his primary concern was 'with the aesthetics of hearing'.[2] Gurney takes hearing in the musical sense of the 'enjoyment of a series of notes perceived as forming a connected group',[3] perception being in this case a concentration of attention on a small segment of melodic progression rather than a process of understanding a large-scale development which may extend beyond the segment of music constituting the 'now' of perception.

Gurney accepts the word 'form' to signify a large-scale structure, but only inasmuch as the usage has been affirmed by convention. Indeed, one feels that it is only convention and custom which compel him to regard form as embodying an interdependence of sections over a larger time-span (pp. 205–6), as his real inclination is to minimize the importance of any large-scale unities which cannot be explained by the retention of a fragment in

[1] E. Gurney, *The Power of Sound* (London 1880), p. vi.
[2] Gurney, p. v.
[3] Gurney, p. 194.

immediate memory. For him the immediacy of mental representation is primary and all other large-scale suggestions of interdependence are secondary: they can be thought of but not momentarily experienced, and the length of a composition eventually contributes towards the weakening of the feeling of unity. This contradiction between the definition of form in its traditional meaning and in the new one which stems from Gurney's own understanding of music is inevitable when one bears in mind that his whole theory is based on the psychology of hearing. It could, of course, be argued that *The Power of Sound* is not primarily a study in psychology because in sheer volume those sections of the book in which the attention is directed towards the work of art outweigh the portions devoted to the study of experience.

Gurney's insistence on the psychological aspect of aesthetics is wholly understandable within the confines of the theories of art then prevalent in England. Both Spencer and Darwin, in spite of the disagreements between themselves, stressed the psychological approach to art. In his interpretation of organic growth Gurney comes close to a Darwinian interpretation which also extends to an endorsement of Darwin's belief that in its earliest stages articulated sound was associated by man's ancestors with mating calls.[4] This later point may in itself be of little importance in Gurney's work, but it is again the implications of such a premiss that are more strongly felt in the development of Gurney's argument. Intuitively Gurney is on the side of the autonomists in the aesthetics of music: music does not convey the emotions or content, it exists in its own right. Above this, however, is superimposed the view that, stemming from experience, music must in some sense embody and transmit that experience. It is both 'expressive' and 'impressive', to use Gurney's terminology. Music is a form of utterance and as such may be understood in relation to language.[5] But the mention of language brings into play the quality of intentionality, which Hanslick tried so hard to avoid. By letting it in Gurney somewhat confuses the whole issue of the relationship of content and form and arrives at an interpretation which claims that the acknowledgement of the expressive power of music, the suggestion of some content, signifies a lower degree of understanding, above which then stands another level – one of the appreciation of the purely musical quality of music – its impressiveness. Thus the old dichotomy of form and content is, possibly unintentionally, endorsed by Gurney although elsewhere he tries to arrive at an interpretation of the essence of music which could function without a reference to either of these concepts. It is possibly for this purpose that he introduces the notion of the 'ideal motion'. It is introduced in order to surpass the static quality of form, recognize the importance of the process of hearing, and yet in a way retain the suggestion of shaping which is inherent in the word 'form'. This brings Gurney close to Hanslick who, too, endeavoured to link form and motion in his famous dictum. Yet, Hanslick did not try to qualify his concept of the form in motion, failing to explain what it is that actually

4 Gurney, pp. 124–5.
5 Gurney, pp. 125–6.

moves. Gurney, whether he knew Hanslick's work or not, was attentive to the fact that movement may in music be taken only in a certain symbolic sense: it is an image that is somehow applied to music. 'Ideal motion' is in Gurney linked to the imagination, always the starting point for him, which removes the need for an explanation of the role of motion in music itself and the centre is switched to the listener's mental activity.

In this respect Gurney is perhaps more successful than Hanslick, but in other instances his insistence on the primacy of experience and memory leads him towards a one-sided view of music. His contention that melody can be divorced from harmony and that harmonic structure is in a way only an accompanying, secondary factor which simply 'colours' the music is a serious shortcoming, but an understandable one. It is a necessary outcome of his reliance on memory and experience: in a simple sense of understanding music one is able to retain in the memory and recall a stretch of melody, but not apparently in the same way to recall the harmonic structure. Pleasure and impact are by him given priority over the structural implications and this, when accepted as a general principle, represents the most serious weakness of a work otherwise full of interesting insights.[6]

---

[6] For a more extensive account of this aspect of Gurney's thought see B. Bujić, 'Musicology and Intellectual History – A Backward Glance to the Year 1885', *Proceedings of the Royal Musical Association*, vol. 111 (1984–5), pp. 139–54. For a different, and an altogether more sympathetic approach see M. Budd, *Music and the Emotions* (London 1985).

# Edmund Gurney (1847–88)
## The power of sound (1880)

English author on musical and psychological subjects. He read classics at Cambridge between 1866 and 1871 but for a long time entertained hopes of becoming a concert pianist. On graduating from Cambridge he settled first at Harrow and then in 1875 moved to London. Apart from playing and composing he read widely in philosophy and psychology and contributed articles on musical and psychological subjects to various periodicals. It may have been his interest in the problems of perception that influenced him to take up the study of medicine in 1877, at the age of thirty. Between 1877 and 1881 he went through the usual course of medical studies only to abandon them altogether shortly before his final examination. A restless and inquisitive mind, he took up law in 1881 but abandoned that too after studying it for two years. During the last seven years of his life he became increasingly absorbed in the studies of extra-sensory perception, hypnotism, and hallucination, and was in 1882 one of the founder members of the Society for Psychical Research.

# The power of sound

*Source:*

*The Power of Sound* (London 1880). Chapter iii: The elements of a work of art, pp. 45–7; chapter viii: Melodic forms and the ideal motion, pp. 164–8; chapter xiv: Music as impressive and music as expressive, pp. 312–14.

*For further reading:*

See Bibliography under Budd, *Music and the Emotions*; Bujić, Gatens, and Mackerness.

## Chapter III: The elements of a work of art

[.  .]

In many products of man's labour and ingenuity, there is such a relationship and adjustment of parts as results in a definite whole, recognized as a unity either in aspect or in purpose; and these individual products or objects we at once distinguish from any purposeless and incoherent agglomeration of things which cannot be co-ordinated under one idea. But however complicated be the structure of these products, we should hardly think of calling them organisms merely on the ground of that complexity, unless indeed our imagination was so excited by the wonderfulness of the work as to justify a rhetorical exaggeration. We may say of Cicero's prose or of Mr Tennyson's later blank verse that it is written in a highly organized style, meaning that the sentences are often complicated structures, in which many parts and clauses are duly subordinated and interwoven: but we connote some quality over and above this structural complexity; we should not use the term of even complicated sentences which expounded the state of the share-market. Or, to take another example, a scientific treatise frequently presents a most complex arrangement and interdependence of parts: how, then, is this less organic than the arrangement of material in a work of the imagination? The answer is involved in the special differentia of the imaginative work, that its life and growth is from within; that it does not appear as an external result, bearing to its author's activities the relation merely of a manufactured article to a machine; but as an actual picture of the activities themselves, of the author's living ideas and emotions, whose only result is to be reborn as part of other's lives. A scientific or mechanical work may, of course, have been laboured at under the influence of ideas and emotions of a lofty and even of a poetical kind; but the result is a work of which, however much the excellence may be due to such ideas and emotions, the object and nature are external to them: the author of a mathematical demonstration may be all on fire for Truth, and worship her as a goddess, but the direct aim of his work is to prove his theorem. In the imaginative work the ideas and emotions are embodied as such, to be again and again reawakened as such.

And the application of this to the question of construction is obvious. The arrangement in a scientific treatise is imposed, as it were, by the subject-matter; it is at the mercy of unalterable and perhaps intractable facts: while the dealings of the artistic worker with his subject-matter, whether in invention, selection, or treatment, are determined by his particular imaginative nature, and the whole fabric of his work is suffused with elements which have made a portion of his inner life. The development of the complete work of science of utility finds a true analogy in the growth of the crystal. All the material that is to appear is in actual existence, in the shape of facts and things already known or in the process of being disentangled and becoming known; and the skilled arrangement of it may be compared to the striking and symmetrical form under which the material of the crystal is solidified and agglomerated. In both cases the supplies of the material, whether large or small, are data, independent of any individual activity or any modifying vital principle, and adjusted, but not conditioned or penetrated, by the forces at work. An imaginative product may also rest, it is true, and in many cases must rest, on a basis of facts: but these are assimilated in the mind of the author under the distinct influence of emotion, and the vital principle which governs their selection and co-ordination is of a wholly individual kind.

The same comparison holds in respect of the individual and self-conditioned completeness of the imaginative work. Any sort of production depends, as in structural arrangement, so in growth and arrival at the final completion, on merciless physical and logical necessities. The size and scope of the whole are a result of these necessities, not of vital processes in the author's mind: its material and conditions are given it, and its completeness just means that it comprises and embraces them, as a crystal will comprise all of its material that is there for it. In imaginative production, the rounding into completeness, the conception of the work as a whole, and the pervading influence of this conception in the development of the subject-matter, are as much matters of internal and individual activity as any of the separate ideal or emotional elements. A true organic unity, not conceived as just comprising the parts or conditioned by them, but as the natural form in which their vital qualities find fullest realization, is that towards which the whole process of development tends: and the artistic faculty must find the secret of such unity in itself. Slightness and fullness of detail are alike compatible with this perfect and independent completeness. The one condition which we attach to the scope of the imaginative work is one which, as it happens, we find to hold in the organisms of Nature, in spite of her very common indifference to our comprehension and pleasure; namely, that it shall not be too vast, nor the relations of its parts too complicated, for the sense and the mind to apprehend. [pp. 45–7]

[.    .]

## Chapter VIII: Melodic forms and the ideal motion

[.    .]

We must now turn to the actual process by which Music is followed, to the facts connected with the evolution of melodic form moment after moment in time. The translation which this will involve of the phraseology of form into the phraseology of motion will make clearer the essential difference of this experience where form and motion are blended – where form is perceived by continuous advance along it – from perceptions both of visible form and of physical motion. It is the *oneness of form and motion* which constitutes the great peculiarity of melody and of the faculty by which we appreciate it. As we derive our primary ideas of sensible form from visible objects, a form which presents the character of motion in that it advances or is advanced along, in one order at one pace from end to end, is a novelty; as we derive our primary ideas of motion from physical motion, a motion which presents the character of form, in that bits of it separated by other bits and by wide distances are yet felt as indispensable parts of one unity, is a novelty. When a melody is familiar to us we realize it by a gradual process of advance along it, while yet the whole process is in some real manner present to us at each of the successive instants at which only a minute part of it is actually engaging our ears.[1] Melodic form and the motion in question are aspects of the same phenomenon; and no confusion need attend the use of the two sets of terms, as long as it is recognized that our sense of the characteristics of melodic forms cannot be abstracted from the continuous process by which alone we perceive them, or rather which constitutes our perception of them. I can think of no better term to express this unique musical process than *Ideal Motion*; ideal not just as giving a refined and idealized and glorified version of something already known, in the sense that a painter may often be said to glorify and idealize the objects he represents – not an idealized quintessence of any sort of physical motion – but ideal in the primary Greek sense of ιδεα, ideal as yielding a form, a unity to which all the parts are necessary in their respective places. The common use of the term *idea*, in relation to music, to express some special bit of striking form is thus entirely accurate, in spite of the extraordinary bungling to which it often leads, as though the idea were one thing and the music another.

It may be well to give one rough specimen of a description of this process by which the course of musical form is perceived, if only for the sake of realizing how essentially indescribable it is. The melody, then, may begin by pressing its way through a sweetly yielding resistance[2] to a gradually foreseen climax; whence again fresh expectation is bred, perhaps for another excursion, as it were, round the same centre but with a bolder and freer sweep, perhaps for a fresh differentiation whereof in turn the tendency is surmised and followed, to a point where again the motif is suspended on another temporary goal; till after a certain number of such involutions and evolutions, and of delicately poised leanings and reluctances and yieldings, the forces so accurately measured just suffice to bring it home, and the sense of potential and coming integration which has underlain all our provisional adjustments of expectation is triumphantly justified. One such piece of description (which to a person without melodic experience means about as much as a description of the sensations of figure-skating to a person who lacked the muscular sense) serves as well as a hundred, to show in what sort of remote way the Ideal Motion lends itself to terms of physical motion; somewhat as we have already

[1] The indispensableness to one another of the different and separated parts of a melodic motion, essentially involved in all perception of coherent music, may be brought home at once to anyone with ear enough to remember a simple tune after sufficient repetition. Let him hear some beautiful slow melody which he does not know; the first bar or two, heard for the first time, will probably be felt as quite neutral by the waiting ear; whereas, when once the tune is known and liked, the full pleasure of its beauty will be felt in going over those very bars, so that the apprehension of them must be entirely dependent on the consciousness of what is to follow. The concluding bars may afford a similar illustration; music-lovers will realize how a perfectly familiar cadence, so ordinary as to be reckoned the common property of composers, may be entirely glorified by occurring at the end of a fine melody, while capable of sounding quite banal elsewhere.

[2] Expressions of this kind are unavoidable in description, and I should think that most lovers of melody would recognize the feeling which the words represent. At the same time different people may receive this and kindred experiences at quite different places in music, and the same melody may certainly be felt in different ways even by people who all keenly enjoy it. [. . .]

described certain characteristics of melodies, regarded as forms, in terms of physical bodies and forces, by the help of such words as strength, weakness, balance, support, and so on.

There is one characteristic of melody which attention to its aspect as motion brings out with special clearness; and that is our own sense of entire oneness with it, of its being as it were a mode of our own life. We feel in it, indeed, an objective character, inasmuch as we instinctively recognize that it has for others the same permanent possibilities of impression as for ourselves; but our sense of it nevertheless is not as of an external presentation, but of something evolved within ourselves by a special activity of our own. Thus it would be a very fair description of [the following] opening subject of Beethoven's trio in D, to say that it was left poised in suspense at the end of the fourth bar; but the poising and suspense are entirely matters of our own experience – it is we who are momentarily left to hang, and we who come toppling gently down again with the bass against us.

One more point, which was mentioned above, should be noticed again in connection with the Ideal Motion, namely, that in it the characteristics of purely physical motion remain undisturbed. The fusion of the rhythmic and the pitch-elements which is essential to the melodic form in no way disguises the rhythm pure and simple; that is to say, the rhythm of a melody is as marked as though the pitch-element were eliminated, and the notes produced correctly in all that regards their time, but in monotone. The result is that the physical stimulation, which one sees so perpetually indicated during the performance of music in gentle tappings of feet and fingers and unconscious swayings of the head, seems woven into the very substance of the musical motive; and a similar delight is given by watching good dancing (when it accompanies fine melody instead of being accompanied by trivial melody), the value of another sense here relieving as it were the pent-up yearning for motion. These physical events of course have not the slightest power to express melodies; precisely the same movements may accompany melodies of the highest and the lowest rank. Physical motion can no more express ideal motion than the movements of a dancer or of a conductor as watched by a deaf person could convey the individual impression of the particular music as heard. But when the ideal motion is surging and swaying through one's head, the accompanying of it with rhythmical physical motion, real or imagined, seems to fuse the sense of the physical movement into the essence of the other; the body seems as if itself endowed with the power of expressing perfect beauty, in a mode comparable to that experienced in the actual delivery of beautiful music by the voice; or, if a very risky expression may be pardoned in the description of what is indescribable, body and spirit seem literally one. Owing to the physically stimulating power of musical sound and the extreme distinctness and determinateness of the physical sense of rhythmic motion, our corporeal life is brought before us in the most direct and striking manner, while at the same instant raised into a new region by its fusion with a quite incorporeal activity.

It is necessary now to point out a special danger which the very use of the word motion in connection with music involves. The danger is of forgetting that the essential characteristic of the complete Ideal Motion is an absolutely unique beauty perceived by an absolutely unique faculty, and of unduly emphasizing the external aspects of musical motion,[3] the aspects of it which physical motion can follow and imitate, and which therefore may seem to follow and imitate (or, as it is more usually put, to idealize and improve on) physical motion; aspects which include not only matters of pace and rhythm, but of range in pitch, such as the steady and quiet keeping within comparatively narrow limits, sudden changes and jumps over a wider space, and so on. In other words, motion naturally suggests motion of bodies in space; whence people are led to attribute the effect of music to those points in which a parallelism to motion in space is undoubtedly presented, forgetting that the complete Ideal Motion has no parallel outside music, and that these points may be just as much presented in compositions which produce no pleasurable emotion as in those which produce the maximum of pleasurable emotion;

[3] I am compelled to use the word *external* in a sense which can only be understood by the reader's meeting me half-way. Nose, eyes and mouth are not external to a beautiful face; but the mere fact that such features are present is external to the quality of beauty, inasmuch as they are present in ugly and unimpressive faces. So any particular music which presents features of pace, amount of range etc. suggestive of a parallelism with physical motions and measurements, presents them as an inseparable part of itself; but the mere possession of such features, as in the other case, is external to, and in no way implies, the quality of beauty or musical impressiveness.

that such features, indeed, are in themselves no more adequate to account for the beauty of any particular music than the possession of a nose and a mouth and two eyes to account for the beauty of any particular face. [pp. 164–8]

[.  .  .]

## Chapter XIV: Music as impressive and music as expressive

[. . .] So far we have been considering music almost entirely as a means of impression, as a presentation of impressive (or, as too often happens, unimpressive) phenomena. We have now to distinguish this aspect of it from another, its aspect as a means of expression, of creating in us a consciousness of images, or of ideas, or of feelings, which are known to us in regions outside music, and which therefore music, so far as it summons them up within us, may be fairly said to express. The chief difficulty in getting a clear view of this part of the subject lies in the vagueness and looseness of thought which is apt to run in the track of general and abstract terms: and this being so, I can only make my argument clear by insisting on the clear separation of the sets of conceptions which come under the heads of impression and expression respectively, or at any rate may be justifiably so classified after due definition.

The distinction is made very simple by considering that expression involves two things, one of which is expressed by the other. The expression may take the form of imitation, as when an appearance or a movement of anything is purposely suggested by some aspect or movement given to something else. Or the thing expressed may be an idea, as when a fine idea is expressed by a metaphor; or a feeling, as when suffering is expressed by tears; or a quality, as when pride is expressed by a person's face or demeanour. As regards expression of qualities, some preliminary explanation is necessary. When a quality is so permanent and general and familiar an attribute of anything that our idea of the thing comprises the quality, the latter does not seem separable enough for us to conceive of it as expressed; and thus we should not naturally say that a tree expressed greenness, or a dark night darkness, or a church-steeple height. In a word, a thing is expressive of occasional attributes, not of the essential attributes of its class. There is a doubtful region where such phrases might be used even of very general qualities with reference to some special idea in the speaker's mind: thus a Platonist might say that the face of nature expressed beauty, conceiving of beauty as a single principle, which is one thing; capable of manifesting itself in this or that form, which is another thing: but should not, in an ordinary way, say that a flower expresses beauty, or a lion strength, but that the flower is beautiful and the lion strong. So with respect to musical forms or motions; they are so familiarly conceived as aiming at being beautiful and vigorous, such qualities are so identified with our idea of their function, that we do not naturally think of them as expressing beauty and vigour. So with qualities identified with the most general effects of impressive sound on the organism; we do not conceive of any sounds, musical or non-musical, as expressing soothingness or excitingness. But we do not quarrel with the description of music as having a romantic or passionate or sentimental expression, even though the analogy of the effect to modes of feeling known outside music may be of the dimmest and most intangible kind; and when some more special and distinctive quality appears, such as agitation or melancholy, when a particular feeling in ourselves is identified with a particular character in a particular bit of music, then we say without hesitation that such a particular bit expresses the quality of feeling.[4]

It is true that there is a very important method of using words like *expressive* in relation to music, in the absence of particular describable qualities or particular suggestions of any sort; a usage which has been more than once adopted in this book, and which it seems to me impossible to forego. Thus we often call music which stirs us more expressive than music which does not; and we call great music significant, or talk of its import, in contrast to poor music, which seems meaningless and insignificant; without being able, or dreaming we are able, to connect these general terms with anything expressed or signified. This usage was explained, at the end of the sixth chapter, as due to the inevitable association of music with utterance, and of utterance with something external to itself which is to be expressed,[5] as our ideas are external to the sounds in which we utter them. But even those who take the transcendental view that something is so expressed or signified by all beautiful music – whether the something be the 'Will of the World', as Schopenhauer taught, or any other supposed fundamental reality to which our present conceptions are inadequate – may still perfectly well accept the

[4] The necessary connection of quality and feeling should be noted: for there being no personality in music, the qualities it can be in itself expressive of must be identified with some affection of ourselves. Thus we should not say that quick or slow music expressed such impersonal qualities as speed or slowness, but possibly hilarity or solemnity. Music may present even decided qualities which are not suggestive of any special and occasional mode of feeling in ourselves. Thus a melody may be simple, but as it does not make us feel simple, and as we have no definite mode of feeling identified with the contemplation of so general a quality, we should not naturally say that it expressed simplicity; unless there were some simplicity external to it, in some words or person associated with it. The feeling in ourselves need not necessarily be the same as the quality attributed to the music: the special feeling corresponding to melancholy music is melancholy, but the special feeling corresponding to capricious or humorous music is not capriciousness or humorousness, but surprise or amusement: clearly, however, this mode of feeling is sufficiently identified with the contemplation of the quality.

[5] Quite apart from the notion of such a something to be expressed, our habitual projection either of the composer's or of the performer's or of some imaginary personality behind the music we hear may naturally lead to such phrases as that someone expresses himself or expresses his personality or expresses his soul in the music; in the same sense e.g. as a theist may hold the Creator to express himself in the beauties of Nature: such a use need not at all confuse the distinction in the text. The word expression, again, in such a general phrase as 'playing with expression' does not mean the signification of any thought or feeling external to the music, but merely the making the utmost, the literal squeezing out, of all the beauty which is there *in* the music.

following proposition: that there is a difference between music which is expressive in the sense of definitely suggesting or inspiring images, ideas, qualities, or feelings belonging to the region of the known outside music, and music which is not so expressive, and in reference to which terms of expression and significance, however intuitive and habitual, could only be logically pressed by taking them in a quite peculiar sense, and postulating an unknown something behind phenomena, which the phenomena are held to reveal or signify, or, according to Schopenhauer, to 'objectify'. [pp. 312–14]

[. . .]

# Part 3: Music and positivist thought

# 3.1 Psychology of music and the theory of *Einfühlung* (empathy)

## *Introduction*

The dissatisfaction with the weighty speculative system of German classical philosophy was demonstrated round the middle of the nineteenth century through an increasing amount of attention paid to the exact sciences and the scientific experiment. Science was, of course, needed in the age of increasing industrialization, and it is not easy to establish the causal link: there is no easy or straightforward answer to the question whether the scientific process was made possible by the expansion of industry or whether the important scientific discoveries were directly responsible for the increased activity in the sphere of commerce and industrial production. These questions in any case relate only to the practical aspect of science, to the discoveries which could be easily and quickly applied, whereas the term 'science' covers, somewhat paradoxically, the field of speculation, or at least that area of speculation where the conceptual thought can be supported and illustrated by measurement, experiment and quantifiable data.

A drive towards an objective presentation of facts and a high regard for mathematics were already present in Herbart's philosophy, but Herbart himself did not go as far as to incorporate experiment in his system of philosophy. Besides, in spite of his opposition to Hegelian metaphysics, Herbart still belonged to the tradition of a complete philosophical system of which aesthetics was only a part. Aesthetics thus conceived still concerned itself with the method of defining a work of art rather than with the way in which a work of art is comprehended by the recipient. Unlike the German philosophers, British empiricists were always more interested in the reception of an art-work and tried to define the nature of art from the way it is received by the human mind. The new science of psychology, which was in Germany, as well as in England, developing under the influence of empiricism, concerned itself at that time primarily with the question of sensations, and throughout the second half of the nineteenth century extended its field to encompass the issues relating to art and to the reception of art through the senses. Herbart had, to a degree, prepared the ground, but through his opposition to experiment remained essentially within the speculative tradition. The decisive move in the direction of experiment was made by those scholars who like Gustav Theodor Fechner came to aesthetics via psychology. Aesthetics was only one field of Fechner's interest alongside physics, psychology and literature. To aesthetics he applied deductive, experimental methods of the sciences, transforming in the process some of Herbart's concepts and presenting them in a new light. Up to his time aesthetics was, in Fechner's opinion, thought of and postulated about from the height of a metaphysical system – from above (*von oben*). He saw his task in establishing an aesthetics which would start 'from below' (*von unten*) – from the verifiable single fact – and build its argument from the systematic exploration of facts. This type of thinking coincided and agreed well with the positivist enthusiasm for scientific exactness and the step-by-step progress towards establishing truth. Although neither Fechner himself nor the other German psychologists in aesthetics thought of themselves as positivists, the term may be conveniently stretched to encompass them.

Fechner brought into aesthetics the techniques of measurement which were being developed in the experimental psychology of his time and grounded his method of measurement on the Herbartian premiss that form is of crucial importance in art. But, whereas in Herbart's writing form was still seen in the light of a speculative system, Fechner tried to explain the nature and significance of form from the standpoint of pleasure or displeasure which it gives to a group of individuals whose reactions are then described statistically. Grounding as he did an aesthetic theory on such principles, he completely overlooked the fact that his experiments did not distinguish between artistic and non-artistic phenomena, and with all its novelty and its anti-speculative tendency his aesthetics remained below the intellectual level of the philosophy of his time.

Fechner's argument is developed in such a way that it often finds him in contradiction with some of his basic premisses. Herbartian anti-emotionalism, which inspired his attention to form is, at least in the case of music, abandoned for the sake of establishing a connection between music and the feelings, which Hanslick, himself close to the Herbartians, played down in an argument which is subtler and more successful than Fechner's. This is in fact a danger inherent in the method, for any psychologism is likely to end up in discussing human emotion rather than the work of art – in short, psychologism is always latently anti-aesthetic. Fechner could not avoid another serious inconsistency: realizing that his experimental method, with all the interesting results it offers, does not answer the question of what beauty is, he turned to a theological explanation and simply claimed that beauty is given and ordained by God, thus largely destroying his intention to create an aesthetics 'from below'.

Unlike Fechner, Hermann von Helmholtz had no ambitions to create a theory of aesthetics, yet his researches into sensation of tone (*Tonempfindungen*) exerted a profound influence among the philosophers who adhered to the psychological stream. Helmholtz himself started from Herbartian premisses and it is not surprising that he refers to Hanslick with approval.[1] Hanslick's anti-emotionalist stance suited all those who tried to discuss music as a phenomenon of sound rather than as a carrier of extra-musical meaning,

[1] See below, p. 280.

although neither he nor any of the psychologists reached the level of understanding of the problem of interaction between form and content, psychology and history, or art and emotion, shown by Hanslick. Scientific facts, however true and objectively presented when first arrived at, have the misfortune of being superseded by later, more correct facts; in this respect Helmholtz's theories are no exception, although any discussion of the details of the scientific argument is outside the scope of this volume and beyond the editor's competence. One detail which is worth pointing out is that Helmholtz contributed towards the shattering of the belief that the acoustical system of Western music was 'based on nature'. This reliance on the theory of the 'natural' properties of music, or more precisely, of the tonal system, has always been a strong weapon of conservatism. Even in our own days it is not rare to find objections to the twelve-note technique being somehow 'unnatural'. Helmholtz demonstrated that, whatever the raw acoustical material of music may be, it was throughout the history of Western civilization subjected to various conscious adaptations: 'The construction of scales and of harmonic tissues is a product of artistic invention, and by no means furnished by the natural formation or natural function of our ear, as it has been hitherto most generally asserted.'[2] It may be added that the nineteenth century still read in Helmholtz what it wanted to read and pursued the discussion of the degree of pleasure or otherwise in the perception of consonance and dissonance with the simplification characteristic of at least some of the exponents of psychologism. It is only in exceptional cases, like the one of Busoni, that the 'progressive' implications of Helmholtz's observation of the nature of our tonal system were understood and developed further.[3]

Whereas both Fechner and Helmholtz were empirical scientists first and foremost, Carl Stumpf came into psychology through philosophy, where the influence on him of Franz Brentano (1838–1917) was of decisive importance. Brentano opposed the excessive reliance on experiment in psychology, represented at that time by the school of physiological psychology of Wilhelm Wundt. According to Brentano, the psychical act is not self-contained but characterized by intentionality, by being directed towards an object. From this follows a distinction between sensation and the physical object that causes it, which in Wundt's teaching tended to be blurred, with the main stress being placed on the mental process. In his *Tonpsychologie* Stumpf, who was more of a psychologist than Brentano, and a better philosopher than Fechner, carried into psychology Brentano's finely argued distinction between the mental act and the physical stimulus, avoiding both Fechner's emotionalism and Wundt's overemphasis on the mental act alone. In relating time-flow, sensation, and memory and maintaining Brentano's distinction between mental and physical phenomena, Stumpf helped to prepare the ground for the systematic criticism of psychologism undertaken at the turn of

[2] H. von Helmholtz, *On the Sensations of Tone*, tr. A. J. Ellis (London 1885, repr. New York 1954), p. 365.
[3] See below, pp. 391 and 393.

the century by his pupil Edmund Husserl. Significantly, it is to Stumpf that Husserl dedicated his first major work, *Logische Untersuchungen* (1900–1). Certain indebtedness to Stumpf may also be detected in Husserl's *Vorlesungen zur Phänomenologie des inneren Zeitbewusstseins*.[4]

The relationship of the mental process and the physical object assumed central importance for a school of psychologism in aesthetics which concerned itself with the phenomenon of *Einfühlung* (empathy, outward projection of the self).[5] The term itself was used already in the eighteenth century by Christoph Meiners (1747–1810), but it was given prominence by F. T. Vischer who towards the end of his life took more interest in psychology, abandoning some of his earlier Hegelian convictions. The aesthetic relationship between the individual and the external world, Vischer claimed, is established through an outward projection of the self. Vischer's son Robert (1847–1933) was largely responsible for the dissemination of the term, but its application in aesthetics is mainly the achievement of Johannes Volkelt (1848–1930) and Theodor Lipps. It may be said that the adherents of the theory of *Einfühlung* wanted to explain Kant's statement that judgement of taste 'finds a reference in itself to something in the Subject itself and outside it',[6] but undertook the explanation from the standpoint of psychology. Aesthetics was thereby reduced to the aesthetic act alone, and the infusion of the aesthetic object with our own experience and feelings became the primary mode of discussing the philosophy of art. From this follows that in the particular case of music *Einfühlung* was the theory which radically intensified the heteronomous approach. Theodor Lipps went as far as to regard aesthetics as 'the psychology of beauty' and even denied its separate existence by regarding it as 'a discipline of applied psychology'.[7]

In the theory of *Einfühlung* it is possible to detect a late flowering of the romantic tendency towards ascribing a certain aesthetic significance to the whole material world, but on the other hand, the insistence on experience, which was radicalized through an enthusiastic application of psychology to philosophy, meant that the work of art itself was neglected. The reversal of this, and the return to the work of art as the central issue became then in the first half of the twentieth century of primary importance in the phenomenological aesthetics.

Gurney's thoughts on the psychology of music are only a part of the complex web that holds together his *The Power of Sound*.[8] Although he saw himself as independent from the disputes then in evidence in German psychol-

---

[4] These were lectures delivered by Husserl between 1905 and 1910, later edited by Martin Heidegger and published under the above title in 1928; English translation by James S. Churchill, *The Phenomenology of Internal Time-Consciousness* (Bloomington and London 1964).

[5] Victor Basch, in *Essai critique sur l'esthétique de Kant* (Paris 1896), translated the term as: *l'acte de symbolisation sympathique* (p. 307).

[6] I. Kant, *The Critique of Judgement*, tr. J. C. Meredith (Oxford 1952), §59, p. 224.

[7] T. Lipps, 'Ästhetik' in *Systematische Philosophie*, ed. Paul Hinneberg (Berlin and Leipzig 1907), p. 349.

[8] See above, pp. 260–71.

ogy, one can see that, perhaps through an intuition that led him to the issues that mattered at the time, he touched in an unsystematic way on several of the themes close to psychologism. His insistence on the primacy of form brings him close to the Herbartians, yet his succinct description of the projection and subsequent assimilation of the mind's activity reminds one of the argument of the adherents of the theory of *Einfühlung*.

# Hermann von Helmholtz (1821–1894)
## Die Lehre von den Tonempfindungen (1863)

German physiologist, physicist and psychologist. He graduated in medicine in 1842 and after a brief career in the army was appointed to the chairs of physiology and anatomy first at Königsberg (now Kaliningrad, USSR) and then at Bonn. His research took him more and more in the direction of physics: in 1858 he got the chair of physiology in Heidelberg and in 1871, having declined an invitation to come to Cambridge, moved to the chair of physics at Berlin. Here he built his famous institute of physics which in subsequent years produced an array of illustrious scholars.

Helmholtz undertook to explain the nature of physiological stimuli and to connect them to a firm scientific basis in which system and measurement were of primary importance. He distanced himself from the speculative German psychology of the first half of the nineteenth century and moved in the direction of British empiricists. His *Lehre von den Tonempfindungen als physiologische Grundlage für die Teorie der Musik* (Braunschweig 1863) seemed to some nineteenth-century philosophers to offer a way of explaining music – a vain hope, as it was subsequently shown, since all it did was to explain the physical attributes of sound and the mechanism of receiving acoustical stimuli. Although he was primarily a scientist, Helmholtz showed a constant interest in the philosophical issues of his time.

# On the sensations of tone

Source:

*On the Sensations of Tone as a Physiological Basis for the Theory of Music,* tr. and ed. A. J. Ellis, 2nd edn (London 1885). Introduction, pp. 2–4.

The title-page of the 1885 edition states that it was 'thoroughly Revised and Corrected, rendered conformable to the Fourth (and last) German Edition of 1877, with numerous additional Notes and a New additional Appendix bringing down information to 1885 . . .'. The first edition of Ellis's translation was published in 1875.

[. . .] Musical esthetics has made unmistakable advances in those points which depend for their solution rather on psychological feeling than on the action of the senses, by introducing the conception of movement in the examination of musical works of art. E. Hanslick, in his book *On the Beautiful in Music* (*Ueber das musikalisch Schöne* [sic!]), triumphantly attacked the false standpoint of exaggerated sentimentality, from which it was fashionable to theorize on music, and referred the critic to the simple elements of melodic movement. The esthetic relations for the structure of musical compositions, and the characteristic differences of individual forms of composition, are explained more fully in Vischer's 'Esthetics' (*Aesthetik*).[1] In the inorganic world the kind of motion we see, reveals the kind of moving force in action, and in the last resort the only method of recognizing and measuring the elementary powers of nature consists in determining the motions they generate, and this is also the case for the motions of bodies or of voices which take place under the influence of human feelings. Hence the properties of musical movements which possess a graceful, dallying, or a heavy, forced, a dull, or a powerful, a quiet, or excited character, and so on, evidently chiefly depend on psychological action. In the same way questions relating to the equilibrium of the separate parts of a musical composition, to their development from one another and their connection as one clearly intelligible whole, bear a close analogy to similar questions in architecture. But all such investigations, however fertile they may have been, cannot have been otherwise than imperfect and uncertain, so long as they were without their proper origin and foundation, that is, so long as there was no scientific foundation for their elementary rules relating to the construction of scales, chords, keys and modes, in short, to all that is usually contained in works on 'Thorough Bass'. In this elementary region we have to deal not merely with unfettered artistic inventions, but with the natural power of immediate sensation. Music stands in a much closer connection with pure sensation than any of the other arts. The latter rather deal with what the senses apprehend, that is with the images of outward objects, collected by psychical processes from immediate sensation. Poetry aims most distinctly of all at merely exciting the formation of images, by addressing itself especially to imagination and memory, and it is only by subordinate auxiliaries of a more musical kind, such as rhythm, and imitations of sounds, that it appeals to the immediate sensation of hearing. Hence its effects depend mainly on psychical action. The plastic arts, although they make use of the sensation of sight, address the eye in the same way as poetry addresses the ear. Their main purpose is to excite in us the image of an external object of determinate form and colour. The spectator is essentially intended to interest himself in this image, and enjoy its beauty; not to dwell upon the means by which it was created. It must at least be allowed that the pleasure of a connoisseur or virtuoso in the constructive art shewn in a statue or a picture, is not an essential element of artistic enjoyment.

It is only in painting that we find colour as an element which is directly appreciated by sensation, without any intervening act of the intellect. On the contrary, in music, the sensations of tone are the material of the art. So far as these sensations are excited in music, we do not create out of them any images of external objects or actions. Again, when in hearing a concert we recognise one tone as due to a violin and another to a clarinet, our artistic enjoyment does not depend upon our conception of a violin or clarinet, but solely on our hearing of the tones they produce, whereas the artistic enjoyment resulting

[1] [See above, pp. 82–9.]

from viewing a marble statue does not depend on the white light which it reflects into the eye, but upon the mental image of the beautiful human form which it calls up. In this sense it is clear that music has a more immediate connection with pure sensation than any other of the fine arts, and consequently, that the theory of the sensations of hearing is destined to play a much more important part in musical esthetics, than, for example, the theory of *chiaroscuro* or of perspective in painting. Those theories are certainly useful to the artist, as means for attaining the most perfect representation of nature, but they have no part in the artistic effect of his work. In music, on the other hand, no such perfect representation of nature is aimed at; tones and the sensations of tone exist for themselves alone, and produce their effects independently of anything behind them.

This theory of the sensations of hearing belongs to natural science, and comes in the first place under physiological acoustics. Hitherto it is the physical part of the theory of sound that has been almost exclusively treated at length, that is, the investigations refer exclusively to the motions produced by solid, liquid, or gaseous bodies when they occasion the sounds which the ear appreciates. This physical acoustics is essentially nothing but a section of the theory of the motions of elastic bodies. It is physically indifferent whether observations are made on stretched strings, by means of spirals of brass wire (which vibrate so slowly that the eye can easily follow their motions, and, consequently, do not excite any sensations of sound), or by means of a violin string (where the eye can scarcely perceive the vibrations which the ear readily appreciates). The laws of vibratory motion are precisely the same in both cases; its rapidity or slowness does not affect the laws themselves in the slightest degree, although it compels the observer to apply different methods of observation, the eye for one and the ear for the other. In physical acoustics, therefore, the phenomena of hearing are taken into consideration solely because the ear is the most convenient and handy means of observing the more rapid elastic vibrations, and the physicist is compelled to study the peculiarities of the natural instrument which he is employing, in order to control the correctness of its indications. In this way, although physical acoustics as hitherto pursued, has, undoubtedly, collected many observations and much knowledge concerning the action of the ear, which, therefore, belong to physiological acoustics, these results were not the principal object of its investigations; they were merely secondary and isolated facts. The only justification for devoting a separate chapter to acoustics in the theory of the motions of elastic bodies, to which it essentially belongs, is, that the application of the ear as an instrument of research influenced the nature of the experiments and the methods of observation.

But in addition to a physical there is a physiological theory of acoustics, the aim of which is to investigate the processes that take place within the ear itself. The section of this science which treats of the conduction of the motions to which sound is due, from the entrance of the external ear to the expansions of the nerves in the labyrinth of the inner ear, has received much attention, especially in Germany, since ground was broken by Johannes Mueller. At the same time it must be confessed that not many results have as yet been established with certainty. But these attempts attacked only a portion of the problem, and left the rest untouched. Investigations into the processes of each of our organs of sense have in general three different parts. First we have to discover how the agent reaches the nerves to be excited, as light for the eye and sound for the ear. This may be called the physical part of the corresponding physiological investigation. Secondly we have to investigate the various modes in which the nerves themselves are excited, giving rise to their various sensations, and finally the laws according to which these sensations result in mental images of determinate external objects, that is, in perceptions. Hence we have secondly a specially physiological investigation for sensations, and thirdly, a specially psychological investigation for perceptions. Now whilst the physical side of the theory of hearing has been already frequently attacked, the results obtained for its physiological and psychological sections are few, imperfect, and accidental. Yet it is precisely the physiological part in especial – the theory of the sensations of hearing – to which the theory of music has to look for the foundation of its structure. [pp. 2–4]

# Gustav Theodor Fechner (1801–1887)

## Vorschule der Aesthetik (1876)

German psychologist, physicist and philosopher. He studied medicine and physics at Leipzig and started lecturing in physics there in 1834, but retired from teaching on health grounds in 1840. He then devoted himself to an intense study of philosophy, psychology and 'psychophysics', and returned to university teaching in 1846. He was married to a sister of Friedrich Wieck, Clara Schumann's father.

Fechner's philosophy has two aspects. On the one hand he wanted to subject philosophy and psychology alike to scientific exactness and introduced into psychology several techniques of measurement which subsequently gained a wide acceptance. On the other hand he firmly believed that the material world is only one aspect of reality, the other being represented by the appearance of spiritual forces in the whole of nature. This essentially pantheistic approach led him to formulate the discipline of 'psychophysics'. His teaching about the interaction of matter and spirit, later named 'psychophysical parallelism', influenced a number of nineteenth-century psychologists, and its echo may be found in the work of the Scottish psychologist Alexander Bain, the founder of the periodical *Mind*. Fechner is now mainly remembered for his interpretation of Weber's experiments dealing with the strength of stimuli, now known as the Weber–Fechner law: 'If sensation is to increase in arithmetic progression, the stimulus which relates to it should increase in geometric progression.'

## An introduction to aesthetics

*Source:*

*Vorschule der Aesthetik*, vol. 1, 3rd edn (Leipzig 1925). [Chapter] xiii: Vertretung des directen Factors ästhetischer Eindrücke gegenüber dem associativen – [section] 2. Der directe Factor in der Musik, pp. 158–60; 161–3; 164–8; 169–70. Translated by Martin Cooper.

### Chapter XIII: The representation of the direct factor of aesthetic impressions in comparison with the associative

#### Section 2: The direct factor in music

The impression made by music consists of each distinguishable moment that goes to make up that impression and the sum of which together forms that impression. Each plays a distinguishable part in the sum total of that impression inasmuch as any change in that part would cause a change in the sum total. Language, however, has no means of denoting all the modifications and nuances of expression satisfactorily and exhaustively, except by listing the causal moments on which the impression in fact depends.

In the meantime it is possible, in order to obtain a general view of the matter, to group together under the heading musical moods [*Stimmungen*] the modes or aspects of the impression which depend on modifications of tempo, metre, rhythm and changes in the rise and fall of dynamics and pitch. Under another heading we can then group those modes and aspects which depend on the sound-relationships effected by overtones as perceptions of melody and harmony, and consequently distinguish an element of mood, or atmosphere, and an element that is specifically musical, inasmuch as the latter is more proper to music than the former.

It is on these two, fundamentally collective elements that the essential effects of music depend. They are independent of imaginative associations; and any images or memories (or results of these) of extra-musical objects or circumstances are merely incidental to these essentially musical effects. Such images and memories vary in the music itself according to fortuitous and inessential circumstances and within definite limits.

What we have spoken of as musical moods partly coincides with these or they have some kind of assonance with moods that are common enough without any musical cause – such as light-heartedness, seriousness and even depression; excitement or tranquillity; vigour or gentleness; sublimity or charm, in fact the whole gamut of our psychic activity. Let us, for want of a better term, call such moods simply 'life-associated' [*lebensverwandte Stimmungen*]. In so doing we shall by no means exhaust the list of musical moods, since many of these can only be characterized by the musical figure or passage on which they depend. These 'life-associated' moods are nevertheless particularly important because they form one of the bridges between music and the other arts, and with life outside music.[1]

In speaking of these life-associated moods one may well state it as a principle that the actual musical provisions and relationships [*Bestimmungen und Verhältnisse*] which stimulate such moods are in all essential points identical with the active expression of the same mood in the tone of voice and type of gesture used in everyday life, always taking into consideration the different construction of musical instruments and the human body. Cheerful and tragic pieces have different tempi and different rhythms, and there is an analogous difference between the tone of voice and the gestures used to express gaiety and grief. In this connection, however, we should by no means

[1] It is an open question whether what we have called 'life-associated moods' are not influenced, at least in part, by the melodic and harmonic relationships between notes. This need not in any case be presupposed. There can on the other hand be no doubt that they are influenced by ascending and descending figures and changes in pitch, and melodic relationships themselves are mostly referred to these. If Helmholtz is right in this matter, as seems probable, it is not pitch-relationships in themselves that form melodies, but the relationship between the accompanying overtones, without which pitch-relationships simply cannot exist.

assume that our being transported into any given mood by a piece of music implies our remembering some active expression of that mood in everyday life. It would be truer to say that the similarity between the rhythmic and other characteristic motions aroused in us by music and those prompted by the moods occurring in our everyday lives provides evidence of the identical nature of these moods. The fact that the active expression of our moods in everyday life is neither melodic nor harmonic in character is still further evidence against explaining these musical expressions of mood as memory of any kind. [pp. 158–60]

[.    .    .]

Of course rhythmic and other features of music, such as contrasts of *piano* and *forte* and even the actual sound of some notes, can remind us of many extra-musical circumstances – the play of waves, the roar of the sea, the gurgling of a stream, the splashing of a waterfall, the sighing or howling of the wind, the roll of thunder, the falling of snowflakes, the gallop of a horse, the flight of a bird, the lark's trilling and the blackbird's song and so on. Thus we may admit the subsidiary play of imaginative associations of this kind in listening to music. In the same way the sight of any yellow, red, convex or concave object may be accompanied by memories of any number of other objects that are yellow, red, convex or concave, but these memories will be only incidental to the main impression. It is now clear why man's first impulse was to explain the overall impression of musical relationships as being an imitation, or a memory, of something else; and why musical relationships were not granted the right of making their own specific impression independently, for the most part, of such memories, which may indeed play a subsidiary role but are never essential and are for the most part mere assonances. After all, no fully developed musical composition is a complete representation of the sea on a calm day or a galloping horse; and indeed it would be truer to say that any memories of such things that the music may arouse are as easily dispelled or distorted as they entered the listener's consciousness, if indeed they did so. Our non-musical world of experience provides only the most imperfect analogies with specifically musical sensations that depend on concatenations of melodic and harmonic relationships between actual notes. Such analogies as there are give no idea of the magical power of music, or of why one should point to such analogies in order to explain that magic as the result of memory.

Lotze makes use of a very common comparison that we may, I think, accept when he says that

Keys represent those infinite relationships, comparisons, affinities, and degrees of variance that are characteristic of the universe as a whole and account for the fact that the diversity of reality, which is everywhere subject to general laws, at the same time forms an ordered whole of categories which suggest each other's existence, merge into, or mutually exclude each other.[2]

    [2] H. Lotze, *Geschichte der Ästhetik in Deutschland* (Munich 1868), p. 490.

I should not, however, agree with Lotze when he says that it is the 'memory' of these universal relationships that gives musical figures, rhythms and relationships their value to us.[3] I should prefer to say that it is precisely because music itself is the best example of that articulation, mutual involvement, and hierarchical organization [*Abstufung*], characteristic of the universe as a whole, that we have no need to suppose a memory of something other than music itself in order to explain the fact that it makes an impression of value. Nor do I think that Mozart or Schubert were people who, when writing their symphonies, were influenced by memories of cosmic events [*Weltgang*] outside the world of music; and indeed it is questionable whether a mental awareness of the large-scale harmonious relationships that exist in real life, and in the life of the mind other than that of music, promotes the creation of such relationships in music itself. In this case the relationship may just as well be antagonistic as sympathetic.

What is unquestionable, on the other hand, is that the whole spiritual wealth of a person can be set vibrating by the irruption of music; and it will depend on the significance or insignificance, the mental structure of that person (which depends in its turn on his previous cultural development) whether the outer effects produced in him by the vibrations or 'attuning' caused by music are significant or insignificant, and whether they take this form or that. It is still possible for a person of relatively small general culture to experience stronger and profounder direct musical impressions – in fact to understand and enjoy music, in the narrowest sense, better than a person of wide general culture, if the former has more experience of grasping and pursuing musical relationships and has a greater natural aptitude for music. This is so despite the difference in scope and quality between the powers of association that each possesses; it merely means that what is in fact a by-product of music is more significant in the person of wider culture. [pp. 161–3]

[.    .]

On pages 32–3 of his book, Hanslick[4] compares the impression made by music to that made by an arabesque, and later on to that made by a kaleidoscopic figure. As far as they go both are very apt and illuminating, though only within certain limits. There are two points of resemblance. The first lies in the fact that in both cases the figures, like those in music (if one may speak of 'figures' in music), make their aesthetic effect without any subsidiary association, though this only applies to arabesques consisting exclusively of serpentine, intertwining lines without the common suggestion of plant, animal or human shapes. The second point of resemblance lies in the circumstance that

---

[3] 'We believe that the value of such things does not reside in themselves, but that they seem to us beautiful because they stir memories of the many good things that are only thinkable in a similar vital rhythm.' (Lotze, *Geschichte*, p. 487.) See also *Über die Bedeutung der Kunstschönheit*, p. 21.

[4] E. Hanslick, *Vom Musikalisch-Schönen* (Leipzig 1854), pp. 32–3 [*HMS*, pp. 74–5; this volume, p. 19].

the reason why these figures are pleasurable – in one case to the eye and in the other to the ear – is to be found in the principle of 'multiplicity in unity'. Even so, graphic shapes of this kind are very far from making a musical impression; and this is explained by more general differences that distinguish the visual arts from music. It is true that the fact the arabesque and kaleidoscopic figures present themselves to the eye as stable whereas musical figures exist in time does not constitute an essential difference. After all, it is quite possible to follow arabesques with an attentive eye, and the course of music in time has a parallel in the play of changing colours obtained by the colour-keyboard and even more notable in the superb spectacle of the *Kalospinthechromokrene* which provides the nearest visual equivalent to musical experience.[5] Even so, this closest possible approximation only emphasizes the gap between these two kinds of impression. What is the reason for this? The following points immediately suggest themselves.

[a] Every musically appreciable note (sound) that we hear is composed of a fundamental and a series of overtones. These consist of distinctly graduated sounds differing in vibrational proportions by simple whole numbers and distinguishable within certain limits to an attentive listener.[6] By means of these, as already remarked, a number of pitch-distinguished relations of equality and inequality are established between the different notes in a manner that has no parallel in the field of colours. There are of course compositions of colours just as there are compositions of sounds (notes), and indeed it is very probable[7] that even every objectively simple and homogeneous ray of colour in the optic nerves or the bundle [*Verbindung*] of optic nerves, which it strikes, produces a mixture of colours, with one colour predominant. But the components of a colour-mixture are absolutely indistinguishable to the naked eye:[8] all that can be said of them is that they lie within the range of an octave and a fourth, since that constitutes the full

---

[5] [*Kalospinthechromokrene* – possibly a type of colour-mixing wheel at which the ratio of the component basic colours may be varied.]

[6] This is true even of notes created as simple outside the range of the human ear; they all produce in our ears – once these have adapted themselves to the fundamental produced externally – the series of so-called 'harmonics'. These are the overtones produced at the same time as the fundamental when a string is set vibrating, though in that case they are not so clearly audible as when the objective conditions needed to produce them are present. Since in ordinary music these harmonics are constantly present, and objectively produced, in all works for voice and strings, it may be that association plays a part and, when these harmonics are in fact absent, it supplies them unconsciously in the listener's consciousness. See Helmholtz, *Tonempfindung*, 3rd edn, pp. 248–9 [*On the Sensations of Tone*, tr. Ellis, pp. 197–8] and a treatise by J. J. Müller in the *Berichte der Sächsischen Societät* (1871), p. 115. The well-known separation of the overtones from the fundamental without recourse to special aids is of course only possible after much practice and with great care. See my *Elemente der Psychophysik*, vol. 2, p. 272. But doubtless the theoretical possibility of such a separation exercises an influence on the comparison of two notes, or rather, sounds, inasmuch as a sound [*Klang*] is accurately defined as a note [*Ton*] with overtones.

[7] See *Elemente der Psychophysik*, vol. 2, p. 304.

[8] This probably depends on the fact that, unlike those of a sound-mixture, they are not perceived by means of different nerve-endings.

extent of colour visibility, and even so the second overtone lies outside.[9] In general terms, indeed, compositions of colours are more analogous to compositions of noises than of a musical sound (note). With corresponding sonorous means it would not be possible to create any music; and the foregoing differences make it clear why the spectacle provided by the *Kalospinthechromokrene* gives the impression of a magnificent succession and juxtaposition, rather than of something immediately and closely related, as do melody and harmony. It remains questionable, however, whether the foregoing points constitute, and exhaust, the list of the most fundamental differences between colours and sounds, as these concern us; in any case there exist still more profound differences that have not as yet been sufficiently elucidated. Why, for example, in the case of notes, does the sensation of pitch rise steadily with the number of vibrations without any change in the character of the sound, while in the case of colours a change of impressions differing in character produces red, yellow or blue in a way that has nothing in common with differences in our sensations of pitch? Why does the simultaneous sounding of all the notes in the octave make an unpleasant noise, while we expect a correspondingly pleasant impression from white light etc.?[10] I do not propose to go any deeper into these hitherto unsolved problems.

[b] Musical impressions are communicated to the mind through the nerves, but external musical vibrations stimulate corresponding internal vibrations of the nervous system; and therefore every attempt to explain the psychic effects of music return repeatedly to these internal vibrations of the nervous system. That is indeed reasonable – only it brings us no whit nearer to an explanation than referring back to the external vibrations; for why do these internal vibrations have these psychic effects? This is a question of internal psychophysiology, which, however, can give no clearer answer than external psychophysiology can give to the question why – that is to say, in obedience to what laws – external vibrations have these effects. Any eventual answer provided by internal psychophysiology must inevitably be based on experiences in the field of external psychophysiology; and we have on several occasions referred to the fact that hitherto aesthetics has not felt able to tackle questions concerning internal psychophysiology. The incidental remarks relevant to the whole question are in fact to be considered strictly as incidental.

Let us now for the moment lay aside all fundamental questions that have hitherto proved intractable and turn our attention to some that are more superficial and therefore more easily debatable. These have been so far touched on rather than discussed; but they have recently engaged the atten-

---

[9] [The ratio of the highest to the lowest visible electromagnetic frequency is about 7:4 and so in fact less than an octave. See E. G. Boring, *Sensation and Perception in the History of Experimental Psychology* (New York, 1942), p. 126ff.]

[10] A thorough compilation and discussion of the relationships of affinity and difference between notes and colours may be found in my *Elemente der Psychophysik*, vol. 2, p. 267ff.

tion of the musical world, which has been of widely differing opinions. For the sake of brevity let us henceforward speak of the 'life-associated' moods (light-heartedness, seriousness, excitement, tenderness etc.) which music is able to stir or, as we say, 'express' simply as moods, and give the name of feelings to the emotions of love, longing etc. which, owing to the complex nature of their special associations, cannot be unambiguously evoked by music. Then let us look more closely at the relationship between music and each of these two groups.

Music which has a certain given mood, or character, can display this character in four different ways; and to say that a work affords the expression of a certain mood is virtually equivalent to saying

1. that any musically sensitive person who is not in any particular frame of mind will be put into that mood by this music;
2. that if the same person already finds himself in that mood, it will be prolonged and increased by this music;
3. that if such a person finds himself in an opposite frame of mind, though to no extreme degree, this music will overcome such a frame of mind and substitute its own specific atmosphere;
4. that if the opposite frame of mind is too strong to be overcome by the music, the contradiction between the two is unpleasurable to the person concerned, whereas a harmony between the two is felt as pleasurable; and this occurs when the original frame of mind vanishes and is replaced by the mood of the music.

In fact quite apart from the aesthetic effect produced by the music without reference to any existing state of mind in the listener, the consonance or contradiction between the music and this state of mind must be taken into account as an element in the aesthetic effect. [pp. 164–8]

[.   .   .]

Music is not completely indifferent to the feelings, which it cannot evoke so definitely as it can evoke moods. For these feelings, though they do not consist entirely of moods, do indeed partake of the same character, and are influenced by music in the manner described above, according to the nature of the mood in which they appear. But while there may be a change in mood without a change in the fundamental feeling, the influence of the music will change. If we take the feeling of love, for example, this may be either tender or ardent, that is to say it may rise to the highest pitch of excitement. Anger, too, may be either cold or intensely excited; so that once again we see that the listener cannot tell with any certainty whether a piece of music is intended to express love or anger – always supposing it is intended to 'express' anything.

In the meantime not all feelings are equally open to all variations of mood – hate and fear, for instance, have no place for moods of light-heartedness or charm, and sorrow has no place for violent excitement. Indeed it may be said that although love is compatible with a high pitch of excitement, and anger with a mood of cold fury, these will never be more than exceptional cases. So too with music – not every work of a distinct emotional mood will fit every feeling equally well and with equal regularity. The melodies of songs expressing love, hope, longing, or sorrow may seem equally suited to each of these feelings and may easily be confused. There will, however, be no confusion between these melodies and those of songs expressing anger, hate, vengefulness, or rage because the character of these moods is never, or only rarely, confused. In feelings that involve different varieties of mood not every variety will offer the same aesthetic advantages, so that the artist will find himself faced with a choice from this point of view. In fact we may say that, by means of moods expressible in music and related to more clearly defined feelings, these same feelings will be able to find musical expression, of varying aptness and of course within limits that must always remain vague. [pp. 169–70]

# Edmund Gurney
## The power of sound (1880)

Source:

The Power of Sound (London 1880), chapter xiii: The two ways of hearing music, pp. 304–6.

### Chapter XIII: The two ways of hearing music

[.   .   .]

Music may be described as having a definite or indefinite character, for any particular person on any particular occasion, according as the individuality[1] of what is presented is or is not perceived; according as the person does or does not grasp something which can be recognized as itself and nothing else when the presentation is repeated, and can be reproduced in memory not as the mere knowledge of a past fact, but with some vital realization of the actual experience. This definition at once recalls the distinctions already drawn between form and colour. It is indeed obviously natural that any matter presented to the higher senses should exhibit the definite aesthetic character just described, in proportion to the degree in which striking form is perceived in it. It is only another way of stating the same fact to say that the mind naturally assimilates and makes completely its own that on which it has brought its own activity to bear; and activity of mind, whether appearing as unconscious and semi-conscious comparison, contrast, and association, or in Music as a unique process of active co-ordination, demands an order of some kind in the matter on which it works. And just as we have seen form to be a primary and constant and colour a secondary and shifting quality of objects – for 'a dahlia is a dahlia whether it be yellow or crimson', and God save the Queen is God save the Queen whether played on an organ or a Jew's harp – so we may say that form or relation of parts gives permanence to our own

[1] Definiteness and indefiniteness of a certain kind may of course belong to mere species of sensation, under which head the formless taste of a strawberry or the formless tone of a bassoon are as definite and unmistakable as anything in the world. But the definiteness of individuality described in the text is confined to the domain of the higher senses; to the visible and audible phenomena which are peculiar in constituting not mere sorts of sensation, like strawberry-taste common to all strawberries and bassoon-tone common to all bassoon-passages, but an infinite number of separate and persistent groups of coherent sensations.

impressions of objects, and is the element which the mind makes its own and retains; while most people will find that colour (to which may be added the qualities of size and mass)[2] demands for its appreciation the actual presence of the object or scene, and is apt to become comparatively ineffective in subsequent reflection. Thus for one person whose inward eye can dwell with prolonged delight on a vanished sunset, a hundred will find pleasure in recalling a face or even a photograph or engraving. The rule, however, as we saw to some extent in the last chapter, applies very much less completely to the visible objects of Nature than to Music; partly because the refined enjoyment of visible colour, being so much a matter of harmony and grada-tion, often does demand a large amount of the mental elements of comparison and co-ordination, and reaps the benefit of these in memory; partly owing to the constant association, in the visible world, of the same familiar colours with the same familiar forms; but chiefly on the more radical grounds that visible colours are, as a pretty universal fact, easier to recall, and also that they are very often actually seen and enjoyed apart from distinct or noticeable form, which facilitates the habit of recalling them on their own account. Sound-colour, on the other hand, we have seen to be almost always presented in connection with form which at any rate claims attention as form, as having an individuality of its own which is foreign to many fortuitous and unordered contours of the outer world. And the mere musical colours are practically never recalled by themselves with independent enjoyment, the enjoyment of them, apart from the form they should clothe, being too purely sensuous to lend itself to any sort of continuous after-meditation; while a person whose lack of musical ear leads him habitually to hear them as mere agreeably-toned sounds, with no perception of the form they invest, is if anything specially incapable of reviving the sense of them. It is thus in the case of Music that the two modes of effect, as above defined, connect themselves clearly and conve-niently with perception and non-perception of form; the definite character of Music involving the perception of individual melodic and harmonic com-binations, the indefinite character involving merely the perception of succes-sions of agreeably-toned and harmonious sound. [pp. 304–6]

---

[2] Size and mass in visible things are primary qualities, and are essentially involved in the impressiveness of any object in which they are noticeable features, so that a mountain or a pyramid would lose in proportion as these qualities were reduced: their effect, however, not being essentially connected with form, is very hard to reproduce strongly in memory. The natural representative of size and mass in Music might seem to be mass of sound, amount of sonorous clang filling the ear: but this, it should be noted, is a secondary quality of Music, and one which, though often greatly enhancing the splendour of presentation, can be reduced or abstracted without destruction to the essential value and significance of the forms. Loudness or mass of clang belongs, in fact, properly to the colour-region, excess of it overpowering the ear as disagreeably as excess of light dazzles the eye: and the nearer musical analogue to impressions of visible mass and size, the musical experiences which prompt words like vast and stupendous, lie far more in true musical magnificence, in some superb motive, however presented or imagined; but this, being in its very essence form, is most vividly reproducible in memory, unlike the vaguer impressions of glorious size in the visible world.

# Carl Stumpf (1848–1936)
## Tonpsychologie (1883)

German philosopher, psychologist and musicologist. Having embarked upon the study of law at Würzburg, he came under the influence of the philosopher Franz Brentano and abandoned law in favour of philosophy and natural sciences. In 1868 he graduated in philosophy at Göttingen as a pupil of Hermann Lotze. After a year in a theological seminary he returned to philosophy and psychology and was further resolved to pursue these two disciplines having come into contact with G. T. Fechner. He became professor in Würzburg in 1873, Prague in 1879, Halle in 1884, where Edmund Husserl was one of his pupils, Munich in 1889, and finally Berlin 1894. In Berlin he founded the Institute of Psychology as well as the Phonogramm-Archiv, a library of recordings of folk and 'primitive' non-European music and a centre for the study of ethnomusicology.

Psychology was, according to Stumpf, the basis on which all philosophical disciplines have to be founded, although he avoided Lipps's concept of *Einfühlung*.

## The Psychology of Musical Sounds

Source:

*Tonpsychologie*, vol. 1 (Leipzig 1883). Zweiter Abschnitt: Beurteilung aufeinanderfolgender Töne, pp. 134–7; 178–81. Translated by Martin Cooper.

### Part 2: The judgement of successive notes

In order to give a more accurate account of the subject it should first be made clear that all judgements relating to consonance, and the characteristics of notes derived from consonance, are for the moment outside our field of observation. For reasons of method they will not be dealt with until section 4, after our investigation of judgements of notes heard simultaneously.

According to the textbooks notes are distinguished by pitch, volume and timbre, though timbre appears not to be a characteristic of sensation as such but rather a feeling comparable to the pleasure derived from a colour or a scent. [. . .] On the other hand notes can plainly be distinguished both spatially and temporally. Notes of the same pitch may be heard together or in succession and judged accordingly, and also according to their duration. Similarly, the same note may be heard on the right or the left of the listener and recognized as coming from different positions. Investigations of these spatial and temporal characteristics, and their implications, will be better conducted if included in the section devoted to judgements of quality. [. . .] Only one question presents itself as of major importance viz. whether a number of notes can be experienced and distinguished simultaneously, and this question coincides with that of analyzing simultaneous tone-qualities (timbres). Furthermore judgements of time and volume are connected with our understanding of rhythm, and this is best treated in association with our study of the feelings. Thus the chief object in our study of note-judgements remains simply the characterization of notes according to timbre and volume. In the present section the final paragraph will be devoted to judgements of volume and the rest to judgements of timbre.

In this section 'note' is to be understood to mean a simple note i.e. without overtones, although what we have to say of such notes will be applicable – unless otherwise stated – to notes in the wider and more popular sense i.e. sounds in which the fundamental is so strong that its overtones are indistinguishable, and the listener is aware only of the pitch of the fundamental.

### §8    Immediate judgement of timbres

1. Anyone asked to mention different notes will provide examples that differ in pitch, not in volume. It is therefore pitch that is felt to distinguish one note from another. Pitch is also the characteristic by which notes are most clearly distinguished from other sense-impressions. Colours and notes may be compared with reference to their duration and location and in part to their volume, but hardly with reference to their quality. Generally speaking, therefore, we may say that pitch is the most characteristic of the distinguishing marks in our sensations of notes, and judgements of pitch and pitch-relationships are accordingly fundamental in music if not in everyday life.

We have now established pitch as an idea of quality. 'Tone-quality' is a term rarely used in practice and not common in theoretical works, where it is equivalent to timbre. In psychology, on the other hand, if the word occurs at all, it is used nowadays as a synonym for pitch, and this makes clear that the impact of a note on the listener's ear [*das bezügliche Moment der Tonempfindung*] is regarded as analogous to the shade of a colour, to a specific taste or smell.[1] From the psychological point of view this definition and approach are

---

[1] Until Aristotle notes were not characterized by their quality (ποιόν) but by their volume (ποσόν). This was due to the fact that the Pythagoreans treated music as a branch of mathematics, overlooking in this case (as in many others) all differences of quality. Aristotle, starting from a more general psychological standpoint, had no difficulty in recognizing qualitative distinctions as such, and this insight was inherited by Aristoxenos, who was an exceptionally fine musical theorist. He was followed in this matter by Porphyrius, who thought that the difference between notes resembled the difference between black and white rather than the difference between the numbers five and three. On the other hand Ptolemy and others inclined more to the Pythagorean view of the matter. For further discussion of this subject see: *Aristoxenus' harmonische Fragmente*, ed. Paul Marquard (Berlin 1869).

so clearly right that they need no defence here, just as it is unnecessary to prove that the terms high and low, when used of notes, are metaphorical, although they have become firmly established in the language, and that very fact – which makes it hard to understand any but these spatial terms – is worth investigation. [. . .] It is not quite superfluous, however, to say something about an opinion connected with these spatial metaphors, and in fact encouraged by them – namely the purely relative nature of notes. Today it is commonly held that it is no more possible to conceive a note in isolation i.e. unrelated to other notes, than to conceive a place except in relation to other places. The identity of each depends on its position in a series. For this reason, like with a place, it is not possible to take a note out of its position and put it into a higher octave, without by that very fact transforming it into another one.

[. . .] No sensation is in itself relative, though all sensations give rise to relationships. If space seems to consist simply in relationships, it is either not a sensation or appearances are deceptive and there exist absolute sensations of space prior to the sense of spatial relationships. Imagine a stone-deaf man who suddenly regains his hearing: will his first sensation not be a musical sound? And if it were something quite different, then his second sensation would not be a musical note either, if one note can only exist in relation to another, and so on *ad infinitum*. From the impossibility of changing the position of a note without changing its identity it follows that notes do not exist simply in relation to each other, since it is precisely relationships that can be transposed. There might even be creatures in whom periodical vibrations produced sensations with exactly the same relationship but whose content was as different as the contents of sounds and scents.

The presupposition of every sensible psychological theory that does not involve putting the cart before the horse is therefore this – that musical sounds make their first appearance in the human consciousness simply as a sum of absolute qualities, exactly like colours, scents and tastes. [pp. 134–7]

[.    .    .]

## §10    Infinity and stability of the tonal spectrum

We must here consider two characteristics generally attributed, with varying degrees of consciousness, to the tonal spectrum and we shall be testing how far, and in what sense, this belief is founded in the material of the sonorous imagination, how far it may be just an illusion and, if so, what is its psychological explanation.

1. It is possible to ascribe to the tonal spectrum an outer and an inner infinity – the first representing the possibility of an extension into increasingly higher or increasingly lower pitches, and the second relating to a possible existence of ever decreasing distances between notes. Of course our imagination does not ever in fact call up an infinite number of notes, an infinite height or depth of pitch, or infinitely small intervals. But the mere possibility of imagining such things requires an interpretation. The human ear cannot receive im-

pressions beyond certain limits at the top and bottom of the tonal spectrum. Beyond these limits it seems to me that even a deliberate act of the imagination cannot travel but remains blocked. I can, for example, still hear a note in the octave eight lines above the stave, but I am not able to hear it accurately in my mind unless I have just heard it in fact. If I make the attempt, I inevitably hear the same note an octave lower. Similarly within the scale itself it is not, I believe, possible infinitely to extend the power of hearing intervals. In any case if we gradually reduce the intervals between notes, we arrive at what is, for us, a minimal interval. If the vibrations are brought closer, the resulting notes seem to us not different but the same. Here, too, it is impossible for the musical imagination to go beyond the limits of these noticeably different sensations, or to become actually conscious of differences that our imagination has conceived. Here again the imagination is blocked. I cannot hear clearly in my mind two notes that are less than a quarter-tone apart, though their difference is quite clear to my sense of hearing [*Empfindung*] in the middle register. No doubt it would be possible to train oneself to hear finer distinctions in one's mind, though never so fine as those one actually hears in the flesh.

What we have established does not of course mean that if there is a limit to the observable differences in actual sensation and imagined sensations, there must of necessity be a limit to the differentiations that we can hear in our minds. Sensations, real or imagined, might still in themselves be potentially infinite [*inners Unendlichkeit besitzen*]. It is difficult to determine with certainty whether this is in fact the case – that is to say, whether between each different pair of notes there is the possibility of an infinite number of notes existing for the ear and the imagination. According to Helmholtz's almost universally accepted theory of the aural isolation of notes the opposite would seem to be the case, as far as the ear is concerned.

Is it then impossible to speak of the tonal spectrum as infinite, in any sense that is intelligible and capable of factual definition? Must we follow Aristoxenus and declare it to be, in both senses, finite?[2]

There will be those who say that although it is impossible to continue the tone-spectrum to infinity in our concrete imaginations, it is still possible to do so in theory; we have in fact the concept of an infinite tone-spectrum although we cannot actually perceive it. But is a concept possible without a corresponding perception? And what, even if we have this concept, can be its application in the realm of actual sonorities? What justification have we for imagining musical sounds to be infinite in number, while scents or colours are not?

There need be only two notes in order to establish a direction and we can abstract the idea of this by taking a number of such groups of notes. Now no idea, of whatever nature it may be, is restricted to a definite number of

---

[2] *Antiquae musicae auctores septem*, ed. Marcus Meibom (Amsterdam 1652), vol. 1, pp. 13–15. This is characteristic of Aristoxenos's extreme positivism and sensualism. He appeals simply to the inner and outer limits of the voice.

instances. In the ideas 'human being', 'district', 'red', 'twenty-four', 'similar', 'mathematical power' we find no distinguishing mark that restricts their application to a certain number of instances. In this sense we may ascribe infiniteness to every content of any idea. In this sense, therefore, we can ascribe it to the idea of progression in any one direction – as we have just spoken of two notes in succession moving either up or down. Here, however, we must take into consideration something of essential importance, and it is this – we can imagine other creatures seeing a thousand colours that we do not see, but it does not seem to us that, should these colours become visible to our eyes, they need necessarily, by their quality, belong within our familiar system of colours – there might be new 'primary' colours. On the other hand it seems to us that any notes that we can imagine, though we have never heard them, must necessarily belong within the musical spectrum that we know. Every imaginable note i.e. every sense-content that we should call a note, must be either higher or lower than the notes which are within our present aural range, or else occupy a position between them. Should such a note become audible to our ears, thanks to some corresponding enrichment or refinement of our present sense of hearing, it would take its place in the system like any of the notes with which we are at present familiar.

We make this supposition as a fact which is part of our general consciousness and of our conception of the tonal spectrum as each individual. Is there any characteristic of notes as we hear them that justifies this supposition? Can we not equally well imagine that a prolongation of the note-series might eventually prove to be circular in character, and that as pitch grew higher we might find ourselves back in the familiar tonal sphere, like the traveller who travels westward in what he supposes to be a straight line, though he is in fact describing a circle? It is clear that we are being led in the tonal sphere to confront a question analogous to that which has often been asked in relation to space: is space (in Riemann's definition) truly infinite or is it merely unlimited, like a circle or a ball? Here we are considering this question only from the psychological point of view. [pp. 178–81]

# Theodor Lipps (1851–1914)

## Ästhetik, Psychologie des Schönen und der Kunst (1903–6)

German philosopher. He studied in Erlangen, Tübingen, Utrecht and Bonn. After a period as a *Privatdozent* in Bonn he was appointed to the chair of philosophy there in 1884, moving to Breslau (now Wrocław) in 1890, and then to Munich in 1894. In Munich he succeeded Carl Stumpf and founded there an institute of psychology which later gained a high reputation.

Lipps's philosophy was founded entirely on psychology. According to him 'inner experience' is the foundation of all aspects of philosophy including logic and aesthetics. Husserl's phenomenology was largely conceived as a critique of psychologism as advocated by Lipps, and it is interesting that towards the end of his life the latter took an interest in Husserl's philosophy.

## Aesthetics, the psychology of the beautiful and of art

Source:

*Ästhetik, Psychologie des Schönen und der Kunst*, vol. 1, *Grundlegung der Ästhetik*, 3rd edn. (Leipzig 1923). Zweiter Abschnitt – Der Mensch und die Naturdinge. Erstes Kapitel: Einleitendes zur Frage der Einfühlung, [section 1:] Selbstwertgefühle, pp. 96–7; [section 6:] 'Einfühlung' in die Affektlaute, pp. 105–7. Fünfter Abschnitt – Farbe, Ton und Wort. Viertes Kapitel: Anfangsgründe der Musikästhetik: [section 13:] Musik als Ausdruck; [section 14:] Innere Bewegung und Stimme, pp. 478–81. Translated by Martin Cooper.

### Part II, chapter 1: An introduction to empathy

#### Section 1: Personal sense of value

When dealing in our first section with 'aesthetic principles of form' our first consideration was concerned with sensory forms – spatial forms as perceived by the senses, in fact. It was only incidentally that we included aesthetic content i.e. the life which finds expression in forms; or, this life was presupposed in individual expressions.

Aesthetic principles of form, however, are not merely principles of a sensory [*sinnlich*] form. In the aesthetic object the sensory element is always 'symbol' of a spiritual content: the object is infused with life or soul, and it is by this infusion, and by this alone, that it becomes an aesthetic object, possesses aesthetic value. This content also has its form, and this determines the general aesthetic principles of form themselves. Furthermore, in the last resort these principles are determined wholly and entirely by that spiritual content. The first question that we must ask ourselves, therefore, is what we mean by 'spiritual content'. Spatial forms, colours and sounds are spiritual contents insofar as they are perceived by us, but it is, of course, not of them that I am thinking when I contrast 'spiritual contents' with the sensory. What I have in mind are modes of vital activity. Nor is this sufficient, for it is not the spatial figures, colours and sounds as perceived by us that can be called spiritual 'vital activities', but our actual perceiving of them. If the vital activities alluded to here are to be differentiated, we must define them more closely as modes of our action and as ways in which we live out our own innermost being in what we experience.

Spatial forms, colours and sounds are data in our lives, events or accidents, and clearly distinct from my actions or my mental activity [*innere Aktivität*].

I have earlier described such accidents or events as pleasurable in so far as the experiencing of them is an 'acting-out of the self' or in so far as the nature of the soul achieves confirmation, authority and expression in their 'fulfilment' or their apperception. Now it is clear that in so far as my actions are really mine – willed and performed by me, not forced upon me but proceeding from my own volition – they must always be an expression of my nature and my being. It is this that makes my actions really mine and distinguishes them from those forced on me.

For this reason my actions are at all times a cause of pleasurable feeling. But pleasurable feeling, as a feeling of my own action, is a pleasurable consciousness of the self, or in other words a self-awareness of a value. The pleasurable feelings discussed in the previous section are pleasurable feelings associated with objects, and I am anxious to distinguish the awareness of one's own worth as belonging to a different species. [pp. 96–7]

[.    .    .]

### Section 6: Empathy with the expression of the emotions

[. . .] Human beings represent to each other the highest form of beauty, or can do so, for the very reason that they are human beings. Human beings, as we may put it, are not beautiful because of their forms, but forms are beautiful because they are human forms, and are therefore bearers – for us – of human life.

Even the symmetry that marks the two halves of the human face and the human body have aesthetic significance because they have meaning i.e. because their symmetrical structure enables the body to act similarly to the right and the left and this has an immediately manifest value for human existence and for all human activity. In the same way these 'homologous structures' are significant because the functions and potentialities of these homologous features – precisely in the form that they now possess – play a felicitous part in the whole process of human activity.

The beauty of the human exterior is due to the human being encased within it, and this beauty exists for us because this exterior is a human exterior i.e. it is a form whose content is what we understand as a human being.

Just as there is no doubt that we can see the exterior of a human being, so there is no doubt that we cannot see 'the human being' itself i.e. the personality capable of sentience, imagination, thought, feeling, volition and action. No trait of this personality is perceptible to our senses, but we construct it from traits of our own personalities. Our neighbour – the 'other' person – is our own personality as imagined and modified according to his outward appearance and his vital actions as perceived by us, our own self with modifications. The human being who is not myself but of whom I am conscious is both a duplication and a modification of my own self.

The primary material, however, and the occasion of our constructing the personality of another are his vital actions, whether audible or visible, the sounds and facial expressions or gestures – in short his expressive movements. Since we are now concerned with the beauty of the visual forms of the human exterior, it is these expressive movements that we must consider next. I will, however, first discuss sounds, especially those which reveal in the most primitive and immediate manner the inner life of the human being. I mean sounds denoting feelings. We manifest directly by sounds a whole variety of feelings, emotions and different varieties of interior excitation; and we do this automatically and by instinct, not because we have learned to do so. So that if I hear a sound that resembles one by which I make some emotional state of my own audible, I immediately recognize this emotional state, not by association but by instinct. This may seem at first to be nothing more than a case of 'shared imagination' [*Mitvorstellen*], but in fact it is more than that. I do not merely imagine that the sound proceeds from an emotional state, but I actually experience that emotion myself. I share the experience and I do so all the more certainly and completely according to my own natural inclination. I incline naturally to join in other people's rejoicing, to share that rejoicing emotionally. And I do this in fact unless something prevents me from giving my whole attention to what I hear. This factual content – this emotional sharing in the sound of rejoicing that strikes my ear – must be subsumed under the idea that we shall encounter repeatedly in what follows, the idea which is indeed fundamental to the considerations which follow – namely that of empathy [*Einfühlung*]. [pp. 105–7]

[.    .    .]

## Part V, chapter 4: The foundations of the aesthetics of music

### Section 13: Music as expression

[. . .] Music is something more than sounds and successions of sounds, melody, harmony and rhythm. Like everything else that is beautiful, music is an expression of life.

Every sound that is pitched, or indeed in any sense a musical sound, is an expression of life. We spoke earlier of 'strong' colours and added there that what was true of these was also true of 'strong' notes and sounds. 'Strength' here means the strength of my own volition or action, mysteriously conveyed by empathy into notes or colours. In the case of musical sounds, however, attention should be drawn to one particular moment. Inner excitement of any kind is given immediate expression not by colours but by sounds, and these sounds are related – some more, and others less closely – to musical notes and sounds. These in their turn appear, and more immediately than do colours, to express an inner something. They seem to give immediate audible expression to that something; a moment of feeling, an inner impulse, an attempt of desire to be discharged or to be drawing breath. Thus it appears that the strength of the note or the sound is equivalent to the strength of this impulse or volition.

This impulse or volition, however, this discharge or explosion of energy is again something quite different depending on the nature of the sound, whether pitched or unpitched. It is not only more intense in a louder sound and more relaxed in a softer, but it is also stiller, broader and heavier in a deep-pitched sound and quicker, lighter, but more 'pointed', more evanescent in a high-pitched sound. It presents itself to my feelings as more simple or more copious, more single or more complex according to the timbre of the individual sound. I may well feel the sound as something exultant or plaintive etc.

And this impulse, this volition, this discharge is something quite different according to whether the sound or note diminishes steadily in volume, or swells and diminishes, and according to its duration.

We have already entered the realm of 'mood' with the predicates which we have assigned to the life which we experience, or could experience, in a single note or sound. The nature of the psychic excitation represented by the sound or note seeks to 'irradiate' the soul in general, or to bring it into rhythmic accord. The rhythmic character of psychic excitation in general – in fact, the atmosphere surrounding this note or sound – therefore appears to reside in the note or sound itself.

### Section 14: Interior movement and mood

This whole life of notes and sounds becomes more intense and develops endless variations if we consider them in their many connections. As I move from sound to sound, passively receptive or actively intelligent, there is a movement going on within me which may be one of many different kinds. This movement is before all else mine, my act of apperception. But it is tied to the sounds and the results of those sounds, and therefore appears – like the movement of apperception that I make when confronted with a spatial form or in experiencing the rhythm of a poem – as something inherent in the result of the sounds, a self-contained movement.

And this movement is very varied in kind and rhythmic character. And furthermore this rhythmic character gives a general psychic resonance to this movement.

The movement in question may be in itself either more or less simple in character, more consonant or more dissonant. It may proceed by consonances or by longer or shorter spells of dissonance, it may be more or less complete – but it always leads to a consonant resolution. At the same time the sounds in this movement may be louder or softer, they may swell or fade, they may unite to form richer or simpler harmonies; they may proceed faster or slower, in larger or smaller contrasts, with smoother or rougher transitions between them.

The psychic resonance of the listener adapts itself to all this. Indeed all moments and modes of experience mentioned above occur in our external, everyday lives. We experience, for example, the resolution of dissonance in a thousand different forms – when the sun breaks through the clouds, when a quarrel is made up, when we are relieved of physical need, when doubts are dispelled or an inner conflict resolved. And it is the same in the case of other modes of interior experience associated with movements in sound, also familiar in every sphere of everyday life.

We thus possess, at least potentially, an unlimited store of memories, images, thoughts in whose very nature it lies to work in us and stir us just as do sounds, and the total aggregate of movements in sound. We might say that we possess, at least potentially, a number of 'notes' ready to vibrate in sympathy with the notes that we actually hear. And because they are ready, they will in fact vibrate and be heard, more richly or less richly according to the emotive power of the notes that we hear and their inherent varieties of spiritual movement. None of all this needs to reach our consciousness in detail. These manifold vibrations amalgamate to form an atmosphere which reaches our consciousness in the form of a mood, or the feeling of some definite mode of our general mental activity.

This mood is also tied to the sounds. It is the radiation of the movement that is inherent in the sounds and belongs to them for the sake of that relationship. Hearing the sounds, and according to the intensity of my identification with them and my ability to lose myself in them, I can experience that atmosphere and at the same time experience myself in it – and thus in the sounds.

In this way I find in music passion and tranquillity, longing and joy, exultation and grief, deep determination and light-hearted gaiety, hostility and reconciliation. I find in it my own ideal self, speaking to me from the notes or expressing itself in them, in their harmonies and sequences. I am this self, that is to say the self that has identified itself with the sounds – not simply imagined self, but real i.e. a self actually experienced, a self that experiences a fully-rounded interior history in the sound-structures that occur in succession and form themselves into musical units. The essence of music lies in this interior history. [pp. 478–81]

# 3.2 Theories and speculation about the origin of music

## Introduction

In a narrow sense the term positivism refers to a particular school of French philosophy which sought to minimize the speculative aspect of philosophizing and construct a new system of philosophy based on the methods of the exact and the social sciences, the latter only beginning to develop around the middle of the nineteenth century. Auguste Comte gave this school its name through his *Cours de philosophie positive* (1830–42) and, with a special reference to art, in *Discours sur l'ensemble du positivisme* (1848). However, the anti-speculative, scientific approach to philosophy, aesthetics, and the theory of art is not confined only to the French followers of Comte. Rather, this orientation makes itself increasingly evident in European thought from the third decade of the nineteenth century. It is therefore possible to speak of the spirit of positivism as a foundation of a type of thinking in which theories are constructed on the basis of assembling, verifying and classifying facts which are drawn from the exact sciences or from the historical data, as well as from an observation of social institutions and human behaviour. Such an approach to the sciences and philosophy was undoubtedly attractive, for it played down doubt and uncertainty and in general agreed with the enterprising spirit of the European bourgeoisie, especially in the big industrial countries. The spirit of positivism can be seen equally behind Taine's theory of art and literature, Helmholtz's and Wundt's experimental psychology, Fechner's psychology and experimental aesthetics, Spencer's philosophy and Darwin's theory of evolution.

In the discussion of the arts, social organization and human existence itself, the positivist attitude manifested itself most explicitly in the firm adherence to the principle of evolution. The widely held contention was that history, society, and art progressed towards a greater perfection, from simpler forms towards more complex ones, from imperfect organization or mode of functioning towards the more perfect ones. In this respect the positivist attitude may be seen as a reaction against the introspective attitude of romanticism and the seeking of a lost ideal in a past age: positivists projected the ideal of perfection into the future instead of seeking it in the past. Nevertheless, in order to complete the picture of the progress they had to ask themselves about the origins or the early stages of the phenomena they were studying, and the speculations about the origin and the original function of music became a topic to which numerous authors repeatedly addressed themselves during the second half of the nineteenth century.

The use here of the term 'speculation' seemingly contradicts the description of positivism offered earlier, but it only points to a contradiction inherent in the positivist school. Although 'facts' are given such high standing by the positivists, there always remained the difficulty of selecting the right facts and even of starting from certain presuppositions. That Darwin and Spencer disagreed in their respective theories of evolution is of no particular importance within the scope of this anthology. In a sense their disagreement over the theory of the origin of music is also of no importance in itself. Their discourse is on the one hand an illustration of how the enquiring spirit of the mid-nineteenth century reacted to a particular question, but on the other hand the implications of their method had consequences for the history of the arts, and history of music in particular, which overshadow their effort in discovering the origin of music. Under the encouraging protection of the positivist spirit and with added enthusiasm following the emergence of Darwin's theory of evolution, theories of biological evolution were simply transferred to the arts, with the result that several generations of music historians believed that they were provided with a proven formula. The outcome is a familiar recurring pattern in writing histories of music in which individual achievement of composers and the significance of individual works are seen as parts in a huge developing flow of history: composers are classified as 'forerunners' or 'followers', representing 'the origins of . . .', being 'more complex than . . .', the embryo of the form A is detected in form B. As far as the aesthetics is concerned the danger constantly lurking in such an approach is that a work of art is not understood and experienced for what it is, but only as how it fits into the pattern of development or as a part of some real or imaginary larger whole or process.

In one particular detail theories about the origin of music lent a quasi-scientific proof to the romantic notion that music is an art of expression. As these theories looked back to the early vocal utterances and linked the emission of sound with heightened emotion it was easy to make the inference that all subsequent organization of sound is simply the more complex form of this first principle, and that therefore all music is a form of expression. Aesthetic phenomena are in this way simply equated with other areas of human activity and art thereby loses its identity. This loss of identity is in a somewhat different sense already noticeable in Spencer's general theory that art is a form of play resulting from the feeling of surplus energy.[1] Equating as he did artistic activity with the attainment of ease and gracefulness, Spencer arrived at a conclusion that as the human society progressed towards a more perfect form, there would be more leisure for the effortless reception of art: art had a future. This mode of thinking in fact encourages the attitude to art

[1] Spencer's thoughts on art are to be found mainly in the *Principles of Psychology* (§524–40), as well as in some of the essays ('The Philosophy of Style', 'Use and Beauty', 'Gracefulness').

which sees it only as a commodity to be enjoyed, with a minimum investment of effort, almost as a background to one's existence in moments of leisure. The reduction of art to a level of commodity to be consumed was later identified by Theodor Adorno as one of the ills of modern society and his writing is a powerful, if sometimes overstated, protest against a simplification of aesthetics for which Spencer is at least partially responsible. The narrowness of Spencer's attitude has been noticed quite early. Already in 1892 Bernard Bosanquet remarked that 'Spencer's theory of the vocal origin of music is not even directed to a serious question',[2] whereas Benedetto Croce dismissed the whole 'positivistic and evolutionary metaphysics' as 'a confused substitution of natural for philosophical sciences'.[3]

Theories of evolution within the positivist system of sciences provided an aid towards and a justification for the development of the study of the life of non-European civilizations, of tribes in remote parts of the globe, newly opened to the Europeans by the increased ease of travel and by the expansion of colonial empires. It was believed that the study of life and social organization of these communities would provide an illustration of the early stages of the development of human society. Types of emotional reaction of these 'savages' would also provide answers to the questions about the emotional reactions of men and women unencumbered by civilization and culture as understood by the Europeans. Thus the study of psychology would be given an added dimension for it would be possible to learn about the development of man's emotional life. The discipline of ethnomusicology, or 'comparative musicology' (*Vergleichende Musikwissenschaft*) as it was at first known, can be seen as a combination of impulses coming from the study of evolution, sociology and psychology. Even here one can observe how the positivist attitude to facts was indeed embedded in a contradiction. Alien musical cultures were studied less for themselves and more as paradigms for establishing laws of musical development in the continued quest for establishing the origin of music. A scholar's imagination was often given free rein. Combarieu, who made a serious study of the origin of music in magic rites went even so far as to equate magic significance with some of the German speculative ideas,[4] while Richard Wallaschek tried to combine Wagner's ideas with a discussion of 'primitive music'.[5]

Among the main currents of European thought Marxism concerned itself the least with the arts, at least in the nineteenth century. Nevertheless, one of the few examples of how the populist socialist attitude to work as a moving force in the development of mankind influenced thinking about the origin of music is provided by Karl Bücher's account of the interconnectedness of work, rhythm and song. There is in Bücher's regret about the lost dignity of work and the negative influence of the machine a suggestion of the longing for

[2] Bernard Bosanquet, *A History of Aesthetic* (London 1892), p. 441.
[3] Benedetto Croce, *Aesthetic*, tr. Douglas Ainslie (New York 1922), p. 388.
[4] Jules Combarieu, *Music, its Laws and Evolution* (London 1910), p. 95.
[5] Richard Wallaschek, *Primitive Music* (London 1893), Chapter vii, *passim*.

the past, not unlike that found with William Morris, though in general absent from the theories of social evolution of the time. It is interesting to note that in another work dating from about the same time, *Die Entstehung der Volks-wirtschaft*, Bücher accepted what amounts to a Spencerian idea of play as the basis for the origin of art: 'play is older than work, art is older than the production of goods'.[6] In spite of the implied contradiction both works continued to be reissued in the last decade of the nineteenth and the first two decades of the twentieth century.

---

[6] Karl Bücher, *Die Entstehung der Volkswirtschaft*, 2nd edn (Tübingen 1898), p. 34.

# Herbert Spencer (1820–1903)
# 'The origin and function of music' (1857)

English philosopher and sociologist. The son of a Quaker teacher, he was given an entirely free and unstructured education in which it was left to his own initiative to read and collect knowledge. Between the ages of thirteen and sixteen he was guided rather more formally by his uncle Revd. Thomas Spencer. After a brief spell as an assistant schoolmaster, he worked between 1837 and 1841 as a railway engineer and then as a journalist, becoming in 1848 a sub-editor on *The Economist*. Abandoning journalism in 1853, he lived on a precarious income derived from subscriptions to his books and relying on the support of wealthy patrons.

Spencer's early writings predate the appearance of Darwin's *The Origin of Species*, but already show a strong tendency to interpret social and aesthetic phenomena according to the principles of evolution and manifestations in particular instances of a set of basic principles, endlessly varied and adapted. Darwin's theories provide a strong impetus for the development of Spencer's subsequent thought, expounded in a series of volumes under the general title of *Principles of Philosophy*.

Although differing from Darwin in details and often disagreeing with him, Spencer was the first philosopher to base his arguments firmly on the principle of evolution and to extend principles of biology to the field of sociology. His aesthetic views are intensely subject-orientated since he scrutinized only the psychological reaction ('aesthetic feeling') of the recipient, but not the work of art itself. The views are aptly summarized in his definition of aesthetic feeling: '. . . the highest aesthetic feeling is one having the greatest volume, produced by due exercise of the greatest number of powers without undue exercise of any' (*Principles of Psychology*, vol. 2, §539).

# The origin and function of music

*Source:*

'The Origin and Function of Music' in *Essays: Scientific, Political, and Speculative*, vol. 2 (London 1901), pp. 403–6; 410–14; 422–3. The essay was first published in *Fraser's Magazine* in October 1857, and then included in *Essays: Scientific, Political, and Speculative*, vol 1 (London 1858). An extended version, with a lengthy Postscript containing the polemics with Darwin and Gurney appeared in *Essays . . .*, vol. 2 (London 1891). The 1901 edition reproduces the 1891 version, although the sections included in the present volume do not contain any of the additional material.

[.   .   .]

All music is originally vocal. All vocal sounds are produced by the agency of certain muscles. These muscles, in common with those of the body at large, are excited to contraction by pleasurable and painful feelings. And therefore it is that feelings demonstrate themselves in sounds as well as in movements. Therefore it is that Carlo barks as well as leaps when he is let out – that puss purrs as well as erects her tail – that the canary chirps as well as flutters. Therefore it is that the angry lion roars while he lashes his sides, and the dog growls while he retracts his lip. Therefore it is that the maimed animal not only struggles, but howls. And it is from this cause that in human beings bodily suffering expresses itself not only in contortions, but in shrieks and groans – that in anger, and fear, and grief, the gesticulations are accompanied by shouts and screams – that delightful sensations are followed by exclamations – and that we hear screams of joy and shouts of exultation.

We have here, then, a principle underlying all vocal phenomena; including those of vocal music, and by consequence those of music in general. The muscles that move the chest, larynx, and vocal cords, contracting like other muscles in proportion to the intensity of the feelings; every different contraction of these muscles involving, as it does, a different adjustment of the vocal organs; every different adjustment of the vocal organs causing a change in the sound emitted – it follows that variations of voice are the physiological results of variations of feeling. It follows that each inflection or modulation is the natural outcome of some passing emotion or sensation; and it follows that the explanation of all kinds of vocal expression, must be sought in this general relation between mental and muscular excitements. Let us, then, see whether we cannot thus account for the chief peculiarities in the utterance of the feelings: grouping these peculiarities under the heads of *loudness, quality or timbre, pitch, intervals,* and *rate of variation.*

Between the lungs and the organs of voice, there is much the same relation as between the bellows of an organ and its pipes. And as the loudness of the sound given out by an organ-pipe increases with the strength of the blast from the bellows; so, other things equal, the loudness of a vocal sound increases with the strength of the blast from the lungs. But the expulsion of air from the lungs is effected by certain muscles of the chest and abdomen. The force with which these muscles contract, is proportionate to the intensity of the feeling experienced. Hence, a priori, loud sounds will be the habitual results of strong feelings. That they are so we have daily proof. The pain which if moderate, can be borne silently, causes outcries if it becomes extreme. While a slight vexation makes a child whimper, a fit of passion calls forth a howl that disturbs the neighbourhood. When the voices in an adjacent room become unusually audible, we infer anger, or surprise, or joy. Loudness of applause is significant of great approbation; and with uproarious mirth we associate the idea of high enjoyment. Commencing with the silence of apathy, we find that the utterances grow louder as the sensations or emotions, whether pleasurable or painful, grow stronger. That different *qualities* of voices accompany different mental states, and that under states of excitement the tones are more sonorous than usual, is another general fact admitting of a parallel explanation. The sounds of common conversation have but little resonance; those of strong feeling have much more. Under rising ill temper the voice acquires a metallic ring. In accordance with her constant mood, the ordinary speech of a virago has a piercing quality quite opposite to that softness indicative of placidity. A ringing laugh marks joyous temperament. Grief, unburdening itself, uses tones approaching in *timbre* to those of chanting; and in his most pathetic passages an eloquent speaker similarly falls into tones more vibratory than those common to him. Now any one may readily convince himself that resonant vocal sounds can be produced only by a certain muscular effort additional to that ordinarily needed. If after uttering a word in his speaking voice, the reader, without changing the pitch or the loudness, will sing this word, he will perceive that before he can sing it, he has to alter the adjustment of the vocal organs; to do which a certain force must be used; and by putting his fingers on that external prominence marking the top of the larynx, he will have further evidence that to produce a sonorous tone the organs must be drawn out of their usual position. Thus, then, the fact that the tones of excited feeling are more vibratory than those of common conversation, is another instance of the connection between mental excitement and muscular excitement. The speaking voice, the recitative voice, and the singing voice, severally exemplify one general principle.

That the *pitch* of the voice varies according to the action of the vocal muscles, scarcely needs saying. All know that the middle notes, in which they converse, are made without appreciable effort; and all know that to make either very high notes or very low notes requires considerable effort. In either ascending or descending from the pitch of ordinary speech, we are conscious of increasing muscular strain, which, at each extreme of the register, becomes painful. Hence it follows from our general principle, that while indifference or calmness will use the medium tones, the tones used during excitement will be either above or below them; and will rise higher and higher, or fall lower and lower, as the feelings grow stronger. [pp. 403–6]

[.    .    .]

Have we not, here, then, adequate data for a theory of music? These vocal peculiarities which indicate excited feeling, are those which especially distinguish song from ordinary speech. Every one of the alterations of voice which we have found to be a physiological result of pain or pleasure, is carried to an extreme in vocal music. For instance, we saw that, in virtue of the general relation between mental and muscular excitement, one characteristic of passionate utterance is *loudness*. Well, its comparative loudness is one of the distinctive marks of song as contrasted with the speech of daily life. Though there are *piano* passages in contrast with the *forte* passages, yet the average loudness of the singing voice is much greater than that of the speaking voice; and further, the *forte* passages of an air are those intended to represent the climax of its emotion. We next saw that the tones in which emotion expresses itself, are, in conformity with this same law, of a more sonorous *timbre* than those of calm conversation. Here, too, song displays a still higher degree of the peculiarity; for the singing tone is the most resonant we can make. Again, it was shown that, from a like cause, mental excitement vents itself in the higher and lower notes of the register; using the middle notes but seldom. And it scarcely needs saying that vocal music is still more distinguished by its comparative neglect of the notes in which we talk, and its habitual use of those above or below them; and, moreover, that its most passionate effects are commonly produced at the two extremities of its scale, but especially at the upper one. A yet further trait of strong feeling, similarly accounted for, was the habitual employment of larger intervals than are employed in common converse. This trait, also, every ballad and aria systematically elaborates: add to which, that the direction of these intervals, which, as diverging from or converging towards the medium tones, we found to be physiologically expressive of increasing or decreasing emotion, may be observed to have in music like meanings. Once more, it was pointed out that not only extreme but also rapid variations of pitch, are characteristic of mental excitement; and once more we see in the quick changes of every melody, that song carries the characteristics as far, if not farther. Thus, in respect alike of *loudness, timbre, pitch, intervals*, and *rate of variation*, song employs and exaggerates the natural language of the emotions – it arises from a systematic combination of those vocal peculiarities which are the physiological effects of acute pleasure and pain.

Beside these chief characteristics of song as distinguished from common speech, there are sundry minor ones similarly explicable as due to the relation between mental and muscular excitement; and before proceeding further, these should be briefly noticed. Thus, certain passions, and perhaps all passions when pushed to an extreme, produce (probably through their influence over the action of the heart) an effect the reverse of that which has been described: they cause a physical prostration, one symptom of which is a general relaxation of the muscles, and a consequent trembling. We have the trembling of anger, of fear, of hope, of joy; and the vocal muscles being implicated with the rest, the voice too becomes tremulous. Now, in singing, this tremulousness of voice is effectively used by some vocalists in pathetic passages; sometimes, indeed, because of its effectiveness, too much used by them – as by Tamberlik,[1] for instance. Again, there is a mode of musical execution known as the *staccato*, appropriate to energetic passages – to passages expressive of exhilaration, of resolution, of confidence. The action of the vocal muscles which produces this staccato style, is analogous to the muscular action which produces the sharp, decisive, energetic movements of body indicating these states of mind; and therefore it is that the staccato style has the meaning we ascribe to it. Conversely, slurred intervals are expressive of gentler and less active feelings; and are so because they imply the smaller

---

[1] [Enrico Tamberlik (1820–89). Italian tenor of supposedly Romanian origin. Sang regularly in London in the 1850s and 1860s.]

muscular vivacity due to a lower mental energy. The difference of effect resulting from differences of *time* in music, is also attributable to this same law. Already it has been pointed out that the more frequent changes of pitch which ordinarily result from passion, are imitated and developed in song; and here we have to add, that the various rates of such changes, appropriate to the different styles of music, are further traits having the same derivation. The slowest movements, *largo* and *adagio*, are used where such depressing emotions as grief, or such unexciting emotions as reverence, are to be portrayed; while the more rapid movements, *andante, allegro, presto*, represent successively increasing degrees of mental vivacity; and do this because they imply that muscular activity which flows from this mental vivacity. Even the rhythm, which forms a remaining distinction between song and speech, may not improbably have a kindred cause. Why the actions excited by strong feeling should tend to become rhythmical, is not obvious; but that they do so there are diverse evidences. There is the swaying of the body to and fro under pain or grief, of the leg under impatience or agitation. Dancing, too, is a rhythmical action natural to elevated emotion. That under excitement speech acquires a certain rhythm, we may occasionally perceive in the highest efforts of an orator. In poetry, which is a form of speech used for the better expression of emotional ideas, we have this rhythmical tendency developed. And when we bear in mind that dancing, poetry, and music are connate – are originally constituent parts of the same thing, it becomes clear that the measured movement common to them all implies a rhythmical action of the whole system, the vocal apparatus included; and that so the rhythm of music is a more subtle and complex result of this relation between mental and muscular excitement.

But it is time to end this analysis, which possibly we have already carried too far. It is not to be supposed that the more special peculiarities of musical expression are to be definitely explained. Though probably they may all in some way conform to the principle that has been worked out, it is impracticable to trace that principle in its more ramified applications. Nor is it needful to our argument that it should be so traced. The foregoing facts sufficiently prove that what we regard as the distinctive traits of song, are simply the traits of emotional speech intensified and systematized. In respect of its general characteristics, we think it has been made clear that vocal music, and by consequence all music, is an idealization of the natural language of passion. [pp. 410–14]

[.    .]

[. . .] beyond the direct pleasure which it gives, music has the indirect effect of developing this language of the emotions. Having its root, as we have endeavoured to show, in those tones, intervals, and cadences of speech which express feeling – arising by the combination and intensifying of these, and coming finally to have an embodiment of its own; music has all along been reacting upon speech, and increasing its power of rendering emotion. The use in recitative and song of inflections more expressive than ordinary ones, must from the beginning have tended to develop the ordinary ones. The complex musical phrases by which composers have conveyed complex emotions, may rationally be supposed to influence us in making those involved cadences of conversation by which we convey our subtler thoughts and feelings. If the cultivation of music has any effect on the mind, what more natural effect is there than this of developing our perception of the meanings of qualities, and modulations of voice; and giving us a correspondingly increased power of using them? Just as chemistry, arising out of the processes of metallurgy and the industrial arts, and gradually growing into an independent study, has now become an aid to all kinds of production – just as physiology, originating from medicine and once subordinate to it, but latterly pursued for its own sake, is in our day coming to be the science on which the progress of medicine depends – so, music, having its root in emotional language, and gradually evolved from it, has ever been reacting upon and further advancing it. [pp. 422–3]

# Charles Darwin (1809–1882)

## The descent of man, and selection in relation to sex (1871)

Darwin studied medicine at Edinburgh from 1825 to 1827, but abandoned medical studies and, toying with the idea of becoming a clergyman, went to study at Cambridge. There he developed an interest in geology and on one occasion accompanied the distinguished geologist Adam Sedgwick on a trip to North Wales. This and his earlier medical studies were his only qualifications for the post of 'naturalist' on board HMS *Beagle*, a warship engaged on a cartographical survey of South America (1831–6). It was during this trip that he broadened his knowledge of geology, palaeontology and zoology and made observations which served as a basis for his subsequent work. On his return to England he spent short periods in Cambridge and London before settling in 1842 at Down near Beckenham, then a small village outside London, where he remained until his death.

Darwin wrote on a number of geological, zoological and botanical issues, but his pre-eminence rests on two works of immense importance: *The Origin of Species* (1859) and *The Descent of Man* (1871). In the former he established his theory of evolution on the basis of natural selection, and in the latter presented an account of the principle of sexual selection as an extension of natural selection.

Darwin's theories profoundly altered the course of natural sciences, psychology and medicine, and challenged the hitherto undisputed Judaeo-Christian view of creation. On the other hand, uncritical application of evolutionary principles to sociology, art and aesthetics in the late nineteenth century often resulted in simplistic accounts of social phenomena and art history, whereas the implications of some of the arguments presented in *The Descent of Man*, if pursued radically, led to the theories of white supremacism and racism.

## The descent of man, and selection in relation to sex

*Source:*

The Descent of Man, and Selection in Relation to Sex (London 1871), vol. 2, pp. 330–1; 331–3; 333–7.

## Part II

### Chapter XIX: Secondary sexual characters of man

[.   .]

The capacity and love for singing or music, though not a sexual character in man, must not here be passed over. Although the sounds emitted by animals of all kinds serve many purposes, a strong case can be made out, that the vocal organs were primarily used and perfected in relation to the propagation of the species. Insects and some few spiders are the lowest animals which voluntarily produce any sound; and this is generally effected by the aid of beautifully constructed stridulating organs, which are often confined to the males alone. The sounds thus produced consist, I believe in all cases, of the same note, repeated rhythmically;[1] and this is sometimes pleasing even to the ears of man. Their chief, and in some cases exclusive use appears to be either to call or to charm the opposite sex. [pp. 330–1]

[.   .]

In the class of Mammals, with which we are here more particularly concerned, the males of almost all the species use their voices during the breeding season much more than at any other time; and some are absolutely mute excepting at this season. Both sexes of other species, or the females alone, use their voices as a love-call. Considering these facts, and that the vocal organs of some quadrupeds are much more largely developed in the male than in the female, either permanently or temporarily during the breeding season; and considering that in most of the lower classes the sounds produced by the males, serve not only to call but to excite or allure the female; it is a surprising fact that we have not as yet any good evidence that these organs are used by male mammals to charm the females. The American *Mycetes caraya* perhaps forms an exception, as does more probably one of those apes which come nearer to man, namely, the *Hylobates agilis*. This gibbon has an extremely loud but musical voice. Mr Waterhouse states,[2] 'It appeared to me that in ascending and descending the scale, the intervals were always exactly half-tones; and I am sure that the highest note was the exact octave to the lowest. The quality of the notes is very musical; and I do not doubt that a good violinist would be able to give a correct idea of the gibbon's composition, excepting as regards its loudness.' Mr Waterhouse then gives the notes. Professor Owen, who is likewise a musician, confirms the foregoing statement, and remarks that this gibbon 'alone of brute mammals may be said to sing'. It appears to be much excited after its performance. Unfortunately its habits have never been closely observed in a state of nature; but from the

[1] Dr Scudder, 'Notes on Stridulation', *Proceedings of the Boston Society of Natural History*, vol. 11, (April, 1868).

[2] Given in W. C. L. Martin's *General Introduction to the Natural History of Mammiferous Animals* (1841), p. 432; Owen, *Anatomy of Vertebrates*, vol. 3, p. 600.

analogy of almost all other animals, it is highly probable that it utters its musical notes especially during the season of courtship. [pp. 331–3]

[. . .]

With man song is generally admitted to be the basis or origin of instrumental music. As neither the enjoyment nor the capacity of producing musical notes are faculties of the least direct use to man in reference to his ordinary habits of life, they must be ranked amongst the most mysterious with which he is endowed. They are present, though in a very rude and as it appears almost latent condition, in men of all races, even the most savage; but so different is the taste of the different races, that our music gives not the least pleasure to savages, and their music is to us hideous and unmeaning. Dr Seemann, in some interesting remarks on this subject,[3] 'doubts whether even amongst the nations of Western Europe, intimately connected as they are by close and frequent intercourse, the music of the one is interpreted in the same sense by the others. By travelling eastwards we find that there is certainly a different language of music. Songs of joy and dance-accompaniments are no longer, as with us, in the major keys, but always in the minor.' Whether or not the half-human progenitors of man possessed, like the before-mentioned gibbon, the capacity of producing, and no doubt of appreciating, musical notes, we have every reason to believe that man possessed these faculties at a very remote period, for singing and music are extremely ancient arts. Poetry, which may be considered as the offspring of song, is likewise so ancient that many persons have felt astonishment that it should have arisen during the earliest ages of which we have any record.

The musical faculties, which are not wholly deficient in any race, are capable of prompt and high development, as we see with Hottentots and Negroes, who have readily become excellent musicians, although they do not practise in their native countries anything that we should esteem as music. But there is nothing anomalous in this circumstance: some species of birds which never naturally sing, can without much difficulty be taught to perform; thus the house-sparrow has learnt the song of a linnet. As these two species are closely allied, and belong to the order of *Insessores*, which includes nearly all the singing-birds in the world, it is quite possible or probable that a progenitor of the sparrow may have been a songster. It is a much more remarkable fact that parrots, which belong to a group distinct from the *Insessores*, and have differently-constructed vocal organs, can be taught not only to speak, but to pipe or whistle tunes invented by man, so that they must have some musical capacity. Nevertheless it would be extremely rash to assume that parrots are descended from some ancient progenitor which was a songster. Many analogous cases could be advanced of organs and instincts originally adapted for one purpose, having been utilized for some quite distinct

---

[3] *Journal of the Anthropological Society* (Oct., 1870), p. clv. See also the several later chapters in Sir John Lubbock's *Prehistoric Times*, 2nd edn. (1869), which contains an admirable account of the habits of savages.

purpose.[4] Hence the capacity for high musical development, which the savage races of man possess, may be due either to our semi-human progenitors having practised some rude form of music, or simply to their having acquired for some distinct purposes the proper vocal organs. But in this latter case we must assume that they already possessed, as in the above instance of the parrots, and as seems to occur with many animals, some sense of melody.

Music affects every emotion, but does not by itself excite in us the more terrible emotions of horror, rage etc. It awakens the gentler feelings of tenderness and love, which readily pass into devotion. It likewise stirs up in us the sensation of triumph and the glorious ardour for war. These powerful and mingled feelings may well give rise to the sense of sublimity. We can concentrate, as Dr Seemann observes, greater intensity of feeling in a single musical note than in pages of writing. Nearly the same emotions, but much weaker and less complex, are probably felt by birds when the male pours forth his full volume of song, in rivalry with other males, for the sake of captivating the female. Love is still the commonest theme of our own songs. As Herbert Spencer remarks, music 'arouses dormant sentiments of which we had not conceived the possibility, and do not know the meaning; or, as Richter says, tells us of things we have not seen and shall not see'.[5] Conversely, when vivid emotions are felt and expressed by the orator or even in common speech, musical cadences and rhythms are instinctively used. Monkeys also express strong feelings in different tones – anger and impatience by low – fear and pain by high notes.[6] The sensations and ideas excited in us by music, or by the cadences of impassioned oratory, appear from their vagueness, yet depth, like mental reversions to the emotions and thoughts of a long-past age.

All these facts with respect to music become to a certain extent intelligible if we may assume that musical tones and rhythm were used by the half-human progenitors of man, during the season of courtship, when animals

[4] Since this chapter has been printed I have seen a valuable article by Mr Chauncey Wright (*North Amer. Review* (Oct., 1870), p. 293), who, in discussing the above subject, remarks, 'There are many consequences of the ultimate laws or uniformities of nature through which the acquisition of one useful power will bring with it many resulting advantages as well as limiting disadvantages, actual or possible, which the principle of utility may not have comprehended in its action.' This principle has an important bearing, as I have attempted to shew in the second chapter of this work, on the acquisition by man of some of his mental characteristics.

[5] See the very interesting discussion on the 'Origin and Function of Music', by Mr Herbert Spencer, in his collected *Essays* (1858), p. 359. [See above, pp. 309–14.] Mr Spencer comes to an exactly opposite conclusion to that at which I have arrived. He concludes that the cadences used in emotional speech afford the foundation from which music has been developed; whilst I conclude that musical notes and rhythm were first acquired by the male or female progenitors of mankind for the sake of charming the opposite sex. Thus musical tones became firmly associated with some of the strongest passions an animal is capable of feeling, and are consequently used instinctively, or through association, when strong emotions are expressed in speech. Mr Spencer does not offer any satisfactory explanation, nor can I, why high or deep notes should be expressive, both with man and the lower animals, of certain emotions. Mr Spencer gives also an interesting discussion on the relations between poetry, recitative, and song.

[6] Rengger, *Säugethiere von Paraguay*, p. 49.

of all kinds are excited by the strongest passions. In this case, from the deeply-laid principle of inherited associations, musical tones would be likely to excite in us, in a vague and indefinite manner, the strong emotions of a long-past age.

‹As we have every reason to suppose that articulate speech is one of the latest, as it certainly is the highest, of the arts acquired by man, and as the instinctive power of producing musical notes and rhythms is developed low down in the animal series, it would be altogether opposed to the principle of evolution, if we were to admit that man's musical capacity has been developed from the tones used in impassioned speech. We must suppose that the rhythms and cadences of oratory are derived from previously developed musical powers. We can thus understand how it is that music, dancing, song and poetry are such very ancient arts. We may go even further than this, and, as remarked in a former chapter, believe that musical sounds afforded one of the bases for the development of language.[7],[8] Bearing in mind that the males of some quadrumanous animals have their vocal organs much more developed than in the females, and that one anthropomorphous species pours forth a whole octave of musical notes and may be said to sing, the suspicion does not appear improbable that the progenitors of man, either the males or females, or both sexes, before they had acquired the power of expressing their mutual love in articulate language, endeavoured to charm each other with musical notes and rhythm. So little is known about the use of the voice by the *Quadrumana* during the season of love, that we have hardly any means of judging whether the habit of singing was first acquired by the male or female progenitors of mankind. Women are generally thought to possess sweeter voices than men, and as far as this serves as any guide we may infer that they first acquired musical powers in order to attract the other sex.[9] But if so, this must have occurred long ago, before the progenitors of man had become sufficiently human to treat and value their women merely as useful slaves. The impassioned orator, bard, or musician, when with his varied tones and cadences he excites the strongest emotions in his hearers, little suspects that he uses the same means by which, at an extremely remote period, his half-human ancestors aroused each other's ardent passions, during their mutual courtship and rivalry. [pp. 333–7]

---

[7] I find in Lord Monboddo's *Origin of Language*, vol. 1 (1774), p. 469, that Dr Blacklock likewise thought 'that the first language among men was music, and that before our ideas were expressed by articulate sounds, they were communicated by tones, varied according to different degrees of gravity and acuteness'.

[8] [The passage marked ‹ › and n. 7 were added by Darwin in the second edition (1874).]

[9] See an interesting discussion on this subject by Häckel, *Generelle Morphologie*, vol. 2, 1866, p. 246.

# Charles Darwin

## The expression of the emotions in man and animals (1872)

*Source:*

*The Expression of the Emotions in Man and Animals* (London 1872),
chapter viii: Joy, high spirits, love, tender feelings, devotion, pp. 218–19.

### Chapter VIII: Joy, high spirits, love, tender feelings, devotion

[.    .    .]

With respect to joy, its natural and universal expression is laughter; and with
all the races of man loud laughter leads to the secretion of tears more freely
than does any other cause excepting distress. The suffusion of the eyes with
tears, which undoubtedly occurs under great joy, though there is no laughter,
can, as it seems to me, be explained through habit and association on the same
principles as the effusion of tears from grief, although there is no screaming.
Nevertheless it is not a little remarkable that sympathy with the distresses of
others should excite tears more freely than our own distress; and this certainly is the case. Many a man, from whose eyes no suffering of his own could
wring a tear, has shed tears at the sufferings of a beloved friend. It is still more
remarkable that sympathy with the happiness or good fortune of those whom
we tenderly love should lead to the same result, whilst a similar happiness felt
by ourselves would leave our eyes dry. We should, however, bear in mind that
the long-continued habit of restraint which is so powerful in checking the free
flow of tears from bodily pain, has not been brought into play in preventing a
moderate effusion of tears in sympathy with the sufferings or happiness of
others.

Music has a wonderful power, as I have elsewhere attempted to show,[1] of
recalling in a vague and indefinite manner, those strong emotions which were
felt during long-past ages, when, as is probable, our early progenitors courted
each other by the aid of vocal tones. And as several of our strongest emotions
– grief, great joy, love, and sympathy – lead to the free secretion of tears, it is
not surprising that music should be apt to cause our eyes to become suffused
with tears, especially when we are already softened by any of the tenderer
feelings. Music often produces another peculiar effect. We know that every
strong sensation, emotion, or excitement – extreme pain, rage, terror, joy, or

---

[1] *The Descent of Man*, vol. 2, pp. 336–7.

the passion of love – all have a special tendency to cause the muscles to tremble; and the thrill or slight shiver which runs down the backbone and limbs of many persons when they are powerfully affected by music, seems to bear the same relation to the above trembling of the body, as a slight suffusion of tears from the power of music does to weeping from any strong and real emotion. [pp. 218–19]

[.   .   .]

# Richard Wallaschek (1860–1917)

## Primitive music (1893)

Austrian musicologist and psychologist of Czech descent. He studied law and philosophy at the universities in Vienna, Heidelberg, Tübingen and Berne, and for a period taught at the University of Freiburg im Breisgau. Between 1890 and 1895 he lived in London, and published several papers in British learned journals. On his return to Vienna he wrote his *Habilitationsschrift* working with Ernst Mach and Friedrich Jodl. In 1897 he took up an appointment at Vienna University lecturing there on the psychology and aesthetics of music and inspiring a number of disciples.

He disagreed with Spencer's assertion about the close connection of speech and music, preferring to view music as an outcome of a strong sense of rhythmic drive: 'Men do not come to music by way of tones, but they come to tones and tunes by way of the rhythmical impulse' (*Primitive Music*, p. 235). The polemics between Wallaschek and Spencer was carried out on the pages of *Mind*, vols. 15 (1890), 16 (1891) and new series, vol. 1 (1892).

## Primitive music

*Source:*

> *Primitive Music, an Inquiry into the Origin and Development of Music, Songs, Instruments, Dances and Pantomimes of Savage Races* (London 1893). Chapter viii: Primitive drama and pantomime, pp. 214–16. Chapter ix: On the origin of music, pp. 230; 231–3; 234–5. Chapter ix is closely based on 'On the origin of music', Wallaschek's response to Spencer, originally published in *Mind*, vol. 16 (1891), pp. 375–86.
>
> The second edition of *Primitive Music* appeared in an extended version in German as *Anfänge der Tonkunst* (Leipzig, 1903).

### Chapter VIII: Primitive drama and pantomime

We have seen in the former chapters how intimately music and dancing are connected. Primitive dances have in the most cases a special meaning: they have to represent something and have therefore a position among the other arts quite different from the modern dances. At such representations no words are spoken, but mimicry and gestures are not less a language, far better fitted to explain the action than the primitive language of words. These pantomimes, as we may call them, are indeed a primitive drama, and as music is always connected with dances one may judge how great the importance was that music had on these occasions. Dramatic music, or musical drama, if you like, is not an occasional union of two different arts, it is originally one organism, and at the same time the earliest manifestation of human art in general. Therefore, Richard Wagner's artistic genius again correctly defined the essential character of the drama when he said: 'Long before the epic songs of Homer had become a matter of literary concern they had flourished among the people as actually represented works of art, supported by the voice and gesture, so to speak, as concentrated, fixed, lyric, dancing songs (*verdichtete, gefestigte, lyrische Gesangstänze*), in which the poets' fondness of resting with the description of the action and the repetition of heroic dialogues prevailed.'[1] In one word, the historical order of all the branches of poetry does not begin with the epos – as frequently taught – but with the drama, lyric coming next, the epos lastly. This is the order the ethnologist can trace, this is at the same time the most simple and natural way in the development of poetry. The epos requires for all its psychological details so much polish of language, so much grammar and refined style to follow all the different shades of expression as to render very difficult our expecting this from very primitive people. For the dramatic representation mimicry and gestures are not only quite sufficient but the only effective means for explaining the action to an audience of different tribes, which sometimes do not understand their respective dialects and are accustomed to converse in gesture language.

Unfortunately Richard Wagner lost his advantageous position (just as in speaking of dance and music) when elaborating his intuitive idea. Then he called those dancing songs 'a middleway station from the ancient lyric to the drama', although the pantomime cannot possibly be the very beginning of poetry and a middleway station at the same time. Wagner constantly over-looks the fact that the primitive drama is pantomime only, not poetry as well, no words being spoken in it. It is not until later on that other arts, poetry among them, begin to show their germs, which they unfold and develop in the same proportion as they become independent and separate themselves from the common trunk. This done it would be contrary to all laws of development that the accomplished arts should once more form an organic union as they might have formed in their primitive state. Therefore, the attempt to unite the accomplished arts in equal rank to a single art work is theoretically a contradiction and practically an impossibility. The result of such an attempt was always that the composer either spoiled his art by a theoretical prejudice or practically acted contrary to his rules. Wagner's artistic genius was never in doubt for a single moment which way to go, and therefore his theory has remained an intolerable chaos, while his art has flourished in unrivalled splendour. [pp. 214–16]

[  .  .  .]

[1] Wagner, *Gesammelte Schriften und Dichtungen*, 10 vols. (Leipzig 1871–3), vol. 3, p. 124. [*Das Kunstwerk der Zukunft*, *GS*, vol. 3, p. 104; *PW*, vol. 1, p. 135.]

## Chapter IX: On the origin of music

We have been told until tired of hearing it, that the one essential feature in primitive music was rhythm, melody being of accessory importance. We do not meet with a single instance among savages of melody, fixed according to musical principles; melodic cadences, where they occur, serve only as signals, or as a convenient accompaniment to certain activities, such as rowing, towing, or fighting. Even among savage tribes where some songs have in course of time become traditional, words and melody are varied after a few repetitions by different singers, or even by the same performer. Rhythm, taken in a general sense to include 'keeping in time', is the essence in music, in its simplest form as well as in the most skilfully elaborated fugues of modern composers. To recall a tune the rhythm must be revived first, and the melody will easily be recalled. The latter may be suggested by the former, but never vice versa. Completely to understand a musical work ceases to be difficult when once its rhythmical arrangement is mastered; and it is through rhythmical performance and rhythmical susceptibility that musical effects are produced and perceived. From these several data I conclude that the origin of music must be sought in a rhythmical impulse in man. I do not mean that musical effects consist in rhythmical movement as such; innumerable ideas and feelings become associated with it, and give rise to those emotions which we on hearing it experience. [pp. 230]

[.    .    .]

If it be asked whence the sense of rhythm arises, I answer, from the general appetite for exercise. That this desire occurs in rhythmical form is due to sociological as well as psychological conditions. On the one hand, there is the social character of primitive music, compelling a number of performers to act in concert. On the other, our perception of time-relations involves a process of intellection, the importance of which has been pointed out by Professor Sully, and which I cannot better describe than in his own words: 'This perception of successive or time-ordered impressions is something more than a succession of impressions or perceptions. It involves a subsequent act of reflection, by means of which the mind is able at the same time to comprehend them as a whole.'[2] Now every product which is of the intellect and appeals to the intellect must contain all the particulars which follow from reflection and render it possible. And since music is produced not merely as an auditory impression and expression, but also in order to evoke reflection, it must contain the qualities above alluded to, viz. time-order and rhythm. Such being the grounds for rhythmical expression the question still remains to be answered: Whence does the general desire for exercise arise? Mr Herbert Spencer's theory affords the most valid explanation. It is the surplus vigour in more highly evolved organisms, exceeding what is required for immediate needs, in which play of all kinds takes its rise; manifesting itself by way of

[2] J. Sully, *Outlines of Psychology*, 2nd edn (London 1885), p. 206.

imitation or repetition of all those efforts and exertions which were essential to the maintenance of life (e.g. the war-dance).[3] And it has, moreover, been demonstrated by ethnological research that to bring about bodily fatigue through the manifestation of energy in a perpetually-increasing ratio up to the last degree of lassitude is an indispensable feature of primitive art.[4]

It may be objected that a mere craving for rhythm is far from amounting to a desire for tones and melody, and that, therefore, the question, as to what gives rise to our discriminative pleasure in musical intervals, is not yet satisfactorily answered. The origin of the significance of intervals and our appreciation of them is indeed one of the utmost importance for our present purpose. A simple example, however, will teach us that rhythm and sonant rhythm coincide. Try to play first on a stretched, and then on an unstretched, drum or kettledrum, such as savages use, and you will see that rhythm brings us in and by itself to sound and certain tones, owing to the fact that the rhythmical movement becomes much more distinct and better-marked on the former, than on the latter, instrument. Hence it came about that men did not stop at simply striking on deerskins as they used to do in primitive times, but proceeded to stretch them first i.e. to perform on drums and kettledrums. The same implicit principle prompted the custom, in grammar schools on the Continent, of teaching the rhythms of classic poetry in a kind of chant, not of course for musical purposes, but simply because the rhythms were rendered much more distinct when intoned. Perhaps no other illustration shows so well how a rhythmical design, in and by itself, brings us to musical tones, and, by way of these, to the appreciation of intervals and melody. [pp. 231–3]

[.    .]

That the development of a melody from detached notes is due in the first instance to a certain rhythmical movement is an obvious fact. Detached notes do not as such prompt to further development or variety. Rhythm is the initiative force which leads us on to any arrangement of notes whatever, although it must not be forgotten that the specific form assumed in any such arrangement depends a good deal upon our contingent ideas and feelings. The power exerted over us by any rhythmical movement lies in its being

---

[3] H. Spencer, *Principles of Psychology*, §534.

[4] It is curious, that whereas Mr Spencer and all the other English writers who treat of the so-called *Spieltrieb* (play-impulse), e.g. Messrs Sully and Grant Allen, regard it as an entirely German idea, in Germany it has always been ascribed to English theorists. It did indeed find embodiment in the writings of Schiller, but was, in my opinion, smothered rather than brought to light by the philosophical jargon which he learned from Kant, and by his own obscure metaphysical style. He ran into a great labyrinth of metaphysics, whence nobody can find the way out – nor could the author himself, I should suppose. Hence the theory remained unheeded, though committed to writing nearly a century ago. Put in our times into intelligible form by Mr Herbert Spencer, it has nothing in common with its earlier presentment beyond the name, the grounds being quite different. But just as Schiller was inspired by Pope and Addison in his *Anmuth und Würde* and *Briefe über die ästhetische Erziehung des Menschen*, he likewise found approximations to the *Spieltrieb* theory in Home's *Elements of Criticism*, chapter v (see Zimmermann's *Geschichte der Ästhetik*).

adjusted to the form in which ideas and feelings succeed each other in our mind. A composer may give us a direct imitation of some movement of external nature (a thunderstorm, a waterfall, or the like); but the fact holds good none the less, that the effect produced in us even in such cases is due to our recognizing, in the intensity, strength, velocity, increase and decrease of the movements, forms corresponding to the flow of our ideas and feelings, though the nature of that flow depends entirely on each individual psychical organism. [pp. 234–5]

[.     .     .]

# Karl Bücher (1847–1930)

## Arbeit und Rhythmus (1896)

German economist and sociologist. He studied history and philology in Bonn and Göttingen and after graduation worked in the Verein für Sozialpolitik and as an editor on the *Frankfurter Zeitung*. He obtained his lecturing qualification (*Habilitation*) in 1881 and went to teach at the German–Russian university in Dorpat (now Tartu, Estonia, USSR). During the period 1883–92 he taught at Basle and Karlsruhe, and then 1892–1917 at the University of Leipzig. As an economist he belonged to an older school in which prominence was given to historical speculation and a straightforward application of statistical data.

# Work and rhythm

*Source:*

*Arbeit und Rhythmus*, 2nd edn (Leipzig 1899). [Chapter] ii: Rhythmische Gestaltung der Arbeit, pp. 24–9; [chapter] ix: Der Rhythmus als ökonomisches Entwicklungsprincip, pp. 357–9; 363–5; 379–82. Translated by Martin Cooper.

In its original form the study was presented to the Royal Saxon Society of Sciences and published in Leipzig in 1896, and then included in *Abhandlungen der Königlich Sächsischen Gesellschaft der Wissenschaften*, vol. 39 (*Philologisch-historische Classe*, vol. 17) (Leipzig 1897). The 1899 edition is a considerably expanded version of the original work.

### Chapter II: Rhythmic shaping of the process of work

Every task which human beings set themselves to accomplish has two aspects: a mental aspect and a physical. The mental aspect is not complete when the readiness to undertake the work has been aroused; in fact this is only its first stage. For the essential task of the mind is to recognize the technical means by which the object of the undertaking may best be achieved. This mental operation will be repeated on each occasion of a change of method during the course of the operation, which will accordingly demand more or less thought from those engaged.

A workman's physical contribution can always be reduced to the simple movements of his muscles.[1] Every continuous using of a muscle produces fatigue and this fatigue will vary according to the length of time that muscle is used and the variety of strength required by each individual movement.

The effective performance of any task depends on the workman's correct assessment of the muscle-movement needed and the amount of strength he must use. The truer this is of any task, the more closely related are its mental and physical aspects and the more satisfactory the progress made.

Now it is an everyday observation that children and primitive people seldom persevere long in any activity, that the speed with which they tire is in direct proportion to the amount of simultaneous mental attention and physical effort required. The reason for this doubtless lies not only in the fatigue produced by the continued use of the same muscle, but also in the fact of sustained mental alertness. It is, however, possible to remove this last factor by partially or entirely excluding it. This can be done by substituting an automatic (i.e. purely mechanical) movement for one involving conscious volition.[2] This happens if the expenditure of effort in the work concerned can be so designed that it occurs with a certain regularity i.e. the beginning and end of a movement always falling within the same lengths of time and space. If the same muscular effort is expended at identical intervals, we have what we call 'practice' or 'routine' [Übung]: a physical effort made at definite intervals and of definite volume will continue mechanically without any new exertion of the will, until it is either arrested by a different act of volition or, if necessary, accelerated or made slower.

It is a matter of common experience that the fatigue caused by work diminishes with practice; and this is explained by the fact that the amount of energy expended is [initially] either too great or too small, and this results in an uneconomic use of the powers involved. All practice is a matter of adaptation; muscle-movements are tied to a law; the degree of strength required is not altered if it is tentative; pauses for rest between movements are designed according to the amount of strength expended, like the movements themselves.

Now we have no immediate awareness and no absolute way of measuring the duration of a movement, but we do know that the shorter it is, the easier it is to make a movement uniform. The actual measuring is greatly facilitated if each movement in an operation includes at least two elements, a stronger and a weaker – raising and lowering, pushing and pulling, extending and contracting etc. This gives the movement a shape of its own, with the result that the regular recurrence of movements of equal force at equal intervals of time inevitably suggests to us the idea of rhythm.

We possess evidence to show that any work involving regular relations of measurement tends to take on a rhythmic character. This tendency is shown most clearly in the many operations in which the contact of the workman's

[1] See H. H. Gossen, *Entwicklung der Gesetze des menschlichen Verkehrs* (Braun-schweig 1854) p. 35ff.
[2] See W. Wundt, *System der Philosophie* (Leipzig 1889), p. 584ff.

tool with his material produces a sound. Loud blows or knocks recurring at regular intervals lead us to infer a similar expenditure of energy in the force involved and a similarity in the duration (or distance) of the accompanying movements. The hammer-blows of the smith, the locksmith, the tinker and the brazier follow a regular rhythm. The sounds of the joiner's plane, saw, rasp and scraper follow each other at regular intervals; and we are all familiar with the sounds of the cobbler's hammer, the flax-breaker's break, the weaver's shuttle, the carpenter's axe, the paver's beetle and the stone-worker's chisel!

Such examples could be extended *ad infinitum*. Domestic agricultural operations, for instance, include many involving a sound which regularly punctuates the work. This sound generally marks the end of an individual movement, and there can be no doubt that this makes it easier to maintain a steady rhythm in those movements. This is the hallmark of work-rhythms, but it is not in itself a sound-rhythm, which only arises when sounds differ in strength and pitch or duration; and then the work-rhythm is accompanied by a corresponding sound-rhythm.

Many different kinds of work are accompanied by rhythms of this kind. When a floor is scrubbed, the backward and forward movements involve sounds of alternating strength. In the same way scything produces sounds of different strength and duration, as the scythe cuts and is withdrawn; and the movements of the weaver's shuttle produce different sounds according to the weaver's intention or to the difference in strength between his right and left hands, and these are heard against the regular alternation of the shafts. The cooper's hammer-blows as he fits the hoops to his barrel differ in strength and form a kind of melody, and the butcher's assistant produces a sort of drum-march with his choppers. Even occupations that appear quite unrelated to this kind of rhythmic activity are in fact marked by similar phenomena – winnowing for instance, and sand-loading, with the loading of the shovel and the rejecting of chaff or emptying the shovel-load into the sand-wagon.

In all these instances the sound-rhythm is not of course independent but determined by the rhythm of the work. There is still no doubt that the sound-rhythm, too, is significant for the intensity of the work. Not only does the maintaining of a regular rhythm support the workmen's movements; it also has an encouraging effect, due to its essentially musical character, and gives all those who can hear it an idea of how the work is progressing. It may thus be said that sound-rhythm both facilitates and promotes work. [pp. 24–9]

[.    .    .]

## Chapter IX: Rhythm as a principle of economic development

Our investigations have shown us a mass of lines leading, in the world of today, in many very different directions. But the further back we trace them, the nearer these lines converge, until they all unite in a single common starting-point. This point lies on the borderline of pre-history, a dark and trackless area; and yet if we cast our eyes back over the thousands of years that have elapsed since that time, we can trace a definite process of social evolution. This evolution may be regarded from two angles – the practical and the human – the first showing us the differentiation and integration of human activities and the second the collaboration and subdivision of labour among those engaged in these activities.

At this early stage there was no closer distinction between art and play. There was a single human activity which merged work, play and art together. In this original unity of human activity, both mental and physical, we can discern the seeds of what were later to become agriculture and technology, and the main varieties of games and arts, with their alternation of movement and repose. If we choose to apply these ideas more closely, we come to the following conclusion – arts involving movement (music, dance and poetry) make their appearance simultaneously with the performance of a work-task, and the arts that do not involve movement (sculpture and painting) appear incorporated in the products of that work, though in many cases simply in the form of ornamentation.[3] There is still no idea of economy, only a pure, instinctive vital activity.

The link between these elements, which seem to us so diverse, is rhythm: the organization in time of various movements. Rhythm is something inherent in the human organism, regulating all activities of the animal body according to the law of minimum effort. The motions of a trotting horse and a loaded camel are as rhythmical as those of a boatman steering and a smith hammering. Rhythm arouses pleasurable feelings and therefore makes work easier; but it is also one of the sources of aesthetic pleasure and is the element in art that appeals to all human beings, regardless of their cultural development. In the early days of humanity rhythm appears as the instinctive economic principle by which (according to Schäffle) men instinctively seek a maximum awareness of life and comfort with a minimum expenditure of vital effort and a minimum sacrifice of happiness. [pp. 357–9]

[.     .     .]

Let us for a moment imagine ourselves at that point of time when economic activity actually began in primitive society. On the one hand we have man himself, indigent and undeveloped in mind and body; on the other we have the natural world from which he must satisfy his needs, by means of labour. All that labour will be directed to the transporting or transforming of natural objects. To accomplish these tasks he has nothing at his disposal beyond his

[3] [. . .] According to E. Grosse [*Die Anfänge der Kunst* (Freiburg im Breisgau 1894)], p. 241ff., the decorative art of primitive peoples provides the most widespread evidence for the 'principle of rhythmical arrangement'. This principle would therefore govern not only the different elements of primitive activity treated here, but it would also be applicable to the products of that activity. To pursue this point further would lead us too far afield.

own limbs, which he moves according to the anatomical and physiological relationship to the rest of his body, and thus acts on the raw material of nature. This operation is undertaken with artificial aids to facilitate the employment of his muscles. The expenditure of strength and its effectiveness are at best equal, since mechanical devices that economize effort are still unknown.

In such circumstances the transportation and transformation of objects is an extremely arduous and tedious task, since they can only be accomplished by the direct use of arms, hands, feet, nails and teeth. Not only that, but every movement in every operation is absolutely conscious, determined simply by the natural mechanical aids provided by the body itself. The great majority of these movements must therefore automatically become rhythmical in character.

Even the invention of the first tools does little to change this state of things, as tools are in the first instance no more than improvements of limbs designed to make more effective the action for which that limb is most used in the work-process.[4] Thus the hammer is a tougher and less sensitive fist, the file, the scraper and the spade replace the fingernails, the tiller is only the extension of the hollow hand and the polishing stone replaces the palm of the hand. It is true that tools are objects interposed between the workman and the material on which he is working, but the workman is still working directly on his material. He is still independent in all his movements, which are controlled entirely by his own volition. Their extension, duration and speed are determined entirely by the constitution of his body, his technical intelligence and his mood. They are not subject to any other power.

The whole method of work depends on the individual. Tools themselves become, as it were, parts of the individual, as can still be seen today when each man works most effectively with his own shovel, his own axe, hatchet or mallet.[5] Moreover most of these methods of working are relatively ineffectual. Each individual task demands long uninterrupted effort in order to achieve the desired result. These are all circumstances which, even at this early stage, offer a very wide scope to the rhythmic shaping of work movements. At the same time the use of hard, vibrating metals for fashioning tools produces work-sounds that are rhythmical, and therefore musical, in character. These have an exciting effect on primitive man because they produce feelings of pleasure which he seeks to repeat and to emphasize. Thus it is that we find the sounds made by tools imitated by the human voice, and the 'work-song' eventually emerges. [pp. 363–5]

[.    .    .]

---

[4] See K. D. H. Rau, *Grundsätze der Volkswirtschaftslehre* (Heidelberg 1826), vol. 1, §125, and M. Chevalier, *Die heutige Industrie, ihre Fortschritte und die Voraussetzungen ihrer Stärke* (Berlin 1863), p. 12.
[5] This is the reason why many old guilds demanded that a journeyman should possess his own tools.

At first machines never did more than relieve the workman of a single movement, and it is a remarkable fact in the history of machinery that many of the oldest machines in fact have a rhythmical motion and simply imitate the hand- and arm-movements executed hitherto by the individual. Thus, the earliest planing-machines copy the thrusts of the hand-plane: the earliest machine-saws, or frame-saws are modelled on the hand-saw, the earliest sausage-machines on the cleaver. The first mechanical printing-press closely resembles the old hand-press, and the first machine for polishing leather performs movements like those of the polishing-stone. The next stage in the history of machinery was to abolish the unproductive withdrawing action in these processes, a feature commonly essential to the rhythmical motion of the machine. This was accomplished, wherever possible, by substituting a uniform rotary movement for the original vertical or horizontal gestures of the human workman, thus economizing energy. In this way the frame-saw was replaced first by the circular and then by the band-saw and wood-polishing was done by lathe and roller-lathe machines [*Scheiben- und Walzenhobelmaschinen*], while the rotary press replaced the earlier device. With these improvements there disappeared from the workshop the old music that was still clearly recognizable in the rhythmic action of the first machines. The swift movement of cogwheel-machinery gives out sounds that are simply confused and deafeningly loud. It is of course possible to detect a kind of rhythm in them, but we do not instinctively hear them as rhythmical and they therefore arouse feelings that are the opposite of pleasurable.

In this new world of machinery the tasks that are still accomplished by hand (such as feeding the machine with raw material) do not necessarily exclude rhythmical motions of the body. In fact many machines make rhythmical movements possible at stages where this was not so in the old manual processes. But such new work-rhythms are quite different from the old. The workman is no longer master of his own movements, with the tool acting as his servant and a kind of additional limb. Now it is the machine that dictates the limits of his movements, and the speed and duration of his work no longer depends on him. He is in fact bound by the mechanism, at once so lifeless and so full of energy.

It is this that makes factory-work destroying and oppressive: the human workman has become the slave of a servant who never rests and never tires, he has become almost a part of the mechanism whose work he must complete at certain given points. And it is in this way that work-songs have disappeared. What hope has the human voice against the clatter and hum of machinery and all those indefinable noises that pervade most factories, banishing all delight! Fortunately not all machine-work is factory-work, and in addition to this working the machines themselves remains handwork. And wherever this work demands bodily movements and involves periods of uniform duration, there appears – and will always be present – a tendency to a kind of rhythmical structuring.

If this situation is recognized, does it provide any important practical pointers for the technical development of the work-process? As early as 1835 P. J. Schneider was maintaining that 'the intelligent and judicious use of rhythmical power could effect an economy of as much as twenty-five per cent in the majority of undertakings such as road-building, water-works, civil and military engineering and weaving processes of various kinds, in mining, salt- and sugar-refining, forging, glass, china and tobacco manufacture'. This may sound fantastic, but we should not overlook the fact that rhythmical work, and work songs, have persisted longest in those operations that are heaviest (towing, pile-driving).

We cannot pursue this matter further here, since we are only concerned with discovering the hidden forces that have been active in the social and economic development of humanity for thousands of years. We cannot expect to obtain satisfactory results in every field at the first attempt. We find the life of primitive peoples too alien and remote, both physically and mentally; and we have to take into account the fact that elements originally associated are today so widely dissociated that it is impossible to be sure in every case of their profound correlation. Art and technology have followed very different lines of development, and, more especially, the arts of move-ment have lost all connection with technological science and training and now play virtually no role in a workman's life. On the other hand the arts of repose have for long been trying to restore their link with technology; any organic connection between the two is virtually out of the question in most fields.

The life of the individual has thus become poorer and less interesting. His work no longer includes elements of music and poetry, and production for the market no longer carries with it the personal prestige and satisfaction associ-ated with work done for personal use. Goods have to be produced in quantity and this allows no scope for the artistic sense of the individual worker, even supposing he possessed it. Art itself is subordinate to earning one's living. Professional activity is not a light-hearted sport and involves no element of gratification or satisfaction: it is a matter of stern duty and often involves painful self-denial. Even so, we should not overlook the general benefit achieved by this process of development. The differentiation between art and technology and the separation of their fields of activity have brought an unimagined productivity. Work itself has become more productive and the provision of economic goods greatly increased. We need not, I believe, even despair of art and technology one day achieving a higher rhythmical unity, which might restore the serene contentment of mind and the harmonious physical development characteristic of the best primitive people. [pp. 379–82]

# Carl Stumpf
## Die Anfänge der Musik (1911)

# The origins of music

*Source:*

Die Anfänge der Musik (Leipzig 1911). Chapter v: Entwicklungsrichtungen, pp. 53–61. Translated by Martin Cooper.

## Chapter V: Trends in development

[.   .   .]

Before anything that could properly be called music existed, work- and dance-rhythms were marked by percussion instruments and inarticulate vocal sounds. As an element of music, however, rhythm was first introduced after pitched sounds [*Töne*] had taken the place of noises, and not only sounds but intervals. At first small intervals were employed for signalling or simply for amusement and it was discovered that, by approximately the same means, such intervals could be recreated at other absolute pitches. Intervals of this kind were produced both by the human voice and also by means of primitive instruments (wood-blocks and the like). Music in any deeper sense did not come into existence until the discovery of the consonant intervals, and most importantly the octave, which then provided a solid framework for the smaller intervals. This discovery was based on the ability [of sounds] to blend and on the occasion of a number of individuals simultaneously exchanging signals. Here again the pitched sound could be given by the voice or by instrumental means, but in either case the basic intervals must be the same. In any case any further development of singing also depended on the objective fixing of intervals such as only instruments could achieve. Apart from the phenomena of blending, the similarity of timbre in successive notes – at least in cases where overtones were plentiful – could lead to the basic intervals. In the case of wind instruments the notes produced by over-blowing increased the consciousness of these intervals. These, however, were not the chief cause.

At the same time that small as well as large fixed intervals were introduced the rhythmic characteristics became more sharply differentiated, in the first place as signals but also for purely artistic reasons e.g. in connection with dancing and liturgical language. The long stressing of higher pitches and the

334

use of fixed intervals were also carried over into heightened forms of speech, and speech-song [*Sprechgesang*] became a special kind of music.[1]

Comprehensive analysis and comparison will enable us to discover the chief forms of melodic structure and their gradual perfecting. We shall find that the development of patterns resembling laws in the rhythmic structure of melodies has been partly dependent on metre and partly independent. The different frequency and duration of individual notes, the size of the intervals between them, and their tuning, the purity of their intonation, the length of individual melodic phrases and of the melody as a whole, the details of performance – in short, all the features that distinguish one melody from another – must be examined statistically and psychologically in the material that we shall hope to garner in good time. At the present moment we are a long way from such an understanding of the melodic processes in primitive peoples: a beginning has been made indeed, but it is too early to make any general statement on the subject.

I should like to add a few words suggesting the paths followed in the further development of the whole musical system [*Tonsystem*] itself, from its first beginnings; or – to refer at once to the empirical material at hand – the essential, purely tonal differences to be found among non-European peoples, to help in forming a picture of exactly how [our own] music developed.

The first point worthy of note is an increasing centralization of musical material. Melodies gradually begin to be marked by a predominating note [*Hauptton*], which we now call the tonic. To our ears there can be no melody and no chord that is not related to this tonic. As soon as we relate a note to a different tonic, it changes its musical character. But this rigid centralization, this clear definition of the tonic as the lowest note of the scale and the harmonic and melodic functions arising from this are late developments.

Gradually, too, scales within the octave grow in significance, most notably those having five and seven degrees. The formation of these scales occurs from different angles, of which two are of primary importance. The first is the concern for a logical extension of the principle of consonance, which leads to the use first of open fifths and fourths and much later of pure thirds to add new intervals and to determine exactly their behaviour. After that arose the principle of distance i.e. the question 'which note is to lie between two other given notes?' Thus within two notes forming a fourth or a fifth a third note may be inserted, giving in the one case a whole tone – which is too large an interval – and in the other a neutral third. The discovery that this is in fact the way in which our ancestors did proceed was not established until Siamese and Javanese music was studied.[2] In this way scales arise consisting of equal

---

[1] In the extensive work of Rowbotham's *A History of Music* (vol. 1, London 1885), the pre-history of music was explained in this way: in the first stage one sound was used, in the second two, in the third three sounds (always distanced by a whole tone). [...]

[2] [The results of the early research in non-European scales are conveniently summarized for English-speaking readers in A. J. Ellis's Appendix xx: Additions by the Translator, section K, to his translation of H. Helmholtz's *On the Sensations of Tone* (London 1885, repr. New York 1954), pp. 514–22.]

degrees, without distinguishing tones and semitones. Five- and seven-note scales of this kind exist, which have not a single note in common with our scales and sound out of tune to a trained European ear.[3] However, these are by no means primitive attempts but the creations of an advanced culture, only of a different kind from their own. Scales constructed, as these are, on the principle of mere acoustic distance [*Tonabstand*] may be considered as developments of what we found in a primitive form among the Veda i.e. the formation of small intervals regardless of consonance and simply based on an appropriate estimate of difference in pitch. These seeds have borne fruit, and the ability to distinguish almost identical intervals has become a virtuoso achievement similar to the recognizing and distinguishing of the different degrees of consonance among Western musicians. Not, however, for its own sake and not only unaided [*aus eigener Kraft*]. For both Siamese and Javanese always start at least from the octave, which forms the frame within which the degrees are numbered off according to the principle of distance. It is even probable that the fourth and fifth play an indirect part.[4] There are therefore no fully elaborate scales based simply on the principle of distance.

In the third place we find very different styles of melody-construction appearing. Although among primitive peoples the principles are often similar to our own and the Siamese principle described above is perfectly intelligible to us, phonograph records of music from South China reveal under analysis principles in the construction and variation of melodies that would be unthinkable to us (removal of several bars, replacing of individual notes by their fifths and other things of the same kind).[5] These may be signs of a decadent art, but however that may be they appear to us as wholly alien and strange.

Finally we have differences in the employment of simultaneous notes and phrases. The references that we have made to this earlier applied to still relatively primitive phenomena. On the other hand we find that Asian civilizations have systematized a kind of polyphony that differs from ours in every way. In China, Japan, Upper India and the Sunda Islands[6] whole orchestras perform a melody in a way that suggests several variations of the theme being played simultaneously rather than in succession. One instrument continues playing the theme in its original form, while another performs more or less free variation on it. Although the original melody dominates the whole, there naturally occur what to our ears seem bad discords; but since the feeling for harmony has not been developed in these civilizations, they are not felt as such i.e. as unpleasing. I have called this kind of polyphony – in contradistinction to harmonic music – *heterophony*, after the word used by Plato in describing a certain kind of polyphony practised in ancient Greece. It is in fact quite possible that Siamese and Japanese music may give us an idea

---

[3] These scales have been established with certainty by D. de Land, A. J. Ellis and myself (through observations made together with Dr O. Abraham). (*Berliner Phonogramm-Archiv*, no. 1.) [. . .]
[4] *Phonogramm-Archiv*, no. 1, pp. 96ff.
[5] *Phonogramm-Archiv*, no. 21 (Fisher).
[6] [i.e. Indonesia]

of this same ancient Greek practice.[7] On the other hand, although our modern European music may show occasional isolated resemblances, it is firmly based on the system of chord arising from a logical and exclusive application of the principle of consonance. It is the fact that in our music the original phenomenon which is the source, the kernel and the very breath of music's being finds its purest and fullest expression, and has been assumed as the stylistic principle of the whole imposing structure – it is this fact that enables us without illiberality to claim to have produced what is from the anthropological, psychological and evolutionary point of view the highest form of music yet known.

I should like in this way to counter the misunderstanding to which such comparisons are sometimes exposed, based on the belief that all value-judgements are wrong, or indeed that the primitive should be taken as a model for our imitation. This Rousseauish fallacy still appears in aesthetic as well as ethical discussions, championed by some enthusiasts: but it is in direct contradiction to the whole idea of development. We are surely not asked to develop backwards. The 'golden age' lies not in the past but in the future, or so at least we hope. We may well discover the real hallmarks of man's spiritual activity in what at first seem the rough products of primitive man. A deep and sympathetic study of the simplest objects – a kind of 'devotion to the miniature' – may well reveal a sense of form, a relationship between component parts, a hierarchical system of values, an ability to recognize identical relationships in different materials – in fact all the hallmarks of spiritual penetration. Such knowledge does not destroy the standard by which we judge later cultures: it merely corrects that standard. Understanding and comparison can only increase the stature of anything that is genuinely great. Comparative study of arts, by emphasizing the unimagined multiplicity of possible art-styles, can only lead towards more judicious and more objective judgements. Such study may even feed the imagination of the creative artist himself – think of the stimulus that Goethe and our modern painters received from oriental art – but it also reveals at the same time the astronomical distances between the explorations of methods once adopted and the different potential value of different artistic principles. There are many kinds of artistic principles, all equally possible and with equal claims, but only a few of these lead to the flowering of a great culture. It is in this way that we first come to appreciate the wonders of this latest musical era, and learn to put our trust in that literally unfathomable power of artistic creation which is responsible for the noblest creation of the past and still today employs fresh means to produce fresh marvels. [pp. 53–61]

---

[7] Guido Adler has published a special study of heterophony ('Über Heterophonie', *Jahrbuch der Musikbibliothek Peters für 1908*, 1909). [. . .]

# Part 4: Bridge between music theory and philosophy and the beginnings of musicology as an independent discipline

# Introduction

The ingredients for a systematic study of music in all of its aspects – historical, technical, theoretical, aesthetic – existed before, in some cases well before the nineteenth century, but at no other time in history were conditions so favourable for such a study as was the case during the middle of the nineteenth century. The initiative did not come from the musicians themselves. The romantic image of a lonely, suffering and rebellious artist and the divinely inspired virtuoso performer did not go towards helping a dispassionate study. Indeed, the image clashed with the enquiring spirit of historical study and the increasing application of scientific method in psychology and positivist sociology. It became increasingly apparent that the positivist step-by-step investigation could be applied in order to counter and de-mystify this romantic attitude. The actual task of formulating a programme for a systematic study came from those scholars who occupied the middle ground between philosophical speculation and scientific rigour or, to put it differently, from those whose traditional humanistic learning was influenced by the positivist manner of defining the scope of a discipline and devising sub-disciplines and categories.

Although, as mentioned earlier, positivism in the narrow sense was largely a French phenomenon, positivist attitude to science and philosophy was powerfully felt in Germany and, taking into consideration the weight of German historiography and philosophy, it is not surprising to see that the programme of a systematic study of music was largely a German phenomenon. A characteristic of positivism was a belief in progress and improvement along the line of a constant development of social institutions as well as the arts, but in Germany it had to be modified by a strong surviving romantic yearning for the past. The importance of the past may have been intensified by the desire to define national identity – a task that had to be achieved in the sphere of culture as a substitute for the existence of a nation-state which Germany still lacked throughout the best part of the nineteenth century. Musicology was seen largely as an aid in the process of the rediscovery of the past, and it is not surprising that the discipline was weighted in favour of history.

The situation was somewhat paradoxical. Throughout its history music behaved in the manner of which the positivists would have approved: it was an art in which, more than in any other art-form, the new tended to displace the old to the point of a complete oblivion. The idea of progress had already become evident through the system of notation which was in the state of flux and constant change from the early Middle Ages up to the eighteenth century. The task of discovering the past was therefore seen as being identical with the effort of establishing 'scientifically' the identity of music, and the result was a reverence for the past otherwise uncharacteristic of positivism. Hegel's view of historical progress and Leopold von Ranke's famous dictum 'wie es eigentlich gewesen' both contributed in their own way to the significant achievement of nineteenth-century musicology. The former's view of 'the great men of history, whose own particular purposes comprehend the substantial content which is the will of the world spirit'[1] lies behind the reverence shown towards the great men of Germany's musical past: Bach, Handel, Mozart and Beethoven, whereas the latter's idea of historical reconstruction lent a theoretical justification to the practical need to rescue the works of old masters from neglect into which history had thrown them. Positivism with its systematic approach supplied the method and that is to be seen at a glance in Adler's tabular survey of the entire domain of *Musikwissenschaft*. Friedrich Chrysander had no such extensive programme of study to present in his preface to the first volume of the *Jahrbücher für musikalische Wissenschaft*, but the themes are succinctly and resolutely stated, the intellectual influences readily discernible. The reference to the progress of the human spirit has a definite Hegelian flavour and yet, in common with the feeling of the time, he registers a complaint that the philosophers have failed in their speculative task. It is now up to those who practise the new 'musical science' to supply from within, from the study of the art of music, the answers which the philosophers, approaching the matter from outside, have apparently failed to provide.

The term *Wissenschaft* has always been a difficult one to translate into English. In German it does not denote only the exact, natural or technical sciences, but is also applied to the humanistic disciplines, including the philosophical ones. Of course, anybody stressing the word *Wissenschaft* in Germany in the second half of the nineteenth century wishes to underline the link between the humanities and the exact sciences and to draw attention to the application of scientific method, however loosely defined, to the fields of philosophy and history. Out of the pair of words (*musikalische Wissenschaft*) used by Chrysander, Adler fashions a single composite one, and his *Musik-wissenschaft* is closely allied to the more general term *Kunstwissenschaft*. The latter one was used increasingly towards the end of the century to describe a philosophy of art 'from within' as a substitute for the generalizations of the earlier philosophical speculation.[2] Adler uses the term often, implying that *Musikwissenschaft*, in itself a discipline of many parts, contributes its share to the more general *Kunstwissenschaft*. In the present volume *Musikwissen-*

---

[1] G. W. F. Hegel, *Die Vernunft in der Geschichte*, ed. J. Hoffmeister (Hamburg 1955). Quoted after Charles Taylor, *Hegel* (Cambridge 1975), p. 392.
[2] This approach is evident in Max Dessoir's work. See below, p. 379.

*schaft* has been translated as 'musicology', and *Kunstwissenschaft* as 'general theory of art'.

There seems to be no doubt in Adler's mind about the primacy of history in the system of musicology, and his description of its field, as well as the tabular summary, offer a clear illustration of this.[3] The division of the entire field into historical and systematic musicology prevents him from realizing fully the implications of the term *Kunstwissenschaft* and it is this lack of grasp that later prevented musicology from its share in the system of the 'general theory of art', which remained more strongly influenced by the work of art historians like H. Wölfflin and E. Grosse, their distinction between history, criticism and aesthetics having been less rigid. Adler was perhaps not wrong in criticizing Fétis's terminology: 'The term "philosophy of music" used by Fétis to describe "the study of artistic products and their transformation" is proper neither for the historical nor the aesthetic musicology; terms belonging to different areas of study are here mixed together.'[4] However, by overstressing the division he weakened the chances of an interaction between historical studies and the areas covered by the disciplines forming his 'systematic musicology' and it could be argued that the legacy of this is noticeable in the entire subsequent history of musicology.

Hugo Riemann offered in the early part of his career no programme for musicology, but in his fruitful life practised nearly all the constituent parts of Adler's system. He was primarily a theorist whose thought was directed to practical considerations and it may be for this reason that his stature is considerably greater than his contribution to the intellectual history of his time would warrant. Stumpf's psychology left an impact on him and provided him with a stimulus for an attempt to overcome Helmholtz's insistence on the moment of perception, implicit in the latter's term *Tonempfindung*. Although he felt that Stumpf had stopped short of overcoming the Helmholtzian weakness, Riemann's distinction between *Tonempfindungen* (tonal sensations) and *Tonvorstellungen* (tonal representations) owes a great deal to Stumpf's stress on memory in the process of tonal perception.[5] Riemann's aesthetics, too, has a strong practical bias and is directed towards providing specific answers to problems arising out of performance and listening. He thus appears to fulfil Franz Brendel's hope that aesthetics would become a practical guide,[6] but at a high price of narrowing its scope and trivializing it.

Heinrich Schenker, likewise, had practical considerations in mind and later in his career he too, like Riemann before him, produced editions of Beethoven's piano sonatas. Unlike Riemann, he did not attempt a wide survey of the entire field of music, but concentrated his attention on a theory of compositional process which he developed over more than thirty years of

---

[3] See below, pp. 354–5.
[4] G. Adler, 'Umfang, Methode und Ziel der Musikwissenschaft', *Vierteljahrsschrift für Musikwissenschaft*, vol. 1 (1885), p. 12, n. 1.
[5] See H. Riemann, 'Idee zu einer "Lehre von den Tonvorstellungen"', *Jahrbuch der Musikbibliothek Peters für 1914/15*, vol. 21/22 (Leipzig 1916), pp. 2–3.
[6] See above, p. 130.

intensive activity. His analytical studies belong largely to the period after the First World War, but some premisses of that work, when singled out from the pages of his early *Harmonielehre* show in a concentrated form all the intensity of the speculative and intellectual influences that Germany could offer at the time. Hegel's belief in the spirit of history manifesting itself in the great names of Germany became more pronounced in Schenker's later work, whereas in the early stages biologism, not unlike the one of Spencer, is mixed with the *Lebensphilosophie* of Nietzsche and Dilthey. Whether this philosophical ingredient in Schenker's analytical method can be disregarded, in order to unburden the analysis as a discipline, is not an unimportant question. It resembles the dilemma of whether Wagner's music could be taken in isolation from his ideas. In both cases there have been repeated attempts to make the distinction since this could mean that some obstinate questions and sources of doubt could be conveniently forgotten. It is precisely at this point that aesthetics and philosophy come back, not as aids to some practical goal, but in order to question the premisses of historical and analytical methods. Bosanquet's words that aesthetics 'exists for the sake of knowledge and not as a guide to practice'[7] get a fuller meaning and are applicable in musicology just as they are in philosophy, and suggest that aesthetics in music has perhaps a larger role to play than the one assigned to it by Brendel, Adler or Riemann.

---

[7] B. Bosanquet, *A History of Aesthetic* (London 1892), p. ix.

# Friedrich Chrysander (1826–1901)

## 'Vorwort und Einleitung' from *Jahrbücher für musikalische Wissenschaft* (1863)

Unlike most of the distinguished German philosophers and musicologists of his time, Chrysander had neither a regular university education nor a university appointment. A doctorate awarded to him by the University of Rostock in 1885 was in recognition of his privately pursued work on folksong and oratorio. The life and the music of G. F. Handel were his life-long interests into which he invested hard-earned income as well as enormous personal energy. In collaboration with G. G. Gervinus he founded in 1856 the *Deutsche Händel-Gesellschaft* with the aim of publishing Handel's complete works. Chrysander managed to edit over forty volumes though the series remained incomplete.

Chrysander was one of the founders of musicology as an independent discipline. His views on the general method of musicology, as well as various studies which put his theoretical views into practice, were published in a number of learned journals. He himself was the founder and co-founder respectively of two such publications: *Jahrbücher für musikalische Wissenschaft* (1863, 1867) and (with Guido Adler and Philipp Spitta) *Vierteljahrsschrift für Musikwissenschaft* (1885–94).

## Preface from *Jahrbücher für musikalische Wissenschaft*

*Source:*

'Vorwort und Einleitung', *Jahrbücher für musikalische Wissenschaft*, vol. 1 (Leipzig 1863), p. 10–13. Translated by Martin Cooper.
    The Preface, signed 'Chr.' and dated '20 December 1862' served as an editorial outlining the aims of the publication.

[.  .]

Doubts have often been expressed as to whether musicology will ever attain the profundity and thoroughness [*innere Vollendung*] of the study of the other arts, and these doubts have unconsciously been occasioned by the problems that we have been discussing. It is easy to understand how the mistake has arisen; but we take leave to declare as an error – and one which reveals the underestimation of music right up to the present day – the chief reason commonly given for this opinion, namely that music is in essence far too vague to form a foundation for any science able to fulfil the strictest

345

scientific demands. It is not surprising that writing about music is still, by comparison with writing about other arts, so far from perfection: there are strong grounds for excusing this which can be pleaded. But can we be content with merely justifying the fact? Surely not, for in that case we should surrender the hope which, although it may not assure us of success, yet always inspires our maximum efforts. To recognize problems is the first step towards solving them; and we should never surrender the conviction that what the human spirit has once created over the years, in the natural process of development, will coalesce as a unity following the progress of human knowledge. It is not therefore a case of assaulting impossibilities – simply throwing stones uphill, as it were – but an undertaking based on a great law of the human spirit, if we set out in good hope of penetrating with the light of cognition the almost immeasurable richness of data to be found in this, as in other fields.

We use the word 'science' in the strictest and fullest sense; and we are publishing these yearbooks with the title 'for musicology' [*musikalische Wissenschaft*] to make it clear that it is the territory of science that we are entering, that we submit to the strictest claims of science and hope to serve her, according to our powers, on the widest possible scale. We intend to consider the whole field of music and to devote as equal attention as possible to each subject, with no special preference for the historical side, as might be suggested by my own previous studies and even by the contents of this first number.[1]

Of course the *history* of music would by itself provide sufficient material to fill the yearbooks for an incalculable number of years; but although there is a need in this field for researchers who are both strict and versatile, and although historical essays will no doubt occupy the majority of our space, the Editor believes that a purely historical journal is not so urgently needed as one which aims at discussing the whole field of music according to a single, scientific set of principles.

*Music theory* provides the clearest evidence of this lack of any common sense of direction, and indeed of the absence of any feeling that such a sense would even be desirable. It cannot be said of theory, as we said of musical history and aesthetics, that its study is still in its infancy; indeed the demands of practice have been such that the theory of music has been all but exhaustively elaborated. Yet at the present time the theory still lacks all the main results, which will be achieved if, guided by history, and with a scrupulous attention once more paid to the artistic views, it [theory] examines its whole field.

The relationship between current *aesthetics* – the theory of the beautiful –

[1] [The volume contained the following studies: M. Hauptmann, 'Klang' and 'Temperatur'; H. Bellermann, 'Joannis Tinctoris terminorum musicae diffinitorium'; F. Chrysander, 'Deutscher Volksgesang im 14. Jahrhundert', 'Geschichte der Braunschweig–Wolfenbüttelschen Capelle und Oper vom 16. bis zum 18. Jahrhundert', 'Händels Orgelbegleitung zu Saul, und die neueste englische Ausgabe dieses Oratoriums', and 'Beethovens Verbindung mit Birchall und Stumpff in London'.]

and the art of music is not a very happy one. The whole structure of general aesthetic theory has recently been completed down to the smallest detail without any significant co-operation from musicians, and it is therefore hardly to be wondered at if the place occupied by music in the philosophical home of artistic theories is that of a stranger and an alien. We should ask ourselves, in fact, whether music is really so lowly that she must accept without complaint the place allotted to her, or whether she should insist on her right to make her own choices and her own structures according to her own needs and her own verities. If some 'aestheticians of music' do not even consider this question, it is without doubt because they believe that music, with her scanty spiritual content, should consider herself lucky even to find a place in the philosophers' palace of aesthetics. In defiance of these gentlemen it is our simple and firmly held conviction that we must reject all that has been said in that quarter until we have examined and approved the qualifications of these philosophical architects. Our duty is all the more imperative, we believe, for this reason – philosophers having exhausted the study, or clarification, of poetry and the plastic arts, it remains for musicologists (who have a full right) to undertake similar operations in the field of music and they are the only possible source of aesthetic rectification.

This does not mean that we have even remotely in mind a separation of musicology from the study of the other arts. On the other hand, we are as firmly convinced of the certainty of a common centre of interest as of the necessity of a uniform treatment of all the sciences of the arts. We unhesitatingly relinquish any idea of a separate 'aesthetics of music' in favour of a general 'science of the Ideal' [*Wissenschaft des Ideals*]; for although, in a sense, each true individual work of art contains within itself the whole of aesthetic theory, no single, individual art is capable of developing even one independent section of that theory.

If we seek on every occasion to hold fast to the methods of true science, we may hope in general not to go wrong and to do useful work even in detail. Anyone who wishes to contribute his share to such an undertaking needs no further vocation, no other patent, than that contained in this conviction. The distinction between so-called amateurs and professionals is irrelevant here. That distinction was borrowed from the performing arts considered as a means of livelihood, and was relevant in that context. In our field there is only one distinction – that between scientific and unscientific – and both 'amateur' and 'professional' will stand on different sides of that dividing line in different circumstances. The amateur will have more difficulty in achieving precision and mastery of detail, while the professional will find it more difficult to form clear general opinions and untrammelled overall views. The most inspiring task of any true science of the arts is to build a bridge between the two for mutual information and assistance. [pp. 10–13]

[.    .    .]

# Guido Adler (1855–1941)
## 'Umfang, Methode und Ziel der Musikwissenschaft' (1885)

Adler studied law in Vienna, gaining a doctorate in 1878, and was at the same time a pupil of Bruckner at the Vienna Conservatory, and of Hanslick at the university, obtaining his second doctorate, in musicology, in 1880. In 1885 he was appointed to the chair of music history at the German university in Prague, and in 1898 succeeded Hanslick at Vienna University. There he founded his later celebrated Institute of Musicology where among his pupils were Anton Webern, Egon Wellesz, Otto Haas, Karl Geiringer and numerous other distinguished musicologists. Together with Philipp Spitta and Friedrich Chrysander, Adler founded in 1884 the *Vierteljahrsschrift für Musikwissenschaft*. He was also the instigator of the *Denkmäler der Tonkunst in Österreich* of which he served as the general editor between 1894 and 1938.

Adler is one of the founders of modern musicology. His learning was wide and his taste catholic, embracing Renaissance polyphony, the music of the Viennese Classics, of Mahler and Schoenberg. In formulating his broad concept of musicology he was helped by the intellectual climate of the universities of Prague and Vienna and by the proximity of the distinguished school of art history flourishing at the latter.

# The scope, method and aim of musicology

Source:

'Umfang, Methode und Ziel der Musikwissenschaft', *Vierteljahrsschrift für Musikwissenschaft*, vol. 1 (1885), pp. 5–8; 15–20. Translated by Martin Cooper.

Musicology came into existence at the same time as music itself. While man still simply opened his mouth and sang without thinking, while sound-patterns formed themselves without being ordered or analysed, it was still impossible to speak of an art of music. It was only when the pitch of notes came to be compared and measured (first by the ear and then by instruments designed for the purpose) and when it was realized that there is an organic relationship between a number of notes and phrases forming a unified whole, and that the products of the human imagination do in fact conform to primitive aesthetic norms – only then did it become possible to speak of musicology and an art of working with tonal material. Any people which can be said to have a music [*Tonkunst*] have also a musicology [*Tonwissenschaft*], though they may not have a fully elaborated scholarly system. The more advanced the music, the more elaborate will be the system: the degree of development of the one determines the tasks of the other. At first the task of scholarship was to identify, determine and analyse the actual material of music – hence the importance attached by the Greeks to the mathematical determination of intervals and the subdivision of the *scientia musicae* into arithmetic, geometry and astronomy by many medieval writers. The claims of music were soon raised: it was ranked among the *artes liberales* and students of music and musicology were presented with a complex of theories abstracted from existing compositions. Notation soon became more complicated, pitch and duration more accurately measured and regulated: and for a time these rules and measurements actually controlled and hampered musical performance, until this was eventually liberated again. The demands made on musicology then changed once more: the relationship between music and poetry had to be clarified and the limitations of music defined. While the true creative artist continued his work undisturbed, it became the scholar's task to examine what the artist produced. Scholars today make individual works of art the chief object of their studies. What, then, are the points of distinguishing features of a composition that are of most vital importance to the scholar?

His first concern when presented with a composition may be said to be one of palaeography. If the notation is different from that in general use today, the work must be transcribed, and this itself will provide important information needed to identify and date the work. Next comes the task of examining its construction. The first task is to establish distinguishing rhythmic features – whether, and if so how, the music is barred, what time-relationships are to be found in its different sections and how these are grouped and organized. After this comes tonality, the tonal structure first of individual parts and only later that of the whole – an order or procedure common in the Middle Ages though now rightly no longer usual. Individual parts are next studied with a view to establishing cadences, transitional passages and accidentals in relationship to the piece as a whole. Then the polyphonic structure must be studied: the range and spacing of the parts, the intervals at which imitative passages occur and the sequence of the entries, the appearance of themes in augmentation, diminution, inversion and reversion, the disposition of consonances and dissonances, and whether these are prepared and resolved or free-standing. The movement of the parts in relation to each other is traced, the relationship between main and subsidiary themes, the presence of a cantus firmus and its use and articulation, the development of themes and motifs – all these points are taken into account and definitively established. Should there be an accompanying text, this must be critically examined – in the first place simply as poetry, then with regard to underlay and musical setting. Care must be taken to examine the accentuation and prosody in relation to the rhythms of the music; and this study of the text will provide further valuable assistance in coming to conclusions about the work. If this is purely instrumental, the treatment of the instruments, or the instrument, concerned must be examined i.e. how they are combined or distinguished from each other, the contrasting and combining of the different groups or families of instruments. In association with all these points we shall consider whether performance of the work is a practical possibility: the employment of the instruments required, the execution, the dynamics of different passages, the disposition of various parts etc.

Once the main distinguishing features of the work are determined and any special individual characteristics identified, we can go on to answer questions relating to the artistic genre to which the piece belongs and indeed to general type, depending on its date and our interpretation of its characteristics. In this way we approach the important final decision of dating the piece. Here we must distinguish (a) the period at which it was written – either the general date or the school to which it belongs, with a possible guess at some individual composer and, if so, at the period in his life at which he wrote the work. The older the piece, the more difficult it becomes to date precisely. (b) A work may also date from a period to which, by character, it no longer belongs i.e. it may present features characteristic of an earlier period. The time-spans of artistic periods may be compared, on a minor scale, to those of geological strata. Just as the earth's crust consists of formations belonging to different epochs, so the general outlines of an artistic period present a variegated spectacle. We must therefore make a clear distinction between the date suggested by the internal evidence of the work and the date of its actual composition. There will always be individual features which betray the fact that, despite its outwardly analogous character, the piece does not wholly correspond with the spirit of the period to which it would seem, by structure and texture, to belong. In such a case the work is said to be 'in the manner of' this or that period or school or individual composer.

The critical examination of such a work is completed by determining its emotional or aesthetic content, though of course this is too often the only point considered, the alpha and omega of critical analysis. For the musicologist this question can only be answered after all the foregoing considerations have been concluded. Even then prior importance will be given to the specifically musical content, even though it will in most cases be useless to try to express such a content in words. Even if the composer has used a poetic scheme – whether a programme or a general idea – it will be a bold man who will undertake to explain in musicologically acceptable terms the emotional content of the two component elements – musical and literary – and to demonstrate where they coincide and where they diverge. It may well be comparatively easier in the case of musico-dramatic works, where the dramatic action provides a more reliable point of reference. [pp. 5–8]

[.    .    .]¹

_____

¹ [In the middle portion of the article, pp. 8–14 of the original, Adler discusses in continuous prose the information presented in condensed form in the tabular survey reproduced here on pp. 354–5.]

The methods of musicological research are determined by the subject of that research. In cases involving palaeography the student will make use of the methods of the so-called ancillary sciences associated with historical research in general. He will adopt all the techniques already explored by the diplomatist and the palaeographer, but he will have to explore a number of subsidiary techniques in the case of notation. Here experience will be his guide. In cases involving philology and literary history the musicologist will again have to use techniques proper to each of those areas of knowledge; but here he will have to tread rather more carefully. For while many philologists have achieved splendid results and turned their attention away from the actualities of human life, every historian of an art-form will have rather to take into account the vital essence of the work of art itself and beware of destroying this with his scalpel. His chief task being the study of the artistic laws valid at different periods, and their organic connection and development, the art historian will make use of the same methods as the naturalist, and in particular of the inductive method. He will take a number of examples, that is, and separate what each has in common with the others from what is individual; and he will make use of this abstract, giving preference to some features and leaving others on one side. The making of hypotheses is quite permissible. To give further reasons for this would need a special essay, but the essential fact to be remembered is the analogy between the methods of the art historian and the naturalist.

The stating of the most essential artistic laws and their realization in musical education showed us musicology in close association with the realities of artistic life. Musicology can only achieve its object in the widest sense if it remains in vital contact with art. The spheres of art and scholarship are not separated by any clear line of demarcation but are in reality identical; it is only their cultivation that is different. The artist builds his temple in the grove, whose fragrance is perpetually renewed by the flowers which blossom there in perfect freedom. The theorist of art makes the ground accessible and practicable, educates the neophyte for his life's work and serves as life-companion to the inspired creative artist. Should the scholar see that an artist's work is not benefiting the art, he will point out to him the way that he should go. Once the building is there, it is the art historian's task to guard and defend it, to repair those parts that become damaged and, should it become ruinous, to preserve it for posterity. This, however, is not the full extent of the good friend's activities. He organizes and disposes the whole [building] in order to make it more accessible to the common man. If it is taken by assault or pulled down, he protects it with a fence or removes it to a respectful distance in order to preserve it for future generations who will understand it properly. One of the scholar's finest tasks is to keep the soil of the existing garden fresh and to arouse and increase interest in it, though unfortunately the majority of those who write about art have tried to shrug off this exalted duty. Finally the scholar is the preserver of order, codifying (as we have shown) rights which have become laws, though he must (or rather should) be flexible in his attitude to the demands of life. If an artist leaves the territory of his ancestors in order to annex new territory, the art historian preserves the ancestral territory from neglect and overgrowing, and at the same time undertakes a second task – that of helping the artist in his occupation of the new territory, lending a hand in bringing the newly acquired ground under cultivation and in erecting the scaffolding for the new building. His experience enables him to give advice to the young architect, who may of course in his arrogance refuse his sympathetic co-operation, in which case the new building will either never be finished or will collapse, being built on unsure foundations and unable to stand up to wind and weather. The scholar accompanies the artist from the cradle to the grave; and the artist's spiritual offspring, the element of truth in his mortal pilgrimage, are defended and sheltered by him even after death. It is easy to preserve independence in judging an artist who is dead, but the same independence should also be preserved in judging the living. Voltaire's *mot* – 'on doit des égards aux vivants, on ne doit aux morts que la verité' – may appear very polite, but it conceals a great danger, and it is this: that by respecting the feelings of one artist and ignoring those of another, and thus showing prejudice in both his sympathies and his antipathies, a writer may well produce those caricatures which do in fact disgrace many pages written on the subject of art. Thus our fundamental principle should be 'nothing but the truth, whether it concerns the living or the dead'.

While scholarship pursues her absolute goals, regards her activities as ends in themselves and has no need to concern herself with any further justifying of these from a practical point of view, she will achieve a correct understanding and judgement of the different artistic periods, and thereby the chief aim of her researches i.e. the determination of the primary laws governing each branch of the art. But this is not all. The arts today are in such a precarious condition and there is so much uncertainty in artistic activity that scholarship may well be able to contribute to the improvement of the present situation. It has been said that the spread of the scientific study of any art is a sure sign that that art is in decay. We have clearly demonstrated, however, that no art is possible without artistic knowledge, and if study and research were to gain the upper hand, all that this would prove provisionally would be a growth in historical understanding – and it is a well-established fact that this is of great benefit to the apperception of works of art.

So long as scholarship remains within its natural frontiers and assists artists in clearly defined enterprises such as the restoration, editing and performance of historical works, she can represent no threat to musical production, quite apart from the fact that genuine creative talent may well accept guidance and education but will never accept a subsidiary role. The most important aim of scholarship, however, is to strengthen itself and achieve mastery, by determining the course it should follow and confining itself to that course. As Chrysander writes in his introduction to *Jahrbücher für musikalische Wissenschaft*: 'We should never surrender the conviction that what the human spirit has once created over the years, in the natural process of development, will coalesce as a unity following the progress of human knowledge.'[2] Speaking of musicology in particular, he writes:

The chief reason generally adduced for doubting whether musicology can match the scientific study of the visual arts in depth and precision is that the nature of music is too indeterminate to permit of any scientific study that will satisfy the strictest requirements. This is wholly mistaken.[3]

The same point is made by Spitta in a passage in his lecture on 'Art and the scientific study of art', given in Berlin at the Königliche Akademie der Künste on 21 March 1883:

The general theory of art is still – except in a few branches – wrestling with all the difficulties associated with new beginnings. Lacking the support of any firm tradition, uncertain in method and frequently questionable in results, it is considered even by scholars rather as an appendix to other disciplines and not strong enough to assert its independent existence. There are many different facets to this new branch of scholarship – philosophical, physical–mathematical, and after all historical and philological – so that it perpetually trespasses on a number of different independent fields of study and can only claim a similar independence on the grounds of the object with which it is concerned. Hitherto hardly any attempt has been made to unite the various branches of this study into a single independent unity and thus to gain public acknowledgement in the world of scholarship and in society generally. Nevertheless this acknowledgement must come sooner or later. The material for research is too varied and too important and the qualifications demanded of scholars for its successful mastery too well defined, to permit our doubting that the general theory of art will win an acknowledged place beside its fellow-disciplines. Whichever way this may come about, one thing remains certain – that great problems lie ahead of us in this field, and that they must and can be solved.[4]

May the present attempt to discover a unified conception of musicology play its part towards meeting this need!

Every step taken towards the goal, and every action that brings that goal nearer, means an advance in human knowledge. The more sincere the attempt, the more comprehensive the abilities, the more significant the final product; the larger the number of those engaged in the common enterprise, the profounder its effectiveness in achieving the twin objects – the investigation of the True and the promotion of the Beautiful. [pp. 15–20]

---

[2] [See above, p. 346.]
[3] [Adler here paraphrases rather than quotes Chrysander. For a translation of Chrysanders's actual words see above, pp. 345–6.]
[4] [The address was later published in P.Spitta, *Zur Musik* (Berlin 1892).]

In tabellarischer Übersicht ergiebt sich das Gesammtgebäude also:

## Musik-wissenschaft.

### I. Historisch.

Geschichte der Musik nach Epochen, Völkern, Reichen, Ländern, Gauen, Städten, Kunstschulen, Künstlern).

| A. musikalische Paläographie (Notationen). | B. Historische Grundclassen (Gruppirung der musikalischen Formen). | C. Historische Aufeinanderfolge der Gesetze. | D. Geschichte der musikalischen Instrumente. |
|---|---|---|---|
|  |  | 1. wie sie in den Kunstwerken je einer Epoche vorliegen, 2. wie sie von den Theoretikern der betreffenden Zeit gelehrt werden. 3. Arten der Kunstausübung. |  |

Hilfswissenschaften: Allgemeine Geschichte mit Paläographie, Chronologie, Diplomatik, Bibliographie, Bibliotheks- und Archivkunde. Litteraturgeschichte und Sprachenkunde. Geschichte der Liturgien. Geschichte der mimischen Künste und des Tanzes. Biographistik der Tonkünstler, Statistik der musikalischen Associationen, Institute und Aufführungen.

### II. Systematisch.

Aufstellung der in den einzelnen Zweigen der Tonkunst zuhöchst stehenden Gesetze.

| A. Erforschung und Begründung derselben in der | | | B. Aesthetik der Tonkunst. | C. Musikalische Pädagogik und Didaktik (Zusammenstellung der Gesetze mit Rücksicht auf den Lehrzweck) | D. Musikologie (Untersuchung und Vergleichung zu ethnographischen Zwecken). |
|---|---|---|---|---|---|
| 1. *Harmonik* (tonal od. tonlich). | 2. *Rhythmik* (temporär oder zeitlich). | 3. *Melik* (Cohärenz von tonal und temporär). | 1. Vergleichung und Werthschätzung der Gesetze und deren Relation mit den appercipirenden Subjecten behufs Feststellung der *Kriterien des musikalisch Schönen*. 2. Complex unmittelbar und mittelbar damit zusammenhängender Fragen. | 1. Tonlehre, 2. Harmonielehre, 3. Kontrapunkt, 4. Compositionslehre, 5. Instrumentationslehre, 6. Methoden des Unterrichtes im Gesang und Instrumentalspiel. |  |

Hilfswissenschaften: Akustik und Mathematik. Physiologie (Tonempfindungen). Psychologie (Tonvorstellungen, Tonurtheile und Tongefühle). Logik (das musikalische Denken). Grammatik, Metrik und Poetik. Pädagogik. Ästhetik etc.

Guido Adler's tabular presentation of the field of musicology from *Vierteljahrsschrift für Musikwissenschaft*, vol. 1 (1885)

# A tabular survey of the whole field looks like this

## MUSICOLOGY

### I. Historical

History of music according to period, nationality, state, province, region, city, school, composer

**A. Musical palaeography (notations)**

**B. Basic historical categories (classification of musical forms)**

**C. Principles in their historical succession:**
1. as they are manifest in the works from each period
2. as they were explained by the theorists of the time
3. types of performance practice

**D. History of musical instruments**

### II. Systematic

Establishment of dominating principles in the individual branches of music

**A. The investigation and establishment of these principles in:**
1. Harmony (tonal aspect)
2. Rhythm (temporal aspect)
3. Melody (fusion of the tonal and temporal)

**B. Aesthetics of music**
1. Comparison and evaluation of the principles and their relationship with the subject of apperception with a view to establishing the criteria for the musically beautiful
2. The complex of questions directly or indirectly connected with the above

**C. Musical pedagogy and teaching methods (drawing up of rules for educational purposes)**
1. Elementary music theory
2. Harmony
3. Counterpoint
4. Composition
5. Orchestration
6. Vocal and instrumental teaching methods

**D. [Ethno] musicology** — Research and comparison for ethnological purposes

---

Ancillary disciplines: General history with palaeography, chronology, diplomatic, bibliography, librarianship and archival skills.
Literary history and philology.
Liturgical history.
History of acting and of dance.
Biographical studies of musicians, statistics relating to musical associations, institutions and performances.

Ancillary disciplines: Acoustics and mathematics.
Physiology (the sensation of sound).
Psychology (the conception, judgement and perception of sound).
Logic (musical thought).
Grammar, metrics, poetics.
Aesthetics etc.

Guido Adler's tabular presentation of the field of musicology

# Hugo Riemann (1849–1919)

## Wie hören wir Musik? Grundlinien der Musik-Ästhetik (1888)

Son of an enthusiastic music amateur, Riemann received a thorough instruction in music before going in 1868 to Berlin to study law, philology and history. After a period of active military service he went to study music at Leipzig in 1871, and in 1873 obtained a doctorate at Göttingen with a dissertation on the nature of musical hearing (*Über das musikalische Hören*, Leipzig 1874). After a variety of teaching posts he settled in Leipzig in 1895 teaching at the university.

Riemann was a man of quite exceptional breadth of musical and musicological interests. Between 1872 and 1918 he published an impressive and bewilderingly diverse quantity of books, textbooks, articles and editions, embracing the theory, aesthetics, psychology and history of music. Without stating his aim explicitly he endeavoured to establish a general theory of tonal music and to this end he wrote studies on harmonic logic, counterpoint, form, phrasing and orchestration. The diversity of his interests was almost too wide, and because of it not all of the observations and theories he put forward stood the test of time equally well. In the aesthetics of music Riemann was primarily an eclectic pragmatist seeking to establish aesthetics as an aid to the performance of and listening to music.

## How do we listen to music? Outlines of the aesthetics of music

*Source:*

*Wie hören wir Musik? Grundlinien der Musik-Ästhetik*, 6th edn. (Berlin 1923), pp. 43–7. Translated by Martin Cooper.

The first edition of the work (Leipzig 1888) was in the form of three lectures, and had the subtitle *Drei Vorträge*. It was then included in a series of popular pamphlets, 'catechisms', published by Max Hesse Verlag and appeared under the title *Katechismus der Musik-Ästhetik* (Leipzig 1890). Thereafter both titles, *Katechismus . . .* and *Wie hören wir Musik?* continued to be used side by side, although the books did not differ in their content. An English translation by H. Bewerunge (London 1895) bore the title *Catechism of Musical Aesthetics*, but retained the original division into three lectures.

## §23 Passive and active listening

[. . .]

Once again I must emphasize the fact that to understand a large complicated composition requires both practice and goodwill. Both a grasp of detail and a conscious ability to trace the way in which the whole work hangs together i.e. a good memory and a gift for synthetic thinking are needed if the work is not to disintegrate into a series of loosely-connected single impressions, none of them very powerful, instead of each supporting, highlighting and intensifying the other either by analogy or by contrast. In other words the higher musical forms necessarily demand the listener's co-operation rather than a merely passive surrender – however willing – to his own impressions. It is not that any technical specialist's knowledge is indispensable to the enjoyment of musical masterpieces; such knowledge is no more essential to the enjoyment of the beauty of Beethoven's Ninth Symphony than of Cologne Cathedral. What is essential is practice, preparation by first listening to music of a simpler kind. This is easily demonstrated by observing how people who are not practising musicians – may not even be able to read music, in fact – but who listen to a lot of music, are capable of hitting the nail on the head when they judge a new work. The musically educated listener simply knows the names and significances of a work's technical details, which do not constitute the essence of the work and are therefore perceived by the non-musician – whose only education consists in having listened to a great deal of music – not as formal elements, but simply in relation to the content of the whole work. The visitor to Cologne Cathedral, however, who is not himself an architect, has one great advantage over any listener to the Ninth Symphony who is not a musician. The former stands in front of the cathedral and can spend as long as he likes absorbing in his imagination first the overall structure and then, gradually, more and more detail, first grasping the large-scale symmetries and passing from these to those on a smaller scale. Not so the listener. The music does not wait as it enters his ear, and if he does not succeed immediately in grasping it, he has lost the chance of understanding it better by comparing one passage with the next. Everything therefore depends on clearly grasping the most minute figures and their correct relationship to each other, in fact on understanding the smallest points of symmetry. The difficulty of such a task explains why the double organization [. . .] is indispensable – the organization of time in identical units of a size that the ear can comfortably grasp, and the organization of pitch-changes into a small number of steps provided for us by the harmonic relationships revealed by the actual nature of the sounds.

## §24 The symmetry of successiveness

Listening to music resembles looking at a piece of architecture as far as form is concerned, a tracing of symmetrical designs. But whereas in architecture the symmetrical designs are static and simultaneous, so that the one may even be called the 'counterpart' of the other, but the order in which they are viewed may always be reversed, this is not so in music. There one always precedes the other, the second establishing the symmetry and as it were completing the first and thus forming in a sense a conclusion. Thus passages, or features, of this kind which answer each other always possess a certain cadential character in varying degrees and may be said to bear more weight than passages from which this cadential character is absent. The smallest unit of symmetry in music will clearly be the confrontation of two units of duration [*Zähl-zeiten*] the second of which is felt as matching the first: and I must also add that cadential time-units of this kind are rendered more emphatic if they are in any way protracted or dwelt upon. If such protraction goes as far as doubling the duration of the concluding note-value, it will result in the original form of a triple measure. Just as there are one strong and one or more weak beats in the bar – which is the smallest unit of symmetry – so strong and weak bars can be distinguished at a higher level i.e. bars that complete a symmetrical pattern have a cadential character which increases according to the size of the figure which they complete. It should be carefully noted that the fundamental disposition [*Urgrundlage*] cannot produce the sequence strong–weak but only its opposite – weak–strong – i.e. the upbeat form [*Auftaktsform*] must be responsible for the conclusion [*Ausgang*]. I only refer to this because it is a basic principle of the new theory of rhythm that I have been trying to introduce and contradicts the opposite point of view which has recently become established. This so-called 'theory of phrasing' is being much discussed at the present time and may well result in a number of literary disputes in the future. My so-called phrased editions of Mozart's, Beethoven's and Haydn's sonatas, and sonatinas by Clementi, Kuhlau and others as well as much other piano music by Bach, Schumann, Schubert, Chopin etc. are an attempt to introduce this consistently applied upbeat conception of thematic figures by means of a complete system of markings; and I hope that anyone interested in the subject and not as yet conversant with any of my editions, will give them a careful consideration should they have the opportunity. I have developed in detail the principles underlying these ideas of mine in a number of theoretical works, more especially in my *Musikalische Dynamik und Agogik*,[1] and also in my lectures at the Hamburg and Wiesbaden Conservatories, which contain a logical defence of the opinions in question. [pp. 43–7]

---

[1] [*Musikalische Dynamik und Agogik: Lehrbuch der musikalischen Phrasierung* (Hamburg 1884).]

# Heinrich Schenker (1868–1935)
## *Harmonielehre* (1906)

Schenker came from Galicia, the easternmost province of the Austro-Hungarian Monarchy, inhabited by Germans, Jews, Poles, Ukrainians and Romanians. For a time he was a pupil of the Romanian–Polish pianist, Chopin's pupil Karol Mikuli, then studied with Bruckner at the Vienna Conservatory. Without ever holding an official academic appointment he built for himself in Vienna a reputation as a teacher of piano and theory.

Between 1904 and 1935 Schenker worked on his systematic theory of tonal music, deduced from the basic postulate that musical logic is governed by a fundamental progression of an essentially linear nature. He developed a highly original, and mainly posthumously influential, method of analysis and of graphic presentation of analytical procedure which reduces the need for translating analytical observations into discursive language. Nevertheless, his writings on analysis were often accompanied by assertions of philosophical provenance, combining Hegelian notions with elements of Gestalt psychology, evolutionism, and philosophy of life. His often exaggerated belief in the supremacy of the German musical tradition may have been the result of a subconscious need of a provincial German to prove himself in the heart of the Monarchy.

# Harmony

*Source:*

Heinrich Schenker, *Harmony*, ed. and annotated by Oswald Jonas, tr. Elisabeth Mann Borgese (Cambridge, Mass. 1973); pp. 3–4; 12–13; 84–5.

*Harmonielehre* was the first part of a trilogy of theoretical studies bearing the common title *Neue musikalische Theorien und Phantasien*: Vol. 1, *Harmonielehre* (Stuttgart 1906); vol. 2, *Kontrapunkt*, part 1 (Stuttgart 1910), part 2 (Vienna 1922); vol. 3, *Der freie Satz* (Vienna 1935).

## Division I
## Tonal systems: their origin and differentiation with regard to position and purity

### Section I: The origin of tonal systems

### Chapter I: The natural tonal system (major)

#### §1    *Music and nature*

All art, with the exception of music, rests on associations of ideas, of great and universal ideas, reflected from Nature and reality. In all cases Nature provides the pattern; art is imitation – imitation by word or colour or form. We immediately know which aspect of nature is indicated by word, which by colour, and which by sculptured form. Only music is different. Intrinsically, there is no unambivalent association of ideas between music and nature. This lack probably provides the only satisfactory explanation for the fact that the music of primitive peoples never developed beyond a certain rudimentary stage. Against all traditional and historical notions, I would go so far as to claim that even Greek music never was real art. It can only be ascribed to its very primitive stage of development that Greek music has disappeared without leaving any traces or echoes, while all other branches of Greek art have been preserved as inspiration and paradigm for our own arts. It seems that without the aid of association of ideas no human activity can unfold either in comprehension or in creation.

#### §2    *The motif as the only way of associating ideas in music*

But whence should music take the possibility of associating ideas, since it is not given by nature? Indeed, it took a host of experiments and the toil of many centuries to create this possibility. Finally it was discovered. It was the motif.

The motif, and the motif alone, creates the possibility of associating ideas, the only one of which music is capable. The motif is a primordial and intrinsic association of ideas.[1] The motif thus substitutes for the ageless and powerful associations of ideas from patterns in nature, on which the other arts are thriving. [pp. 3–4]

---

[1] [Oswald Jonas's note:] During a later stage of his development Schenker would hardly have defined the motif as an association of ideas *intrinsic* to music. It is undeniable that the motif introduced into music the principle of repetition in its pure form. This had already happened during the epoch of imitative music. But the only principle intrinsic to music is the chord as presented by Nature in the overtone series [...] According to Schenker, music was elevated to the rank of an art only by the unfolding of the chord in *Auskomponierung* and the theory of *Auskomponierung* constitutes the essential part of Schenker's theories [...]

## §6  The biological nature of form

[.    .    .]

For what is the fundamental purpose of the turns and tricks of the cyclical form? To represent the destiny, the real personal fate, of a motif or of several motifs simultaneously. The sonata represents the motifs in ever-changing situations in which their characters are revealed, just as human beings are represented in a drama.

For this is just what happens in a drama: men are led through situations in which their characters are tested in all their shades and grades, so that one characteristic feature is revealed in each particular situation. And what is character as a whole if not a synthesis of these qualities which have been revealed by such a sequence of situations?

The life of a motif is represented in an analogous way. The motif is led through various situations. At one time, its melodic character is tested; at another time, a harmonic peculiarity must prove its valor in unaccustomed surroundings; a third time, again, the motif is subjected to some rhythmic change: in other words, the motif lives through its fate, like a personage in a drama.

Obviously, these destinies, in drama as well as in music, are, so to speak, quantitatively reduced and stylized according to the law of abbreviation. Thus it would be of no interest at all to see Wallenstein having lunch on the stage regularly during the whole process of dramatic development. For everyone knows anyhow that he must have lunched daily; and the poet could therefore omit the dramatic presentation of these quite unessential lunches in order to concentrate the drama on the essential moments of his hero's life. In an analogous way the composer applies the law of abbreviation to the destiny of the motif, the hero of his drama. From the infinity of situations into which his motif could conceivably fall, he must choose only a few. These, however, must be so chosen that the motif is forced to reveal in them its character in all its aspects and peculiarities.

Thus it is illicit, according to the law of abbreviations, to present the motif in a situation which cannot contribute anything new to the clarification of its character. No composer could hope to reveal through overloaded, complicated, and unessential matter what could be revealed by few, but well-chosen, fatal moments in the life of a motif.[2] It will be of no interest at all to hear how the motif, metaphorically speaking, makes its regular evening toilet, takes its regular lunch etc. [pp. 12–13]

[2] Incidentally, it seems to me that the cyclical compositions of our days (as well as the so-called 'symphonic poems') are largely failures precisely for this reason. On the one hand, they indulge in all too many unessential situations which do not reveal anything worth hearing; on the other hand, the choice among possible situations is made so awkwardly that the motif is never given a chance for a full manifestation of all its character traits. The composers of our generation, as well as of the next, will have to go to the school of the great old masters if they want to relearn the art of describing the fate of a motif succinctly and through a strict choice of really essential fatal moments.

## Chapter II: Combinations

### §38    The biologic foundations of the process of combination

I have repeatedly had occasion to show the truly biologic characteristics displayed by tones in various respects. Thus the phenomenon of the partials could be derived from a kind of procreative urge of the tones; and the tonal system, particularly the natural [major] one, could be seen as a sort of higher collective order, similar to a state, based on its own social contracts by which the individual tones are bound to abide. We are now entering another field of consideration which will further reveal the biologic nature of the tones.

How do the vitality and egotism of man express themselves? First of all, in his attempts to live fully in as many relationships as the struggle for life will permit and, second, in the desire to gain the upper hand in each one of these relationships – to the extent that his vital forces measure up to this desire.

What we call 'vitality' or 'egotism' is directly proportionate, then, to the number of relationships and to the intensity of the vital forces lavished on them. In other words, the more numerous the relationships cultivated by a human being and the more intense the self-expression within these relationships, the greater, obviously, is his vitality.

Now what meaning are we to ascribe to 'relationships' in the life of a tone, and how could the intensity of its self-expression be measured? The relationships of the tone are established in systems. If the egotism of a tone expresses itself in the desire to dominate its fellow-tones rather than be dominated by them (in this respect, the tone resembles a human being), it is the system which offers to the tone the means to dominate and thus to satisfy its egotistic urge. A tone dominates the others if it subjects them to its superior vital force, within the relationship fixed in the various systems (cf. §18 and 20 above). In this sense, a system resembles, in anthropomorphic terms, a constitution, regulation, statute, or whatever other name we use to grasp conceptually the manifold relationships we enter. Thus the tone A, for example, may subject all other tones to its domination in so far as it has the power to force them to enter with it into those relationships which are established in our major and minor systems (to mention, for the time being, only these two). The vitality of the tone A will be measured by its ability to enter with the other tones not only that relationship which is determined by the major system but simultaneously those other relationships created by the minor system. In other words, the tone lives a more abundant life, it satisfies its vital urges more fully, if the relationships in which it can express itself are more numerous; i.e. if it can combine, first of all, the major and the minor systems and, second, if it can express its self-enjoyment in those two systems with the greatest possible intensity. Each tone feels the urge, accordingly, to conquer for itself such wealth, such fullness of life. [pp. 84–5]

# Part 5: New tendencies at the turn of the century

# Introduction

The ever-increasing impact of the exact sciences on psychology, philosophy and aesthetics evident throughout the second half of the nineteenth century produced in its turn a reaction against the domination of humanistic disciplines by scientific modes of thought. The reaction, which was evident in the work of several philosophers and influential intellectual figures, could be divided into two streams: in the one are to be found the philosophers whose ideas took a long time to assert themselves, while in the other stand those whose presence was initially felt quite strongly although later their importance appeared to decline. Edmund Husserl belonged to the first stream, and, as it was only in the 1920s that phenomenology extended itself to aesthetics in the works of Moritz Geiger, Roman Ingarden, and Nicolai Hartmann, this group stands outside the scope of this volume. A more immediate impact was made by two representatives of the second group, Wilhelm Dilthey and Max Dessoir. At first the influence of the former was felt largely through his lectures, as some of his important writings became accessible only after his death.

In the case of Dilthey non-German speakers are confronted by a difficulty characteristic of nearly all German philosophical writing of the last hundred or so years. Dilthey, like Husserl, and later Heidegger, uses a specially constructed terminology and gives individual words specific meaning often extremely difficult to render into English adequately. Dilthey's first important work had the title *Einleitung in die Geisteswissenschaften* (Leipzig 1883), and already here in the term *Geisteswissenschaften* an English translator is confronted with his first problem.

Although the German word *Geist* is perhaps best rendered into English as 'mind', a literal translation as 'the sciences of the mind' would not do. H. P. Rickman has suggested 'the human studies'[1] which seems the correct way of describing what Dilthey meant, namely, 'all the humanities and social sciences, all those disciplines which interpret expressions of man's inner life, whether the expressions be gestures, historical actions, codified law, art works, or literature'.[2]

[1] Wilhelm Dilthey, *Meaning in History*, tr. and ed. H. P. Rickman (London 1961), pp. 22–4.
[2] R. E. Palmer, *Hermeneutics. Interpretation Theory in Schleiermacher, Dilthey, Heidegger, and Gadamer* (Evanston, Illinois, 1969), p. 98.

Starting from the premiss that on the one hand the natural sciences, which largely dominated the philosophy of his time, were not suited to deal with the issues arising from the study of the works of art or institutions created by the human intellect, and on the other that the deterministic, rigid structure of Hegelian historicism overlooked the fact that philosophy must take into account the concrete, lived experience first and foremost, Dilthey conceived of 'hermeneutics' as a basis on which to found 'the human studies'. The word 'hermeneutics' was before Dilthey taken to mean either the art of elucidation in biblical studies, or the method of explanation in philology and linguistics. Following F. E. D. Schleiermacher (1768–1834), who wanted to extend the term beyond the disciplines with which the term was associated, Dilthey, himself a biographer of Schleiermacher, defined hermeneutics as an art of understanding, thus broadening the previous concept of 'explaining'. 'Explaining' was for him in any case a term more suited to the natural sciences where scientific truths which suggest a definite or static quality, are concerned. 'Understanding' is directed towards grasping the many-sidedness of man's experience through history, it is a way of re-experiencing the dynamic, changing quality of life embodied in the human soul (*Seelenleben*).[3] This insistence on life rather than metaphysics or science is responsible for the term *Lebensphilosophie* (philosophy of life, life philosophy) used to describe Dilthey's philosophy. The idea of the experience of life as a foundation of philosophy is noticeable in the nineteenth century already in Kierkegaard and later in Nietzsche, but it was Dilthey who developed it into a more substantial system joining it to his concept of history as a form of the flow of life. The formula which is necessary for this understanding of life-through-history is by Dilthey defined in the triad Experience–Expression–Understanding (*Erlebnis–Ausdruck–Verstehen*). The first of these – *Erlebnis* – is deliberately chosen by Dilthey instead of the more familiar German word *Erfahrung*, since its origin from the verb *erleben* (literally 'to live through') gives it both the necessary dynamic quality and the connection with 'life'. Experience in Dilthey's sense includes the immediacy of living through an act of experiencing as well as the process of reflecting on it, thus implying a flow and a constant change of direction. Added to this is the point that experiences may consist of many such acts and processes spread in time: all the repeated hearings of a Mozart quartet during one's life make up such an experience. R. E. Palmer suggests the word 'objectification' as an alternative translation of the term *Ausdruck* (expression).[4] Dilthey's 'expression' is far from the expression in the aesthetics of the psychologists. It is not a gesture or a feeling, but rather an appearance in art of lived experience, the experience itself being not a momentary phenomenon but something laid out in time. Finally 'understanding' (*Verstehen*) is not a purely conceptual process, but a composite act

---

[3] 'Die Natur erklären wir, das Seelenleben verstehen wir.' See Dilthey, *Ideen über eine beschreibende und zergliedernde Psychologie* (1894), in *Gesammelte Schriften*, ed. G. Misch, vol. 5 (Stuttgart 1957), p. 144.

[4] Palmer, *Hermeneutics*, p. 112.

in which all mental powers are engaged in the process of grasping and re-living the experience of the other person. This is not done in order to understand the private emotional ingredients that went into making a work of art, but in order to grasp the importance of the 'objectification of what was, in the composer, a state of mind'.[5] The original state of mind is not interesting in itself, it enters the world through its objectification in a work of art, becomes a part of experience which lives through history. Man's understanding and knowledge of himself is strongly conditioned by his understanding of history – this is the main weight beyond Dilthey's concept of 'historicality' (*Geschichtlichkeit*).

Dilthey exerted a strong influence on German historians during the first three decades of the twentieth century but the over-insistence on the primacy of history and the strong accent on the division between *Geisteswissenschaften* and the exact sciences both contributed to a decline in his importance. However, his advocacy of hermeneutics as a basic method was later taken up and transformed by Martin Heidegger and Hans-Georg Gadamer, and his influence continues in the contemporary German philosophy in this indirect manner.[6]

Max Dessoir had none of Dilthey's breadth, yet his work signals an important development in the direction of specialized aesthetic theories, to be seen as a marked tendency in the philosophy of art throughout the twentieth century. Dessoir reacted against the psychological interpretation of aesthetics and the theory of *Einfühlung* by proposing a re-definition of the scope of aesthetics. If understood as reaction to beauty and the sense of harmony, aesthetics deals with taste and investigates the sensations of pleasure and satisfaction. The theorists of *Einfühlung* were particularly keen to point out that aesthetic experience arises wherever one encounters emotional response, and the scope of aesthetics was thereby widened. Dessoir's criticism of *Einfühlung* (offered mainly in chapters 2 and 3 of his *Ästhetik und allgemeine Kunstwissenschaft*) consisted not so much in again narrowing the scope of aesthetics but in re-defining the disciplines that deal with emotional response, beauty and art. The criticism is not marked by a negation of the position of the psychologists: all Dessoir is attempting is to weaken their case by constantly and deliberately changing his own stance. He will look at a problem from the point of view of emotionalist aesthetics only to continue his argu-

---

[5] See below, p. 373.

[6] It has recently again been claimed (article 'Dilthey' in the *New Grove Dictionary of Music*) that Dilthey's influence appears in the work of Hermann Kretzschmar. Kretzschmar may have been inspired by Dilthey's 'Entstehung der Hermeneutik', in *Philosophische Abhandlungen, Christoph Sigwart zu seinem 70. Geburtstag* (Tübingen 1900) to adopt the term (see above, p. 114), but if so, he totally misunderstood and trivialized Dilthey's ideas. For Kretzschmar 'hermeneutics' is a method of interpreting, or explaining, as understood in the nineteenth century before Dilthey, and his step-by-step procedure of linking musical themes with moods and affections has none of the subtlety which characterizes Dilthey's thought. Kretzschmar has therefore in the present volume been classed not as a follower of Dilthey but simply as a representative of a particular type of the aesthetics of content.

ment from the other side of the bridge which in his theory connects the emotional reaction of the subject to the work of art itself.

Although beauty is applicable to art it also exists in nature, outside the realm of art, and aesthetics, dealing as it does with our response to beauty is not adequate to embrace the complex set of issues arising from art. Also, philosophical speculation deadens the live immediacy of art. The categories which philosophy imposes are not suited to the many-sidedness of art, which comprises spiritual, social and moral issues as well as the traditionally 'aesthetic' ones. Thus, according to Dessoir, the discipline appropriate to art is not aesthetics but *Kunstwissenschaft* ('general theory of art').

Although the distinction may remind one of Hegel, the link with Dilthey is stronger here since Dessoir is keen to stress the primacy of the aspect of life rather than aprioristic categories, but unlike Dilthey he does not sharply divide humanistic disciplines from the exact sciences. In the concrete case of music this leads him to a qualified emotionalist interpretation of the sense of music, but in more general terms his *Kunstwissenschaft* implies a possibility of establishing specialized fields within the general theory of art, each field developed round a particular art form and bringing together studies in philosophical aesthetics, art history, psychology and even ethics. Dessoir was, of course, not original here: on the one hand this composite investigation is reminiscent of the positivists, though far from giving any importance to the social sciences, and on the other hand certain tendencies in the history of art and music of the time already pointed in the direction of *Kunstwissenschaft*. Adler's systematic presentation of musicological disciplines was one of such pointers,[7] and in the history of art A. Schmarsow's *Grundbegriffe der Kunstwissenschaft* (Leipzig 1905) is almost exactly contemporaneous with Dessoir's work. The rise of specialized aesthetics and art theories in the twentieth century, signalling the weakening of the traditional general aesthetics was thus prophetically envisaged by Dessoir and this gives him in the intellectual history of the twentieth century a prominence greater than his stature and achievement would have otherwise accorded him.

Dilthey's and Nietzsche's philosophy of life and Dessoir's notion of the study of art detached from a philosophical system find an echo in Busoni's *Entwurf einer neuen Aesthetik der Tonkunst* (1907). It is unlikely that Busoni was writing in direct response to either Dilthey's or Dessoir's philosophy – he was merely receptive to the ideas then current in the intellectual world. It is, however, worth pointing out that all three men, Dilthey, Dessoir and Busoni, were active in Berlin at the same time. His *Entwurf* is an example of a fine artistic intuition rather than of systematic thought. There is, indeed, no system or plan in the *Entwurf*. Some inherited romantic notions close to the ideas and the type of overblown rhetoric characteristic of Liszt's writings are found side by side with reflections of an eminently practical musician and with an almost Pythagorean belief in the eternal presence of music ('musical

[7] See above, pp. 354–5.

art-work exists, before its tones resound').[8] This contradicts, and in its forcefulness overshadows the statement that 'all arts [. . .] ever aim at the one end, namely, the imitation of nature and the interpretation of human feelings'.[9] This changing of position and constant looking at both aspects of the aesthetic dilemma is close to Dilthey but rings more genuine, the more so as it is not employed as a basis of a theory. The experience of the past which is projected into the future is reminiscent of Dilthey's approach but is characterized by an immediacy of feeling. Finally, the assertion that the tonal system of Western music is not given by nature, but is capable of being re-shaped for future use is vindicated by subsequent history of Western music. This gives an added vividness to Busoni's ability to combine artistic sensibility with the power of speculation – something that was often denied to many of those who otherwise were better philosophers than himself.

[8] F. Busoni, *Sketch of a New Esthetic of Music* (New York 1911), p. 18; see below, p. 390.
[9] Busoni, p. 3.

# 5.1    Historical understanding
## Wilhelm Dilthey (1833–1911)
## 'Das musikalische Verstehen' (c. 1906)

German philosopher. After three semesters' study of theology in Heidelberg, where the Hegelian philosopher Kuno Fischer awakened his interest in philosophy, he went to Berlin in 1853 and came under the influence of Hegel's critic Friedrich Adolf Trendelenburg and the historian Leopold von Ranke. Following the wish of his father, a Protestant pastor, he graduated in theology in Wiesbaden in 1856. For a while he was a schoolmaster and then a free-lance writer in Berlin, and in 1864 produced his *Habilitationsschrift* on Schleiermacher's ethics. Between 1864 and 1882 he held various university appointments in Berlin, Basle, Kiel and Breslau (now Wrocław). In 1882 he returned to Berlin to occupy the chair of philosophy from which he retired in 1905.

His intention to construct a system of 'human sciences' which would overcome the division between the natural and philosophical sciences remained unfulfilled in the sense that Dilthey's own leaning was pronouncedly in the direction of philosophy (which thus becomes, in Dilthey's own terms, 'Wissenschaft der Wissenschaften'). Some of his important ideas were to be found in his lecture notes, isolated fragments and sketches intended for further development, and became accessible only after his death through the efforts of the editors of his complete works who had to grapple with his near-illegible handwriting.

Dilthey was a grandson of a court kapellmeister from whom he received early instruction in music, broadening his knowledge of music theory during his student days in Berlin. Apart from writing on music in his philosophical works, he published in the 1870s a number of articles on musical subjects and reviews of musicological works of the time.

## On understanding music

Source:

'Das musikalische Verstehen' from *Plan der Fortsetzung zum Aufbau der geschichtlichen Welt in den Geisteswissenschaften*, in Wilhelm Dilthey, *Gesammelte Schriften*, ed. B. Groethuysen, vol. 7 (Leipzig and Berlin 1927), pp. 220–4. Translated by Martin Cooper and the editor.

The title *Plan der Fortsetzung* ... was given by B. Groethuysen to a collection of Dilthey's unpublished papers and derives from *Der Aufbau des geschichtlichen Welt in den Geisteswissenschaften*, the first part of a projected large work, first published in 1910 in the *Abhandlungen der Königlich Preussischen Akademie der Wissenschaften*. Various short sketches, among which 'Das musikalische Verstehen', were intended for further revision and extension. Their precise dating is not possible and they may have been written at any time between 1906 and 1910.

*For further reading:*

W. Dilthey, *Meaning in History* (London 1961); C. Dahlhaus, *Foundations of Music History* (Cambridge 1983).

It proved to be impossible to grasp the self itself in the experience, either in the way it flows or in the depth of its content.[1] It is only the small area of our conscious lives that rises, like an island, out of these unfathomable depths. But we are raised from these same depths by means of expression; for expression is a form of creation. Life itself becomes accessible to our understanding, intelligible as an imitation of creation. True, we have before us only a single work and this, if it is to endure, must somehow be given an existence in space – in a musical score, in printed characters, on a gramophone record and, in the first place, in memory itself. But what is preserved is the ideal representation of a process in time, of a complex musical or poetic experience. And what is it that we are in fact perceiving? Parts of a whole, unfolding in time. In each of these parts, however, there is what we call a 'tendency' at work. One note follows another, or accompanies it according to the laws of our musical system; but within that system there lie innumerable possibilities, and it is in the direction of one of these possibilities that music progresses, in such a way that earlier musical events are qualified by those that come later. The rising phrases of a melody appear to flow in the same direction. In such a case those phrases that appear later are conditioned by those that have gone before, but in the case of, say, one of Handel's rising melodies, what appears latest is at the same time rooted in what came first. Similarly the falling line of a melody moves towards its conclusion, which both conditions it, and is conditioned by it. In every case all possibilities remain open. Nowhere is there a necessity in this conditioning. The situation resembles a free agreement between figures moving first towards, and then away from each other. There is never any suggestion of our knowing why the second phrase of a melody follows the first precisely as it does, with precisely this new harmonic nuance, or re-shaped into precisely this variant, ornamented with this figure rather than any other. There is no kind of necessity that determines why these things should be precisely as they are: they are thus a realization of an aesthetic value; and there is no feeling of necessity, in any particular passage, compelling one idea to follow another: what in fact follows could have been something else. Here, too, there is a tendency inherent in all [artistic] creation towards what appears to the thinking mind as beautiful or noble. Let us look further: we shall find that understanding depends on the memory's ability to retain what has just occurred and on taking this information into account in considering what follows.

---

[1] [In the original the sentence reads: 'Im Erleben war uns das eigene Selbst weder in der Form seines Abflusses, noch in der Tiefe dessen, was es einschliesst, erfassbar.' It is desirable to retain the stress on 'das *eigene* Selbst', hence the wording 'the self itself' in the translation. 'Form' has been translated as 'way' since the context suggests a process rather than a static property.]

The object of historical musical studies is not the search for some psychological event in the composer's life: it is rather something objective – the musical complex arising in the composer's imagination as expression. The historical study of music deals therefore with comparisons – it is in fact a 'comparative' science, undertaken in order to discover the musical means employed to achieve individual effects.

There is a further sense in which music is the expression of an experience – experience here meaning any larger unit composed of separate experiences at the present moment or retained in the memory, and 'expression' meaning an event in the imagination in which the experience throws its reflection [*hineinscheint*] into the world of music as it has developed in history – a world in which all means of expression have been brought together in a continuous historical tradition. In this creation of the imagination, then, there is no rhythmic figure and no melody that is not related to experience, and yet the whole is something more than expression. For this world of music, with its inexhaustible possibilities of beauty and significance, is always in existence, always continues in history and is always capable of endless further development. It is in this world, and not in the world of his own feelings, that the musician lives.

It is useless to enquire of the music historian how human experience is converted into music. It is precisely this transmutation that is the highest achievement of music – the fact that what takes place in the composer's imagination as something opaque, indeterminate, often unconscious involuntarily achieves limpid expression in musical figures. There is no division between music and experience, no question of two worlds or of any transformation from one world to another. Genius means living in the world of music as if it alone existed: it means forgetting all existence, all suffering in this world of sound, yet including all this. One does not deal with a single, determined, progression from experience to music. The listener who experiences and as it were assimilates music – some memory, some floating image, some vague mood from the past reaching over into the ecstatic moment of creation – may find that what initiates the process is some rhythmic invention or some sequence of harmonies, or perhaps some experience. In the whole world of the arts musical creation is the most rigorously tied to technical rules and at the same time the freest form of emotional expression.

This interplay [of art and experience] is the natural sphere of the creative faculty and at the same time the most profound mystery – the mystery of how a succession of sounds and rhythms can have a significance beyond themselves. It is not a question of psychological relationship between emotional states and their representation in the imagination – anyone who embarks on that line of explanation is pursuing a will-o'-the-wisp. It is rather the relationship between an objective composition – its component parts as a creation of the imagination – and the meaning which is to be found in each melodic strand, that is, what the work tells the listener about a spiritual something that exists in the link between rhythm, melody, harmonic relations and the impact of an emotional message. It is not psychological, but musical relationships that form the study of musical genius, musical composition and musical theory. The artist has innumerable methods of working. The relationship of any musical event to what a listener understands by that event – and thus what it actually expresses to him – is quite definite: it is capable of being understood and represented [in the mind]. We speak of a conductor or performer 'interpreting' a work, but the relationship of each and every listener to a composition is in fact an interpretation. It is concerned with something objective. What prompts the composer, psychologically speaking, may be a passage from music to experience or vice versa, or both alternatively, and the fundamental spiritual experience does not need to be (and for the artist himself is often not) actually something that can be experienced. What begins as a movement deep in the unconscious only finds expression as a dynamic relationship in the finished work, and it is only from the finished work that we can discover it. This is in fact the value of music – that it is the expression, the objectification, of what was, in the composer, a state of mind. This complex in which quality, duration, motoric form, and content all combine will be analysed in a composer's mind, then presented as a relationship between rhythm, sound-sequences, and harmony, and brought to its full existence as a relationship between sonorous beauty and expression.

The point of departure is the actual world of sound itself, with all its various potentialities of beauty and expressiveness, historically developed in music, seized on by the musician while he is still a child, something always present to him, something into which all his experiences are transformed, something that he repeatedly encounters – a world into which his innermost being enters in order to find expression so that life, with all its joys and sorrows, exists for the artist primarily in his music. Here again memory presents itself as current meaning. Life's miseries, as such, are too overwhelming to allow his imagination to range freely, but echoes and dreams of the past are the airy material – remote from the solid earth – from which the gossamer shapes of music issue.

There are aspects of life that can find expression as rhythm, as melody, as harmony, as forms of succession [Ablauf], rising and falling temper of mind, continuity, durability, the extension in depth of the interior life subsisting in harmony.

The existing foundations of musical history must be completed by a theory of musical meaning. This is the connecting link between the other departments of musicology with the creative activity (and eventually the life) of the artist, and the development of the different schools of music – a system relating the two to each other. This is the heart of the secret of musical imagination.

Let us take some examples. In the first act finale of Don Giovanni rhythms may be heard which are different from each other not only in speed but in metre. The effect of this is a combination of quite different aspects of human life, dancing and so forth, so that the variety of the world finds expression.

This is exactly what music, more generally speaking, can effect, depending as it does on the possibility of presenting simultaneously different characters or even different musical entities such as choruses etc. whereas poetry is tied to dialogue etc. This accounts also for the metaphysical character of music. Take a Handel aria, for example, in which a simple figure repeats itself in ascending motion. Thus arises in the memory a single, easily comprehensible unity: a growth of this kind becomes an expression of strength. But in the last resort this impression rests on the fact that the memory retains a succession of notes in time as a single unity, owing to the fact of its simplicity. Or take a chorale based on a folk-song, in which a simple melodic unity expresses very clearly a single succession of feelings. Here we have a new situation – the slow, even sequence and the harmonic progressions based on the organ part emphasize a single sublime object which subsists through all the changing emotional moods. It resembles a religious communion, a relationship in time to what is suprasensual, of what is finite to what is infinite, which thus achieves expression. Or take one of the exchanges between the trembling sinner and his Redeemer in a Bach cantata. Here the restless, swiftly moving music with its strongly-marked intervals, high notes and florid passages signifies a definite religious type, while that of the Saviour is suggested by deep, tranquil music, moving mostly in small intervals, and combined with patterns that suggest comfort or consolation. No one can doubt the existence of such meanings.

Musical meaning develops in two opposite directions. Here it is as the expression of a poetic text with a definite object, in the direction of interpreting something clearly identified by words. Instrumental music has no definite object – only something infinite and therefore indeterminate, something that can only be found in life itself. Thus instrumental music in its highest forms has life itself as an object. A musical genius such as Bach is stimulated by every sound in nature, every gesture and every vague noise. These suggest to him corresponding musical figures, as it were motoric themes whose character breathes the breath of life itself. Thus we can see that programme music is in fact the death of true instrumental music. [pp. 220–4]

# Wilhelm Dilthey

# 'Mozart' (c. 1906)

*Source:*

'Mozart' in *Von deutscher Dichtung und Musik*, ed. H. Nohl and G. Misch (Leipzig and Berlin 1933), pp. 277–82. Translated by Martin Cooper.

The volume consists of a number of Dilthey's previously unpublished essays on various aspects of German poetry and music. The essays on music, dating from *c.* 1906–7, were grouped together by the editors under the common title 'Die grosse deutsche Musik des 18. Jahrhunderts'.

[.　.　.]

## 1. The principle of musical construction

Following the practice of Italian composers, Mozart constructs his characters, situations and action purely musically. Character is expressed at a low emotional level, and is shown in relation to others by means of recitative. So in this relationship the life of the emotions becomes intensified into action in the traditional forms in which musical discourse alternates with concerted numbers such as duet, trio etc. Intensified emotional states arising from the dramatic action are expressed in the aria. The chief characters of the drama are thus developed by means of these closed forms and so achieve perfect expression in their changing attitudes to existence. In each of these forms the connection between the inner life of a character and its expression in mime and gesture is completed in the musical form; and it thus becomes possible to give complete expression, by miming the expression, to something that the drama is incapable of expressing – the deep emotional coherence of a character, including natural temperament, normal physical habit and emotional quality. This side of human character can be made clearer [in opera] than in spoken drama.

Here, too, we may see the close connection between the lyrical drama and the special nature of the German poetry of the day, which was not content to show human beings simply in their actions and their speech as means of those actions. By the flood of their eloquence the poets sought to give expression to the emergence of both words and actions from the inner consciousness. And it is immediately evident that the unrealistic style of the drama enables it to achieve this end far more completely than it could be achieved in *Iphigenie* or

375

*Wallenstein.*[1] Here we become aware of the opposing claims of realism and style. In the pure musical atmosphere of the opera this opposition simply vanishes.

In just the same way the relationship of the characters to the stage and the action is purely musical. The effects of the musical principle are even more noticeable here. The emotional character of each scene is enormously affected by the orchestra, which prepares the atmosphere of each scene from the overture onwards, and can preserve it unchanged even through changes of scenery. The most astonishing advantage of the sung over the spoken drama lies in the possibility of two characters speaking simultaneously. Mozart makes each of his characters express themselves with complete naturalness and, by linking this with the unity of musical form, produces one of the aesthetically greatest emotional effects imaginable, viz. the union between the many-sidedness of human nature and the unity of human life. Thus we have a direct way of making the listener conscious in a single moment of the richness of life. Thanks to his contrapuntal skill Mozart achieves altogether extraordinary effects by this means. In the very first scene of *Don Giovanni*, as we hear the voices of the Commendatore, the Don and Leporello – a veritable incarnation of both mortal tragedy and plebeian instincts – it is as though we were raised to an awareness of that mosaic of feelings that is the emotional basis of our very existence. This same effect is repeated on a heroic scale in the last act, where we hear the voices of Elvira, Don Giovanni and Leporello and once again feel the presence of a preternatural power – the struggle of a heroic will on the one hand and the trembling of a trivial soul on the other, uniting to form a consciousness of life's unimaginable variety, with its recurrent counterpoint of strong fundamental emotions. In this way the highest musical effects approach metaphysical consciousness more nearly than is ever possible in the spoken drama. There, similar effects may be produced – as in the scene with the three fools on the heath in *King Lear* – but only in succession. In the spoken drama, too, the emotional tone of a scene is set suddenly, by the actual scenery, instead of being sustained as a unity, as the orchestra does in opera. Another even more effective combination occurs in the entertainment scene in Don Giovanni's castle. There we find a contradiction between the festive atmosphere expressed by the music on the stage and the element of tragedy introduced by the Three Masks and Don Giovanni's lordly reception of them; and the different attitudes of all the characters – from Masetto, Leporello and Zerlina to Don Giovanni himself and Donna Anna – find expression in complex shiftings of emphasis. This gives the listener the feeling of experiencing the whole world as a single web of sound in a characteristic counterpoint of primitive emotional attitudes; and the inexhaustible richness of the scene, combining unity with variety and harmony with dissonance, gives it a definitely metaphysical note.

There are a number of historical connections here. Mozart found in the

---

[1] [*Iphigenie auf Tauris*, a dramatic poem by Goethe; *Wallenstein*, a dramatic poem by Schiller.]

secular drama the same effects exclusively characteristic of vocal music as had reached, in the religious sphere of cantata and oratorio, their highest point in the vocal music of J. S. Bach. And a musicianly poet like Jean Paul sought to achieve similar effects by bringing disparate sound-effects into a single unity, creating as it were a landscape – the verbal expression of feeling – of distant sounds. In this way he created a feeling of expanding a moment in the life of the individual to a cosmic wealth of meaning and profound significance.

Another effect which goes far beyond those obtainable by spoken drama is produced by Mozart's artistic principle of continuity, the steady building up of an artistic whole. This consists in showing the vital essence of each of the chief characters expressing itself in different situations in which it takes on different forms, though remaining fundamentally unchanged. This union, as it were, of modulations in a single human will, and of the expressive possibilities arising from those modulations, has only once been presented with such forcefulness in musical terms, namely in the character of the Don himself and on a smaller scale in the words and actions of Donna Anna, the two protagonists of this great drama. This was of course only possible because the subject itself contains the remains of a great dramatic work of art, and these contained for Mozart the possibility needed for the purely musical construction of these two characters.

This principle of musical construction explains Mozart's relatively free handling of his text, a point in which he stands in strong contrast to both Gluck and Wagner, and resembling Bach. His melodies give the trivialities of that text a wealth of expression that is by no means to be found in the words.

## 2. Mozart's vital consciousness and its expression by means arising from his musical principle

Mozart is the greatest dramatic genius of the eighteenth century, and this fact is explained by his temperamental ability to identify himself objectively with every event, every situation, every character. He had no didactic ambition, no vocation to maintain an unbroken nobility of tone by sheer moral energy, like Handel or Beethoven; and in this fact lay the essential character of his dramatic genius. All circumstances confirm this – his brilliance and vivacity as an actor, his letters, his nimbleness and volubility. He must have been a wonderful mimic, and of course every situation and every character immediately had for him its own individual musical 'voice'. Everything expressed itself to him in terms of music. His whole attitude to life was purely aesthetic. He seized on the musical kernel of every situation. Music was his language. He was like a child expressing himself in words, and there could be no greater mistake than to judge his power of comprehension by his words. He was always an observer, a connoisseur. Only music was for him a serious matter.

Thus it was that he had that sense of richness, the plenitude of existence that is the hallmark of such dramatic geniuses as his. In this he resembled Shakespeare. He did not come to set the world to rights but simply to express in musical terms the world as it is. And in this he was helped by the stage that music had reached in his day. Just as vocal is always conditioned by instrumental music, so the quartet and the symphony contained the means to express certain fundamental human moods. Mozart himself played an important part in the musical development of these means of expression. There is a close affinity between his instrumental Andantes and the melting airs of Octavio or Cherubino, between his scherzo movements and the music of Figaro, Leporello and some of Don Giovanni's moods.

Thus Mozart's achievement is supreme where his text suggests the infinite variety of human existence. Heroic opera was alien to him and his *Idomeneo* was a failure. What he felt the need to express was precisely the simultaneous counterpoint of comedy and tragedy, in fact the universal human chorus [*alle Stimmen in allen Dingen*]. It was this that determined his choice of texts, insofar as we have any historical grounds for supposing an influence on that choice. It was this that determined the manner in which he understood these different voices and gave them expression. For such a nature as his creation could only mean presenting every vital nuance in the drama. This is the most individual feature of the opera that he created, if we consider subject and material. Nothing human was alien to Mozart's genius. He had to choose subjects that range from the world of transcendent contemplation to the most primitive sensual activity; he had to bring into a single picture masters and servants, honour and elegance, sensual appetite, trivial commonplace. It was only thus that he could be himself.

Add to this the naturalness and simplicity of expression possible at that particular moment in the history of music, for at no other moment of history could Mozart's lyric drama have come into existence. With the growth of subjectivity and the final intensification of expression in the following generation it was no longer possible.

Let us finally compare him with Richard Wagner! Wagner returns to the German past and creates characters each of which represents a definite emotional mode [*Gefühlston*], a dramatic structure dominated by human passions and based on metaphysical relations. His very choice of material completes the process of musical abstraction. He has no knowledge of the humble reality in which all human life is rooted. [pp. 277–82]

[.    .    .]

# 5.2 Criticism of the theory of *Einfühlung*

## Max Dessoir (1867–1947)

## *Ästhetik und allgemeine Kunstwissenschaft* (1906)

German philosopher and psychologist. He studied philosophy in Berlin between 1885 and 1889 and obtained a doctorate as a pupil of Wilhelm Dilthey. Wishing to understand and explain the nature of artistic creativity he became interested in occult phenomena and observed mediums. This led him to the study of and a doctorate in medicine in Würzburg in 1892. He started teaching philosophy at Berlin University in 1897, becoming in 1920 a full professor. The Nazis first suspended him from his post and then dismissed him in 1936.

In 1906 he founded the *Zeitschrift für Ästhetik und allgemeine Kunstwissenschaft* and edited it until 1937. He was also the founder, in 1909, of the Gesellschaft für Ästhetik und allgemeine Kunstwissenschaft. Dessoir was an able violinist and for a while studied with Carl Flesch.

## *Aesthetics and general theory of art*

*Source:*

*Ästhetik und allgemeine Kunstwissenschaft* (Stuttgart 1906), [chapter] vii: Tonkunst und Mimik; [section] 3. Der Sinn der Musik, p. 329–38. Translated by Martin Cooper and the editor.

The second, revised edition (Stuttgart 1923) contains small changes of wording throughout, as well as some new material. For a complete English translation of the second edition see Max Dessoir, *Aesthetics and Theory of Art*, tr. S. A. Emery (Detroit 1970). Pages 290–300 in Emery's translation contain an extended version of the text included in the present volume.

*For further reading:*

Max Dessoir, *Buch der Erinnerung* (Stuttgart 1946).

### Chapter VII, section 3: The meaning of music

[.    .]

What we are concerned with is the particular meaning of music. This does not of course arise for those unable to distinguish notes of different pitches, nor even for those unable to grasp the unity of clearly perceived sounds or to distinguish one sequence of notes from another of the same kind. In fact such a question arises only for those who are 'musical', and by musical – in the higher sense – we mean those for whom music is a familiar language, we might almost say a second mother tongue. But more generally speaking 'musical' applies to anyone who enjoys rhythmic and harmonic sounds in the same way that he enjoys beautiful shapes and bright colours. A melody that delights the ear and a simple, brisk rhythm that immediately suggests bodily movement are a source of bodily well-being, like a warm bath. No music that fails to satisfy these conditions can really be called pure art: it remains fundamentally a refined and organized form of noise. There is something dead, something unnatural in prolonged silence. Those who enjoy plays on words might call silence disturbing [*die Ruhe beunruhigend*] and disturbance reassuring [*die Unruhe beruhigend*]. For disturbance is evidence of life, and this sensation of life surging round one is beneficial and reassuring. There is no need to distinguish the component parts of noise: any complex roar or clatter, any continuous din assures us that we are alive and surrounded by life. This delight in sound as a sign of life is at the very origin of our delight in music. We are all familiar with this from our own experiences, walking pleasantly in the park surrounded by giggling girls or chatting idly at the dinner table, our ears charmed by the sounds of light music. On such occasions music is no more than a pleasant noise, something that we hear but to which we do not listen. The pleasure derived from rhythms and timbres is hardly to be distinguished from the pleasure we derive from natural sounds, only everything is stylized, composed according to definite laws and therefore more pleasurable to our almost unconsciously-receiving ears than are the sounds and rhythms of the natural world. The effect of music that is hardly noticed, and certainly not 'understood', is of extraordinary importance for man's whole life-awareness: we feel liberated and vitalized by music, the hum and the rhythm of a dance-melody make us feel happy and carefree and the primitive energy of military music seems to restore something of our youthful alertness. Music as an art of social noise means a uniform movement of the air, and this does us good. It penetrates simultaneously all our surroundings and rouses, at the same moment and with the same inevitability, everyone present.[1]

The meaning of music is extended as soon as we include a practical concern with its production. Let us consider in the first place the whole mechanical aspect of performance. It is important here to think of performing music as a technique of movement – as a time-consuming training of the fingers or the throat muscles, sometimes painful and sometimes pleasurable. This purely physical schooling is as essential to the amateur as to the artist, and not too much should be made of it – the artist in fact (like the scholar) should be spared any offensive praise for the hard work involved, since work must always be taken for granted. It can, on the other hand, present a danger, if it is

[1] See Oskar Bie, 'Von der dekorativen Musik', *Der Kunstwart*, 15 Sept. 1894.

falsely mistaken for the content of a whole life, when in fact there is no such content. An insatiable passion for listening to music may well distract a person from more serious tasks, but the actual practice of music may be an even stronger temptation to neglect urgent duties and lead to a life that is spiritually empty and idle. The never-ceasing struggle with a recalcitrant hand or voice may come in the end to occupy the whole personality. No sport, no amusement and no profession carries with it such a threat to true breadth of vision. This apparent ability of musical technique to absorb all a man's energies is not enough to explain the attraction of participating in musical performance. Still deeper lies another reason for our finding this interest such an exclusive one. This is the fact that in musical performance we live out our personalities, absolutely untrammelled and completely our own. Every flight of imagination that we bring to the music recalls the heroic life of the senses lived by our forefathers: every muscle does its work, we raise our heads proudly, shudders go down our backs as though we were confronted with a decision that can only lead to triumph. A boy plays a poor little piece of his own with a *fortissimo* dissonance before the final cadence. 'He would not allow himself the final resolution, he held it in reserve for himself and his listeners. What would it be – this resolution, this ecstatic liberation into B major? An unparalleled joy, a satisfaction of ineffable sweetness. Peace . . . bliss . . . heaven . . . but not yet, not yet! Postpone it one minute longer, a minute of hesitation, of an excitement which must become unbearable so that the satisfaction may be the keener . . . One more final savouring of this urgent, impulsive longing, this desire of the whole being, this ultimate convulsive effort of the will, which still refuses fulfilment and deliverance because he knows that happiness is momentary . . .'[2] Yes, we become kings, masters of the world, when we make sounds swell and fade and weave harmonies and rhythms in contrasting patterns. By a mere accentuation we form a new creation which we then annihilate with a gesture of indifference, we have the most marvellous adventures, rush forward, shrink back, set enchanted princesses free – who can recount all that we do and suffer? Added to that is the awareness of having plumbed the very depths of the composer's soul, and still more the fusing with the soul of one's partner, as it is at that very moment – a marvellous coming together in the details of interpretation, the sharing in short pauses for breathing, it may be, and the mutual support at every moment of the performance. Anyone who has played in an orchestra knows the feeling, like the comradeship of the battlefield. Above one stands the conductor, interpreting the music by his facial expressions and his gestures, as an actor interprets his role. All around are one's colleagues, inspired by a single purpose. By one's side are players whom one knows to be inalienable confederates. Out there is the enemy, sometimes victorious and sometimes beaten, sometimes aggressive and superior, sometimes cowed and submissive. The violinists' bows are poised for the downbeat – and is it not as though

---

[2] Thomas Mann, *Buddenbrooks*, vol. 2 (1901), pp. 168–9, compare also vol. 2, pp. 522ff.

the lances of a squadron of uhlans were glittering in the sun? Are not the deep social origins of all art being rediscovered?

Effects such as these make themselves felt even in the greatest music and with sophisticated players and listeners. There are always some passages in which our first concern is not with the actual work but with the instinctive excitement aroused in us by the sheer movement and beauty of the sounds, or with purely subjective images of our own. The march-rhythms of military music seem to compel our feet to imitate the movement of the music and participation in movement may even on occasion be prompted by the abstract conversation [*Geistersprache*] of a string quartet. If one listens to a delightful Bach suite – say the Flute Suite in B minor – one will find that the pleasure derived from the sounds and rhythms will be interwoven with conscious associations e.g. images of a rococo minuet. 'Social' light music and serious music are of course fundamentally different in nature and in effect. One is a pleasant way of spending time and the other deadly serious, the one a blessing for the poorest and simplest and the other something outside the reach of those who have to struggle for their existence. Light music is emotionally the simplest and most popular of the arts, serious music the most abstract and impenetrable. And yet, when we observe composers, performers, and music-lovers we find that at every degree of their activity the two types of music remain connected. Thus those for whom all art immediately becomes reality and takes on the character of drama automatically make the rhythms of *Parsifal* as spritely as those of a street song. They have no need to know what is happening in the purely musical sense: they simply allow themselves to be elated or calmed by the sounds they hear. Everyone is familiar with Shakespeare's frequent praising of music and with Nietzsche's account of how he reacted to the music of Bizet's *Carmen*.[3] Stendhal writes in much the same vein in chapter 16 of *De l'amour*:

Yesterday evening I came to understand that a perfect musical work has the same effect on the heart as the presence of the beloved i.e. it causes what appears to be the most intense happiness possible to mortals. If this were universally true, nothing in the world could more dispose human beings to love. But only last year, in Naples, I realized that a perfect musical work, like a perfect pantomime, makes me think of whatever is at the moment the chief object of my reveries, and gives me wonderful ideas: in Naples it was the question of how to arm the Greeks.

It must be admitted that for anyone who enjoys music in this way music itself must eventually disappear. Art that is austere and disciplined gives us no freedom to ponder political questions. Fundamentally music remains, for amateurs of this kind, at the early stage of stylized noise, only it is enjoyed as a narcotic or an intoxicant rather than as an after-dinner amusement of a kind of aural titillation.

Where to look for the other 'meaning' of music is indicated by a well-known phenomenon – I mean the incredibly early appearance of musical

---

[3] [F. Nietzsche, *The Case of Wagner*. See above, p. 103.]

genius. Children of eight can perform prodigies of understanding, performing, even creating music, and even a people as completely uncultivated as the gypsies show quite remarkable musical powers. There is virtually no parallel to this in the other arts, since even the most gifted can only gradually acquire that understanding of the world and of humanity which is needed by the poet and the painter. Music, on the other hand, has no essential need of any relationship with reality. Very early in human history it became the centre of a profound symbolism, thanks to the seemingly supernatural character of its origins. In fact musical 'events' are unique by the virtue of creating their own values and not by being, like shapes and colours, qualities attached to objects. Music obeys its own inherent laws and does not refer to models in nature or in the human spirit. It reveals itself, with all its rules, to spirits attuned to it by nature, and often remains a closed book to the most refined aesthetic taste. Good music is in many ways simply an interrelation of forms moving in sound.[4] I cannot conceive of any images of the real world or any emotional drama that a listener would be objectively justified in associating with a Bach fugue. Masterpieces such as these express no mood: who could gather from them the composer's state of mind when he wrote them? They make their effect by the systematic organization of their component parts and in accordance with the laws of part-writing. The delightful, convivial sounds affect the listener in the same way as physical charms, but the art of the mind and the spirit is something solitary, something that requires understanding and must be understood. The listener must know whether the key and the mode, rhythm and beat change or not, he must remember the theme and recognize it in the variations, grasp the disposition of the parts and follow the movement to be ready to welcome its climax – in fact he must keep his attention always on the alert. In so doing he will have the pure enjoyment of the music in all its complexity – the return of a melody, the reappearance of earlier motifs, developments, combinations, transitions, the entries of the different instruments and the myriad other charms which can hardly be comprehended by a listener who simply sits comfortably in his seat or has his mind taken up with other matters. In order to do full justice to a work of art, it is not only the music that must fulfil certain conditions but the listener as well.

We have said something about the power of music over senses and its formal self-sufficiency; but there is a third element which we can recognize in a very familiar example, namely Beethoven's 'Pastoral' Symphony. Here the peasants' dance suddenly breaks off, and we hear in the bass instruments of the orchestra a shift of key. This sudden interruption offends the ear and disturbs the formal structure of the music [see example, p. 384]. It cannot be justified according to any of the familiar musical conceptions, and yet it is one of the most miraculous passages in the whole work. The theory by which its solemn beauty is explained equates music with expression. According to this the listener hears and appreciates what is happening by identifying

---

[4] [In the original: 'ein Zusammenhang tönend bewegte Formen'. Here and later (see below, p. 384) Dessoir obviously refers to Hanslick's words (see above, p. 19).]

himself with the interior life that communicates itself in the music, which he interprets as symbolic of a deeper meaning.[5] Of course a good composer is in the first place a master of the world of rhythms and sounds and an expert in that of forms, but he is also someone able to discover sounds that release his own feelings. And since we all have an innate ability to express the changes in our emotional states by means of sounds, we are able to follow sympathetically the emotional excitement and even the general spiritual direction of many compositions, though not all. Meanwhile our particular problem remains unsolved. It lies in the following question: whether, and if so to what extent, basic mental conditions [*seelische Unterlagen*] and activities are determined by the specific nature of music and how far besides a significance is transferred to what charms our senses and to the forms moving in sound.[6] Not every excitement caused by sound can be made the subject-matter of the general theory of art. Rather, one is dealing here with the mind demonstrably seized by the object [the work of art], or the puzzle of how an interior mental state can achieve an exterior existence by means of an interaction of rhythms and harmonies. Much that is directly or indirectly relevant to the explanation of this fact has already been said, and we will therefore fix our whole attention simply on the main point.

If one turns to the history of music for help one is at first quite at a loss to find that some melodies were used with widely dissimilar texts, and that in all

    [5] [Dessoir here refers to the theory of *Einfühlung*.]
    [6] [See above, p. 383, n. 4.]

cases the use was taken to be valid in terms of expression and characteristic detail. The helplessness increases as soon as one asks the listeners about the impression left by a piece. The information gained appears uncertain and contradictory. If by some chance the mood of the music is known explicitly and if the composer has done something in order to communicate it, there exists in turn scarcely one amongst a thousand listeners able to put himself onto the right track.

The metaphorical language of music is beyond question extremely ambiguous, but why should this be made a subject of complaint? The character of every art is after all determined by its limitations or deficiencies: and if the fact that the same music can correspond to two diametrically opposed states of mind constitutes a weakness in the art's power of definition, what shall we say of poetry, which is obliged to reduce to words the ineffable, which is by definition inexpressible? On the other hand, consider the advantages of music. It is thanks to its fluid nature that music is able to overcome the barriers with which we are inclined to partition off the different areas of human consciousness and to enable the basic unity of the individual personality to appear in all its many manifestations. Lotze has suggested the reason for this complaisant character of music in the following examples:

Music cannot represent justice, but it can represent the irreversible consequence of an action, which stands as its formal symbol. It cannot represent the untiring striving of the human spirit towards some definite goal, but it can represent the alternation of vigour and exhaustion and the untiring return to the same, ever-growing aspiration. It cannot represent hope or benevolence, but it can represent the ready reconciling in circumstances hostile to the original direction of development, yet used in order to create a higher harmony . . .[7]

In other words, sequences of notes cannot imitate feelings in all their dimensions. Instead of this they are content to hint at what may be called the form, or essence, of those feelings i.e. at stillness and movement, fastness and slowness, wealth of component parts and emptiness, to give only a few examples. In referring to such things as these music can be extremely precise. If one compares Beethoven's 'Eroica' Symphony with the programme attributed to it by Wagner, it is undeniable that Beethoven's melodies have more character than Wagner's shapeless explication of them. Of course, it is possible to describe how a melody goes straight to the point or gets lost on the way thither, how it slowly dies away or is suddenly interrupted. It is possible to envelop that melody in profound meditations or to caress it with the most delicate metaphors, but we are still a very long way from its precise character. That character, however, is something quite different from a visual apprehension or an idea. Robert Schumann wrote of his piano piece *In der Nacht*:

Later, when I had finished composing it, I was delighted to discover in the music the story of Hero and Leander. Now, when I play the piece, the whole story forces itself

[7] H. Lotze, *Kleine Schriften*, vol. 3 (Leipzig 1891), p. 213.

upon my mind – Leander plunging into the sea – Hero calling and he answering – his safe arrival on the opposite shore – then the lovers' cantilena – his forced departure and his reluctance – and then the darkness of the night veiling the whole scene. Tell me whether you find this picture seems to you to suit the music, as it does to me.[8]

J. D. Rogers, in his invaluable appendix to Bosanquet's *A History of Aesthetic*, tells us that before he had any knowledge of Schumann's letter he had imagined quite a different scene for *In der Nacht*. He saw, as it were, a stormy night-sky in which the moon and the clouds were engaged in a kind of battle – the moon appearing and disappearing, at one moment visible behind a silvery veil and at another hidden by an impenetrable bank of clouds, still visible at moments but eventually altogether covered.[9] A comparison of the two 'programmes' reveals the equal aptness of each – the clouds corresponding to the waves, the moon to the swimmer. It is just what they have in common that is the life of the music.

If there were a scientific term for the emotional counterpart of a general concept, we should be able to say: it is this that music expresses. The general concept of 'merchandise' includes innumerable different meanings, since there are innumerable kinds of merchandise, and one meaning is as good or as bad as another. But the actual meaning of the concept develops simply from an act of judgement i.e. in the logically precise determination of its content. In the same way I can attach the most brilliant images to a piece of music, but its real significance as expression resides in the musically precise development of its emotional shape. If we look more closely, we shall recognize two circumstances which will make this statement clear. Our wonderful language contains a number of instances in which the presence of an umlaut changes the meaning entirely: *achten* [to respect] and *ächten* [to outlaw], for example. In music it happens much more frequently, when minute modifications of a single thematic cell reveal diametrically opposite potentialities; nor need this be a matter of chance, for the skilful composer can deliberately emphasize the basic unity of apparent opposites. If, for instance, the same musical idea, only very slightly modified, is used to depict the high hopes with which the hero embarks on his career and the melancholy of its conclusion, the listener is aware of the deep affinity between the pride of youth and the self-denial of old age; and this is indeed a fact of human nature. Who can define exactly where passionate love turns to hatred? Where does high-minded loyalty become mere habit? When is action the nobler course and when is it nobler to refrain from action? Which of our feelings are manly or womanly, which are objective and which subjective?

In Brahms's 'German Requiem' there is a fugal movement which begins with the words: 'Der Gerechten Seelen sind in Gottes Hand und keine Qual rühret sie an.'[10] Here the protecting hand of God is suggested by the low D in

---

[8] R. Schumann, *Jugendbriefe* (Leipzig 1885), 21 April 1838.

[9] [B. Bosanquet, *A History of Aesthetic* (London 1892), p. 488.]

[10] ['The souls of the righteous are in the hand of God, and there shall no torment touch them.']

the basses and timpani, which persists throughout the fugue. In this way music can express the belief that God is the beginning and end of all things, that He is omnipresent and that He is the ground of all being, that His nature knows nothing of struggle and repose, growth and decay – this and much more. From this example we can not only see once more how a formal musical event can touch a sympathetic chord in the human spirit: we can also obtain a further insight. It is more or less a personal matter whether, in listening to music, we pursue such considerations or not; but what is of objective importance is the fact of that sympathetic vibration of similar trains of thought in absolute accord with what is happening in the music itself. Images and ideas which must, by their very nature, remain outside music, cannot constitute the psychological core of music. The decisive fact is that psychological impulses – memories, thoughts, feelings and associations – take on a certain colour when listening to music, and that this does not occur in the case of the other arts. These impulses are rendered fluid and irresistibly absorbed into the musical texture. It is only by this means that they establish a connection with the formal characteristics of a work as perceived by the senses and seize, as it were, a fraction of the total experience which originally filled the composer's whole consciousness. It is difficult to give a precise verbal account of this transmutation of the listener's mental activity; but it is always possible to point to its occurrence in the listener's consciousness. Like the descent of the Holy Spirit at Pentecost, music seizes us and enables us to speak in foreign tongues. Thus the power of music, as the expression of joy and sorrow, extends from physical excitement to that realm which is not of this world, from organized noise to 'the art of sonorous silence'.

# 5.3 The past and the future of music

## Ferruccio Busoni (1866–1924)

## *Entwurf einer neuen Aesthetik der Tonkunst* (1907)

An international piano virtuoso, prolific composer, conductor and teacher, Busoni was also a man of a refined literary taste, author of librettos for his own operas and a skilful and dignified polemicist.

Busoni was bilingual, expressing himself with ease in Italian and German. E. J. Dent said in 1909 that Busoni wrote German 'with a certain Tuscan directness and clarity'. He felt himself close to German culture, though by no means accepting it uncritically. He settled in Berlin in 1894 and remained there for the rest of his life, withdrawing to Switzerland during the First World War.

The first edition of his *Entwurf*, published in 1907 in Trieste, then a city in the south-western corner of the Austro-Hungarian Monarchy, had only a limited impact as it was read by a small circle of friends and associates. An English translation, published in New York in 1911, helped to make the work better known. However, it was the revised German edition of 1916 that was responsible for the full impact of the work in Europe. It was met with both enthusiasm and hostility, and the ripples of the controversy it caused continued to be felt for a few years after Busoni's death. The full story of the reception of Busoni's *Entwurf* lies thus outside the period covered by this volume, but its roots are firmly in the first decade of the twentieth century.

## *Sketch of a new aesthetics of music*

Source:

*Sketch of a New Esthetic of Music*, tr. Th. Baker (New York 1911), pp. 7–10; 17–19; 23–5; 26–7; 29–34. A reprint was included in *Three Classics in the Aesthetic of Music* (New York 1962). The reprint orders into numbered groups the unnumbered paragraphs of the original edition. Our edition follows the layout of the original.

[.   .]

Is it not singular, to demand of a composer originality in all things, and to forbid it as regards form? No wonder that, once he becomes original, he is accused of 'formlessness'. Mozart! the seeker and the finder, the great man with the childlike heart – it is he we marvel at, to whom we are devoted; but not his Tonic and Dominant, his Developments and codas.

Such lust of liberation filled Beethoven, the romantic revolutionary, that he ascended one short step on the way leading music back to its loftier self: – a short step in the great task, a wide step in his own path. He did not quite reach absolute music, but in certain moments he divined it, as in the introduction to the fugue of the Sonata for Hammerclavier. Indeed, all composers have drawn nearest the true nature of music in preparatory and intermediary passages (preludes and transitions), where they felt at liberty to disregard symmetrical proportions, and unconsciously drew free breath. Even a Schumann (of so much lower stature) is seized, in such passages, by some feeling of the boundlessness of this pan-art (recall the transition to the last movement of the D minor Symphony); and the same may be asserted of Brahms in the introduction to the Finale of his First Symphony.

But, the moment they cross the threshold of the *Principal Subject*, their attitude becomes stiff and conventional, like that of a man entering some bureau of high officialdom.

Next to Beethoven, Bach bears closest affinity to 'infinite music'.[1] His Organ Fantasias (but not the Fugues) have indubitably a strong dash of what might be overwritten 'Man and Nature'.[2] In him it appears most ingenuous because he had no reverence for his predecessors (although he esteemed and made use of them), and because the still novel acquisition of equal temperament opened a vista of – for the time being – endless new possibilities.

Therefore, Bach and Beethoven[3] are to be conceived as a *beginning*, and not as unsurpassable finalities. In spirit and emotion they will probably remain unexcelled; and this, again, confirms the remark at the beginning of these lines: that spirit and emotion remain unchanged in value through changing years, and that he who mounts to their uttermost heights will always tower above the crowd.

What still remains to be surpassed is their form of expression and their freedom. Wagner, a Germanic Titan, who touched our earthly horizon in orchestral tone-effect, who intensified the form of expression, but fashioned it into a *system* (music-drama, declamation, leading-motive), is on this account incapable of further intensification. His category begins and ends with himself; first, because he carried it to the highest perfection and finish; secondly, because his self-imposed task was of such a nature, that it could be

---

[1] [Translator's note:] 'Die Ur-Musik', is the author's happy phrase. But as this music *never has been*, our English terms like 'primitive', 'original' etc. would involve a *non sequitur* which is avoided, at least, by 'infinite'.

[2] In the recitatives of his Passions we hear 'human speech'; *not* 'correct declamation'.

[3] As characteristic traits of Beethoven's individuality I would mention the poetic fire, the strong human feeling (whence springs his revolutionary temper), and a portent of modern nervousness. These traits are certainly opposed to those of a 'classic'. Moreover, Beethoven is no 'master', as the term applies to Mozart or the late Wagner, just because his art foreshadows a greater, as yet incomplete. [. . .]

achieved by one man alone.[4] The paths opened by Beethoven can be followed to their end only through generations. They – like all things in creation – may form only a circle; but a circle of such dimensions, that the portion visible to us seems like a straight line. Wagner's circle we can view in its entirety – a circle within the great circle. [pp. 7–10]

[.    .    .]

'Notation' ('writing down') brings up the subject of Transcription, nowadays a term much misunderstood, almost discreditable. The frequent antagonism which I have excited with 'transcriptions', and the opposition to which an oft-times irrational criticism has provoked me, caused me to seek a clear understanding of this point. My final conclusion concerning it is this: every notation is, in itself, the transcription of an abstract idea. The instant the pen seizes it, the idea loses its original form. The very intention to write down the idea, compels a choice of measure and key. The form, and the musical agency, which the composer must decide upon, still more closely define the way and the limits.

It is much the same as with man himself. Born naked, and as yet without definite aspirations, he decides, or at a given moment is made to decide, upon a career. From the moment of decision, although much that is original and imperishable in the idea or the man may live on, either is depressed to the type of a class. The musical idea becomes a sonata or a concerto; the man, a soldier or a priest. That is Arrangement of the original. From this first transcription to a second the step is comparatively short and unimportant. And yet it is only the second, in general, of which any notice is taken; overlooking the fact, that a transcription does not destroy the archetype, which is, therefore, not lost through transcription.

Again, the performance of a work is also a transcription, and still, whatever liberties it may take, it can never annihilate the original.

For the musical art-work exists, before its tones resound and after they die away, *complete and intact*. It exists both within and outside of time, and through its nature we can obtain a definite conception of the otherwise intangible notion of the Ideality of Time.

For the rest, most of Beethoven's piano compositions sound like transcriptions of orchestral works; most of Schumann's orchestral compositions, like arrangements from pieces for the piano – and they are so, in a way. [pp. 17–19]

[.    .    .]

What we now call our Tonal System is nothing more than a set of 'signs'; an ingenious device to grasp somewhat of that eternal harmony; a meagre pocket-edition of that encyclopedic work; artificial light instead of the sun. –

---

[4] 'Together with the problem, it gives us the solution', as I once said of Mozart. [In 'Mozart: Aphorisms', see F. Busoni, *The Essence of Music and other Papers*, tr. Rosamond Ley (London 1957; reprinted New York 1965), p. 105.]

Have you ever noticed how people gaze open-mouthed at the brilliant illumination of a hall? They never do so at the millionfold brighter sunshine of
noonday. –

And so, in music, the signs have assumed greater consequence than that
which they ought to stand for, and can only suggest.

How important, indeed, are 'Third', 'Fifth', and 'Octave'! How strictly we
divide 'consonances' from 'dissonances' – *in a sphere where no dissonances
can possibly exist*!

We have divided the octave into twelve equidistant degrees, because we
had to manage somehow, and have constructed our instruments in such a
way that we can never get in above or below or between them. Keyboard
instruments, in particular, have so thoroughly schooled our ears that we are
no longer capable of hearing anything else – incapable of hearing except
through this impure medium. Yet Nature created an *infinite gradation –
infinite*! who still knows it nowadays?[5]

And within this duodecimal octave we have marked out a series of fixed
intervals, seven in number, and founded thereon our entire art of music. What
do I say – *one* series? Two such series, one for each leg: the Major and Minor
Scales. When we start this series of intervals on some other degree of our
semitonic ladder, we obtain a *new key*, a 'foreign' one, at that! How violently
contracted a system arose from this initial confusion,[6] may be read in the law
books; we will not repeat it here. [pp. 23–5]

[.    .    .]

Upon the two Series of Seven, the major key and the minor key, the whole
art of music has been established; one limitation brings on the other.

To each of these a definite character has been attributed; we have learned
and have taught that they should be heard as contrasts, and they have
gradually acquired the significance of symbols: – Major and Minor – Mag-
giore e Minore – Contentment and Discontent – Joy and Sorrow – Light and
Shade. The harmonic symbols have fenced in the expression of music, from
Bach to Wagner, and yet further on until today and the day after tomorrow.
*Minor* is employed with the same intention, and has the same effect upon us
now, as two hundred years ago. Nowadays it is no longer possible to
'compose' a funeral march, for it already exists, once for all. Even the least

[5] 'The equal temperament of twelve degrees, which was discussed theoretically as early
   as about 1500, but not established as a principle until shortly before 1700 (by Andreas
   Werkmeister), divides the octave into twelve equal portions (semitones, hence 'twelve-
   semitone system') through which mean values are obtained; no interval is perfectly
   pure, but all are fairly serviceable' (Riemann, *Musik-Lexikon*). Thus, through
   Andreas Werkmeister, this master-workman in art, we have gained the 'twelve-
   semitone' system with intervals which are all impure, but fairly serviceable. But what
   is 'pure', and what 'impure'? We hear a piano 'gone out of tune', and whose intervals
   may thus have become 'pure, but unserviceable', and it sounds *impure* to us. The
   diplomatic 'twelve-semitone system' is an invention mothered by necessity; yet
   nonetheless do we sedulously guard its imperfections.
[6] It is termed 'The Science of Harmony'.

informed non-professional knows what to expect when a funeral march –
whichever you please – is to be played. Even such an one [*sic*] can anticipate
the difference between a symphony in major and one in minor. We are
tyrannized by Major and Minor – by the bifurcated garment.

Strange, that one should feel major and minor as opposites. They both
present the same face, now more joyous, now more serious; and a mere touch
of the brush suffices to turn the one into the other. The passage from either to
other is easy and imperceptible; when it occurs frequently and swiftly, the
two begin to shimmer and coalesce indistinguishably. – But when we recognize that major and minor form one Whole with a double meaning, and that
the 'four-and-twenty keys' are simply an elevenfold transposition of the
original twain, we arrive unconstrainedly at a perception of the UNITY *of our
system of keys* [tonality]. The conceptions of 'related' and 'foreign' keys
vanish, and with them the entire intricate theory of degrees and relations. *We
possess one single key*. But it is of most meagre sort. [pp. 26–7]

[.    .    .]

That some few have already felt how the intervals of the Series of Seven
might be differently arranged (graduated) is manifested in isolated passages
by Liszt, and recently by Debussy and his following, and even by Richard
Strauss. Strong impulse, longing, gifted instinct, all speak from these strains.
Yet it does not appear to me that a conscious and orderly conception of this
intensified means of expression had been formed by these composers.

I have made an attempt to exhaust the possibilities of the arrangement of
degrees within the seven-tone scale; and succeeded, by raising and lowering
the intervals, in establishing *one hundred and thirteen different scales*. These
113 scales (within the octave C-C) comprise the greater part of our familiar
twenty-four keys, and, furthermore, a series of new keys of peculiar character. But with these the mine is not exhausted, for we are at liberty to *transpose*
each one of these 113, besides the blending of two such keys in harmony and
melody.

There is a significant difference between the sound of the scale *c-db -eb -fb -
gb -ab -bb -c* when *c* is taken as a tonic, and the scale of *db* minor. By giving it
the customary C-major triad as a fundamental harmony, a novel harmonic
sensation is obtained. But now listen to this same scale supported alternately
by the *A*-minor, *Eb*-major, and C-major triads, and you cannot avoid a
feeling of delightful surprise at the strangely unfamiliar euphony.

But how would a lawgiver classify the tone-series *c-db -eb -fb -g-a-b-c,
c-db -eb -f-gb -a-b-c, c-d-eb -fb -gb -a-b-c, c-db -e-f-gb -a-bb -c?* – or these, forsooth: *c-d-eb -fb -g-a#-b-c, c-d-eb -fb -g#-a-b-c, c-db -eb -f#-g#-a-bb -c?*

One cannot estimate at a glance what wealth of melodic and harmonic
expression would thus be opened up to the hearing; but a great many novel
possibilities may be accepted as certain, and are perceptible at a glance.

*    *    *

With this presentation, the unity of all keys may be considered as finally pronounced and justified. A kaleidoscopic blending and interchanging of twelve semitones within the three-mirror tube of Taste, Emotion, and Intention – the essential feature of the harmony of today.

The harmony of *today*, and not for long; for all signs presage a revolution, and a next step toward that 'eternal harmony'. Let us once again call to mind, that in this latter the gradation of the octave is *infinite*, and let us strive to draw a little nearer to infinitude. The tripartite tone (third of a tone) has for some time been demanding admittance, and we have left the call unheeded. Whoever has experimented, like myself (in a modest way), with this interval, and introduced (either with voice or with violin) two equidistant intermediate tones between the extremes of a whole tone, schooling his ear and his precision of attack, will not have failed to discern that tripartite tones are wholly independent intervals with pronounced character, and not to be confounded with ill-tuned semitones. They form a refinement in chromatics based, as at present appears, on the whole-tone scale. Were we to adopt them without further preparation, we should have to give up the semi-tones and lose our 'minor third' and 'perfect fifth'; and this loss would be felt more keenly than the relative gain of a system of eighteen one-third tones.

But there is no apparent reason for giving up the semitones for the sake of this new system. By retaining, for each whole tone, a semitone, we obtain a second series of whole tones lying a semitone higher than the original series. Then, by dividing this second series of whole tones into third-tones, each third-tone in the lower series will be matched by a semitone in the higher series.

Thus we have really arrived at a system of whole tones divided into sixths of a tone; and we may be sure that even sixth-tones will sometime be adopted into musical speech. But the tonal system above sketched must first of all train the hearing to thirds of a tone, without giving up the semitones.

To summarize: we may set up either two series of third-tones, with an interval of a semitone between the series; or, the usual semitonic series *thrice repeated* at the interval of one-third of a tone.

Merely for the sake of distinction, let us call the first tone C and the next third-tones C#, and Db ; the first semitone (small) *c*, and its following thirds *c#* and *db* ; the result is fully explained by the table below:

A preliminary expedient for notation might be to draw six lines for the staff using the lines for the whole tones and the spaces for the semitones:

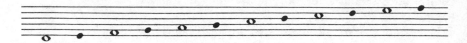

then indicating the third-tones by sharps and flats:

etc.

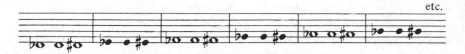

The question of notation seems to me subordinate. On the other hand, the question is important and imperious, how and on what these tones are to be produced. Fortunately, while busied with this essay, I received from America direct and authentic intelligence which solves the problem in a simple manner. I refer to an invention by Dr Thaddeus Cahill.[7] He has constructed a comprehensive apparatus which makes it possible to transform an electric current into a fixed and mathematically exact number of vibrations. As pitch depends on the number of vibrations, and the apparatus may be 'set' on any number desired, the infinite gradation of the octave may be accomplished by merely moving a lever corresponding to the pointer of a quadrant.

Only a long and careful series of experiments, and a continued training of the ear, can render this unfamiliar material approachable and plastic for the coming generation, and for Art.

And what vista of fair hopes and dreamlike fancies is thus opened for them both! Who has not dreamt that he could float on air? and firmly believed his dream to be reality? – Let us take thought, how music may be restored to its primitive, natural essence; let us free it from architectonic, acoustic and aesthetic dogmas; let it be pure invention and sentiment, in harmonies, in forms, in tone-colours (for invention and sentiment are not the prerogative of melody alone); let it follow the line of the rainbow and vie with the clouds in breaking sunbeams; *let Music be naught else than Nature mirrored by and reflected from the human breast*; for it is sounding air and floats above and beyond the air; within Man himself as universally and absolutely as in Creation entire; for it can gather together and disperse without losing in intensity. [pp. 29–34]

[7] 'New Music for an Old World.' Dr Thaddeus Cahill's Dynamophone, an extraordinary electrical invention for producing scientifically perfect music. Article in *McClure's Magazine* [vol. 27] for July 1906 [p. 291], by Ray Stannard Baker. Readers interested in the details of this invention are referred to the above-mentioned magazine article. [An alternative name for this instrument was 'telharmonium'. See the entry 'Electronic instruments' in *The New Grove Dictionary of Music*.]

# Select bibliography

Abegg, W., *Musikästhetik und Musikkritik bei Eduard Hanslick* (*Schriften zur Musikgeschichte des 19. Jahrhunderts*, 44, Regensburg 1974)

Adler, G., 'Umfang, Methode und Ziel der Musikwissenschaft', *Vierteljahrsschrift für Musikwissenschaft*, vol. 1 (1885), pp. 5–20

'Musik und Musikwissenschaft', *Jahrbuch der Musikbibliothek Peters für 1898*, vol. 5 (1899), pp. 27–39

'Über Heterophonie', *Jahrbuch der Musikbibliothek Peters für 1908*, vol. 15 (1909), pp. 17–28

Adorno, T. W., *Ästhetische Theorie*, ed. Gretel Adorno and R. Tiedemann (Frankfurt am Main 1970); English transl. *Aesthetic Theory* (London 1984)

Allen, G. (Charles Grant Blairfindie), *Physiological Aesthetics* (London 1877)

Allen, W. D., *Philosophies of Music History* (New York 1962)

Ambros, A. W., *Die Grenzen der Musik und Poesie. Eine Studie zur Ästhetik der Tonkunst* (Leipzig 1855, reissued Prague 1856, repr. Hildesheim 1976); 2nd edn. (Leipzig 1857); English transl. *The Boundaries of Music and Poetry*, tr. J. H. Cornell (New York 1893); Italian transl. in *I confini della musica e della poesia* (*Instituta et monumenta pubblicate dalla Scuola di paleografia e filologia musicale dell'Università di Pavia, Serie ii. Instituta no. 6*, Cremona 1978). [The Italian edition contains also reprints of the German original and the English translation]

Austin, L. J., *L'univers poétique de Baudelaire. Symbolisme et symbolique* (Paris 1956)

'Mallarmé on Music and Letters', *Bulletin of the John Rylands Library, Manchester*, vol. 42 (1959), pp. 19–39

Basch, V., *Essai critique sur l'esthétique de Kant* (Paris 1896); 2nd edn. (Paris 1927)

'Les grands courants de l'esthétique allemande contemporaine' in Andler, C., Basch, V., Benrubi, J. *et al.*, *La philosophie allemande au XIXe siècle* (Paris 1912), pp. 69–125

Baudelaire, C., *Oeuvres complètes*, ed. C. Pichois (Paris 1961)

*Art in Paris, 1845–1862, Salons and other Exhibitions*, tr. and ed. by J. Mayne (London 1965)

*Selected Writings on Art and Artists*, tr. P. E. Charvet (Harmondsworth 1972, repr. Cambridge 1981)

Baumer, F. L., *Modern European Thought. Continuity and Change in Ideas 1600–1950* (New York and London 1977)

Beardsley, M. C., *Aesthetics from Classical Greece to the Present* (New York 1966)

*Aesthetics. Problems in the Philosophy of Criticism*, 2nd edn. (Indianapolis 1981)

Beauquier, C., *Philosophie de la musique* (Paris 1865)

*La musique et le drame, etude d'esthétique*, 2nd edn. (Paris 1884)

Becker, Martha, 'Der Einfluss der Philosophie Schellings auf Richard Wagner', *Zeitschrift für Musikwissenschaft*, vol. 14 (1931–2), pp. 433–47

Beckerman, M., 'Janáček and the Herbartians', *The Musical Quarterly*, vol. 69 (1983), pp. 388–407

Berlioz, H., *A travers chants* (Paris 1862). [Contains the essay 'Concerts de Richard Wagner, la musique de l'avenir']

    *Mozart, Weber and Wagner with Various Essays on Musical Subjects*, tr. E. Evans (London 1918, repr. 1969)

    *Oeuvres littéraires*, eds. R. Dumesnil, H. Barraud, J. Chailley, *et al*. (Paris 1968– )

    *The Memoirs*, tr. D. Cairns (London 1969)

Bernard, Suzanne, *Mallarmé et la musique* (Paris 1959)

Boring, E. G., *Sensation and Perception in the History of Experimental Psychology* (New York 1942)

    *A History of Experimental Psychology*, 2nd edn. (New York 1950)

Bosanquet, B., *A History of Aesthetic* (London 1892)

Brendel, F., *Geschichte der Musik in Italien, Deutschland und Frankreich von den ersten christlichen Zeiten an bis auf die Gegenwart* (Leipzig 1852)

    *Die Musik der Gegenwart und die Gesamtkunst der Zukunft* (Leipzig 1854)

    *Zur Geschichte und Kritik der neueren Musik* (Leipzig 1888)

    'Die Aesthetik der Tonkunst', *NZM*, vol. 46 (1857), pp. 185–6

Brock, W., *An Introduction to Contemporary German Philosophy* (Cambridge 1935)

Bücher, K., 'Arbeit und Rhythmus' (*Abhandlungen der Königlich Sächsischen Gesellschaft der Wissenschaften*, 39, Leipzig 1897); 2nd extended edn. *Arbeit und Rhythmus* (Leipzig 1899)

Budd, M., *Music and the Emotions. The Philosophical Theories* (London 1985)

    'The Repudiation of Emotion: Hanslick on Music', *The British Journal of Aesthetics*, vol. 20 (1980), pp. 29–43. Incorporated into *Music and the Emotions*

Bujić, B., 'Musicology and Intellectual History: A Backward Glance to the Year 1885', *Proceedings of the Royal Musical Association*, vol. 111 (1984–5), pp. 139–54

Busoni, F., *Entwurf einer neuen Aesthetik der Tonkunst* (Trieste 1907); 2nd extended edn. (Leipzig 1916); English transl. *Sketch of a New Esthetic of Music*, tr. Th. Baker (New York 1911); translation reissued in *Three Classics in the Aesthetic of Music* (New York 1962)

    *The Essence of Music*, tr. Rosamond Ley (London 1957)

    'Music: A Look Backward and a Look Forward', *Monthly Musical Record*, vol. 62 (1932), p. 100

    'On the Nature of Music', *The Music Review*, vol. 17 (1956), pp. 282–6. [A translation different from the one in *The Essence of Music*]

Byrnside, R. L., 'Musical Impressionism: the Early History of the Term', *The Musical Quarterly*, vol. 66 (1980), pp. 522–37

Calvocoressi, M. D., 'Esquisse d'une esthétique de la musique à programme', *Sammelbände der Internationalen Musikgesellschaft*, vol. 9 (1907–8), pp. 424–38

Caramaschi, E., *Essai sur la critique française de la fin-de-siècle: Émile Hennequin* (Paris 1974)

Charlton, D. G., *Positivist Thought in France during the Second Empire, 1852–1870* (Oxford 1959)

Chrysander, F., 'Vorwort und Einleitung', *Jahrbuch für musikalische Wissenschaft*, vol. 1 (Leipzig 1863), pp. 9–16

Coeuroy, A., *Wagner et l'esprit romantique* (Paris 1965)

    'Musical Aesthetics of Comte de Gobineau', *The Musical Quarterly*, vol. 16 (1930), pp. 305–13

Cohen, H. R., 'Hector Berlioz, critique musical', *Revue de musicologie*, vol. 63 (1977), pp. 5–16

Cohn, A. W., 'Das Erwachen der Ästhetik', *Zeitschrift für Musikwissenschaft*, vol. 1 (1918–19), pp. 669–79

'Hugo Riemann als Systematiker der Musikwissenschaft', *Zeitschrift für Musikwissenschaft*, vol. 3 (1920–1), pp. 46–50

Collingwood, R. G., *The Principles of Art* (London 1937)

Combarieu, J., *Les rapports de la musique et de la poésie considérées au point de vue de l'expression* (Paris 1894)

*La musique, ses lois, son évolution* (Paris 1907); English transl. *Music, its Laws and Evolution* (London 1910)

*La musique et la magie* (*Études de philologie musicale*, 3, Paris 1909)

Comte, A., *Discours sur l'ensemble du positivisme* (Paris 1848); English transl. *A General View of Positivism*, tr. J. H. Bridges (London 1865)

Cooperman, H., *The Aesthetics of Stéphane Mallarmé* (New York 1933)

Croce, B., *Aesthetic as Science of Expression and General Linguistic*, tr. D. Ainslie, 2nd edn. (New York 1922)

*L'estetica della 'Einfühlung' e Roberto Vischer* (Naples 1934)

Dahlhaus, C., *Grundlagen der Musikgeschichte* (Cologne 1967); English transl. *Foundations of Music History*, tr. J. B. Robinson (Cambridge 1983)

*Musikästhetik* (Cologne 1967); English transl. *Esthetics of Music*, tr. W. W. Austin (Cambridge 1982)

*Zwischen Romantik und Moderne. Vier Studien zur Musikgeschichte des späteren 19. Jahrhunderts* (*Berliner musikwissenschaftliche Arbeiten*, 7 Munich 1974); English transl. *Between Romanticism and Modernism. Four Studies in the Music of the Later Nineteenth Century*, tr. Mary Whittall (Los Angeles and London 1980)

*Musikalischer Realismus. Zur Musikgeschichte des 19. Jahrhunderts* (Munich 1982); English transl. *Realism in Nineteenth-Century Music*, tr. Mary Whittall (Cambridge 1985)

'Eduard Hanslick und der musikalische Formbegriff', *Die Musikforschung*, vol. 20 (1967), pp. 149–53

'Formästhetik und Nachahmungsprinzip', *International Review of the Aesthetics and Sociology of Music*, vol. 4 (1973), pp. 165–73

'Chronologie und Systematik? Probleme einer Edition von Wagners Schriften', in Dahlhaus, C. and Voss, E. (eds.), *Wagnerliteratur – Wagnerforschung* (Mainz 1985), pp. 127–30

'Studien zur romantischen Musikästhetik', *Archiv für Musikwissenschaft*, vol. 42 (1985), pp. 157–65

Dahlhaus, C. (ed.), *Musikalische Hermeneutik* (*Studien zur Musikgeschichte des 19. Jahrhunderts*, 43, Regensburg 1975)

Dahlhaus, C. and Voss, E. (eds.), *Wagnerliteratur – Wagnerforschung* (Mainz 1985)

Dahlhaus, C. and Zimmermann, M. (eds.), *Musik-zur Sprache gebracht* (Munich and Kassel 1984)

Danz, E.-J., *Die objektlose Kunst. Untersuchungen zur Musikästhetik Friedrich von Hauseggers* (*Kölner Beiträge zur Musikforschung*, 118, Regensburg 1981)

Darwin, C., *The Descent of Man, and Selection in Relation to Sex* (London 1871) 2 vols.

*The Expression of the Emotions in Man and Animals* (London 1872); 2nd edn., ed. F. Darwin (London 1890)

Deathridge J. and Dahlhaus, C., *The New Grove Wagner* (London 1984)

Debussy, C. A., *Monsieur Croche et autres écrits*, ed. F. Lesure (Paris 1971); English transl. *Debussy on Music: The Critical Writings*, tr. and ed. R. Langham Smith (London 1977)
Delfel, G., *L'esthétique de Stéphane Mallarmé* (Paris 1951)
Della Corte, A., *La critica musicale e i critici* (Turin 1961)
Delsemme, P., *Teodor de Wyzéwa et la cosmopolitisme litteraire en France* (Paris 1967)
Dent, E. J., 'Busoni on Musical Aesthetics', *Monthly Musical Record*, vol. 39 (1909), pp. 197–8
    'Busoni: a Posthumous Paper', *Monthly Musical Record*, vol. 62 (1932), pp. 99–100. [Contains an introduction by Dent and his translation of Busoni's 'Music: a Look Backward and a Look Forward']
Dessoir, M., *Ästhetik und allgemeine Kunstwissenschaft* (Stuttgart 1906); 2nd revised edn. (Stuttgart 1923); English transl. *Aesthetics and Theory of Art*, tr. S. A. Emery (Detroit 1970)
    'The Contemplation of Works of Art', *Journal of Aesthetics and Art Criticism*, vol. 6 (1947–8), pp. 108–19
    'Art History and Systematic Theories of Art', *Journal of Aesthetics and Art Criticism*, vol. 19 (1960–1), pp. 463–9
Dilthey, W., *Gesammelte Schriften*, ed. G. Misch, B. Groethuysen, *et al.* (Leipzig, etc. 1921–74) 17 vols.
    *Von deutscher Dichtung und Musik*, ed. H. Nohl and G. Misch (Leipzig and Berlin 1933)
    *The Essence of Philosophy*, tr. S. A. and W. T. Emery (*University of North Carolina Studies in the German Language and Literature*, 13, Chapel Hill 1954)
    *Meaning in History. Wilhelm Dilthey's Thoughts on History and Society*, tr. and ed. H. P. Rickman (London 1961)
    *Selected Writings*, tr. and ed. H. P. Rickman (Cambridge 1976)
    *Poetry and Experience*, tr. and ed. R. A. Makkreel and F. Rodi (*Selected Works*, 5, Princeton 1986). [Part of a projected six-volume set]
Dömling, W., 'Musikgeschichte als Stilgeschichte. Bemerkungen zum musikhistorischen Konzept Guido Adlers', *International Review of the Aesthetics and Sociology of Music*, vol. 4 (1973), pp. 35–50
Dujardin, E., '"La revue wagnérienne"', *La revue musicale*, Numéro spécial (1923), pp. 141–60
Dukas, P., 'L'influence wagnérienne', *La revue musicale*, Numéro spécial (1923), pp. 1–9
Eckart-Bäcker, Ursula, *Frankreichs Musik zwischen Romantik und Moderne. Die Zeit im Spiegel der Kritik* (*Studien zur Musikgeschichte des 19. Jahrhunderts*, 2, Regensburg 1965)
Eggebrecht, H. H., 'Musik als Tonsprache', *Archiv für Musikwissenschaft*, vol. 18 (1961), pp. 73–100; also in Eggebrecht, H. H., *Musikalisches Denken* (Wilhelmshaven 1977)
Ehrlich, H., *Die Musikästhetik in ihrer Entwicklung von Kant bis auf die Gegenwart. Ein Grundriss* (Leipzig 1881)
Eisley, I. R., 'Some Origins of Music: Communications and Magic', *The Music Review*, vol. 32 (1971), pp. 128–35
Elssner, Mechtild, 'Hegel und Vischer über Gegenstand, Inhalt und Form in der Musik', *Bericht über den internationalen musikwissenschaftlichen Kongress Leipzig 1966*, ed. C. Dahlhaus (Kassel and Leipzig 1970), pp. 391–6
Emmanuel, M. *Histoire de la langue musicale* (Paris 1911) 2 vols.

Engel, G. E., *Aesthetik der Tonkunst* (Berlin 1884)
  'Der Begriff der Form in der Kunst und in der Tonkunst insbesondere', *Vierteljahr-sschrift für Musikwissenschaft*, vol. 2 (1886), pp. 181–233
Epperson, G., *The Musical Symbol* (Ames, Iowa 1967)
Fechner, G. T., *Vorschule der Aesthetik* (Leipzig 1876) 2 vols.; 2nd edn. (Leipzig 1897–8) 2 vols.; 3rd edn. (Leipzig 1925) 2 vols.
Ferchault, G., 'La musique dans l'oeuvre de Charles Lalo', *Revue d'esthétique*, vol. 6 (1953), pp. 153–62
Fétis, F.-J., 'Richard Wagner', *La revue et gazette musicale*, vol. 19 (1852), pp. 185–7; 193–5; 201–3; 209–11; 225–7; 242–5; 257–9
Foerster-Nietzsche, Elizabeth, 'Wagner and Nietzsche – Beginning and End of their Friendship', *The Musical Quarterly*, vol. 4 (1918), pp. 466–89
Frank, P., 'Wilhelm Dilthey's Contribution to the Aesthetics of Music', *Journal of Aesthetics and Art Criticism*, vol. 15 (1956–7), pp. 477–80
Fubini, E., *L'estetica musicale dal settecento a oggi* (Turin 1964)
  *Les philosophes et la musique* (Paris 1983)
  'Il linguaggio musicale nel pensiero di Jules Combarieu', *Rivista di estetica*, vol. 7 (1962), pp. 423–41
  'L'estetica crociana e la critica musicale', *Analecta musicologica*, vol. 12 (1973), pp. 1–22
Galli, A., *Estetica della musica* (Turin 1900)
Gardiner, P. L., *Schopenhauer* (Harmondsworth 1963)
Gatens, W. J., 'Fundamentals of Musical Criticism in the Writings of Edmund Gurney and his Contemporaries', *Music and Letters*, vol. 63 (1982), pp. 17–30
Gatz, F., *Musikästhetik in ihren Hauptrichtungen* (Frankfurt and Stuttgart 1922)
Gautier, Judith, *Richard Wagner et son oeuvre poétique, depuis 'Rienzi' jusqu'à 'Parsifal'* (Paris 1882)
Gervinus, G. G., *Geschichte des neunzehntes Jahrhunderts seit den Wiener Verträgen* (Leipzig 1855–66) 8 vols.
  *Händel und Shakespeare. Zur Ästhetik der Tonkunst* (Leipzig 1868)
*Gesamtverzeichnis des deutschsprachigen Schrifttums (GV) 1700–1910*, ed. P. Geils and W. Gorzny (Munich 1979–)
*Gesamtverzeichnis des deutschsprachigen Schrifttums (GV) 1911–1965*, ed. R. Oberschelp (Munich 1976–81) 150 vols.
Gilbert, K. E., and Kuhn, H., *A History of Esthetics*, 2nd edn. (Bloomington 1954)
Glatt, Dorothea, *Zur geschichtlichen Bedeutung der Musikästhetik Eduard Hanslicks* (*Schriften zur Musik*, 15, Munich 1972)
Goethe, J. W. von, *Werke (Hamburger Ausgabe)*, ed. E. Trunz, *et al.*, 5th edn. (Hamburg 1960) 14 vols.
Graf, M., *Composer and Critic. Two Hundred Years of Musical Criticism* (London 1947)
Groth, J. H., 'Willamowitz-Möllendorf on Nietzsche's *Birth of Tragedy*', *Journal of the History of Ideas*, vol. 11 (1950), pp. 179–90
Grunsky, K., *Musikästhetik* (Leipzig 1907)
Guichard, L., *La musique et les lettres au temps du romantisme* (Paris 1955)
  *La musique et les lettres en France au temps du wagnérisme* (Paris 1963)
Gurney, E., *The Power of Sound* (London 1880)
  *Tertium Quid. Chapters on Various Disputed Questions* (London 1887) 2 vols.
Guyau, J.-M., *L'art au point de vue sociologique*, 3rd edn. (Paris 1895)
Hall, R. W., 'On Hanslick's Supposed Formalism in Music', *Journal of Aesthetics and Art Criticism*, vol. 25 (1966–7), pp. 433–6

Hand, F., *Aesthetik der Tonkunst*, 2nd edn. (Leipzig 1847) 2 vols.; English transl. of vol. 1 only, *Aesthetics of Musical Art*, tr. W. E. Lawson (London 1880)

Hanslick, E., *Vom Musikalisch-Schönen. Ein Beitrag zur Revision der Aesthetik der Tonkunst* (Leipzig 1854, repr. Darmstadt 1965); *Vom Musikalisch-Schönen* . . . *Zweite verbesserte Auflage* (Leipzig 1858); 7th edn. (Leipzig 1885); English transl. *The Beautiful in Music*, tr. G. Cohen (London 1891, repr. Indianapolis and New York 1957)

    *Vom Musikalisch-Schönen* . . ., 8th edn. (Leipzig 1891)

    *Vom Musikalisch-Schönen, Aufsätze, Musikkritiken* (Leipzig 1982)

    *Du beau dans la musique* (Paris 1986). [Contains the text of C. Bannelier's 1982 translation revised by G. Pucher and with an introductory essay, 'Introduction à l'esthétique de Hanslick', by J.-J. Nattiez]

    *Aus meinem Leben* (Berlin 1894) 2 vols.

Harding, F. J. W., 'Notes on Aesthetic Theory in France in the Nineteenth Century', *The British Journal of Aesthetics*, vol. 13 (1973), pp. 251–70

Hare, W. F., *see* Listowel, Earl of

Harrell, Jean G., 'Issues of Music Aesthetics', *Journal of Aesthetics and Art Criticism*, vol. 23 (1964–5), pp. 197–206

Hartmann, E. von, *Philosophie des Unbewussten* (Berlin 1869); English transl. *Philosophy of the Unconscious*, tr. W. C. Coupland (London 1884)

    *Aesthetik* (Leipzig 1886–7) 2 vols. Vol. 1: *Die deutsche Aesthetik seit Kant* (1886); vol. 2: *Philosophie des Schönen* (1887); 2nd edn. of vol. 2 ed. R. Müller-Freienfels (Berlin 1924)

Hauptmann, M. *Die Natur der Harmonik und Metrik* (Leipzig 1853); English transl. *The Nature of Harmony and Metre*, tr. and ed. W. E. Heathcote (London 1888)

Hausegger, F. von, *Die Musik als Ausdruck* (Vienna 1885); 2nd extended edn. (Vienna 1887)

    *Gedanken eines Schauenden*, ed. S. von Hausegger (Munich 1903)

    *Frühe Schriften und Essays*, ed. R. Flotzinger (*Grazer musikwissenschaftliche Arbeiten*, 7, Graz 1986)

Hegel, G. W. F., *Ästhetik* (Frankfurt 1965) 2 vols.

    *Aesthetics. Lectures on Fine Art*, tr. T. M. Knox (Oxford 1975–6) 2 vols.

Heinen, M., *Die Konstruktion der Ästhetik in Wilhelm Diltheys Philosophie* (Bonn 1974)

Heinz, R., *Geschichtsbegriff und Wissenschaftscharakter der Musikwissenschaft in der zweiten Hälfte des neunzehnten Jahrhunderts. Philosophische Aspekte einer Wissenschaftsentwicklung* (*Studien zur Musikgeschichte des 19. Jahrhunderts*, 11, Regensburg 1968)

Helmholtz, H. von, *Die Lehre von den Tonempfindungen als physiologische Grundlage für die Teorie der Musik* (Braunschweig 1863); 2nd edn (Braunschweig 1865); English transl. *On the Sensations of Tone as a Physiological Basis for the Theory of Music*, tr. and ed. A. J. Ellis, 2nd edn. (London 1885, repr. New York 1954)

    *Populäre wissenschaftliche Vorträge* (Braunschweig 1865) 2 vols.; English transl. *Popular Lectures on Scientific Subjects*, tr. E. Atkinson (London 1873–81) 2 vols.

Herbart, J. F., *Sämtliche Werke*, ed. K. Kehrbach and O. Flügel (Langensalza 1887–1912) 19 vols.

Hodges, H. A., *Wilhelm Dilthey. An Introduction* (London 1944)

    *The Philosophy of Wilhelm Dilthey* (London 1952)

Holborn, H., 'Dilthey and the Critique of Historical Reason', *Journal of the History of Ideas*, vol. 11 (1950), pp. 93–118

Hollinrake, R., *Nietzsche, Wagner, and the Philosophy of Pessimism* (London 1982)

Hostinský, O., *Das Musikalisch-Schöne und das Gesamtkunstwerk vom Standpunkte der formalen Aesthetik* (Leipzig 1877); Czech transl. in *O hudbě* (Prague 1961), pp. 23–124

Hueffer, F., *Richard Wagner and the Music of the Future* (London 1874)

*International Review of the Aesthetics and Sociology of Music* (Zagreb 1970–)

Jäckel, K., *Richard Wagner und die französische Literatur* (Breslau 1931–2) 2 vols.

Jensen, E. F., 'Adventures of a French Wagnerian: the Work of Villiers de l'Isle-Adam', *The Music Review*, vol. 46 (1985), pp. 186–98

Jones, Patricia C., 'Richard Strauss, Ferruccio Busoni and Arnold Schonberg: "Some Imperfect Wagnerites"', *The Music Review*, vol. 43 (1982), pp. 169–76

Jůzl, M., *Otakar Hostinský* (Prague 1980)

Kahn, S. J., *Science and Aesthetic Judgment. A Study in Taine's Critical Method* (London 1953)

Kaminsky, J., *Hegel on Art. An Interpretation of Hegel's Aesthetics* (Albany 1962)

Kant, I., *The Critique of Judgement*, tr. J. C. Meredith (Oxford 1952)

Kivy, P., 'Herbert Spencer and a musical Dispute', *The Music Revue*, vol. 23 (1962), pp. 317–29

Klein, J. W., 'Nietzsche and Bizet', *The Musical Quarterly*, vol. 11 (1925), pp. 482–505

'Nietzsche's Attitude to Bizet', *The Music Review*, vol. 21 (1960), pp. 215–25

Knox, I., *The Aesthetic Theories of Kant, Hegel and Schopenhauer* (London 1958)

Kohn, H., *The Mind of Germany* (London 1961)

Köstlin, H. A., *Geschichte der Musik im Umriss für die Gebildeten aller Stände* (Tübingen 1875)

*Die Tonkunst, Einführung in die Aesthetik der Musik* (Stuttgart 1879)

Kravis, Judy, *The Prose of Mallarmé. The Evolution of a Literary Language* (Cambridge 1976)

Kretzschmar, H., 'Anregungen zur Förderung musikalischer Hermeneutik', *Jahrbuch der Musikbibliothek Peters für 1902*, vol. 9 (1903), pp. 47–66. [Later included in Kretzschmar, H., *Gesammelte Aufsätze aus den Jahrbüchern der Musikbibliothek Peters* (Leipzig 1911, repr. 1973)]

'Neue Anregungen zur Förderung musikalischer Hermeneutik: Satzästhetik', *Jahrbuch der Musikbibliothek Peters für 1905*, vol. 12 (1906), pp. 73–86. [Later included in *Gesammelte Aufsätze*.]

Kropfinger, K., '*Oper und Drama*. Die Schrift und ihr Kontext', in Dahlhaus, C. and Voss, E. (eds.), *Wagnerliteratur–Wagnerforschung*, pp. 131–7

Kunze, S., *Der Kunstbegriff Richard Wagners. Voraussetzungen und Folgerungen (Forschungsunternehmen der Fritz-Thyssen-Stiftung, Arbeitsgemeinschaft "100 Jahre Bayreuther Festspiele"*, 1, Regensburg 1983)

Lalo, C., *Esquisse d'une esthétique musicale scientifique* (Paris 1908)

Langer, Susanne K., *Philosophy in a New Key: A Study in the Symbolism of Reason, Rite, and Art*, 2nd edn. (New York 1948)

*Feeling and Form* (New York 1953)

Large, D. C., and Weber, W. (eds.), *Wagnerism in European Culture and Politics* (Ithaca, N.Y. 1984)

Laurencin d'Armond, Count F. P., *Dr. Eduard Hanslicks Lehre vom Musikalisch-Schönen. Eine Abwehr* (Leipzig 1859)

Laurila, K. S., 'In Memory of Max Dessoir', *Journal of Aesthetics and Art Criticism*, vol. 6 (1947–8), pp. 105–7

Lehmann, A. G., *The Symbolist Aesthetic in France 1885–1895*, 2nd edn. (Oxford 1968)

le Huray, P. and Day, J., *Music and Aesthetics in the Eighteenth and Early-Nineteenth Centuries* (Cambridge 1981)

Leibniz, G., *The Monadology and other Writings*, tr. R. Latta (London 1898, 7th reprint 1971)

Leroy, M., *Les premiers amis français de Wagner* (Paris 1925)

Lippman, E. A. (ed.), *Musical Aesthetics: A Historical Reader*, vol. 1: *From Antiquity to the Eighteenth Century* (*Aesthetics in Music*, 4, New York 1986)
  'Esthetic Theories of Richard Wagner', *The Musical Quarterly*, vol. 44 (1958), pp. 209–20

Lipps, T., *Psychologische Studien* (Heidelberg 1885)
  *Ästhetik, Psychologie des Schönen und der Kunst* (Hamburg and Leipzig 1903–6) 2 vols; 2nd edn. (Leipzig 1914–20) 2 vols.; 3rd edn. of vol. 1 only (Leipzig 1923)
  'Ästhetik' in *Systematische Philosophie*, ed. P. Hinneberg (*Die Kultur der Gegenwart, ihre Entwicklung und ihre Ziele*, vol. 1, part 6) (Berlin and Leipzig 1907)

Listowel, Earl of (William Francis Hare), *A Critical History of Modern Aesthetics* (London 1933); 2nd revised edn. as *Modern Aesthetics: an Historical Introduction* (London 1967)

Liszt, F., *Lohengrin et Tannhäuser de R. Wagner* (Leipzig 1851)
  *Gesammelte Schriften*, tr. La Mara and L. Ramann, ed. L. Ramann (Leipzig 1881–99) 6 vols.

Loncke, Joycelynne, *Baudelaire et la musique* (Paris 1975)

Lotze, H., *Geschichte der Aesthetik in Deutschland* (Munich 1868)
  *Grundzüge der Aesthetik* (Leipzig 1884); English transl. *Outlines of Aesthetics*, tr. and ed. G. T. Ladd (Boston, Mass. 1886)

Mackerness, E. D., 'Edmund Gurney and "The Power of Sound"', *Music and Letters*, vol. 37 (1956), pp. 356–67

Makkreel, R. A., 'Toward a Concept of Style: an Interpretation of Wilhelm Dilthey's Psycho-Historical Account of the Imagination', *Journal of Aesthetics and Art Criticism*, vol. 27 (1968–9), pp. 171–82

Mallarmé, S., *Oeuvres complètes*, ed. H. Mondor and G. Jean-Aubry (Paris 1945)
  *Correspondance*, ed. H. Mondor and L. J. Austin (Paris 1959–85) 11 vols.

Marcel, Odile, 'Nietzsche musicien manqué', *Revue philosophique de la France et de l'étranger*, vol. 102 (1977), pp. 3–26

Masur, G., 'Wilhelm Dilthey and the History of Ideas', *Journal of the History of Ideas*, vol. 13 (1952), pp. 94–107

Mauser, S., 'Strawinskys "Musikalische Poetik" und Hanslicks "Vom Musikalisch-Schönen"', *Igor Strawinsky* (*Musik-Konzepte*, 34/35, 1984), pp. 89–98

Mercier, A., 'Douze lettres inédites de R. Wagner à E. Schuré (23 janvier 1869–6 février 1878)', *Revue de musicologie*, vol. 54 (1968), pp. 206–21

Mersmann, H., *Angewandte Musikästhetik* (Berlin 1926)
  'Versuch einer Phänomenologie der Musik', *Zeitschrift für Musikwissenschaft*, vol. 5 (1922–3), pp. 226–69

Meumann, E., *Untersuchungen zur Psychologie und Aesthetik des Rhythmus* (Leipzig 1894)
  *Einführung in die Ästhetik der Gegenwart* (Leipzig 1908)

Mies, P., *Über die Tonmalerei* (Stuttgart 1912)

Montinari, M., 'Die Entstehungsgeschichte von Nietzsches vierter *Unzeitgemasser Betrachtung: Richard Wagner in Bayreuth*', in Dahlhaus, C. and Voss, E. (eds.), *Wagnerliteratur–Wagnerforschung*, pp. 143–7

Moos, P., *Moderne Musikästhetik in Deutschland. Historisch-kritische Übersicht* (Leipzig 1902); 2nd revised edn. as *Die Philosophie der Musik von Kant bis Ed. von Hartmann* (Stuttgart 1922)

*Richard Wagner als Ästhetiker* (Berlin and Leipzig 1906)

Morawski, S., 'Value and Criteria in Taine's Aesthetics', *Journal of Aesthetics and Art Criticism*, vol. 21 (1962–3), pp. 407–21

Morpurgo Tagliabue, G., *L'esthétique contemporaine* (Milan 1960)

de la Motte, Helga, 'Über die Gegenstände und Methoden der Musikpsychologie. Ein geschichtlicher Überblick', *International Review of the Aesthetics and Sociology of Music*, vol. 1 (1970), pp. 83–9

Müller, U. and Wapnewski, P. (eds.), *Richard-Wagner-Handbuch* (Stuttgart 1986)

Mundt, E. K., 'Three Aspects of German Aesthetic Theory', *Journal of Aesthetics and Art Criticism*, vol. 17 (1958–9), pp. 287–310

Munro, T., 'Evolution and Progress in the Arts: A Reappraisal of Herbert Spencer's Theory', *Journal of Aesthetics and Art Criticism*, vol. 18 (1959–60), pp. 294–315

'The Psychology of Art: Past, Present, Future', *Journal of Aesthetics and Art Criticism*, vol. 21 (1962–3), pp. 263–82)

'"The Afternoon of a Faun" and the Interrelation of the Arts', *Journal of Aesthetics and Art Criticism*, vol. 10 (1951–2), pp. 95–111

Negri, A., 'Comte e l'estetica positiva', *Rivista di estetica*, vol. 10 (1965), pp. 386–416

*Neue Zeitschrift für Musik* (Mainz 1834–1955; repr. Scarsdale, N.Y. 1963–71)

*The New Grove Dictionary of Music and Musicians*, ed. S. Sadie (London, Washington DC and Hong Kong 1980), 20 vols.

Nietzsche, F., *The Case of Wagner* and *Nietzsche contra Wagner*, tr. A. M. Ludovici in *The Complete Works of Friedrich Nietzsche*, vol. 8, ed. O. Levy (Edinburgh and London 1911)

*The Portable Nietzsche*, tr. and ed. W. Kaufmann (New York 1954, reissued London 1971). [Contains *Nietzsche contra Wagner*]

*Werke*, ed. K. Schlechta (Munich 1954–65) 3 vols.

*The Birth of Tragedy* and *The Case of Wagner*, tr. W. Kaufmann (New York 1967)

*Werke. Kritische Gesamtausgabe*, ed. G. Colli and M. Montinari (Berlin 1967–)

*Untimely Meditations*, tr. R. J. Hollingdale (Cambridge 1983)

*Human, All-Too Human*, tr. R. J. Hollingdale (Cambridge 1986)

Nowak, S., *Hegels Musikästhetik* (Studien zur Musikgeschichte des 19. Jahrhunderts, 25, Regensburg 1971)

Oelmüller, W., *Friedrich Theodor Vischer und das Problem der nachhegelschen Ästhetik* (Stuttgart 1959)

Oersted, H. C., *The Soul in Nature*, tr. L. and J. Horner (London 1852)

Offer, J., 'An Examination of Spencer's Sociology of Music and its Impact on Music Historiography in Britain', *International Review of the Aesthetics and Sociology of Music*, vol. 14 (1983), pp. 33–52

Palmer, R. E., *Hermeneutics. Interpretation Theory in Schleiermacher, Dilthey, Heidegger, and Gadamer* (Evanston, Ill., 1969)

Partsch, E. W., 'Von der Historie zur Empirie. Richard Wallascheks Entwurf einer reformierten Musikwissenschaft', *Studien zur Musikwissenschaft*, vol. 36 (1985), pp. 87–109

Pastille, W. A., 'Heinrich Schenker, Anti-Organicist', *19th-Century Music*, vol. 8 (1984–5), pp. 28–36

Patmore, C., *Principle in Art* (London 1889)

Payzant, G., 'Hanslick, Sams, Gay, and *Tönend bewegte Formen*', *Journal of Aesthetics and Art Criticism*, vol. 40 (1981–2), pp. 41–8

'Eduard Hanslick and the "geistreich" Dr. Alfred Julius Becher', *The Music Review*, vol. 44 (1983), pp. 104–15

'Eduard Hanslick's *Vom Musikalisch-Schönen*: a Pre-publication Excerpt', *The Music Review*, vol. 46 (1985), pp. 178–85

Philipson, M., 'Dilthey on Art', *Journal of Aesthetics and Art Criticism*, vol. 17 (1958–9), pp. 72–6

Pinkus, H., *Friedrich Hebbels und Richard Wagners Theorie vom dramatischen Kunstwerk im Zusammenhänge mit ihren Weltanschauungen* (Marburg 1935)

Piselli, F., *Mallarmé e l'estetica* (Milan 1969)

Plantinga, L. B., *Schumann as Critic* (*Yale Studies in the History of Music*, 4, New Haven and London 1967)

Podro, M., *The Manifold in Perception. Theories of Art from Kant to Hildebrand* (Oxford 1972)

Portnoy, J., *The Philosopher and Music. A Historical Survey* (New York 1954; repr. New York 1980)

Raessler, D. M., 'The "113" Scales of Ferruccio Busoni', *The Music Review*, vol. 43 (1982), pp. 51–6

Raitt, A. W., *The Life of Villiers de l'Isle-Adam* (Oxford 1981)

Rand, C. G., 'Two Meanings of Historicism in the Writings of Dilthey, Troelsch, and Meinecke', *Journal of the History of Ideas*, vol. 25 (1964), pp. 503–18

Reckow, F., 'Richard Wagner und der esprit d'observation et d'analyse. Zur Charakteristik aufgeklärter Operntheorie', *Archiv für Musikwissenschaft*, vol. 34 (1977), pp. 237–59

Reilly, E. R., 'Mahler and Guido Adler', *The Musical Quarterly*, vol. 58 (1972), pp. 436–70

*Revue wagnérienne* (Paris 1885–8; repr. Geneva 1968)

Riemann, H., *Wie hören wir Musik? Drei Vorträge* (Leipzig 1888); 6th edn. as *Wie hören wir Musik? Grundlinien der Musik-Ästhetik* (Berlin 1923). English transl. *Catechism of Musical Aesthetics*, tr. H. Bewerunge (London 1895)

*Die Elemente der musikalischen Ästhetik* (Berlin 1903)

'Wurzelt der musikalische Rhythmus im Sprachrhythmus?', *Vierteljahrsschrift für Musikwissenschaft*, vol. 2 (1886), pp. 488–96

'Ideen zu einer "Lehre von den Tonvorstellungen"', *Jahrbuch der Musikbibliothek Peters für 1914/15*, vols. 21–2 (1916), pp. 1–26

'Neue Beiträge zu einer Lehre von den Tonvorstellungen', *Jahrbuch der Musikbibliothek Peters für 1916*, vol. 23 (1917), pp. 1–22

Rodi, F. and Lessing, H.-U. (eds.), *Materialen zur Philosophie Wilhelm Diltheys* (Frankfurt 1984)

Rowell, L., *Thinking about Music* (Amherst, Mass. 1983)

Rummenhöller, P., *Musiktheoretisches Denken im 19. Jahrhundert* (*Studien zur Musikgeschichte des 19. Jahrhunderts*, 12, Regensburg 1967)

Schafer, R. M., *E. T. A. Hoffmann and Music* (Toronto 1975)

Schäfke, R., *Geschichte der Musikästhetik in Umrissen* (Berlin 1934; repr. Tutzing 1964)

Schenk, H. G., *The Mind of the European Romantics. An Essay in Cultural History* (London 1966)

Schenker, H., *Harmonielehre* (*Neue musikalische Theorien und Phantasien*, 1, Stuttgart 1906); English transl. *Harmony*, ed. and annotated O. Jonas, tr. Elisabeth Mann Borgese (Cambridge, Mass. 1973)

Schnädelbach, H., *Philosophy in Germany 1831–1933*, tr. E. Matthews (Cambridge 1984)

Schnauss, F., *Die Grundlagen der Hartmannschen Ästhetik* (Cologne 1914)

Schopenhauer, A., *The World as Will and Representation*, tr. E. F. J. Payne (New York 1966) 2 vols.

   *Parerga and Paralipomena. Short Philosophical Essays*, tr. E. F. J. Payne (Oxford 1974) 2 vols.

Schumann, E., 'Die Förderung der Musikwissenschaft durch die akustisch-psychologische Forschung Carl Stumpfs', *Archiv für Musikwissenschaft*, vol. 5 (1923), pp. 172–6

Schumann, R., *Gesammelte Schriften über Musik und Musiker* (Leipzig 1854) 4 vols.; 2nd edn. (Leipzig 1871) 2 vols.; 3rd edn. (Leipzig 1875) 2 vols.; English transl. *Music and Musicians. Essays and Criticisms*, tr. and ed. Fanny Raymond Ritter (London 1877–80) 2 vols.

   *Jugendbriefe*, ed. Clara Schumann (Leipzig 1885); 2nd edn. (Leipzig 1886)

Schuré, E., *Le drame musical* (Paris 1875), 2nd edn. (1886)

Servières, G., *Richard Wagner jugé en France* (Paris 1886)

Siegel, Linda, 'Wagner and the Romanticism of E. T. A. Hoffmann', *The Musical Quarterly*, vol. 51 (1965), pp. 597–613

Silk, M. S. and Stern, J. P., *Nietzsche on Tragedy* (Cambridge 1981)

Simon, W. M., 'Saint-Simon and the Ideas of Progress', *Journal of the History of Ideas*, vol. 17 (1956), pp. 311–31

Spencer, H., *Essays: Scientific, Political and Speculative* (London 1858–74) 3 vols.

   *Principles of Psychology*, 4th edn. (London 1899) 2 vols.

Spitta, P., 'Kunstwissenschaft und Kunst' in *Zur Musik. Sechzehn Aufsätze* (Berlin 1892), pp. 3–14

Sponheuer, B., 'Zur ästhetischen Dichotomie als Denkform in der ersten Hälfte des 19. Jahrhunderts. Eine historische Skizze am Beispiel Schumanns, Brendels und Hanslicks', *Archiv für Musikwissenschaft*, vol. 38 (1980), pp. 1–31

Steinbrück, K., *Grundzüge der Musikästhetik Hermann Lotzes* (Berlin 1918)

Strunk, O., *Source Readings in Music History* (New York 1950)

Stumpf, C., *Tonpsychologie* (Leipzig 1883–90) 2 vols.

   *Beiträge zur Akustik und Musikwissenschaft* (Leipzig 1898)

   *Geschichte des Consonanzbegriffes* (Munich 1898)

   *Die Anfänge der Musik* (Leipzig 1911)

   'Musikpsychologie in England', *Vierteljahrsschrift für Musikwissenschaft*, vol. 1 (1885), pp. 261–349

Suarès, A., 'La première lettre de Baudelaire à Wagner', *La revue musicale*, vol. 4 (1922–3), pp. 1–10

Sully, J., *Sensation and Intuition: Studies in Psychology and Aesthetics* (London 1874)

   Review of E. Gurney, *The Power of Sound* in *Mind*, vol. 6 (1881), pp. 270–8

Suppan, W., 'Franz Liszt – zwischen Friedrich von Hausegger und Eduard Hanslick', *Studia musicologica*, vol. 24 (1982), pp. 113–32

Svoboda, K., 'The Contribution of Emil Utitz to Aesthetics', *Journal of Aesthetics and Art Criticism*, vol. 16 (1957–8), pp. 519–24

Taine, H., *Philosophie de l'art* (Paris 1865); English transl. *The Philosophy of Art*, tr. J. Durand (London 1865)

Taylor, C., *Hegel* (Cambridge 1975)

Tiersot, J., *Lettres françaises de Richard Wagner* (Paris 1935)

'Hector Berlioz and Richard Wagner', *The Musical Quarterly*, vol. 3 (1917), pp. 453–92

Torrefranca, F., *La vita musicale dello spirito* (Turin 1910)

Tschulik, N., 'August Wilhelm Ambros und das Wagner-Problem. Ein Beitrag zur Geschichte der Musikkritik und der Wagner-Rezeption', *Studien zur Musikwissenschaft*, vol. 29 (1978), pp. 155–69

Venturi, L., 'The Aesthetic Idea of Impressionism', *Journal of Aesthetics and Art Criticism*, vol. 1 (1941), pp. 34–45

Vischer, F. T., *Aesthetik oder Wissenschaft des Schönen* (Reutlingen etc. 1846–57) 3 vols.; 2nd edn. ed. R. Vischer (Munich 1922–3) 6 vols.

*Altes und Neues* (Stuttgart 1881–2) 2 vols.

Volkelt, J., *System der Ästhetik* (Munich 1904–14) 3 vols.

Wagner, R., *Gesammelte Schriften und Dichtungen* (Leipzig 1871–7) 9 vols., vol. 10 (1883); 2nd edn. (Leipzig 1887–8, repr. Hildesheim 1976) 10 vols. in 5. English transl. *Richard Wagner's Prose Works*, tr. and ed. W. A. Ellis (London 1892–9, repr. New York 1966) 8 vols.

*Dichtungen und Schriften*, ed. D. Borchmeyer (Frankfurt 1983) 10 vols.

*Oper und Drama*, ed. K. Kropfinger (Stuttgart 1984)

*Wagner-Handbuch*, see Müller, U. and Wapnewski, P. (eds.), *Richard-Wagner-Handbuch*

Wallaschek, R., *Primitive Music, an Inquiry into the Origin and Development of Music, Songs, Instruments, Dances and Pantomimes of Savage Races* (London 1893, repr. New York 1970); expanded German edition as *Anfänge der Tonkunst* (Leipzig 1903)

Weber, C. M. von, *Sämtliche Schriften*, ed. G. Kaiser (Berlin 1908); English transl. *Writings on Music*, tr. M. Cooper, ed. J. Warrack (Cambridge 1981)

Welch, Liliane, 'Mallarmé and the Experience of Art', *Journal of Aesthetics and Art Criticism*, vol. 30 (1971–2), pp. 369–75

Wellek, R., *A History of Modern Criticism 1750–1950* (New Haven, Conn. and London 1955–86, 6 vols.; vols. 1–4 repr. Cambridge 1981 and 1983)

Weyers, R., *Arthur Schopenhauer's Philosophy of Music* (Regensburg 1976)

White, D. A., 'Who is *Parsifal's* "pure fool"?: Nietzsche on Wagner', *The Music Review*, vol. 44 (1983), pp. 203–7

Wilhelmer, A., *Der junge Hanslick. Sein 'Intermezzo' in Klagenfurt, 1850–1852* (Klagenfurt 1959)

Wintle, J. (ed.), *Makers of Nineteenth Century Culture* (London 1982)

Wiora, W., 'Historische und systematische Musikforschung', *Die Musikforschung*, vol. 1 (1948), pp. 171–91

Wolfenstein, Marta, 'Social Background of Taine's Philosophy of Art', *Journal of the History of Ideas*, vol. 5 (1944), pp. 332–58

Wolff, H. M., *Friedrich Nietzsche. Der Weg zum Nichts* (Berne 1956)

Wölfflin, E. von, 'Zur Geschichte der Tonmalerei', *Sitzungsberichte der Münchener Akademie* (*Philosophische Klasse*, 2, 1897), pp. 221–58

Wundt, W., *Grundzüge der physiologischen Psychologie* (Leipzig 1874) 2 vols.; English transl. from the 5th edn. (1902–3) *Principles of Physiological Psychology*, tr. E. B. Titchener (London 1904)

Wyzéwa, Isabelle de, *La revue wagnérienne. Essai sur l'interprétation esthétique de Wagner en France* (Paris 1934)

Wyzéwa, T. de, *Beethoven et Wagner. Essais d'histoire et de critique musicales* (Paris 1898)

Zimmermann, M. *'Träumerei eines französischen Dichters'. Stéphane Mallarmé und Richard Wagner* (Berliner musikwissenschaftliche Arbeiten, 20, Munich and Salzburg 1981)

Zimmermann, R., *Aesthetik* (Vienna 1858–65) 2 vols. Vol. 1: *Geschichte der Aesthetik als philosophischer Wissenschaft* (1858); vol. 2: *Allgemeine Aesthetik als Formwissenschaft* (1865)

# Index

## BY FREDERICK SMYTH

Bold figures (**234**) indicate the more important references; 'n' ('nn') directs attention to footnotes.